1820

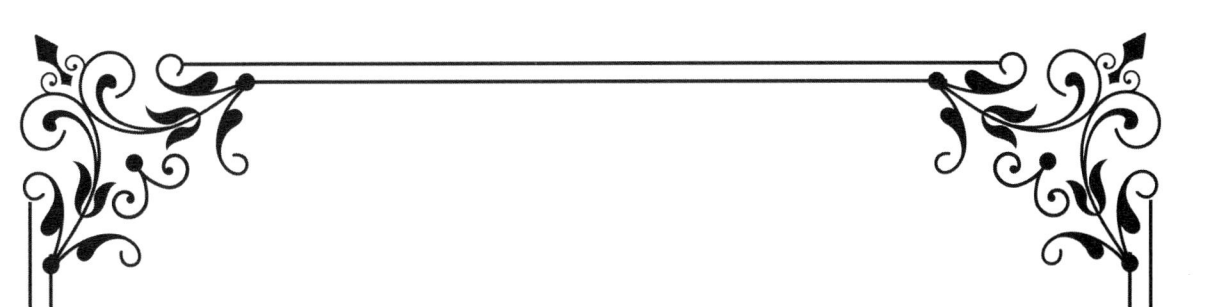

1820

DAWNING OF THE RESTORATION

RICHARD E. BENNETT

RSC
BYU

DESERET BOOK

Published by the Religious Studies Center, Brigham Young University, Provo, Utah, in cooperation with Deseret Book Company, Salt Lake City.
Visit us at rsc.byu.edu.

© 2020 by Brigham Young University. All rights reserved.

Printed in the United States of America by Sheridan Books, Inc.

DESERET BOOK is a registered trademark of Deseret Book Company.
Visit us at DeseretBook.com.

Any uses of this material beyond those allowed by the exemptions in US copyright law, such as section 107, "Fair Use," and section 108, "Library Copying," require the written permission of the publisher, Religious Studies Center, 185 HGB, Brigham Young University, Provo, UT 84602. The views expressed herein are the responsibility of the authors and do not necessarily represent the position of Brigham Young University or the Religious Studies Center.

Cover and interior design by Emily V. Strong
Endsheet images: *Brother Joseph*, courtesy of David Lindsley; *The Emperor Napoleon in His Study at the Tuileries*, by Jacques-Louis David

ISBN 978-1-9443-9494-3

Library of Congress Cataloging-in-Publication Data

Names: Bennett, Richard E. (Richard Edmond), 1946- author.
Title: 1820 : dawning of the Restoration / Richard E. Bennett.
Other titles: Eighteen twenty : dawning of the Restoration
Description: Provo, Utah : Religious Studies Center, Brigham Young University ; Salt Lake City : Deseret Book, [2020] | Includes bibliographical references and index. | Summary: "This volume examines the "four cornerstones" of the early nineteenth century: revolution and reform, Romanticism, emancipation, and religious revivalism. The book focuses on remarkable figures in each of these movements during this era, including people such as Napoleon Bonaparte, Alexander von Humboldt, Ludwig van Beethoven, and Charles Wesley. The author weaves together the biographies of these extraordinary people in order to give readers a glimpse into the spirit of the age. Readers will gain greater insight into the exciting and dynamic era of 1820, the year of the restoration of Christ's church on the earth"-- Provided by publisher.
Identifiers: LCCN 2019056285 | ISBN 9781944394943 (hardback)
Subjects: LCSH: Church of Jesus Christ of Latter-day Saints--History--19th century. | Mormon Church--History--19th century. | Biography--19th century. | LCGFT: Biographies.
Classification: LCC BX8611 .B327 2020 | DDC 289.309/034--dc23
LC record available at https://lccn.loc.gov/2019056285

CONTENTS

vii Introduction

xv Acknowledgments

1. Le Petit Caporal: Napoléon Bonaparte — 1

2. "Je Tiens Mon Affaire!": Jean-François Champollion, the Translator and the Stone — 31

3. Tsar Alexander I: The King of the North and His Holy Alliance — 57

4. "Who Can Ever Surpass These Inexpressible Heights?": Ludwig van Beethoven — 81

5. Théodore Géricault, Romantic Artists, and *The Raft of the Medusa* — 105

6. "An Archangel a Little Damaged": Samuel Taylor Coleridge and the Romantics — 125

7. Pandora's Box: King George IV, Queen Caroline, and the Industrial Revolution — 153

CONTENTS

181   8. Of Prophets, Preachers, and Poets: William Wilberforce,

207   9. El Libertador: Simón Bolívar and the Spanish American Independence Movement

231   10. "To Extend the Boundaries of Zion": The London Missionary Society and Rev. John Williams, "Apostle of Polynesia"

259   11. "We Never Had So Ominous a Question": Henry Clay, The Rise of America, and the Value of Political Compromise

287   12. "He, Like Another Sun, Illumines Everything I Behold": Alexander Von Humboldt and the New Age of Scientific Inquiry

317   13. From Plymouth Rock to Palmyra: Joseph Smith Jr., the Second Great Awakening, and the Quest for Divine Truth

343   Bibliography

000   Index

000   About the Author

INTRODUCTION

For members of The Church of Jesus Christ of Latter-day Saints, the year 2020 holds sacred significance: it marks the two hundredth anniversary of Joseph Smith Jr.'s First Vision near his boyhood home in upstate New York. This theophany will likely be remembered in songs and sermons as well as pageants and performances of various kinds throughout this year—a time of celebrations and commemorations. It is in this joyful spirit of remembering and reflecting upon that memorable event in the year 1820 that I have chosen to write this history. One major purpose of this work is to expand the stage of that visionary experience from merely a local Palmyra setting to a more global environment. If, as the late Latter-day Saint historian B. H. Roberts once insisted, there were "earlier lights in the morning than the outburst of the rising sun," that is to say other cast members who "caught the spirit of the [incoming new] dispensation," then this work also aims at identifying who some of those "earlier lights" may have been.[1] Their contributions to the age of 1820, of which many played a significant, if unwitting, role in the rise and early progress of the Church, will form the basis of this work.

When I began this work several years ago, I was of the naive opinion that writing about the year 1820 would be a fun, relatively straightforward project. A few events here and a few interesting stories there—that should just about do it. However, I learned very early on that

---

1. Roberts, *Comprehensive History*, 6:252.

INTRODUCTION

the once-upon-a-time approach may work well for fairy tales and historical novels, but it poses several challenges for the writer of history. Most sane historians write about people, events, places, or even ideas that become understandable only with the passage of time. Where I once believed that 1820 could be captured by merely chronicling key events that occurred during that not-so-long-ago year, I soon realized that such an approach would be a lazy, grossly simplistic short circuiting of a vast, magisterial complexity. The fact is, the year of our Lord 1820 was but one of an age, as is every other year in time. It cannot be understood or explained in isolation from those nearby years before and after it; rather, it must be seen as part of a continuum, a portion of the relentlessly moving train of history. There are so many ongoing streams of human thought and expression developing simultaneously that to say "this is what happened in 1820" or "this is what's most important" makes very little sense and can offend those with differing priorities and viewpoints. It is not fundamentally a question of what was happening but rather why, not merely a matter of what was developing but more a question of cause and effect that occurred in so many different fields of human endeavor.

There are even more serious challenges to writing a history of this sort. One surely is interpretation. In attempting to place the Restoration into a wider context, there is the temptation of some Latter-day Saint readers to see all of history pointing to Palmyra, that so many of those gifted in song were singing to a chorus of "Oh, How Lovely Was the Morning," when in fact it just wasn't so. A worldwide history cannot be artificially bent to fit a narrow, preconceived, faith-promoting paradigm of interpretation and self-fulfilling prophecy, that everyone and everything were somehow all part of a divine Latter-day Saint hymnbook. Seeing history through such a narrow prism would give lie to one of the essential purposes of this book, which is to place Joseph Smith's First Vision story within a worldwide context, not the other way around. A world history cannot be made the captive of any one interpretation. Some of what was happening elsewhere did indeed impact the unfolding of the Restoration, and where that was the case, I have briefly made comments thereon. However, this was not always so. The astute reader will have to make his or her own connections and conclusions.

Yet another challenge is that of creating a justifiable historical context, or of placing the story line in its proper sequence of development. This may explain why each one of the following thirteen chapters has a historical on-ramp leading up to, and sometimes past, the year 1820. While some may take exception with how long each run-up may be, please be patient; it takes time to get up to speed with the fast traffic lanes of history. Thus, I have chosen to start the chapter on Napoléon with the French Revolution of 1789, the chapter on Henry Clay with the American Revolution of 1776, and the study of Joseph Smith as far back as the Puritans of 1620.

Another obstacle to writing a work of this kind is that of scope. David McCullough, in his prizewinning, highly acclaimed study of the year 1776, enjoyed the benefit of writing about a single year in just one nation's colorful history—the beginnings of America.[2] He masterfully presented his characters and events primarily within a political and military context and, in the process, made sense of a specific year for the United States in particular. In contrast, the canvas upon which this book is painted is worldwide in scope, more akin to John E. Wills Jr.'s lesser-known attempt to capture an earlier age with his *1688: A Global History*.[3] It is a daunting, if not Herculean, task to make sense of an entire world history in so short and so selective a work as this is. Nevertheless, this work promises to be an exciting journey in time as it moves primarily from east to west over lands and seas before ending in upstate New York.

Further to the challenge of breadth and scope, this tries to be an encyclopedic work, spread across many countries, climates, and fields of endeavor. It is almost out of fashion these days to be like George Bancroft in the sense of writing a sweeping, ten-volume comprehensive history of America. To do so requires a breadth of understanding that taxes the limits of any one person's knowledge. It is virtually impossible nowadays to be an expert generalist in an age of specialties, even in the writing of history. I can already hear the reviewers criticizing the efforts of one, who is fundamentally a church historian, to venture into unknown worlds and never-before-seen panoramas. Such audacity and bold ambitions certainly have their serious limitations. While comprehensive in design, what follows is highly restrictive in scope, size, and content. The publishers would have it no other way. Wide swaths of human history are inevitably missing from the pages that follow. For instance, so much more could have been written about the domestic, Asia and the Far East, medicine, and philosophy, to name but a few of many missing fields. A single volume of the age can at best be only selective. It would take a library of books to do it all justice. Still, this work will try to be more than representative of the time; its purpose is to capture the essence of its fundamental meaning.

It was also a formidable challenge to decide how to approach this kind of study and how to even come close to capturing an accurate understanding of the main currents of thought in a given age. There are so many ways of doing so—the subjective and the objective, the quantitative and the qualitative, the analytical and the statistical, the theoretical and the practical. This may explain why I have deliberately chosen to approach the study of this age through writing a series of somewhat interconnected biographies. Admittedly, biography may not be either the most complete, the most interpretive, or the most analytical approach to understanding the past. However, it certainly is the most intimate form of history and arguably the most compelling to read for the simple reason that it is people, individually and collectively, who make history what it so unforgettably is. I have chosen the historical biographical approach not because it is the most thorough but because it is the most manageable. Like viewing a sprawling construction site spread over several blocks, one sees and comprehends it more fully from different angles and viewpoints. Through the

---

2. McCullough, *1776*.
3. Wills, *1688*.

lens of biography, we will attempt to view the age of 1820 as if it were, if you will, under construction. The devilishly difficult challenge will be to create an interconnectedness of meaning, to bring seamlessness out of compartmentalization, to recognize the building rising from its foundation.

If, then, biography, the inevitable questions arise: why these particular biographies, and what is the thread that binds them together? There are, after all, so many to choose from, so many to investigate. After years of research and study, I carefully selected the actors to this play because they made stellar, unforgettable contributions to their fields of activity. Whether it be Beethoven in music, Coleridge in literature, or Hannah Moore in religion, these men and women exercised a degree of predominance in their respective spheres of influence and are, to this day, universally acclaimed for having done so. Furthermore, by reaching into their lives, we can also look upon many of their contemporaries and fellow sojourners in a way that gives a fuller appreciation of the age. As Thomas L. Hankins has so well argued, "Biography provides the cross-sectional view" and "gives us a way to tie together the parallel currents of history at the level where the events and ideas occur." Such biography, he continued, well-crafted and carefully researched, "can be the ruin of all kinds of historical generalities."[4]

As to their interconnectedness, I readily admit to a degree of subjectivity and bias on my part. However, in researching one chapter after another, I began to notice commonalities of thought, interest, and ambition among such notable figures as Bolívar and Napoléon, explorers such as Humboldt and Williams, and artists such as Gericault and Coleridge. Sometimes such figures crossed paths, as with Beethoven and Elizavita at the Congress of Vienna or with Napoléon and Champollion. And they often looked to one another for inspiration. Some made discoveries and contributions so pertinent to the rise of The Church of Jesus Christ of Latter-day Saints that they begged inclusion in this work.

The danger in approaching history in this biographical manner is that it may come perilously close to hagiography, or the "great man theory," of explaining history, a short-circuiting excuse to understanding the complexities of the past that is anathema to so many historians today. Those who are antibiographical rigorously resist the idea that any one man or woman, or even a small cluster of people, could make much of a difference when in fact there were so many other causal factors, so many trends and tides and peoples that led to this or that change or development. They insist that this heroic mode of writing history is but foam tossed upon the ocean's surface as compared to the deeper currents of human history that transcend the personal and the biographical.

Robert J. Richards of the University of Chicago in his 2017 study on "The Role of Biography in Intellectual History" believes differently. He maintains that biography is critical to understanding the past. "The focus of an individual allows a coherent representation of science and of intellectual development at a moment in history." Biography is the "meeting

---

4. Hankins, "In Defense of Biography," 5–6.

place of psychological dispositions, political attitudes, religious beliefs and worries about theory and evidence. In such a mind," he contends, "one encounters a complex of interacting causes that offers the basis for realistic explanation."[5] Those so critical of biography would be hard pressed to dismiss the enormously negative consequences of the character, viewpoints, and prejudices of an Adolph Hitler or a Joseph Stalin in more contemporary times. The deliberate choices they made mattered enormously to the lives—and deaths—of millions of people; likewise, the positive consequences of such personalities as Winston Churchill and Abraham Lincoln.

Biography can also introduce something far beyond the cold calculations of cause and effect. That something else is emotion. The Prussian scientist Alexander von Humboldt, one of the characters we will be studying later in this work, once stated that the task of the historian is "to execute the task of his craft, [and to] compose the given events so as to move the reader's emotions in a way similar to that of reality itself."[6] Human beings are not always predictable or even reasonable in their actions. There are deep-seated psychological, spiritual, and emotional realities borne out of trials and difficulties, unique circumstances, and impressions that contribute to the decisions people make in their everyday lives. Capturing these conflicts and emotions, making them real to the reader who is subject to the same, creates not merely a believable tale but an unspoken truth. Thus, I maintain that some incredibly gifted men and women did indeed change the world and that a study of their lives, decisions, feelings, and emotions speaks to us today in powerful, very understandable ways.

If these individuals featured so prominently herein were, in one way or another, forerunners to the Restoration. They were very much human. They were not always of noble character, perfect in every way. Each one had serious flaws, yet each made, or at least supervised, significant contributions to the age.

Last but certainly not least is the challenge of writing in such a way as to give a book on a specific time period the quality of timelessness, to transcend the barriers of time by making it interesting to you, the reader—in short, to make it a good read! Regardless of whether the contributions of the many men and women discussed later on can be directly tied to Palmyra, the life stories of those selected for study must be both fascinating and instructional. Readers deserve nothing less.

These many challenges notwithstanding, a book such as this promises much to the careful reader who seeks to understand the qualities and essential meanings of the age. The many stars in this work will cluster around the following four dominant constellations in the skies of early nineteenth-century history. These four cornerstones are first, revolution and reform; second, Romanticism in its many literary and artistic forms and expressions; third, emancipation and the rebirth of freedom and independence; and lastly, religious revivalism as expressed in many different ways on both sides of the Atlantic. If the specific

---

5. Richards, "Role of Biography in Intellectual History," 2.
6. Humboldt, *Gesammelte Werke*, 1:6; as cited in Richards, "Role of Biography," 6.

year 1820 was one not known for revolution, the years leading up to it certainly were. The French, American, and Spanish American revolutions launched a series of independence movements that changed the world. Likewise, the impact of the industrial revolution, which began in England in the late eighteenth century, continued to be felt worldwide. With the shouts and slaughters of the French Revolution and the Napoleonic wars fading into history, 1820 was also a welcomed time of peace, a forward-looking time when many collectively sighed in hearty relief after the din of a war-torn world and in eager anticipation of the renewed forward march of progress. The age was a time of fledgling political independence and rising nationalism, with many a nation shaking off its long-held chains of colonial rule. It was also a time when artists were expressing themselves in nontraditional and less classical, rule-bound ways in what many scholars call the rise of Romanticism. Religious movements were defining anew what it meant to believe in God and in his word. With similar optimism that filled the air after the conclusion of the Second World War in the mid-twentieth century, "the year of our Lord 1820," as every almanac spoke of it, broke upon a weary world that was cautiously seeking new hopes, new dreams, and bold new visions—including Joseph Smith's.

The curtain will rise on Napoléon Bonaparte—"the dear corporal"—representing the spirit of the age. His star is once again on the ascendancy as scholars have begrudgingly reevaluated his efforts to spread the liberalizing and liberating reforms of the French Revolution. Hobbled by egotism and ultimately doomed by overarching ambition, Bonaparte nevertheless spread the spirit and the aims of the Revolution across countries and continents and in the process, changed the world. Despised by many yet adored by multitudes, Napoléon was more than a conqueror; he was a principle, and his life affected many others who follow in his train in this book.

Napoléon's invasion of Egypt paid an unexpected but enduring dividend in the discovery of the Rosetta Stone in 1798 as well as other remarkable archaeological wonders along the Nile. Jean-François Champollion's "Lettre a Monsieur Dacier," in which he proved he had decoded the ancient Egyptian hieroglyphs, signaled a linguistic triumph unparalleled in modern history. In the process, "the man from Grenoble" ushered in a new age of biblical archaeology and the study of Egyptian and other Middle Eastern ancient civilizations and their many secrets. His pioneering work had an enormous and surprising impact on Latter-day Saint history.

From Russia came that enigmatic Tsar Alexander I, Napoléon's worthy contender, who, while finally defeating Napoléon, admired his adversary almost as a god. Twisted in soul and spirit to his wandering end, Alexander Daniel's "king of the north," never escaped the haunting shadow of his father's murder. The "morning star of freedom" stumbled in self-acrimony and squandered a splendid opportunity to reform a serf-bound and suspicious imperial Russia. Yet his Holy Alliance, forged in the furnace of the Congress of Vienna, redrew boundaries and established the foundations of a profound peace, a peace that if not universally enjoyed, would endure for a century.

In the constellation of the arts, a cadre of geniuses redefined the boundaries of music, literature, art, and dance by rebelling against the classical, more rigid forms of expression. All were expressing themselves with the guns of Napoléon still being heard in the background. The Romantics were rewriting all the old rules by insisting on capturing the emotions, feelings, inspirations, and the human in all their manifestations. Theirs was a majestic, liberating portrayal of both the devil and the divine in human nature, a movement that broke older, more static modes of presentations. Beethoven's stirring Ninth Symphony, Coleridge's "Rime of the Ancient Mariner," and Géricault's enormous *Raft of the Medusa* are all enduring representations—embodiments might be the better word—of the transcendent artistic spirit of an age that produced masterpieces of music, literature, and art.

Meanwhile, Great Britain experienced a revolution of a different kind that was no less far-reaching in its consequences than the political eruptions that were then transforming Europe, South America, and the United States. Simultaneous with the courtly distractions of King George IV and the "tatterdamalion caravan" of his wife, Queen Caroline, was the Industrial Revolution. With the advent of the steam engine, the rise of factories, railroads, steamships, and the harnessing of hydro- and steam-generated power, this wrenching transformation not only profoundly altered how people worked, thought, traveled, and discovered, but it also, in the words of Paul Johnson—a master scholar of the age of 1820—marked the "birth of the modern": a tectonic economic shift away from an agricultural society to a new social and world order.

Napoléon also inspired Simón Bolívar. Bolívar's indomitable efforts led to a spirit of revolution that liberated much of South and Central America from the hated tyranny of Spanish rule that had corrupted itself seeking gold at enormous human cost. His daring marches across the Andes, his personal bravery and incredible victories on the battlefield, and his search for love are the stuff of legend and parallel the daring exploits of Napoléon. He may have fallen short in his dream to galvanize South America into a single, unified nation, but he did much to ensure the independence of many new nations from Spain.

The time also witnessed a new age of scientific inquiry as captured by that Prussian prince Alexander von Humboldt. In so many ways the father of modern science, Humboldt traveled the world, climbing mountains and volcanoes, navigating torturous rivers and endless streams, and describing ancient civilizations with such colorful detail and captivating descriptions that the whole world wondered in awe. In the process, Humboldt inspired and supported whole new constellations of scientists in their endless pursuit of truth, from Faraday to Darwin. He was indeed the great illuminator, one of the finest naturalists this world has ever known.

Meanwhile, the United States of America, after fighting a successful revolutionary war of its own against Great Britain, declared its independence and through the efforts of many gifted men, established a fitting and lasting constitution. America's remarkable westward expansion resulted from Napoléon's sale of the Louisiana Purchase and the stalemate with

Great Britain in the War of 1812, a conflict that emboldened the new republic while giving rise to Canada, America's northern neighbor. Yet had it not been for the brilliant skills of that great compromiser Henry Clay, the United States probably may well have dismembered itself in 1820 in a bitter sectional conflict between the North and the South over the matter of slavery.

Another main current of thought coursing through much of this study will be the religious spirit of the age. I am, after all, a church historian, and this book is written primarily to a believing audience. It will pursue the rise of religious revivalism, beginning with Charles Wesley, George Whitefield, and the Methodist revivals in Great Britain that challenged the supremacy of the established Church of England and inspired the conversions of Reverend John Newton and his protégé William Wilberforce. With "amazing grace"[7] and persistent tact and political pressure, Wilberforce, Hannah Moore, and the Clapham Sect finally succeeded in persuading the British Parliament to abolish the slave trade in 1807. Additionally, the remarkable conversion of Coleridge, that "archangel a little damaged," and the rise of the Broad Church Movement show a religious theme that resisted any narrow prescriptions of Christian thought. This religious impulse also gave rise to the British Foreign Bible Society, the American Bible Society, and the remarkable, worldwide dissemination of the Holy Bible from Polynesia to Palmyra. This religious tenor of the time also led me to study the life of Reverend John Williams and others of similar sterling faith in the London Missionary Society, with its relentless efforts to spread the Christian gospel in the South Pacific, Asia, and Africa.

That same spirit of revivalism and revelation prompted the likes of Jonathan Edwards, in the American colonies, to initiate the Great Awakening. Later came the Methodist camp meetings and a Second Great Awakening that began in Kentucky and quickly reached northward. Spreading across upstate New York like Halley's Comet in the midnight sky was a spirit of religious revivalism so dramatic and intense that scholars still refer to it as the burned-over district, a place and time of unparalleled religious enthusiasm and devotion.

Inheriting this atmosphere of religious inquiry and excitement was young Joseph Smith Jr., who retired to his own sacred grove near Rochester, New York, in the spring of 1820 in a determination to ask his God which of all the many faiths he should join. While the answer to his prayer led to the sunrise of a new world religion, his quest must also be seen as part of a time that was changing old ways, mannerisms, and streams of thought in a wide range of human endeavor. It was a time that fostered new revolutions in politics, economics, the arts, science, and religion.

We will commence our study with a lonely little man living out his life on a remote island of the South Atlantic Ocean—an enormous personality that time will never let us forget.

---

7. Newton, "Amazing Grace."

ACKNOWLEDGMENTS

I first conceived of the idea of writing a book to commemorate the two hundredth anniversary of Joseph Smith's First Vision shortly after joining the faculty of Religious Education at Brigham Young University more than twenty years ago. It has been an on-and-off again project ever since, with two other book publications and several published articles consuming my attention along the way. During several of those years, I continued to teach a full load of four-to-five classes per semester, filled my share of various committee assignments, and served as department chair and associate dean, which, as most academic administrators will quickly attest, cam be detrimental to serious publication efforts. Consequently, the work limped along at a frustratingly slow pace. Indeed, this book has been so many years in the making that I may have forgotten some of those who helped me along the way.

 This book would not have been possible without the support of my employer, Brigham Young University. Former deans Robert Millet, Andy Skinner, Terry Ball, Brent Top, and currently Dan Judd of Religious Education were consistent in their support of this endeavor. Thanks also to Paul Peterson, Arnie Garr, and Alex Baugh, former and present chairs of the Department of Church History and Doctrine, who supported my labors with indispensable study leave opportunities, fellowships, and other forms of substantial financial support. I wish also to thank the Office of Research and Creative Activities (ORCA) for granting me a sizable mentoring grant with which I was able to hire several student research assistants for an entire semester. I thank Patty Smith of the Faculty Support Center for typing several chapters. I thank Susan Bettis and Josh McDaniel, our former and present college comptroller, who have helped handle the financial intricacies of paying research help outside the country. Linda Godfrey and Connie Brace, department secretaries past and present, have also been very helpful.

I want to give especial thanks to Scott C. Esplin, director of the Religious Studies Center, who committed to publishing this work. He arranged to have the manuscript reviewed by seasoned scholars who gave me invaluable feedback, constructive criticisms, and encouragement. Several members of my own faculty read one or more chapters and likewise provided helpful suggestions. Scott's capable team of professionals, including Joany O. Pinegar, R. Devan Jensen, Emily V. Strong, Brent R. Nordgren, Emily Cook, Julie Newman, Andrew Johnson, Sarah Johnson, and Meghan Wilson were remarkably helpful—Devan and Emily Strong especially so. Rachel Lyon was the indexer. Deseret Book has also been encouraging of the project since it was first proposed.

Thanks to financial support from the Frederick W. and Jolene Edmunds Rockwood Family Foundation, the Religious Studies Center has been able to print a beautiful book of unusual quality, worthy of the highest expectations, and something of which I am proud. Their financial support has also enabled me to hire excellent research assistance.

Several undergraduate students here at Brigham Young University have served as research assistants through the years. These have included David Choules, Grant Eckstein, Chontal Green, Nate Irvin, Sheri Rowley, Nick Valetta, Lisa Love (Snyder), Beth Lott, Amber Siddell, Megan Shumway, and Christian Solomon. Others who have assisted me include Arran Wytinck in Canada, Hugh Hannesson, Dr. Giovanni Tata, and my research assistants overseas, who have included Sam Stoumont and Eleanor Balmy in Paris and Andrea and Stefano Raimondi in Turin, Italy. I am happy to report that Sam and Eleanor, who did not know each other before working for me, are now married to one another, which shows how lively and romantic staid and stuffy archives and libraries can become. Huguette Tornar of Paris has been particularly helpful as a researcher both in Paris and Geneva, Switzerland, and in translating French documents into English.

I wish to once again thank Wendy Top, my loyal and longest-serving research assistant, who has helped me in so many ways over the past few years, not only with this project but with others along the way. Her research expertise, patience, and abiding cheerfulness have been indispensable.

A work of this magnitude could not have come about without the support of archival and library staff at the following institutions—in the *United States*: the Huntington Library in San Marino, California where I wrote most of the chapters; the Harold B. Lee Library (Brigham Young University), especially Interlibrary Loan and Document Delivery Services; the Church History Library of The Church of Jesus Christ of Latter-day Saints; the New York Historical Society (New York City); the New York Public Library; the American Philosophical Society (Philadelphia); the American Antiquarian Society (Worcester, Massachusetts); the Library of Congress (Washington, DC); the National Archives and Records Services (Washington, DC); the Newberry Library (Chicago); the Beinecke Library, Yale University (New Haven, Connecticut); and the Schaffer Library, Union College (Schenectady, New

York); in *France*: Les Archives Nationales in Paris, France; Le Centre Historique des Archives (Militaire) at Vincennes, France; Le Centre des Archives Diplomatiques de Nantes; the Archives of the Louvres Museum (Paris); La Bibliotheque Nationale de France; in *England***:** the British Library (London); the British National Archives (Kew, England); Bodleian Special Collections, the Sackler Library, and Harris Manchester College, Oxford University; the John Rylands University Library, the University of Manchester; in *Italy*: the State Archives of Turin (Italy); the Egyptian Museum (Turin); Cittadi Torino (City Archives of Turin); the city archives of Castellamonte, Italy; and in *Switzerland*: La Bibliotheque de Geneve.

Finally, to my wife, Patricia, I will ever owe my love and gratitude for putting up with my academic pursuits. She has often traveled with me on research trips and been my loyal amanuensis and careful researcher at various times and several places. She had also been a careful first editor of much of my writings. Furthermore, she has patiently endured my long ramblings, my living in the past when so much in the present has been neglected, and my long absences researching here and there and everywhere from hearth and home. She has ever been my constant first support and encourager. Thank you, sweetheart.

The Emperor Napoleon in His Study at the Tuileries, by Jacques-Louis David.

LE PETIT CAPORAL

NAPOLÉON BONAPARTE

By the spring of 1820, Napoléon Bonaparte's health had begun to wane. Banished to the tiny, windswept island of St. Helena, far from anywhere in the South Atlantic, the former emperor of France languished in exile, reduced to the petty disciplines of a third-rate British officer. Napoléon spent his declining days riding horseback under the gaze of an uneasy regiment of British redcoats, gardening at Longwood—his small villa residence—and dictating his memoirs. He could only hope for better news from Europe—perhaps a release and safe passage to America.

What had brought him to this? And what is it about Napoléon that has since caused more biographies to be written about him than any other person in history except Jesus Christ? Napoléon's story is one for the ages, but the year 1820 can claim him as one of its most celebrated figures and the dominant spirit of the age, one forged in the fiery furnace of the French Revolution who went on to change the history of not only France but also the world.

"PUSS IN BOOTS"

Having just returned from attending mass, Letizia Buonaparte gave birth to her fourth child, her second son, in her small home in Ajaccio, on the island of Corsica, on 15 August 1769. Her husband, Carlo Buonaparte, though "very far from rich," had gained a reputation for himself, having been elected to the council of twelve nobles in Corsica, which had only recently been wrested by the French from the hated Genoese. Ironically, they named their new son Nabulion, later christened Napoléon Bonaparte, after an uncle who had recently fought against the conquering French forces.[1]

As the second oldest son of a family of eight children—five brothers and three sisters—Napoléon grew up in an Italian-speaking, Roman Catholic home. Letizia was a strict disciplinarian whose deep maternal affections instilled in him a love for his mother that would last a lifetime. Although she tried to develop religious faith in the lad, his interests were ever more inclined to the military than to the church. While his brothers were drawing "grotesque figures on the walls of a large empty room which she had set apart for them to play in, Napoléon drew only soldiers ranged in order of battle."[2] She encouraged his interests by securing for him a toy drum and a wooden saber. All through his growing up years, Letizia tried hard to teach him and all her other children a Christian sense of faith and morality as well as honor, fidelity, courage, and a strong sense of justice.

Meanwhile, Napoléon became increasingly aware of his father's library, numbering over one thousand titles. No one knows just what books he read as a boy, but they were obviously instrumental in providing him an early worldview and in introducing him to some of the world's greatest minds in politics, art, and literature. His greatest loves were history and geography.

When Napoléon was only nine years old, his watchful father determined to enroll him and his older brother Joseph in the Brienne Military Academy in Autun, France, if for no other reason than to help his sons become more proficient in French. Run by friars of the Roman Catholic Church, this elementary-school–like experience taught Napoléon far more than French (though he ever afterward spoke French with a thick Corsican accent, much to his embarrassment), for it was while at Brienne that he showed surprising skills in mathematics and military maneuvers. An "obedient, affable, straight forward and grateful" student, Napoléon fancied a career in writing by the time he graduated (middle of his class) and had come to believe less in God and more in France and its place of supremacy in the world.[3]

Upon graduation, Napoléon was one of only five chosen to continue military training at l'Ecole militaire de Paris in 1784. He was then only fifteen years old. Initially inclined to the navy, Napoléon later gravitated toward an interest in artillery warfare, and by the time he was commissioned a second lieutenant the following year, he had selected a career in the army. Never more than 5 feet, 6 inches tall, Napoléon took more than enough ribbing from

---

1. Cronin, *Napoleon*, 21–22. "An analysis of Napoleonic autographs, of which thousands exist, shows that he always signed himself Buonaparte, then later Bonaparte. This was the name by which all his friends, and even his first wife, Josephine, knew him and addressed him, both officially and familiarly. . . . When he became emperor, he reluctantly adopted Napoleon as his name." Johnson, *Napoleon*, 4.
2. Williams, *Women Bonapartes*, 39.
3. Cronin, *Napoleon*, 34. There is some evidence to show that a Breton nobleman, the comte de Marbeuf, may also have played a role in funding the young boy's early education. See Johnson, *Napoleon*, 7–8.

his fellow officers as well as the teasing of his young female admirers, who called him "puss in boots."[4]

With the death of his father in 1785, Lieutenant Bonaparte assumed the financial obligations of the family. As he read ever more seriously, including Plato, Rousseau, Voltaire, and James Macpherson, he concluded that what most ailed France was the virtually unlimited, absolute power of the king and the excessive privileges of the aristocracy and clergy. What France needed most urgently, he came to believe, was a new constitution, one that would ensure greater liberties, freedoms, and economic opportunities for the so-called third estate—the common people. Soon he was composing such essays as "Man Is Born to Be Happy" and "Morality Will Exist When Governments Are Free."[5]

In 1789 his regiment was called up to quell some of the winter food riots that were then erupting in various parts of the country. Although he disliked King Louis XVI's abuse of executive power, Napoléon deplored chaos, anarchy, and mob rule even more. Before long, he found himself in the middle of a violent political upheaval that was rapidly spinning out of control, one destined to change modern European society forever.

NAPOLÉON AND THE FRENCH REVOLUTION

The seeds of the French Revolution may be traced to the embedded injustices of ancient feudal times. Over the centuries, French society had become stratified into three categories: "clerics who prayed, nobles who fought, and commoners who labored."[6] Known as the first, second, and third estates respectively, the first two—the Roman Catholic Church clergy of bishops, priests, nuns, and friars and the landed gentry and nobility—came to be regarded as the "privileged orders," which, if not above the law, certainly enjoyed a disproportionate share of benefits. These included much lower taxation rates, feudal powers over laborers, and immunity from many forms of legal prosecution.[7]

The third estate—the commoners—made up 98 percent of the nation's population of twenty-seven million people (a true superpower in its time)[8] but enjoyed little, if any, individual power and only a small voice in the three-chambered French legislature. This old way of doing things—the so-called *ancien régime*—included a cumbersome judicial order, an inefficient system of local governments, an excessively complicated method of road tolls, and a porous, unfair, and punitive system of taxation. It also handicapped enterprising

---

4. Markham, *Napoleon*, 18–19.
5. Cronin, *Napoleon*, 52. In these formative years, Napoléon was a strong supporter of the republican (antimonarchist) movement. Once arrested for supporting other young revolutionaries, he later admitted, "When I was young I was a revolutionary from ignorance and ambition." Seward, *Napoleon's Family*, 23.
6. Jones, *French Revolution*, 4. See Hunt, *French Revolution*, 3–5.
7. "Because of their special status as mediators between God and humanity, members of the clergy enjoyed exemption from most taxes." Popkin, *Short History*, 9.
8. Jones, *French Revolution*, 4.

merchants and laborers, perpetuated vested class interests, stubbornly resisted reform, and caused France to lag behind England in enjoying the economic benefits of the Industrial Revolution. Overseeing and superintending it all was the Bourbon absolute monarchy, with its several tiers of overpaid regulators and ministers and a royal army officered by privileged sons of the landed gentry and French nobility.

Aware of the rising popular chorus for change and in desperate need for increased revenue, the French government considered making real reforms in 1787, particularly with respect to fairer taxation. The only way to solve the problem, however, was for the king to reconvene the French Parliament—the Estates General—in 1789.[9] In the meantime, bread riots had broken out all over the country following poor harvests and a punishingly cold winter. In addition, common citizens began promoting a very successful pamphlet campaign aimed at doubling the power of the third estate's voice in government at the expense of the clergy and aristocracy. With such actions, "the time-bomb of revolution . . . started ticking."[10]

The complexities of the French Revolution may be simplified by dividing its history into four distinct phases: (1) the Bastille (1789), (2) the Reform (1789–91), (3) the Reign of Terror (1792–94), and (4) the Restoration (1794–99). When at last the Estates General convened at Versailles on 5 May 1789, the third estate's elected deputies virtually abolished the other two estates and took on the title of National Assembly. Under their spirited leader, Honoré Gabriel Riqueti, comte de Mirabeau, the commoners defied the king's order to disband, and in the famous Tennis Court Oath on 20 June, they refused to dismiss until they had given France a constitution. Thereupon the king called in the army on 27 June to expel the stubborn deputies at the point of gun and bayonet. Instead of disseminating, however, the deputies held firm and on 9 July reconstituted themselves as the National Constituent Assembly. The assembly's courageous action in the face of determined royal opposition inspired all of Paris to arise with indignation. Then on 14 July 1789, Parisians stormed the Bastille, a prison fortress in central Paris and a symbol of everything that was hated about the *ancien régime*. They overpowered and killed the guards and razed the Bastille. As if on cue, all across the country peasants rose up in arms against their feudal masters and seigneurs. They burned fields and chateaux indiscriminately in what came to be known as the "Great Fear."[11]

Truly, the time for reform had given way to a fiery revolution that engulfed France as never seen before. Law and order fell victim to a pell-mell rush for liberty as the awesome, fearful power of the people rose up in anger, rushing everywhere. Men and women throughout the tired, old country were willing to countenance the destruction of an entire way of

---

9. Though on the losing side of the Seven Years' War with England (1756–63), France supported the American War of Independence (1776–83) against England. These wars came at a steep financial price—as most wars invariably do—to the point that King Louis XVI's government fell into virtual bankruptcy. The only solution was to increase revenue by drastically reforming an archaic system of taxation that had plagued the country for centuries.
10. Jones, *French Revolution*, 25.
11. Popkin, *Short History*, 35.

The Storming of the Bastille, or *Prise de la Bastille* (1789), by Jean-Pierre Houël.

life in hopes of a new, if unpredictable, more equitable, more just, more egalitarian world. Napoléon and much of the army could only watch the fires light up the skies all over France.

Within a month of the storming of the Bastille, the National Constituent Assembly convened in what might be called the Reform, or second phase of the Revolution. Painfully aware of the spirit of insurrection engulfing France, the deputies moved swiftly in doing away with all forms of feudal society in what has been termed "the bonfire of privilege."[12]

---

12. Jones, *French Revolution*, 31. Thomas Jefferson was in Paris at the time of the storming of Bastille and at first was wildly in favor of the Revolution. However, unlike the American Revolution, which was a movement of independence from Great Britain, the French Revolution took on a thousand years of privilege from an entire class society that was thoroughly guarded by entrenched special interests. As one historian of the age wrote, "No event in European history ever caused such a change in the political thought of the ruling classes as did the French Revolution." Fueter, *World History*, 16. By nature, the French Revolution would be a far bloodier affair than its American counterpart. As the intensity and bloodletting of the French Revolution unfolded, American support waned. See Kramer, "French Revolution," in Klaits and Haltzel, *Global Ramifications*.

In short order, the National Constituent Assembly abolished a plethora of hated taxes and ordered the nobility to pay its fair share. It then reorganized the country administratively by abolishing the old provinces and establishing a new, more efficient governmental structure, liberalizing the terms of citizenship, mandating the popular election of local officials as well as justices of the peace, and abolishing hereditable nobility altogether with its titles and symbols. No less sweeping and controversial, the National Constituent Assembly passed the "Civil Constitution of the Clergy," which nationalized the Roman Catholic Church by confiscating its vast, tax-free land holdings, abolishing its monastic orders, and mandating the election of its bishops and priests—in short, turning the clergy into employees of the state. Although there was still popular goodwill for the Crown, the National Constituent Assembly envisioned a constitutional monarchy with reduced powers and, looking to the US Declaration of Independence as a model, issued its famous Declaration of the Rights of Man and Citizen on 26 August 1789.

What triggered the violent third stage of the Revolution was the royal family's opposition to the course of the uprising and its clumsy effort to escape the country in 1791. News of the king's written renunciation of the aims of the Revolution and of the royal family's subsequent failed defection, along with the Austrian-born Queen Marie-Antoinette's treasonous correspondence with Austrian military forces, shook the nation to its core. Confidence in the monarchy plummeted everywhere. Captured in June of that year at Varennes just before crossing the border into the Netherlands, the royal family was arrested, paraded in disgrace, and promptly imprisoned without trial.[13]

The Legislative Assembly then voted to suspend King Louis XVI from his royal functions and to call nationwide elections for yet another assembly that would determine the fate of the monarchy, thus in effect scrapping the constitution of 1791. In this newly elected National Convention, the Jacobins, or Parisian radicals—led by such puritanical moralists as Georges Danton, Maximilien Robespierre, and others—seized parliamentary control, abolished the monarchy and every symbol of it, and declared France a republic on 20 September 1792. Condemning the king and queen as traitors to France, the National Convention took the drastic action of executing King Louis "the Faithless" by guillotine on 21 January 1793, followed by the execution of his wife—the hated Marie-Antoinette—on 16 October, in the public square now more euphemistically known as the Place de la Concorde. These actions hurled a ghastly challenge to European monarchists everywhere. Soon afterward, the Jacobins set up a new, powerful executive body ironically called the Committee of Public Safety, which unleashed the Reign of Terror by executing imprisoned noblemen, clergy, and others who were considered even slightly counterrevolutionary.

---

13. King Louis XVI and Queen Marie-Antoinette had "greatly underestimated the extent of popular support for the Revolution" and wrongly believed that a great counter-revolution would restore them back to power. Tackett, *When the King Took Flight*, 56. See also Tackett, *Coming of the Terror in the French Revolution*, chapters 3 and 4 in particular.

Execution of Louis XVI, by Isidore Stanislas Helman.

By 1793 the rebellion had become a veritable civil war waged with "unrelenting cruelty on both sides."[14] The drastic methods used to put down the rebellion, "which included mass drownings of prisoners in the Loire River and the burning down of entire villages, together with the massacre of their inhabitants, were the bloodiest episodes of the revolution. The estimates suggest that the fighting in the Vendée may have claimed over 200,000 lives."[15]

During the second year of the Reign of Terror, "perhaps half a million men and women saw the inside of a cell . . . and around 16,000 mounted the steps of the guillotine. Many more were killed during spectacular acts of collective repression" by both republicans and royalists.[16] Robespierre eventually gained total control over the blood bath that the Revolution was fast becoming, ordering the execution of hundreds of innocent citizens, Danton included.

One of the most bizarre acts of the Committee on Public Safety was its dechristianization campaign. Initiated by "revolutionary militants" in outlying areas, the movement blamed the Roman Catholic Church for abuses and subjugations of all kinds. More to the point, revolutionaries knew that more than half the parish clergymen in France had refused to swear a loyalty oath in the words specified by the National Constituent Assembly and believed that refractory priests, especially in western France, were plotting sedition and counterrevolutionary

---

14. Popkin, *Short History*, 76.
15. Popkin, *Short History*, 76.
16. Jones, *French Revolution*, 8.

activities.[17] This may explain why they closed churches, defrocked priests, transformed church buildings into granaries, and even rechristened the venerable Notre Dame Cathedral a "Temple of Reason."[18] Even the Christian calendar was abolished, and a new secular version was adopted in which Sundays were done away with and years were counted from the birth year of the new republic.[19] It seemed almost everyone was suspected of some treasonable act or another. Robespierre himself became a victim of his own excesses and was executed late in Thermidor year II (July 1794). Meanwhile, the Thermidorian Convention (made up of the legislators who had survived Robespierre) drafted the Constitution of 1795, aimed at preventing the rise of another dictatorial government.

Gradually, under such leaders as Abbé Sieyès, the French citizenry revolted against these excesses of the Reign of Terror. More moderate voices—the Girondists—prevailed and regained control of government, freed thousands of prisoners, reopened many of the churches, tore down the scaffolds of execution, renamed the Place de la Révolution (where the guillotine had once stood) the Place de la Concorde, and drafted yet another constitution calling for the executive power, now void of a king, to be vested in a Directory of five men elected by the legislature, renamed the Chamber of Five Hundred.

"THE WHIFF OF GRAPESHOT"

With the resurgence of royalist influence in the Chamber of Five Hundred and the massing of Austrian and Prussian royalist armies to the east with the British fleet prowling the coastlines of France, the Directory felt threatened from within and without. When an army of twenty thousand royalist national guardsmen took control over much of Paris, the desperate Directory sought help from those in the military who were supportive of the spirit of the Revolution.

Ever the realist, Napoléon knew which way the political winds were blowing, although he was legitimately a supporter of the republican cause.[20] Promoted to the rank of captain in 1792, he had witnessed firsthand the near anarchy of the food riots in Paris, and he sympathized with the overthrow—though not the execution—of the king and queen. His regiment was called up in 1794 to help drive back a British force of eighteen thousand troops that had landed in Toulon, in southern France. As second in command in charge of hillside batteries, Napoléon successfully shelled the British fleet below before leading his men in fierce hand-to-hand combat, during which he suffered a bayonet stab to his left thigh, the only wound of

---

17. Tackett, *When the King Took Flight*, 167.
18. Popkin, *Short History*, 86.
19. Jones, *French Revolution*, 60–62.
20. In the early days of the Revolution, Napoléon Bonaparte was "a ferocious republican" and anti-revolutionary. He was arrested for his close support of Robespierre but was released soon after. Seward, *Napoleon's Family*, 22.

his illustrious military career. Courageous and unflinching in battle, he harbored an almost fatalistic view toward death—"If your number is up, no point in worrying."[21]

Napoléon's valor and successful use of ballistics in the "mathematics of warfare" soon led to his promotion to brigadier general. Word of his prorepublican sympathies and military expertise quickly reached Paris, where the new Directory was contending against mounting opposition. Consequently, the Directory called on Napoléon to rush to the capital and put down the royalist uprising. Soon in command of his own troops in the streets of Paris, Napoléon employed "the whiff of grapeshot," in which he fired both gun and cannon indiscriminately upon Parisians, successfully crushing the "rising of Vendémiaire."[22] With the Parisian uprisings quashed, a desperate Directory immediately promoted Napoléon to general of the French forces in Italy, where enemy forces were massing for war.

On the Italian front, Napoléon's brilliance and daring as a military commander began to shine. Though his forces were significantly outnumbered, Napoléon routed not one but three opposing Austrian and papal armies and earned the zealous admiration of his troops at the Bridge of Lodi, where his personal bravery earned him the title *le petit caporal* (the dear corporal). In quick succession, Napoléon pushed southward, seizing Milan, Turin, Mantua, and other papal state cities and "liberating" most of Italy. Forced to capitulate, a stunned Austria soon surrendered both the Netherlands and the Milanese to the French forces.

When Napoléon returned in triumph to Paris in late 1797, he was lionized everywhere as savior of the Revolution and France, and he then very likely could have seized control of the faltering government, but he cunningly chose not to do so. As one scholar put it, "he knew the pear was not ripe."[23] When asked to seriously consider the advantages of attacking and crippling Great Britain, Napoléon deferred, respecting well the one true lifeline of Britain's sure defense—its glorious navy. Rather, he turned his sights eastward to Egypt, from which he could mount an attack on Asiatic trade routes, thereby disrupting Britain's lucrative cotton trade with India and the Far East. The date of his Mediterranean project was so closely guarded that not even Napoléon's fellow commanders knew of it until the very day of sailing on 19 May 1798. Successfully evading the British fleet and the watchful eye of Admiral Horatio Nelson, Napoléon commanded a force of thirteen ships, four hundred transports, an army of thirty-eight thousand men, and a corps of many of France's leading scientists—"a complete *encyclopédie vivante*, equipped with libraries and instruments"—

---

21. Cronin, *Napoleon*, 76.
22. "Bonaparte preferred musket balls encased in tins, known as canister or caseshot, or in canvas bags, known as grapeshot. The advantage of grapeshot was that it scattered over a wide area, tending to produce a lot of blood and often maiming its victims, but had to be fired at close range. It rarely killed and thus, while effective as drastic crowd control, did not enable opponents to create the myth of a 'massacre.' Its aim was to frighten and disperse. But it ended the attempted coup forthwith, and with it the Revolution itself: the era of the mob yielded to a new era of order under fear." Johnson, *Napoleon*, 26–27.
23. Markham, *Napoleon*, 57.

to further the cause of France, of modern science, and, of course, of Napoléon himself.[24] Though Nelson later destroyed the French fleet at Aboukir Bay at the Battle of the Nile, Napoléon, "who took to the desert as most men do who love the sea,"[25] easily conquered the Mamluks of Alexandria and Cairo and the Turks of Aboukir and likely would have overrun Syria had he been able to retain sufficient naval power.

Upon hearing that the French government was teetering and that the Directory was in jeopardy from yet another Austrian invasion, Napoléon decided to return to Paris, where he captured the hearts of a grateful, adoring nation that heralded his return once again as a conquering hero and the savior of France. At the request of the Directory, now more beholden to him than ever before, Napoléon dissolved the legislature in his famous coup d'état of 18 Brumaire (9 November) 1799. Now holding the full power of the military, he concentrated the executive power of the former Directory into a new three-man consulate or triumvirate with himself as the first, or most powerful, of the consuls. He may have saved the government, but he was a self-serving savior.[26]

CONSOLIDATOR OF THE REVOLUTION

In his meteoric rise to power, Napoléon ever regarded himself as "the consolidator of the Revolution," or, as many called him, its "savior."[27] Blessed with an extraordinary capacity for work, a prodigious memory, and an impressive grasp of the complexities of contemporary politics, Napoléon set out to preserve the ideals and gains of the Revolution. As important as was his Concordat with the Roman Catholic Church in July 1801, in which many of the egregious policies of dechristianization were overturned, his most long-lasting, far-reaching accomplishment was the establishment of the Civil, or Napoleonic, Code of 1804, which "gave legal expression" and safeguards "to the social gains of the Revolution."[28] These included the equality of all under the law, the sanctity of property and individual ownership, freedom of commerce and contract, freedom of career, and the strengthened place of family, particularly the authority of the husband and father. One can well argue that the Consulate, led by Napoléon, secured virtually all the gains of the Revolution—*liberté, égalité, et fraternité*.

Few people, however, seemed to have noticed or even cared that their conquering hero was moving France away from a democracy and toward a dictatorship of his own creation, or as one scholar has stated, "a dazzling embodiment of the enlightened despot in action."[29] But

---

24. Markham, *Napoleon*, 59. See chapter 2.
25. Cronin, *Napoleon*, 152.
26. Crook, *Napoleon Comes to Power*, 3.
27. Jones, *French Revolution*, 76.
28. Jones, *French Revolution*, 83.
29. Markham, *Napoleon*, 95.

once he had declared himself sole consul in 1802 and crowned himself emperor of France in December 1804 in the Cathedral of Notre Dame, few could anymore doubt that the French Revolution was over and that a new form of monarchy was now firmly in control.

Yet, for all the adoring crowds and the fierce loyalty of his troops, Napoléon was a lonely man. His very successes set him apart from many of his military and political colleagues, who feared or were jealous of him, and by others who began to revere him as something almost more than a man. Even his enemies were beginning to see in him as a figure the likes of which the world had not seen in a very long time. Had he married well, his wife may have been his best counselor. The fact is, however, that the first consul of France was suspicious of most women, certainly of women in authority.

Napoléon may have had affairs of his own, but he was not the kind of man to be distracted by sex. It never dominated him, although many women were attracted to him, or at least to his power, and would have been more than willing to be mistresses despite his foul language, quick temper, and dismissive style. His penetrating gaze, fine Corsican skin, and neatness in dress made for an impressive figure.[30]

The first woman he loved—his brother's wife, Désirée—he could not have. But he gave his heart in marriage in 1796 to Josephine, a widow six years his senior with two small children, whose husband had been earlier executed during the Revolution. She admired the way he loved her and also the way he rose in power, but she never fully loved him in return. She had one eye for expensive things and another for handsome young men. News of her torrid extramarital fling with Hippolyte Charles, a handsome, young officer and "accomplished womanizer," made it all the way to Egypt and may well have been a factor in Napoléon's abrupt return to Paris in 1799.[31] Although he captured the hearts of a grateful nation, he never could command Josephine's deepest affections. Their marriage was at best one of tepid affection bordering on distrust. Their marriage ended in divorce in 1809 with Josephine unable to bare a son, and Napoléon married Marie-Louise, an immature, sixteen-year-old schoolgirl and daughter of the Austrian king, in what was a blatant political

Josephine Bonaparte. *Joséphine de Beauharnais vers 1809*, by Antoine-Jean Gros.

---

30. "Napoleon had an established reputation for continence.... It rarely seems that carnal impulse troubled him hardly at all." Aubry, *St. Helena*, 210, 292.
31. Seward, *Napoleon's Family*, 39.

relationship of convenience. Although she bore him a son—Napoléon II—she was as unfaithful to Napoléon as Josephine had been, choosing to love a much younger man.

Thus, even in matrimony, France's favorite son was a lonely figure. The women and men who might have mellowed him were unable, unwilling, and incapable of doing so. And Letizia, his mother, could not dictate to him. The fact is he was too proud for love, "except perhaps, a little, with Josephine," too contemptuous of both men and women, and too involved with the affairs of state rather than with personal relationships.[32]

"VIVE L'EMPEREUR" (1800–1811)

It was on the blood-soaked battlefields of Europe where Napoléon, "the God of Modern War," won the begrudging respect of his enemies and the unending admiration of history.[33] One of his most critical biographers admitted: "[One] cannot refuse to acknowledge that no man ever comprehended more clearly the splendid science of war; [one] cannot fail to bow to the genius which conceived and executed the Italian campaign, which fought the classic battles of Austerlitz, Jena and Wagram. These deeds are great epics. They move in noble, measured lines and stir us by their might and perfection. It is only a genius of the most magnificent order which could handle men and materials as Napoleon did."[34]

What accounts for his successes? One key factor was his early mastering of the element of surprise. Abrupt and impatient to a fault and almost carelessly decisive, he could hardly ever be second-guessed. When Austria redeclared war on France in 1800, he did the unthinkable by marching his army, Carthaginian-like, across the snow-packed Swiss Alps into northern Italy, shocking his enemies by attacking them from the rear. His victory at the Battle of Marengo near Turin was subsequently a most resounding one.

After the collapse of the Peace of Amiens (1802), the British determined to crush Napoléon by bankrolling the armies of Austria and Russia in the so-called Third Coalition against France. In response, Napoléon once more seriously considered invading England, this time at the head of a Grande Armée of 120,000 battle-hardened veterans. Had not Nelson, by this time a mighty legend in his own right, shattered the combined French and Spanish fleet at Trafalgar off the coast of Spain in October 1805 in one of the most brilliant naval victories of all time, Napoléon may well have crossed the English Channel.

Pretending to ignore the British victory, Napoléon, within weeks of Trafalgar, performed, not once but twice, a no less memorable victory on land. First against superior numbers, he launched a daring surprise attack and defeated General Mack and the Austrian armies at Ulm in late October, and thereafter he marched into Vienna without a fight. Next, he routed the Russian armies at Austerlitz in early December 1805. By the end of 1806, Napoléon occupied Berlin.

---

32. Tulard, *Napoleon*, 232.
33. Becke, *Napoleon's Waterloo*, 165.
34. Tarbell, *Life of Napoleon Bonaparte*, 291.

His stunning victories at Ulm and Austerlitz underscore another reason for his success: Napoléon was a master strategist. His "consummate skill," remarked one astute observer, "was . . . in estimating and combining time, distance, and number; in calculating the movements of great armies; . . . with a promptitude that was quite surprising. A single glance through his telescope in the midst of smoke and confusion, gave him instantly the actual state of affairs, at moments of greatest danger."[35] Napoléon, albeit a risk-taker, left little to chance. He planned for victory. In his mind, a campaign was faulty "unless it anticipated everything that the enemy might do and provided the means of outmaneuvering him."[36]

A third factor for success was that he acted courageously and lightning with speed. "My troops have moved as rapidly as my thoughts,"[37] he once declared. He was at his best when outnumbered for he knew well how to divide and conquer. His habit was to spread out his forces when marching, then quickly concentrate them into attacking relentlessly with splendid cavalry rushes and incredibly accurate artillery fire on one column and flank of

The Battle of Austerlitz, 2nd December 1805, by François Gérard.

---

35. Review of *Relation Circonstanciée de la Campagne de 1813 en Saxe* by M. Le Baron d'Odeleben and Aubert de Vitry, 216.
36. Luvaas, "Napoleon on the Art of Command," 31.
37. Cronin, *Napoleon,* 128.

the enemy, then turning with full force on another.[38] Even at night, by the light of torch fire, Napoléon's field headquarters always featured a large table with a large map of the theatre of war spread out upon it with troop positions marked with different colored pens. From there, Napoléon, who seldom slept, would redeploy, amass his forces on another front, and, come the dawn, take full advantage of the situation, surprising his enemy. The elements of speed, surprise, careful strategy, and flexibility, along with his superb use of the cavalry and his deadly use of artillery consistently frustrated and overwhelmed his opposing forces. Indeed he once said, "It is with artillery that war is made."[39]

Napoléon was more than a brilliant tactical strategist. He brought a degree of passion, emotion, and enthusiasm to the front that his men had seldom, if ever, seen before. As one American journalist wrote, "We have never heard of a general who possessed the love and confidence of his soldiers like Bonaparte. . . . Without the love of his army he could have done nothing—with it, everything."[40] As much a father figure as a commander, Napoléon loved his men, and in return many gave their lives for him. Endowed with an incredible memory, he could call many of even the lowest ranking officers by name. Many a time he would scratch out written notes of commendation and affection for those showing true gallantry in battle, and in his famous bulletins, Napoléon reported on their bravery for all the world to read. He constantly rewarded them with advancement or with the Legion of Honour. He ensured their widows were given lifetime pensions; his successful marshals were promised duchies; and surviving children were given the right to use his name.[41]

Napoléon was not immune to the sufferings, brutality, and horrors of war. He wrote in a letter to Josephine, "One suffers and the soul is oppressed to see so many victims."[42] He nevertheless viewed human life as the necessary currency for victory. "A man such as I am does not concern himself much about the lives of a million men," he once remarked.[43] He was ruthless and "did not economize the lives of his men."[44]

Napoléon's very presence was incredibly motivational to his forces. A man of raw courage and indomitable will, Napoléon was always in the forefront of his armies. Wellington once said of him, "His presence on the field made a difference of 40,000 men."[45] Consider the following description of the French victory at Austerlitz:

---

38. "In this way," writes another of his biographers, "he was able to concentrate overwhelming masses of men against opponents whose overall numbers were much greater than his own." Seward, *Napoleon's Family*, 32.
39. Markham, *Napoleon*, 37.
40. "Bonaparte," *Ladies' Literary Cabinet*, 44.
41. Markham, *Imperial Glory*, 5.
42. Emerson, *History of the Nineteenth Century*, 1:190.
43. Strawson, *The Duke and the Emperor*, 15.
44. Becke, *Napoleon's Waterloo*, 21.
45. Roberts, *Napoleon and Wellington*, 283.

> The Emperor, surrounded by all the marshals, wanted only for the horizon to clear to issue his last orders. At the first rays of the sun, the orders were issued and each marshal rejoined his corps at full gallop. The Emperor said, in passing along the front of several regiments, "Soldiers, we must finish this campaign by a thunderbolt that shall confound the pride of our enemies," and instantly hats were placed at the point of bayonets, and cries of "Long live the Emperor" were the true signal of battle. A moment afterwards, the cannonade began . . . and the battle was engaged.[46]

In this, undeniably one of Napoléon's greatest victories, the Russian-Austrian forces suffered thirty thousand fatalities and an equal number of prisoners, compared to a French loss of only fifteen hundred.

Ever the willing improviser, Napoléon also streamlined his forces into smaller combat units or corps of twenty to thirty thousand men led by field marshals who were given surprising autonomy and freedom of action. Each corps was subdivided into four or five divisions, each division equipped with regiments and battalions, cavalry brigades, infantry, and even medical and service units, the latter of which implemented "ambulances," light carriages that removed the wounded and dying quickly from the battle. Napoléon's organization of the Imperial Guard, made up the finest soldiers in the army, created a genuine sense of honor and mystique, a true fighting elite.[47]

Of course, as emperor and supreme head of state, Napoléon had the advantage of calling upon the full financial powers of France and of several conquered nations to support his military exploits. One reason for his selling the Louisiana Territory to the Americans in 1803 was to raise funds to support his military conquests. He was also able to draft conscripts into his Grande Armée from conquered nations.

In 1806, a Fourth Coalition made up of England, Russia, Austria, and Prussia had formed once again, providing the necessary financial backing. But at the battles of Jena and Auerstadt in October 1806 and again at Elyan in 1807, Napoléon once again proved successful. Suing for peace at almost any cost, the Russian tsar Alexander I, who hated the English almost as much as Napoléon did and who wanted to keep Prussia and Austria at bay, met with the French emperor on a raft on the Niemen River (see chapter 3). In the famous Treaty of Tilsit (1807), Alexander I agreed to participate in Napoléon's continental blockade, aimed at closing all European and Asian ports to British trade, thereby forcing England to its knees.[48] The entire continent was now more or less under Napoléon's command. At this, arguably the apex of Napoléon's military fortunes, friends and foes alike were hailing Napoléon as "above human history," declaring, "He belongs to the heroic age."[49]

Portugal's refusal, however, to join in the blockade and its decision to allow British expeditionary forces under Arthur Wellesley (Lord Wellington) to reenter Europe in 1809

---

46. Markham, *Imperial Glory*, 53.
47. Ellis, *Napoleonic Empire*, 74–77.
48. Tulard, *Napoleon*, 148.
49. Emerson, *History*, 1:210.

was the beginning of the bloody Peninsular War, which proved a quagmire for French forces: a constant drain and distraction to Napoléon's eastern European campaigns. The savage fighting in Portugal and Spain—characterized by anti-French guerilla warfare, widespread pillaging and banditry on both sides, bloody city sieges (like that at Saragossa), and wholesale massacres—absorbed the attention of many hundreds of thousands of French troops, although Napoléon himself never bothered to involve himself personally in the eroding conflict.

Sensing its chance, Austria once again declared war on France only to be decisively defeated again at the battle of Wagram in July 1809. In this one battle, 200,000 French soldiers, with Napoléon galloping along the frontline on a white charger, faced an even larger enemy army. Napoléon's twenty-fifth bulletin, though slanted in his favor, provides us with a sense of the terror of that scene.

> Such is the narrative of the battle of Wagram, a battle decisive and ever memorable, in which from 300,000 to 400,000 men, and from 1,200 to 1,500 pieces of artillery, contended for great interest, upon a battlefield, studied, planned and fortified by the enemy for several months. Ten pairs of colours, 40 cannon, 20,000 prisoners, including between 300 and 400 officers, and a considerable number of generals, colonels, and majors are the trophies of this victory. The battlefields are covered with the slain, among whom are the bodies of several generals, and among others, Norman, a Frenchman, traitor to his country, who prostituted his talents against her.[50]

Napoléon lost twenty-seven thousand men and Austria lost twenty-five thousand, but in the end Austria was routed and Archduke Ferdinand sued for peace.

As a teenage cadet back in Brienne, Napoléon had once built so dazzling a fortification of ice and snow, from which he launched magnificent snowball attacks against his fellow cadets, that many local townspeople came out to see it—all in good fun and humor.[51] But there would be nothing fun or kind about the ice, snow, famine, and suffering of the Russian winter of 1812 that ultimately destroyed *la gloire de la France*. Napoléon's tragic defeat, less at the hands of opposing Russian armies and more from the icy grip of a Russian winter, has gone down in history as one of the greatest military tragedies of all time. Yet even his losses, on so vast a scale, have magnified his legend and made of it an epic drama about which grand symphonies and great novels have been written.

---

50. Markham, *Imperial Glory*, 233.
51. Browning, *Boyhood and Youth*, 56–57.

"MY ARMY HAS HAD SOME LOSSES": THE RUSSIAN CAMPAIGN OF 1812

Where once upon a time they had been uneasy allies (Napoléon had even tried to marry Alexander's sister at one time), the two emperors, Napoléon and Tsar Alexander I, had become enemies for at least two reasons: first, Napoléon's desire to extend French imperialism over the Polish territories and into the Baltics; and second, the economic devastation wrought upon Russian trade because of the continental blockade. To these must be added another: Napoléon's overreaching and, by now, unbridled ambition. Never were his military powers so great and never was he so close to bankrupting Great Britain. This was his moment, despite festering problems in Spain, to seize total control of virtually all of Europe. Confident of victory, Napoléon declared war on Russia.

"Since the days of Xerxes no invasion of war had been prepared on so gigantic a scale."[52] Napoléon's Grande Armée of over 610,000 men (made up of French, Swiss, Italian, Polish, Prussian, Austrian, and Bavarian soldiers), 182,000 horses, 1,300 cannons, and 20,000 commissary wagons began crossing the Niemen River at Kovno on 24 June 1812, marching eastward in three parallel columns, an invading force not seen since ancient times. Its purpose was to divide and defeat the two defending Russian armies that Alexander had earlier deployed to Russia's western front. Instead of engaging the enemy, Napoléon kept looking for it, like a shadow boxer, swinging every which way but seldom making contact. While some have argued that the Russian retreat was a clever, calculated strategy designed to entrap the invaders deep inside Russian territory, more likely the Russian commanders feared to confront, at least too early in the campaign, so vast and formidable a foe.[53] Whatever the real Russian strategy, it frustrated Napoléon's desire to end the conflict quickly and drew him ever farther east into the Russian vortex in his chase of an elusive victory.

And the farther eastward they marched, the more apparent became their problems. As we have already seen, Napoléon was at his best when outnumbered and with smaller, not larger and unwieldy, armies. Communication between such a polyglot, cosmopolitan, and multilingual army proved ever problematic. And the farther east the army marched, the longer the necessary supply lines stretched behind and the more difficult it became to maintain and protect them. Bad roads, insufficient harvests, lengthy forced marches, and Russia's scorched-earth tactics all contributed to a rapidly worsening situation.

When Napoléon finally decided to march on Moscow, the combined Russian armies made their long-awaited stand at Borodino, near St. Petersburg, in September 1812, where between five and six hundred thousand men fought for more than fifteen hours within the space of a square league. The losses were staggering on both sides: forty-four thousand Russian soldiers and thirty-three thousand French Imperial Forces soldiers were killed or

---

52. Emerson, *History*, 1:420–21.
53. See Labaume, *Circumstantial Narrative of the Campaign in Russia*, for one of the earliest accounts of the Russian campaign. For one of the most recent and perhaps most remarkable studies of this episode, see Zamoyski, *Moscow 1812*.

Fire of Moscow (1812), by Viktor Mazurovsky.

wounded. The dead were piled up six to eight men deep in spots. It was, Napoléon considered, "the most terrible battle he had ever fought." [54]

Borodino proved a Pyrrhic victory for Napoléon's forces because the Russians adroitly retreated, preventing the rout Napoléon had needed. Weakened, frustrated, and without the knockout blow necessary to claim victory, Napoléon, with one hundred thousand men, at long last entered a deserted, nearly burned-out, Moscow on 15 September. Hoping to have defeated Russia by this time, Napoléon had barely gained the capital, and with Alexander refusing to negotiate or surrender, Napoléon could hardly claim victory. Surprisingly, the evacuating Russian forces had forgotten to destroy warehouses of grain and fodder that were enough to feed the entire French army for six months. Had Napoléon chosen to winter at the capital until the spring, he may well have won the war. However, he was uneasy being so far removed from his Polish bases, worried that news of the war was not going over well back in Paris, and concerned that Russia would strengthen its forces over the winter. Finally, in a pique of rage over Alexander's steadfast resolve not to surrender, Napoléon quit the city late in October and began his inglorious return march to France.

"Now we shall make war in earnest," Tsar Alexander reportedly declared. Thousands of infuriated Russian peasants, feigning food and friendship, butchered the retreating French soldiers with knives and pitchforks. Vicious Cossack attacks eliminated advance parties and sentinels while the Russian armies harassed the rear of the French columns. Then on came the Russian winter and with it famine and disease. Self-preservation became the only motive. Unheard-of calamities began thinning the ranks of a proud army now staggering like a wounded blind man.

---

54. Cronin, *Napoleon*, 318.

The winter was so severe, with nighttime temperatures as low as -25°F, that desperate soldiers, often with their hands, feet, ears, and noses entirely frozen, "burnt whole houses to avoid being frozen [to death]. We saw around the fires, the half-consumed bodies of many unfortunate men, who having advanced too near in order to warm themselves, and being too weak to recede, had become a prey to the flames. Some miserable beings, blackened with smoke, and besmeared with the blood of the horses which they had devoured, wandered like ghosts around the burning houses."[55] Panic replaced discipline, and chaos reigned in a frightful, cannibalistic effort to stay alive.

The French crossing of the Beresina River, with its burned-out bridges and ice-cold water, was but one of many heroic yet tragic stories of the weary march west. Had the Russians been able to pin down Napoléon on its eastern banks, he likely would have been captured. However, the French were able to decoy away and delay their pursuers long enough for some four hundred geographical engineers to wade into the icy river waters and construct a makeshift bridge strong enough to support the retreating army. Almost to a man, the engineers died of exhaustion and exposure.[56]

Impatient and fearful of an attempted plot against him, Napoléon, as he did in Egypt, went ahead to Paris to retain his weakening grip on power, secure help for his men, and raise new armies, for of the 610,000 men who had marched with him to Russia, only 40,000 returned! A wounded Napoléon would muster enough new recruits to fight on, winning several major battles, but the French reversals against Wellington in Spain and the realignment of Russia, Austria, Prussia, and England against him spelled the end of Napoléon's imperial France. "As he returned across the Rhine to Paris, Napoléon found himself an Emperor without an Empire."[57] Weary of war, French forces continually retreated until the victorious allied armies marched into Paris on 31 March 1814.

The subsequent Congress of Vienna (see chapter 3) strove to achieve a lasting peace in the Treaty of Fontainebleau, carved up much of Napoléon's European victories, and banished Napoléon to the island of Elba in the Mediterranean Sea in April 1814, ironically not far from Corsica. The world, so everyone surmised, could finally move forward.

"HERE AM I": THE ONE HUNDRED DAYS

Reduced to "Emperor and Sovereign of the Isle of Elba"—a small island twelve by eighteen miles with a population of only twelve thousand—Napoléon spent his days gardening and his nights plotting a return. He knew that the restored Bourbon monarchy was not playing well in France, and incredibly, despite spies covering the island, Napoléon quietly slipped away with seven ships and 1,150 men, landing in France on 1 March 1815. His destination, Paris. His design, France!

---

55. LaBaume, *Campaign in Russia*, 400.
56. Cronin, *Napoleon*, 328.
57. Cronin, *Napoleon*, 351.

While marching northward, the great testing moment came near Grenoble when he encountered a royal regiment of French grenadiers who had been ordered to shoot him on sight. At that moment, wearing his famous gray coat and three-pointed hat, Napoléon walked out alone in front of the royalist troops, threw open his coat and shouted: "Soldiers of the Fifth of the Line, do you remember me? . . . If there is in your ranks a single soldier who would kill his Emperor, let him fire. Here am I."[58] A deafening silence followed. Instead of a volley there arose a tremendous shout of "Vive l'Empereur!" And he was instantly mobbed with veneration by men still willing to sacrifice their all for him. Playing the stirring strains of "La Marseillaise," the anthem of the Revolution, Napoléon's ever-growing army marched northward. On 19 March, one day after the puppet king Louis XVIII had hurried out of town, Napoléon returned once more in triumph to a Paris wild with jubilation.

Stunned by the incredible news of the vanquished's resurrection, the Austrian prime minister Klemens von Metternich and the Congress of Vienna, which he supervised, moved promptly to counter the revived threat. England, Prussia, Russia, and Austria each pledged to send an army of 150,000 men against Napoléon—600,000 men in aggregate, called the Armies of the Seventh Coalition—all under the command of Wellington, the "Iron Duke." Napoléon knew that his only chance of success was to go on the offensive and, by once again employing the element of surprise, attack and destroy in sequence first the British and then the Prussian armies that were then massing under Wellington's command. He would then move on to Brussels before the advancing Russians and Austrians could join the fray. With incredible dispatch, he soon amassed a new army—*L'Armée du Nord*—to spearhead the assault against the advancing allied armies.

After four days of preliminary skirmishes and heated battles at Quatre Bras in Ligny, in which the French won Pyrrhic victories, Sunday, 18 June 1815, broke bright and beautiful over the Belgian fields near the tiny village of Waterloo, not far from Brussels. Waiting impatiently for the ground to dry sufficiently after days of heavy rain, the overly confident Napoléon once more heard the stirring strains of "La Marseillaise" waft across the tender wheat fields as one hundred thousand French soldiers, dressed in parade uniforms resplendent as the rising sun shouted, "Vive l'Empereur." Less than a mile away, Wellington stood restless yet resolute, poised at the head of a British-Dutch-Belgian, multinational, multilingual army of 93,000, cautiously optimistic that his battle-tested regulars, with the expectant arrival of General Gebhard Leberecht von Blücher and his Prussian army of over 120,000 men would withstand the imminent French onslaught. All sensed it would be a day of days, balanced between an unforgettable past and an unforgiving future.

At about 11:30 a.m. Napoléon's artillery began its fearful, incessant bombardment of Wellington's forces, stretched across a three-and-a-half-mile front. The cannonading from both sides tore down whole rows of advancing columns in fighting that was "so terrible as to strike with awe the oldest veteran on the field."[59] Yet even with this, Wellington knew he

---

58. Becke, *Napoleon's Waterloo*, 2.
59. Becke, *Napoleon's Waterloo*, 191.

The Battle of Waterloo, by William Sadler.

could be swept from the field only by Napoléon's cavalry and infantry charges. Surprisingly unsupported by French artillery—a critical error on Napoléon's part—the French cavalry was cut down by Wellington's blisteringly effective counterattacks. Then, at the Iron Duke's famous command, "Up, guards, at them," the allied forces went on the offensive.

As well as Wellington fought (Napoléon later said of him, "Wellington is a man of great firmness"[60]) and as disciplined as the British foot soldiers were in repelling one wave of Field Marshal Ney's French cavalry after another, what turned the tide that fateful day was Field Marshal Grouchy's tardiness and failure to join in with Napoléon, combined with the sudden, unexpected appearance on the battle field of the determined Prussian columns. When Napoléon heard of it, he said to Ney, "On a perdu la France" ("We lost France"). Wellington then "rode to the crest of the position, took off his hat, and waved it in the air. Forty thousand men came pouring down the slopes in the twilight, the drums beat, and the trumpets sounded the charge."[61] Panic spread like wildfire. By evening, with the dreaded words *La Garde recule* (The Guard retreats), the French were routed, and Napoléon barely escaped to Paris.

Back in Paris, General Gilbert du Motier, Marquis de Lafayette, rose in the chambers to distance France once and for all from Napoléon: "Three million Frenchmen have perished for one man who still wishes to fight the combined powers of Europe. We have done enough for Napoleon; let us now try to save France."[62]

---

60. Bourrienne, *Memoirs*, vol. 16, chapter 13.
61. Becke, *Napoleon's Waterloo*, 227.
62. Emerson, *History*, 1:586–87.

"HOW I AM FALLEN"[63]

Fearing arrest from his own government, Napoléon calibrated his best chances of survival. On the 22 June 1815, the restored French royalist government gave Napoléon a single hour to abdicate before Louis XVIII's imminent arrival in Paris. General Blücher announced "that he would have Napoleon shot at the head of his columns," rather than be captured by the advancing Prussian armies, who entered Paris on 7 July. Napoléon then fled westward for the coast, where he spent a fortnight in hiding, mulling over his next move.[64] Surrender to King Louis XVIII? Flee to the United States? Sail to South America? Finally, on 15 July, knowing the effectiveness of the British naval blockade, he decided to test the good graces of the British government by surrendering himself up to his majesty's ship *Bellerophon* in hopes of securing passage to the United States of America. "I have come to throw myself on the protection of your Prince and your laws," he said to the ship's startled commander, Captain Frederick Maitland.[65] Maitland and his crew, as surprised as anyone at this unexpected turn of events, accepted Napoléon as their worthy prisoner, treated him as a royal personage, gave him and his aides Maitland's private quarters, and immediately set sail for England. The *Bellerophon* anchored in Plymouth harbor for almost two weeks while London wrestled with the question of what to do with the captured emperor.

The news out of London, however, was anything but cheery. Fearing another French uprising if they returned Napoléon to France, yet anxious to banish him far away from England, Prime Minister Lord Liverpool ordered him exiled to the destitute volcanic island of St. Helena, a British East India Company refueling station located in the South Atlantic Ocean five thousand miles away from France and much further away than Elba. Napoléon and his small company of aides were transferred to another warship, the HMS *Northumberland*, and they arrived on the island seventy days later on 17 October 1815 to a small, curious, and admiring crowd.

There at St. Helena for the next six years, General Napoléon (as his captors insisted on calling him) took up forced residence in a small, unpretentious, rather uncomfortable wooden house called Longwood, located on a high table of land looking out over the broad expanse of limitless ocean. Across a deep ravine in the front of the house encamped the British 53rd Regiment, whose twice-daily cannon firings announced day break and sunset. In all, some twenty-five hundred British soldiers encamped on the small island, with two ships constantly patrolling the island's ragged coast lines to ensure against any repeat of what had happened on Elba.

Napoléon, longing for his son and hoping that, with a change in governments, London might change its mind, devoured every newspaper and every bit of letter-borne news and rumors. Determined to make the best of a bad situation, he began dictating his memoirs

---

63. Markham, *Napoleon*, 252.
64. Aubry, *St. Helena*, 43. General LaFayette had offered to take him to America in a merchant vessel.
65. Coote, *Napoleon and the Hundred Days*, 271.

Napoleon in St Helena, by Franz Josef Sandmann, c. 1820.

to Las Cases, one of his personal secretaries, from journals he had kept during his many campaigns. He was determined to make sure his interpretation of his life would outlast him. Consciously playing what one scholar has called his little game of "make believe,"[66] he resigned himself to commanding his little, adoring household while sparring with his British overseers with all the enthusiasm of a royal magistrate. *Le petit caporal* was as much the abrupt and domineering dictator in his island prison as he had ever been in battle or in his Parisian palaces, and his aides would have it no other way.

At the advice of his personal surgeon, Napoléon rekindled his lifelong Corsican interest in gardening and soon put all his household to work planting scores of peach trees, willows, oaks, and vegetables of every kind. He put in water fountains, a fishpond, and an arbor-covered pavilion. Rising before daybreak and dressed in a jacket, large trousers, an enormous straw hat, and sandals, he would "rush outside to plant new seeds, to water the roses and the strawberries, to arrange for trees and bushes to be moved like furniture from one place to another until the correct symmetry had been achieved" in the arboretum of his new empire.[67]

By 1818 his health began to fail. Seriously overweight and feeling the effects of the damp and incessant wind, Napoléon complained of what he termed a "knife turning inside his belly"[68] and around his liver. At the request of his mother, two Catholic priests were permitted

---

66. Ballard, *Napoleon*, 293.
67. Blackburn, *Emperor's Last Island*, 147.
68. Blackburn, *Emperor's Last Island*, 161–62.

to land on the island in September 1819, and, with Napoléon's permission, they transformed Longwood's sparsely furnished dining room into a chapel, where they celebrated mass every Sunday. On those days when their bedridden parishioner was too ill to move, he listened to the service through the open door of his bedroom.

While it is true that in his declining days Napoléon reverted to the Roman Catholic faith of his youth—"I believe in God; I am of the religion of my fathers," he allegedly once declared[69]—he was a man of fate more than faith and was deeply pessimistic about life after death. If not an atheist, he believed Christianity was fundamentally a "man-made edifice."[70]

Throughout the year 1820, his health steadily declined, though on occasion he strolled through his garden and even rode around the island. Toward the end of the year, he was walking with increasing difficulty and needed help even to reach a chair in the garden. Meanwhile Sir Hudson Lowe, the island's new governor, court-martialed Napoléon's surgeon for being too kind. As Napoléon's legs swelled and his appetite waned, the rounds of nausea and sweats increased. He grew increasingly depressed and morose. "How I am fallen!" Napoléon said, "I, whose activity was boundless, whose mind never slumbered, am now plunged into a lethargic stupor, so that it requires effort even to raise my eyelids. I sometimes dictated to

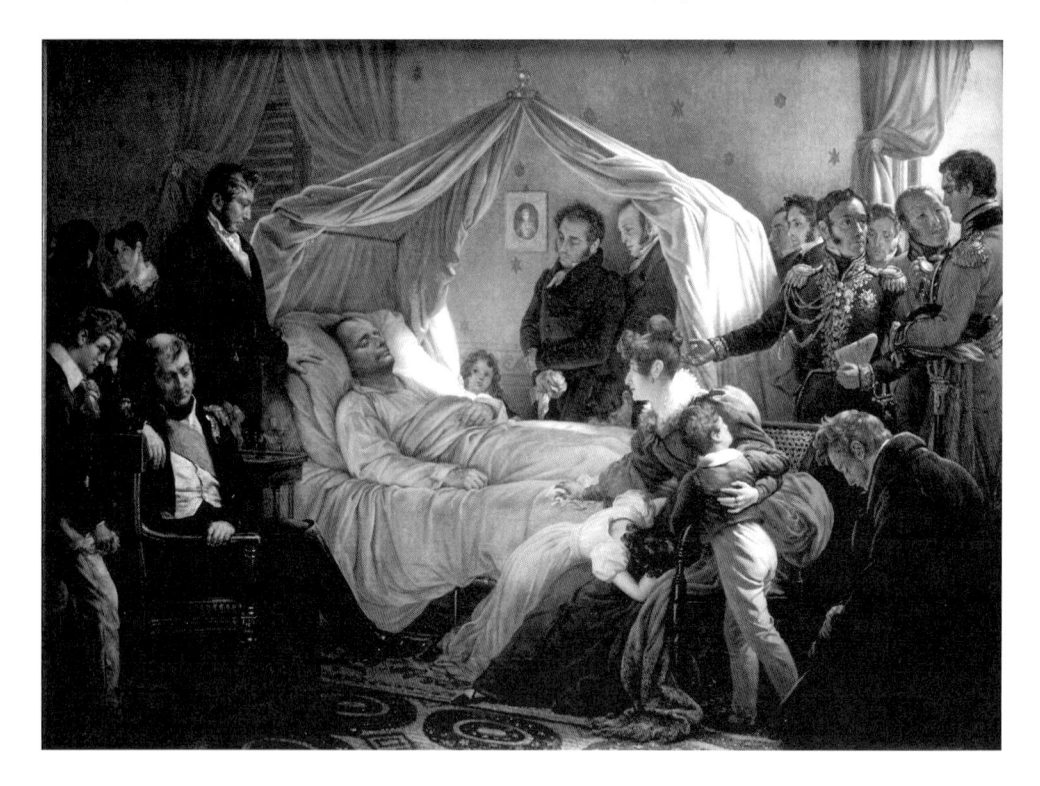

Death of Napoléon, by Charles de Steuben.

---

69. Bourriennne, *Memoirs*, 16.
70. Aubry, *St. Helena*, 314.

four or five secretaries, who wrote as fast as words could be uttered, but then I was NAPOLEON—now I am no longer anything. My strength, my faculties forsake me. I do not live—I merely exist."[71]

The year 1820 was the period of his steepest decline. His last airing came on 17 March 1821. He dictated his last will and testament in which he expressed the wish that "his ashes should repose on the banks of the Seine, in the midst of the French people whom he had loved so well." In the early evening of Saturday, 5 May, while a tremendous storm thundered by overhead and after receiving communion and extreme unction, he spoke his last: "*France, armée, tete d'armée, Josephine*" (France, army, head of the army, Josephine)[72] Though debate continues to swirl to this day over the precise cause of his death, Napoléon almost certainly succumbed to the same malady that took the life of his father and two of his sisters—a painful cancer of the lower stomach.[73]

While Napoléon lay in state, draped in black cloth, in his little bedroom at Longwood, virtually the entire island population filed by his body, which was dressed in the green uniform of the Chasseurs of the Guard with the grand cordon of the Legion of Honour across his breast, long boots with spurs, and three-cornered hat. Many a British soldier bent the knee and kissed the corner of his cloak. At his funeral on 8 May, his last adversary, Governor Lowe, ordered full military honors, and British soldiers bore him to his grave in Rupert Valley while the guns of the Royal Navy, his lifelong enemy, boomed their final salute.[74] The day was beautiful and clear, the islanders crowded the roads, and music resounded from the heights. "Never had a spectacle so sad and solemn been witnessed in these remote regions."[75] His grave was marked by stone with only the words "here lies" engraved thereon, "because the French and the English could not agree on the inscription."[76] Nineteen years later, his body was exhumed and moved to Paris, where a magnificent funeral was held in December 1840. Today he lies encased in marble and enshrined in glory as "the greatest soldier who ever lived"[77] in the historic military hospital of Les Invalides on the banks of the Seine, as he wished.

NOT A PERSONALITY BUT A PRINCIPLE

So what are we to make of this "Ogre from Corsica" (as his enemies called him), this spirit of the age, after a mere chapter of review? Appraisals by some of the world's leading historians are continually changing and defy a simple consensus. Napoléon still refuses to be captured and defined. As Ida Tarbell has written: "No man ever did more drudgery, ever followed details more slavishly, yet who ever dared so divinely, ever played such hazardous games of

---

71. Bourrienne, *Memoirs*, 16.
72. Ballard, *Napoleon*, 290; and Markham, *Napoleon*, 203.
73. "Death of Napoleon Bonaparte," *Saturday Magazine*, 207–8.
74. Ballard, *Napoleon*, 292.
75. Bourrienne, *Memoirs*, chapter 16.
76. Johnson, *Napoleon*, 182.
77. Johnson, *Napoleon*, 183.

chance. . . . No man ever made practical realities of so many of liberty's dreams, yet it was by despotism that he gave liberal and beneficent laws. . . . He was valorous as a god in danger. . . . He was the greatest genius of his time." Yet this same writer could only lament that he lacked "the crown of greatness, that high wisdom born of reflection and integration which knows its own powers and limitations."[78]

Surely he will be continually criticized, if not despised, by many who regard him as nothing less than a dictator in republican clothing, a despot, a tyrant, and even a criminal whose bloody conquests and violent, rapacious conduct created unfathomable suffering on an unbelievable scale and spawned universal hatred and decades of resentment throughout much of Europe. The human toll of his exploits cost the flower of a generation on all sides—an estimated 1.4 million men killed in battle and another 1.6 million wounded or disfigured. He was a man of wars and those who love and promote peace are effusive in their negative estimation of him. They choose to see him as but another dictator on par with such notorious totalitarian rulers as Adolf Hitler, Joseph Stalin, and Mao Zedong. These critics brush aside any of his accomplishments, believing they are meaningless and irrelevant. As the British historian Paul Johnson has said: "The great evils of Bonapartism—the deification of force and war, the all-powerful centralized state, the use of cultural propaganda to apotheosize the autocrat, the marshaling of entire peoples in the pursuit of personal and ideological power—came to hateful maturity only in the twentieth century, which will go down in history as the Age of Infamy. It is well to remember the truth about the man whose example gave rise to it all, to strip away the myth and reveal the reality."[79]

His detractors likewise despise his use of self-promotion, his relentless propaganda machine, his ill treatment of women, and his disregard for the environment. They loathe him for his self-aggrandizement and for fostering the myth that he was a superior being. Even many of his contemporaries, like Alexis de Tocqueville, charged him with being "a political domination unparalleled in modern history."[80] To them, his empire "was in many respects a personal act of vanity."[81] At base he remains for many not a reformer but a cruel, egotistical conqueror and megalomaniac whose tragic human flaw was that he did it all for the glory of self. And because of this "overweening ambition and ego, Napoléon was as much the cause of the wars of 1796–1815 as were the forces unleashed by the French Revolution."[82] At best, his detractors see him as a "tragic hero," one who failed his moment and the test of time for not being all he could have been.

Yet, for all this, the sun is beginning to shine once more on Napoléon, not merely for what he did for France but for Europe and the world. Wellington, his worthy adversary, was probably right when he once said of him: "Napoleon was not a personality, but a principle."[83]

---

78. Tarbell, *Life of Napoleon Bonaparte*, 293–94.
79. Johnson, *Napoleon*, 186.
80. Hazareesingh, "Napoleonic Memory," 748.
81. Hazareesingh, "Napoleonic Memory," 766.
82. Byman and Pollack, "Let Us Now Praise Great Men," 127.
83. Markham, *Napoleon*, 257.

To his lasting credit, Napoléon consolidated, institutionalized, and disseminated the hard-fought gains of the French Revolution. That he did so in a self-aggrandizing fashion and by military conquests that spilled the blood of millions cannot be denied. But the French Revolution, imperfect in its aims and ofttime horrific in its methods, was the bloody, long-coming statement of the common man and woman that the abuses of aristocratic privilege, absolutist royal power, and ecclesiastical paternalism could no longer be tolerated. Inspired in part by the American Revolution, the French Revolution had an even greater effect, throwing off a millennium of European feudalism and cruel domination. Against overwhelming odds and long-established inertia, it won a new world of freedom, equality, and justice. Had the European monarchies and class systems succeeded in preserving their *ancien régime*, their old, tired ways of doing things, more horrific wars with more terrible weapons would inevitably have later arisen. The French Revolution was inevitable; however, its gains may not have been defensible or endurable without a Napoléon to buy a generation of time to let such freedoms take root and survive.[84]

Arguably, Napoléon's greatest reform, at least that closest to the soul of the Revolution, was the establishment of the Napoleonic Code, a code of civil law. Enshrining the spirit of *liberté*, *égalité*, and *fraternité*, his new system of laws proclaimed legal equality, abolished serfdom, established fairer justice and taxation for all, gave new rights to home and family, and guaranteed property rights and the right to choose a career independent of status or rank. He upheld the legal institution of marriage and restricted divorce.

Yet Napoléon not only fought for new principles: he also was a man of practical innovations. Ever concerned with the details of administration and government—indeed, if he made "war with his genius," he made "politics with his passions"[85]—he consolidated hundreds of levels of unwieldy government bureaucracies into a much more merit-based, centrally controlled, and hierarchical administration, much of which is still in operation today. He also reformed the treasury, modernized accounting systems, and created a central bank. Local provincial governments were strengthened into prefects, and administration greatly improved.

Napoléon's reforms were arguably positive in many other areas. In the field of education, he mandated free education; improved the nation's secondary school system with a standardized curriculum, exams, libraries, and uniforms; reorganized the nation's schools under a state model rather than a Roman Catholic model; and established a National University.[86] His interests in furthering the cause of science and research were seen most vividly in his Egyptian campaign and in the establishment of Les Archives Nationale, which have paid lasting dividends. Without the French invasion of Egypt, the Rosetta Stone would likely not have been discovered or decoded by Jean-François Champollion in 1822 (see chapter 2). In

---

84. As one revisionist scholar put it, "Napoleon consolidated many of the Revolutionary changes, giving them fifteen additional years of life beyond the Revolutionary decade, which was crucial in making it impossible for the restored Bourbons to turn the clock back." Grab, *Napoleon and the Transformation of Europe*, 205.
85. Hazareesingh, "Napoleonic Memory," 768.
86. Laven and Riall, "Restoration Government and the Legacy of Napoleon," 3.

the arts, Napoléon improved the Louvre, erected many other museums, and encouraged fine art, architecture, and the opera. Though he feared the power of a free press, the books and pamphlets of the era were relatively free of government censorship. In public works, he built thirty-two hundred miles of new roads, a thousand miles of canals, introduced gas lighting, and beautified the city of Paris with new bridges, boulevards, and monuments.

As for religion, no one can doubt that he was a liberating, albeit secularizing, force. "Faith," he once declared, "is beyond the reach of the law. It is the most personal possession of man, and no one has the right to demand an account for it."[87] Although his own belief in God will ever be a point of debate, his was a force for religious toleration and pluralism. Napoléon declared freedom of religion throughout the regions under his control. He also restored the presence of the Catholic Church, without its dominance and exclusivity, by removing it from its place as the established church. Under his rule, the dreaded Italian laws of Inquisition and the horrors of the Spanish Inquisition were, at least for a time, done away with. Protestants as well as Moors (Muslims) were allowed to worship more freely than ever before and Jewish ghettos were abolished. Several Jews, in fact, looked upon Napoléon as their messiah for liberating them in whatever country he conquered, granting them full citizenship and freedom of worship. One modern scholar even went so far to say, "The encounter of the Jewish people with Napoléon was a turning point in Jewish history. For the first time, a modern statesman had envisaged the Jewish problem as a fundamental issue of international politics."[88]

Napoléon's softening of the absolute power of the clergy over the religious domain of France and several other European nations opened the door for a new kind of religious pluralism and freedom. While slow in coming, such new religious toleration opened the door for evangelistic Protestantism and for a host of other faiths.

If Napoléon consolidated the gains of the French Revolution within France, as a military conqueror he disseminated them beyond its borders in the Frenchification of Europe.[89] He was far more than a mere occupier; he was just as much a force for change in Berlin, Vienna, or Milan as he ever was in Paris. While the inner realms of empire—those countries closest to France—were more influenced by his reforms than those in the outer realms, Europe would never be the same because of him. Even the Congress of Vienna, which was dominated by his adversaries and ushered in almost a century of peace, preserved many of Napoléon's reforms because of their popularity and liberalizing influence (see chapter 3). Thus, even in defeat, Napoléon may be said to have claimed partial victory.

Europeans may have hated the pride, power, and nationalism of Napoleonic France, but they found inspiration in Napoléon's reforms. Little wonder the peasants welcomed him everywhere. The heavy hand of nobility, aristocracy, and privilege was dealt a severe blow

---

87. Weider, "Napoleon and the Jews."
88. Napoléon even wanted to make Palestine an independent Jewish state in 1799, but the British counterinvasion prevented his establishing control over Jerusalem. Weider, "Napoleon and the Jews."
89. Grab, *Napoleon and the Transformation of Europe*, 205.

in the name of the common class all over a Europe that was anxious to enjoy a better life. Clearly, Napoléon "advanced the position of the middle classes and provided an impetus to sound mobility on the basis of wealth, education, and merit, criteria that remained dominant in modern Europe."[90] Governments all across Europe were modernized and made to be more efficient, more open, and, to some greater degree, more answerable to their people. The revolutions of the 1820s and 1830s were ample proof that it was not possible to return to the old order. And as will be shown in a later chapter, his military conquests and political reforms inspired Simón Bolívar, who in turn inspired the independence movement an ocean away that transformed so much of South America.

Thanks to Napoléon, many of the modern German, Polish, and Italian states were formed with far fewer divisions and far greater territorial unity than before. Napoléon radically redrew the map of Germany, reducing the number of sovereign states from over three hundred to approximately fifty, thereby creating the modern German confederation.[91] Good or bad, European nationalism of the modern era owes much to Napoléon.

As for Napoléon's impact on religion, Joseph Smith's vision of an expanding world religion could hardly have been realized, at least not on so grand an international scale, without the liberalizing, liberating religious concepts of Napoléon. If Napoléon hastened the decline of established religions, he heralded a new age of religious pluralism that has benefitted a galaxy of new religions. As will be more amply shown in the following chapter, without Napoléon's invasion of Egypt not only may the famed Rosetta Stone not have been discovered but also the papyri from which the Book of Abraham was eventually translated would likely never have been found.

Napoléon remains a difficult personality to capture and understand, especially in so short a study as this inevitably is. We give the final word to two of his most dedicated detractors. First from the French foreign minister Charles Maurice de Talleyrand-Périgord: "His career is the most extraordinary that has occurred for one thousand years. . . . He was clearly the most extraordinary man I ever saw, and I believe the most extraordinary that has lived in our age." And this from the Austrian prime minister Klemens von Metternich: "By the force of his character, the activity and lucidity of his mind, and by his genius for the great combinations of military science, he had risen to the level of the position which [destiny] had destined for him. Having but one passion, power, he never lost either his time or his means in those objects which might have diverted him from his aim. Master of himself, he soon became master of events."[92]

---

90. Grab, *Napoleon*, 209.
91. Laven and Riall, "Restoration Government and the Legacy of Napoleon," in *Napoleon's Legacy*, 12.
92. Markham, *Napoleon*, 265.

Jean-François Champollion, by Léon Cogniet.

"JE TIENS MON AFFAIRE!"

JEAN-FRANÇOIS CHAMPOLLION, THE TRANSLATOR AND THE STONE

"I believe that the phonetic writing existed in Egypt at a far distant time; that it was just a necessary part of the ideographic (pictorial) script; and that it was then used . . . to transcribe (crudely, it is true) in ideographic texts the proper names of peoples, countries, cities, rulers, and individual foreigners who had to be commemorated in historic texts or monumental inscriptions."[1] So wrote Jean-François Champollion on 22 September 1822 in his famous "Lettre à M. Dacier," secretary of the Académie des Inscriptions et Belles-Lettres in Paris. In what stands as one of the greatest academic revelations of all time, the brilliant, headstrong, thirty-two-year-old linguist who had mastered Coptic and some twenty other languages restored to the waiting world the long-lost knowledge of how to read the language of the ancient Egyptian hieroglyphs. Because of this one single discovery, an entire civilization—its secrets, gods, and pharaohs, dating as far back as 3300 BC—has been brought to light. What follows is the account of several remarkable discoveries made in Egypt by various fascinating explorers and amateur archaeologists in the wake of Napoléon's 1798 invasion followed by the riveting story of how Champollion earned his lasting reputation as the father of Egyptology.

---

1. Champollion to M. Dacier in Fagan, *Eyewitness to Discovery*, 85.

THE ROSETTA STONE

In the words of William Stiebing Jr., a leading archaeology historian, it was only fitting that because "the French had initiated the study of European antiquities . . . a Frenchman finally deciphered the ancient Egyptian script."[2] In his invasion of Egypt in 1798, Napoléon, who was genuinely interested in science and in the histories of Egypt and the Middle East, took with him a "Commission of Arts and Science," consisting of la crème de l'Ecole polytechnique—167 "savants" drawn from the nation's best scientists—"astronomers, geographers, cartographers, architects, engineers, chemists, naturalists, physicians, orientalists, artists and historians."[3] Such a faculty of learning may seem out of place in the midst of an army of conquest—"soldiers of France accompanied by a body of savants, no less ambitious for trophies won in the peaceful triumph of science than were the veteran legions covetous of the bloody trophies of victory"—but so it was.[4]

Many of these men of learning sailed aboard Napoléon's own ship and made for interesting conversation. One night, under a clear Mediterranean sky, Napoléon was listening intently to an argument about the existence of God. Many on board were of the Voltaire school of thought and were seeking to prove by logic and metaphysics that there could not possibly be a God. Bonaparte, "who hated all ideologists, abstract reasoners, and logical demonstrators, no matter what they were demonstrating, would not fence with these subtle dialecticians, but had them immediately on deck, and pointing to the stars in the clear sky, replied by way of counterargument, 'Very good, messieurs! But who made all of these?'"[5]

What came of their late-night ruminations, history does not record, but after taking possession of Malta, Napoléon sailed on and invaded Egypt—then part of a tired, decaying Ottoman Turkish empire. Despite the blistering desert heat, Napoléon's well-disciplined army easily conquered Alexandria. Then, under the very shadow of the Great Pyramids themselves, he virtually annihilated a large Mameluke cavalry army that was totally unprepared to fight against a modern, well-equipped European military force. Further up the Nile, Cairo also fell to the invaders on 24 July 1798. Had not Admiral Horatio Nelson destroyed the French fleet in early August at the Battle of the Nile while it was still in harbor at Aboukir Bay, the Lion of the Desert, as Napoléon was then called, would likely have also conquered Syria and vast regions of the Middle East.

Muslim support contributed much to Napoléon's successful military campaign, at least initially, because of his opposition to Roman Catholicism, autocratic rule, and pledge to modernize and improve Egyptian society. Furthermore, Napoléon made it his habit to read and study the Koran and instructed his army to respect the Muslim faith. As a conqueror, he was greeted as a benevolent one by many, a force for much needed change and toleration.

---

2. Stiebing, *Uncovering the Past*, 70.
3. Stiebing, *Uncovering the Past*, 57.
4. *Ruins of Sacred and Historic Lands*, 145.
5. *Ruins of Sacred and Historic Lands*, 143.

Many Muslim muftis proclaimed him "as God's messenger and the Friend of the Prophet Mohammed."[6]

Once in firm control, Napoléon set out to win over the hearts and minds of the people while pursuing his own military agenda. Calling upon the expertise and resources of his cadre of scientists, he set up the multidisciplinary Egyptian Institute of Arts and Sciences at Cairo. And his far-reaching reforms included the constructing of modern hospitals, irrigation schemes, and sewage systems; establishing Egypt's first newspaper and book-making printing presses; building roads, canals, and an elaborate, new postal network; conducting geographical and geological surveys; and setting up streetlamps in Cairo and Alexandria. Of particular interest to Napoléon was the feasibility of rebuilding and greatly expanding the ancient canal through the strategic isthmus of Suez. Such a waterway between the Mediterranean and the Red Sea would prove a highly attractive alternative to that of circumnavigating half the globe by sailing around Africa's southerly Cape of Good Hope to India and the Far East. It would also surely pose a "devastating trade problem" for the hated English.[7]

Of chief interest to the many French scientists was their pursuit of a systematic survey of the lower and upper Nile River regions, at least to the second cataract, and where possible, archaeological excavations of Thebes, Luxor, Karnak, and other ancient sites. In January 1799, when Napoléon's troops first saw the panorama of ancient Thebes, "in sheer amazement [they] halted and burst into spontaneous applause."[8] Vivant Denon's wonderfully illustrated *Voyage dans la Basse et la Haute Egypte*, published in 1802, sold by the tens of thousands and fired the imagination of the Western world. It was superseded in grandeur and in popularity by the far greater, more majestic work commissioned by the emperor himself—the twenty-volume masterpiece *Description de l'Egypte*, published in installments between 1809 and 1828.

This "gain of a great book," as the editors of the *Quarterly Review* called it, was a superbly illustrated, heavily researched, and official publication of the French government consisting of some twenty volumes and 794 illustrated plates. It told of the many discoveries in Egypt, from ancient hieroglyphs to modern zoology, "everything worth knowing about Egypt past

---

6. Cronin, *Napoleon*, 152. However, the longer the occupying French Army remained in Egypt, the more suspicioned and disliked it was. Eventually, rebellions erupted in Cairo and elsewhere as European customs and morals interfered with local religious convictions and traditions.
7. Hallberg, *Suez Canal*, 23–33. Long a dream of kings and pharaohs, the approximately hundred-mile long Suez Canal, or "Gate to the East," has a long and difficult history. Under Necho II (ca. 600 BC), a partial canal—the so-called "Canal of the Pharaohs"—was built at the cost of some 120,000 lives. The Persian ruler Darius I tried to rebuild it around 500 BC. Ptolemy II and the Roman ruler Trajan tried their hand as well. However, for centuries no serious progress was made because of formidable obstacles as well as the Portuguese discovery of the great Cape route to India late in the fifteenth century. Under Charles Le Pere, Napoléon's engineers revived the efforts to rebuild it, but miscalculations, cost overrides, and other insurmountable difficulties led to yet again another abandonment. The dream proved impossible until, under the direction of an international commission, the Suez Canal was finally completed in 1869.
8. Adkins and Adkins, *Keys of Egypt*, 31.

Image from *The Memnon Colossi, Thebes. (1884)*, unknown. From *Description de l'Egypte*.

and present."[9] Europe was soon caught up with Egyptomania and would remain so for a generation or more, with Napoléon decorating much of Paris with obelisks and monuments. Even the new symbol of the empire became the bee, the hieroglyphic symbol for Lower Egypt.

As fate would have it, of all their careful studies and excavations, their most significant discovery came by way of sheer accident. In July 1794, while reinforcing a decaying Arab fortification near the town of Rashîd (or as the French called it, Rosetta), near the mouth of the Nile River and some forty miles east of Alexandria, a French soldier by the name of Colonel d'Hautpoul stumbled across a most extraordinary stone. He immediately notified his superior officer, Pierre-François Xavier Bouchard (Boussard), an officer of the engineers, who ordered an abrupt halt to their efforts. There, carelessly embedded in the wall, was a peculiar, irregular-shaped stone, three feet nine inches long by two feet four inches wide by eleven inches thick (114 by 72 by 28 centimeters) and weighing 1,500 pounds. Obviously once part of an ancient monument (it originally was part of an Egyptian temple erected in 196 BC by the Macedonian Greek king of Egypt, Ptolemy V, to commemorate the first anniversary of his reign), the polished black asphalt slab featured three different writings in parallel columns: one in ancient Egyptian hieroglyphics, one in Greek, and the third in some unknown language. The inscription found between the hieroglyphics and the Greek was soon identified as some sort of cursive, but no one could begin to decipher either one of the two Egyptian transcriptions. Sensing its potential value as a tool for translation and decipherment, Bouchard carefully secured the stone and delivered it to Cairo, where it was immediately placed in the newly established Institut d'Egypte. Napoléon himself showed great interest in the discovery and promptly ordered a number of impressions be made of it for distribution across Europe.[10]

Had the French occupying forces moved with more dispatch, the world famous Rosetta Stone would likely be on display at the Louvre in Paris today. However, Napoléon abruptly quit Egypt for Paris, leaving an infuriated General Jean-Baptiste Kléber to face the invading Ottoman–British coalition army, which overpowered the outnumbered French forces that were decimated by disease. Under terms of the Treaty of Capitulation, France reluctantly

---

9. Cronin, *Napoleon*, 165.
10. Stiebing, *Uncovering the Past*, 57–58.

The Rosetta Stone.

surrendered many of its plunders, including the Rosetta Stone, which, after considerable French protest, eventually made its way to England, arriving in Portsmouth in February 1802. For several months it resided at the Rooms of the Society of Antiquaries in London before its eventual transfer to the British Museum, where for the next twenty years it silently defied decipherment by some of the world's greatest minds.[11]

The discovery of the Rosetta Stone and the publication of *La Description* served only to intensify Europe's increasing fascination with all things Egyptian. Egypt, the so-called granary of the world, with its almost never-ending catalog of kings and pharaohs from 3200 BC to AD 300, had long stood at the very center of ancient civilization in arts, language, commerce, and military might for thousands of years. And no other nation—whether of ancient or modern times—has ever erected such great and durable monuments in the form of the lasting Pyramids and the Great Sphinx of Giza, among others. These stand as testaments

---

11. Fagan, *Eyewitness to Discovery*, 87–89.

to the glories of an ancient civilization that may have known mathematical, scientific, and engineering secrets modern society can even now only guess at and approximate.

Most enticing of all was its ancient hieroglyphic language chiseled into the stone of temples, monuments, and obelisks all over Egypt. If such writings could at last be deciphered, what treasured knowledge would they reveal about ancient civilizations, the Bible, and perhaps even Creation itself? For the wisdom of the ancient Egyptians was considered proverbial.

Nevertheless, Egypt would surrender its secrets jealously. Some two millennia before Napoléon, the "triumphant Christians closed (and often destroyed) the ancient temples, forbade the old religious rites, and banned the use of the traditional hieroglyphic writing."[12] Later, after the Muslim conquests of the mid-seventh century, outside access to Egypt beyond Cairo and Alexandria was restricted. With the addition of Egypt to the Ottoman (Turkish) Empire in the early sixteenth century, more of the interior opened to outsiders, but travel was extremely dangerous because of unstable political conditions, poor transportation, and intense poverty.

In the wake of the Renaissance and the rebirth of interest in the ancient Greek, Roman, and Egyptian civilizations, Europeans set their sights once more on the land of the Nile. The first to come may have been the Frenchman Pierre Belon in 1533, the German Johannes Helferich in 1579, and the Jesuit scientist-priest Athanasius Kircher, who perhaps was the first to hint at the phonetic importance of Egyptian hieroglyphs. Pietro della Valle brought back several mummies in the early 1600s (for centuries many believed such mummies had secret medicinal powers). Others followed, including George Sandys (1610), John Greaves (1638), the Reverend Richard Pococke (1737–38), and Frederick Norden (1738). Despite the many efforts of these intrepid inquirers, by the end of the eighteenth century, what little was known of ancient Egyptian history and civilization was still based primarily on the accounts of Greek and Roman authors.[13]

THE WAR OF THE CONSULS

Napoléon's invasion of Egypt in 1798 inevitably spurred intense European rivalry over the spoils of Egypt. It was, as Donald Malcolm Reid has suggested, "a turning point in confirming Egypt as a cockpit of Anglo-French geographical rivalry" and in heightening public interest in that part of the world.[14] In 1806, Muhammad Ali became pasha, or governor, of Egypt under the nominal authority of the sultan of Turkey, who, after fighting against France, had recognized the superiority of European technology. Ali, an Albanian who had served in the British-Turkish expeditionary force sent by the sultan to fight Napoléon in Egypt, set about "[attempting] to bring Egypt into the modern world by borrowing from the

---

12. Stiebing, *Uncovering the Past*, 55.
13. Stiebing, *Uncovering the Past*, 56.
14. Reid, *Whose Pharaohs?*, 32.

West."[15] Recognizing that his modernization plans needed the goodwill of the major powers, he adroitly played the interests of one against another in what became known as the War of the Consuls, allowing Europeans a virtually free hand to compete with one another, despoil monuments, and carry away antiquities in return for military and scientific upgrades and advancements.

The truth is, however, that Egypt did not need outsiders to rob it of its treasures; Egyptian natives, hungry for food and money, turned to robbing tombs and destroying temples. These native treasure hunters destroyed much and cared little "about the havoc they wreaked on immovable remains."[16] Even the Egyptian government demolished ancient temples for sugar refineries. "The widespread, frantic, and unrestrained deportation of artifacts that ensued was closer to wholesale looting than to excavation, . . . a period of excavation by explosion and coat-closet conservation."[17] It was a time when few people concerned themselves with originality, location, provenance, sequence, and arrangement—in short, the very essence of modern archaeology.

The British Foreign Office appointed Henry Salt as consul general in 1815. With the early support of Joseph Banks, member of the Royal Society and Trustee of the British Museum, Salt set out to represent British interests, if not also to make a tidy fortune of his own to supplement his meager salary. Like his French counterparts, Salt selected his own team of field agents, including Giovanni Caviglia, a Malta-bound sea captain who would dig at Giza; the Swiss adventurer Jean Louis Burckhardt; Giovanni d'Athanasi; and another Italian, Giovanni Battista Belzoni, billed as the "Patagonian Samson."

One of the era's more colorful adventurers, "the Great Belzoni," as his promoters delighted to call him, was born in Padua, Italy, in 1778. This six-foot seven-inch redheaded giant of a man left Italy in 1798 for England to escape Napoléon's invading armies. There, as a circus strongman, he

Giovanni Battista Belzoni. From *Narrative of the Operations and Recent Discoveries Within the Pyramids, Temples, Tombs and Excavations in Egypt and Nubia* by Giovanni Battista Belzoni (London, 1820).

---

15. Armajani and Riches, *Middle East*, 177.
16. Stiebing, *Uncovering the Past*, 60.
17. Muhlestein, "Prelude to the Past," in Harper et al., *Prelude to the Restoration*, 136–37.

awed his audiences with great feats of physical strength. Expert with levers, hydraulics, and weights, the Patagonian Samson, in one of his more famous stage acts, lifted twelve people who had been put into a specially constructed iron frame.

Convinced that he could make more money elsewhere, Belzoni and his Irish wife, Sarah, left for Egypt in 1812, where he tried to persuade Ali that Egypt simply had to buy his new ox-driven hydraulic pumps. Though Ali declined Belzoni's invention, he did give Belzoni a small government pension and permission to work with Salt in his ongoing efforts to unearth additional Egyptian antiquities for the British Museum. Surprisingly gifted at reading landscapes and working with only a handful of the most rudimentary tools, Belzoni, "with a large staff in his hand, . . . commanded his army of Mussulmans, directed their labors, astonished them with his displays of physical strength, learned to speak their language with marvelous facility, and speedily came to be regarded as a superior being, endowed with magical power."[18] In 1816 he discovered, excavated, and successfully removed the colossal granite head and upper torso of Pharaoh Ramses II from a temple at Thebes. Despite fierce opposition from French agents, Belzoni sailed his seven-and-a-half-ton colossus down the Nile to Alexandria from whence it, too, like the Rosetta Stone, eventually arrived at the British Museum.[19]

Soon he was at it again, this time following up on Burckhardt's lead. After sailing up the Nile to the Lower Nubian site of Abu Simbel, Belzoni hired a team of locals to clear away forty feet of sand and then used battering rams to smash in the doors. In doing so, he became the first to discover and crawl inside the temple of Luxor, where he discovered the unfinished sepulcher of Ramses II in his glorious temple carved out of the hillside.[20] The temple of Luxor had been so long lost and so completely buried in sand that its very existence was in doubt. Anciently, it had been dedicated to Isis by the queen of Ramses the Great. Four colossal figures, each sixty-one feet high, are seated in front with eight others, each forty-eight feet high, supporting the roof of the inner hall wherein gigantic bas-reliefs depict the history of Ramses. Sixteen other halls, not much smaller than the first, made up the complex. Belzoni's discovery of this ancient temple alone ensures his reputation in Egyptology. On his return trip, Belzoni explored the Valley of the Kings, discovering the majestic tomb and alabaster sarcophagus of Seti I. Then in 1818 at the second pyramid of Giza, the Pyramid of Khafre (or Chephren), Belzoni once again used his engineering genius and discovered its hidden entrance to the inner chambers, becoming the first man since ancient times to enter in. In all, Belzoni located eight previously unknown burial chambers.

Of Belzoni's methods, one can only wish he had been a bit more careful, for if truth be told, he destroyed almost as much as he discovered. The following is his own account of discovering one set of tombs:

---

18. "The Story of Belzoni," *Harper's New Monthly Magazine*, 751.
19. Stiebing, *Uncovering the Past*, 60–61.
20. "Story of Belzoni," 752.

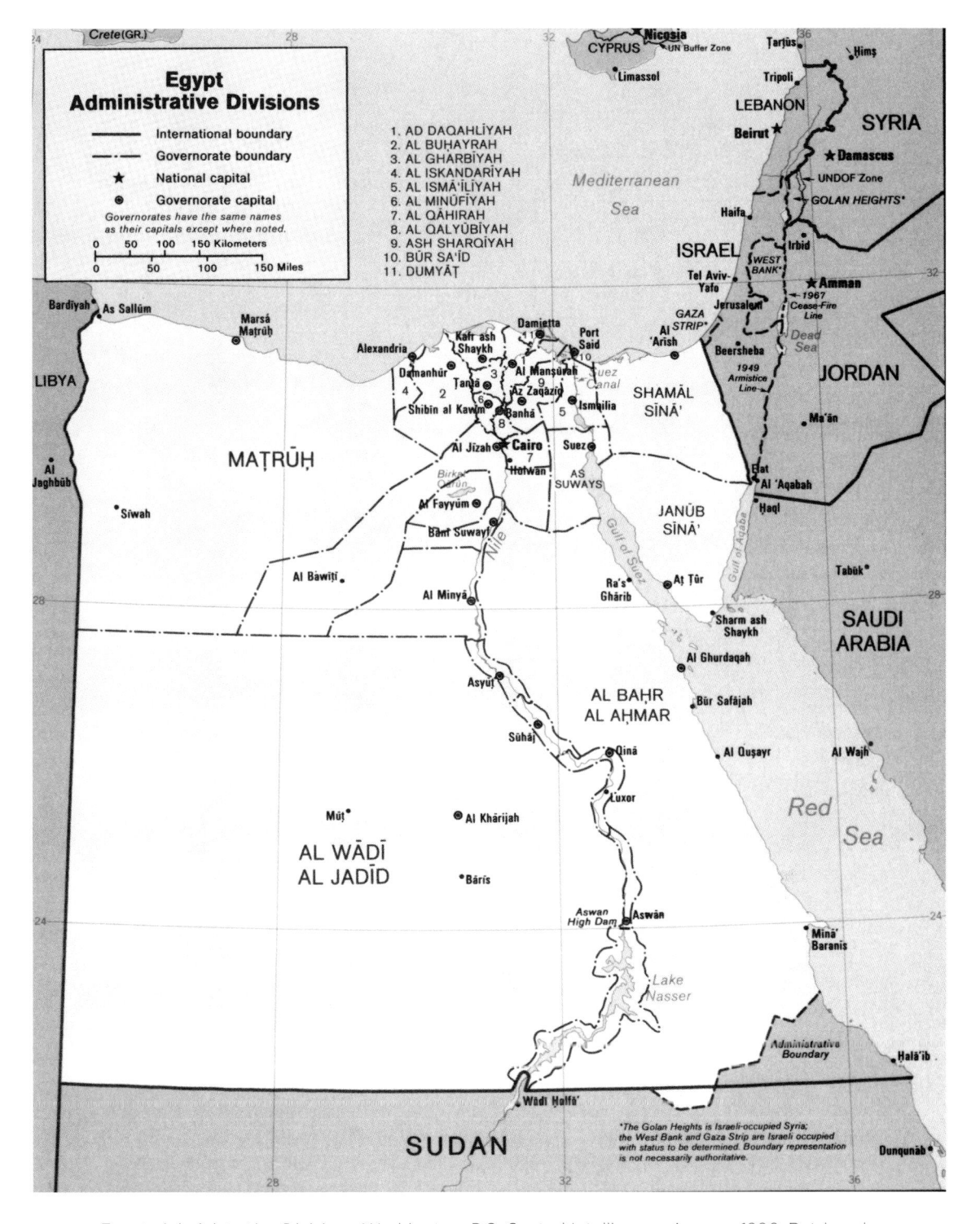

Egypt, Administrative Divisions. Washington, DC: Central Intelligence Agency, 1990. Retrieved from the Library of Congress.

In some places there is not more than the vacancy of a foot left, which you must contrive to pass through in a creeping posture, like a snail, on pointed and keen stones, that cut like glass. After getting through these passages, some of them two or three hundred yards long, you generally find a more commodious place, perhaps high enough to sit. But what a place of rest! Surrounded by bodies, by heaps of mummies in all directions; which, previous to my being accustomed to the sight, impressed me with horror. The blackness of the walls, the faint light given by the candles or torches for want of air, the different objects that surrounded me, seeming to converse with each other, and the Arabs, with the candles or torches in their hands, naked and covered with dust, themselves resembling living mummies, absolutely formed a scene that can not be described. In such a situation I found myself several times, and often returned exhausted and fainting, till at last I became inured to it, and indifferent to what I suffered, except from the dust which never failed to choke my throat and nose. . . . After the exertion of entering into such a place, through a passage of fifty, a hundred, three hundred, or perhaps six hundred yards, nearly overcome, I sought a resting-place, found one, and contrived to sit; but when my weight bore on the body of an Egyptian, it crushed it like a band-box. I naturally had recourse to my hands to sustain my weight, but they found no better support; so that I sunk altogether among the broken mummies, with a crash of bones, rags, and wooden cases, which raised such a dust as kept me motionless for a quarter of an hour, till it subsided again. I could not remove from the place, however, without increasing it, and every step I took I crushed a mummy in some part or other. Once I was conducted from such a place to another resembling it, through a passage of about twenty feet in length, and no wider than that a body could be forced through. It was choked with mummies, and I could not pass without putting my face in contact with that of some decayed Egyptian; but as the passage inclined downward, my own weight helped me on; however, I could not avoid being covered with bones, legs, arms, and heads rolling from above. Thus, I proceeded from one cave to another, all full of mummies piled up in various ways—some standing, some lying, and some on their heads.[21]

While modern readers can only grimace at the indelicate stumblings of a man who, like a bull in an ancient china shop, blundered about robbing and destroying much of the area's portable antiquities, Belzoni was no worse than most of his Egyptian or European contemporaries. However, his efforts to take careful notes of wall paintings and hieroglyphs—even though he could not read them—set him apart from tomb robbers. He was, one might argue, Egypt's first amateur archaeologist. The publication of his *Narrative of the Operations and Recent Discoveries Within the Pyramids, Temples, and Tombs in Egypt and Nubia*, in two volumes that were published in London in 1820, and his great exhibition at the Egyptian Hall in Piccadilly went far to pique the interests of a rising generation of much more respectful,

---

21. "Story of Belzoni," *Harper's New Monthly Magazine*, 752.

professional army of Egyptian archaeologists. An intrepid explorer to the end, Belzoni died of dysentery in 1823 while en route to discover the source of the Niger River.

DISCOVERIES OF THE FRENCH

Meanwhile, the French were making remarkable discoveries of their own. In August 1802, Napoléon's government appointed the twenty-six-year-old Piedmontese, Bernardino Drovetti (1776–1852), to the post of vice-consul in Cairo.[22] Drovetti was a lawyer by profession who had been wounded while serving in the French army in northern Italy. He fought in the Battle of Marengo (in his native Piedmont) in June 1800 and soon afterward became a naturalized French citizen. In 1805 the well-regarded Drovetti became consul general of Egypt, a post he held with distinction until he was dismissed by the restored Bourbon monarchy in late 1814. Deciding not to return to Italy, where his Napoleonic sympathies had fallen out of favor among his native countrymen, Drovetti, with the full permission of Ali, remained in Egypt, where he took to the highly expensive mania of collecting Egyptian antiquities in a quest for personal fortune.

Over the next seven years, Drovetti made four excavation trips up the Nile to Sair, Memphis, and Thebes, gaining the trust of many Arabs in the process. "The Arabs besiege without cease the camp where Mr. Drovetti is," observed one of his most fervent admirers. "Each of them brings mummies, bronzes, money, and sometimes cameos. These inhabitants of the desert know that they deal with the most fair and noble man, that they leave always satisfied with the prices that he fixes, and often to his disadvantage. . . . Mr. Drovetti showed me richly ornamented cedar wood boxes, used by women; tables, needles, scissors, textiles of different kinds, pallet charged with vibrant colors, and a precious batch of papyrus."[23] In the course of his work, Drovetti hired a number of field agents to help him excavate and collect antiquities, including Jean-Jacques Rifaud, Antonio Lebolo, and Joseph Rosignana. Drovetti's formidable knowledge of Egypt, his positive relationships with Ali, and his shrewd diplomatic skills eventually led to his reappointment as consul general on 25 June 1821.[24]

---

22. Bernardino Drovetti became a corporal in the Twenty-seventh Legion in June 1796. He was promoted captain in February 1799 and then "premiere Officeur a Ministere de la Guerre in Piemont" in July 1800. In March 1801, he was again promoted, this time to Major "de la Division des Troupes Piedmontaines." Personal Dossier of Bernardino Michel Marie Drovetti: Centre Historique des Archives (Militaire) à Vincennes, Paris, France, GR 2 YE 1242. See also GR 28 YC 441.
23. M. Le Comte de Forbin, *Voyage dans Le Levant*, 28, author's translation.
24. As to Drovetti's character, Monsieur Louis Nicolas Auguste de Forbin, director of the Louvre, strongly recommended his reappointment in 1821 as consul general: "Mr. Drovetti, ex-lieutenant colonel of cavalry, wounded in the Army of Italy, was sent on a mission in Egypt, where the power and goodness of his character, helped him have many friends who became very useful to French commerce and gave to M. Drovetti the esteem of the actual Pasha. Named Consul General [in 1805] he used his credit with the Vice King only to rectify his ideas, to moderate the excess of his despotism and to satisfy without dangers his taste for antiquity."

LEBOLO, DROVETTI, CAILLIAUD, AND RIFAUD

Lebolo is pictured standing on the far left; Drovetti is the man with his arm outstretched. *Portrait of Drovetti near Colossal Head*, by Godefroy Engelmann (1788-1839).

Like Drovetti, whom he had likely known from earlier times (they grew up only nine miles apart), Lebolo also hailed from the Piedmont of northern Italy (Castellamonte), where he had served as a gendarme during the French occupation. He likewise had enlisted in the French Army, preferring to support rather than resist the French occupation. Had he returned home immediately after Napoléon's defeat, Lebolo likely would have been considered a traitor, certainly by the Carbonari, who were secret revolutionary Italian patriots. He thus left his wife and young son and came to Egypt in 1815—perhaps as an invitee of Drovetti—for his personal safety, to make a small fortune, and to begin a new life. At the time he worked with a still shadowy figure named Josef Rosignana, and the two men soon entered into the employ of Drovetti. Rosignana was also a French Army veteran from the Piedmont (Turin) and, along with some four hundred other cavaliers (dragomans), had stayed on in Egypt after the French defeat. Having learned Arabic, Rosignana—or as the Arabs called him, Youssef Kachef—proved a most helpful partner.

For the next several years, Lebolo and Rosignana worked the upper Nile as adventurers, excavators, and amateur archaeologists. Their most important discoveries were in Luxor, near Thebes, where their findings did not go unnoticed. Their British adversary, Henry Salt, tells of buying mummies, papyri, and other "purchases of antiquities . . . of a certain Antonio Lebolo, a countryman of Drovetti, who had just been buying up all the antiquities the Arabs had to sell."[25] Some of the more exquisite mummies then being found in this vicinity were of young virgins, their bodies covered from head to foot "with very beautiful papyrus, in

---

"Recommendation de M. de Forbin pour la Nomination de M. Drovetti, Consul General de France en Egypte," 19 May 1819. Archives Nationales de France, FD 20144775/24.

25. D'Athanasi, *Brief Account*, 51. It would seem that Lebolo was less the excavator himself and more the purchaser of scrolls, mummies, and other such materials that others brought and sold to him. He had sold a significant collection of materials to the Imperial Museum of Vienna as early as 1820.

Ebers Papyrus. *Papyros Ebers (1875)*, by Georg Ebers Wellcome.

twelve folds, and containing hieroglyphics and colored figures of extremely good execution. Their colors are so fresh, that one would almost say they had been traced only a few days previously. The length of the papyrus is about 60 feet."[26]

---

26. D'Athanasi, *Brief Account*, 78. The papyri were usually found between the legs of the corpse, often "in such good condition . . . that it may be unrolled without difficulty or danger." *Brief Account*, 57. Some papyri were letters, others biographies, contracts, even funeral representations. The

Two other, much more careful contemporary French excavators were Frédéric Cailliaud (1787–1869) and Jean-Jacques Rifaud (1786–1852). Both men had extensive scientific training and had been making invaluable finds of their own. Rifaud made some of his finest excavations and discoveries in Thebes in September 1816. In fact, no other contemporary excavated as many sites in Thebes as he did. By the time he returned to France in 1825, Rifaud had sold a good many of his own discoveries and antiquities. It is entirely possible that Rifaud either found the mummies and scrolls that would later be translated into the Book of Abraham and sold them to Lebolo and Rosignana or directed Lebolo and Rosignana to the destination they were discovered. Eventually, Lebolo sold off parts of his collections, which made their way to America, eventually to be translated into the Book of Abraham by Joseph Smith. This work has had an enormous impact on the history, doctrines, and temple practices of The Church of Jesus Christ of Latter-day Saints. Thus without Lebolo and, by extension, without Napoléon, so much of the core beliefs and practices of the Church would have gone missing.

Cailliaud, who was more a naturalist and anthropologist than he was an archaeologist, made numerous trips of his own to the Theban necropolis to search for antiquities, amassing a rich collection in the process. However, his intent was less financially motivated and more anthropologically oriented. Drawing heavily upon the talents and connections of Lebolo and Rosignana's skills as interpreter, Cailliaud intended to understand the daily life of ancient Egyptians as found in their garments, eating utensils, jewelry, and tools.[27]

Unfortunately, wherever Lebolo went, troubles followed in his wake. Rifaud and Lebolo, once field work colleagues, soon became jealous antagonists, if not bitter enemies, each man charging the other with stealing goods and other various criminal activities.[28] Then later, in yet another confrontation, Belzoni and Lebolo came to blows over the ownership of certain properties and antiquities.[29] Both Lebolo and Belzoni returned to their native Italy in about 1823 with the intentions of suing each other in a court of law, a course of action that appar-

---

wooden masks that often encased the mummies were to protect them from worms and insects whereas the bodies themselves were almost always wrapped in linens.

27. For a fuller understanding of the contributions Cailliaud made in Egypt and which until recently were relatively unknown, see Bednarski, *Lost Manuscript*, 3–25. See also Cailliaud, *Travels*.
28. In an 1827 letter to Drovetti, Rifaud speaks very critically of Lebolo—a disgraceful cheat, thief, and obvious criminal: "He was tearing me apart by his incurable jealousy while deceiving you to obtain some pieces. . . . Mr. Lebolo ha[s] not been for you and for me the man that he should have been as a compatriot." Jean-Jacques Rifaud to Bernardino Drovetti, 6 December 1827, Papers of Jean-Jacques Rifaud, Book MS supplement 112, Fonds Rifaud, Bibliotheque de Geneve, Switzerland. In defense of Lebolo, it must be admitted that Rifaud, a staunch French patriot, was highly critical of most everyone in Egypt at the time, Drovetti included, especially if they were of Italian extraction.
29. James, *Egypt Revealed*, 92. See also Halls, *Henry Salt*, 2:23. Halls speaks of the "shameful attack made upon Belzoni by Messrs. Lebolo and Rosignana, at Carnak, which led him [Belzoni] to quit the place." Belzoni threatened Lebolo with a lawsuit for his interference in shipping obelisks down the Nile.

ently never occurred. Meanwhile, Lebolo, whose first wife had died, married—allegedly—a second wife, a native black woman from Egypt.[30] Lebolo would die in 1830 but not before selling off a variety of his antiquities, some of which eventually made their way to America and into the hands of Michael Chandler, who in turn sold them to Joseph Smith for the impressive sum of $2,400 in July 1835 (approximately $100,000 in 2019 purchasing power).[31]

In 1824, Drovetti made a fortune selling off most of his remarkable collection of Egyptian artifacts—some 5,200 pieces in all, including mummies of all kinds, sarcophagi, statues, stelae, scrolls, jewelry, monuments, weapons, money, tools, pieces of art and furniture, and cases of other items—to Charles Felix, king of Sardinia in Turin, for 400,000 lire—where they became the foundation of the famed Museo Egizio, or Egyptian Museum.[32] Jean-François Champollion deciphered the writings on Drovetti's many papyri, which were most often collections of plans, spells, and sayings designed to protect the survival and glorification of the dead in the afterlife. Drovetti's remarkable collection—arguably the most impressive assemblage of Egyptian antiquities outside of Egypt—remains on display to the present day. In his correspondence with Drovetti, Champollion himself validated the authentic antiquity of so much of Drovetti's collections, having determined that many of the discoveries dated back 4,000 years ago to the time of Abraham in Egypt.[33]

THE CHALLENGE

Meanwhile, despite the flurry of discoveries along the Nile, the Rosetta Stone, seemingly disdainful of its captors, defied the world's greatest linguists in their continuing, though unsuccessful, attempts at deciphering its ancient engravings. While its Greek letterings were translated easily enough, the other two writings, both Egyptian, could not be deciphered.

---

30. Peterson, *Story of the Book of Abraham*. See also notes in the possession of the author of an extended conversation he had with local Castellamonte historian, Emilio Champagne, 16 May 2018. Lebolo and his second wife arrived in Italy with their two small children, who were baptized in Venice before the family finally decided to risk their return to Castellamonte sometime in 1821–22.
31. There is evidence to show that as early as 1824, Lebolo and Drovetti's nephews were planning on buying some of Drovetti's antiquities and selling them to America, where they could get "double the price." Bernardino Drovetti to Pierre Balthalon, 4 February 1824, in Buichard, *Lettere di Bernardino Drovetti*, 483–84.
32. Porter, "Antonio Lebolo: His Life and Contributions to Egyptology" (unpublished paper in possession of the author), 6.
33. From a handwritten statement by Jean-François Champollion, signed 5 July 1827, regarding a second Drovetti collection of antiquities eventually sold to the Louvre. As shown above, Drovetti sold his first and much larger collection to Turin, Italy. As found in the file "Acquisition de la Collection Drovetti Transport Paiement," Les Archives Nationales de France, Paris, France, file 20144775/8. If Drovetti's collection found the support of the greatest linguist of his age, Lebolo's collections, many taken from the same areas at Thebes as Drovetti's, may well have been from the time of Abraham in Egypt.

The first was in the form of ancient Egyptian hieroglyphs, a religious or formal text, and the other was in a cursive adaptation of hieroglyphs, a so-called Demotic text. They both proved entirely unreadable. Part of the reason for this lay in the fact that the three different writings of the same event were not identical, word-for-word transliterations but phrases that were only roughly comparable in meaning. A second complication was the scarcity of characters on the stone, particularly in the hieroglyphs, to allow for a larger, more comprehensive study. A third problem was that the Demotic text, a long-lost Egyptian style of writing, was almost as difficult to translate as the hieroglyphs. The Demotic text, looking like nothing more than a scribble to linguists, gave way, historically, to a form of the Coptic language when the Christians overran Egypt around AD 250. A language that included elements of the Greek, Coptic was the first Egyptian language to use vowels. Thus, reading the Rosetta Stone was somewhat akin to a modern student of English or French trying to read Latin without a knowledge of either old English or old French and with no understanding whatsoever of the parent language—Latin.

The earliest serious study of hieroglyphs preceded the discovery of the Rosetta Stone by almost three hundred years. The Italian Pierio Valeriano published his *Hieroglyphica* in 1505. Almost two hundred years later, Athanassius Kircher, in an argument well ahead of his time, postulated that a knowledge of Coptic was a prerequisite to understanding hieroglyphs but continued to foster the long-held misconception that hieroglyphs were symbols and not script. In 1741, William Warburton concluded that the hieratic owed its origins to the ancient hieroglyphs. The hieratic was later superseded in about the seventh century BC by an Egyptian language derivative of hieroglyphs called the Demotic, a more secular language used for business and literary purposes. A generation after Warburton, the French abbé Jean-Jacques Barthélemy pioneered the argument that those hieroglyphs circled in ovals (the French "cartouches") usually contained names of royalty. Then in 1783, the great Danish scholar, Georg Zoëga, compiled a massive listing of 958 different hieroglyphs, classifying them by various symbols—plants, mammals, and so forth. Most, even at this late date, believed Egyptian hieroglyphics was, like Chinese, a language of pictographs, with each character representing a certain word, name, or larger meaning.

In the same year that the Rosetta Stone went on display in London, the French Oriental scholar Antoine Isaac, Baron Silvestre de Sacy, and his brilliant Swedish student, Johan David Åkerblad, began in rapid order to read proper nouns—like Ptolemy—in the ancient Demotic. Why Åkerblad and Sacy failed to apply their knowledge of Demotic to hieroglyphs still remains a puzzle.[34] By 1802 the world was still totally incapable of deciphering ancient Egyptian.

All this was destined to change. On 23 December 1790, in the small town of Figeac and at the height of the French Revolution, a baby boy was born, the last child of a forty-six-year-old mother and a struggling bookseller father. Raised in a small home just yards away from the town guillotine, Jean-François Champollion grew up in a family that was fearful of

---

34. Adkins and Adkins, *Keys of Egypt*, 59–65.

most everything and everyone. Refusing to send her children to nearby schools, his illiterate mother tried to teach Jean-François things she knew only from the schools of hard knocks and common sense. Drawn, Napoléon-like, to his father's library, the young Champollion, impatient, quick-tempered, and inclined to unsociable behavior, taught himself to read out of a passion for copying and drawing words over and over again. In his young and highly impressionable mind, he came to associate script to a collection of drawings and was as fascinated at the appearance of letters and words as he was their meanings.

What his parents could not teach him, his older brother, lifelong mentor, and personal hero, Jacques-Joseph Champollion, began to do. Passionate about books and ancient history, Jacques-Joseph was the one who opened his younger brother's mind and insatiable intellectual appetite to the world of higher learning. When he saw his younger brother's unhappiness with the strict disciplines and sterile, rote learning as taught at a local primary school, Jacques-Joseph sent for him to come and study with him and with a tutor, Abbé Oussert, at Grenoble in southeast France. The younger Champollion—"Champollion Le Jeune," as he came to be called—soon showed such promise in studying the classics that he also took to studying Hebrew, Arabic, Syrian, and Chaldean, showing a prodigious and remarkable linguistic capability in one so young.

In another fortunate twist of fate, the school prefect was none other than Jean-Baptiste-Joseph Fourier, one of Napoléon's leading Egyptian scientists, or savants, who was at that precise moment writing the Introduction to the *Description de l'Egypte*. Impressed with Champollion's linguistic aptitude and his consuming interest in all things Egyptian, Fourier invited his young protégé to his home to view his collection of Egyptian antiquities, drawings, and hieroglyphs. At first speechless at seeing such incredible things, Champollion left the house filled with a youthful fire that sparked an undying determination to someday decipher the ancient scripts, which many people then believed would reveal the whys and whens of creation, the true chronologies of the Bible, and secrets of subsequent civilizations. At the end of the school year, the seventeen-year-old Champollion received an invitation to speak before the academy in Grenoble. His essay on the geography of ancient Egypt received a standing ovation and Champollion was invited on the spot to become a member of the Grenoble Academy.

Moving to Paris with his brother later that year, Champollion resumed his linguistic studies at the Institut de France and the Collège de France under the tutelage of some of the country's greatest minds. These included the above-mentioned Professor Silvestre de Sacy, the foremost Oriental scholar in Europe; Professor Louis-Mathieu Langlès, who taught Champollion Persian; Prosper Audran, an expert in Hebrew and Aramaic; and Dom Raphaël de Monachis, who continued teaching Champollion in Coptic and Arabic. By the end of the following year, Champollion had reworked his earlier Grenoble essay into a draft of a book, which he tentatively called *L'Egypte sous les Pharaons*, a geographical study of Upper and Lower Egypt that ultimately was published in two volumes in 1814. Favoring Coptic over any other language, Champollion also embarked on writing a Coptic grammar and dictionary.

During all this time, his foremost worries were first, his deteriorating health; and second, the fear of conscription. Champollion sensed what his brother more fully realized—that such intense study made him both weak and irritable. Paris, with its relatively cold and damp climate, was not agreeable to him. He worked with such abandon that he spent himself. Had he developed more friends and a healthier social life, he may well have learned how best to pace himself and preserve his energies. Instead, tied up within himself as tightly as the bowstrings of a new violin, he continually drove himself to ill health. Yet his course was set—master Coptic before turning to the Demotic found on the Rosetta Stone.

His other fear was that of being conscripted into Napoléon's Grande Armée. At a time when French soldiers were dying at the alarming rate of well over 100,000 men per year, with even worse years soon to come, avoiding military service appeared almost impossible. Had it not been for the continuing intercessions of Fourier and other scholars, Champollion may well have been doing his duty in some garrison outpost on the outskirts of Napoléon's empire—or worse!

In May 1810, both he and Jacques-Joseph once more moved to Grenoble, this time to teach at one of Napoléon's new universities that had recently opened there. The year 1812, as we have seen, meanwhile turned out to be a nightmare for Napoléon and all of France, and Grenoble itself was only spared massive bombardment by advancing Austrian forces because of Napoléon's surrender. Ever more inclined to openly support Napoléon, Champollion and his brother were constantly creating enemies. On hearing of Napoléon's escape from Elba and his approach to Grenoble at the head of an expanding army on its way to Paris, Champollion prepared to meet his hero for the first time. The two men met only briefly between Napoléon's hurried dispatches, with the emperor saying, "It's a good omen—he has half my name."[35] Napoléon, on his way northward, showed genuine interest in Champollion and promised to see his manuscript published in Paris. The two men, one bound for Waterloo, the other for a destiny of a different kind—never met again.

With Napoléon's subsequent defeat and banishment to St. Helena, the restored Bourbon monarchy shut down the University of Grenoble and all but exiled the Champollion brothers to Figeac. Fortunately, however, Jacques-Joseph soon afterwards received an appointment as secretary of the Académie des Inscriptions et Belles-Lettres back in Paris, while Champollion returned to Grenoble to accept a history professorship at a new Royal College. Because of continuing intrigues and opposition by his political enemies, Champollion was, however, soon dismissed and almost jailed for alleged treason before his ever more tactful and diplomatic brother rescued him yet again by bringing him back to Paris to work in the Institut. Forever poor, in precarious health, and continually on the run from one place to another, Champollion—who by now had married a young woman named Rosine Blanc in December 1818—was an outcast in his own country. Unable to relate well even to his closest friends, Champollion was never the best of husbands. Though his wife deeply loved him, he seemed incapable of forming a healthy relationship with her. To the end, Champollion's

---

35. Adkins and Adkins, *Keys of Egypt*, 123.

closest confidante and emotional support was his older brother, although he once fancied himself in love with a much older woman. His life was learning, not loving. Yet despite these obstacles, his prodigious talents as a linguist were real and his personal commitment to decipher the Rosetta Stone was unflagging—a task he renewed with increasing devotion aware now, more than ever, that he was in a race with time.

An Englishman almost solved the Rosetta puzzle before Champollion did. The brilliant English physician, mathematician, and scientist Thomas Young, a man seventeen years Champollion's senior who was financially independent and revered by his government and countrymen, had already earned a reputation for his study of optics. Having convinced himself that the hieratic script was a derivative of the hieroglyphs, Young began to turn his energy and prodigious language talents to deciphering the Rosetta Stone in 1814. Applying his remarkable mathematical skills (precisely what Champollion lacked) to the challenge, Young made impressive progress, soon identifying numbers and plural forms in hieroglyphs. Before long, Young was able to read the word *Ptolemy* in the Rosetta Stone, and he correctly deciphered at least a half a dozen hieroglyphic letters by careful comparison with the Demotic. Most importantly, he concluded—rightly, as time would tell—that hieroglyphs were not primarily pictographs but representations of distinctive sounds, like an ancient alphabet. Had he a better command of Coptic, he would have been able to read more of the Demotic and, by extension and comparison, decoded more of the ancient language of the hieroglyphs.

Back in France, whereas Champollion first naively believed that a thoroughgoing knowledge of Coptic would allow him to directly decipher the hieroglyphs, he gradually came to the realization that, dauntingly, such was not the case. Hieroglyphics were not a single alphabet; rather, they had a wide variety of spellings for the same person or place, and they had no vowels but plenty of shorthand contractions, such as in English one might write "pkg" for "parking," "unvsty" for "university," or "∴" for "therefore." Furthermore, ancient scribes assumed the reader knew the combinations of right vowels and contractions, "but this knowledge had been lost, although Coptic gives clues to it."[36]

After long and painstaking effort, Champollion concluded that hieroglyphs could not be read alone but in groups or clusters. Intently comparing the Greek to the Coptic, the Coptic to the Demotic and, by extension, the Demotic to the hieroglyphs, Champollion noted that there were three times as many hieroglyphic signs as there were Greek words and, therefore, that there had to be a combination or grouping of signs to convey a single meaning—in other words, consonants and syllables, essential components to phonetic expressions. Hieroglyphs were a combination of phonetics and pictures. Unlike Young, Champollion was now looking not just for more clues between the hieroglyphic and the Demotic but also for the ability to read the hieroglyphs themselves.

An important, contributing discovery, one that confirmed if not enhanced both Young and Champollion's interpretations of the Rosetta Stone, was the arrival in England in the

---

36. Adkins and Adkins, *Keys of Egypt*, 84.

winter of 1820–21 of the so-called Bankes's obelisk, with its own set of Greek and hieroglyphic inscriptions. The obelisk was discovered in Philae in 1815 by the aforementioned Belzoni and turned over to William John Bankes, the British antiquarian and collector, who believed the obelisk should add much to human understanding. Young mistakenly concluded that the obelisk's hieroglyphs and Greek writings must represent the same text and meaning. Young jealously refused to publish or disseminate the writings on the obelisk for almost a year. When Champollion finally obtained a copy of its inscriptions, he deciphered the word "Cleopatra," which Bankes had also deciphered, and painstakingly and methodically expanded his understanding of several other hieroglyphic signs.[37]

Then, on the morning of 14 September 1822, while living with his brother on 22 Rue Mazarine in Paris, Champollion received yet another indispensable piece to the puzzle. Drawings of hieroglyphs from the temple of Abu Simbel, done by Jean-Nicolas Huyot—architect of the famous Arc de Triomphe—arrived in the post. Thanks to the recent excavation work of Burckhardt and Belzoni, Huyot had gained entrance to the temple and made faithful drawings and replications of the temple's monumental writings. Historians Roy and Lesley Adkins explain what happened next:

> Poring over the drawings in his attic room in the rue Mazarine, Champollion soon noticed names within cartouches—names that he had never seen before. The first sheet contained ⊙🅜🅟, and he immediately recognized the first sign ⊙ as a picture of the sun. He knew that in Coptic the word for sun was Re or Ra, which also happened to be the name for the ancient Egyptian sun god. From his earlier work he knew the last two signs 🅜🅟 would transliterate as 's' in Ptolemaic or Roman names, which if applied to this cartouche would give 'Ra . . . ss,' or more likely 'Ra . . . ses' because vowels were not normally shown in hieroglyphs. At once he saw that if the other sign 🅜 was 'm,' it would represent 'Rameses,' a name known to have been used by several pharaohs well before the Greek and Roman rule in Egypt–which is nowadays spelled as Ramses, Rameses or Ramesses. With mounting excitement and joy as he began to understand what was happening, yet still fearful that he would find proof that his system was totally wrong, he searched the rest of the Abu Simbel drawings and found the name 🅘🅜🅟. Once again he read 🅜🅟 as 'mes,' and he recognized the sign in front as a picture of an ibis, recorded by ancient writers as the symbol of the god Thoth who was revered by the Egyptians as the inventor of hieroglyphs and god of scribes. The name on the cartouche therefore read 'Thothmes,' better known nowadays by the ancient Greek version of the name, Tuthmosis—another name used by several pharaohs well before Greek and Roman times. . . . Champollion

---

37. Bankes, a friend of Young and a scornful critic of Champollion, believed that Champollion had stolen from Bankes's scribbled annotation on a lithograph of the inscription from the obelisk, where he had deciphered the name Cleopatra. Champollion always denied the accusation and went on to formulate his system of decipherment quite independent of Bankes. See Usick, *Adventures in Egypt and Nubia*, 76–80.

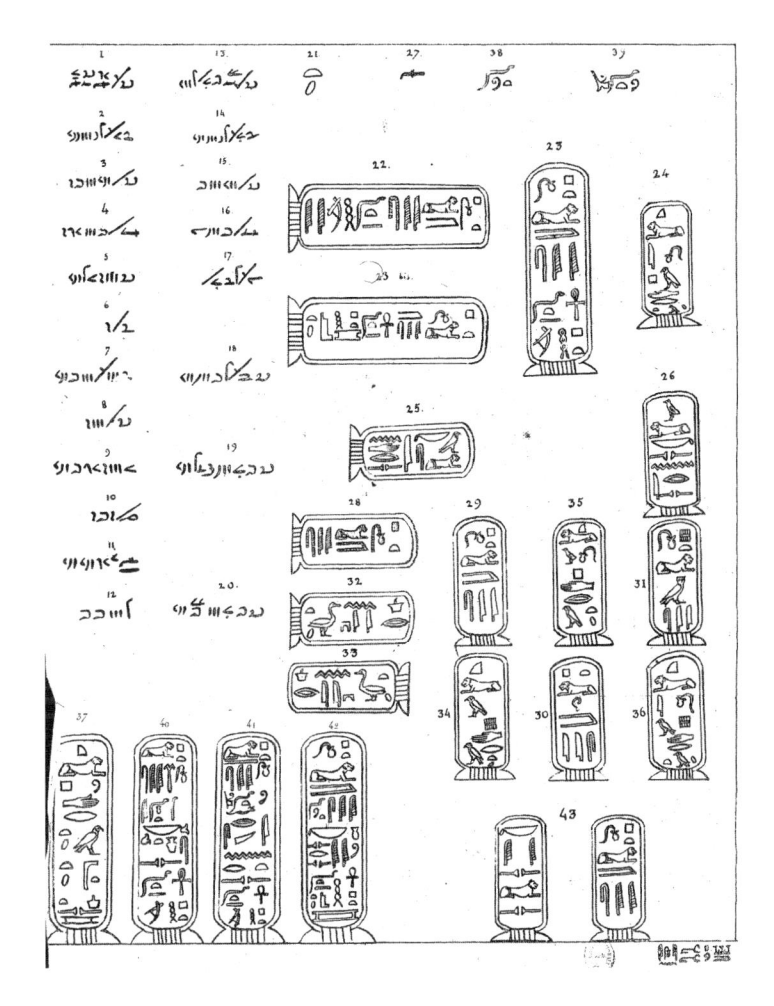

Lettre à M. Dacier relative à l'alphabet des hiéroglyphes phonétiques, p. 54, by Jean-François Champollion. Courtesy of Bibliothèque Nationale de France.

instantly saw the underlying principle, and it confirmed the system of decipherment that he had been painstakingly putting together, piece by piece, over the last few months.[38]

What finally enabled Champollion to do what neither Young nor any others were able to accomplish was to apply his mastery of Coptic to the problem. "His knowledge of Coptic enabled him to deduce the phonetic values of many syllabic signs, and to assign correct readings to many pictorial characters, the meanings of which were made known to him by the Greek text on the Stone."[39] The system of decipherment that Champollion had been

---

38. Adkins and Adkins, *Keys of Egypt*, 180–81.
39. Budge, *Rosetta Stone*, 4.

methodically developing over several years and now verified was that hieroglyphic script was mainly phonetic but not entirely so. It also contained logograms that were used to write native names and common nouns from the pharaonic period. The combination of both constituted an ancient alphabet that he now could prove and sufficiently read or decipher. Champollion thus came to the rightful conclusion that the hieroglyphic writings within cartouches were not only of the later periods of Egyptian history but also of the every earliest pharaonic era, thus proving the ability to read the ancient transcriptions as well as the much later ones. The system was, therefore, decoded and proved that hieroglyphic, hieratic, and Demotic all corresponded to the same language. Whereas Young may well have discovered parts of the alphabet, it was "Champollion [who] unlocked an entire language."[40]

In a state of exhaustion mingled with euphoria, Champollion gathered up his papers, rushed downstairs into the street, before heading out to find his brother, then working at the nearby Institut de France. As the story goes, by the time he found his brother, Champollion was totally out of breath. Falling to the floor, he cried out, "Je tiens mon affaire!" (I've done it) and collapsed in a dead faint.[41]

Champollion's subsequent letter of discovery dated 22 September 1822 and written to M. Dacier was read at the *Academie des Inscriptions at Belles Lettres* just five days later on 27 September, with none other than Champollion's rival, Thomas Young, in attendance. His British counterpart refused, at first, to accept many of his rival's decodings, assuming they were false, if not borrowed from him. However, he admitted that Champollion's findings "appear[ed] to be gigantic." Running out of research time and money, Young, jealous to the end, more or less abandoned the field to Champollion and died in May 1829.[42]

What Champollion merely hinted at in his "Lettre à M. Dacier," he later elaborated upon in his classic work *Précis du Système Hiéroglyphique des Anciens Egyptiens par M. Champollion le jeune*, published in Paris in March 1824. A later edition followed in 1828.

Champollion's reputation extended far beyond the decoding of the Rosetta Stone. While this remarkable feat earned him an almost instant reputation as the leading expert on Egyptian writings and antiquities, he was soon to make other contributions as well.[43] In 1824, Champollion traveled to London, where he gazed upon the Rosetta Stone for the first time, the translator and the stone finally face to face. From there he journeyed to Italy to catalog the various Egyptian monuments at Naples, Florence, and Rome. Authenticating Drovetti's collection of antiquities as worthy of purchase and preservation, Champollion played a positive role in the sale of Drovetti's magnificent collection to Turin. In March 1825, Champol-

---

40. Parkinson, *Cracking Codes*, 40.
41. Parkinson, *Cracking Codes*, 35; and Adkins and Adkins, *Keys of Egypt*, 181. There is some slight disagreement between the above scholars as to precisely what Champollion said: either "je tiens l'affaire" *or* "je tiens mon affaire."
42. Adkins and Adkins, *Keys of Egypt*, 204.
43. British consul Henry Salt wrote, "You will be surprised to hear that I have become a complete convert to Monsieur Champollion's file system of explaining the hieroglyphics." Henry Salt to William Hamilton, 4 October 1824, in Halls, *Life and Correspondence*, 2:239.

lion moved on to Florence and Rome, deciphering what he could in one great museum after another. Appointed curator of the Egyptian Museum at the Louvre, as well as professor of Egyptian Antiquities at the *Collège de France* in 1827, Champollion soon embarked on an eighteen-month expedition to Egypt—his one and only journey to the land that had dominated his life. He departed in the summer of 1828, thirty years after Napoléon's invasion, to confirm his system of decipherment and to make more accurate maps and drawings. Greeted as "the man who could read the writings and the old stones,"[44] Champollion urged Ali to put an end to all looting and desecration of Egyptian tombs, temples, and antiquities, a recommendation that was put into law in 1835. Furthermore, he made extensive and careful field notes and meticulous drawings wherever he went, most of which were later published posthumously. Dying tragically far too young, at the age of forty-one, of a stroke brought on by overexertion on 4 March 1832, Champollion will ever be regarded as the father of modern Egyptology.

SINCE CHAMPOLLION

Thanks in large measure to the prodigious work of the leading German archaeologist Karl Richard Lepsius, with his studies of other trilingual decrees found at Tanis, Champollion's hypothesis was finally proven a generation after his death.[45] In America, the first complete translation of the Rosetta Stone, based solely on Champollion's methods, appeared in 1858 as the *Report of the Committee Appointed by the Philomathean Society of the University of Pennsylvania to Translate the Inscription*, authored by C. R. Hale, S. H. Jones, and H. Morton. However, Professor Samuel Latham Mitchill, the foremost American naturalist of Columbia University, knew of Champollion's work as early as 1828.[46]

---

44. Adkins and Adkins, *Keys of Egypt*, 247.
45. David, *Experience of Ancient Egypt*, 81.
46. Of further interest to the Latter-day Saint reader is the fact that Martin Harris, seeking linguistic and scientific corroboration for the characters and engravings Joseph Smith had found on the plates of gold, which Joseph had received from the angel Moroni in September 1827, traveled to Columbia University in February 1828. After Harris visited with Professor Charles Anthon, who was a learned classicist but who knew virtually nothing about Egyptian, Anthon then referred him to his older, more esteemed, and much more approachable colleague, Professor Samuel L. Mitchill, whom even President Thomas Jefferson called "the Congressional Dictionary" because of his vast knowledge of ancient American antiquities and languages. A member of the prestigious American Philosophical Society in Philadelphia, Mitchill "perlitely" received Harris and began to examine carefully the engravings Harris had brought with him. Mitchill then "made a learned dissertation on them" and "compared them with the hieroglyphics discovered by Champollion in Egypt and set them down as the language of a people formerly in existence in the East, but now no more." Bennett, "Mormon Religion—Clerical Ambition," 362. For a more complete study of this fascinating episode, see Bennett, "'Read This I Pray Thee,'" 178–216.

The immediate interest among many in Champollion's decipherings and Belzoni's discoveries was an early endeavor to show that all such things proved the historicity and validity of the Holy Bible, especially its Old Testament accounts of ancient peoples. At the time, the Bible was very much in ascendency because of the incredible dissemination efforts of the British and Foreign Bible Society (see chapter 10) and its later counterpart the American Bible Society. The birth of Egyptology was, as so many then assumed, evidence of God's holy writ. The pope even wanted to make Champollion a cardinal because his discoveries seemed to substantiate the chronology of the Bible. Newspapers and journals throughout the world published scores of articles showing how all such findings—the references to and experiences with Egyptian whirlwinds, mirages, locusts—all proved the accuracy of biblical accounts.[47]

Today, scholars seem less interested in proving the validity and chronology of the Bible and more committed to integrating the study of Egypt with such other disciplines as anthropology, writing, archaeology, art history, and literature. "There is a general movement away from socio-functional approaches towards attempting to reconstruct individual lives and contexts in more plausible shapes and detail."[48] Modern scholars still strive to understand what remains, in fact, an entirely different culture from that of modern civilization, with its different mindsets and alphabetic languages.

The systematic study of the language has continued ever since under such scholars as the Irish Reverend Edward Hincks, Heinrich Brugsch, Adolf Erman, Kurt Sethe, Francis Griffith, Battiscombe Gunn, and Sir Alan Gardiner. Yet, for all this, Champollion's achievement remains the key "turning point of a study which is still progressing." And the Rosetta Stone still maintains its supreme place in the pantheon of Egyptian discoveries, a silent, ever-beckoning, always fascinating "bridge between our world today and the ancient Egyptian [which] seems too vast to contemplate."[49]

The history of Napoléon's invasion of Egypt in 1798, the resultant discovery and Champollion's incredulous deciphering of the Rosetta Stone, the publication of *La Description de*

---

47. Note the following argument as quoted in the *British Review* and reprinted in the American publication *Saturday Magazine* in August 1821: "The account of the invasion of Judea, by Pharaoh-Necho, King of Egypt, related in 2 Kings 23:29–34 . . . is confirmed by the sculptures discovered by Mr. Belzoni in the tomb of his son Psammethis. Necho conquered Jerusalem and Babylon, and Psammethis made war against the Ethiopians. In one of the halls of this tomb is a military procession consisting of a great number of figures, all looking towards a man who is greatly superior to them in size, and who faces them. At the end of this procession . . . are three different sorts of people . . . evidently Jews, Ethiopians, and Persians. . . . Behind the Persians are some Egyptians without their ornaments, as if they were rescued captives returning to their country. Among the hieroglyphics, contained in his drawings of this tomb, Dr. Thomas Young (who is preeminently distinguished for his successful researches in archaeology) has discovered the names of Nichas (Necho) and Psammethis." From "Belzoni's Discoveries in Egypt and Nubia," 124.
48. Parkinson, *Cracking Codes*, 177.
49. Parkinson, *Cracking Codes*, 42–43.

l'Egypte, and the incredible discoveries by a host of fascinating excavators along the Nile—some of which led to the translation of the Book of Abraham—continue to fascinate readers two hundred years later. It was a time of amazing finds and the unfolding of unknown ancient worlds of knowledge. While remarkable excavations and discoveries were indeed made, and whereas Champollion brilliantly decoded the ancient hieroglyphs of Egypt in our era of 1820, it seems entirely possible that much of the life and culture of the pattern of human thought among Egyptian ancients remains to be discovered.

Equestrian Portrait of Alexander I (1777–1825), by Franz Krüger (c. 1837, Hermitage).

TSAR ALEXANDER I

THE KING OF THE NORTH AND HIS HOLY ALLIANCE

With Napoléon encamped in Moscow in October 1812, waiting impatiently for terms of surrender, and with General Kutuzov and the Russian army hunkered down just fifty miles to the southwest, Russia's thirty-five-year-old emperor, Tsar Alexander I, stared outside his St. Petersburg palace window, wondering what his next move should be. Stung by his staggering losses at Borodino, saddened by those who now called him a coward, and secretly tormenting himself for Russia's steep decline, Tsar Alexander was a discouraged, almost defeated, man.

In this moment of despair, he once more reverted to studying the Holy Bible while listening intently to the counsel of his lifelong, boyhood friend Prince Alexander Golitzen, now procurator of the Holy Synod and effective leader of the Russian Orthodox Church. As the story goes, Golitzen was in the act of opening a huge, folio-sized Bible in front of Alexander when it suddenly slipped from his grasp, fell to the floor, and opened to the book of Psalms, the ninety-first chapter: "I will say of the Lord, He is my refuge and my fortress, my God; in him will I trust. . . . He shall cover thee with his feathers and under his wings shalt thou trust: Thou shalt not be afraid for the terror by night; nor for the arrow that flieth by day. . . . A thousand shall fall at thy side, and ten thousand at thy right hand; but it shall not come nigh thee" (Psalm 91:2, 5, 7).

Upon hearing the same verse read at church the following day, Alexander took it as a heaven-sent sign and immediately plunged headlong into an intensive study of the Old Testament prophets. "I simply devoured the Bible," he later admitted, "finding that its words poured an unknown peace into my heart and quenched the thirst of my soul."[1] Feeling that Russia's defeat was a personal condemnation for his past sins, Alexander gained a new level of inspiration and sense of forgiveness from searching the scriptures. He gained a resolve to continue the conflict against the conqueror. When the French emperor demanded terms, an emboldened Alexander thundered back his now famous retort, "Peace? We have not yet made war!"[2] As history has shown, Alexander, more than any other man, would become responsible for defeating the French and for the restructuring of the new European order.

So who was this enigma of St. Petersburg? Who were the ghosts that haunted him and the men and women who inspired him? What role did he eventually play in refashioning Europe after the end of the Napoleonic Wars? And what contributions would he make to the era of profound peace that followed the Congress of Vienna and that came to characterize the age of 1820, our continuing focal point of study?

"SOMETHING IS MISSING IN HIS CHARACTER"

Alexander was his grandmother's son—or at least he seemed to be. Catherine the Great, who had wrested the empire from her husband in 1762, would rule Russia until 1796. A powerful, often ruthless, woman whose life was her country, Catherine expanded the Russian Empire by force of conquest to the Black Sea and the Crimea, transforming Russia into a true superpower. While expanding Russia's vast and seemingly limitless borders, she initiated important liberalizing reforms that endeared her to her people, such as reducing the powers of the clergy, improving education at all levels, establishing a system of local governments, supporting the arts, and modernizing a country and society still slow and almost boorishly backward by modern European standards. She desperately sought to continue such liberal reforms and territorial expansions through her successor son, Paul, but concluded that by disposition and deportment, he would utterly fail her and the Empire. She disdained him for his pedantry, his lack of vision and intelligence, and instead fastened her attention on her grandsons, Alexander (born in 1777) and his younger brother, Constantine (born in 1779), both sons of Paul and his wife, Maria Feodorovna. With no law of primogeniture in place, it was the reigning Russian monarch's right to choose his or her own successor.

Catherine came to favor Alexander as much as she disdained her own son. She saw in her grandson, who was indeed precocious, gifted, and startlingly handsome, the very qualities her son lacked, and she actively planned for Alexander to succeed her to the throne.

---

1. Troubetzkoy, *Imperial Legend*, 105. See also Zorin, "'Star of the East,'" 317. Alexander himself recorded: "I read the Psalms, which again and again gave me new courage to withstand the dark hours of the trial sent to me, I was sure of this, from above. I read in the prophets Isaiah, Jeremiah, Ezekiel; and I knew that I would withstand the hour of tribulation. I had not thought much of religion in previous years, but now, having reached the depth of despair and not knowing what would happen next, I had no other support or comfort than religion. The God of the Old Testament prophets was also my God." Klimenko, *Notes of Alexander I*, 196.
2. Troubetzkoy, *Imperial Legend*, 106.

Denying his parents of their rightful role, Catherine assumed the rearing and governorship of Alexander and resolved to mold him into the kind of leader she believed Russia needed in the coming nineteenth century.

Although Alexander was born in a palace, Catherine raised him in austere conditions so he would know the hardships of his people. His bedroom window would always be left open so that he would feel the cold of a Russian winter. His bed was never comfortable; it was one made of straw and thick leather. She purposely ordered regimental batteries nearby to fire their cannons and shout their orders so loudly that Alexander would easily hear them and sense early on the rhythm and sounds of military life. Because of this, he lost the hearing in his left ear in his early youth. On the other hand, she insisted that he wear the finest clothes and the best in silk stockings, that he be exposed to fine art and great literature, and that he learn to appreciate high society and the fineries of royalty and high court living.

Catherine II, by Franz Krüge, after Roslin (c. 1770, Hermitage).

After Alexander turned twelve years old, Catherine entrusted his education to the noted Swiss tutor Frédéric La Harpe. A liberal and republican by training and a friend of Rousseau, La Harpe emphasized the arts and the humanities over math and science and taught his young pupil in the principles of the Enlightenment, exposing him to such writers and thinkers as Plato, Demosthenes, Plutarch, Tacitus, Locke, and Descartes. If not a gifted student, Alexander soon gained "a comfortable command of five languages," including English but especially French, the language of international diplomacy. Soon it became his favored language. Ironically, he was never able to communicate thoroughly in his native Russian. La Harpe's influence upon Alexander was profound and contributed much to his developing sense of egalitarianism, needed liberal reforms, social justice, and careful diplomacy. Until La Harpe's death in 1838, the two men carried on a warm and friendly correspondence, a godfather–godson type of relationship.

Catherine also selected the woman Alexander would marry. After searching everywhere in royal courts all across Europe, she finally settled on the young and beautiful fifteen-year-old German princess Louise of Baden—the Grand Duchess Elizaveta Alexeyovna, as she came to be called. Elizabeth was a charming and intelligent, though not forceful, woman.

Elizaveta Alexayovna. *Portrait of Empress Elisabeth Alexeievna of Russia*, by Louise Élisabeth Vigée Le Brun (1795, Castle of Wolfsgarten).

She and Alexander were married in a grand royal wedding ceremony in St. Petersburg on 28 September 1793 to the applause of thousands and the thundering peals of a twenty-one-gun salute.

Alexander had a romantic longing that he never satisfied in the marriage bed. He enjoyed being around beautiful and intelligent women "in whose company he found greater comfort than he ever did with men." Scandalously unfaithful, he took on a succession of mistresses, his lifelong favorite being the beautiful and seductive Polish countess Maria Naryshkina (1779–1854), who bore him at least one daughter. As one scholar wryly noted, "Sex to him was a many-roomed mansion."[3]

Arranged marriages seldom spoke of love and rarely succeeded, but the marriage of Alexander and Elizabeth came to be one of true friendship that deepened through the years. She gave birth to a daughter, Lisinka, who died when only eighteen months old, and never produced a male heir. Alexander, though not quite sixteen years of age when he married, was already smarting under the dominance of his demanding, overly controlling grandmother. Gradually he asserted his independence and reverted more and more to the influences of his own parents—his father teaching him a love for military drill, parade dress, and procession and his mother cultivating a sense of tenderness and dealing mercifully with others.

So the future emperor learned contrasting worlds—absolutism and brute force on the one hand, liberalism and a spirit of kind forgiveness on the other. He was, as the Russian romantic poet Aleksandr Pushkin once called him, "a Sphinx who carried his riddle with him to the tomb."[4] A born diplomat, astute politician, and dramatist who knew how to handle people in virtually every situation, Alexander was inconsistent and secretive, as one who never really knew himself nor the full consequences of his actions. Said Napoléon, who

---

3. Troubetzkoy, *Imperial Legend*, 62.
4. Palmer, *Alexander I*, xvii.

Alexander ever admired as the greatest man of the age, "Something is missing in his character, but I find it impossible to discover what it is."[5]

AN AMBIVALENT HAMLET

But there was much more to Alexander's troubled soul. With the unexpected death of Catherine the Great by a stroke in November 1796, her son Paul, the "mad tsar," became emperor of Russia's forty million people. Unprepared for leadership, poorly taught, and ill-disposed by personality and training to handle the rigors of a position his mother never believed he could fulfill, Paul proved a dismal failure as Russia's new petty tyrant and Romanov emperor. In his short three-year rule, he reversed many of the reforms and policies of his mother, viewed the French Revolution as an invidious threat, restricted freedoms of speech and literature, and increased the powers of the hated secret police. His reign was marred by his ruthlessness and paranoia of virtually everyone around him and his misjudgments in diplomacy and international affairs. As a result, a mood of military mutiny developed, and many feared that, like England's King George III, Paul was losing his mind. Surely, he was Russia's most uncomfortable emperor, totally unsuited for power. Even his closest advisers came to believe that something drastic had to be done to save the motherland—a forced abduction, banishment, or worse. His son, Alexander, could then reign and rule as Russia's regent, as George IV would do for many years in England.

If Alexander agreed to the plot to arrange his father's banishment, he never consented, at least not explicitly, to the conspiracy that took his life. "All along he had truly, perhaps, naively, believed that a peaceful abdication was possible."[6] A palace murder, however, was exactly what transpired when late on the night of 23–24 March 1801 in the supposed safety of his own chambers, Paul was cruelly bludgeoned to death by his own guards and honored advisers. The news given out to Russia was that he had died of natural causes, most likely of an apoplectic seizure. His wife, Maria Feodorovna, almost immediately blamed her son Alexander for the murder, though she later changed her mind as more details of the killing emerged. Alexander, however, was stunned by the tragedy and seemingly unaware of how far this deadly turn of events had gone. He came to blame himself, if not for killing his father, then for not saving his life. He soon began to torment himself for his father's death and more particularly for the cruel manner in which he had been killed. Alexander was driven to moments of deep despair and anguish for being an unwitting accomplice in the affair. "It imposed upon him an ineffaceable stain," wrote one of his more recent biographers, "and it could never be wiped from his soul. . . . It settled like a vulture on his conscience and paralyzed his best intentions and faculties from the beginning of his reign, . . . plung[ing] him

---

5. Troubetzkoy, *Imperial Legend*, 65. François-René Chateaubriand, French author and diplomat, once said of him, he "had a strong soul and a weak character" (65).
6. Troubetzkoy, *Imperial Legend*, 57.

into a somber reflection and mysticism, sometimes degenerating into superstition."[7] "His mental tortures never ceased thereafter," as another of his biographers phrased it. "As the months passed into years, with the murderers themselves unpunished, it became clear that Alexander was haunted, not by the crime he never witnessed, but by the conspiracy of which he had known too much and too little."[8]

He was anointed Emperor Tsar Alexander I by the Metropolitan of the Russian Orthodox Church at elaborate ceremonies in St. Petersburg on 15 September 1801. The young and handsome twenty-three-year-old emperor, with Empress Elizabeth at his side, spoke the Orthodox Confession, prayed aloud for guidance and forgiveness (a most positive sign to the throngs of clergy attending the ceremony), and sought for the well-being of the Holy Russian Empire. Gathering in the streets of St. Petersburg, men and women bowed in reverence or thronged him eagerly to catch a passing glance as he rode by. Elegant as he was affable, the new tsar carried the hearts and hopes of Russia with him. Surely, they thought, he would usher in the needed reforms for which so many were praying.

Few reigns began so promisingly. Seeing himself as the protector of the weak and oppressed, Alexander in a single command restored the freedoms of the press and of the rights of assembly and travel, released thousands of political prisoners, and curtailed the excesses of the dreaded "secret chancellor," or state police. He also founded the Society of Russian History and Antiquity, which began the collection of ancient documents and manuscripts that would prove helpful to later generations of scholars.

Surrounded by his "committee of friends," consisting of gifted, liberal-minded young reformers who were encouraged by Thomas Jefferson and inspired by the 1789 French Declaration of the Rights of Man, Alexander also streamlined government bureaucracies and gave careful consideration to establishing a form of constitutional monarchy and an elected representative assembly. And, in the revolutionary spirit of the time, Alexander and his advisers likewise considered abolishing that most deadening of all Russian institutions—serfdom! Had it not been for the vested powers of the influential privileged classes—the nobility and the clergy—he would likely have gone much further.

Unfortunately, the tradition-bound, ritualistic, and overly conservative Russian Orthodox Church was never comfortable with the free-spirited religious nature of the new emperor. Since at least 1789, Russia had been experiencing a revival of Christian religion not seen in centuries. Taking many different forms, this rebirth of piety was "stimulated by a rejection of the decayed formation of official churches" and by "the excesses of rationalism and skepticism."[9] Whether English evangelicalism, German Pietism, or simple English Quaker-style spirituality, there was at this auspicious time a widespread, genuine hunger for new modes of religious experience.

---

7. Klimenko, *Tsar Alexander I*, 85.
8. Palmer, *Alexander I*, 46.
9. Zacek, "Russian Bible Society," 418.

In Russia, despite the opposition of the church, mysticism had become very popular. Increasingly uncomfortable with dogmas, ancient creeds, and liturgical ritual, these Christian mystics sought the "internal church," a kind of spiritual rebirth by which men lived in Christ and Christ in man, a true mystical union and communion with God.[10] Freemasonry—with its long-standing emphasis on brotherhood and equality, on secret oaths and sacred lodges, and on Christian service and virtuous living—became "a comforting social anchor" and religious expression for many. It would flourish all across Russia until it was eventually repressed in the religious retrenchments of the late 1820s.[11]

Above all, in this short-lived window of religious freedom and opportunity that existed from about 1790 to 1825, the Russian Bible Society virtually swept the country. Established in 1813 as an extension of the British Foreign Bible Society (see chapter 10), the Russian Bible Society was a favorite of Alexander; Golitzen (Golitsyn), his minister of Foreign Creeds; and even, least initially, the Russian Orthodox Church. More than a mere mechanism for distributing the Bible into the homes of millions who had never before possessed scriptures in their home, the Russian Bible Society was an ambitious, enthusiastic, Christian crusade involving the energies of hundreds of thousands of loyal supporters in disseminating the Bible. In the repressive years that followed Alexander's reign, as historian Judith Cohen Zacek has noted, Russia "settled back into its age-old formalism, narrow-mindedness, and theological stagnation," and in 1826 the Russian Bible Society was abolished, though not without leaving an indelible impression upon the Slavic soul.

Meanwhile, in 1807 Mikhail Speransky, one of the country's most revered reformers, became Alexander's governor-general, closest confidant, and financial adviser, a power behind the throne. Within only two years, Speransky became secretary of state and effectively prime minister of Russia. A deeply religious, highly intellectual personality with both conservative and progressive views, Speransky was a firm believer in the state's active role in directing the progress of the nation while at the same time wishing

Portrait of M. M. Speransky, by unknown artist.

---

10. Zacek, "Russian Bible Society," 422.
11. Smith, *Working the Rough Stone*, 177. One reason for the repression of the Freemasons was the suspicion that they fostered a spirit of revolution.

to promote "the untrammeled activity and free enterprise of individuals."[12] Speransky was a true agent for change. He proposed such far-sweeping liberal reforms as a limited constitutional monarchy, a system of much-improved education, the cautious reduction of serfdom, the establishment of luxury taxes on the rich, and entrance exams for potential civil servants. One of his most lasting achievements was to codify Russian law and to infuse into government bureaucracy a sense of the spiritual and of greater morality.[13]

Tragically for Russia and its future, Speransky's jealous enemies successfully portrayed him as a traitor to Mother Russia and a defender of French political ideals and freedoms as the shadow of Napoléon loomed ever larger and more menacingly across Europe. Speransky's tragic fall and dismissal in 1811 by a tsar who ever loved him but was too weak to sustain him marked the end of Alexander's age of reform—it had been a sacrifice to the vested interests of selfish landowners, the nobility, and the church. Had Alexander possessed the strength of his own convictions, a less divided personality without the weaknesses of character that played into the hands of powerful detractors, his reign might have ended far more successfully than it did. Had he shown the courage to transform society as he once daringly set out to do, his reforms may well have saved Russia and the whole world from the bloody atrocities of the Russian Revolution and the scourge of Communism a century later.[14] So it is that the great door of history turns on such tiny human hinges.

A TALE OF TWO EMPERORS

By 1804 the insatiably ambitious and unstoppable Napoléon had already overrun Italy, Belgium, Holland, Switzerland, Spain, the Rhine states, the Duchy of Warsaw (Poland), Denmark, Norway, and much of Prussia and Austria. As we have seen previously, the emperor of the West had no desire to invade Russia then but instead sought to overpower Great Britain, one way or the other. Similarly, Alexander, the emperor of the East, had no desire to confront the French juggernaut. Only because of his previous alliances with Prussia and Austria, now staggering under the weight of Napoléon's blows, was Alexander finally drawn into open warfare at Austerlitz (in present-day Czechoslovakia) in December 1805.

With a flair for the theatrical and a naive, exaggerated, and untested belief in his own abilities as a military commander, a bewildered Alexander overruled his top generals and rode to the front of the Russian armies against a far more experienced, savvy, and formidable opponent. With the combined Russian, Austrian, and Prussian lines divided too thinly at the center, Napoléon waited cat-like for the opportune moment to pounce. Constantine, Alex-

---

12. Raeff, *Michael Speransky*, 306. In his political biography of Speransky, Raeff argues for a much more cautious, more conservative, reformer than do other students of Speransky. Nevertheless, even he concludes that despite his weaknesses of character and mystical personality, Speransky "helped to bring about a fundamental break with the past" and "brought order, lawfulness and stability into government machinery" (366).
13. Raeff, *Speransky*, 362.
14. Palmer, *Alexander I*, 87.

ander's brother, led a foolish cavalry charge in which he was almost killed. What Alexander hoped would have been a great victory soon turned into a murderous rout, with Alexander himself almost being captured. The Russian Army retreated, badly bruised but unbroken. Napoléon once again carried the day, while a shattered Alexander, shedding tears of humiliation, retreated in disgrace to St. Petersburg. It was a cruel and bloody lesson in the heartless realities of war. Public reaction to Alexander's bungling of the battle soon turned bitter and angry, and those who had once shouted his praises now jeered in derision. For months, as became his custom, Tsar Alexander turned inward and noncommunicative, full of remorse, self-condemnation, and regret.

In the meantime, Napoléon kept on coming, winning at Jena, Auerstadt, and Friedland in June 1807. With neither man wanting to take on the other at this time, Napoléon sued for a peace that Alexander was more than eager to accept. In their famous Treaty of Tilsit, signed on a raft in the middle of the Niemen River, the two men countersigned what essentially became a treaty of distrust, where each promised to leave the other alone—at least long enough for Napoléon to carve up Europe and Alexander to do the same with Turkey and the Ottoman Empire. Alexander agreed to join Napoléon's continental embargo of Great Britain on the condition that Napoléon would let Alexander expand into Finland, Sweden, and Constantinople. Both agreed to divide Prussia between themselves. While Napoléon thought he was charming his Russian counterpart into believing he was Russia's foremost ally, he never fully gauged Alexander's political astuteness and unyielding loyalty to the motherland. The fact is, the two men never did understand one another—Napoléon underestimating Alexander's resolve and Alexander overestimating Napoléon's political savvy.

But the continental system proved ruinous to the Russian economy. And Napoléon's excesses and brutality galvanized opposition in virtually every sphere and segment of Russian society. Despite his setbacks, Tsar Alexander was now regarded by serf and noble alike as Russia's only true hope and the only force strong enough to counter the "Corsican anti-Christ." An absolute frenzy of Russian patriotism and religious fervor swept over the land, destroying any attempts at reconciliation with France. When Napoléon and his Grande Armée attacked that fateful summer of 1812, never was Mother Russia more united against its advancing foe.

Psalm 91 was not the only scripture from the Bible to catch Alexander's eye that forlorn day in St. Petersburg. Drawn to the eleventh chapter of the book of Daniel, he took courage and renewed determination to fight from the following passage:

> And the king of the south shall be moved with choler, and shall come forth and fight with him, even with the king of the north: and he shall set forth a great multitude; but the multitude shall be given into his hand. . . .
>
> For the king of the north shall return, and shall set forth a multitude greater than the former, and shall certainly come after certain years with a great army and with much riches. . . .

> So the king of the north shall come, and cast up a mount, and take the most fenced cities: and the arms of the south shall not withstand, neither his chosen people, neither shall there be any strength to withstand. . . .
>
> And at the time of the end shall the king of the south push at him: and the king of the north shall come against him like a whirlwind, with chariots, and with horsemen, and with many ships; and he shall enter into the countries, and shall overflow and pass over.
>
> He shall enter into the glorious land, and many countries shall be overthrown. (Daniel 11:11, 13, 15, 40–41)

With help from the spiritual advisers and mystics about him, Alexander began to see himself as God's divinely appointed agent to fulfill prophecy, especially after Napoléon's occupation of the holy city of Moscow and the desecration of the Kremlin, the sacred center of Russia. No matter how one chooses to see it, there can be no disputing the fact that the Russian defeat of Napoléon's Grande Armée, with the help of Russian "Generals January and February," was nothing less than a remarkable campaign, a stunning, undeniable victory. Not content to stop at Poland or Prussia, Alexander and his Russian Army followed in close pursuit of the retreating Napoléon like a hound on the chase. After Leipzig and the Great Battle of Nations, one battle followed after another until finally Alexander rode triumphantly into Paris on 31 March 1814—the first foreign conqueror to enter Paris in four hundred years—stunning even his Austrian and British allies with the speed of his incredibly successful westward march.

But "Freedom's Morning Star," as Alexander came to be called, was not hell-bent on vengeance. How could he be, since he believed God had given him a victory? The fact was, Alexander truly admired Napoléon and thought seriously of creating a regency for Napoléon's three-year-old son; however, working with the duplicitous French foreign minister, Talleyrand, who had served every French regime for the past twenty-five years, Alexander changed his mind. After signing the Treaty of Fontainebleau, which restored the Bourbon king Louis XVIII to the French throne, and exiling Napoléon to Elba, the charming Alexander enjoyed Paris's famous night life, at one time dancing with none other than Marshal Michel Ney's wife and even with Josephine herself, Napoléon's first wife. Alexander insisted in the First Treaty of Paris that France be treated most leniently, because Napoléon, not France, had been his enemy. He did not even demand indemnities of France—the payment of reparations for the costs of war. France therefore retained many of her expanded borders and escaped without even paying reparations. In retrospect, one wonders what the wars had all been about.

THE CONGRESS OF VIENNA

Such stupendous events as those described above—when emperors, armies, and millions of people were on the march, forever changing boundaries, perceptions, and nation states—

inevitably required cool heads and diplomatic reasoning to bring new order out of war-torn chaos.

Alexander's rapid march westward across Europe in the wake of his enemy's rapidly receding armies and his eventual triumphal entry into Paris positioned the Russian emperor as the sole "arbiter of Europe's destiny."[15] Yet his victories worried many of his allies who believed that he had gone much too far and much too fast. Forty-two-year-old Klemens von Metternich—Austria's astute, calculating foreign minister from 1809 to 1848 and arguably the mastermind behind the eventual restructuring of postwar Europe—feared Russia with its standing army of almost one million men almost as much as he did France. Representing a composite state of diverse loyalties (Germans, Magyars, Slovaks, Poles, Slovenes, and Italians) whose borders on all sides could be easily overrun by enemy armies, Metternich feared that one empire was merely replacing the other. A supreme realist and a shrewd judge of human nature as well as of foreign affairs, the conservative Metternich distrusted Tsar Alexander's enigmatic character, his vanity, and his religious, almost mystic motivations, choosing to see the Russian leader as an unstable visionary and dreamer. Thus, even before the fall of Paris, he was busily planning a congress of power to convene at his invitation in Vienna.

Meanwhile, the other architect of Europe's future—Great Britain's Irish-born Viscount Castlereagh, foreign secretary from 1812 to 1822—was as cumbersome and inarticulate as Metternich was smooth and eloquent. Icy and aloof, Castlereagh was nevertheless astute and immensely intelligent, and he signaled England's intention to participate—indeed to take a leading role—in preventing the rise of Napoléon or anyone else like him from ever taking power again. An island nation defended by its formidable navy, England ambitioned to protect itself from future French invasions through the formations of strong alliances, to remain free from European entanglements, to preserve and extend its far-flung colonies through the formations of such alliances, and to gain wealth from overseas trade. The safeguard of its maritime power and prominence was England's highest priority. Less concerned with far-away Russia, Castlereagh sought a new balance of powers to ensure a lasting peace.

Both Metternich and Castlereagh—along with Prussia's Hardenberg, who was anxious to restore as much of the constantly overrun Prussia as he could—wanted to negotiate a European peace as soon as possible. Alexander, however, stubbornly and defiantly insisted on marching to Paris, believing that it was "his mission to destroy the Napoleonic state and then seek revelation of what was to take place."[16]

In June 1814, in company with his sister Catherine, Alexander visited England, where he was thronged by vast and adoring crowds who hailed him as "the Christian conqueror who saved Europe."[17] Given an honorary degree by Oxford University as "Liberator of Europe" and "Freedom's Morning Star," Alexander agreed not to use Russia's entrenched military

---

15. Palmer, *Alexander I*, 286.
16. Palmer, *Alexander I*, 272.
17. Palmer, *Alexander I*, 290.

position to gain undue influence. Instead, he promised to negotiate with the other allied powers in formulating a lasting European peace—in other words, to go to Vienna.

The Congress of Vienna that opened 1 October 1814 and lasted the following seven months went down in history as the first, and certainly one of the most important, assemblies of world powers ever convened. Its purpose was multiple: to redraw the political map of Europe, to protect the autocratic rule of the great powers against the rise of future revolutions of the kind and scale of the French Revolution, to keep Napoléon from ever rising again, and above all, to establish a fair balance of powers in Europe that would ensure a lasting peace. Alexander hoped the conference would agree to one other action: a provision wherein the big four powers would form a Holy Alliance and a system of future congresses that, like the later League of Nations, would bring leaders of the great nations together to avert a further calamity like the one they had just witnessed.

Every European nation, sovereign state, principality, and power, small and great, that had any interest whatsoever in postwar Europe was invited. Thus, Vienna that winter of 1814–15 witnessed a glittering gaggle of kings and queens, prime ministers and potentates, emperors and empresses on a scale the civilized world had never before seen. Austria's host emperor, Francis I, spent vast sums of money—some thirty million florins—lavishly dressing up the city and preparing it to host a hundred thousand people, providing a social life of banquets and balls, concerts and symphonies, festivals and festoons, and a night life of rus-

Congress of Vienna (1819), by unknown engraver, after Jean-Baptiste Isabey.

tling gowns and squeaking shoes. Little wonder it has gone down in history as "le Congrès qui danse" (the dancing Congress)!

Even before they formally convened, the Great Four Powers—Great Britain, Austria, Russia, and Prussia—had secretly agreed among themselves to be the directing committee, running the show on their terms and to their own advantage. Lesser powers such as Spain, Portugal, Holland, and Sweden would be kept informed but take a much lesser role. Going into the Congress, the most immediate question was what to do with France, its place in postwar Europe, and more immediately, what position would its foreign minister, Talleyrand, be allowed to play in the negotiations.

At the risk of simplifying a most complex affair, the Congress of Vienna was a mixture of Alexander's idealism, Metternich's materialism, and Castlereagh's pragmatism. Russia, with a population of forty-three million, wanted all of Poland and access to the Mediterranean Sea. Prussia, with its ten million, wanted more land on the east and on the west to better defend itself. Great Britain, with its eighteen million, eyed the port of Antwerp and wanted France out of Belgium. Austria, with its eight million, sought much of northern Italy and, above all, a political equilibrium where no one power could overrule Austria or the rest of Europe. The emphasis would not be on punishing France but rather on establishing a balance of force. If lands—and after all, land represented people, industry, and money—could be properly distributed to the winning sides, and if a new balance of power could be implemented, then perhaps the Congress might be successful. As for France, Talleyrand quietly maneuvered behind the scenes to minimize French losses and to regain the country's status as a major power.

The Congress was also as much concerned about turning back the clock as it was in realigning the future boundaries of Europe. The peacemakers of 1815 were, as Tim Chapman has argued, "backward looking and conservative"—wanting to put the genie of revolution back into the bottle of autocratic rule.[18] However, those key ideals of the French Revolution—liberty, equality, and fraternity—along with belief in a constitutional monarch, representative government, and such basic civil rights as freedom of religion and speech would not be easy to contain or resist, especially in those countries closest to France and longest occupied. Prussia, the Rhineland, the Low Countries, and the northern Italian states had been deeply influenced by such French reforms as the abolition of serfdom, curtailing the power of the trade guilds, and improving education. While the new power brokers "absolutely opposed the idea of countries being ruled without a hereditary ruling family,"[19] they found some of Napoléon's reforms impossible to resist. As one scholar has argued, "The Napoleonic Codes were, for the most part, retained, and the rulers realized that the limited progress that had been achieved under the French could not be undone."[20] If a new age of nationalism was not yet the issue, a new era of liberalism certainly was. While Austria sought for the authority

---

18. Chapman, *Congress of Vienna*, 2.
19. Chapman, *Congress of Vienna*, 15.
20. Shinn, *Italy*, 24.

to intervene in other nation-states' affairs in order to resist revolutionary impulses, Great Britain was more or less content to let each nation do as it deemed best, unless of course its own commercial interests were at stake.

The peculiar nature of the Congress of Vienna did not agree with Alexander but was tailor-made to fit Metternich's manipulative style of back-room diplomacy. Accustomed to poring over copious memoranda and to taking the lead in conferences, Alexander was ill-prepared for corridor communications, sideline conversations, and dealings made on the sly at the symphony or in the parlor. A constant beat of nightlife and carefully arranged meetings with mistresses sank the whole affair almost to "the level of a cheap farce."[21]

But a farce it was not. The Congress of Vienna was far more than a meeting of diplomats; rather, it was a gathering of nations and of national and cultural expressions, something akin to a carnival of nations. And women played far more than a passive role in this colorful consortium of political, cultural, and national interests. During the Congress, "it was the ladies as mavens of society who took the lead and set the tone for sociability in general and political sociability in particular, providing informal political contacts and exchanges."[22] Friendly and informal salon gatherings—where representatives and diplomats learned of each other's favorite foods, music, literature, and customs of the various cultures and nations—probably did more to lessen tensions and increase understandings between delegates than anything else. In short, social gatherings were highly significant to bridge-building between peoples and to the ultimate success of the Congress.

Likewise, such gatherings lessened religious misunderstandings and prejudices. Brian Vick, in his new study of the Congress, makes it clear that religion and religious freedom and toleration were hot topics of discussion, especially in light of the fact that new national boundaries meant millions of people were now living under new confessionals of faith. "The idea of protecting the rights of religious minorities"—though a very prickly issue—"found much support at the Congress."[23]

Throughout the Congress, Metternich clearly knew what he was doing and patiently played his hand. At the outset, he felt Alexander held the upper hand, with his armies still occupying most of Europe. Thus, he purposely dallied and delayed to wear down Alexander's patience. The two men quite honestly despised one another and never met in open conference or spoke with each other until the very last day of the conference. As one described, "Le Congrès danse, mais il ne marche pas" (The Congress dances, but it doesn't walk/work).[24]

The negotiations stalemated and nearly ruptured over Poland. Prussia demanded the return of its lost eastern provinces, while Alexander insisted on retaining what Rus-

---

21. Palmer, *Alexander I*, 309.
22. Vick, *Congress of Vienna*, 14.
23. Vick, *Congress of Vienna*, 162.
24. Kissinger, *World Restored*, 160.

sia had overrun. Sensing that France—the conquered, ostracized power—was the key to achieving a lasting balance, Metternich feigned one illness after another to buy time and public support. And while the British cabinet signaled little interest in repositioning France as an equal power, its clever foreign minister, Lord Castlereagh, quietly maneuvered for France to play a leading role, fully realizing his position would not play well back in London.

The fact was that both Metternich and Castlereagh realized that this was a conference less designed to punish France and more designed to establish a lasting European peace. To achieve a stable future, France had to be included with a strong voice and as an equal power. Sensing such determination, Prussia threatened a new war and almost pulled out of Vienna, yet reluctantly realized it had little choice but to compromise. A new alliance, with France now included, was ultimately signed 3 January 1815, with the Big Four becoming the Big Five.

THE PROPHETESS

Two widely different events broke the logjam of continuing intrigue and stalemate: one close at hand, the other hundreds of miles away. In one of those life-changing moments, like that of the Bible falling on the palace floor three years before, a determined old woman banged so loud and so long on Alexander's castle door in Heilbronn late one night during a recess in the conference that his imperial guards finally had to allow her entrance. Believing God had sent a messenger to him (she had sent him letters well in advance), Alexander allowed the woman—Baroness Julie von Krüdener—into his chambers. In short order, this Livonian prophetess, a widow of a Russian diplomat and an evangelical Protestant who had earlier taken up spiritualism, begged his pardon for her intrusion. She then, however, scolded the emperor for his sinful ways and called upon him to repent and surrender his soul to God and to accept the formidable destiny and divine calling God had given him. She went on to call him to surrender his soul to Christ and to fulfill the God-given, predestined mission she had been sent to remind him of—to establish a Christ-centered peace in Europe and, as "the chosen one of the Lord," to lead God's people to the promised land. Impressed by her boldness and stung by his own punishing conscience for his many past sins, Alexander listened intently to every word this haggard, mission-driven Joan of Arc had to say. She chastised him as no one had ever done, but because of the peace she brought to his hankering, troubled soul, he instantly fell under her will as his spiritual guide, conscience, and personal prophet.

In what came to be a bizarre relationship that lasted the year, Baroness Krüdener became his trusted spiritual adviser who would later claim for herself many of his accomplishments. Believing that Alexander was the "one upon whom the Lord has conferred a much

Baroness Barbara Juliane von Krüdener (1764-1824), by unknown artist.

greater power than the world recognizes," she stroked his ego while calling him to repentance.[25] Because she was hated by the Russian Orthodox Church, Alexander felt compelled to banish her in 1822.

Having been reminded of the divine calling he had long believed he owned, Alexander returned to Vienna with renewed energy, determined to change his approach with Metternich and the Congress. Preferring now to play the role of a benevolent overseer and of the more compromising superpower, he softened his position on Poland and signaled his intent to negotiate in return for the realization of his new Holy Alliance.

Meanwhile, on 7 March 1815, Vienna heard the seemingly impossible news that Napoléon had somehow escaped Elba and was then on his way back to France. No one knew then what kind of reception he would receive, but Metternich rightly judged he would head straight for Paris and for power. The allies immediately pledged an army between eight hundred thousand and one million men. With most of the Russian army still stationed in Poland, everyone agreed that Wellington would be the supreme commander of the British, Prussian, and other nearby armies to join with Alexander's overwhelming force and put down the revived French threat once and for all. "It is for you to save the world again," said Alexander to Wellington.[26] And as we have already seen, three months later Napoléon lost at Waterloo, outmanned and outgunned by superior allied forces.

The height of Krüdener's influence over Alexander came after Waterloo when she accompanied Alexander to Paris, where the allied powers signed the Second Treaty of Paris.

---

25. Palmer, *Alexander I*, 310, 322. Krüdener's influence on Russia's leader has long been debated by historians and biographers alike. Some insist she was a dominating, mystical force who changed history forever; others prefer to see her as a mere confirmer of Alexander's own deep religious convictions. Alan Palmer may be as accurate in his evaluations as any other scholar in his saying, "There remains in Julie's exaltations and Alexander's agonies of the soul a passionately compulsive power of conviction, . . . a genuine attempt to rend the veil of mortality and achieve a state of mind whence would emerge . . . Revelation."
26. Palmer, *Alexander I*, 322.

On 11 September 1815, dressed in a blue serge dress and straw hat, she stood beside the Russian emperor as they reviewed an immense military parade of 150 squadrons of cavalry, over 100 battalions of infantry, and 600-plus pieces of artillery march through the town of Vertus, near Paris. After the heavy march had passed, 150,000 Russian troops assembled in seven gigantic squares and kneeled in unison around seven large altars: "the mystic number of the Apocalypse," in reference to John the Revelator's seven churches. Then the bishops and priests celebrated mass according to the Russian Orthodox liturgy and offered thanksgiving prayers for their recent victory over Napoléon. Convinced that he was witnessing the fulfillment of prophecies from the book of Revelation and that the "Christian Russian forces were equated with the new Israel,"[27] Alexander, with the baroness beside him, moved in procession from altar to altar. Filled with love for his enemy, "in tears, at the foot of the cross, [he] prayed with fervor that France might be saved." For Alexander, it was "the most beautiful day in his life."[28] But for others, like Castlereagh, they worried about the deeply religious spirit that had come over him, while Metternich and Emperor Francis I thought him mad.

Both Alexander and Krüdener and those other religious mystics of the time saw in this magnificent occasion and grandiose spectacle not only a fulfillment of biblical prophecy but also the herald of the latter days. As the German mystic Eckartshausen put it, "That time when the great veil concealing the Holy of Holies shall be drawn back, the ushering in of the last times on earth before Christ's Second Coming."[29] As Eckartshausen and many other mystics believed, the last days truly began with the first decades of the nineteenth century.

It was shortly thereafter, while in Paris, that Alexander presented his counterparts with his Holy Alliance, a "Sacred treaty," "a new Dispensation of Holy Writ," a moral statement sent from God to bind all Europe's rulers in a "union of virtue, peace, forgiveness, and Christian brotherhood."[30] Though influenced by Krüdener, the document was of Alexander's own making—a reflection of years of religious thinking. Long on virtues and short on specifics, the Holy Alliance was not a treaty per se but a declaration of policy, a promise of a future policy. All but the pope, the leaders of Great Britain, and the sultan of Turkey signed it on 26 September 1815, not because they supported it in principle but because it held no binding power over them. Castlereagh called it "a piece of sublime nonsense" and Metternich "a loud-sounding nothing."[31] As Henry A. Kissinger argued, Castlereagh and Metternich, whatever their differences, "sought a world of intermeshing nuance, Alexander one of immediate perfection."[32] The one strong suit of the treaty, and perhaps its lasting significance, was its binding invitation to all the powers to meet regularly thereafter whenever world

---

27. Zorin, "'Star of the East,'" 327.
28. Palmer, *Alexander I*, 333.
29. As cited in Zorin, "'Star of the East,'" 327.
30. Palmer, *Alexander I*, 334.
31. Kissinger, *World Restored*, 189.
32. Kissinger, *World Restored*, 187.

peace was threatened. Believing that he had fulfilled his divine appointment, Alexander seemed to have lost interest and delegated the details of further negotiations with the allies to his ministers and ambassadors.

The negotiations at Vienna accelerated during Napoléon's One Hundred Days that ended with his defeat at Waterloo. With the sixty-year-old, notoriously immoral Talleyrand (Napoléon had once called him "filth in silk stockings") at the table, no longer representing Napoléon but the French Bourbon government, the Big Five powers hammered out the terms of a final agreement in what clearly was "an uneasy compromise."[33] Alexander acquiesced and contented himself with the Duchy of Warsaw and eastern Poland, promising the Poles something the Russian people themselves would not be allowed—a constitutional monarchy and a representative government (though in truth Russia would rule Poland with an iron hand). Austria retained Hapsburg rule and acquired much of northern Italy, including dependent dynasties in Parma and Tuscany. Great Britain held on to Ireland, Holland, the free part of Antwerp (Belgium), and of most importance—all its colonies. Prussia, in many ways the winner of Vienna, obtained much of Saxony, Swedish Pomerania, much of the Rhineland, and the Duchy of Westphalia. A new German Confederation, a loose union of sovereign princes, came into being and reduced the number of states and free cities from 350 to 16—a giant step forward toward the ultimate creation of modern Germany. France escaped without being reduced in size, but several buffer states—Bavaria, Piedmont, Holland, and the Rhineland, the so-called "cordon sanitaire"—were placed between it and the other great powers.[34]

The Final Acts of Vienna were ratified 9 June 1815. As Kissinger has argued, Vienna, for all its intrigue, social glitter, immorality, and corridor diplomacies, created a new European order, a successful balance of powers, and a lasting, "just equilibrium." Not "a fortunate accident" but a deliberate effort, "there existed within the new international order no power so dissatisfied that it did not prefer to seek its remedy within the framework of the Vienna settlement rather than in overturning it."[35]

In the Second Treaty of Paris, signed after Waterloo, the allies were furious with Napoléon and, had it not been for Castlereagh's astute diplomacy, would have tried to dismember France altogether. Napoléon was banished to St. Helena, and Marshal Ney, "the bravest of the brave," was executed for supporting Napoléon's return to power. Although more punitive terms were placed on France—slightly reduced territories, fewer overseas colonies, a smaller standing army, the forced return of art seized abroad, and an indemnity of seven hundred million francs (a sum France paid back in just three years)—this second peace treaty was

---

33. Vick, *Congress of Vienna*, 240.
34. Chapman, *Congress of Vienna*, 41, see map. Despite his brilliance as a compelling negotiator and superb strategist, Talleyrand was far from master of the Vienna conference. His "actions were always too precisely attuned to the dominant mood" for him to have played the lead role. Kissinger, *World Restored*, 136. Yet it must be admitted, the sly fox defended the interests of France superbly well.
35. Kissinger, *World Restored*, 173.

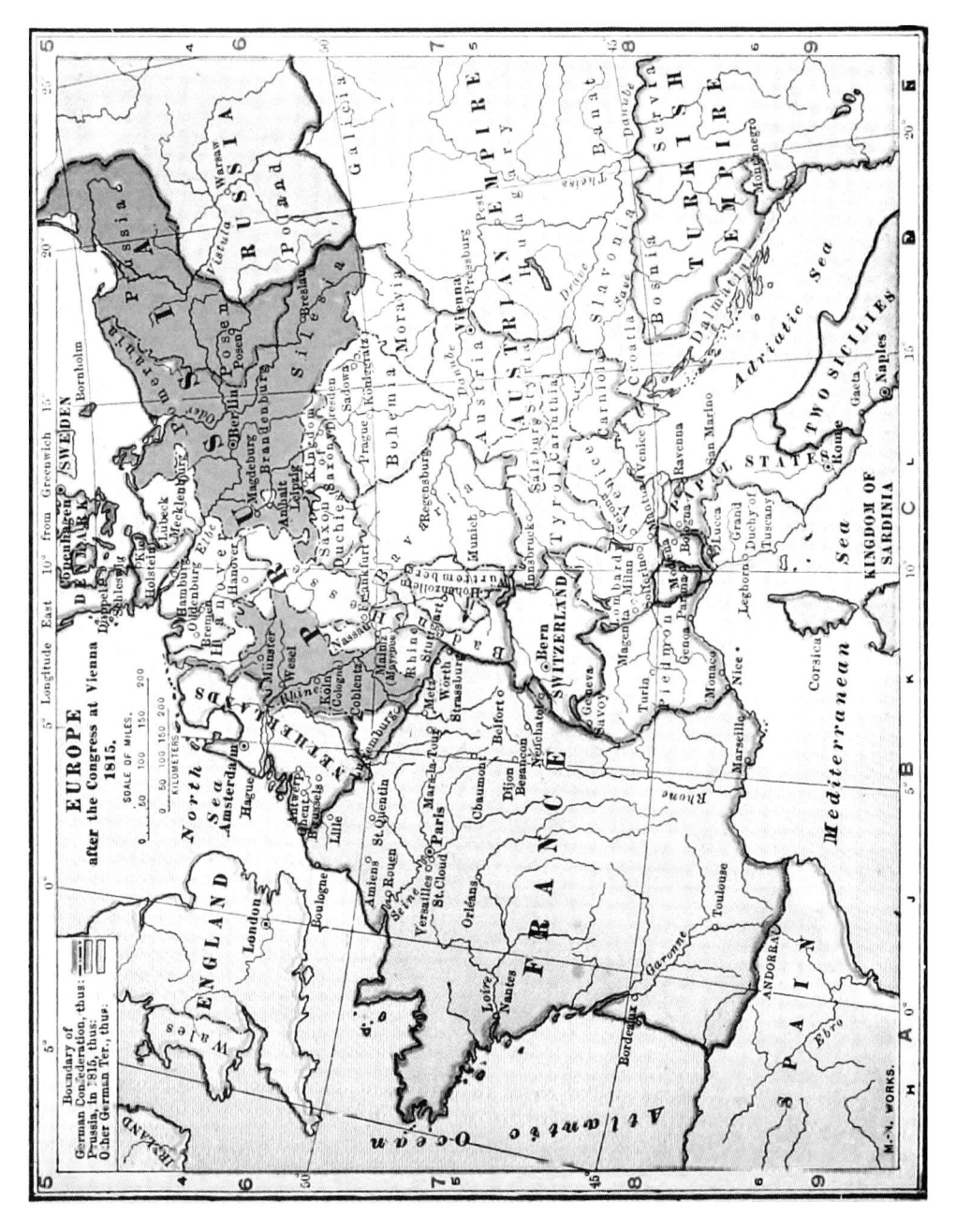

Europe after the Congress at Vienna 1815. From *The New International Encyclopædia*, vol. 7, facing p. 290 (New York: Dodd, Mead & Company, 1903).

surprisingly lenient in its treatment of France, a recognition that the enemy had not been the country but rather its emperor. If it lacked the magnanimity of the first Peace of Paris, "it was nevertheless not so severe as to turn France into a permanently dissatisfied power."[36] Thus out of Paris came the two instruments that would guide Europe for several decades—the Quadruple Alliance and the Holy Alliance: "the hope for a Europe united by good faith and the quest for a moral consensus, [and] the political and the ethical expressions of the equilibrium."[37]

The peace that followed the Congress of Vienna and its resultant treaties and systems of congresses (Aix-la-Chapelle, Carlsbad, Trappau, and Laibach) would last the better part of a century. Save for such glaring exceptions as the wars of independence in South and Latin America, the American Civil War (1861–65), Bismarck's Franco-Prussian War and hostilities of the 1870s, and scattered, various revolutions, the modern world sat upon a relatively stable course of peace. Thus unlike the Versailles Treaty of 1918 a century later, which, while ending the terrible conflict of the First World War, nevertheless gave rise to the Second World War a generation later because of its harsh and punitive demands upon Germany, the skillful, forward-looking diplomats of 1815 set in place a lasting, fair, international peace.

This ensuing peace engineered by the Congress of Vienna and the rising spirit of religious freedoms allowed for the expansion of religious missionary work throughout Europe and, indeed, the world, on a scale perhaps unseen before. Certainly, for missionary-minded religions such as The Church of Jesus Christ of Latter-day Saints, the relative stability of world politics, the guarantee of peace, and increased tolerance for religious diversity were indispensable to their successful missionary efforts in the mid-to-late nineteenth century and lasting well into the second decade of the twentieth.

And while Alexander's Holy Alliance, like Woodrow Wilson's League of Nations a century later, was long on dreams and ideals but short on specifics and binding contracts, it contributed nevertheless to fostering a spirit of future, ongoing negotiation and compromise. As World War II historian O. J. Frederickson has concluded, Alexander's efforts, despite all the scorn and ridicule heaped on them, were "faltering steps toward a lofty goal." It may well be that "Alexander will go down in history not as the victor over Napoléon but as the far-sighted initiator and champion of the World Federation which was finally achieved after World War II."[38] So it was that the years which followed—the very age of our study—have gone down as an era of negotiated peace.

---

36. Kissinger, *World Restored*, 184.
37. Kissinger, *World Restored*, 190. The Quadruple Alliance of Russia, Prussia, Austria, and Great Britain was signed 15 November 1815 and claimed the right to interfere with French internal affairs if further revolutions broke out.
38. Frederickson, "Alexander I and His League to End Wars," 22.

IN SEARCH OF PEACE

Although Alexander helped secure a lasting European peace, he never found peace for himself. The final decade of his life was marred by bouts of severe depression, aimless and excessive travels, profound disappointments, and personal frustrations. A reign that had begun so promisingly with its anticipation of change and needed liberal reform ended in despair and a hint of mystery that remains intriguing in the present day. Europe's widely acclaimed "Liberator" never escaped the chains of his own personal bondage.

For all of Krüdener's efforts at saving his soul and for all the praise Mother Russia bestowed upon its favorite son, Alexander was an unhappy wanderer. He seemed to lose interest at a critical moment of his life and, instead of heading home directly to pomp and glory, he dallied all the way back to Russia, spending a week here or two weeks there. Clearly bored with life and possibly suffering from venereal disease, he seemed to be a man without home or hope, no longer wanting to govern, more inclined to run and hide than to take the helm. At one point in late 1812, he even hinted at abdication: "The throne is not my vocation, and if I were able to change my condition I would do it willingly."[39]

Consequently, he let others do what he should have done. The efficient yet brutal guardian of feudal Russia—General Alexai Arakcheyev—soon took over the daily matters of government business. The very opposite of the more enlightened Speransky in outlook and personality, Arakcheyev was, as one called him, as "industrious as an ant, venomous as a tarantula," turning back those impulses of reform that top Russian Army officials had first tasted in "free-thinking Europe." There they had seen the enemy, and the enemy turned out to be not all that bad. In other words, "serfdom was not necessary to national prosperity," and a constitutional government, a free press, and an open society were hallmarks of the new West.[40] Pushkin and a host of other hopeful Russian intellectuals and activists soon became disillusioned at Alexander's failure to inspire on the one hand and Arakcheyev's repressive measures on the other.

Arakcheyev's repressive influence on domestic policies was most extensive during Alexander's final decade. He organized a highly unpopular system of military colonies, enhanced the powers of the secret police, suppressed the intelligentsia, and with unnecessary force and brutality put down even the hint of riots and revolt (for example, the Decembrist revolt). While Alexander did encourage the promotion of the Russian Bible Society and the expansion of Russian Freemasonry, he never displayed the kind of hands-on, superintending style of leadership so many liberals yearned to see in Russia. Ever the idealist, he was always outmaneuvered by the materialists and those who resisted real change.

One of his most poignant failures and personal disappointments came with the Greek insurrections of 1821. Tailor-made for Russian intervention, the Christian Greek revolt, led by the Russian Orthodox Alexander Ypsilanti, a former Russian general, aimed at putting down the inhuman, barbaric dominance of the aging Ottoman Empire and the Turkish sul-

---

39. McConnell, *Tsar Alexander I*, 179.
40. McConnell, *Tsar Alexander I*, 169.

tan's control and making an independent Greek state that was Christian and free. At the critical moment, Metternich persuaded Alexander not to interfere, though he himself had intervened all over Italy to put down similar revolutionary stirrings. While eventually Great Britain intervened in 1826–27 and supported the successful Greek war of independence and the establishment of a semi-independent state, Alexander's dallying cost the lives of thousands. Ever after, Alexander blamed himself for his failure to take leadership in a cause he felt was right.

Delving even more deeply into mysticism, scripture study, and soul-searching, Alexander was a tormented man trying to escape himself. Although Alexander's religious quest has been seen by some as a pose, there can be "no question of his sincerity; he prayed so long and often that his knees became calloused."[41] His father's murder cast a shadow that followed him over the vast steppes and mountain ranges of Russia. When his recently married sister, Catherine, died in January 1819 at the age of thirty, Alexander blamed her death on his sins. When his daughter, Maria, born of his early mistress Sophia, died at eighteen, it was to him a crushing blow, and he once again blamed himself—this time on his earlier immoralities. And when St. Petersburg was flooded in 1824 by the rising spring run-offs from the Baltic Sea, which resulted in the loss of many lives, he again reproached himself for inciting the wrath of God. And while it is true that he and his long-suffering wife, Elizabeth, rediscovered one another in a marriage of true friendship, Alexander never found lasting peace at home.

Finally, when his wife took sick with tuberculosis and a high fever in 1820, he moved the entire royal household from the damp and dismal climate of St. Petersburg to Toganrog, a city on the Azov far to the south. There, he contracted a fever and died 1 December 1825 at age forty-seven. Elizabeth followed him to the grave just six months later. His brother Nicholas (Alexander and Elizabeth never had a son) was more like their father than Alexander was. He outmaneuvered his brother Constantine to the throne, where followed thirty years of reactionary rule—"autocracy, orthodoxy, and nationality"—setting the country back a century.[42]

Today the location of Alexander's body, which was thrice exhumed, is unknown, leading some to speculate that Alexander feigned his death to secretly abdicate and become a wandering prophet and monastic—Feodor Kuzmich—who would live on in Siberia for another thirty years.[43] While the truth is more likely that he died as emperor and was buried in some unknown tomb in southern Russia, Alexander's death remains a mystery.

The great defender of Russia, liberator of Europe, self-proclaimed fulfillment of God's prophecies, and king of the North returned from whence he came. Ever tormented by his past sins, he never found peace. One raised to rule, he sank into obscurity, a tragic figure who never really knew himself. A reformer early on, he gradually succumbed to his passion

---

41. McConnell, *Tsar Alexander I*, 177.
42. McConnell, *Tsar Alexander I*, 200.
43. For a further discussion of this debate, see Klimenko, *Tsar Alexander I*, 7–21.

for order and paternalism. Although he saved Russia at one moment, he failed it at another. Yet, to his lasting credit, he overcame the conqueror. Working with those other men of Vienna—most notably Metternich and Castlereagh—Alexander hammered out a just peace, a Holy Alliance, that transcended themselves and their combined abilities and would endure for a century.

Portrait of Ludwig van Beethoven When Composing the Missa Solemnis, by Joseph Karl Stieler.

"WHO CAN EVER SURPASS THESE INEXPRESSIBLE HEIGHTS?"

LUDWIG VAN BEETHOVEN

A hush of anxious, silent anticipation settled over the small, candlelit crowd that cold winter night of 25 January 1815. Seated in the center of the front row of the drawing room in royal evening attire was the beautiful Russian princess Elizaveta. She was accompanied by her attendants and a handpicked audience of Vienna's finest and best. She had been waiting years for this magical moment. Suddenly he appeared, slipping through the curtains. All eyes strained to see; all ears yearned to listen, including those of Metternich's hated secret police. A short, stocky man with a large head, a pockmarked face, and ruddy complexion, Ludwig van Beethoven was smartly dressed in powder blue evening attire. His appearance belied his long-established reputation as a slovenly dresser, one who was as clumsy, awkward, and ill-tempered as the princess was elegant, poised, and good-natured. Rather than convey the impression that this was just another unwanted demand on his hectic schedule, the forty-five-year-old Beethoven filled the room with graciousness. After bowing before the audience and kissing the outstretched hand of the waiting empress, Beethoven sat down at the piano to his left and began to play.

As shown in the preceding chapter, the Congress of Vienna was as well known for its pageantry as it was for its politics. Concerts and symphonies, dances and balls, operas and plays lasted well into the night, and Vienna—the city of Haydn and of Mozart—would boast its finest. But its finest had been reluctant to come. Suffering from advanced deafness, acute colitis, and possibly cirrhosis of the liver, a sullen, reclusive, and overworked Beethoven was facing a pending physical breakdown. Persuaded to capitalize on the patriotic fervor of the time, if only to pay his mounting debts, Beethoven had hurriedly composed two rather bombastic pieces in line with his earlier nationalistic "Wellington Song," "You Wise Founders of Happy Nations" and a cantata in praise of the Congress entitled "The Glorious Moment." All three pieces were faint echoes to the greatness of his more established works. Of all the artists performing and conducting that Viennese winter, Beethoven was by far the one most in demand, yet he was the one least anxious to perform.

His stirring and majestic Seventh Symphony, completed just three years before and first performed in 1814, had already gained enormous popularity and renown across war-torn Europe as a stirring and majestic musical celebration of Napoléon's Russian defeat. Many recent veterans wept publicly upon hearing it, so stirred were they by the force and power of Beethoven's Seventh. Having dedicated the symphony to the empress—who in company with her husband, Tsar Alexander I, had become one of his most famous patrons and financial supporters—Beethoven accepted her invitation to perform, knowing full well it would not be his best showing. The tragedy was that he could not hear what he would now play.

Other than himself and his sternest critics, everyone in attendance, the empress included, thoroughly enjoyed the performance. Beethoven, however, knew it had fallen short of his accustomed best. Disgusted with himself, he was barely able to remain civil, and when his performance ended, he almost bolted from the room in a state of anger, depression, and frustration. He left as brusquely as he had entered graciously, determined never to play the piano in public again.

While the focus of this chapter will be Beethoven, the man and his works, some attention must inevitably be given to other musical geniuses of his time, many of whom knew and respected Beethoven as one of the most masterful composers of all time. Together, they made music that has endured since and that will continue to enthrall music lovers for centuries yet to come.

"I HAD SOME TALENT FOR MUSIC": A CHALLENGING CHILDHOOD, 1770–92

Ludwig van Beethoven's childhood and adolescence have been a source of unending scholarly debate. Born 17 December 1770 into a musical family in the electorate of Cologne, Beethoven grew up in Bonn (West Germany). Of his mother, Maria Magdalena Leym (1746–87), he once said she was his "best friend" and his "kindest supporter, protector, and most affectionate influence." Even though he later gained the friendship of the widow Frau von Breuning, the untimely death of his mother when he was sixteen years old devastated him and left a vacuum of affection no other person could fill.

On the other hand, his father, Johann van Beethoven (1740–92), a court tenor and music teacher who was in want of a decent education, never reached the towering expectations of his own father and *kapellmeister* and eventually turned to drink to drown his sorrows and failures. When enraged, he often belittled his promising young son, boxing him hard on the ears, berating him in public, and scolding him unmercifully. With his father so often away drinking or suffering from a hangover, young Ludwig, rather than run away, took care of his five younger siblings and did all he could to protect them from the wrath of their tyrant father, whom Beethoven also eventually took care of. Feeling abandoned, unwanted, and unloved by his father but resigned to live out the storm, Beethoven became the protector and guardian of his own brothers and—in time—of his own disconsolate father. A virtual orphan in his own home, Beethoven learned early the solace of isolation and loneliness; what it meant to live in an unkempt, disorganized, and unclean home; and the pain and sorrow of broken family relationships. At the same time, he drew strength from the inner music of his soul, a veritable musical balm of Gilead. As one of his best biographers phrased it, "He seems to have found sustenance in inwardness."[1]

The young Beethoven chose to emulate his musically talented grandfather, also named Ludwig van Beethoven (1712–73), even though his grandfather had died when Beethoven was but three years of age. Beethoven turned first to the piano and organ and later to the violin and the viola as his most trusted friends. Despite his father's discouragement, he began to compose early in his life. A virtuoso at playing the piano, Beethoven was driven towards originality as if to express the yearnings of a tormented soul. He was so proficient, through long hours of daily practice that often lasted past midnight, that he became a deputy court organist when merely fourteen years of age.

Never the best of students in a formal classroom setting and "sadly deficient" in spelling, grammar, and arithmetic,[2] Beethoven "took from the legacy of his elders only what made sense to him in terms of his own inner experience."[3] He learned best from one-on-one instruction. Fortunately, during this dark and formative time of his life, the eleven-year-old Beethoven fell under the influence of a wise tutor. Just as Tsar Alexander I had developed and matured under Frédéric La Harpe, Beethoven stood to gain much from Christian Gottlob Neefe (1748–98), a composer, organist, and conductor with rigorous standards of performance. Neefe recognized at once the genius in his young student's talent and encouraged him to compose and play sonatas and lieders (songs). Far more than a mere music teacher, Neefe also inculcated in Beethoven a philosophy of learning and of viewing the world; a love of great literature—especially of Shakespeare but also of Kant, Schiller, Rousseau, and Goethe; and an appreciation of the romanticist ideals of the European Enlightenment. Thus, from his adolescence, Beethoven developed a love of freedom, a hatred of tyranny, and a desire to reach for the divine in the human soul.

As Neefe taught Beethoven a love for the harmonics of Bach and the operatic magnificence of Mozart, he saw far more than a gifted musician. He saw one who, while emulating others, could also follow his own creative voice. As another biographer put it, Beethoven had an "inner, self-critical drive toward originality."[4] Beethoven regarded Mozart, whom he

---

1. Solomon, *Beethoven*, 27.
2. Forbes, *Thayer's Life of Beethoven*, 59.
3. Siepmann, *Beethoven*, 6.
4. Lockwood, *Beethoven*, 15.

Wolfgang Amadeus Mozart, c. 1780, by Johann Nepomuk della Croce. Courtesy of *Encyclopædia Britannica*.

likely met while visiting Vienna in 1787, "as his early musical god" and may well have studied under him had not Mozart died so tragically young in 1791.[5] Much in Beethoven's finest musical compositions would hearken back to both Mozart and Bach.

By the age of fourteen, Beethoven had already written three quartets for piano and strings and a large number of lieders, including the so-called "Dressler Variations."[6] These early Bonn compositions, though not emotionally powerful, showed many of those elements that would go on to characterize his music: dynamic contrasts, abrupt pianissimos and fortissimos, broad rhythms, eight-measure groupings, and an overriding "absolute" or overarching melody that entwined itself throughout the work.[7] William Kinderman, a musician and scholar, argues that from Beethoven's earliest compositions in Bonn, there is a "progressive unification" in all his works and that his earlier works "were eventually absorbed into the mainstream of his creative enterprise."[8] Constantly writing down themes, patterns and melodies, Beethoven developed ideas early on for entire concertos and symphonies and could transform a very simple melody into a symphony.

In the era before the Congress of Vienna, Bonn was the central city of the electorate of Cologne, one of over three hundred German feudal territories, or *kleinstaaten* (ministates), and all part of the decaying Holy Roman Empire. Bonn, although a local center for culture and theater, never rivaled the cultural splendor of Vienna or even Berlin. Although he was financially supported by local royalty and aristocrats, most notably the elector Max Franz (Marie-Antoinette's brother), Beethoven yearned to move on from Bonn. With the death of his father in 1792, he seized his opportunity and, at age twenty-two, accepted the invitation to study for at least a year under one of Vienna's finest musicians—Franz Joseph Haydn (1732–1809). He would never return.

There was another, very practical and pressing reason for Beethoven's move east to Vienna—the growing fear of Napoléon. Even at this early date, Prussian and Austrian royalties

---

5. Some believe that Beethoven, when seventeen, played for Mozart and that Mozart said of him: "Keep your eyes on him; some day he will give the world something to talk about." Forbes, *Thayer's Life of Beethoven*, 87. See also Landon, *Beethoven*, 52.
6. Lockwood, *Beethoven*, 59. Throughout his life, Beethoven, never good at handling money, earned his living by way of commissions.
7. Solomon, *Beethoven*, 70.
8. Kinderman, *Beethoven*, 1, 27.

Vienna in the early nineteenth century. *Wien, Michaelertor der Hofburg und altes Burgtheater, Aquarell* (1888), by Rudolf von Alt.

worried over the rising influence of the republican ideals of the French Revolution and of the reputation of its militant son, Napoléon. Were Napoléon to advance eastward to Berlin, Bonn stood squarely in his path. Beethoven would develop a love-hate attitude toward the French general—on the one hand, Beethoven had an undying admiration for Napoléon's personal courage, military prowess, and allegiance to the republican ideals of the French Revolution; on the other, he later had a repugnance against Napoléon's rising ambition, ruthlessness, and self-admiration. While Beethoven despised tyranny, he was a political moderate, advocating neither the abolition of royalty nor aristocracy but also ever in search of expanding personal liberties. Much of his music would be written either in praise or in criticism of Bonaparte, though to his dying breath, Beethoven ever retained a powerful admiration for the man. And Metternich's spies and secret police knew it.

AN AGE OF MUSIC

Of all the arts at the end of the eighteenth century, music was the least esteemed. Musicians were low- or middle-ranking servants in the households of the great or minor cathedral functionaries. Immanuel Kant, summing up prevailing sentiment, admitted that music could "move the mind in a variety of ways, and very intensely" but that its impact was fleeting and "[did] not, like poetry, leave anything over for reflections."⁹ By 1800, however, the emotive power of music was becoming more valued in an age that was learning to prize individual expression, emotions, and personal inspirations. As Paul Johnson has noted, emotion created forms of knowledge as "serious as reason, and music, as a key to it, became more serious" and respected as a way "to enhance serious meaning."¹⁰ By the turn of the century, music was becoming more popular among the masses, and the concert began to rival the opera in popularity.

Vienna had long been the musical and operatic center of Europe. It was there that Joseph Haydn, who had known and admired Johann Sebastian Bach (1685–1750), composed most of his 104 symphonies, 68 string quartets, and 20 concertos. And it was also in Vienna that Haydn met young Wolfgang Amadeus Mozart (1756–81). A child prodigy, Mozart had composed his first minuet at age five, his first symphony at eight, his first oratorio at eleven, and his first opera at twelve. Mozart went on to write more than six hundred musical compositions, the likes of which have never been equaled for their joyful, uplifting songs and melodies. A lover of the stage, Mozart's finest operas were *Marriage of Figaro* (1786), *Don Giovanni* (1787), and *The Magic Flute* (1791). Mozart and Haydn's operas, symphonies, and sonatas came to epitomize the classical style in music.¹¹

To think of music in the early nineteenth century was to think of opera, particularly comic opera, and no one had popularized the opera more by 1820 than the outstanding Italian composer Gioachino Rossini (1792–1868). So ardent an admirer of the music of both Haydn and Mozart that he was called "the little German," Rossini wrote his first opera at age fourteen and went on to compose more than forty more. A man of sparkling wit, corpulent stature, and exuberant personality, by age twenty-one Rossini had become the idol of Italian opera. Some were even then calling him "the first composer in the world" and "the god of modern music." In 1816 at age twenty-four, Rossini produced *The Barber of Seville* in just a three-week period, which

Portrait of Joseph Haydn, by Thomas Hardy.

---

9. Johnson, *Birth of the Modern*, 118.
10. Johnson, *Birth of the Modern*, 117–19.
11. For two excellent studies on Mozart, see Gutman, *Mozart*; and Deutsch, *Mozart*.

almost immediately earned him both fame and fortune. His immense popularity followed him all across Europe, and when he met Beethoven, whom he greatly admired, in 1822, Rossini heard the older man say, "So you're the composer of 'The Barber of Seville'! I congratulate you. It will be played as long as Italian opera exists." Rossini's other great works included *Cinderella* (1817), *Semiramide* (1823), and *William Tell* (1829). In contrast to Mozart, who died in undeserved poverty and obscurity in 1791, Rossini lived in fame and fortune until his death in 1868. Music scholars maintain that he helped to push opera into the age of Romanticism, breaking down one convention after another.[12]

The age was also one that saw the piano replace the harpsichord in popularity. A transitional musical figure between the more classical style music of Mozart and Haydn and the more Romantic music of Beethoven was the Austrian composer Franz Schubert (1797–1828), the "Prince of Song." Though he, like Mozart, died prematurely, he also was a prolific composer, producing more than six hundred lieder (written to the words and poetry of Goethe, Mayrhofer, and Schiller), ten symphonies, and more than a score of piano sonatas and duets, which Felix Mendelssohn (1809–47), Franz Liszt (1811–86), and Johannes Brahms (1833–97) later made memorable. His Unfinished Symphony of 1822 and his Symphony No. 9 are still frequently performed and are highly regarded by music lovers the world over. Schubert, a fervent admirer of Beethoven whom he first met in 1822, insisted on being buried next to the "Master's" grave in the village of Währing.[13]

"NO LONGER A PROPHECY BUT A TRUTH"— HIS FIRST MATURITY (1792–1802)[14]

As generous and courteous as his young student was irascible and often obstinate, Haydn was for Beethoven more an inspiration than a hands-on instructor. A careful student of Haydn's symphonies, Beethoven copied many of his ideas and innovations and embarked on tours of his own, albeit to more local sites such as Leipzig and Berlin. Soon he became regarded as one of the finest young composers and pianists of his time. Though Haydn never warmed to the aloofness of Beethoven, Haydn proudly saw in him his protégé. Maynard Solomon has summarized Haydn's influence on Beethoven as follows: "To study with Haydn was to learn not merely textbook rules of counterpoint and part writing, but the principles of formal organization, the nature of sonata writing, the handling of tonal forces, the techniques by

---

12. Two of the many excellent works on Rossini include Osborne, *Rossini*; and Weinstock, *Rossini*.
13. In 1888, both Schubert's and Beethoven's graves were moved to Zentralfriedhof, where they can now be found next to those of Johann Strauss II and Johannes Brahms. For more on Schubert, see Kreissle, *The Life of Franz Schubert*; Newbould, *Schubert*; and Gibbs, *Life of Schubert*.
14. Dividing Beethoven's life into three distinct periods called "maturities" was first proposed in 1828 and has since settled into something of a consensus. Though attacked by various critics as overly simplistic, such a scheme refuses to die because, in spite of all, it obviously does accommodate "the bluntest style distinctions" in Beethoven's output. Sadie, *New Grove Dictionary of Music and Musicians*, 3:95.

which dynamic contrasts could be achieved, the alternation of emotional moods consistent with artistic unity, thematic development, harmonic structure—in short, the whole range of ideas and techniques of the Classical style."[15]

It is not, however, sufficient to discuss merely the techniques or even the dynamics of Beethoven's music. What is important to show is that he felt deeply compelled, if not driven, to compose. "Beethoven the pupil may have honestly and conscientiously followed the precepts of his instructors in whatever he wrote, . . . but Beethoven the composer stood upon his own territory, following his own tastes and impulses, [and] wrote and wrought subject to no other control."[16] He was a man born with a mission, a calling, an unquenchable drive to write from the inner depths of his being and not the mere reflections of the age. He wrote from within. A deeply sensitive and spiritual man, though a Catholic only nominally, he loved nature and the conformities and uniformities of creation. Often depressed but still believing, he held to the fatherhood of God and the essential brotherhood of man. He loved his art and revered the talent he believed Providence had given him. As he once said, "Strength is the morality of those who distinguish themselves from the rest, and it is mine too."[17]

His foremost patron in Vienna was Prince Karl Lichnowsky (1761–1814), a longtime financial supporter of Mozart who looked upon Beethoven almost as a son. Though Beethoven wanted to be free of aristocratic sponsorship, he needed the funds to pursue his lessons, travels, and tutorships. Mastering the skills of both harmony and counterpoint, between 1798 and 1802 Beethoven composed several piano sonatas, three piano concertos, and several chamber works. His boldly independent sonatas, especially for piano with cello or violin accompaniment, illustrated his budding genius and power of invention. For the first time, the piano assumed an essential, virtuoso role.[18] At a time when piano music was gaining in popularity and improvements were being made to the piano itself, the forcefulness and assertiveness of his music found growing favor with increasingly large audiences. Ever desirous of writing an opera to equal the likes of Mozart's *Magic Flute*, Beethoven studied vocal composition under the imperial court *Kapellmeister* and opera composer Antonio Salieri (1750–1825). Salieri found Beethoven "self-willed and difficult" and was bewildered at his ingratitude, stubbornness, and multiplicity of compositions, wondering what other directions his restless student would take.

Haydn and Salieri were not alone in finding Beethoven a difficult young man to teach. Goethe regarded him as "an utterly untamed personality."[19] Beethoven held powerful views and opinions and never took criticism gracefully. Short but powerfully built with a face scarred by an early attack of smallpox, Beethoven was awkward and clumsy and always seemed to be knocking things over. He would have been an utter failure on the dance floor.

---

15. Solomon, *Beethoven*, 93.
16. Forbes, *Thayer's Beethoven*, 150.
17. Hamburger, *Letters*, 29; hereafter referred to as *Letters*.
18. Kinderman, *Beethoven*, 45.
19. Solomon, *Beethoven,* 106.

He often lost his temper and would brood in sullen moodiness for days. As a housekeeper, there were few bachelors worse. When ill-tempered, he would often throw his inkwell into the piano or up against the wall. No piece of furniture was safe with him, least of all a valuable one. "Imagine all that is most filthy and untidy," remembered a visitor to Beethoven's apartment. "Puddles on the floor, a rather old grand piano covered in dust and laden with piles of music, in manuscript or engraved. Beneath it (I do not exaggerate) an unemptied chamber pot. The little walnut table next to it was evidently accustomed to having the contents of the inkwell spilled over it. A mass of pens encrusted with ink—and more musical scores. The chairs, most of them straw chairs, were covered with plates full of the remains of the previous evening's meal and with clothes."[20]

He loved women from afar. "Beethoven was always glad to see women," the famous pianist Ferdinand Reis once remarked, "especially beautiful, youthful faces, and usually when we walked past a rather attractive girl, he would turn around, look at her again sharply through his glasses, and laughed and grinned when he found that I had observed him. He was very frequently in love, but usually for a very short time."[21] Distrusting deeply personal relationships, he was attracted physically but seldom emotionally. He had a fondness for women he could not have—either those married or engaged to be—as if he most enjoyed what he knew deep inside he would never have. Beethoven was not given to the women of the street, and nightlife for him meant composition, not moral dissolution. Most women were put off by his shoddy appearance and ungainly demeanor, believing he would be too much of a handful to train in the domestic arts.

However, if his home life and relationships with others were less than endearing or ideal, his music was becoming more powerful, more accomplished, more unforgettably beautiful and compelling as time went by. In the ten years between 1782 and 1792, he composed at least forty pieces, the most substantial being piano sonatas and quartets, many of which were never published. Two of his most famous works, composed in 1795, were his Sonata

Beethoven in His Study, by Carl Schloesser.

---

20. From the Memoirs of Baron de Tremont, *Letters*, 77.
21. From the "Biographical Notes" of Ferdinand Ries, *Letters*, 59.

in C Minor ("Pathetique") and his Opus 27, the hauntingly beautiful and utterly unforgettable "Moonlight Sonata." In 1801 he composed his First Symphony and his first ballet, *Prometheus*. No longer a mere copyist, Beethoven was finding his own voice. While writing within the formal musical conventions and constraints of his time, he was pouring new musical wine into old bottles at such a pace and with such force and beauty that his role as Mozart's successor was "no longer a prophecy but a truth."[22]

"I SHALL SEIZE FATE BY THE THROAT"— THE SECOND MATURITY, 1802-12

Beethoven's Second Maturity was characterized by a flurry of compositions in the new heroic style of music's Romantic age, his finding but not securing the one woman he most deeply loved, the deterioration and ultimate loss of his hearing, and finally, despite all these bitter and profound disappointments, an abiding determination to write music even more majestic than before.

Key to understanding Beethoven as composer is his custom of using sketchbooks from as early as 1798 to capture melodies and bring sense, order, and continuity to his work. Almost always carrying blank composition books, he would compose several new pieces simultaneously and while on the go as his many moods and circumstances changed.[23] Such style of creation was in his nature. "I carry my thoughts about with me for a long time, often for a very long time, before writing them down," he once confided to a friend, sharing profound insights into his creative process.

> I can rely upon my memory in doing so, and can be sure that once I have grasped a theme I shall not have forgotten it even years later. I change many things, discard others, and try again and again until I am satisfied; then, in my head, I begin to elaborate the work in its breadth, its narrowness, its height, and its depth, and as I am aware of what I want to do, the underlying idea never deserts me. It rises, it grows up, I hear and see the image in front of me from every angle . . . and only the labour of writing it down remains, a labour which need not take long but varies according to the amount of time at my disposal, as very often I work at several things at the same time, but I can always be sure that I shall not confuse one with the other.[24]

Beethoven went on to comment on the origins of his ideas and the provenance or the source of his inspiration. "They come unevoked, spontaneously or unspontaneously. I could grasp them with my hands in the open air, in the woods while walking, in the stillness of the

---

22. Lockwood, *Beethoven*, 174.
23. Johnson, Taylor, and Winter, *Beethoven Sketchbooks*, built upon the earlier work (1865) of Nottebohm, *Two Beethoven Sketchbooks*, to bring to greater light some eight thousand pages of Beethoven's sketchbooks and loose sketch leaves.
24. From "An Account by Louis Schlosser," 1823, *Letters*, 194–95.

night, at early morning, stimulated by those moods which the poets turn into words, in[to] tones within me, which resound, roar and rage until at last they stand before me in the form of notes."[25] He often made several revisions and refinements to each of these works over long periods of time, a continuing process of improving upon earlier themes and melodies, what Kinderman and others have called his "aesthetic project." Thus Beethoven's music ripened and matured, like vintage wine, over time through various moods and conditions, "a blend of the rational and sensuous achieved in a prolonged process of critical reflection."[26]

Eventually Beethoven fever swept the continent, and he began making a very good living from commissions and the sale of his printed music. Besides piano sonatas such as Waldstein, he composed several violin sonatas including his Kreutzer Sonata (one of his finest violin sonatas), his Second Symphony, his Mass in C, and at least three piano concertos—all of which demanded the finest in keyboard virtuosity. Though he often played his own pieces, he was never considered a concert soloist. Beethoven's only opera, *Fidelio*, a story of daring, imprisonment, and rescue in the heroic style, was first performed in Vienna in 1804 at the same time the city was occupied by French forces. Panned by critics for being far too long and much too difficult to play, *Fidelio* was one of his rare failures. Some wondered if Beethoven, as much as he wanted to write opera, ever really understood the theater.[27]

Though given to writing in the formal classical style of Haydn, Mozart, and Handel, Beethoven was influenced by the rigor, power, and nationalistic fervor of postrevolutionary French music that was very much in vogue. Such music featured stirring military marches and songs, all designed to stroke nationalistic fervor and pride, and was perhaps best epitomized in the new French national anthem, "La Marseillaise," composed by a young French lieutenant in 1792. However, it is also recognizable in such other contemporary patriotic works as "Rule Britannia," "Finlandia," and the enormously popular "God Save the King," This genre of music, written for the masses, has been called the heroic style.

Yet Beethoven's music was far more than heroic; it was romantic and free in the sense that it exhibited much more passion and emotion than Haydn's would ever allow. Beethoven's music spoke of tragedy and death, anxiety and aggression, vitality and victory. That may explain, at least in part, why his music is also called tragic—not because it is unhappy, indeed quite the reverse, but because, while recognizing the desperate struggles and disappointments of human existence individually and collectively, it nevertheless rises to a glorious, crowning celebration of the human soul.[28]

If Beethoven's Second Symphony overwhelmed his critics with its strong contrasts, stirring military marches, tumultuous force, and "manic" finale, few were prepared for his Eroica, or Third Symphony. Filled with bewildering originality and far greater emotion than

---

25. From "An Account by Louis Schlosser," 1823, *Letters*, 194–95.
26. Kinderman, *Beethoven*, 64.
27. Opera was not Beethoven's strong suit. Most musical scholars consider *Fidelio* (originally titled *Leonore*) as falling far short of Beethoven's best efforts, even though he revised it in 1814. Kinderman, *Beethoven*, 102–7.
28. Solomon, *Beethoven*, 252.

most of his earlier works, this enormously energetic piece owed everything to Napoléon, who was then proudly on the march. Despite Austria's secret police, Beethoven spoke publicly in favor of Napoléon at every opportunity and took thinly veiled inspiration from an emperor many yet hoped would overthrow despotism and tyranny. Napoléon was, as Lockwood has well written, "a worldly counterpart of what Beethoven imagined his own role in the world of music could become."[29] Beethoven initially dedicated his heroic-styled Third Symphony to Napoléon. "In writing this symphony," one of his students recorded, "Beethoven had been thinking of Buonaparte, but Buonaparte while he was still First Consul. At that time Beethoven had the highest esteem for him and compared him to the greatest consuls of ancient Rome. Many of Beethoven's closest friends saw this symphony on his table, beautifully copied in manuscript, with the word, 'Buonaparte' inscribed at the very top of the title page and 'Luigi von Beethoven' at the very bottom.

However, in 1804, upon learning that Napoléon had crowned himself emperor, Beethoven exclaimed, "So he is no more than a common mortal! . . . He will tread under foot all the rights of man, indulge only his own ambition and . . . become a tyrant." Angrily he tore the top of the symphony's title page in half and thrust it on the floor. Eventually he retitled it "Sinfonia Eroica."[30] Another heroic work of this time was his *Egmont* overture, written from his admiration of a great Belgian warrior. In contrast, his Fourth Symphony, written in 1805 and 1806, was much slower and majestic, almost lyrical, manifesting his ability to write in other styles than the heroic.

Meanwhile, still longing for love, Beethoven proposed marriage to a nineteen-year-old countess, Giulietta Guicciardi (1782–1856), but she spurned him, as did Josephine von Brunsvik (1779–1821), a widow with four children. Later he met his "Immortal Beloved," who was likely Bettina Antonie Brentano (1780–1869), a talented married woman with several children who was long out of love with her husband.[31] Of all the women in his life, she was arguably his only true love, the only woman who captured his deepest affections and fully reciprocated his love, the one woman more than any other he yearned to have. "I must live with you entirely, or not at all," he pleadingly wrote, sensing the impending hurt he would bring upon himself. "Never shall another be able to possess my heart, never—never! Oh, God, why is one forced to part from her whom one loves so well. My life, my all!"[32]

Yet at the crucial moment Beethoven backed away, unwilling to destroy her marriage and unable, as Solomon writes, "to overcome the nightmarish burden of his past and set the ghosts to rest."[33] The truth is, at the deepest level Beethoven could not share his life with anyone. He was too much the artist, too self-sufficient, too independent, too used to creative solitude to give himself away. An ancient Egyptian inscription that he kept on his desk said

---

29. Lockwood, *Beethoven*, 187.
30. From the "Biographical Notes" of Ferdinand Reis, *Letters*, 47.
31. Sadie, *New Grove Dictionary of Music and Musicians*, 3:85.
32. Beethoven "To His Immortal Beloved," 7 July 1806 [or 1807], *Letters*, 113.
33. Solomon, *Beethoven*, 246.

it well—one translated by Champollion, another of Beethoven's heroes—"He is of himself alone, and it is to this loneliness that all things owe their being."[34]

Exacerbating everything at this time of life was the highly disturbing fact that Beethoven had been losing his hearing for some time. Precisely when he began to go deaf has not yet been determined. Whether brought on by childhood beatings from his father or, as is more likely, from a disease of the inner ear, his hearing was fading as early as 1796. Writing to his close friend Karl Amenda in 1801, Beethoven painfully admitted the problem: "You must be told that the finest part of me, my hearing, has greatly deteriorated [and] has grown progressively worse. Whether it can ever be cured, remains to be seen." For one who lived by his music, for whom music was his profession and his deepest consolation and inspiration, his increasing deafness was a most terrifying affliction. Though he was at first desperate for some kind of cure, he sensed early on that little could be done. "Illnesses of this kind are most incurable," he plaintively wrote. "How miserably I must now live, and avoid all that is dear and precious to me.... Oh, how happy I should be if only I had the full use of my ears."[35] As his condition worsened, it made him more of a misunderstood recluse than ever before. "I have been avoiding all social functions simply because I feel incapable of telling people," he said to another friend.

> In the theatre I have to keep quite close to the orchestra, lean against the railings, in fact, to understand the actors. The high notes of instruments, singing voices, I do not hear at all if I am at some distance from them. As for conversation, it is a marvel that there are people who have never noticed my deafness; as I have always been absent-minded, it is attributed to this.... Heaven only knows what will come of it ... already I have cursed the Creator and my existence. Resignation! what a wretched refuge, and yet it is the only one left for me.[36]

For a time, Beethoven thought seriously of taking his life, believing that God had scorned and punished him. "I might easily have put an end to my life," he admitted in 1802:

> Only one thing, Art, held me back. Oh, it seemed impossible to me to leave this world before I had produced all that I felt capable of producing, and so I prolonged this wretched existence.... My determination to hold out until it pleases the inexorable Fates to cut the thread shall be a lasting one.... Recommend virtue to your children, for virtue alone, not money, can grant us happiness. I speak from experience. It was virtue that raised me up even in my misery.... How glad I am at the thought that even in the grave I may render some service.[37]

---

34. Solomon, *Beethoven*, 206.
35. Beethoven to Karl Amenda, 1 June 1801, *Letters*, 34–41.
36. Beethoven to Franz Wegeler, 29 June 1801, *Letters*, 41–42.
37. From Beethoven's "Heiligenstadt Testament" (a small village near Vienna), 1802, *Letters*, 50.

Then, at this critical turning point and deepest crisis of his life, he made peace with his condition and decided to go on as never before. "I shall seize fate by the throat," he declared.[38] Beethoven managed to hold on to some of his hearing until about 1812, but the loss became so progressive thereafter that by 1818 he could hear virtually nothing at all.

As was his life's pattern, there followed after this crisis a period of intense creativity—much of the music of Beethoven's Second Maturity came in response to his loss of hearing. Indeed, one scholar has argued that his deafness proved ironically beneficial. Although he came to terms with his infirmity "only very gradually," "his art actually became richer as his hearing declined."[39] A key to understanding why this was so was his aforementioned use of sketchbooks in which melodies from years past, complete with his several revisions and self-criticisms, would find later melodic expression and fulfilment. This may well explain the origins of his incomparable Fifth Symphony.

We writers and biographers, for all our best efforts, will always do a disservice to Beethoven and place him at a terrible disadvantage to the visual arts by trying to capture in writing the art and majesty of his music, a music that defies and transcends the power of pen and paper to re-create. Certainly that is the case in so short a study as this is. Like describing the beauties of a painting to one who cannot see, or the deliciousness of a Thanksgiving dinner to one who cannot taste, Beethoven must be heard, not read. The power of the pen simply cannot describe it. His majestic strains are for the ear, not the eye, and are to be experienced, not merely heard. His work transcends time and place. He is to music what Shakespeare is to literature—unforgettable, timeless, without peer.

Some passionately assert that his Symphony No. 5 in C Minor, Opus 67, which he wrote simultaneously with the Sixth Symphony, remains his most famous work. Written in 1807 and 1808 at the time of the Treaty of Tilsit, his Fifth Symphony is a stirring revolutionary anthem not in praise of Napoléon but of his enemies—Tsar Alexander and the allied powers. Filled with patriotic and military energy, the Fifth Symphony is a classic example of thematic unification, how Beethoven took a very simple, magnificent opening melody, a single four-note (short-short-short-long) motif and wrote an entire symphony around it. It begins in C minor, ends in C major, and covers a wide range of moods from deep despair to near ecstasy. The last movement, featuring piccolo and trombone, culminates in a note of transcendent triumph. First performed in the Theater an der Wien in December 1808, it quickly attained a reputation as a prodigious, enduring anthem of magnificent music. Beethoven produced his Eighth Symphony and Quartet in F Minor, Op. 95, in 1812.

---

38. Beethoven to Franz Wegeler, 25 June 1801, *Letters*, 41–42.
39. Kinderman, *Beethoven*, 61.

Beethoven's 5th Symphony No. 5—opening bars of the printed score for full orchestra instruments. Courtesy of Alamy Stock Photo.

"GOD HAS NEVER FORSAKEN ME"—THE FINAL MATURITY, 1813-27

At the same time Napoléon was suffering his ignominious Russian defeat, Beethoven was enjoying enormous success. Outside Vienna, he had "moved into a position of extraordinary preeminence and popular appreciation, unmatched by any nonoperatic composer of the era, and even surpassing the great popularity of Mozart and Haydn."[40] Especially popular were his Third, Fifth, Sixth, and Seventh Symphonies—particularly the Fifth and Seventh because of the perception that they celebrated Napoléon's defeat. Also popular were his *Fidelio* overture, *Egmont* overture, "Wellington's Song," and "Adelaide."

Adored far more by the British than the French, Beethoven probably would have fulfilled his lifelong desire to visit England had it not been for certain diversions. He had become so popular and so highly revered that the many visitors became a distraction. A steady stream of students and admirers knocked at his Vienna residence, anxious to catch a glimpse or talk to the man many were now calling the "master." Rossini, Schubert, and many other great composers all came in praise of him and his work. Yet he managed to keep his success in proper perspective. Writing to a friend in April 1815, he said, "Have you heard at all of my great works? Great, I say—compared with the works of the Supreme Creator, all things are small."[41]

Lucky were the favored few, like the dazzling young eleven-year-old pianist, Franz Liszt, who managed to play for him and to receive personal instruction. After playing a piece by Bach, Liszt looked up, noting that Beethoven's

> darkly glowing gaze was fixed upon me penetratingly. Yet suddenly a benevolent smile broke upon his gloomy features, Beethoven came quite close, bent over me, laid his hand on my head and repeatedly stroked my hair. "Devil of a fellow!" he whispered, "such a young rascal!" I suddenly plucked up courage. "May I play something of yours now?" I asked cheekily. Beethoven nodded with a smile. I played the first movement of the C Major Concerto. When I had ended, Beethoven seized both my hands, kissed me on the forehead and said gently, "Off with you! You're a happy fellow, for you'll give happiness and joy to many other people. There is nothing better or greater than that."

Remembering this moment with fondness, Liszt later called it "the palladium of my whole artistic career."[42]

Liszt's own teacher, Carl Czerny (1791–1857), himself an accomplished pianist, went on to describe Beethoven at the keyboard: "No one equaled him in the rapidity of his scales, double trills, skips, etc. . . . His bearing, while playing was perfectly quiet, noble, and beautiful, without the slightest grimace—but bent forward low, as his deafness increased; his fingers were very powerful, not long, and broadened at the tips from much playing, for he told

---

40. Solomon, *Beethoven*, 324.
41. Beethoven to "Amanda," 12 April 1815, *Letters*, 137.
42. From "Franz Liszt's Account of His Visit to Beethoven," 1823, *Letters*, 197–98.

me that in his youth he generally had to practice until after midnight. . . . He could scarcely span a tenth. . . . He was also the greatest sight reader of his time."[43]

Maria von Weber described him as follows: "His hair [was] dense, grey, standing up, quite white in places, forehead and skull extraordinarily wide and rounded; high as a temple, the nose square, like a lion's, the mouth nobly formed and soft, the chin broad with those marvelous dimples. . . . A dark ruddiness coloured his broad, pock-marked face; beneath the bushy and sullenly contracted eyebrows, small, shining eyes were fixed benevolently upon the 'visitors.'"[44]

As a piano teacher, he could be both surprisingly patient and incredibly demanding but for reasons not immediately obvious. "When Beethoven gave me a lesson, he was unnaturally patient," Ferdinand Reis once recalled.

> He would often have me repeat a single number ten or more times. . . . When I left out something in a passage, a note or a skip, which in many cases he wished to have specially emphasized, or if I struck a wrong key, he seldom said anything; yet when I was at fault with regard to the expression, the crescendi or matters of that kind, or in the character of the piece, he would grow angry. Mistakes of the other kind, he said, were due to chance; but these last resulted from want of knowledge, feeling or attention. He himself often made mistakes of the first kind, even when playing in public.[45]

Goethe saw, perhaps better than most, the strengths and the weaknesses of his fellow countryman. "I have never seen an artist more concentrated, energetic and intense," he wrote in 1812.[46] Amazed at Beethoven's talent, Goethe gave this insightful premonition of Beethoven's uncomfortable evening with the empress at the Congress of Vienna, an insight into how his deafness was warping his personality and how Beethoven may have often been misunderstood by others: "His is a personality utterly lacking in self-control; he may not be wrong at all in thinking that the world is odious, but neither does such an attitude make it any mere delectable to himself or to others. On the other hand, he much deserves to be both excused and pitied, for his hearing almost failed him, which probably does more harm to the social part of his character than to the musical part. He, who in any case is laconic by nature, is now becoming doubly so because of this defect."[47]

Visitors, however, were not nearly as much a distraction as family concerns soon became. At what surely would have been a most productive time in his life, Beethoven became embroiled in a highly charged emotional tug-of-war over the guardianship of his young nephew. For the next five years, his music suffered noticeably. Even before his father's death

---

43. From C. Czerny, Uber den richtingen Vortrag der samtlichen Beethoven's schen Klavierwerke, in Lockwood, *Beethoven*, 284–85.
44. From "Max Maria Von Weber's Biography of His Father," *Letters*, 208.
45. Siepmann, *Beethoven*, 38.
46. From a letter to Christine von Goethe, 19 July 1812, *Letters*, 116.
47. From a letter to Zelter, 2 September 1815, *Letters*, 116.

in 1792, Beethoven had taken on a paternalistic, even possessive interest in his younger siblings. Later, he became particularly incensed with his brother, Caspar Carl, and his marriage to Johanna Reiss, whom Beethoven disdainfully regarded as little more than a criminal and a street prostitute. When Carl died young in 1815, Beethoven became fretful and obsessive over his nephew, Karl, and—convinced that Karl's mother was totally unfit to raise the child—launched into a long series of legal challenges to win guardianship. While no doubt Reiss's reputation was a tainted one, something more must explain Beethoven's implacable hatred toward her and the enormous emotional and monetary expense he endured in promoting his case. While it is true that his brother Carl had wanted Beethoven to have at least a share in the custody of his child, Beethoven sought for more—the chance to be the father he had always wanted to be. Losing his first legal custody battle, he turned sullen, depressed, ever angrier. He began to look worse than ever before, pale and frightful in his long, dark overcoat and low top hat, wandering the streets until late into the night. While he turned to drink, Beethoven was not an alcoholic; however, the secret police would surely have arrested him for wandering alone at nights had he not been so popular a figure. Some even thought he was going mad.

When in early 1820 the courts reversed their ruling (after Johanna had become pregnant out of wedlock) and gave Beethoven co-guardianship of his nephew, his moods considerably brightened. He soon oversaw the boy's education and development, and though he loved his nephew, he interfered too much and was far too possessive, demanding to know his every move, even spying on the young man's romantic interests. Only after Carl had threatened suicide and demanded that his uncle back away did Beethoven finally surrender such tight control. Eventually Beethoven and his sister-in-law reconciled, and he would will more than half his estate to his nephew and a considerable amount to Johanna.

With the conflict resolved, Beethoven gravitated back to his music, but this time with an unequalled determination and passion. Absolutely "every thing was subordinated to his work." Some argue that his emotional struggles may have even served as "catalysts" to bring his deepest feelings to the surface, thereby helping to set the scene for a "breakthrough of his creativity into hitherto imagined territories."[48]

Some of his finest string quartets and piano sonatas (Opp. 109–11), including the Hammerklavier Sonata, can be dated to 1818–20. Early in 1821, he composed and compiled his "Eleven Bagatelles for Piano" (Opus 119), which included his famous "Für Elise." These bagatelles (literally meaning "trifles") were short piano pieces, either cast-offs from more advanced sonatas or concertos, some going back forty years to his earliest childhood compositions. Often the delight of today's piano students, his bagatelles feature unforgettably haunting melodies and "convey a sense of completeness within the smallest boundaries."[49]

---

48. Solomon, *Beethoven*, 327.
49. Lockwood, *Beethoven*, 397.

In these later years, Beethoven became increasingly religious, not in the denominational mode of the avid churchgoer but in the spiritual sense of recognizing and worshipping a loving, omnipotent, supernatural being, a benevolent Father in Heaven. In February 1820, he penned one of his most famous citations: "The moral law within us, and the starry heavens above us."[50] His faith had matured to the point of believing in a God who had intervened and overruled man's politics for good in the past and would so again in the future, that nature was his sublime handiwork, and that humankind was his crowning accomplishment. In the words of the Psalmist, "For thou hast made him a little lower than the angels, and hast crowned him with glory and honour" (Psalms 8:5). At this time, Beethoven's most earnest inspiration did not come from Napoléon or Alexander, kingdom or nationality, but the fatherhood of God and the humanity of man. At the deepest personal level Beethoven believed God had blessed him beyond measure with talent, and despite his deafness—indeed, perhaps because of it—Beethoven would now write perhaps his greatest pieces of music in praise of him. "God has not forsaken me," he wrote just two years before his death.[51]

This shift in spirituality accounts for the composing of what Beethoven thought was his finest piece, his immense Missa Solemnis in D Major, written in four parts: Gloria, Credo, Sanctus, and Agnus Dei. This mass was originally intended for the installation ceremony of his friend and pupil Archduke Rudolf of Austria as bishop of Olmutz in 1821, but it was not completed until three years after. It first performed in St. Petersburg in March 1824. Beethoven's chief aim in writing it was to awaken and permanently instill spiritual feelings not only within the singers but also within the listeners. For at least a year, he had studied meticulously Handel's *Messiah* and Mozart's *Requiem Mass*. Beethoven's work demonstrates its composer's mastery of the highest forms of liturgical music. Born out of his entire life's experience, Missa Solemnis depicts the death, Resurrection, and victorious ascension of Christ and the inner peace of the soul. Written on his original score were his words "Brothers, above the starry text of heaven, a beloved Father must dwell."[52]

THE NINTH SYMPHONY—"ODE TO JOY"

With his Missa Solemnis completed by mid-1823, Beethoven returned to his last and most glorious composition—a culmination of a lifetime of musical creation—a veritable climax of talent. Written over an eight-month span between July 1823 and February 1824 while at his retreats in Hetzendorf and Baden, Beethoven's Ninth Symphony—"Ode to Joy"—stands as his grandest symphony and one of the finest pieces of music ever written. Louis Schlösser, a contemporary musician, said of Beethoven's efforts in composing it, "The Ninth Symphony

---

50. Kinderman, *Beethoven*, 238.
51. Ludwig von Beethoven to Karl B., 14 September 1825, *Letters*, 240.
52. Lockwood, *Beethoven*, 407, 411.

filled his imagination, at home and in the highest spheres and the composition of this gigantic work displaced every other occupation at this time."[53]

If it was his finest work, it came at a time of his most intense physical afflictions. By 1823, Beethoven was almost totally deaf, although it is true that at odd moments he could hear the faintest of sounds. Furthermore, his eyes had become so weak after years of strain working late by candlelight that he was visually impaired. His lifelong colitis had worsened to the point of acute pain and discomfort. He likewise suffered from jaundice and increased liver disorder. Yet he remained surprisingly cheerful, determined to complete his life's work. Having been composing this piece for over thirty years but never taking the time to write it down, Beethoven's Ninth was his life's most fulfilling work.

Since his youth, Beethoven had been drawn to the writings of the great Romantic poets, most notably Friedrich Schiller and his "Ode to Joy," which he wrote in 1785. Schiller's views and writings on the brotherhood of man were a deep well of inspiration to Beethoven, and as the years passed, these feelings intensified. Beethoven had witnessed Napoléon Bonaparte's rise and subsequent decline and applauded the enduring values of the French Revolution and its assault on those forces that put down man's liberty, and he was now ready to write a colossal objection to tyranny of all kinds, including Metternich's petty secret police. This piece would be an anthem to liberty, an optimistic tribute to humanity, a musical ode to joy, and a sacred rendering to God. Though he had failed to compose a great opera, Beethoven was still anxious to put to music Schiller's unforgettable words and phrases, believing no instrumentation could match the power of the human voice to portray such lofty human sentiments. He would write what is essentially a choral anthem on the grandest possible scale, with Schiller's poem sung in the stirring climax of the fourth movement. Translated into English, the text reads as follows:

> Joy, beautiful spark of divinity,
> Daughter of Elysium,
> We enter thy sanctuary
> Heavenly one, drunk with fire;
> Your magic binds again
> What custom rudely divided;
> All mankind becomes brothers,
> Where your gentle wing abides.

The Ninth Symphony owes less to Haydn and Mozart and far more to the supernal harmonies of Bach and the Baroque era. Written in the key of D major, the opening of the overture connects thematically with the finale's climax; indeed the finale, in chorus form, reconnects with the introduction, giving the piece a certain wholeness and completeness. Some have called this device the art of "foreshadowing, early in the work, important musical

---

53. From an account by Louis Schlösser, 1823, *Letters*, 193.

The Kärntnertor Theater. *Das Kärntnertortheater in Wien*, by Carl Wenzel Zajicek.

events come."[54] At times, it stops almost in midsentence; dramatic and compelling pauses signal new waves of majestic music. Incredibly complex in its entirety, a score written for a gigantic orchestra and deliberately designed to test the finest talents of the greatest violinists, cellists, and other instrumental musicians and singers of the age, it at one point features the voice of a single baritone, placed perilously close to the climax. Then, with an avalanche of onrushing sound of orchestra and chorus combined, the Ninth Symphony reaches its unforgettable choral climax in everlasting tribute to the unrelenting joy of man, in the liberty of soul, and in coming into the presence of God—a musical vision of humanity's unconquerable spirit and of God's everlasting majesty! As one musical scholar said, it is "an enduring monument to the compatibility of beauty and truth."[55] In this stirring musical vision of God and his creations, could even prophets have asked for anything more?

The piece was originally commissioned by London's Royal Philharmonic Orchestra, which was fully aware that Beethoven's fortunes had been decimated by currency devaluations and years of legal wrangling. Beethoven, however, decided late in the composition

---

54. Kinderman, *Beethoven*, 240.
55. Kinderman, *Beethoven*, 283.

to have it initially performed in his beloved Vienna. On what surely must have been an unforgettable, four-and-a-half-hour evening of music, both the Missa Solemnis and the Ninth Symphony—each with four movements—premiered together at the Kärntnertor Theatre on the evening of 7 May 1824. The much-enlarged orchestra and chorus only had time to practice these pieces two or three times before the opening performances, and from what the critics said, it showed.

The mass went first, and after a shortened intermission most returned to hear the Ninth Symphony and to participate in a moment never to be forgotten in music history. In the audience were many of the finest of Vienna's musicians, composers, and critics, as well as royalty. Kapellmeister Michael Umlauf (1781–1842) was the principal conductor, assisted by the world-renowned violinist Ignaz Schuppanzigh (1776–1830). At their side and simultaneously turning the pages of his score while beating time, stood Beethoven. Umlauf had previously warned the choir and orchestra to pay little attention to Beethoven since he was too deaf to know precisely where they were in the score. The music, despite a flawed performance, electrified the audience. Either at the end of the scherzo or, as is more likely, at the end of the entire symphony, amid deafening applause, Beethoven—who we must remember could not hear and who could barely see—still stood poring over his score, his back to the audience, until the contralto soloist, Caroline Unger, plucked at his sleeve and pointed him to the cheering audience. Whereupon the master turned and bowed to the weary but adoring audience, jubilant in its encores of applause.

Although not a financial success, the Ninth Symphony was met with positive critical reviews. E. T. A. Hoffman, perhaps the most renowned critic of his age, called it a "masterpiece," praising it "for its capacity to transport the listener into the realm of the infinite."[56] Another critic stated: "Art and truth here celebrate their most brilliant triumph. . . . Who can ever surpass these inexpressible heights?"[57] Most German composers afterward, including Mendelssohn, Schumann, Brahms, Buchner, and Mahler, described the Ninth Symphony as the "central bulwark of musical experience."[58] Performed in London the following year (1825) but not in America until 1846, the Ninth was not an instant worldwide success. The world only gradually caught up to that night in Vienna in 1824. However, by the late nineteenth century, the Ninth Symphony had taken on mythic proportions as one of Europe's finest musical compositions, transcending time and place. Interpreted in so many ways and by so many different musicians and conductors, it remains a modern favorite of classical music and has been played at such memorable occasions as Olympic performances and in celebration of the tearing down of the Berlin Wall.

Beethoven continued to compose after 1824, including his last quartets, but nothing on so grand a scale. Opus 135, another string quartet, was his final piece. When he finally died of a liver complaint on 26 March 1827, ten thousand Viennese turned out in a steady

---

56. Lockwood, *Beethoven*, 306.
57. Solomon, *Beethoven*, 351.
58. Lockwood, *Beethoven*, 418.

downpour to pay their last respects. The Austrian dramatist and poet Franz Grillparzer (1791–1872) delivered the oration. Of all the swelling words and phrases, this remains: "He was an artist, and who can bear comparison with him? . . . Thus he lived, thus he died, thus he shall live forever."

Théodore Géricault. *Jean-Louis-André-Théodore Gericault*, by Horace Vernet.

THÉODORE GÉRICAULT,

ROMANTIC ARTISTS, AND
THE RAFT OF THE MEDUSA

Beethoven was not the only one gifted with artistic genius that revolutionized the world. There were other "earlier lights" in the morning of the Restoration whose genius and talent have stood the test of time and who expressed themselves in light of the revolutionary ideals of liberty with a certain newfound freedom of expression.[1] This chapter will examine such a person, a deeply tormented soul whose paintings of suffering and portraits of madness nonetheless speak of hope, rescue, and the indomitable spirit of humankind. His life—and death—will provide us with yet another vantage point to view the age of 1820, this time from the painter's brush.

The aspiring twenty-six-year-old French artist Jean-Louis André Théodore Géricault read the tragic story of the loss of 150 passengers of *La Méduse* soon after his return to Paris in September 1817 after a yearlong visit to Italy, where he had systematically studied the paintings of Michelangelo, Raphael, and several other leading Renaissance painters. What baited his interest even more than the tragedy itself was the French Bourbon government's attempt to cover up the whole affair. It became Géricault's mission to expose the tragic episode.

On 2 July 1816, the French frigate *La Méduse*, flagship of a convoy carrying soldiers and settlers to the colony of Senegal on Africa's west coast, ran aground on the reefs of Arguin, an island off the coast of Mauritania. Two hundred fifty of the ship's four hundred passengers

---

1   Roberts, *Comprehensive History of the Church*, 6:252.

and crew, including the cowardly captain, crowded onto six lifeboats, leaving the unfortunate others to fend for themselves on a makeshift raft. This crude floating device, made from the ship's masts and beams that those left behind had hurriedly lashed together, measured sixty-five feet long by twenty-eight feet wide. As these unfortunate 150 castaways, including one woman, were herded onto the slippery beams, the raft sank at least three feet below the surface of the sea under the weight of the panic-driven assembly. Sensing that the weight of the raft would drag them under, those in the lifeboats cut the towing ropes, leaving the heaving raft and its doomed passengers to the mercies of the wind-tossed Atlantic.

That first nightmare at sea served as notice of the calamities that awaited them. The ship's surgeon, Jean Baptiste Henri Savigny, one of the mere handful who survived the horrors of the "raft of the *Medusa*," recalled the following: "A great number of our passengers who had not a seaman's foot tumbled over one another; after ten hours of the most cruel sufferings, day arrived. What a spectacle! . . . Ten or twelve unfortunate creatures having their lower extremities entangled in the interstices left between the planks of the raft, had been unable to disengage themselves, and had lost their lives. Several others had been carried off the raft by the violence of the sea, so that by morning we were already twenty fewer in number."[2]

Come daybreak, panic ensued as all hands pushed to the center of the raft, and several mutinied against the officers among them, throwing several overboard before they, in turn, were quieted by the charge of surviving armed soldiers. Sixty-five more died that second day. By the third day, weakness, fatigue, and raw hunger had driven the remaining survivors to that basest act: "Those whom death had spared in the disastrous night which I have just described threw themselves ravenously on the dead bodies with which the raft was covered, cut them up in slices which some even that instant devoured. A great number of us at first refused to touch the horrible food; but at last . . . we saw in their frightful repast our only deplorable means of prolonging existence; and I proposed . . . to dry these bleeding limbs in order to render them a little more supportable to the taste."[3]

This dreadful scene of hunger, thirst, and insanity repeated itself day after weary day until by the sixth day at sea only twenty-eight survivors remained. When there was too little drinking water left, the strongest resolved to practice survival of the fittest by throwing their weaker comrades into the sea in a blatant act of murder.

The fifteen ruthless men now in sole command of the raft managed to survive another seven days when, on the morning of 17 July, after virtually all hope for rescue had been lost in an abject spirit of delirium and despair, "Captain Dupont, casting his eye towards the horizon, perceived a ship, and announced it to us by a cry of joy; we perceived it to be a brig, but it was at a very great distance; we could only distinguish the top of its mast. The sight of the vessel spread amongst us a joy which it would be difficult to describe. . . . We did all we

---

2. *The Times* (London), 17 September 1816, 2.
3. *The Times*, 17 September 1816, 2.

could to make ourselves observed; we piled up our [wine] castes, at the top of which we fixed handkerchiefs of different colours."[4]

When, however, the distant ship disappeared over the horizon, the shipwrecked crew members fell in utter despair and lay down together in a makeshift tent, which they had rigged beneath the mast to await an almost certain death. To their disbelief, two hours later, the ship *Argus* of the original convoy sent out to search for survivors returned, miraculously spotted them, and turned sail for their deliverance. Of the fifteen starving, sunbaked men rescued from the raft, five died soon afterward, leaving only ten to tell the sordid tale.

Géricault could hardly have chosen a topic more in tune with his own inclinations to the violent and the macabre, his own self-condemnation and guilt over a tortured love affair, and his own artistic talent for painting scenes of grandeur in the neoclassical style. A colossal painting that mirrored Géricault's inner talent and distress, a masterpiece of political art that captured the decline of Napoléon's military power, and a robust transitional piece of Romantic art, *The Raft of the Medusa* continues to elicit critical acclaim. In fact, Géricault's life and his many other works have been eclipsed by the very grandeur of this one enduring, monumental piece. This enormous painting, which is sixteen by twenty-four feet and still on display on the walls of the Louvre in Paris, speaks to the universal themes of suffering and death, tragedy and triumph, hopelessness and redemption.

A SELF-TAUGHT ARTIST

Géricault was born 26 September 1791 in Rouen, France, to forty-seven-year-old Georges-Nicolas Géricault (1743–1826), a wealthy and well-established lawyer, and thirty-seven-year-old Louise-Jeanne-Marie Caruel (1753–1808), who was from a well-known merchant family with connections to the slave trade. He moved with his wealthy parents to Paris when only four years old. There he spent a troubled childhood in the turbulent, terrifying Reign of Terror. What psychological impact the chilling atrocities of the French Revolution and the death of both his mother and father had upon him when he was still relatively young has not been sufficiently analyzed, but his parents left him an annuity that freed him from financial cares for most of his life. He never painted by commission; he was free to paint "fully at the mercy of his temperament."[5] If not a brilliant student, Géricault was keenly perceptive and blessed with an exquisite talent to draw and a remarkable memory for detail.

During his formative years, he spent days visiting the Louvre and studying paintings of every sort. He also looked forward to vacations with relatives in rural Normandy, where he developed his taste for high-bred horses and a love and skill for horsemanship. Never close to his rather quaint and unimaginative father, who failed to understand his son, Géricault gravitated to his kinder, more affectionate, and much more supportive uncle, Jean-Baptiste Caruel—his mother's brother. Things were going quite well indeed until Caruel married the

---

4. *The Times*, 17 September 1816, 2.
5. Vaughan, *Romantic Art*, 232.

young and beautiful Alexandrine-Modeste. It did not take long for Géricault to see in his new aunt the sister he never had and, as time went on, someone much more than that.

His first lessons in art came at the Lycée Impérial at the hands of Pierre Bouillon (1776–1831), a winner of the prestigious Prix de Rome in 1787, an award that provided talented young artists fame and prestige. Soon afterward Géricault decided to travel to Italy to study Renaissance art—a rite of passage for aspiring French artists. There he began visiting the studio of the affable Carle Vernet (1758–1836), who was well known for his remarkable equestrian paintings but who, like most other struggling artists of the day, had accepted commissions from the French Directory to draw glorified paintings of Napoléon and his military conquests. Vernet's drawings of Napoléon's Italian campaign had won him acclaim, as did his *Battle of Marengo*. For his *Morning of Usterlitz*, Napoléon had also awarded him the Legion of Honour.

Sensing his own developing interests and talents and the need for more earnest artistic training, nineteen-year-old Géricault later enlisted as a pupil of the better-known Pierre-Narcisse Guérin (1774–1838), whose 1799 painting *Marcus Sextus* had earned him fame and a little fortune. Although he studied under Guérin for six months and occasionally thereafter, the independent-minded Géricault would always regard himself as a self-taught artist. After studying the mechanics of monumental painting with Guérin, Géricault studied at the Louvre, where from about 1810 to 1815 he copied the works of Peter Paul Rubens (1577–1640), Diego Velázquez (1590–1660), and Rembrandt (1606–69). While at the Louvre, he explored a wide range of emotion and choice of subjects common to the budding Romantic school of art that the prevailing classical art forms lacked. And all the while he gave the appearance of "a gentleman-artist, an outsider, by habit and temperament, to the professional world of art."[6]

ART AND THE ROMANTICS

Géricault was very much a pioneering product of his time and in company with several other developing Romantic painters and artists. The Romantic impulse in art, as we have already seen in music and will also see in literature, was a self-conscious cultural movement, a highly individualized, emotional reaction to the perceived formalized, rule-bound rigidities of the earlier Enlightenment era. It was a highly popular, more democratic movement of expression than the top-down, aristocratic, state- or Church-commissioned art that had for so long subsidized and dominated the world of art. Although Romanticism was not a religious movement, it was certainly an emotional (some even say spiritual) trend—a deeply moving yearning of the soul and a revolt against the enveloping materialism and increasing mechanization of the industrial age. Marcel Brion, in his study of Romanticism, described its

---

6. Eitner, *Gericault's* Raft of the Medusa, 12.

principal elements in terms of feelings—a "feeling for nature, for the infinite and far distant pastures, for solitude, for the tragedy of Being and the inaccessible ideal."[7]

Admiration for the Gothic had been growing in European art circles since at least 1750. This "medieval revival" soon became widespread, not only in art but also in literature. However, in no small part, Romanticism owed its true beginnings to the French Revolution, which, in overturning the established political, religious, and economic orders of the time, permanently cast doubts on those earlier strains of classical artistic thought and expression. The French and American Revolutions and the Napoleonic Wars all showed the unpredictability of human history and of how humanity reacts in difficult circumstances.

The Romantic impulse in art viewed men and women as highly emotional as well as rational beings, capable of the grand and the noble as well as the base and the

Self-Portrait, by Jacques-Louis David.

deplorable. Whether they chose to see humanity in positive hues, like Wordsworth, or in more pessimistic strokes, as did Francisco de Goya and Géricault, the Romantics believed in giving full rein to their emotions. To the Romantics, truth was more a subjective than objective reality, and inspiration and emotion were the most dependable arbiters for understanding and capturing life's moods, ideals, and meanings whether in music, on paper, or on canvas. As another noted scholar succinctly phrased it, "Romanticism sought to express ideals which could be sensed only in the individual soul and lay beyond the bounds of logical discourse."[8]

The most significant visual interest among the Romantic painters was that of color and illusion. This led many to see painting—in particular the portrayal of the heroic, the picturesque or landscape, the spiritual, and the portraiture—as the quintessential Romantic visual art, far more so than with sculpture or architecture.

Arguably the most famous artist of the age was Jacques-Louis David (1748–1825). Destined to live through the tumultuous times of the French Revolution, the rise and fall of Napoléon's empire, and the restoration of Bourbon authority, David honed his skill of captur-

---

7. Brion, *Art of the Romantic Era*, 13.
8. Honour, *Romanticism*, 16.

ing the defining moments and dominating personalities of his time in majestic, neoclassical style paintings. As astute politically as he was gifted artistically, David managed to survive through a most tumultuous political era.

Having studied in Rome for several years, David understood "the classicing art of the Italian Renaissance," with its catalogue of pomp and magnificence, and the prevailing sentiment that the highest beauty was Greek art as expressed in the human figure. "Antiquity," David once said, "has not ceased to be the great school of modern painters, the source from which they draw the beauties of their art. We seek to imitate the ancient artists, in the genius of their conceptions, the purity of their design, the expressiveness of their features, and the grace of their forms."[9]

Upon returning to France after a temporary, self-imposed exile, David continued his formal training at the Royal Academy of Paintings and Sculpture, created by Louis XIV. Following the standard sequence of training for French schools, David spent long years of drawing from prints, plaster casts of ancient sculptures, and live models. A republican and avid supporter of Robespierre and the aims of the French Revolution, the "Robespierre of the Brush"—as David was sometimes called—was elected to the National Convention, where he acted almost as dictator of art for all of France. After Robespierre's death in 1794, David spent a year in prison, and upon his release he kept a low profile. Knowing of David's artistic genius, Napoléon visited his studios before becoming emperor and enlisted his artistic support.

Painting with astonishing clarity, color, detail, and with "personal determination and passion," David produced heroic historical paintings with stunning, photograph-like style.[10] In demand by republicans, royalists, and emperors alike, David memorialized the Revolution and immortalized Napoléon, bequeathing to the world of art such timeless patriotic classics as *Belisarius* (1781), *Oath of the Moratir* (1784–85), *The Oath of the Tennis Court* (1791), *The Death of Marat* (1793), *Napoleon Crossing the Alps* (1801), and *The Coronation of Napoleon* (1806).[11] With the post-Waterloo Bourbon restoration in 1815, David fled to Brussels, where he lived his declining years in exile.[12]

David also encouraged his better pupils to express their own style and individuality. Under David's direction in 1791, the Salon, an annual public exhibition of paintings at the Louvre, was open to most every artist and not just servants of the state. More than ever before, artists were being commissioned by wealthy sponsors and less by the Church itself. Among David's more notable disciples was Anne-Louis Girodet (1767–1824), François Ge-

---

9. From the foreword of David's *The Painting of the Sabines*, as exhibited to the Republic at the National Palace of the Sciences and the Arts, Hall of the Former Academy of Art by The Citizen David, member of the National Institute, Paris, Year VIII, as cited in Holt, *From the Classicists to the Impressionists*, 4.
10. Vaughan, *Romantic Art*, 61.
11. Rosenblum, *19th-Century Art*, 24–30.
12. Crow, "Classicism and Romanticism: Patriotism and Virtue: David to the Young Ingres," in Eisenman, *Nineteenth Century Art*, 18–20.

The Coronation of Napoleon, by Jacques-Louis David.

rard (1770–1837), Jean-Germain Drouais (1763–1788), and Jean-Auguste-Dominic Ingres (1780–1867), whose hero-worship painting of *Napoleon on His Imperial Throne* (1806) stunned even David with its majestic colors and deification overtones.[13] It was in France that the controversy between Romantic art and classicism became "most vociferous," even violent. Art became the surrogate of political action. Romantic art was a school of painting so aberrant and "full of drama and emotional complexity" that only the word Romantic captures its essence.[14]

One clearly begins to detect the bedrock meaning of Romantic heroic art in the paintings of yet another one of David's loyal disciples, Antoine-Jean Gros (1771–1835). In his *Napoléon on the Battlefield of Eylau* (1808), Gros shows not just the conquering Napoléon but also focuses, in the forefront of that painting, on the dead and dying. Attuned more to expressing feelings and raw emotions than to following slavishly the formalities of style, the French Romantics tended to be less worshipful of military and spiritual heroes and more observant of the common soldier, of human suffering, and of the best and worst in humanity, while not abandoning the classical forms of art.[15] They exhibited, as Robert Rosenblum puts

---

13. For more on David, see Robert, *Jacques-Louis David*.
14. Vaughan, *Romantic Art*, 222.
15. Honour, *Romanticism*, 36–38.

it, "a condition of emotional unrest" and explored "new dimensions of irrational experience that are couched in images of awe, terror, hallucination [and] mystery."[16]

Eugène Delacroix (1798–1863) was a close friend and artistic heir to Géricault and, in many ways, a later leader of the French Romantic school. Delacroix's impressive use of brush-strokes and the optical effects of color and movement prepared the way for the later Impressionist School of Art. Like Géricault, Delacroix had studied the great Renaissance artists and had also painted scenes of death and dissolution (for example, *The Barque of Dante* in 1822 and *The Massacre at Chios* in 1824) and emotional scenes of stirring nationalism, but he did so with more emotional control than Géricault. His most renowned painting, *Liberty Leading the People* (1830), portrayed a bare-breasted female symbol of Republican Liberty marching under the banner of the tricolor flag, representing liberty, equality, and fraternity. Over 9,000 works have been attributed to Delacroix, including 850 paintings, 1,500 pastels, and more than 6,600 drawings.[17]

No study of Romantic art would be complete without considering William Blake, the so-called prophet of his age, who stands defiantly outside all formal schools of training. His work tended to the mystic and the spiritual, exploring the problem of evil in a God-created world. An English Jacobin, Blake opposed royal and sectarian subjugation and authority and yearned for an English revolution like that in France or America (see his "Albion Rose"). He was, to borrow Brian Luhacher's phrase, a countercultural Romantic poet, painter, and engraver.[18] He decorated his books of poetry—including *Songs of Innocence* ("The Lamb," 1789) and *Songs of Experience* ("The Tiger," 1794)—in the medieval fashion of illuminated manuscripts complete with relief etchings and woodcuts. Blake was a mystic, an enigma, and a believer in the Swedenborgian tradition of prophecies, visions and dreams, and an imminent apocalypse. His inspiration came not from nature's landscapes but, as he believed, the voice of God speaking to him from within. His art, what one scholar called "the super-reality of the visionary," is brilliantly colored and unique in symbolism, bordering on the sublime and the surreal.[19]

With England being spared the traumas and terrors of the French Revolution and the scourge of conquering armies, the Romantic impulse there took a more graceful turn. More a nostalgic response to the intrusion of the Industrial Revolution on English agricultural life and society, the English art of this period favored the picturesque landscape paintings of William Gilpin (1724–1804), Humphry Repton (1752–1818), and the watercolorist Thomas Girtin (1775–1802), with his famous *The White House at Chelsea*. This generation of painters took Romantic landscape painting to new heights. In England, an early precursor of Romantic artists was the Swiss-born Henry Fuseli (1741–1825), who was as prolific with the pen of

---

16. Rosenblum, *19th-Century Art*, 62.
17. For a good, recent study of Delacroix and the French Romantic School of Art, see Johnson, *David to Delacroix*.
18. Brian Lukacher, "Blake and His Contemporaries," in Eisenman, *Nineteenth Century Art*, 102.
19. Vaughan, *Romantics*, 82.

an art critic as he was with the brush. Many of his early paintings were inspired by the works of John Milton. Fuseli favored the supernatural and grotesque humor, as evidenced in *The Nightmare* (1781) and *Horseman Attacked by a Giant Snake* (1800).

Perhaps the three most famous English artists of the rustic landscape school were John Constable (1776–1837), John Martin (1789–1854), and that renowned painter of light, J. M. W. Turner (1775–1851). These artists sought to portray insensate nature in a way that was emotionally compelling to the viewer. They believed that "the contemplation of nature can provide the deepest moments of self-discovery," which has led some scholars to refer to this expression as "transcendent landscape art."[20] Constable is well remembered for his pure and unaffected paintings of pastoral England. His *The Hay Wain* and *The Clouds*, for example, are pure and unaffected efforts to feel the simple, peaceful, and enduring beauty of nature in a way that is spiritually uplifting and wholly unforgettable.

As much a traveler as Constable was a stay-at-home idyllic artist, J. M. W. Turner painted oil landscapes of grandiose historical themes (*Battle of Trafalgar*, 1822) but more especially nature's many moods and sublime or terrifying indomitability and mastery over man, as best seen in his *Shipwreck* (1805) and *Snow Storm: Hannibal and His Army Crossing the Alps* (1812). Disaster pictures, especially shipwrecks, were favorite topics of many Romantic artists. And in the best Romantic tradition, Turner's *Rain, Steam and Speed: The Great Western Railway* (1844) blended reality with imagination as it captures an intruding, oncoming train of the Industrial Revolution into the once idyllic, picturesque English landscape with impressionistic-like mood and vitality. Turner is properly called the painter of light because of his transcendent visions of color and its effects. Turner captures the brilliance of the sun and the ghostly effect of moonlight in his paintings of Venice and Rome. Through this skill, Turner speaks of a divine spirituality and a wonderful optimism of a benevolent, shining nature that, when all is said and done, promises more light and truth. As bright and optimistic as Goya tended to the dark and pessimistic, Turner captured the brightness of day like no other contemporary artist.

The Romantic landscape impulse likewise found expression in Germany, where a longing for German unification and budding nationalism found full sway in the Blake-like mystic landscape art of Phillip Otto Runge (1777–1810) and was more darkly manifested in the works of Caspar David Friedrich (1774–1840). Both artists strenuously opposed French occupation and showed a more Christian-centered, melancholy theme. Well known are Friedrich's *Procession at Dawn* (1805), *The Cross in the Mountains* (1808), and more particularly his *Abbey in the Oakwood* (1809–10), with its Gothic overtones and stark landscapes. He seemed to show that the era when God revealed himself directly to man may have passed, that nature, and not sectarian religion, was the sublime way to gaining true spirituality and

---

20. Vaughan, *Romantic Art*, 134.

Rain, Steam and Speed: The Great Western Railway (1844), by J. M. W. Turner.

oneness with God and Christ. Many of Friedrich's paintings of lonely, barren landscapes and of Arctic shipwrecks reflect his "fading hope of a united German nation."[21]

In America, the mood was much brighter and far more optimistic than in Europe. The recent American Revolution, the declaration of independence from Great Britain, and the beckoning of a magnificent western wilderness all filled the new republic (see chapter 11) with a hope and vibrancy that was in stark contrast to the gloom and despondency of many post-Napoleonic European Romantic artists. Inspired by the works of John Constable, J. M. W. Turner, and other English Romantic artists, Thomas Cole (1801–48, leading artist of the Hudson River School), Asher B. Durand (1796–1886), and Frederic E. Church (1826–1900) boldly presented vast panoramic vistas of America's promised land. A notable example of this is Cole's *View of the Round-Top in the Catskill Mountains* (1827). This school of art presented intoxicating spectacles of national power and of America's destiny in successfully taming a new and seemingly endless wilderness of opportunity. Depicting scenes along the Hudson River in the 1820s and later of New England, Niagara Falls, and more westward

---

21. Lukacher, "Landscape Art and Romantic Nationalism in Germany and America," in Eisenman, *Nineteenth Century Art*, 150.

places, these vivid paintings depicted America as a new and bountiful Garden of Eden, an idealistic manifestation of sublime peace and wonder where both humans and nature could coexist in majestic beauty and everlasting harmony.

Another notable innovation associated with Romanticism was the emergence of political caricature in the graphic arts. In Great Britain, James Gillray (1756–1815) pioneered exaggerated portraiture, particularly in his satirical representations of King George III. In France the political cartoonist of the day was Honoré Daumier (1808–79). Etching was also becoming an acceptable creative medium.

In portraiture painting, one sees the influence of early Romanticism. Probably the most famous portrait painter of the eighteenth century, certainly in England, was Thomas Gainsborough (1727–88). Remarkably proficient technically, he had developed a style of portrait in which he integrated the sitter into the background landscape, as in his famous *Blue Boy* (1770). Thomas Lawrence (1769–1830) followed suit with his equally famous *Pinkie*, painted in much the same fashion in 1794.

On the continent, the most famous portrait painter was the inimitable and highly imaginative Spanish painter, Francisco de Goya (1746–1828)—at least he started out as such. As with David in France, Goya was royalty's "first painter" (in this case for Spain's King Charles V) and a magnificent portrait painter of the aristocracy. Goya's portraits captured much more than likeness: they expressed the psychology and the deepest sentiments and slightest nuances of emotion and heightened feelings in his subjects—especially fear. Privately he was inclined to paint the troubled waters of the grotesque, the nightmarish, and the mysterious. An eyewitness to the horrors of the French occupation of Spain from 1808 to 1814, he turned his attention from mere portraits to capturing on canvas the panic, chaos, and awful brutalities of the Iberian Peninsula War. Unforgettable are his *Third of May, 1808* (1814), in which he painted Spanish insurgents being executed by French occupational forces, and his scores of drawings entitled *The Disasters of War* (1810–20). Like Beethoven, Goya became deaf near the end of his life. Nevertheless, he emotionalized his

The Third of May, 1808, by Francisco de Goya. Detail.

art by dramatizing his way through to the awful truths of inhumanity and the ignobleness of war.

Although the Romantic impulse was harder to see in sculptures, the most prominent sculptor of the age was likely Pierre-Jean David D'Angers (1788–1856), who made very enthusiastic studies of the most prominent figures of his time, as evidenced by his *Wounded Philopoemen*. Along with such other contemporary French practitioners as August Préault (1809–79), Johan de Seigneur (1808–66), Antoine Louise Barye (1796–1875), and François Rude (1784–1855), D'Angers moved somewhat away from the smooth surfaces of classical sculpture to rougher, more individualistic, more emotional effects.

And in architecture, the Romantic once again found its finest expression in recapturing the past of the Medieval Age, most particularly in Gothic representations on both sides of the Atlantic. This was most evident in the building of churches and universities. James Wyatt's Fonthill Abbey (1807), Alexander Davis's Blithewood Estate in Fishkill, New York (1834), and Richard Upjohn's Trinity Church in New York City all come to mind as examples of this reclaimed, artificial Gothic. And in the field of landscape gardening, there were grandiose redevelopments in major capital cities. Napoléon set the new standards for this expression in Paris, and the Prince Regent (later George IV) commissioned John Nash (1752–1835) to do the same in London.

GÉRICAULT IN ITALY

The factors that led up to Géricault's decision to go to Italy and the influence his study of Roman and Florentine art had upon him are central to understanding the troubled genius of the man. As with David, Delacroix, and other contemporary French painters, most serious artists of the time believed that a season in Italy studying the classics of antiquarian art was a necessary rite of passage, an essential prerequisite for professional advancement and state appointments. Still somewhat of an outsider to the academic art establishment, Géricault may never have won the Prix de Rome, but he was financially secure enough to spend a year in Italy.

Géricault sought to escape the stagnant depression that gripped Paris and all of France in the wake of Napoléon's crushing defeat at Waterloo and his subsequent exile to the island of St. Helena. To one as fervently patriotic and republican as Géricault was (he briefly served in the army), *la gloire de la France* was a painful memory. Two of his earlier paintings, *Chasseur de la Garde* (*The Charging Light Cavalryman*) of 1812 and *Le Cuirassier Blessé Quittant le Feu* (*The Wounded Heavy Cavalryman*), which he painted only two years later, are vivid studies in emotional contrasts, capturing the rise and fall of France's once-feared cavalry. The former is a glorification of French triumphant military might and ascendancy, with a cavalry officer on the back of a charging steed. It was well received. The latter, a much more forceful and original work in more subdued shades and leaden tones, shows a wounded, dismounted, and defeated cavalryman solemnly retreating from the scene of battle, a sober testament to Napoléon's devastating defeat. Considered a transitionalist artist, Géricault sought to capture the drama, expressive force, and feelings of war among the anonymous men who fought in it, both victors and victims. Inclined as he was to the violent, macabre, and pessimistic, Géricault sensed a prolonged stay in Italy would do good for his mental and physical health.

There was also another reason for his extended visit. By 1816, now aged twenty-five, Géricault had fallen passionately in love with his aunt, Alexandrine-Modeste Caruel, wife of his uncle Jean-Baptiste Caruel, head of the family business. At the time, she was already mother to two sons who were six and seven years old. Unlike her husband, she was drawn to art. Charles Clément, Géricault's biographer, called the relationship with Alexandrine a "reciprocated, irregular stormy love that he could not acknowledge but to which he saw all the vehemence of his character."[22] While his kind and trusting uncle continued to support and sustain him, Géricault secretly carried on with his liaison. Afflicted by contrasting feelings of love and guilt, joy and remorse, and with an agonizing fear of being discovered, Géricault tore himself away from the only woman he ever loved, crossing over the Alps.[23]

The Wounded Cuirassier, by Théodore Géricault, study (ca. 1814).

In Italy, first in Florence and then in Naples and Rome, Géricault entered into what one might call his second period of creativity. While studying the paintings of Michelangelo and Raphael, Géricault found his own inner artistic expression and creativity, not a mere mimicking of classical art but, as Wheelock Whitney describes it, a capturing of the "antique manner" of great classical art without its rigid classical forms.[24]

Learning to go deeper than outward appearance by capturing underlying human emotion, Géricault blended "the solemn, timeless qualities of the art of antiquity, and the High Renaissance with the excitement and energy of ideas from everyday life, . . . a synthesis of the Rome of the Caesars and the Rome of the Popes."[25] Drawn to the common rather than the heroic,

---

22. Clément, *Géricault*, 77.
23. Eitner, *Géricault*, 75.
24. Whitney, *Géricault in Italy*, 3.
25. Whitney, *Géricault in Italy*, 43, 49.

he gained his greatest inspiration from everyday occurrences such as parades, street rallies, and carnivals. He shared the Romantic fascination with the horse as an image of superhuman energy. In all of Géricault's equestrian paintings, he captured not only differences in breeds but also differences in personality, with something almost human in their expressions.[26]

He was also fascinated by the violent, the gruesome, and the macabre, as evidenced by his many Italian notebook sketches of men injured in the streets, the butchering of cattle, and public executions and decapitations—a "brutal realism undiluted by literary, mythological, historical or political associations."[27] And he owned that unique ability of capturing the spontaneous and the extreme or climactic moment of virtually any event before him without the clutter of detail or distraction.

His self-imposed absence from Alexandrine may go far in explaining the turbulent erotica and rampant sexuality evident in his later Italian paintings of 1817. Géricault was a passionate, troubled young man who often used brush and canvas to work out the warring emotions that bedeviled him. From out of this cauldron of heightened emotions, he produced such exquisite art as *Young Woman Holding a Child* (1816–17) and *Leda and the Swan* (1816–17). His most important Italian project was *Start of the Barberi Race* (1817), inspired by the carnivals and horse races of Naples. In many of the eighty-five preliminary drawings and paintings he drew before completing his central piece, there are mass groupings of many human figures in pyramidal form, showing a collective sense of impending danger and a severe juxtaposition of darkness and light—all painted in the grand scale that presaged his *Raft of the Medusa*. Men and horses were shown in classic Apollo form as he combined neoclassical and Romantic expressions.[28]

THE RAFT OF THE MEDUSA

Upon his return to Paris in the fall of 1817, a hapless Géricault renewed his secret love affair with Alexandrine, no matter the shame and regret it would inevitably cause. She soon became pregnant, and when it was discerned that his uncle could not possibly have been the father, family suspicion turned frowningly on Géricault, who, painfully and reluctantly, admitted to it all. To prevent further reproach and dishonor, Alexandrine sought privacy in a country estate, where in November 1818 she gave birth to their son, Georges-Hippolyte (d. 1882), a secret kept hidden from sleuths and scholars for over 150 years.[29]

Such was the troubled and tormented life of Théodore Géricault when he stumbled across the story of the sinking of the *Medusa*. Immediately captivated by its enormous human drama of suffering and death, Géricault sequestered himself, monk-like, in his private

---

26. Berger, *Gericault*, 11.
27. Whitney, *Géricault in Italy*, 55–57.
28. For instance, see *Start of the Barberi Race* (1817).
29. If Charles Clément, Géricault's nineteenth-century biographer, knew of this episode, he conveniently kept it quiet to guard the reputation of those involved. Only recently and quite by accident did researchers stumble across evidence of the episode in papers found in a Normandy attic.

studio, where he embarked upon the painting of his life in February 1818. He spent the next eight months at work, occasionally visiting morgues and hospitals to study body parts of the sick and dying but mostly secluding himself at home, where he painted series of episodes relating to the mayhem and mutiny of the disaster. Over time, he painstakingly sketched out on a colossal canvas, some twenty feet high, one larger-than-life figure after another. Visitors were few and infrequent, although Delacroix posed for one of the dying figures. Géricault worked at a feverish pace, sleeping and eating only intermittently, seldom stopping for visitors or relaxation. Gradually, his enormous painting began to emerge.[30]

A painting of such power that was so blatantly critical of the ruling governing authorities would inevitably stir controversy, if not intervention. And with the secret of his love affair now out in the open and his aunt forced far away, Géricault drowned his sorrow and his guilt in secrecy and in a torrent of activity. So he toiled on in tormented seclusion. His love for Alexandrine was one he took to his early grave, for in truth he almost worked himself to death painting his masterpiece.

Le Radeau de la Méduse (*The Raft of the Medusa*) is a timeless drama. Its series of diagonals moving up from the foreground toward the sky captures the climactic moment of both hope and despair, that precise time when several in that collection of writhing sailors and survivors were at the point of death. The positioning of Géricault's human figures into four distinct groupings—the dead and dying at the stern, the more alert and watchful on the other side of the mast, the struggling men who drag themselves to the far edge of the raft, and the three men who mount some barrels at the raft's forward end to signal the distant ship—is "so precisely thought out, so clearly described, that the conflicting gestures are held in a coherent pattern that has the powerful simplicity of truly monumental art."[31]

The Raft of the Medusa defies simple explanation but is considered an important bridge between the neoclassical and Romantic styles. Géricault's human figures, nearly twice life-size, though pale and apparently emaciated, are portrayed in a powerful, classical, superhuman style, like Olympic deities. The lines in the painting direct the eye upward, pyramid-wise, to a pinnacle where a black man, signaling the hope not only of their rescue but also of emancipation for an entire race, reaches above the rest, savior-like, seeking for the redemption of his ship and of all humankind. The contrasts in mood are remarkable between the disconsolate father—grasping the partly cannibalized body of his dead son, whose left arm is stretched out in invitation for all viewers to understand—and the jubilation of another man, turning in excitement to tell the news of the distant ship with his left arm pointing upward in contrast to the dead son below. It is a dense, crowded, and graphic scene of contrasts: hope and despair, young and old, life and death, and past and future. It is almost biblical—certainly Romantic—in its vivid portrayal of abject suffering, utter despair, and unexpected joy—a kaleidoscope of human emotions all tossed together in a storm on a single raft in a roiling sea.

---

30. Zerner, *Géricault*, 28–33.
31. Vaughan, *Romantic Art*, 240. For a discussion of the four groupings, see Eitner, *Géricault's Raft*, 29.

The Raft of the Medusa (1818–1819), by Theodore Gericault.

When unveiled to the public at the Salon of 1819, it stirred immediate controversy. Reaction to it was muted and mixed. Some critics adored; others deplored it or were at least disturbed. King Louis XVIII gazed at it for several long moments, not sure at first what to make of it. The royal word, however, is said to have been: "Mr. Gericault, you have just made a shipwreck that is not one for you," although the king did award him with a medal.[32] Other government officials, who by then had tried and court-martialed the ship's captain, were less condemning than Géricault thought they might be. But no royal commission was forthcoming, and Géricault, discouraged over a less-than-enthusiastic response, left for England in the fall where the painting, on display at the Egyptian Hall in Piccadilly in June 1820, generated a much more favorable public response—a case of a prophet without honor in his own country.[33] Géricault's share of the receipts amounted to almost twenty thousand francs, a most considerable sum. Although Géricault was arguably "the purest incarnation

---

32. Eitner, *Géricault's Raft*, 6.
33. Appearing in the *Literary Gazette* was this comment: "Taken all together, his work is, as we before observed, one of the finest specimens of the French school ever brought to this country." *The London Literary Gazette and Journal of Belles Lettres, Arts, Sciences, etc.*, 1 July 1820, 427.

of Romantic art in France,"[34] it took the stilling of a thousand prejudices before his painting could ever be accepted as the masterpiece it has become.

The Raft of the Medusa has since gained universal renown as a classic metaphor for humankind. Contemporary journalists saw in it the obvious condemnation of the naval ministry, which surely it was, while others viewed it as Géricault's chastisement of the Bourbon royalty. Jules Michelet later said of it, "*C'est la France elle-même; c'est notre societé toute entiére qu'il embarqua sur ce radeau.*" (It is France itself and all of our society, that embarked upon that raft.)[35] Still others have seen in it a religious motif symbolizing the fall of man, his apostasy from truth, and his desperate need for rescue, restoration, and redemption. For our purposes, however, Géricault's painting may well have captured the spirit of the age of 1820. It too was a time of searching and of revolution, of prophets and of revelation, of coming out of the despair born out of the ancient regimes of the past, and of being rescued by the emerging light of a new age. A long, dark night of death and despondency was finally coming to its close.

HIS FINAL YEARS

Géricault lived for only four years after returning home from England in this the third and final creative period of his short life. Until recently, most scholars believed that this was his least productive time. Although he gave serious thought to painting another mighty mural on yet another political and humanitarian theme such as the injustices of the slave trade or the cruelties of the Spanish Inquisition, nothing ever came from such plans, likely on account of the severe depression that overtook him. Some believe he may have even considered suicide, a realistic possibility, considering the fact that there was a history of mental illness in his family. His maternal grandfather had committed suicide, and an uncle on his mother's side had died insane in 1805.[36]

Surely, he had every reason to be depressed. He was almost daily haunted by the guilty memory of the one who died in his place. When Géricault was drafted into Napoléon's army some years before, his father had paid for a substitute to serve in his place, a young man by the name of Claude Petit. Tragically, Petit had died from wounds he suffered in 1812 at the Russian front, along with three hundred thousand other men. Furthermore, the man who sat for Géricault's painting of the *Chasseur de la Garde*, Lt. Alexandre Dieudonné, had also perished while fighting in Russia that same year. The fact that both men died in a losing cause hurt Géricault even more. Surely Napoléon's inglorious defeat and the return of the French monarchy was a bitter pill to swallow.

To add to his troubled spirit was the disappointment of never having won the much-coveted Prix de Rome and the fame it surely would have brought him. Perhaps the strain of painting the *Medusa* and the less-than-positive response it initially received also discouraged

---

34. Rosen and Zeiner, *Romanticism and Realism*, 39.
35. Honour, *Romanticism*, 41.
36. Snell, *Portraits of the Insane*, 39–41.

The Mad Woman, by Théodore Géricault (ca. 1819/1822).

him from going further. Nor did he ever recover emotionally from the loss of his star-crossed lover, the erosion of family respect, and the wall of separation the family erected between him and his infant son. Such grief and guilt led to moral lassitude, which at times laid him low with syphilis, likely being the cause of his many illnesses late in life.[37] Compounding his misery was a foolish investment in a failed factory enterprise that led to personal bankruptcy in 1823.

During these final years, Géricault was driven to painting the poor, the alcoholic, the sick, and the insane in a series of portrait sketches unique for their subject matter. It was almost as if he were painting his own despair. In his *Portrait of a Kleptomaniac* (1822), *Monomaniac of Child Abduction* (1823), *Monomaniac of Military Command* (1823), *Monomaniac of Gambling* (1823), and *The Madwoman* or *Monomaniac of Theft* (1824), Géricault displayed a profound psychological penetration uncommon in other painters, a morbid empathy for the outcast and the ignored. This series of maniacal paintings, originally ten in all, were rejected by the Louvre, set aside, and virtually lost for some forty years before they were rediscovered piecemeal, sold to various buyers, and all but forgotten. In time, five of the lot were eventually tracked down and once more exhibited together in Paris in 1924, a century after their creation.

The plight of the mentally challenged had for centuries been an uncelebrated cause. Conditions in hospitals, asylums, and prisons, even in the late eighteenth century, were still horrible. Locked up, chained, crammed together in the most filthy and squalid conditions imaginable, treated as animals, and displayed as curiosities, and wild beasts, those with mental illness were viewed as a derangement to be feared, forgotten, and forsaken.

It took the pioneering efforts of Dr. Philippe Pinel (1745–1826) to take up the cause of the mentally ill in a serious, scientific manner. Working in concert with others of similar interests, most especially Jean-Etienne Dominique Esquirol (1772–1840), the most eminent specialist of the day in insanity, Pinel set about ordering and classifying the various levels of madness, such as distinguishing melancholics from maniacs and separating the curable from the incurable. Interviewing hundreds of the insane, he founded a new form of "moral" psychotherapy: "to engage the patient in dialogue during periods of lucidity, and establish a relationship of trust, in what would now be called a therapeutic alliance."[38] As a doctor who

---

37. Michel, Chenique, and Laveissiere, *Géricault*, 34.
38. Snell, *Portraits of the Insane*, 70–78.

would listen to rather than mock his patients, Pinel unchained many of his patients and discarded the long-popular equation of mental illness with demon possession. Taking careful and voluminous notes and compiling statistical summaries of his work, he set about publishing his results and making highly informed and enlightened recommendations on the treatment of the mentally ill. Many today regard him as the father of modern psychiatry.[39]

Géricault likely knew both Pinel and Esquirol. He may have even been a patient. Whether that is true or not, Géricault also went about visiting various asylums and hospitals, interviewing many of the insane who resided there. As a "painter-analyst," to borrow Robert Snell's phrase, Géricault forced his viewers to reflect upon such people and their conditions and to register a sense of their unique personhood. His surviving portraits of anonymous inmates are "powerful, startling works, . . . far from voyeuristic or prurient. They show ordinary, recognizably individual idiosyncratic people" and offer viewers even today an indispensable aid to understanding the subject matter of mental illness. They therefore provide "critical reflection for our own uneasy times."[40]

Art historians have since come to see Géricault's efforts as unique, a serious probing of a long taboo subject, a penetrating effort to try to understand the mentally ill and challenged. His painting of such subjects was "not through a diabolical lack of feeling but for the value of such scenes as unique documentation for their monstrous strangeness, for their anomalousness."[41] In taking interest in such lost souls onboard rafts or bound in asylums and in capturing on canvas their likeness and pain, Géricault was a morning light with a newfound vision of what could and should be done for them. In that regard, he was a pioneer painter-analyst, decades ahead of his time.

France's tormented artist died in relative obscurity on 18 January 1824 from injuries suffered, ironically, after falling from a horse. Quietly and without fanfare, the Louvre set about purchasing his mighty *Medusa* only afterward. A monument was finally erected in his memory at the Père Lachaise Cemetery, Paris's largest cemetery, seventeen years later in 1841, just after Napoléon's remains were returned to France.

For over a century, Géricault's reputation has languished behind that of several other leading Romantic painters of his time, particularly Delacroix, who was always more emotionally controlled than Géricault.[42] Gradually, however, as several more of his sketches and paintings have come to light and as many more details of his life have been uncovered, Géricault has been reclaimed and his reputation reestablished. Considered a tragic figure still, Géricault is now esteemed as a key transitional painter of his age. His masterpiece painting, with its powerful penetration and presentation of a struggling humanity but with hope and light on the horizon, will surely stand as one of the finest artistic expressions of the Romantic era.

---

39. Pinel, *Treatise on Insanity*.
40. Snell, *Portraits of the Insane*, xv.
41. Brion, *Art of the Romantic Era*, 154.
42. Thomas Crow, "Classicism in Crisis," in Eisenman, *Nineteenth Century Art*, 77–81.

Portrait of Samuel Taylor Coleridge (1772–1834), Peter Vandyke.

"AN ARCHANGEL A LITTLE DAMAGED"

SAMUEL TAYLOR COLERIDGE AND THE ROMANTICS

He prayeth best, who loveth best
All things both great and small;
For the dear God who loveth us,
He made and loveth all.[1]

"If I should leave you restored to my moral and bodily health, it is not myself only that will love and honour you. Every friend I have (and thank God! Spite of this wretched vice I have many and warm ones who were friends of my youth and have never deserted me) will think of you with reverence."[2] So admitted one of England's favorite literary sons in April 1816, less than a year after the Battle of Waterloo. What had brought this giant of a critic, philosopher, and poet, this friend of William Wordsworth, Robert Southey, Charles Lamb, and a host of other literary figures of his age, on bended knee to an obscure surgeon at Highgate, North London? And what were the lasting contributions this tortured soul made to our unfolding understanding of the age of 1820?

The careful reader will find much in Coleridge's late but remarkable conversion to Christianity to stir the soul. Like a C. S. Lewis of an earlier century, his was more than a remarkable transformation: Coleridge was one of the few literary geniuses of his time to proclaim his conversion to the gospel of the New Testament. And he did so in a way that his critics

---

1. Coleridge, "The Rime of the Ancient Mariner," lines 614–17.
2. Samuel Taylor Coleridge to James Gillam, 13 April 1816, in Griggs, *Collected Letters*, 4:630.

could not easily dismiss. If not the prophet of his age, Coleridge may well have been its poet, writing a modern style of scripture that many are only now beginning to appreciate.

The youngest of thirteen children, Samuel Taylor Coleridge was born 21 October 1772 at Ottery St. Mary in Devonshire. His father, John Coleridge, whom he loved dearly, was a Cambridge graduate, a schoolmaster, and an Anglican vicar who called the scriptures "the immediate language of the Holy Ghost."[3] "My father was fond of me," Coleridge remembered, "and used to take me on his knee, and hold long conversations with me. I remember that at eight years old I walked with him one winter evening . . . and he told me the names of the stars, and how Jupiter was a thousand times larger than our world and that the other twinkling stars were suns that had worlds rolling round them, . . . and I heard him with a powerful delight and admiration. . . . From my early reading of Faery Tales and Genii etc. my mind had been habituated to the vast."[4] Coleridge later called his father a perfect Parson Adams, an allusion to the benevolent character in Henry Fielding's novel *Joseph Andrews*.

On the other hand, his mother, Ann Bowden, was an unimaginative, uneducated, and rather strict and distant parent who seemed to begrudge his very existence. Coleridge never found in her the love he yearned to have from a mother. Being part of a very large and lively family, he learned early in life to assert himself. Although six of his siblings died during his childhood, Coleridge developed fortitude and faith in God.

A dreamer and an imaginary, young Coleridge learned early on to love the outdoors and its resplendent beauties through his many nature walks in the nearby countryside, and, though given to books, he was gregarious and amiable and made friends freely. As one later said of him, "He was a creature made to love and be loved."[5] From all accounts, his was a happy childhood. "Visions of childhood! Oft have ye beguiled lone manhood's cares, yet waking fondest sighs; Oh! that once more I were a careless child."[6] But everything changed for the worse when his father died. His penniless mother shipped him off to London to go to boarding school. Mother and son seemed satisfied not to have to live under the same roof and seldom corresponded thereafter. In London, Coleridge's maternal uncle, a tobacconist by trade, fortunately got him into Christ's Hospital, a renowned charity school on Newgate Street, founded two hundred years before to educate the orphaned sons of poor gentry. Famous for its blue coats and yellow stockings and its academic rigor and strict discipline, Christ's Hospital left an indelibly forlorn impression upon the young, untidy, and unkempt scholar, who studied there until age eighteen.

Headmaster Reverend James Bowyer more than once flogged Coleridge, as he did most other boys, for want of this or that—harsh experiences that Coleridge remembered in vivid nightmares for the rest of his life. Yet Bowyer saw in the lad real academic promise, for Coleridge was a veritable "library cormorant"—having already read so much of

---

3. Caine, *Life of Samuel Taylor Coleridge*, 12.
4. Samuel Taylor Coleridge to Poole, 16 October 1797, in Griggs, *Collected Letters*, 1:354.
5. Caine, *Life of Samuel Taylor Coleridge*, 16.
6. Caine, *Life of Samuel Taylor Coleridge*, 15.

Shakespeare, Milton, Voltaire, and other great writers. From Bowyer, Coleridge learned that poetry "had a logic of its own, as severe as that of science; and more difficult, because more subtle, more complex and dependent on more and more fugitive causes." Of the truly great poets, he would say, "There is a reason assignable, not only for every word, but for the position of every word."[7] Bowyer successfully instilled in Coleridge precision in writing, logical thinking, economy of words, and "a deep sense of [his] . . . moral and intellectual obligations."[8]

While at Christ's Hospital, Coleridge "immersed himself in metaphysics and in theological controversy" and found the old poetry of Pope and other eighteenth-century classical writers "insipid, lifeless, and artificial." Alternatively, the sonnets of Reverend W. L. Bowles, with his love of fancy, nature, and "the sense of beauty in forms and sounds," impressed Coleridge deeply.[9] Prone to loneliness, Coleridge combined "an advanced intelligence with emotional immaturity."[10] "There was something awful about him," a contemporary recalled, "for all his equals in age and rank quailed before him."[11]

While still at boarding school, Coleridge met Charles Lamb, who was destined to become a lifelong friend, and Tom Evans, who, in turn, introduced Coleridge to his widowed mother and his five sisters. Coleridge soon preferred to spend his weekends and holidays with the Evans family. It was there that he found the maternal love in Mrs. Evans that he never found in Devonshire. Coleridge also soon fell in youthful love with Mary, the oldest Evans daughter, whom he admired "almost to madness."[12]

Admitted to Cambridge in 1781, Coleridge began attending Jesus College in the fall. Although training to become an Anglican clergyman, he could never quite see himself in that pastoral role. His theology was much freer and more expansive, almost Unitarian, than Anglicanism would allow. He also preferred the spontaneous writing of creative poetry and the company of friends. His room was ever a clutter of conversations. Moreover, his youthful political radicalism set him apart from—if not at odds with—the staunch, conservative Cambridge political and religious culture. Praising the French Revolution and condemning Britain's war with France at a time in England when it was politically inexpedient to do so, he identified himself with the cry for liberty, equality, and fraternity, a stance which many of his countrymen perceived as radical.

> When France in wrath her giant limbs upreared,
> And with that oath, which smote air, earth, and sea,
> Stamped her strong foot and said she would be free,
> Bear witness for me, how I hoped and feared!

---

7. Coleridge, *Biographia Literaria*, 1:4.
8. Coleridge, *Biographia Literaria*, 1:6.
9. "To the Reverend W. L. Bowles," lines 1–3 in Perry, *Coleridge*, 52.
10. Ashton, *Life of Samuel Taylor Coleridge*, 18.
11. Perry, *Coleridge*, 10.
12. Perry, *Coleridge*, 12.

> With what joy my lofty gratulation
> Unawed I sang, amid slavish band.
> . . . For ne'er, O Liberty! With partial aim
> I dimmed thy light or damped thy holy flame;
> But blessed the paens of delivered France,
> And hung my head and wept at Britain's name.[13]

Unhappy and unfulfilled, Coleridge suddenly quit Cambridge, preferring to beg on the streets of London, quoting Greek and Latin to all who would listen. Hungry for food, lodging, and companionship, Coleridge was driven to enlist in the very thing he despised most—the army, specifically, the 15th Company of Dragoons, under the fictitious name of Silas Titus Comberbach (though retaining his initials S. T. C.). As clumsy a horseman as he was gifted a poet, Coleridge would have been laughed to scorn by his illiterate comrades had he not enthralled them with his gift of telling ancient Greek and Roman warfare stories and more especially his skills of writing eloquent love letters to their wives and girlfriends back home. It was also during his four-month stay in the military that he discovered his love for alcohol and for medicine. He spent time bandaging the wounded, caring for those with smallpox, and nursing others back to health. Undoubtedly, he would have made a most capable surgeon. Thanks to his brothers, George and James, Coleridge was able to quit the military in April 1794 after only four months' service when they bought out his contract. He returned to Cambridge wiser and humbler than before.

Back in school, he met a fellow pupil destined to become a future poet laureate of England who would greatly influence his life—Robert Southey (1774–1843). Like brothers, the two shared much in common ideologically, politically, and poetically. Southey invited Coleridge to his hometown of Bristol and into his circle of influential literary friends and intellectuals, which included George Burnet, Hannah More, Ann Yearsley (the literary milkwoman), Robert Lovell, and William Gilbert. It was in Bristol that Coleridge, spurred on by Southey and his newfound friends, began writing his earliest sonnets.

Southey shared Coleridge's disdain at becoming a priest; in fact, he was distinctly and radically Unitarian in his Godwinian belief that the real sin in the world was not the Fall of Adam but the depravity of society, the crime of inequity in private property and the consequential social inequality, and the hypocrisy of the judicial system. William Godwin had espoused in his *Enquiry Concerning Political Justice* (1793) that humanity was an optimistically good creature who sinned only because of the repressive laws of bad government. What was needed was a new society with entirely different values, a new utopia.

Quite conveniently, Southey introduced Coleridge to his future wife. Southey was engaged to Edith Fricker, and when Coleridge was introduced, he began meeting with Sara Fricker, Edith's older sister. Within just two weeks they were engaged. Coleridge subse-

---

13. From "France, An Ode" (1797–98), lines 22–27, 39–42, as found in Bernbaum and Jones, *Blake, Coleridge, Wordsworth, Lamb, and Hazlitt*, 86–87.

quently married Sara, a clever, stylish, quick-witted young lady, on 4 October 1795 in Bristol's St. Mary Redcliffe Church, just weeks before Southey and Edith Fricker were married in the same building. Another fellow writer, Robert Lovell, married a third sister, Mary Fricker. Coleridge later described his new wife as "an honest, simple, lively-minded, affectionate woman but without meretricious accomplishments; a comfortable and a practical wife for a man of somewhat changeable temper."[14]

The young married couple first moved into a small, comfortable cottage but soon relocated to Nether Stowey in Somerset, closer to Bristol, where their first child, Hartley, was born in 1796. While there, Coleridge launched his own weekly literary magazine called *The Watchman*. Designed to be a commentary on current affairs and parliamentary debates and a forum for his poetry and that of like-minded associates, it provided Coledrige with an opportunity to express his liberal, if not radical, political views, which were often aimed at Prime Minister William Pitt's foreign policy, and to show off the latest in literature. But the pressures of finding and collecting information, the challenges of composition, and the rigors of meeting publishing deadlines all proved far too daunting a task for a one-man operation. Consequently, *The Watchman* folded after only ten issues, throwing its proprietor and his family deep into debt. Had it not been for the timely financial assistance from Josiah and Thomas Wedgwood, the famous potters, who admired his poetry and established an annuity for him, Coleridge would have faced bankruptcy.

Such financial blunders became a pattern in his life as he darted from one financial crisis to another, for Coleridge was not so much a mismanager of funds as he was philosophically opposed to accumulating wealth. As Cottle put it in more delicate terms, he was "too well disciplined to covet inordinately nonessentials."[15] Such financial carelessness put an enormous strain on his marriage because his wife, Sara, never really understood him or appreciated his impracticalities.

Reluctantly, Coleridge came to admit that he was still in love with Mary Evans, whose image was "in the sanctuary of his bosom."[16] Not surprisingly, he soon found reasons to be lecturing and writing back in London, and only at the persuasions of Southey did he find time to write home. His marriage to Sara was at best a sentimental relationship, a union of duty, and though they would have several children together, they later separated. However, like Tsar Alexander and Elizabeth, they rejoined as friends in much later years.

ROMANTICISM:
A REVOLUTION IN LITERARY AND ARTISTIC THOUGHT

Literary scholars today place Coleridge squarely in the camp of Romantic poets. As with music and art, Romanticism in literature was essentially a reaction against constraint,

---

14. Caine, *Life of Samuel Taylor Coleridge*, 48.
15. Cottle, *Reminiscences*, 30.
16. Campbell, *Coleridge*, 34.

against rigid and artificial formalities of style and format. It defied the openly didactic and pedagogical styles of the neoclassical era of Pope, Dryden, and Johnson. It was, as Henry Beers wrote over a century ago, "the effect of the poetic imagination to create for itself a richer environment, . . . a reaching out of the human spirit after a more ideal type of religion and ethics than it could find in the official churchmanship and formal morality of the time."[17]

More recent commentators, like literary critic Northrop Frye, argue that Romanticism was a "new kind of sensibility," a new "mythology" in the broadest sense of a paradigm shift in how to view creation. Before, all was seen through the lenses of God as supreme Creator, the Fall of Man, Christ's Atonement, and mankind's ultimate redemption. But in the minds of many of the Romantics, humanity is its own agent of creation, not fallen from God but from nature. And redemption comes through a sensory reconnection, as Wordsworth taught, with the beauty, laws, and profundity in nature. It was, in a sense, a new religion no longer tied, as Milton had done, to a moral responsibility. Little wonder that in much of Romanticism on both sides of the Atlantic there were strong strains of deism, Pantheism, Universalism, and Unitarianism.[18]

Romanticism was also a more optimistic view of the nature of humankind than what had been portrayed for centuries. Resisting classical atheism on the one side and rejecting the Calvinist view of man's total depravity on the other, many Romantic writers believed the beauties and glories of nature attested to an exalted creation, not a fallen one. They also believed in the power of the human will to reason and overcome afflictions and in the divinity within humankind that was so well expressed in the beauties of nature.

Writing his famous poem "Elegy Written in a Country Churchyard" in 1751, Thomas Grey popularized the early Romantic's love for twilight, solitude, "the darkening vale" of melancholy, and Gothic castles, architecture, and the antiquarian spirit. Others, like Clara Reeve and Anne Radcliffe, protested against "the emotional coldness of the classical age."[19] Near the end of the century, Thomas Percy's "Reliques of Ancient English Poetry" made known the ancient ballads and songs of Scotland, Wales, and North England, including those of King Arthur and of Robin Hood, providing the indispensable groundwork for Sir Walter Scott and his incredibly popular Waverley novels. Thomas Chatterton, that "exalted genius" who died at age seventeen, captivated the attention of a generation of poets, including Coleridge and Wordsworth. Jane Austen (1775–1817) authored *Sense and Sensibility* in 1811 and *Pride and Prejudice* two years later and through her exquisite development of character, explored the affections of the heart in a compressed domestic setting in ways that none of her peers could match.[20]

---

17. Beers, *History of English Romanticism*, 32.
18. Frye, *Study of English Romanticism*, 3–14.
19. Beers, *English Romanticism*, 252.
20. In Germany, the transition came later and much faster through the writings of Lessing, Herder, Goethe, and Schiller, but in France barely at all. In America the Romantic impulse came later in the form of the Transcendentalism of Ralph Waldo Emerson and Henry David Thoreau.

It was Sir Walter Scott (1771–1832) who best captured the Gothic sentiment of the treasures of Scottish legend on a grand scale. The author of *The Heart of Midlothian* (1818), *Ivanhoe* (1819), *The Legend of Montrose* (1819), and scores of other novels, Scott fathered the historical novel as its own genre and popularized the Gothic novel as no one had before—or has since.

COLERIDGE AND WORDSWORTH

Coleridge's early poetry was didactic, simple, and lifeless. All that changed, however, when he read Wordsworth for the first time. In Wordsworth he immediately sensed a philosophical and poetic bond. Wordsworth's powerful, though simple verse was a mirror to the soul and stirred in Coleridge a spiritual awakening and a yearning to compose his finest poetry. He was therefore delighted when Wordsworth and his sister, Dorothy, a woman of education and refined feelings, deliberately came to Bristol in 1797 to see him.

The son of an attorney and two years older than Coleridge, Wordsworth had taken notice of several of Coleridge's so-called conservative poems, including "The Nightingale," "The Eolian Harp," and "Religious Musings," works that interwove natural objects with deep personal religious feeling. Like Coleridge, Wordsworth had quit Cambridge and had separated himself from the Anglican Church. Likewise, he sympathized with the aims and ideals of the French Revolution. He had even visited France in 1790, where he fell in love with a French army surgeon's daughter, Annette Vallon of Orleans, and fathered a daughter, Caroline, born in 1792. They considered marriage, but the outbreak of war between France and England and the atrocities of the Reign of Terror prevented his return to France.

In addition to these similarities, Coleridge and Wordsworth discovered in one another an ideal harmony of philosophical and poetic viewpoint. The two men shared an appreciation for the beauty of nature, a reverence for the immortal and marvelous mystery or soul of life, and the talent to capture such sentiments in sublime poetry. Thus began one of the most creative, synergistic friendships in all of literary history. Their mutual admiration for each other and for one another's poetry was virtually

William Wordsworth, 1873 reproduction of an 1839 watercolor by Margaret Gillies.

boundless and would last a lifetime. While Wordsworth esteemed Coleridge as "the best poet of the age," Coleridge saw in his new friend "the only man to whom at all times and in all modes of excellence I feel myself inferior."[21] "I feel myself a little man by his side," he once confided.[22]

Dorothy Wordsworth was also highly impressed: "Coleridge is a wonderful man; his face beams with mind, soul and spirit. He is so benevolent, so good-tempered and cheerful. . . . At first I thought him plain, that is for about three minutes. He is pale, thin, has a wide mouth, thick lips and not very good teeth, longish loose-growing, half-curling, rough black hair. . . . His eye is large and full, . . . fine dark eyebrows and over-hanging forehead."[23]

Unlike Coleridge, who was very much cut off from his own family, Wordsworth enjoyed the love, companionship, and keen support of his devoted and intelligent younger sister, Dorothy, who encouraged and supported his literary interests. Wordsworth's marriage in 1802 to Mary Hutchinson proved to be long and happy, in sharp contrast to that of Coleridge, who seemed seldom at peace with himself or others—a ship without a harbor.

Wordsworth spurned the rigid, intellectual approach to poetry in favor of simple, free-flowing verse. Wordsworth loved to take long walking tours, often for hundreds of miles, over hill and valley, mountain and seacoast, all the time ruminating on the beauties and lasting truths of nature, on the immortality of the soul, and the innocence of childhood. From these he penned such lines as:

> My heart leaps up when I behold
> A rainbow in the sky:
> So was it when my life began;
> So be it when I shall grow old,
> Or let me die!
> The Child is father to the Man![24]

And in his unforgettably beautiful "Ode to Intimations of Immortality," published in 1807, he penned these lines:

> But for those first affections,
> Those shadowy recollections,
> Which be they what they may,
> Are yet the fountain-light of all our day,
> Are yet a master-light of all our seeing;
> Uphold us, cherish, and have power to make

---

21. Perry, *Coleridge*, 41.
22. Cottle, *Reminiscences*, 107.
23. Caine, *Life of Samuel Taylor Coleridge*, 62.
24. William Wordsworth, "My Heart Leaps Up When I Behold" (1807), in Bernbaum, *Anthology of Romanticism*, 217.

> Our noisy years seem moments in the being
> Of the eternal silence: truths that wake
> To perish never;
> Which neither listlessness, nor mad endeavor,
> Nor man nor boy,
> Nor all that is at enmity with joy,
> Can utterly abolish or destroy!
> Hence is a season of calm weather
> Though inland far we be,
> Our souls have sight of that immortal sea
> Which brought us hither,
> Can in a moment travel thither,
> And see the children sport upon the shore,
> And hear the mighty waters rolling evermore.[25]

Like Coleridge and most other Romantics, Wordsworth decried the advances of the Industrial Revolution with its disregard for the environment and the spreading disease of unchecked commercialism:

> The world is too much with us; late and soon,
> Getting and spending, we lay waste our powers:
> Little we see in nature that is ours;
> We have given our hearts away, a sordid boon![26]

Ever more financially comfortable than Coleridge, Wordsworth published ten thousand other lines of rich poetry, including *The Excursion* (1814), *The White Doe of Rylstone* and *Miscellaneous Poems* (1815), *Peter Bell* and *The Waggoner* (1819), *Yarrow Revisited, and Other Poems* (1835), and *Poems Chiefly of Early and Late Years* (1842).

Later in his life, again like Coleridge, his liberal political views died with the ruthless ambitions of Napoléon. Wordsworth became increasingly conservative with age. He never returned, as Coleridge did, to the orthodoxy of Anglican Christianity, preferring to see God everywhere, manifested in the harmony of nature. Much more acclaimed in life than Coleridge ever was, Wordsworth succeeded Southey as poet laureate of England, receiving honorary degrees from Oxford and Durham Universities before his death in 1850. His simplicity of verse, his careful descriptions, his ability to touch the deepest human emotions, aspirations, and inner religious convictions and blend them into memorable and beautiful verse made Wordsworth arguably the greatest poet of his age.

---

25. William Wordsworth, "Ode: Intimations of Immortality from Recollections of Early Childhood" (1807), in Bernbaum, *Anthology of Romanticism*, 233–34.
26. William Wordsworth, "The World Is Too Much with Us: Late and Soon" (1807), in *Anthology of Romanticism*, 236.

Wordsworth and Coleridge blended philosophically and poetically so very well together that they decided to publish a combined collection of their early poetry in a simple, thin volume entitled *Lyrical Ballads*, which their bookseller friend Joseph Cottle published in Bristol in 1798. Coleridge contributed his "Rime of the Ancient Mariner," "Christabel," "The Nightingale," and other poems, to which Wordsworth added "The Dungeon," "The Idiot Boy," and "Lines Written a Few Miles above Tintern Abbey," plus several others.[27] Coleridge later looked back at this time as the high tide of happiness in his life.

Though dual in authorship, the purpose of *Lyrical Ballads* was one: to write a wholly new kind of poetry in search of the enduring truth of who man is and of what constitutes the soul. Coleridge wrote about supernatural persons and characters, such as the ancient mariner, whose fantastic voyage of death and redemption nevertheless taught profound truths, so long as the reader gave it "poetic faith"—"that willing suspension of disbelief" so essential to understand all his poetry.

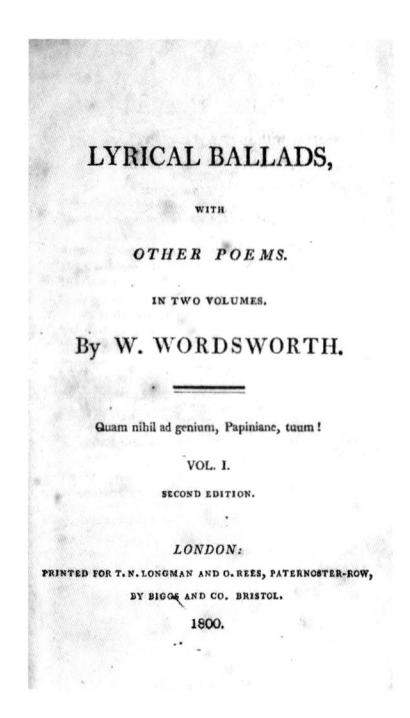

Title page of *Lyrical Ballads* (1800).

For his part, Wordsworth meant "to give the charm of novelty to things of every day" by awakening attention to "the loveliness and wonders" of the everyday world and encouraging others to see and learn from nature "truths which perish never."[28] His poetic vision was to give nature a meaning it had never taken before.

These few lines from "Tintern Abbey" may capture his intent: "For I have learned to look on nature," he penned:

> ...Therefore am I still
> A lover of the meadows and the woods,
> And mountains; and of all that we behold
> From this green earth;... well pleased to recognize
> In nature and the language of the sense,
> The anchor of my purest thoughts, the nurse,
> The guide, the guardian of my heart, and soul
> Of all my moral being.[29]

---

27. A second edition came out two years later with an explanatory preface and Wordsworth as the sole author.
28. Wordsworth and Coleridge, *Lyrical Ballads*, xix.
29. Wordsworth, "Lines Written a Few Miles above Tintern Abbey," lines 89–112, 114–15.

Few poems are so easy to read and yet so difficult to comprehend as "Rime of the Ancient Mariner."[30] Though Coleridge and Wordsworth set out together to write it, Wordsworth soon deferred to the supernatural and fantastic imagination of Coleridge, whose ancient mariner taps a passerby on his way to a wedding feast. The Mariner's story or dream ballad was so spellbindingly interesting that his listener soon forgot all about the wedding feast; he and others fell into its trance.

> The wedding guest sat on a stone;
> He cannot choose but hear;
> And thus spake on that ancient man
> The bright-eyed Mariner.
>
> The ship was cheered, the harbor cleared,
> Merrily did we drop
> Below the kirk, below the hill,
> Below the lighthouse top.
>
> The sun came up upon the left,
> Out of the sea came he!
> And he shone bright, and on the right
> Went down into the sea.[31]

The Albatross, engraving by Gustave Doré (1876).

Far down into the southern sea, they sailed into the "copper sky" of the tropics until an albatross flew across the sky and followed them for days. The mariner's killing of the bird, soon perceived by his fellow sailors as "a hellish thing to do," cast a shadow over the voyage and brought misery, misfortune, and death upon the crew.

> Day after day, day after day,
> We stuck, nor breath nor motion;
> As idle as a painted ship
> Upon a painted ocean.

---

30. The storyline owes much to George Shelrocke's "Voyage Round the World by the Way of the Great Sea" (1726), which Coleridge had previously read and which tells of a sailor killing an albatross, an act his fellow sailors regarded as an ill omen. Perry, *Coleridge*, 44.
31. Bernbaum and Jones, *Blake, Coleridge, Wordsworth, Lamb, and Hazlitt*, 64, lines 17–28.

Water, water, everywhere,
And all the boards did shrink;
Water, water, everywhere,
Nor any drop to drink.[32]

Becalmed one moment and frozen in ice "as green as emerald" the next, the ship sailed on from one misfortune to another, all in punishment for the mariner's sinful act. Eventually after a ghost ship passed by, all two hundred of his fellow sailors died at sea, but upon his remorse and repentance, they mysteriously returned to life, "a ghastly crew" to sail with him back northward.

They groaned, they stirred, they all uprose,
Nor spake, nor moved their eyes;
It had been strange, even in a dream,
To have seen those dead men rise.[33]

Chastened and unforgetting, the mariner concluded his tale with these famous lines:

Farewell, farewell! But this I tell
To thee, thou Wedding Guest!
He prayeth well, who loveth well
Both men and bird and beast.

He prayeth best, who loveth best
All things both great and small;
For the dear God who loveth us,
He made and loveth all.[34]

Coleridge's haunting dream-poem can be understood on many different levels. Through his imaginary, supernatural archetype, he speaks to humankind's earthly odyssey: the inevitable fall from grace through the sinful act of killing the albatross and the ultimate redemption and resurrection, "almost restoration." "Almost" is the appropriate term, because Coleridge never tells a fully happy ending. Neither the mariner nor his listener went to the wedding feast. There is always a sense of disappointed resolution in his writings, at best a damaged redemption. "The Rime of the Ancient Mariner" is, at base, a deeply Christian poem. Whereas Wordsworth found new meaning and salvation in nature, Coleridge found them in Christianity—not in the narrow confines of evangelical revivalism or Anglican ritualism and denominationalism, but in a deeply personal Christian conversion. This, however, is getting ahead of our story.

---

32. Lines 115–21.
33. Lines 331–34.
34. Lines 610–17, 85.

"SINKING, SINKING, SINKING": COLERIDGE'S SLIDE INTO DARKNESS, 1799–1816

While *Lyrical Ballads* was being published, Coleridge, Wordsworth, and Dorothy Wordsworth traveled to Germany on yet another of their trips together, walking, as was their custom, hundreds of miles through the countryside.[35] While Wordsworth and Dorothy were writing an explanatory "Prelude" to a second edition of *Lyrical Ballads*, Coleridge spent three months as a guest in a home at Ratzeburg, where he learned to converse and write in German. Then from February to June, fulfilling the design of his trip, he studied the writings of Friedrich Schiller and other German philosophers and writers at Gottingen University. Coleridge would soon translate Schiller's *Wallenstein* into English.

On their return to England in May 1799, Coleridge went on yet another long walking tour with the Wordsworths through their childhood countryside in the Lake District near Afton, England. Coleridge became so enamored with the astonishing beauty of the place that he convinced his wife to move with him into a new cottage at Greta Hall near Keswick, only thirteen miles away from where the Wordsworths took up their residence at Dove Cottage. Coleridge felt more the genius of creation when around Wordsworth and the Lake District than anywhere else. It was here the Coleridge's third son, Derwent, was born in late 1800.[36]

There was, however, another attraction, this time in the form of yet another Sara—Sara Hutchinson, the younger sister of Mary Wordsworth. Coleridge found in her the love he never felt for his wife: a companionship of mind and spirit he longed to have. His unfulfilled marriage, acute poverty, proneness to drink, and his acute sciatica, likely brought on by his exceedingly long walks and climbs, led Coleridge to experiment with "Kendal Black Drop," another name for laudanum. Coleridge first began taking it with good results, but he soon began consuming it in ever greater quantities. Laudanum, a preparation of opium, eventually wrought its devastatingly addictive powers on Coleridge until he was secretly taking a pint of opium every day—the "accursed drug," as he put it.

The change in him was noticeable as he missed, without explanation, many appointments and lectures. His hands began shaking so that he could not lift a glass of wine without spilling it all over the floor, although one hand supported the other. His efforts at quitting caused "intolerable restlessness, incipient bewilderment." "You bid a man paralytic in both arms," he wrote to a close friend who was wondering at his inability to quit, "to rub them briskly together, and that will cure him. 'Alas!' he would reply, 'that I cannot move my arms,

---

35. When it was republished in 1800, with Wordsworth inexplicably listed as the sole author, the "Ancient Mariner," which Wordsworth felt was hard for readers to understand, was placed at the back of the book.
36. A second son, Berkeley, had died in infancy, and a fourth son, Thomas, would die in 1812.

is my complaint and my musing."[37] "Sinking, sinking, sinking!" he wrote Humphrey Davy in April 1801, "I feel that I am sinking."[38]

Putting into poetry the growing agony of his soul, Coleridge, otherwise an optimist, wrote "Dejection: An Ode" in 1802, wherein he lamented the downward course his life was taking:

> A grief without a pang, void, dark, and drear,
> A stifled, drowsy, unimpassioned grief,
> Which finds no natural outlet, no relief,
> In word or sigh, or tear. . . .
> There was a time, when though my path was rough,
> This joy within me dallied with distress,
> And all misfortunes were but as the stuff
> Whence fancy made me dreams of happiness:
> For hope grew round me, like the twining vine,
> And fruits, and foliage, not my own, seemed mine.
> But now afflictions bow me down to earth:
> Nor care I that they rob me of my mirth;
> But oh! such visitation
> Suspends what nature gave me at my birth,
> My shaping spirit of imagination.[39]

In search of a better climate and in hopes of recovery, Coleridge set out for Malta in 1804 with a new friend, John Stoddart. In so doing, Coleridge left his wife and children once again in the "trusty vice fathership" of his brother-in-law, Robert Southey, who was now more than ever critical of his brother-in-law's repeated moral misjudgments in leaving his family "to chance and charity."[40] So too was Wordsworth critical of Coleridge spending much more time with the unmarried Sara Hutchinson than with his own wife.

While at Malta, Coleridge accepted one of the only regular paying positions of his life, as public secretary to the British governor of the island. However, after only a few months, he moved on to Sicily, Etna, and finally to Rome. At this same time Napoléon, having just won the Battle of Austerlitz, was on the march through Italy. With England now at war with France, no Englishman was safe, especially one who had recently condemned Napoléon in the *Morning Post* as "a remorseless invader, tyrant, usurper."[41] Coleridge fortunately found passage on an American ship for England.

---

37. Cottle, *Reminiscences*, 273.
38. Perry, *Coleridge*, 65.
39. "Dejection: An Ode," (1802), lines 21–24, 76–86, in Bernbaum and Jones, *Blake, Coleridge, Wordsworth, Lamb, and Hazlitt*, 131–32.
40. Caine, *Life of Samuel Taylor Coleridge*, 110.
41. Campbell, *Coleridge*, 175.

Not anxious to return home, though his wife dearly wanted him back, and in agony of self-reproach, a virtually penniless Coleridge went instead to London, where he moved into a tiny one-room apartment in the upstairs offices of the *Courier*, a newspaper owned by Daniel Stuart, his former employer at the *Morning Post*. Thanks to the financial windfall of some three hundred pounds from a young admirer, the future famous essayist Thomas de Quincey (yet another in a long list of benefactors), Coleridge eventually returned to his wife and family in August 1806 after a three-year absence from home, having written no more than a handful of letters to his wife in all that time. Still hoping to preserve at least a semblance of a marriage, his long-suffering Sara tried to welcome him back. By now, their third child and only daughter, Sara, had been born. And while their feelings one for another were obviously strained, the Coleridges did love and enjoy their children. Young Sara, who far exceeded her brothers in intellect and literary skills, would edit and publish a great many of her father's unpublished works.

Meanwhile, Coleridge was undergoing a profound change in outlook. As his poetic powers and interests faded and Wordsworth's increased, he became more and more the literary critic, philosopher, and, eventually, theologian. He accepted an ever-increasing number of invitations to return to London to lecture on literature, specifically on Shakespeare, Milton, Homer, Dryden, and several other great writers. Showing a mastery of Shakespeare's dramas, especially *Hamlet*, and the character and structure of his many plays and sonnets, Coleridge spoke of essential meanings of Shakespeare not often heard. Speaking extemporaneously and often without written notes, his green eyes darting wildly, he soon found himself in increasing demand. Here at last he had found, as one of his most recent biographies has noted, "a forum ideally suited to his extemporizing genius."[42] Wrote one of his listeners, "It was unlike anything that could be heard elsewhere; the kind was different, the degree was different, the manner was different. The boundless range of scientific knowledge, the brilliancy and exquisite nicety of illustration, the deep and ready reasoning, the strangeness and immensity of bookish lore."[43]

Coleridge was a gifted orator and lecturer, "like a being dropped from the clouds,"[44] as Cottle once described him. Said the critic William Hazlitt, "He talked on forever, and you wished him to talk on forever."[45] He took scarce attention to dress or appearances but enthralled his listeners at this time as much as he had done in his early years in the army and at Cambridge. He was always planning more than he could ever accomplish, but his listeners loved him regardless and considered it almost a "profanation to interrupt so impressive and mellifluous a speaker."[46] However, Madame Germaine de Staël, a well-known contemporary

---

42. Perry, *Coleridge*, 101.
43. Cottle, *Reminiscences*, 224.
44. Cottle, *Reminiscences*, 53.
45. Caine, *Life of Samuel Taylor Coleridge*, 11.
46. Cottle, *Reminiscences*, 57.

critic of the arts, said that Coleridge was "great in monologue, but he has no idea of dialogue."[47]

Coleridge enthralled his listeners with his exciting and enthusiastic probes into the life and thought of Aristotle, Milton, Shakespeare, Christ and his Apostles, Wordsworth, Kant, Schelling, and other German philosophers. He quite literally talked his way into developing his own philosophy of life, so much so that he earned the title "The Great Conversationalist," or as one described him, "an intellectual exhibition altogether matchless."[48] In the process, Coleridge created an ever-expanding circle of friends who kept coming back for more. What he lacked with home and family he made up for with friends.

In 1810 he decided on yet another ill-fated publishing project, this time *The Friend: A Literary, Moral, and Political Weekly Paper*, a rather highbrow enterprise aimed at London's intelligentsia. Unlike *The Watchman*, *The Friend* set out to be an entirely literary journal of poetry, prose, and criticism. With the indispensable help of Sara Hutchinson as collaborator, Coleridge managed to publish twenty-seven issues. It became a vehicle for much of his thought, literary criticism, and poetry, but it could not, however, survive the competition, his continuing proneness to drink, his addiction to opium, and of course, his habitual fiscal irresponsibility.

Coleridge's personal habits and addiction and his continued emotional attachment to Sara Hutchinson led not only to an inevitable separation from his wife but also to an unfortunate estrangement from the Wordsworths, a loss Coleridge took particularly hard. Long tolerant of his best friend's weaknesses, Wordsworth deplored what Coleridge was doing to himself and the shame he was bringing upon others.

> Oh! piteous sight it was to see this man
> When he came back to us a withered flower,
> Or, like a sinful creature, pale and wan.
> Down would he sit; and without strength or power
> Look at the common grass from hour to hour.[49]

The two men said things about one another that they later regretted. And though they later tried to patch up their differences, their friendship never quite recovered, and it left a wound on both men's souls.

Coleridge returned to London, this time for good, in 1810. After being asked to leave his apartment at his old Bristol friends' house, the Morgans, he once again begged scant room and board from his associates at the *Courier* in exchange for freelance writing and editing. By this time the Wedgwood brothers had revoked their pledged annuity, convinced that Coleridge was squandering the funds for no good purposes. Despite the fact that his

---

47. Perry, *Coleridge*, 97.
48. Cottle, *Reminiscences*, 221.
49. Caine, *Life of Samuel Taylor Coleridge*, 104.

one attempt at drama, the tragedy *Osoric*, was accepted and ran for twenty performances, Coleridge was so poor he couldn't even buy issues of the paper he worked for!

De Quincey described Coleridge's descent as follows: "I called upon him daily, and pitied his forlorn condition. There was no bell in the room which for many months answered the double purpose of bed-room and sitting-room. Consequently I often saw him picturesquely enveloped in night caps surmounted by handkerchiefs indorsed upon handkerchiefs, shouting . . . down three or four flights of stairs, to a certain 'Mrs. Brainbridge,' his sole attendant, whose dwelling was in the subterranean regions of the house."[50]

In these, his darkest hours, this "Archangel a little damaged"—as his lifelong friend Charles Lamb called him—wrote on. Sometime between 1808 and 1810, due largely to his "boundless power of self-retrieval," he managed to write one of his greatest pieces of prose and literary criticism: *Biographia Literaria*.

Still, his hapless addiction only worsened until even his beloved Sara Hutchinson left him to his nighttime agonies and howls. In his poem "The Pains of Sleep," he offered this glimpse at his sufferings and nightmares, or what he called "the unfathomable hell within," for Coleridge looked at his drinking and opium addiction not merely as human weaknesses but abominable sins in the sight of God. "You bid me pray," he responded to one of his well-meaning friends. "O, I do pray inwardly to be able to pray."[51]

> But yester-night I prayed aloud
> In anguish and in agony,
> Up-starting from the fiendish crowd
> Of shapes and thoughts that tortured me
> A lurid light, a trampling throng,
> Sense of intolerable wrong,
> And whom I scored, those only strong!

He ended the poem with this expression of love:

> To be beloved is all I need
> And whom I love, I love indeed.[52]

In a letter to an old Bristol friend, Coleridge penned the following painful picture of himself: "Conceive a poor miserable wretch, who for many years has been attempting to beat off pain by a constant recurrence to the vice that produces it. Conceive a spirit in hell, employed in tracing out for others the road to that heaven, from which his crimes exclude him! In short, conceive whatever is most wretched, helpless and hopeless, and you will form a

---

50. Campbell, *Coleridge*, 167.
51. Cottle, *Reminiscences*, 274.
52. "The Pains of Sleep" (1816), lines 14–20, 51–52, in *Guide to Anthology of Romanticism*, 137–38.

tolerable notion of my state."[53] On hearing one of Coleridge's rambling lectures, Lord Byron took pity on him and gave him a hundred pounds to live on and publish a small volume of his more recent poetry.

One of Coleridge's biographers summed up his situation most powerfully: "It was a terrible conflict. No struggle more awful played a part in the life of any man. That fearful conflict day by day, night by night, between remorse and appetite, the heartrending appeals for mercy, and forgiveness for genius wasted, the anguish of powerlessness, the sense of extinguished vigour, the thought of what might have been, and is not, and never can be."[54]

Coleridge was truly a pitiable specimen of human nature, seeking and praying for help and asylum from whatever quarter he could find it. He had, as one might say today, hit rock bottom and had nowhere else to turn. Suicide—or, as he put it, "annihilation"—may well have been the one alternative left. At this moment of deepest distress, salvation came in the form of a friend, Joseph Adams, who put him in touch with Dr. James Gillman, a surgeon, apothecary, and naturalist, who would prove a good Samaritan to Coleridge for the rest of his life. Adams' importuning letter to Gillman is worth citing:

> Halton Garden, 9 April 1816
>
> Dear Sir:
>
> A very learned, but in one respect an unfortunate gentleman has applied to me on a singular occasion. He has for several years been in the habit of taking large quantities of opium. For some time past, he has been in vain endeavoring to break himself off it. It is apprehended his friends are not firm enough, from a dread, lest he should suffer by suddenly leaving it off, though he is conscious of the contrary; and has proposed to me to submit himself to any regimen, however severe. With this view, he wishes to fix himself in the house of some medical gentleman, who will have courage to refuse him any laudanum, and under whose assertions, should he be the worse for it, he may be relieved. As he is desirous of retirement, and a garden, I could think of no one so readily as yourself. Be so good as to inform me, whether such a proposal is absolutely inconsistent with your family arrangements. I should not have proposed it, but on account of the great importance of his character, as a literary man. His communicative temper will make his society very interesting, as well as useful. Have the goodness to favour me with an immediate answer; and believe me, dear sir, your faithful humble servant.[55]

Five days later, the forty-three-year-old Coleridge moved in with the good doctor and his kindly wife at their Highgate residence and began a slow, painful, and cautious recovery. A stay that was meant to have lasted one month stretched out for eighteen years until Coleridge's death in 1834. At last he had found a home, and he began to rediscover himself.

---

53. Samuel Taylor Coleridge to Josiah Wade, 26 June 1814, cited in Cottle, *Reminiscences*, 292.
54. Caine, *Life of Samuel Taylor Coleridge*, 125.
55. Griggs, *Collected Letters of Samuel Taylor Coleridge*, 4:628–29.

"IT IS BETTER THAN I DESERVE": HIS FINAL YEARS

The concluding years of Coleridge's life at Highgate from 1816 to 1834 provide the ideal opportunity to contemplate three legacies of his life and thought; first, a physical and mental recovery more wonderful than his fall; second, his rising reputation among scholars as perhaps the towering literary figure, critic, and philosopher of his time; and finally, his odyssey into Christianity, a religious sojourn tempered by the agony of his own personal tragedies. For, of all the major English romantics, many of whom believed Christianity to be a cultural and philosophical irrelevancy, Coleridge found in Christ, the Bible, and the Holy Spirit the redemption of his sufferings, the revelation to his inquiries, and the purpose to his ponderings. These three factors, in addition to the recent recovery of so much of his thought and writings, go far to explain why Coleridge has been rediscovered by many modern scholars and why much has recently been written about his life, thought, and faith.

As to his recovery, none of his recent biographers claim that he quit opium entirely, but all agree that he reduced the use of it so dramatically that the drug no longer dominated his life. That he was in near constant pain is also clear; however, he fought his way on not merely to a physical recovery but also to a profoundly spiritual recovery. And it was the Gillmans

Samuel Taylor Coleridge, English Poet and Critic in His Room at Gillman's House, The Grove, Highgate, London. Chronicle / Alamy Stock Photo.

to whom he gave full and constant credit. "The fortunate state of convalescence I am now in," he wrote three months into his recovery in a tone of cherished optimism, "I owe to the unrelaxed attention, the professional skill, and above all the continued firmness and affectionateness of Dr. Gillman, his wife, and their two sons."[56]

Thomas Carlyle came to know and greatly admire Coleridge at Highgate and tells this touching remembrance of one of his many visits: "'Ah, your tea is too cold, Mr. Coleridge!' moaned the good Mrs. Gillman once, in her kind, reverential and yet protective manner, handing him a very tolerable though belated cup. 'It's better than I deserve!' said Coleridge, in a low hoarse murmur. 'It's better than I deserve.'"[57]

The Gillman's benefited from Coleridge's presence as well. The good doctor and his wife adopted him into their daily family routine, even taking him with them on annual vacations to the coast, thoroughly enjoying his kindness and lively conversations. "His manner, his appearance, and above all, his conversation, were captivating," Gillman once remarked. "I felt indeed almost spell-bound."[58]

A recovering Coleridge set out to mend his broken family life. He tried hard to see his oldest and favorite son, Hartley, now at Cambridge, and to help him recover from his own propensities to alcohol, an inclination that unfortunately led to his ruin. Coleridge took much of the blame on himself and wished for a happier day. The blighted life Hartley chose for himself became very painful to a profoundly disappointed, self-recriminating father, a "peal of thunder," as he called it in his declining years. After 1822 father and son never met again, despite Coleridge's several written overtures.

With the encouragement of Coleridge, Derwent, one of his younger sons, went on to become an Anglican minister. Meanwhile Coleridge's wife and daughter moved to nearby quarters to spend more time with him. Coleridge and his estranged wife soon recovered a semblance of friendship not felt in almost forty years, and as grandparents they came to enjoy one another's company and that of their extended family. Sara, their daughter, of a strong literary bent herself, loved and admired her father and spent much of her adult life compiling, cataloging, and publishing his writings, as did his nephew (William Hart Coleridge) and grandson, Carl Woodring.

Meanwhile friends, younger writers, and admirers of all kinds gravitated to the "sage of Highgate" in ever-growing numbers. These included such luminaries as Thomas Carlyle, Sir Walter Scott, the American novelists James Fenimore Cooper and Ralph Waldo Emerson, the Scottish divine Ernest Irving, the German poet Ludwig Tieck, the businessman Thomas Allsop, the founder of the Swendenborgian Society—Charles Tulk, his constant friend Charles Lamb, and hosts of others. Lamb could not withhold the excitement he felt at seeing his old friend rejuvenated. "The world has given you many a shrewd nip and gird," he said, "but either my eyes are grown dimmer, or my old friend is the same who stood before

---

56. Coleridge to John Gale, 8 July 1816, as cited in Campbell, *Coleridge*, 221.
57. Carlyle, as cited in Hennelling, *Coleridge's Progress to Christianity*, 33.
58. Cited in Perry, *Coleridge*, 110.

me 23 years ago, his hair a little confessing the hand of time, but still shrouding the same capacious brain, his heart not altered, scarcely where it 'alteration finds.'"[59] Coleridge's so-called "Highgate Thursdays" became a lively forum of literary, philosophical, and religious musings. Much of what he said others eagerly jotted down, and his writings were later published by his grandson in two volumes of *Table Talk*.[60]

John Keats—another giant of the Romantic age and an exquisite observer of nature, as seen in his "Ode to a Nightingale" and "Ode on a Grecian Urn"—visited Coleridge just before his own untimely death in 1819. Keats was drawn captive into the writings of Coleridge, especially his *Biographia Literaria*. Within days of their meeting, Keats wrote his "La Belle Dame Sans Merci," and "Ode to a Nightingale." Roundly criticized by William Hazlitt, a critic and an old protégé, for its unsystematic ramblings, *Biographia Literaria* struck a resonant chord with Keats, especially Coleridge's account of Shakespeare's "protean" imaginative powers and the idea of poetry demanding "a willing suspension of disbelief." Meanwhile, Byron, for all his sarcasm and witty criticism, loved Coleridge's "Christabel" and referred to him as "a genuinely prophetic writer."[61] Coleridge's "growing sense of security"—as one of his finest biographers, Richard Holmes, has phrased it—resulted in his bringing more of his finest work into print than ever before. These included *Biographia Literaria* (1817) and *Sibylline Leaves* (1817). Highgate was a harvest, a second birth, and Coleridge became a national figure.[62]

One of his greatest joys was a partial reconnection with Wordsworth. In the summer of 1828 the two men, along with Dorothy Wordsworth, who was then experiencing the early onset of dementia, spent a wonderful six weeks together touring the Rhineland, striving to rekindle the joys of a youthful friendship.

Coleridge continued to write poetry and at last received recognition of his rising reputation from the Crown in the form of a public pension. In 1819 he delivered his final series of lectures, focusing on Shakespeare (of whom he had devoted some sixty lectures in his lifetime) and the reconciliation of philosophy and religion. Coleridge distinguished the Bard from all other writers and poets by seeing in his plays expectation placed above surprise, an unfailing and remarkable development of strong and memorable characters, and a keeping to what Coleridge called "the high road of life"—that there are no innocent adulteries, no virtuous vices. Shakespeare never "rendered amiable" that which religion and reason teach one to detest. Shakespeare succeeds because he expresses human emotions so brilliantly, vengeance and revenge, passion and love.[63]

Literary scholar René Wellek has argued Coleridge's place as follows: "Coleridge is the intellectual centre of the English Romantic Movement. Without him, we would feel that

---

59. Ashton, *Life of Samuel Taylor Coleridge*, 325.
60. Woodring, *Collected Works of Samuel Taylor Coleridge*.
61. Holmes, *Coleridge*, 457.
62. Holmes, *Coleridge*, 432.
63. Coleridge, *Biographia Literaria*, 423.

English Romanticism, glorious as its poetry and prose is in its artistic achievements, remained dumb in matters of the intellect. We can extract a point of view, a certain attitude from the writings of Shelley and Keats, we find an expression of a creed in Wordsworth, but only in Coleridge we have thought which can be expressed in logical form and can claim comparison with the systems of the great German philosophers of the time."[64]

Coleridge sought to overcome the dualism that had separated the philosophies of past centuries essentially into the two camps of spirit and body, mind and matter, and reason and understanding that had prompted pantheism, deism, and atheism.[65] In his philosophical lectures, which filled 123 pages of a brown leather-bound notebook, he covered all of Western philosophy from Plato and Aristotle, to medieval Christian thought, the Reformation and the Enlightenment, and eventually Kant and Schelling. Praising the new spirit of science, he argued that it was compatible with religion and urged the rejection of the philosophy of materialism. In his brand of metaphysics, reason stood outside of mechanistic, logical thought and was the domain of knowledge learned by the inner soul of man. As much, if not more, would be learned from the inner man and the nature within than from deductive reasoning, science, and logic.

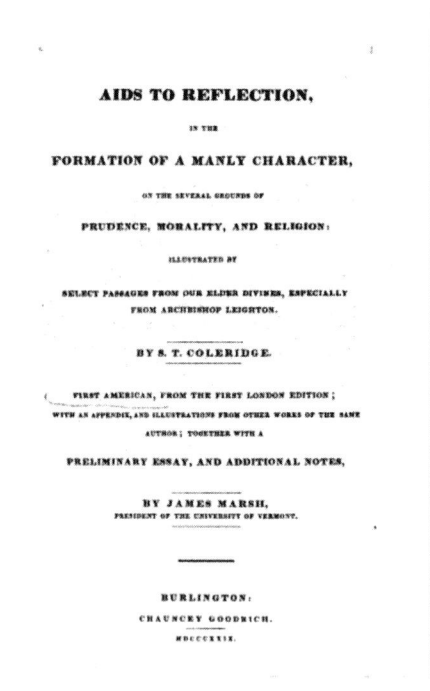

Title page of *Aids to Reflection: In the Formation of a Manly Character on the Several Grounds of Prudence, Morality, and Religion* (1825), by Samuel Taylor Coleridge.

In these later years, Coleridge also recognized the pressing need in postwar England for social change and urgent political action to minimize the "tremendous economic gaps between classes," which he termed in his *Lay Sermons* the "anti-magnet of social disorganization." In a series of political pamphlets, he criticized not only Parliament for doing too little to address economic problems, child exploitation, insufferably long work hours, and the negative impact upon the family therefrom, but he also condemned the clergy for "sleeping with their eyes half-open."[66]

---

64. From René Wellek in *Kant in England, 1793–1938*, as cited in Blunden and Griggs, *Coleridge Studies by Several Hands on the Anniversary of His Death*, 181.
65. Ashton, *Life of Samuel Taylor*, 328.
66. Holmes, *Coleridge*, 449.

Thomas Carlyle may have best captured Coleridge's rising public reputation and magnetic literary force:

> Coleridge sat on the brow of Highgate Hill, in those years, looking down on London and its smoke-tumult, like a sage escaped from the inanity of life's battle, attracting towards him the thoughts of innumerable brave souls still engaged there. His express contributions to poetry, philosophy, or any specific province of human literature or enlightenment, had been small and sadly intermittent; but he had, especially among young enquiring men, a higher than literary, a kind of prophetic or magician character. He was thought to hold, he alone in England, the key to German and other Transcendentalisms . . . to the rising spirits of the young generation he had this dusky sublime character; and sat there as a kind of Magus, girt in mystery and enigma.[67]

Highgate may best be remembered as the setting for the 1825 publication of Coleridge's *Aids to Reflection*, which stands as a testament to his philosophy that the greatest truths of the soul are not obtained through logic and deductive reasoning or even through communing with nature. Rather, the deepest truths, those which he believed were found in orthodox Christianity, come through "Reason" which he defined as an imputation of the logos, or spirit, and specifically, the spirit of Christ within. Above all, *Aids to Reflection* amounted to a series of carefully reasoned arguments or, better, "reflections" on why he had come to Christianity and what in Christianity stands above all other philosophies: (a) a belief in a risen Christ who redeems mankind, (b) a belief in the necessity of repentance and faith, (c) a belief in the immortality of the soul, (d) a belief in the awakening of the spirit and its communion with the Holy Spirit, (e) a belief that by the gifts of that Spirit one will manifest works of love and obedience, (f) a belief that such works "are the appointed signs and evidences of our faith," and (g) a belief in a "kind and gracious Father in Heaven, who may grant forgiveness of our deficiencies by the perfect righteousness of the Man, Christ Jesus, even the Word that was in the beginning with God."[68]

It would be both simplistic and erroneous to argue that Coleridge was here, in the twilight of his life, returning to his childhood Anglican beliefs. However, what he believed as a child laid the foundation of the later discovery of his life. "Christianity is not a theory, or a speculation," he wrote, having learned much from his own self-imposed sufferings, "but a life, not a philosophy of life, but a life and a living process."[69]

Besides asserting his own deep Christian convictions, Coleridge tangled with many of the greatest theological and philosophical questions facing Christianity since the Reformation. What had happened to Christianity through the ages? What is the origin of the devil? What is the nature of man and the Trinity? What is reason and its relationship to understanding and faith?

---

67. Carlyle, *Life of John Sterling* (1851), as cited in Holmes, *Coleridge*, 488.
68. Coleridge, *Aids to Reflection*, aphorism 7, 130–31.
69. *Aids*, 134.

After the deliberate renunciation of early Christianity, and "across the night of Paganism, philosophy flitted on, like the lantern-fly of the Tropics, a light to itself, and an ornament, but alas! No more than an ornament of the surrounding darkness."[70] "This was the true and first apostasy," he continued, in words that would have resonated with Joseph Smith, "when in Council and synod the Divine Humanities of the Gospel gave way to speculative systems, and religion became a science of shadows under the name of theology, or at best a bare skeleton of truth, without life or interest, alike inaccessible and unintelligible to the majority of Christians. For these therefore there remained only rites and ceremonies and spectacles, shows and semblances."[71]

The result of this apostasy was a decrease in willingness to consider God in his "personal attributes," and from thence came a distaste of all the peculiar doctrines of the Christian faith, the Trinity, the Incarnation, and redemption. Coleridge says of this, "I speak feelingly; for I speak of that which for a brief period was my own state."[72] Coleridge condemned pantheism and deism as impersonal religions, prone to the secularism he saw as encroaching upon the world. He even condemned the nature god of his fellow Romantics, Wordsworth included. "The last and total apostasy of the Pagan world, when the faith in the great I AM, the Creator, was extinguished in the sensual polytheism which is inevitably the final result of Pantheism or the worship of Nature, . . . that the material universe [is] the only absolute Being."[73]

Yet Coleridge was also highly critical of the evangelical Christian movement then coursing through Great Britain, which he denounced as fanatic literalism, a sordid "Bibliolatry" in its attempt to see in every word and phrase therein the infallible word of God. Not that Coleridge denied the supreme place of the Bible. In fact he once wrote, "in the Bible there is more that finds me than I have experienced in all other books put together." The "words of the Bible find me at greater depths of my being; and that whatever finds me brings with it an irresistible evidence of its having proceeded from the Holy spirit."[74] However, he believed the Bible was not the sole source of truth. It "is the appointed conservatory, an indispensable criterion, and a combined source and support of true belief. But that the Bible is the sole source; that it not only contains, but constitutes the Christian religion; that it is, in short, a creed, consisting wholly of Articles of Faith, . . . I, who hold that the Bible contains the religion of Christianity . . . dare not say."[75]

Thus, Coleridge believed that revelation was an ongoing necessity, that it was both objective, coming from the prophets and the Bible as the law, and subjective, emanating from the Holy Spirit within man. "Without that spirit in each true believer, whereby we know the spirit of truth and the spirit of error in all things pertaining to salvation, the consequence

---

70. *Aids*, 125.
71. *Aids*, 126.
72. *Aids*, 70–71.
73. *Aids*, 188.
74. "Confessions of an Inquiring Spirit," in *Aids to Reflection*, 296.
75. Letter 4, "Confessions," 315.

must be 'so many men, so many minds!'"[76] "Revealed religion is in its highest contemplation the unity, that is, the identity or co-inherence of subjective and objective."[77] Coleridge's Christianity was too broadly conceived to be straightjacketed by sectarianism and too narrowly perceived to allow for godless secularism. Little wonder his views later gave rise to what in Anglican Church history is known as the "Broad Church Movement" of the latter nineteenth century.

On the matters of the fall of man and original sin, he felt the weight of that terrible reality in his own life: "which I feel and groan under, and by which all the world is miserable." Fallen as he believed himself to be, however, he wrote that humankind is not predestined to heaven or hell, as the Calvinists insisted, nor is the will of humankind a captive of fallen nature, as Luther indicated. "The least reflection will convince even man that he is a responsible being" and that his will is the "condition of his personality." "Evil is not something imposed on man," he argued.[78] "The corruption of my will may very warrantably be spoken of as '*consequence*' of Adam's fall," he went on to clarify, "even as my birth of Adam's existence. . . . But that it is on *account* of Adam, or that evil principle was, *a priori*, inserted or infused into my will by the will of another, . . . this is nowhere in scripture."[79] "Sin is an evil which has its ground or origin in the agent, and not in the compulsion of circumstances."[80] Little wonder that he opposed infant baptism.

One of Coleridge's lasting contributions to philosophy was his carefully developed differentiation between reason and understanding. In his mind, to mix the two led to hopeless mysticism and atheism. Understanding pertains to sensory perception of the external realities around us, including nature, science, and all other "experimental notices," and is "the faculty by which we reflect and generalize." Even animals have understanding, at least to some degree.

Reason, on the other hand, is neither cold logic nor a form of mysticism; rather, it is essentially spiritual and comes from within. He described it as "the power of universal and necessary convictions, the source and substance of truths above sense, having their evidence in themselves." It is "the light that lighteth every man's individual understanding," "an influence from the Glory of the Almighty, . . . the Messiah, as the Logos."[81] Reason, therefore, is a God-sponsored, Christ-given endowment and "affirms truths which no sense could perceive, nor experiment verify, nor experience confirm."[82] Likewise, such reason leads the true Christian to a belief in the Holy Spirit.

The remedy to fallen humankind, he argued, lies outside of oneself, much like a sick patient who cannot nurse or cure him or herself. Coleridge had arrived at a point in his life

---

76. Letter 7, "Confessions," 334.
77. Letter 7, "Confessions," 335.
78. "Confessions," 189–91
79. "Confessions," 194.
80. "Confessions," 175.
81. *Aids*, 143–44.
82. *Aids*, 154.

when he was asking "the most momentous question a man can ask: . . . Have I a Savior? . . . Have I any need of a Savior? For him who needs none, . . . there is none, as long as he feels no need."[83] Redemption, or rescue through Christ, is the great design of religion, a truth many past philosophers and contemporaries did not or would not see. Drawing this lesson from art, Coleridge concluded:

> As in great maps or pictures you will see the border decorated with meadows, fountains, flowers, and the like, represented in it, but in the middle you have the main design; so amongst the works of God is it with the foreordained Redemption of Man. All his other works in the world, all the beauty of the creatures, the succession of ages, and all the things that come to pass in them, are but as the border to this as the main piece. But as a foolish unskilled beholder, not discerning the excellency of the principal piece in such maps or pictures, gazes only on the fair border and goes no further, so thus do the greatest part of us as to the great work of God, the redemption of our personal Being, and the reunion of the Human with the Divine, by and through the Divine Humanity of the Incarnate Word.[84]

Cottle recalled that Coleridge spoke of Christ "with an utterance so sublime and reverential, that none could have heard him without experiencing an occasion of love, gratitude, and adoration. . . . a truth incontestable to all who admitted the inspiration and consequent authority of scripture."[85]

CONCLUSION

Coleridge's health took a dramatic turn for the worse in 1830, and for his last three and a half years he was almost entirely bedridden. Yet his mind remained lucid and surprisingly active right up until the end. He died on 25 July 1834 at Highgate in the company of those who had nursed him back to health and sanity the last several years of his life. He is buried in Highgate Village churchyard. Less than a fortnight before his death, in one of his final letters to an old German friend, he summed up his life as follows: "I now on the eve of my departure, declare to you and earnestly pray that you may hereafter live and act in the conviction that health is a great blessing; competence, obtained by honorable industry, a great blessing; and a great blessing it is, to have kind, faithful and loving friends and relations. But the greatest of all blessings, as it is the most ennobling of all privileges, is to be indeed a Christian."[86]

---

83. *Aids*, 165–66.
84. *Aids*, 200–201.
85. Cottle, *Reminiscences*, 246.
86. Samuel Taylor Coleridge to Adam Steinmetzkinnaird, 13 July 1834, as cited in Cottle, *Reminiscences*, 245.

Bronze plaque erected by St Pancras Borough Council.

    Charles Lamb—the one who knew him at his best times and at his worst—may well have said it best when he called Coleridge "an Archangel a little damaged": "Never saw I his likeness, nor probably the world can see again."[87]

---

87. Charles Lamb, in Perry, *Coleridge*, 121.

Coronation Portrait of George IV, by Thomas Lawrence.

Caroline of Brunswick (1768–1821) When Princess of Wales, by Gainsborough Dupont.

PANDORA'S BOX

KING GEORGE IV, QUEEN CAROLINE, AND THE INDUSTRIAL REVOLUTION

The central feature of this chapter is to assess the wrenching impact the Industrial Revolution made on British society in the late eighteenth and early nineteenth centuries. While some insist that it eventually resulted in an age of improvement, such growing pains came with a steep price. These profound changes shook English society to its very core, scarring an agrarian landscape, disrupting patterns of family living, replacing men with machines, and improving the lives of some while impoverishing those of many others. Like a pot of water about to boil over, the heat was turned up on an England now bubbling and steaming over for radical change. Such changes, while falling short of causing an English-styled French Revolution, were revolutionary in and of themselves and led to much-needed reforms that ultimately changed a nation and eventually transformed the world.[1] However, this study will begin—and end—with what some might consider window dressing, an interesting royal sideshow between two selfish, self-centered personalities whose inconsiderate actions toward one another riveted the attention of the nation, sparked the beginnings of popular journalism, and ironically contributed to many necessary reforms and genuine improvements in society. And certain it was that the Industrial Revolution would affect the Restoration and the rise of the Church of Jesus Christ in ways not yet fully appreciated.

---

1. The terms *England* and *Great Britain* are not synonymous. As a result of the Act of Union in 1801, England, Wales, and Scotland together became the nation of Great Britain. When Ireland was added, the term United Kingdom came into being.

PANDORA'S BOX

Early in the spring of 1820, King George IV received the jarring news from his royal couriers that his estranged wife, Caroline, had defied his decree and left Rome for London. After a six-year, self-imposed absence abroad, she had determined to return to take her rightful place as England's queen at her husband's impending coronation ceremony, whether or not it ruined the monarchy or ruptured the nation. "My mind is in a state that is not to be described," the king admitted in a mood of profound melancholy and disbelief. Confided his foreign secretary, Lord Castlereagh, "If she is mad enough or so ill-advised as to put her foot upon English ground, I shall from that moment, regard Pandora's box as opened."[2]

When Caroline reached the outskirts of London on 6 June 1820, rays of sunlight broke through the cloudy skies, and her carriage top was thrown open so that the princess could be clearly seen dressed in a black gown with a fur ruff and a black satin hat adorned at the front with a few high, luxuriant feathers. "It was a look," wrote one of her biographers, "that during the coming months, she was to make her own."[3] All of London seemingly turned jubilant at the news of her pending arrival.

Come nightfall, however, the mood turned sinister. For three consecutive nights, mobs with torches in hand roamed the streets, knocking on doors, demanding that residents illuminate their houses "for the queen," and smashing windows of every government cabinet minister and known King George supporter. The Austrian countess Dorothea Von Lieven (1785–1857) described the city in a letter to Metternich: "What a stir, what excitement, what noise! The mob streamed through the streets all night making passers-by shout 'Long live the Queen.'"[4] Several soldiers mutinied, and it seemed the furious crowds were "careering towards rebellion." The cry "No Queen, no King" was heard on every corner. Arthur Wellesley (1769–1852), the Duke of Wellington, expressed his "greatest anxiety" respecting the state of the military in London, and Lady Frances Jerningham (1747–1825) believed that England "[was] nearer disaster than it [had] been since the days of Charles 1st."[5] Lord Charles Grey (1764–1845), the Whig leader in the House of Lords, feared "a Jacobin Revolution more bloody than that of France."[6] Never had England so revered a blemished royal, and never had it so despised its king.

The immediate cause of Caroline's return was the king's insistence that they divorce, that she be degraded from her royal rank, and that her name be expunged from the Anglican Church Litany and no longer prayed for. Having indignantly refused an annual pension of £50,000 on condition of her not using the title of queen of England or any other royal title, she had courageously decided to return, knowing full well Parliament would immediately put her on trial for adultery, if not high treason, which, if proved, would be sufficient

---

2. Fraser, *Unruly Queen*, 353.
3. Robins, *Trial of Queen Caroline*, 123.
4. Robins, *Trial of Queen Caroline*, 123.
5. Robins, *Trial of Queen Caroline*, 123.
6. Robins, *Trial of Queen Caroline*, 126.

grounds for the king's desired divorce. Her plan was, however, to put the king on trial in the court of public opinion, for if she were far from perfect, King George was far more so, with more mistresses on call than government ministers at bay. She would play the role of the victim for all it was worth and win over the hearts of women and men everywhere until her husband would be forced to relent, bow the knee, and accept her back as the rightful princess of Wales, queen consort of England.

A MEDLEY FOR THE MOST OPPOSITE QUALITIES: THE PRINCE OF WALES

Born in 1762 as the oldest of the fifteen children of King George III and Queen Charlotte, George Augustus Frederick, first Prince of Wales and Duke of Cornwall, was indeed in a royal predicament, although one not all of his own making. He has received more than his share of criticism. Upon his death in 1830, *The Times* thundered out this verdict: "There never was an individual less regretted by his fellow creatures, . . . an inveterate voluptuary, . . . of all known beings the most selfish." Charles Grenville (1794–1865), clerk to the privy council and famous diarist, wrote of him: "A more contemptible, cowardly, selfish, unfeeling dog does not exist. . . . There have been good and wise kings but not many of them, . . . and this I believe to be one of the worst." Even Lord Wellington, who served him as prime minister from 1828 to 1830, could muster only muffled praise: "The most extraordinary compound of talent, wit, buffoonery, obstinacy, and good feeling—in short a medley of the most opposite qualities with a great preponderance of good—that I ever saw in any character in my life."[7]

When George IV, or "Prinny" as he was called for being the Prince of Wales, was fifteen years old, his tutor said, "He will be either the most polished gentleman or the most accomplished blackguard in Europe—possibly both."[8] Although at heart a good and decent man, by his early teens he had already rebelled against the strictness of his father and the overbearing nature of his mother. King George III reigned over England for sixty years, presiding over the disastrous American Revolutionary War (1776–83) as well as the triumphant victory over Napoléon. A deeply religious, very moral man, "Farmer George," as King George III was sometimes called because of his love for agriculture and the simple things of life, firmly believed his mission was to spread the Protestant faith and to save the rapidly expanding British Empire from moral collapse. But he could not do so without his sons. King George III often punished his oldest son, fearing that he lacked the inner discipline, industry, good manners, and integrity he so ardently wished for in his successor. This drove the prince closer to his more tolerant mother. King George III always favored his second son, Frederick, Duke of York, and Prince George knew and resented it. Whatever the cause for his flagrant misbehaviors, the volatile prince of Wales rebelled against his father and turned

---

7. Baker, "George IV," 30.
8. Delderfield, *Kings and Queens*, 114.

to bad company, drink, and an extravagant lifestyle. A quick learner who loved music, the fine arts, and architecture and a student of several languages, his accomplishments were more "elegant than necessary."[9] He was a handsome, overweight young man whose love for all things equestrian was eclipsed only by his love for wine, women, and waging bets. At age sixteen, he fell in love—or at least in lust—with Mary Hamilton, one of his sister's governesses, who, seven years his senior, set the pattern of loving older women. He next fell in love with actress Betty Robinson and at age eighteen fathered a child with a married woman.[10]

King George IV, by Thomas Lawrence.

E. A. Smith, one of King George IV's finest biographers, noted that it was "a licentious age, when young and adolescent sprigs of nobility sowed wild oats with reckless abandon." Drunkenness was "the vice of the age," and during the middle to later years of the eighteenth century, "attitudes towards sex in England, especially in London, were unusually relaxed." But Prince George, "a man of a thousand loves," was more "relaxed" and easily persuaded than most others.[11] Among the aristocracy, women were frequently as free as men in their social flings and illicit sexual behavior. "Pleasure was king, and for a time George was its prince."[12]

At age twenty-one, the prince moved out of the royal palace and took up residence at Carlton House on Pall Mall, where he pursued his lifelong habits of constantly remodeling his living quarters, hosting wildly expensive balls, and entertaining lavishly, all at a cost he could ill afford. The future king never understood the value of a pound, shilling, or crown and racked up debts that only Parliament and his father could pay off.

Then in 1785, at age twenty-three, he found the one true love of his life. Maria Fitzherbert (1756–1837), already twice widowed, was his senior by six years and was as virtuous as he was promiscuous, a noble and highly religious woman of rosebud complexion. The prince tried everything—feigning even suicide—to win over her affections. Finally, after reading her own emotions, she agreed to secretly marry him. But there was one fundamental

---

9. Richardson, *Disastrous Marriage*, 13.
10. Jenner, *Royal Wives*, 226.
11. Smith, *George IV*, 19.
12. Smith, *George IV*, 20.

problem: Maria was a Roman Catholic, while he was committed as the future leader of the Church of England to uphold Protestantism at all costs throughout the realm. Given five hundred pounds for agreeing to perform the ceremony, a Catholic priest married the couple in Maria's drawing room on Parte Street in December of that year. Although they lived apart and in secret, the star-crossed lovers lived happily as husband and wife. Eventually, however, Maria, unwilling to be seen as another mistress, moved away and loved him from afar.

The sad fact is that "he never found anyone whom he loved as he had loved her."[13] Incapable of giving the same devotion she conferred on him, Prince George had affairs with Lady Jersey (1753–1821), Lady Hertford (1759–1834), and Lady Conyngham (1769–1861), to name but three of many—some married, some not. When King George III finally learned of Prince George's marriage to Maria, he invoked the Royal Marriage Act, revoking his son's clandestine union and declaring it null and void and without effect because no royal consent had been given. If he persisted in his marriage to Maria, he would be forced to forfeit the crown, something the prince was not disposed to do. But all of England knew who his real love was.

Torn between the woman he loved and the crown he craved, what was he to do? Some maintain that Lady Jersey had concocted a plan for him to marry a German princess while she, Lady Jersey, stayed on the royal payroll as chambermaid and mistress. More likely it was his father's decision for an arranged marriage that saw his son marry—sight unseen—his first cousin, a German Protestant, Princess Caroline Amelia Elizabeth (1768–1821), daughter of the Duke and Duchess of Brunswick. In exchange for the arranged marriage, Parliament paid off the prince's debt of 375,000 pounds.

AND THEY LIVED HAPPILY NEVER AFTER

James Harris, 1st Earl of Malmesbury (1746–1820) and a highly regarded British diplomat, was sent to prime and prepare the princess and escort her back to England for the wedding. He sensed from the start that the proposed marriage would prove disastrous. Caroline, he soon discovered, was a loud, uncouth, scatter-brained chatterbox who lacked discrimination, tact, sound judgment, and common sense. She was "a creature of impulse" and was "carried away by appearances and enthusiasms."[14] She spoke English poorly and cared little about education and learning the great matters of the day. And although she had her physical charms, she had little sense of fashion and cared even less about personal hygiene. One would have to get over the initial sense of repulsion before beginning to enjoy her company. In short, Caroline was "one of the most unattractive and almost repulsive women for an elegant-minded man that could have been found amongst German royalty."[15] Although a mismatch of minds and hearts, brought together by circumstances not of their choosing,

---

13. Smith, *George IV*, 39.
14. Richardson, *Disastrous Marriage*, 28–29.
15. Richardson, *Disastrous Marriage*, 33.

Caroline Amelia Elizabeth of Brunswick, by James Lonsdale.

the two were equally selfish, self-centered, undisciplined, and rebellious.

At the first meeting of Caroline and the prince, he is reported to have turned and said to an apprehensive Lord Malmesbury, "I am not well; pray get me a glass of brandy." It was contempt at first sight. Never was a prince dragged more reluctantly to a wedding than Prince George was that fateful 8 April 1795. Even the archbishop of Canterbury who officiated at the ceremony laid down his book and looked earnestly at the groom, who was as forlorn and disconsolate as the bride was giddy and full of high spirits, smiling and nodding to everyone. Others were mortified. On hearing news of the marriage, Maria Fitzherbert fainted. The queen mother, Charlotte, who abhorred Caroline from the start, vowed never to talk to her new daughter-in-law and resolved to hate her till her dying day. Even King George III now recognized the impossibility of a lasting union but urged them to live at least for a time under the same roof. Prince George spent his wedding night drunk on the floor. Their honeymoon, with his mistress Lady Jersey "in constant malicious attendance," was an awkward catastrophe, and the prince and bride never lived as man and wife for more than a few days.[16] Put simply, they lived happily never after.

The marriage, however, did solve some immediate problems. As promised, Parliament paid off the prince's debts and increased his annual income to 125,000 pounds, hardly enough to support his lavish style of living. In early 1796, nine months after the wedding, Caroline gave birth to their only child, a daughter, whom they named Charlotte Augusta. Recognizing the futility of their marriage, Prince George wrote Caroline a famous letter, essentially dictating their own standards of morality by attempting to absolve each of fidelity, with neither "to be left answerable to the other."[17]

Meanwhile, the prince begged Maria to return to his side, beseeching her, in his words, to "save me . . . from myself," and Caroline, pursuing old habits of her own, moved to Blackheath, where she found comfort with other men. The scorned princess decided to get even with her unfaithful husband by dressing provocatively and acting eccentrically. "What a pity she has not a grain of common sense, not an ounce of ballast to prevent high spirits, and a

---

16 Richardson, *Disastrous Marriage*, 33–35.
17 Richardson, *Disastrous Marriage*, 37.

The Wedding of George, Prince of Wales, and Princess Caroline of Brunswick Officiated on 8 April 1795 in the Chapel Royal of St. James's Palace, London, by Gainsborough Dupont. The Picture Art Collection / Alamy Stock Photo.

coarse mind without any degree of moral taste," said one woman at court. Another stated: "She was a nasty, vulgar, impudent woman that was not worth telling a lie about."[18]

Their daughter, Charlotte, was as high-spirited and independently minded as her parents. She proved to be an unhappy scapegoat of contention between two quarreling parents. Fearful that she would follow after her mother, Prince George treated her sternly and did all he could to keep mother and daughter apart. He chose one governess after another to look after the young girl, intercepted correspondence between Caroline and Charlotte, and limited their visits to only twice a week. Charlotte came to distrust both of her parents and detested their constant selfish bickering and machinations. Anxious to set out on her own, she married at age nineteen in 1815, but to everyone's utter dismay she died two years later while giving birth to a stillborn son, throwing all of England into deep mourning over the

---

18   Richardson, *Disastrous Marriage*, 74–75.

deaths of both of Prince George's lawful successors. Caroline, then away on the continent, was not even told of the tragedy until sometime afterward. More than any other factor, Charlotte's untimely death spurred the prince toward getting a divorce.

Meanwhile, Prince George's path to the throne was a much delayed and twisted one. Not only did his father live for a very long time, but in 1788 King George III suffered his first bout of madness. If not caused by a form of manic depression (to which his own arguably failed marriage may have contributed), it stemmed more likely from acute intermittent porphyria, a physical disorder that may have also affected his son and even Caroline, his niece and daughter-in-law.[19] Although he recovered, King George III's unhappy malady reoccurred in 1804 and then again permanently in 1810. For the last ten years of his life, he wandered the halls of Windsor castle in insanity, a blind old man with a long white beard and a violet dressing gown. Only the "Star of the Order of the Garter" pinned to his chest was a reminder "that this wreck of a man was King of England."[20] Prince George was subsequently appointed regent—acting king—with unrestricted royal prerogatives in 1811 and served as such until his father's death on 29 January 1820.

Distanced from her own daughter and barred from celebration and other royal festivities at St. James's Palace, Charing Cross, and Temple Ben, Princess Caroline gained increasing sympathy in the public eye for what seemed to be unnecessary persecution of a woman deprived of her place and of her daughter. Shrewdly guided by Lord Minto (1751–1814), Sir Matthew Wood (Lord Mayor of London, 1768–1843), and especially Sir Henry Peter Brougham (a Whig leader in Parliament and a highly regarded barrister, 1778–1868), Caroline fought back, firing Lady Jersey and many other unfriendly ladies at court. Why she then foolishly decided to leave her daughter and go abroad on an open-ended tour of Europe just when her popularity was rising is still not entirely clear. Perhaps it was a desire to go home to Prussia, to get away from the king, to see the world, or to find happiness away from England—whatever the cause, she departed in August 1814. With peace restored and Napoléon in Elba, now was her moment to travel.

For the next six years, Europe was her unwilling playground. With a small train of chambermaids and chamberlains in tow, "the tatterdemalion caravan," to borrow Joanna Richardson's phrase, frolicked across Europe.[21] After spending several months in Brunswick, she stopped at Milan, Bologna, Florence, and Rome before reaching Naples, her intended destination. Unwilling to stay too long in any one place, the restless princess traveled on to Africa, Constantinople, the Holy Land, and back again through Europe. She was a woman without a home and on the loose, lavishly spending money on balls, clothing, and food. A traveling embarrassment to England, she soon met Bartolomeu Pergami, a handsome Italian security guard, whom she assigned to her entourage and upon whom she conferred the title

---

19. Smith, *George IV*, ch. 5.
20. Fraser, *Lives of the Kings and Queens of England*, 285.
21. Richardson, *Disastrous Marriage*, 93.

Baron de la Francino. All of England was atwitter with accounts of the German-born English queen under the spell of her Italian dandy.

With his daughter now dead and his wife away carousing on the Continent, Prince George determined to divorce, believing, at fifty-nine years of age, that it might not yet be too late to sire another legitimate heir. However, obtaining such a divorce would not come easily. Constitutionally, adultery would have to be proven; it was an act potentially seen as tantamount to high treason against the state and often punishable by death. As for Caroline, although she was willing to grant a separation, she resolutely opposed divorce, which would remove her royal privileges and the chance to be queen. If not for reasons of privilege, style, and wealth, she would have resisted out of spite. Once a royal commission—the so-called Milan Commission—had been established to spy on and prove her activities, Caroline began to fear for her life. All such things, coupled with the news of King George III's death, induced her to return to England, where she would test the levels of popular support and fight it out with the new king. It was a fateful decision, for the new king and the queen neither cared about nor understood the economic, social, and political unrest then gripping the nation.

AN AGE OF IMPROVEMENT?

As interesting as the warfare between these two quarreling monarchs may have been, by far the more important story of the age was the mighty changes wrenching their way throughout Great Britain that shook society to its core, arguably improving the everyday standard of living for millions of people and laying the groundwork for our modern era. The specific post-Waterloo years from 1815 to 1819 were especially painful and led England to the cusp of a political revolution on the eve of Caroline's return. "From all parts of the country came reports of violence and crime," as the British historian J. A. R. Marriott has contended. "In the Eastern countries there was an alarming amount of unrest and disorder. Barns and bricks were burnt to the ground; threshing machines and other agricultural implements were publicly burned; bakers' and butchers' shops were attacked, and angry mobs demanded 'bread or blood.' . . . Immense damage was inflicted upon property. . . . Nor was the unrest confined to the agricultural countries. The Tyneside colliers, the Preston cotton-weavers, the Wiltshire cloth-workers, the Monmouthshire and Staffordshire iron-workers, the jute-workers of Dundee—all alike were in turmoil, demanding more employment, higher wages, and cheaper food."[22]

The immediate postwar era constituted a cold, wintry period in an otherwise warming spring. Just as the French Revolution heralded a time of new freedoms and the Congress of Vienna ensured a century of peace, so likewise did the Industrial Revolution ensure the promise of a better age, but only over time. Life in Great Britain was rapidly improving for the majority of people, and while not every improvement or change can or ought to be attributed to the Industrial Revolution, it gradually and inexorably changed daily life for

---

22. Marriott, *England Since Waterloo*, 25–26.

millions and surely stands as the gateway to a new and better day, the foundation of modern society.

In the words of historian Asa Briggs, "If France had a political revolution in 1789, England had an industrial revolution already in progress."[23] Simplifying the incredible complexity of the Industrial Revolution and the new enabling economic order ushered in by the economist Adam Smith (1723–90) with his pathbreaking work *Wealth of Nations* (1776) is no small order. It might be better to tell of three simultaneous, interlocking revolutions rather than one. It was a trinity of change in one essential union of societal reformation, with gradual, uneven stops and starts that occurred between 1760 and 1830. The first was demographic; the second agricultural; and the third, industrial and economic. While these changes were certainly not confined to Great Britain (they followed hard thereafter in Europe and in North America), they were at first most concentrated in an England, Scotland, and Wales untouched by the recent ravages of war. Furthermore, Great Britain was blessed with such other unique advantages as naval supremacy, a developing colonial empire of abundant raw resources, a rapidly improving system of roads and canals, an improving banking system, relatively low taxation, a government that ensured freedom and encouraged innovation, a seemingly endless supply of keen inventors and curious engineers (men with the "mechanical hobby," to borrow J. H. Clapham's term), a growing amount of food, and an enormous supply of coal and iron located in close proximity one to another.

Two important points must be made about population: first, unparalleled growth and second, movement. Between 1750 and 1820, the population of Great Britain grew extraordinarily fast—it doubled, in fact—in what J. H. Clapham called "the flood of life." From 7.3 million in 1751, the population in Great Britain increased to 11 million in 1801, to 12.6 million ten years later, and to 14.4 million in 1821, despite an ever-increasing exodus to Canada, Australia, and the United States, a trend that dramatically increased during the second quarter of the century.[24] Such rise in population drove Thomas Malthus (1766–1834), in his ponderous study on the sources of poverty, to gloomily predict in his *Essays on Population* (1798) widescale famine, death, and self-destruction in a world unable to feed so many mouths. What Malthus failed to anticipate were the twice as many hands available to plant and harvest, which led to the dramatic increase in agricultural yields of the later nineteenth and twentieth centuries. He also failed to take into account the twentyfold increases in average real per capita gross domestic product since his time, allowing for more to be spent on nutrition, sanitation, and health care.

This population growth was more the effect of a dramatic decrease in death rates starting in the mid-eighteenth century than a rising birth rate. Advances in medicine—including the conquest of smallpox, the disappearance of scurvy (at least on land), improvements in obstetrics (leading to less death among infants and mothers in childbirth), the growing

---

23. Briggs, *Age of Improvement*, 30.
24. Clapham, *Economic History of Modern Britain*, 54–55.

number of better trained doctors and midwives, and the spreading and improving of hospitals, dispensaries, and medical schools—were definitely mitigating factors.

Improvements in sanitation and personal hygiene also contributed to population growth. With better soaps and purer water supplies, people washed their clothes and themselves more regularly. The number of cesspools decreased as water closets improved drainage and public sewer systems increased. Dirty and antiquated farmhouses and putrid privies were steadily replaced. Newer, cheaper, and cleaner cotton clothing became available, allowing for more frequent changes in wardrobes. It was, to be concise, a cleaner, healthier age, a breath of fresher air. People looked better, smelled better, ate better. Vegetables were more readily available, as even the most common laborers had small gardens and a potato patch. And with improvements in travel and communication, some of the more fortunate escaped to the lake events or to coastal towns and villages—resorts in embryo—although the masses could ill afford to travel too far away from their village hovels.

The result of such change and improvements was, as N. F. R. Crafts has carefully pointed out, a dramatic shift in labor. In 1750, 55 percent of the workforce was concentrated in agriculture, and by 1850 that figure had dropped to merely 22 percent. Similarly, in 1750 some 21 percent of the population lived in towns, compared to 54 percent a century later.[25] The shift to urbanization was in full swing.

The agrarian revolution likewise contributed to making life more bearable, sustainable, and attractive. Heavy remnants of feudalism, such as open field farming in the form of narrow strips of land with bulks of uncultivated land separating them—what might simplistically be called subsistence agriculture—were giving way to more efficient and profitable techniques. These included husbandry of larger farms and land enclosures, specialization in better summer and winter crops, improved crop rotations, more durable breeds of cattle and sheep, improved top drainage, and better farm implements. Large farm holders and landed proprietors dramatically increased the amount of enclosed or fenced land, especially after 1760, and also increased the number of tenant farmers by buying up large amounts of common pasture and wastelands previously in possession of the village as a whole. This had the unfortunate result of driving many yeoman and peasant poor from their tiny family holdings. Dispossessed and often living on the verge of starvation, these cottagers either became the hired laborers of their new landlords or left to work in collieries (coal mines), factories, or foundries. The net demographic result, as already shown, was a steady shift from rural hamlets and villages to the urban towns and cities.[26] Difficult and traumatic as these changes were for common people, crop yields dramatically improved, as did the supply of meat, cheese, and milk, which permitted the feeding of a rapidly growing and increasingly urbanized population.[27] This agrarian

---

25. Crafts, *British Economic Growth*, 4, 65–69.
26. Cole and Postgate, *British People*, 120–23.
27. Briggs, *Age of Improvement*, 34–36.

Machines of the Industrial Revolution. *Hartmann Maschinenhalle* (1868), by unknown artist.

revolution fed the increase in population that in turn fueled the fire of the Industrial Revolution.

The essence of the Industrial Revolution was the harnessing and specialized application of steam power and with it, the invention of new tools and machines that transformed and greatly enhanced methods of production. Such advances led to a rapid rise in industrial output, especially in the textile, coal, iron, and transportation industries, all of which led to increased productivity, rapid urbanization, the proliferation of factories, and the relentless relocation of labor. The Industrial Revolution demanded the new economics of competitive capitalization or, as Arnold Toynbee phrased it, the "substitution of competition for the medieval regulations which had previously controlled the production and distribution of wealth."[28] The new machines and the rise of the forge and the factory gradually replaced the domestic system so long in vogue, although many of the greatest changes did not occur until after 1820, by which time Great Britain had become the workshop of the world.

The introduction of steam power as the "all-powerful agent," as Briggs has phrased it, afforded two indispensable advantages: first, the necessary power to manufacture vastly increased volumes of materials in virtually every branch of production, and, second, freeing

---

28. Toynbee, *Lectures on the Industrial Revolution*, 85.

industry from its dependence on water power and having to locate mills and factories near rivers or falls.[29] There was as much geographical change as there was economic, for now factories of production could be built closer to the necessary resources of coal and iron, thereby ensuring the rise of company towns such as the new industrial cities of Manchester, Sheffield, and Birmingham. Manchester alone grew from 75,000 in 1801 to 303,000 fifty years later, and Sheffield grew from 46,000 to 135,000.[30]

James Watt (1736–1819), a Scottish-born inventor and son of an architect, was a key figure in the birth of the new age. Thomas Newcomen, a Cornish mechanic, had previously invented steam pumps—or "fire-engines," as they were more commonly called—long before Watt's day and had pioneered water pumping operations needed for mines, floods, and the regulation of urban water supplies. In 1781 Watt, with the financial backing of Matthew Boulton, invented something of far greater importance. What he designed was a new and more efficient piston, combined with a rotary motion that, through a watch-like mechanism of interlocking gears, enabled his steam engine to be used directly to supply machine power, thereby giving "an immense impetus" to the growth of the factory system.[31]

The first massive application of Watt's steam engine technology came in the textile industry. Improvements had been made to automate the spinning and weaving process, including John Kay's (1704–79) "flying shuttle" (1733), James Hargreaves's (1720–78) multiple spinning wheel or "spinning jenny" (1765), and Reverend Edmund Cartwright's (1743–1823) "power loom" (1785). But it was Sir Richard Arkwright's (1732–92) new water frames and cotton mills—first water-driven but soon geared to steam power—that quickly made cotton king. This allowed for the production of an entirely new line of clothing that soon far surpassed the traditional wool and silk industries in terms of volume, size of the labor force, and number of factories. The first Manchester steam-driven cotton loom factory was built in 1806. By 1818 there were over 2,000 such establishments, and by 1830 there were no less than 55,000. The wool industry was older and more resistant to modernization in part because they worked with heavier products such as broadcloth, blankets, and carpets, which defied simple mechanized procedures. Yet even with wool, mechanization predominated after 1820, as it did in the flax and silk-spinning industries.[32] Between the accession of King George III and the death of George IV, the output of the cotton industry increased an astonishing hundredfold.[33] Christopher Daniell argues that between 1760 and 1800, cotton cloth production rose in value from 227,000 pounds in 1760 to 16,000,000 pounds in 1800, a staggering 7,000 percent increase![34]

---

29. Briggs, *Age of Improvement*, 21
30. Eastwood, "Age of Uncertainty: Britain in the Early Nineteenth Century," in *Transactions of the Royal Historical Society*, 8:100.
31. Cole and Postgate, *British People*, 133.
32. Clapham, *Economic History of Modern Britain*, 143–47.
33. Trevelyan, *British History in the Nineteenth Century*, 155.
34. Daniell, *Traveller's History of England*, 168.

The second area where steam power came quickly into play was in iron making. John Wilkinson (1728–1808) was the first ironmaster to replace charcoal from burnt wood with coke from purified coal in blast furnaces. He also pioneered the use and manufacture of cast iron, thereby removing the need to access ever-depleting timber supplies. With new steam-powered machinery, blast furnaces became much bigger, hotter, and more efficient, producing larger volumes of cast iron and cast-iron goods than ever before. In 1788 Great Britain's twenty-six charcoal furnaces produced a mere sixty-eight thousand tons of pig iron; by 1830 almost all had been replaced, and between 250 and 300 coke furnaces (many in Wales) were putting out some seven hundred thousand tons of pig iron annually—a tenfold increase in less than fifty years.

Thanks to the Scottish ironmaster Henry Cort (1741–1800) of Portsmouth and Peter Onions (1724–98) of Merthyr Tydfil, Wales, who simultaneously developed what is known as the puddling and rolling process, pig iron could now be smelted and refined into more malleable and usable wrought iron. Whereas pig iron was used in building cast-iron objects such as pots, kettles, cannons, stoves, nails and such, the stronger, more purified wrought or malleable iron was used to make tougher metal for rails, plates, and chains and finer applications such as gates, bridges, machines, and tools. With the proximity of coal to iron ore in northwest England, the iron industry inevitably congregated there.

The new demand for iron caused a commensurate growth in the coal and iron mining industry, especially in the northeast. In Yorkshire alone, the number of collieries increased from one to forty-one between 1800 and 1830 and from an annual production of 160,000 tons to almost 3,000,000 tons of coal. The number of workers, both above and below ground, climbed to 12,000.[35]

In the field of transportation and communication, through the work of John Loudon McAdam (1756–1836), a Scottish engineer, and Thomas Telford (1757–1837), a canal builder, the nation's bumpy and often impassable muddy roads were vastly improved. McAdam pioneered the use of small, broken stones in much smoother road construction ("macadamization"). The era of canal building lasted from 1790 to 1830, and networks of such waterways coursed through most of England, carrying manufactured goods, raw resources, and an increasing number of passengers. George Stephenson's (1781–1848) invention of the steam-driven iron horse earned him the title "Father of Railways." His steam locomotive, called the "Rocket" (1829), set a new standard for speed and efficiency. Prior to Stephenson, a railroad was merely a horse-drawn feeder line connecting coalfields and factories with nearby rivers and canals. Come the invention of the iron horse, however, railways began connecting cities and towns, with the first railway being the Liverpool and Manchester Railway, which opened in September 1830.

With steam engines and iron came the age of steam on the water, first on river and then at sea, with the first iron steamship built by the American Robert Fulton (1765–1815), which sailed up the Hudson River in 1807.

---

35. Clapham, *Economic History of Modern Britain*, 186.

Catharine Akerly Mitchill (1778–1864), wife of Senator Samuel L. Mitchill (1764–1831) of New York, witnessed the inaugural voyage of Mr. Fulton's steamboat:

> I had the opportunity of seeing her pass our house. She moved very rapidly through the water, with the high tide rather against her, without aid of sails. It was a novel and interesting sight. The experiment succeeds perfectly, and you may suppose that Mr. Fulton is much elated with his success. I walked up to the Hook to look at her before she started, and had an invitation to take a sail in her; but declined the honor. The machinery is so complicated, and I understand it so little, that I shall not attempt a description, but it is certainly a very ingenious piece of workmanship. You would have been pleased to have seen her rolled along through the water by her two great arms, resembling the wheels of a grist mill.[36]

Henry Bell (1767–1830), Fulton's tutor, returned to Glasgow in 1811, where he constructed the *Comet*, a steamboat that weighed twenty-five tons. The first passenger steamboat to sail the Thames was the *Margery* in 1815. In 1818 the first steam ships began making scheduled voyages at sea.[37]

If the changes in agriculture displaced the poorer segments of population, industrialization eventually scaled back the so-called domestic or putting-out system, where workers collected the raw materials, worked on them at the capitalist's premises, and then sold them back to the supplier. Knitting and hosiery were essentially outwork industries where craftsmen and their helpers worked for the commercial entrepreneur. With the invention of the spinning jenny and looms run by steam power, machines became concentrated in mills and factories and demanded a far larger workforce of men, women, and even children.

The theoretical foundation to this changing economy lay in the writings of that apostle of capitalism, global growth, and the potential for accumulation of wealth—the Scottish-born Adam Smith. Smith was influenced by the ideas and events of the Protestant Reformation that resisted Catholic authority, the divine right of kings, and the status quo, and he wrote at a time when market forces were lessening the rigidities of the remaining feudal and medieval practices and the mercantilism that followed them. He saw the potential of individuals to act, as economist Alan Greenspan has argued, "independently of ecclesiastic and state restraint" and in an era of economic freedom. A "whole new system of enterprise" was now possible.[38] As Smith wrote in *An Inquiry into the Nature and Causes of the Wealth of Nations*, every man should be "free to pursue his own interest in his own way and to bring both his industry and capital into competition with those of . . . other . . . men."[39] He also recognized the enormous "productive powers of labor" and argued that freedom, capital, vision, and labor, when combined with the above-described principles would promote the public good

---

36. Catherine Mitchill to her sister, 17 August 1870, Catherine Mitchill Papers, Library of Congress, MSS Division, Washington, DC.
37. *Account of the Origin of Steam-boats*, 29–37.
38. Greenspan, Adam Smith Lecture, Fife College in Kirkcaldy, Scotland.
39. Smith, *Wealth of Nations*, 687.

by developing a whole new system of enterprise and would increase the wealth and the standards of living in potentially every nation and in virtually limitless ways. His argument provided for a whole new class of merchants, traders, and manufacturers. "Perhaps if the *Wealth of Nations* had never been written, the Industrial Revolution would still have proceeded . . . at an impressive pace," Greenspan further argued. "But without his demonstration of the inherent stability and growth of what we now term free-market capitalism, the remarkable advance of material well-being for whole nations might well have been quashed."[40]

Of course, not everyone agreed with Adam Smith, and some elements of his arguments were later modified. He naively believed in the unselfishness of men. Social reformers like Robert Owen (1771–1858) and Lord Shaftesbury (1801–85) campaigned hard against unrestrained laissez-faire that, if left unchecked, led to poverty, child exploitation, disease, and premature death. Owen criticized the religions of the day for emphasizing too much the state of the soul hereafter and too little the fair treatment and improvement of the worker's plight in the present world. Improving one's environment improved one's character as much as going to church or reading the Bible ever did. His school of utopian socialists and new villages of cooperation, such as his 1826 New Harmony experiment in Indiana in the United States, were failed attempts to rectify what he perceived to be untrammeled capitalism.

The cost of all this economic progress and of the age of improvement, as well argued by Briggs and other scholars, came at a terrible price. The very conditions that brought wealth to the landed interests and manufacturers often brought misery to the laboring class. As historian Alfred Henry Sweet has pointed out, cotton spinners who were working seventy-four hours a week in 1801 were paid a meager thirty-six shillings and six pence, and weavers were paid only seven to eleven shillings a week.[41] The hardships of poverty, dislocation, family rupture, inhumane working conditions, child exploitation, fractious employee-employer relationships—to name but a few—were all too painfully real. Not all were necessary, and few can be defended in the name of economic progress. Whenever technology changes and advances, human nature remains doggedly the same. Greed, selfishness, and corruption have never been vanquished simply by changing technologies.

Historian William Cunningham has noted that while many in the rising ranks of entrepreneurs believed the "production of increased quantities of material goods" was the only valid means by which to improve society, "they seemed to attach very little importance to measures for the direct protection of human life."[42]

In the textile industry, at least in the early years, women, youth, and children predominated because they could be paid less than male adults, especially handloom weavers and framework twitters. Pay was minimal, and working conditions were dismal, if not frightful. In the textile mills, for instance, because of the nature of the material, it was best to spin and

---

40. Greenspan, Lecture.
41. Sweet, *History of England*, 597.
42. Cunningham, *Growth of English*, 775.

Women in the Industrial Revolution. *Power Loom Weaving*, by unknown artist. Courtesy of Wellcome Collection.

weave flax when it was wet. Consequently, workers labored all day standing up in a continual cold, wet spray, their hands constantly sore from never being dry.

Factory children fared little better. Parents were known to carry their children to the mills in the morning on their backs and then carry them back again at night. Both girls and boys, some no more than six years old, often worked thirteen- to fourteen-hour days, starting work at three or four in the morning, with little time off for meals or rest breaks. Reported one young man: "Am twelve years old. Have been in the mill twelve months. Begin at six o'clock, and stop at half past seven. Generally have about twelve hours and a half of it. Have worked over-hours for two or three weeks together. Worked breakfast time and teatime and did not go away till eight." Another worker stated, "We only get a penny an hour for over-time.... We used to come at half-past eight at night, and work all night, till the rest of the girls came in the morning. They would come at seven. Sometimes we worked on till half-past eight the next night, after we had been working all the night before. We worked in meal-hours, except at dinner.... It was just as the overlooker chose."[43]

---

43. Report of the Minutes of Evidence taken before the Select Committee on the State of Children employed in the Cotton Manufactures of the United Kingdom (1816), as cited in Cunningham, *Growth of English Industry and Commerce*, 779–82, 785–86.

It was only in the 1830s that factory reforms and establishing ten-hour days for children were initiated by Robert Owen. The smaller mills were decidedly the worst, with children often severely punished by tyrannical supervisors for tardiness, lack of performance, or even illness. Sanitation was often wholly lacking, and the frequency of accidents was especially shocking because of overcrowded conditions, overworked machinery, and tired and underpaid laborers.

The employment of women and children in the collieries was a particularly disgusting and brutalizing state of affairs that had negative impacts on families. As more and more women left their homes to work in such places, as well as in factories, infants were neglected. To what extent sexual immorality increased because of families under economic stress is debatable. Yet, as one witness declared before a Parliamentary Factory Commission in 1833: "It would be no strain on his conscience to say that three-quarters of young women between fourteen and twenty years of age were unchaste" and that "some of the married women were as bad as the girls."[44]

The stress on family life was increasingly exacerbated. Farm laborer families were torn asunder in the tiring efforts to make a barely subsistent living. The accounts of pregnant women, covered in coal dust, lugging bags of coal over their heads and on their backs while climbing up broken ladders to the mine's surface are easy to find. Boys and some girls—some only six or seven years old—would go down with the men at four o'clock in the morning and remain in a stope or pit, six hundred feet deep, for up to twelve hours. One six-year-old child had the forlorn duty of opening and shutting the traps or doors to prevent flammable drafts whenever the coal wagons would pass and repass.[45]

Looking over the bustling city of Birmingham now so dramatically transformed by such economic 'progress', Robert Southey saw it as little better than a new blight on English society: "A heavy cloud of smoke hung over the city, above which in many places black columns were sent up with prodigious force from the steam-engines . . . the contagion spread far and wide. Every where around us . . . the tower of some manufactory was seen at a distance, vomiting up flames and smoke, and blasting everything around with its metallic vapours. The vicinity was as thickly peopled as that of London. . . . Such swarms of children I never beheld in any other place, nor such wretched ones."[46]

Defenders of the new order said that families worked no harder in factories, workshops, and mines than they had on farms, where they had eked out an even worse standard of living. But, given the overwhelming evidence and the eventual reforms mandated, it seems clear that many were exploited. Young mothers especially were deprived of caring for their infants and children, and infant mortality rates were markedly higher, sometimes as much as 50 percent or more.[47]

---

44. Perkin, *Origins of Modern English Society*, 150.
45. Cunningham, *Growth of English Industry and Commerce*, 805.
46. Southey, *Letters from England*, 203.
47. Perkin, *Origins of Modern English Society*, 154–55.

Perhaps the worst examples of child exploitation existed in London when chimney sweeps were in constant demand. With many flues no bigger than nine inches square, very small boys (and a few girls), no more than five or six years old, were sent out to work. Many got stuck and were then beaten. Some died. Even worse than sweeping a normal chimney was to clean a hot chimney. "Did your master or the journeymen ever direct you to go up a chimney that was on fire?" a young boy was once asked. "Yes, it is a general case." "Do they compel you to go up a chimney that is on fire?" "Oh yes, it was the general practice for two of us to stop at home on Sunday to be ready in case." The soot often remained on their unwashed bodies for a week or two. There is even evidence that some parents, especially poor single parents, sold their children as chimney slaves. Samuel T. Coleridge (see chapter 6) called them "our poor little white-slaves." William Blake also spoke of this notorious trade in his "Songs of Innocence:"

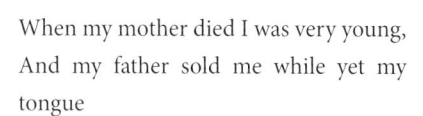

A postcard of a young chimney sweep. *Little Savoyard Chimney Sweep*, photographer unknown.

> When my mother died I was very young,
> And my father sold me while yet my tongue
> Could scarcely cry "'weep! 'weep! 'weep! 'weep!"
> So your chimneys I sweep, and in soot I sleep.[48]

While some went up chimneys, others of these so-called street children —untutored, independent urchins—took on every job imaginable, including tumbling, fetching cabs, and even finding prostitutes for "gentlemen." Tiny "nightmen" were let down holes and into privies, where they forlornly splashed about fetching watches and other lost articles. Such dirty, young, and barefoot lads were often employed by a master who forced them to sleep in cellars without a bed.[49]

---

48. "The Chimney Sweeper" (1789), in Bernbaum, *Anthology of Romanticism*, 115.
49. From *An Account of the Proceedings of the Society for Superseding the Necessity of Climbing Boys*, as cited in the *Edinburgh Review* 32 (1810): 309–14.

A combination of interrelated factors in postwar England from 1815 to 1819 created an "unprecedented stagnation of every branch of commerce and manufacture," or in today's parlance, a perfect storm. The rapid demobilization of over 330,000 sailors and soldiers after Napoléon's defeat flooded an already saturated labor market and led to widescale and massive unemployment. Continental buyers were impoverished by the great war. Price inflation had greatly increased the cost of living, while taxation was at an all-time high in order to pay off the nation's enormous war debts. Antistrike legislation made workers powerless to organize. To make matters worse, crops were almost ruinous in 1816 and 1817, and Parliament had recently passed Poor Laws and Corn Laws at the behest of landowners, which placed artificially high tariffs on imported grain and encouraged idleness and the dole. All these factors resulted in the economic depression of 1819, with its tell-tale signs of tight and shrinking credit, sharp declines in property values, a spike in the number of bank failures and bankruptcies, massive unemployment, and all-around economic turmoil and suffering. The following extract of an 1818 letter from a village in Scotland puts the dire situation of the common laborer into perspective:

> This county is still in a miserable state, for although trade is getting rather better, yet numbers are still out of work and the landed proprietors taking advantage of this, endeavor to reduce the price of labor as much as possible.... A laborer's wages are from one shilling to one shilling three pence per day. Oatmeal from one shilling and eight pence, to two shillings per peck. Indeed you will be hardly able to imagine how a poor man can manage to keep himself and family alive from this pittance.... Many families have nothing but potatoes three times a day.[50]

Add to this distressing scene the rise in contagious fevers such as typhus, scarlet fever, and whooping cough, in part contracted by returning soldiers (much like how the Spanish influenza killed millions worldwide a century later), and one begins to question the term "age of improvement."[51]

The end result of all such discomfitures was a series of mass meetings, a rise in radical agitation, assassination attempts, and worker-inspired riots that rocked the nation. William Cobbett (1763–1835), a brilliant labor pamphleteer, demanded such political reforms as universal suffrage and annual Parliaments, and Lord Byron used his sarcasm to pour contempt on Parliament. Most notable were the Greenock riots in Scotland, the Spa Field riots of 1816, the Pentridge's rising in 1817, and the Scottish insurrection of 1820 and with it the execution of James Wilson. In Manchester, which was not even represented in Parliament, a crowd of over fifty thousand amassed in protest on 16 August 1819 at St. Peter's Field. Henry Hunt (1773–1835) and other radical labor orators received a hero's welcome, and their highly inflammatory speeches fanned discontent. Fearful of a riot, authorities ordered

---

50. "Foreign Affairs," *National Register*, 21 November 1818, 6.
51. *Edinburgh Review* 31 (1819): 415–19. See also Marriott, *England Since Waterloo*, 24–26.

the dispersal of the protesters. When the crowds resisted, a cavalry charge ensued with sabers in hand. Eleven people, including two women, were hacked to death, and four hundred others were injured in the ensuing stampede. The Peterloo Massacre, as it became known, greatly frightened the nation. Parliament reacted repressively and failed to ease the tension when it sentenced Hunt to two and a half years' imprisonment and forbade future public meetings in the name of preserving peace and public safety.[52]

In 1820 a group of radicals from their headquarters in Cato Street in London, conspired to murder the entire cabinet while dining at a house in Grosvenor Square and then seize the Bank of England, but the plot was betrayed at the very last moment. This "Cato Conspiracy" resulted in the execution of several conspirators and placed the government on a near-panic footing. There can be little doubt that the nation was in despair, and many feared an imminent revolution, which might well have occurred had not crops and employment dramatically improved in 1820.

At this turbulent time, the wandering Queen Caroline decided to return to capitalize on the seething, widespread unrest aimed at a Parliament and a king too preoccupied and oblivious to the crises of working men, women, and children.

"WHAT A STIR, WHAT EXCITEMENT, WHAT NOISE"

Quitting Rome on 8 April and crossing the Alps into Switzerland, Caroline, "like any general on the move," resolutely formed her plans on the go.[53] She traveled swiftly in a "miserable half-broken down carriage covered with dust" to Geneva and thence down the Rhone valley to Lyon, Villeneuve, and St. Omer, eventually reaching Calais in early June, where hundreds of curious French onlookers crowded the pier. Her request for a royal yacht denied, she and her small traveling party embarked directly onboard the *Prince Leopold*. At six o'clock on the morning of 5 June, she set sail, crossing the Channel in seven hours. Disembarking at one in the afternoon, she was greeted by a royal salute in the form of a roar of cannon from Dover Castle, accompanied by lusty cries of "God Bless Queen Caroline" from some ten thousand cheering well-wishers. Waving to all her jubilant supporters as if running for election, she sped westward to London, traveling through Canterbury, Sittingbourn, Chatham, Deptford, Greenwich, and other towns, where rumors of her impending arrival had spread like prairie wildfire. In every town and hamlet, the locals insisted upon drawing "Her Majesty" through the town, displaying royal insignia and Union Jack flags from building windows on each side of her route. Some were even strewn across the road. Well-dressed ladies were seen everywhere waving their handkerchiefs and joining in the general exclamations of "Long Live Our Gracious Queen. Long Live Queen Caroline." Wrote one *London Times* reporter, "The bells of the churches were set ringing, and all was joy and exultation."[54]

---

52. Babbington, *Military Intervention in Britain*, 46–58.
53. Fraser, *Unruly Queen*, 355.
54. *London Times,* 7 June 1820, 3.

As she traveled further west, so many new horsemen and carriages joined her royal entourage that by the time she reached London, like another William the Conqueror or a triumphant Napoléon returning from Elba, she presided over a veritable army of devoted, cheering followers. It seemed like all of England had stirred to support her return. "The Queen of England now occupies all thoughts," this same reporter observed, "and is at present every thing with every body."[55] Robert Peel (1788–1850) spoke more perceptively of "a feeling, becoming daily more general and more confirmed . . . in favour of some undefined change in the mode of governing the country. . . . Public opinion never had such influence on public measures, and yet never was so dissatisfied with the share it possessed. It is growing too large for the channels that it has been accustomed to run through."[56] And wrote the editors of the *Ladies' Literary Cabinet*, "From the obstinacy of the King and his ministers, and the strength of the new queen's party, it would not be surprising if a civil war were to grow out of this affair."[57]

Shortly after Caroline's return to London (without Pergami), by order of the king, Lord Liverpool (1770–1828), his Tory prime minister, reluctantly introduced to Parliament a "Bill of Pains and Penalties against her Majesty," charging Queen Caroline with "an adulterous intercourse with Pergami, her menial servant" and proposing that she should be "degraded" from the title and station of queen and that her marriage with the king should be "dissolved."[58] Liverpool's reluctance stemmed not from any lack of evidence in the king's "Green Bag" of documentation but from his sense that the king would lose in winning, especially among the masses. A guilty verdict might well result not merely in a loss of Tory support but also in a revolution against the monarchy and the establishment of a republican form of government that many radicals and some of his Whig counterparts had been clamoring for ever since the French and American Revolutions. At stake were not merely the whims of a highly unpopular king and a troubled, embarrassing queen, but the very form of future British governments. Civil war might well erupt.

The ensuing trial lasted almost three months. The crown had enough witnesses and sufficient evidence, but the queen, who often attended the court in person, was masterfully represented by Henry Brougham, the ablest of the young Whigs, who admitted the queen's faults but still fully played up the king's unfairness to her through the years, his double standard of behavior, and his 1797 letter granting her, in effect, license for what he was now trying to condemn. After a long, hot summer, the bill passed first, second, and third and final readings in the House of Lords, though with steadily eroding support with each successive vote. Well aware that popular opinion was rising in support of the victim queen ("The Queen forever! The King in the River!") and that a verdict against her might result in a tidal wave of anger, especially among her many female supporters, Prime Minister Liverpool astutely

---

55. *London Times*, 7 June 1820, 3.
56. Fraser, *Unruly Queen*, 365.
57. *Ladies' Literary Cabinet* 2 (1820): 16.
58. Campbell, *Lives of the Lord Chancellors*, 7:367.

called for a time out. Instead of moving "that this bill do pass" for consideration in the lower House of Commons, he postponed further action for a period of six months. The London mobs erupted with joy. "Caroline the Glorious" was granted an annuity of fifty thousand pounds but no castle.[59]

Popular support for Caroline, however, proved fickle and short-lived. The evidence produced at trial had proven the baseness of her character and her subsequent drunken parties, outlandish dress, and uncouth behavior at theaters and balls in London disgraced her dignity and was an affront to her supporters. If she had successfully counted on public favor, she was now squandering it. Said Lady Cowper, "There never was such an Apple of Discord as that woman has been."[60]

Surely one of the most pathetic moments in the annals of British Royalty occurred on 19 July 1821, the day George IV was crowned in a glory of unsurpassed pomp and ceremony at Westminster Abbey. His new crown featured 12,532 diamonds, and his coronation robes, trimmed with gold, took nine pages to support, while Caroline, uninvited and unwelcomed, was twice barred from entering. The great hall had begun to fill up as early as one o'clock in the morning. Caroline arrived at 5:30 in a morning already lit by the rising summer sun and knocked personally at the door at Poet's Corner but was refused entrance because she had no ticket. In tears, she climbed back into her carriage amid such insults from the crowd as "Go home, you common disturber" and "Go back to Pergami." She circled about and tried yet a second time to enter Westminster Hall, only to have a hunched red-robed page bang the door shut in her face. Demanding a coronation of her own in two or three weeks' time, her reputation sullied, and whatever little dignity she had left now in tatters, Caroline returned to her rented residence where she took sick, and died three weeks later on 7 August 1821, if not from an overdose of laudanum and excessive blood-letting, then surely of acute depression and a broken heart. There was little mourning at her private funeral, and she was quietly laid to rest in Harwick, eighty miles away from her few remaining London supporters.

A SORDID LEGACY

Queen Caroline was an unhappy figure, ill-equipped for her royal role. She may well have had the same afflictions that robbed her father-in-law of his sanity. She managed to offend even her most ardent supporters as she, unloved and essentially unappreciated, wore out her welcome. Seldom before had anyone galvanized public opinion so quickly, then lost it so decidedly. Her escapades both home and abroad, her fateful return to England, and her subsequent trial and sorry end all contributed to the birth of a popular press that spun off hundreds of thousands of pamphlets, broadsides, squibs, and penny-a-yard ballads that re-

---

59. Churchill, *History of the English-Speaking Peoples*, 17–21.
60. Richardson, *Disastrous Marriage*, 198. Some people chanted, "Gracious Queen, We thee implore: Go away, sin no more. Or if the effort be too great, go away at any rate." Richardson, *Disastrous Marriage*, 86.

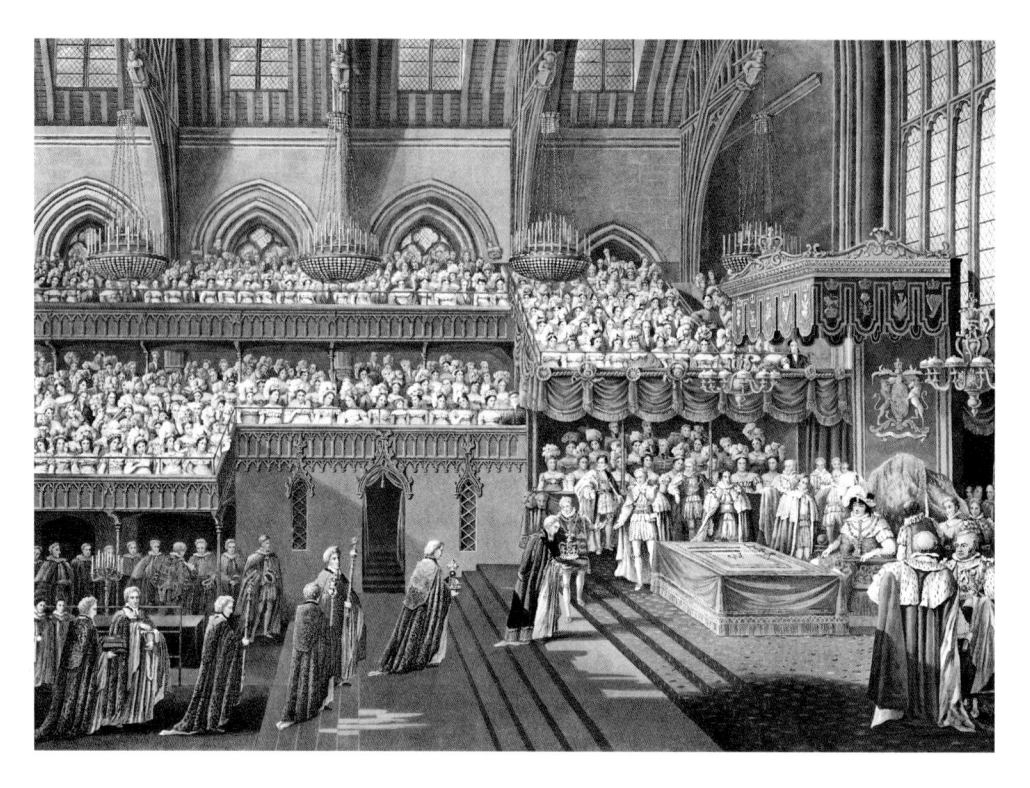

Coronation Banquet of King George IV of Great Britain, by Sir George Naylor, 19 July 1821.

sulted in the divorce bill being dropped.[61] It may well be argued that the trial of Queen Caroline was "the spark that set Britain on the road to political reform."[62] Certainly it sparked the rise of a truly popular press with the London *Times* and William Cobbett's pamphleteering, which all demand change and reform.

By 1822 the worst of the postwar adjustment had passed. The economy was rapidly improving in what might be called the first boom of the industrial era. Soon public tensions eased. With the suicidal death of the foreign secretary Castlereagh in 1822, King George IV appointed the generous-minded George Canning (1770–1827) in his place and Sir Robert Peel (1788–1850), son of a cotton spinner, as home secretary. Both Tories under Liverpool, Peel and Canning practiced a brand of social or Tory liberalism, being much more attuned to the suffering and welfare of the middle and lower classes than aligned with the aristocracy. Peel took up the cause of penal and prison reform, greatly reduced the number of capital (death penalty) offenses, and sought for and obtained Roman Catholic emancipation. Fearful of another Peterloo Massacre debacle, Peel established the London Metropolitan Police, an unarmed but highly trained force soon nicknamed "bobbies," after him. In the

---

61. "A Right Royal Scandal," *Economist*, 381.
62. Robins, *Trial of Queen Caroline*, 319.

hopes of lessening support for the radical cause, working class claims were more fully entertained and trade unionism grew steadily, especially in the shipbuilding, manufacturing, and mining industries, with John Doherty as a leading figure. In foreign affairs, Canning's new Navigation Act permitted freer trade between the colonial empire and Europe, and tariffs were reduced. After a short, more conservative reign under Prime Minister Wellington from 1827 to 1830, during which time Parliament passed the long overdue Catholic Emancipation Act, Charles Grey became prime minister in 1830 and, under the new Whig government, passed the famous Reform Bill of 1832, which put resolutions to the grievances of a generation into law.

The great Reform Bill of 1832, a major turning point in British history, owed much to many people, including many reform-minded souls already discussed—William Cobbett, Robert Peel, Robert Owen, Anthony Ashley-Cooper (Lord Shaftesbury), William Wilberforce (see chapter 8), and Charles Grey. The rising middle class of merchants and industrial employees in the Midlands and the North also wanted policies and laws less favorable to the interests of the landowners. Jeremy Bentham (1748–1832), the philosopher and famous social reformer, believed that government existed to ensure the greatest happiness of the greatest number, and the more Parliament listened to the voice of the majority and less to the vested interests, the better life would be for all.[63]

Among other things, the Reform Bill disenfranchised scores of boroughs, more than doubled the number of people entitled to vote, increased representation from counties and cities heretofore unrepresented, and increased Scottish and Irish representation. This important piece of legislation took power from the upper social class and gave it to the strongly emerging middle classes; there was more democratic power for the people. And the very next year Lord Shaftesbury succeeded in finally passing his Factory Act, forbidding child labor for those under nine years of age and limiting the hours of women and children to ten a day.

And as for Prinny, finally King George IV, he would reign over England for the next decade. A man of style, he did not follow fashions; he set them. A patron of the arts and of literature, he donated his father's library to form the basis of the British Museum Library. He loved the writings of Jane Austen, Sir Walter Scott, and Samuel Taylor Coleridge. He encouraged the renaissance of the ballet with such new brilliant dancers and choreographers as Lise Noblet, Fanny Bias, François Decombe, Charles Vestris, and James d'Egville.[64] His greatest legacy was in architecture: he built the Brighton Pavilion and Carlton House, extensively renovated and extended both Windsor Castle and Buckingham Palace, and, with the help of architect John Nash (1752–1835), transformed and beautified the heart of Regency London by remodeling and replanting St. James's and Regent's Parks. His taste in furniture

---

63. Sweet, *History of England*, 615–16.
64. Although ballet was still essentially a man's art, the place of women was becoming increasingly center stage in the 1820s. The display of a ballerina's legs was something recent in ballet as was the cultivation of the "pointe," a female dancing on the very tips of her toes.

and ornamentation is still known as the Regency style. And, as "the greatest common scion ever to sit on the British throne, he acquired the works of Rembrandt, Reubens, Cuyp, and Pietrde Hooch, making it one of the finest art collections in the world. He commissioned every leading English painter, including Gainsborough, Reynolds, Lawrence, Stubbs, and Turner. His state visits to Ireland and Scotland set a new precedent and drew the monarchy closer to the people.

Of perhaps greater significance, his refusal to dismiss his Cabinet ministers if they disagreed with him during such crises and setbacks as the failed divorce trial was a major step toward a constitutional monarchy with more power vested in Cabinet and Parliament than ever before.[65]

For all his accomplishments, King George IV lived out his life a lonely and tragic figure. At his death in June 1830 he was buried with a picture of Maria Fitzherbert around his neck, who died on a dark and windy day seven years later. He was little more than an entertaining shadow, and a very expensive one at that. Concluded one leading scholar of British royalty: "It is sad that one of the most gifted of British monarchs was, by the time of his death, also one of the most despised. George IV's undoubted charm, his evident wit, his innate aesthetic sense, his enthusiasm and his imagination ultimately left him insufficiently equipped to rise to the challenge of a nation daily growing in self-confidence and wealth. His self-indulgence and short attention span, together with his evident ability to abandon political principles and to forget friendships with barely a backward glance, won him few encomiums after his death."[66] And, as the royal historian Sir Owen Moreshead concluded: "George IV had melted like a snowman: only the clothes remained."[67]

When King George IV died in June 1830, few mourned his passing. He was neither loved nor respected. He had grown so enormously fat and increasingly out of touch with his subjects that he was enveloped by the disdain that had followed him since before Caroline. His childless second brother, the Duke of Clarence, had already predeceased him. Next in line was his third brother, William, Duke of Clarence, who became king in 1830. Upon William's death in 1837, and that of two of his oldest daughters, the scepter fell on one few had ever imagined would ascend—Queen Victoria (1819–1901)—the unlikely monarch who would reign over England and the British Empire for the next sixty-three years.

It is nigh impossible to measure or assess how the Industrial Revolution influenced religion generally. But certainly advances and improvements in land and sea transportation, communication, capitalization, and rapid urbanization changed faithful missionary work, the gathering impulse, publishing efforts, and inter-city communication. And the effects which the Industrial Revolution had upon the later arrival of The Church of Jesus Christ of Latter-day Saints beginning in 1837 would be substantial. It is a well-established fact that most Latter-day Saint converts came mainly from the laboring classes in the industrial re-

---

65. Baker, *George IV*, 32.
66. Parissien, "George IV," 9–11.
67. As cited in Parissien, "George IV," 9–11.

gions of northwest England.[68] Dislocation, rapid urbanization, displacement of workers and their families, poor working conditions for many, child labor, unequal distribution of wealth and services, and the economic depression of the late 1830s and early 1840s—all these and other related factors "helped create an atmosphere for success" when Latter-day Saint missionaries began spreading their message of faith and hope. Between 1837 and 1848, the number of British Latter-day Saint converts skyrocketed from a mere handful to about 31,000.[69] Likewise, their invitation to new converts to emigrate to America would play well at a time when the total annual figures of British emigrants bound mainly for America and Canada reached as high as 250,000, some of them Latter-day Saints. It marked a new harvest of emigrant converts that continues to bless the Church into the twenty-first century.

---

68. Allen, Esplin, and Whittaker, *Men with a Mission*, 18–19.
69. Allen, Esplin, and Whittaker, *Men with a Mission*, 321.

William Wilberforce, c. 1790, by Stephen C. Dickson.

Hannah More, by Henry William Pickersgill.

OF PROPHETS, PREACHERS, AND POETS

JOHN WESLEY, WILLIAM WILBERFORCE, HANNAH MORE, AND THE ABOLITION OF SLAVERY

Amazing grace, how sweet the sound
That saved a wretch like me.
I once was lost, but now am found,
Was blind, but now, I see.

'Twas grace that taught my heart to fear.
And grace, my fears relieved.
How precious did that grace appear
The hour I first believed.

—John Newton (1725–1807)

The purpose of this chapter is to investigate yet another kind of revolution contemporary to, and descriptive of, the age of 1820—a revolution in religious belief, practices, and social thought that set a conservative tone in the social mannerisms and religious behavior of the coming Victorian era, the effects of which are still being felt. Our study has given ample space thus far to studying the French, the Industrial, the Romantic, and the Agricultural Revolutions with all their many characteristics and consequences. What now begs our attention is the Methodist and evangelical revival that spared England and its expanding overseas empire from what many Britons saw as the godless secularism then engulfing France. This religious revolution eventually culminated in that long, arduous, and eventually successful effort of two "earlier lights" in the morning of the Restoration, to cite B. H. Roberts once again, that eventually ended the scourge of slavery throughout the British Empire.[1]

Of all the many personalities on this religious stage, we have time to study but two, without either of whom this transformation would have been impossible: William Wilberforce (1759–1833) and Hannah More (1745–1833). If Napoléon was the spirit of the age, Wilberforce became its moral conscience first by spearheading the long but ultimately successful campaign to rid England and its empire of slavery and second by establishing a new and renewed sense of "vital Christianity," especially among the higher ranks of society. And if Wilberforce was the prophetic voice of this great humanitarian and religious revival, then Hannah More, with her persuasive pen, was its poet, transcribing Christian beliefs, customs, and convictions into a compelling popular literature that spoke to the millions of poor and barely educated men and women. Wilberforce's and More's deeply held convictions and combined efforts revitalized British Christianity and the efforts to eliminate slavery in the British Empire. This momentous accomplishment later inspired Abraham Lincoln to push for the same in an America slow to divest itself of this moral curse. Without the persistent influence of Wilberforce, slavery may have endured decades longer than it did, and without his Christianizing influence, Great Britain may well have gone the secular route of France.

"THE CHURCH MILITANT": JOHN WESLEY AND THE EARLIER METHODIST REVIVALS

To understand why Wilberforce became such a transforming figure, we must once again travel further back in time to appreciate the foundations that later bore such positive fruit. Over a century ago, Elie Halévy (1870–1937), the noted French scholar of British religious history, argued that the revival of evangelical religion in the late eighteenth century spared England of a French-style Jacobin Revolution.[2] As discussed in the previous chapter, surely all the makings of a class struggle were evident: the economic disruption and unemployment brought on by the Industrial Revolution; family displacements; the despair and riots of the working classes, or proletariat; rising class envies and agitations; a weak, increasingly distant, and unsympathetic established church; and a conservative government intent on repressing violence and resisting the growing democratic demands of the commoner. By 1800, Great Britain was at a crossroads but, instead of turning against the established order, reasserted itself religiously in a way unlike any other European nation.

What happened in England in the era of 1820 with Wilberforce and More had its roots some eighty years before in 1739 with John Wesley (1703–91), Charles Wesley (1707–88), George Whitefield (1714–70), and the great Methodist revivals. This highly spirited religious reformation was a reaffirmation and a rekindling of England's long-standing, deeply felt Christian convictions. Another famous French historian, Hippolyte Taine, once described

---

1. Roberts, *Comprehensive History of the Church*, 6:252.
2. Halévy, *Birth of Methodism in England*, 1–3.

the English as possessing a "naturally serious, meditative, and sad" temperament that can be traced back as far as the Protestant Reformation.[3] Generally uneasy, if not distrustful of the clergy and of its priestly ordinances, the English, despite the Glorious Revolution of 1689 and the reestablishment of a Protestant monarchy, had never warmed to its own established Church of England. It was more "a country of voluntary obedience" than of imposed religious prescriptions and creedal directives.[4]

Capitalizing on economic discontent, the Methodist movement gained rapid popularity for at least four reasons: (1) the inability of the Church of England to satisfy the deep religious cravings of its people; (2) the rise of vice and popular degradation and the fear over what English society was becoming; (3) the outstanding courage, spiritual command, doctrinal understandings, powerful preaching, and organizational skills of John and Charles Wesley and George Whitefield; and (4) the give-and-take doctrine of man's condemnation for sin on the one hand and Christ's willing forgiveness on the other.

The seeds of this religious outburst were sown in large part by a static, state-supported church that was never too popular and in a society "no longer constrained to accept its leadership."[5] Financially supported by the state rather than by its parishioners, the Anglican clergy was perceived as overpaid, out of touch, and indifferent to the needs of its membership, a profession of inheritance and prestige rather than a call to service. Many parishes suffered from absentee clergy, due in part to the wrenching demographic changes brought on by the Industrial Revolution. While England's population grew from 5.5 million in 1740 to 13.1 million in 1831, the number of Anglican churches remained static, and the Church of England declined from monopoly to minority status.[6] Tightly bound by prayer book formality, the church was perceived by many as class-bound, aristocratic, apathetic, nepotistic, and out of touch with the everyday needs and problems facing most English families living in poverty from day to day. Consequently, just after its formation, it lost favor with the modern urban working class.

The Methodist movement came also as a response to a perceived decline in societal morals and conduct. "The superstitions of Popery were disregarded and despised, but the licentiousness of infidelity covered the land," wrote one nineteenth-century scholar of Methodism. "The rich were wholly regardless of the claims of religion, and even considered vital godliness as the height of fanaticism. The poor were sunk into the lowest depth of vice and degradation," a state of "spiritual putrefaction." He added, "Wickedness flourished, piety languished, and God was forgotten."[7]

The clerical spark plug to the Methodist movement was John Wesley. Born in 1703, educated at Christ Church, Oxford, and ordained an Anglican clergyman in 1725, Wesley

---

3. Semmel, in the introduction of Halévy, *Birth of Methodism in England*, 14.
4. Halévy, *Birth of Methodism in England*, 12.
5. Gilbert, *Religion and Society in Industrial England*, 12.
6. Gilley, "The Church of England in the 19th Century," in Gilley and Shields, *History of Religion in Britain*, 293–94.
7. Harwood, *History of Wesleyan Methodism*, 20–21.

Statue of John Wesley in Melbourne, by Paul Raphael Montford.

underwent a crisis of faith after returning from a mission tour to the colony of Georgia in America. Having witnessed there the personal assurance of salvation among the German Moravian missionaries, he prayed for and received a life-changing spiritual certainty and conversion to Christ. "I felt my heart strangely warmed," he wrote. "I felt I did trust in Christ, Christ alone, for salvation; and an assurance was given me that he had taken away *my* sins, even *mine*, and saved *me* from the law of sin and death."[8]

Convinced that his own Church of England was lacking the spiritual enthusiasm or power to change hearts and bring souls to Christ, he set out on a new path. In company with his more musically talented and poetic younger brother, Charles, whose hymns portrayed the spiritual majesty of the movement, and encouraged by his former pupil George Whitefield, John Wesley took the unprecedented and courageous step in 1739 of preaching beyond parish boundaries, not in the churches and cathedrals, which were closed to him, but in the barns and byways of England. "I look upon all the world as my parish," he said and began spreading the good news from Bristol to Norwich and from London to Glasgow. An enormously commanding speaker with a highly compelling message, Wesley was soon attracting audiences that numbered in the tens of thousands.

Eyewitness accounts of the preaching of John Wesley and George Whitefield, sometimes to outdoor crowds as large as eighty thousand people, attest to the awesome power of their presence. Dressed in long black gowns with his locks flowing around his neck, Wesley usually spoke extemporaneously with fiery emotion about sin and hell, followed by a message of hope and a mood of blissful peace.

> No sooner would he commence his sermon, than every eye involuntarily gazed with fixed attention upon the holy man of God. In fact, if you once fixed your eye upon him you could not take it off again. His musical voice conveyed the word with such power and effect that seldom was a sermon heard without the heart being touched, mellowed, and affected. The voice of Mr. Wesley was not so strong as it was fine, clear, and distinct, so much so that even . . . at the distance of one hundred and forty yards, persons . . . heard and understood the sounds of his voice.[9]

---

8. Baker, "Wesley Brothers," in Eliade, *Encyclopedia of Religion*, 15:370.
9. Walker, *History of Wesleyan Methodism in Halifax*, 84.

Whitefield, who had followed Wesley to Georgia, where his passionate and thunderous preaching sparked an American Great Awakening of religion in the 1740s (see chapter 13), was more Calvinist than Arminian in his theology but readily joined his former teacher in the great English Methodist crusade of bringing souls to Christ. The following account of his outdoor preaching in 1756 captures, if not his preaching style, then surely the popularity of his preaching:

> When Mr. Whitefield arrived at Bristol, a platform was erected at the foot of a hill adjoining the town, whence he addressed the immense concourse of twenty thousand people. . . . Much as he was in the habit of public speaking and preaching to large and promiscuous multitudes, when he cast his eyes on the vast assemblage around him, and was about to mount the temporary stage, he expressed to his surrounding friends a considerable degree of timidity; but when he began to speak, an unusual solemnity pervaded the vast assembly. Thousands during the sermon, as was often the case, vented their emotions in tears and groans, and "Fools, who came to mock, remained to pray."[10]

Not content to follow normal ecclesiastical channels, Wesley began to ordain a lay clergy of field preachers, "a church militant"—an itinerant ministry of zealous though untrained followers—and organized societies, or bands, of believers. Soon Methodist conferences, or parish districts, were organized with their characteristic systems of discussions, questions, and minutes, forming a new society or "a circle within a circle, a church within a church." Condemned by the Anglican Church for exceeding his authority and for preaching a gospel of justification by faith detached from salvation through priesthood sacraments, Wesley, like Luther two centuries before, had never intended to start his own church. Though he ever considered himself an ordained clergyman of the Church of England, his labors eventually gave rise to the Methodist churches, so named in part because of their method of organization and desire to re-create the life and method of salvation as seen in the early apostolic church.

Traveling thousands of miles and preaching hundreds of times each year, visiting the sick, and organizing prayer groups wherever he went, Wesley became the "poor people's friend."[11] Beginning in 1769, Methodist preachers traveled overseas to America, the West Indies, Upper and Lower Canada, and soon afterward to Europe.

Ironically, the pessimism of Methodist doctrine—that man is innately evil and worthy of eternal damnation, if not utterly depraved, as Calvinism taught—was counterbalanced by the optimism of the free and proffered grace of Christ that brought peace, the warmth of forgiveness, and a surety of salvation that many longed for but could not find in the cold formality of Anglican liturgy and dogma. It was at once a personal and more approachable

---

10. Walker, *History of Wesleyan Methodism in Halifax*, 84, 95.
11. Aspland, *Rise, Progress, and Present Influence of Wesleyan Methodism*, 23.

doctrine, more spiritual and hopeful and certainly more pertinent to daily living than what many had ever heard before.

Methodism found its most responsive audiences among England's poor. As Halévy has further observed, "The despair of the working class was the raw material to which Methodist doctrine and discipline gave a shape."[12] Wesley deliberately packaged his preaching and tailored his message to reach the collier and the factory worker, the fisherman and the farmer, often teaching in the fields before sunrise and then again at eventide. Soon bonfires of religious revival were aflame all over Britain. In many towns, preaching and prayer meetings were held every night and continued at times until two o'clock in the morning in what one observer called "a sin-killing, soul-saving, and spirit-quickening time."[13] On some occasions, "all work ceased, whole families were brought under the influence of God's Spirit; night and day the voice of prayer was heard to ascend from the dwellings of the people."[14] And in many coastal villages, "fishermen held prayer meetings on board their vessels while anchored in the bay and even the sea resounded with the praises of the Most High."[15]

A supremely gifted sermonizer, Wesley popularized the gospel message by bringing the church to the people where they lived and in what they did, meeting their spiritual, emotional, and physical wants rather than waiting for them to come to church to hear an erudite but distant sermon. As one early Methodist directive put it, "We strongly advise the preachers in their respective circuits, particularly in the more populous districts, . . . to avail themselves of every opportunity to preach in private houses, especially in the cottages of the poor . . . in order to obtain access to the more neglected part of our people."[16] The persecution that these early Methodists suffered—false arrests, riots, unjustified jailings, mob violence, and senseless beatings, and these often at the initiation of the local parish priest—only fanned the flame of devotion higher.

While France was undergoing a secularizing revolution, Methodism rose so rapidly in popularity among the poor, the disenfranchised, and the working classes all over Great Britain that it remains difficult to refute Halévy's thesis that Methodism was the antidote to revolutionary Jacobinism, a sort of anti-revolution, the influence of which "contributed a great deal . . . to preventing the French Revolution from having an English counterpart."[17] More recent historians agree that popular evangelicalism did indeed make "a fundamental difference to the political stability of industrial England" and "produced a profound shift of allegiance in the nation as a whole."[18]

---

12. Halévy, *Birth of Methodism*, 8.
13. Brownsword, "Extracts of Journals," 19.
14. Ward, *Brief Sketch of Methodism in Bridlington and Its Vicinity*, 25.
15. Ward, "Brief Sketch of Methodism," 25.
16. From "Minutes or Journal of the Conference of the People Called Methodists," vol. 2.
17. Halévy, *Birth of Methodism*, 51.
18. Hampton, "Evangelicalism and Reform, c. 1780–1832," in Wolffe, *Evangelical Faith and Public Zeal*, 24–28.

Yet, for all of its successes, there developed a strong backlash to these Methodist advances. Albeit in a weakened state, the Church of England was still the dominant, established religion and began to actively resist Wesley's advances. Not all its clergy were ravenous wolves or scribes and Pharisees. Many were good and noble men who cared deeply about their parishioners. Some serviced more than one parish but did so to eke out a living. Its bishops, while denouncing the Methodist fanatics, slowly but surely realized improvements had to be made. Moreover, the ruling class, the nobility, and the rich were deeply offended by the puritanical morality of Methodism and felt themselves too often the target of Wesley's preaching. Others openly questioned how patriotic Methodism really was, how committed it was to England's national and global interests. While succeeding among the lower classes, Methodism offended the rich and the powerful who were put off by religious piety and fanaticism and thus alienated itself from the very ones who could have transformed a stirring movement into a true societal reformation. After sixty years of Methodist revivals (1740–1800), there was not a single Methodist in Parliament, and very few were in business or among the gentry.[19]

Likewise, Christianity's fight with sin and corruption among the high and the low, the princes and the prostitutes, was a never-ending war. Although there was arguably a general improvement in the moral tone of England in the latter half of the eighteenth century, Christian evangelicals focused on the corruption still so evident. "Sin wears a front of brass among us," the *Christian Guardian* newspaper lamented in 1809, and a "veritable tide of evil," as one person put it, engulfed the nation, particularly London, where at least thirty thousand female prostitutes, averaging age sixteen, roamed the streets—"the open female debauchery of the age," as one put it. With prostitution came increased crime, violence, abortion, infanticide, and the breakdown of family values. Even the Church of England, while anxious to blame it all on the notoriously promiscuous French, admitted that it was an age of "luxurious habits, dissipated manners, and shameless profligacy. . . . Bastardy is now scarcely deemed a disgrace. . . . Adultery and concubinage in the lower classes of society are unhappily most prevalent."[20] The age of elegance had deteriorated into the triumph of sin. One had only to look at the immorality of Prince George IV and Princess Caroline and others in the royal court to see what examples royalty cared about setting (see chapter 7).

"MEASURES, NOT MEN"

Onto this conflicted stage came one destined to change British society more profoundly than any reigning head of state and who in time became one of the foremost moral figures of the world. Born after his father's death in the port city of Hull in 1759 into a nominally Christian home, William Wilberforce was raised by a childless uncle and aunt who had been previously evangelized by George Whitefield. In their careful religious enthusiasm,

---

19. Brown, *Fathers of the Victorians*, 16, 22–24.
20. Brown, *Fathers of the Victorians*, 46.

they introduced young William to one of the more remarkable men of the age: the kind, old Calvinist divine—the Reverend John Newton (1725–1807). Author of the classic Christian hymn "Amazing Grace," Newton firmly believed that God had a "controversy" with England because of its corrupt state. Wilberforce, an unassuming young man of small stature, was as humble as he was full of good humor. He endeared himself to the older Newton, who in turn enthralled his young pupil with exciting tales of maritime adventure. Newton had gone to sea at age eleven, deserted the navy, and eventually became the overseer of a slave depot on the Plantain Islands off the coast of Africa. A slave himself for two years until rescued by his father, Newton became a captain of a slave ship in 1750 and made several transatlantic voyages with human cargo, witnessing firsthand the awful inhumanities and cruel injustices of the slave trade. Pressed down with guilt for his sins and deep regret for the "wretch" he felt he had become, Newton—the "old African blasphemer," as he called himself—saw his subsequent Christian conversion and call to the ministry as a miraculous rescue and a merciful personal redemption. He came to view his time with the young and impressionable Wilberforce as providential. Their friendship, built on trust, mutual admiration, and respect, would last a lifetime.

At age seventeen, Wilberforce set off to Cambridge, where, like so many of his contemporaries, he enjoyed the new and unrestrained life of a partygoer. A talented singer and an easy conversationalist, but with a serious turn of mind, young Wilberforce made friends easily. Of all his Cambridge associates, none would come to play so great a role in his life as William Pitt (1759–1806), a son of the Earl of Chatham who was even then being groomed for a life in politics. In just seven years' time, Pitt would rise to become prime minister of Great Britain at age twenty-four, the youngest in British history.

Portait of William Wilberforce (1794), by Anton Hickel.

With Pitt's election to Parliament, Wilberforce felt compelled to follow suit, a decision made possible by the death of his uncle William Alderman, who left him a sizable fortune (£30,000/year). So, at the tender age of twenty-one, Wilberforce found himself elected a member of Parliament from Hull and at the beginning of a parliamentary career destined to span his lifetime.

The two young Tory parliamentarians greatly complemented one another. Pitt was the brilliant debater, gifted speaker, and astute and respected politician, whereas Wilberforce was developing his own depths of passion, principle, and persuasive powers. The dynamic pair became animated in their youthful opposition to Lord North and

England's involvement in the American Revolutionary War (see chapter 11), which they both considered ruinous, cruel, and unwinnable.

While at times capable of vicious satire, Wilberforce was given to hospitality and the art of the gentle compromise. He also became known for his sterling integrity, unassailable personal morality, and independent thinking. Gaining the respect of friend and foe alike, Wilberforce was never predictable, never a safe bet to vote purely along Tory Party lines. In 1783, he and some other members of Parliament formed a rump, or subparty of independents who renounced patronage and vowed never to be "raised" (bought out) to peerage in the upper chamber of the House of Lords.[21]

The following year changed Wilberforce's life. While touring Europe with the openly Christian Isaac Milner (1750–1820), a Cambridge don, Wilberforce began a thorough study of the scriptures, a daily habit that would last a lifetime. Between their visits to various sites, the two men also read and discussed works such as Sir Francis Bacon's (1561–1626) *Essays* and Philip Doddridge's (1702–51) *Rise and Progress of Religion in the Soul*. In due time, Wilberforce experienced the need for personal salvation and underwent a conversion so deep and soul-stirring that he returned to England a changed man. Upon visiting with Newton and listening to his sage advice, Wilberforce determined against a career in the clergy and decided to remain in politics and mingle with high societies of influence where he might effect change at the highest levels. "Measures, not men" became his personal motto, and he set about to reform society incrementally by living a life of personal holiness in a world of political vice and economic compromise.[22]

THE "AFRICAN EMANCIPATOR"

Perhaps it was Newton's riveting stories of slave ship abuses or Wilberforce's own innate sense of justice and mercy now quickened by his Christian conversion. Whatever the cause, Wilberforce, in 1787, began in earnest his unrelenting campaign to abolish England's involvement in the African slave trade and to eventually free African slaves throughout the British Empire. It would prove to be a long and oftentimes discouraging fight against both the propertied and the prejudiced.

The Atlantic slave trade had begun with the Spanish and Portuguese as early as 1502 when conquered natives in Brazil and elsewhere in the Americas were understandably slow to accept slavery status and were dying off in very large numbers (see chapter 9). Consequently, frustrated overseers began to import enslaved Africans to do their bidding. The other colonial powers (British, French, and Dutch) had followed suit by midcentury, with England importing enslaved people to support its labor-intensive plantations in its Caribbean islands and southern colonies of North America. The importation of enslaved people soon became part of a highly lucrative triangular trade, consisting of carrying liquor and

---

21. Belmonte, *William Wilberforce*, 18–65.
22. Belmonte, *Wilberforce*, 70–94.

supplies from Europe to West Africa, then shipping enslaved people westward across the Atlantic and finally returning to Europe with ships now filled with sugar, lumber, and other produce—a three-part round trip that took up to eighteen months.[23] British defenders of the trade called it "the foundation of our commerce, the support of our colonies, the life of our navigation, and the first cause of our national industry and riches."[24]

But some connected to this sordid business, such as the Reverend Newton, found it difficult, if not impossible, to defend so reprehensible a traffic in human suffering. Between 1760 and 1820, a minimum of almost four million enslaved Africans, both male and female, were forcibly uprooted from their tribal lands in the Congo and bought by slave ship captains. They were then chained and crammed into poorly ventilated lower decks (some only three feet high), where they endured unspeakable heat, filth, and squalor and the occasional flogging during their eight-week voyage across the Atlantic. Although fed reasonably well so that they, like cattle, could later fetch a decent price, many enslaved people mutinied, only to be tortured, wounded, or drowned. Upon arriving at Barbados or some other Caribbean port, ship captains sold enslaved people at scramble sales, or auctions, to plantation owners for the highest possible price, usually without concern for preserving family ties. During the entire 350 years of importation, some forty thousand ships brought over as many as eight to ten million black slaves!

One of the very few slaves who could write later recounted his reaction to living in a slave ship:

> The first object which saluted my eyes when I arrived on the coast was the sea, and a slaveship which was then riding at anchor and waiting for its cargo. These filled me with astonishment, which was soon converted into terror when I was carried on board. I was immediately handled and tossed up to see if I were sound by some of the crew, and I was now persuaded that I had gotten into a world of bad spirits and that they were going to kill me. . . . Indeed such were the horrors of my views and fears at the moment, that, if ten thousand worlds had been my own, I would have freely parted with them all to have exchanged my condition with that of the meanest slave in my country. When I looked round the ship and saw a large furnace or copper boiling and a multitude of black people of every description chained together, every one of their countenances expressing dejection and sorrow, I no longer doubted of my fate; and quite overpowered with horror and anguish, I fell motionless on the deck and fainted. . . . Soon after this the blacks who brought me on board went off, and left me abandoned to despair.[25]

---

23. Anstey, *Atlantic Slave Trade and British Abolition*, 34–37.
24. An African Merchant [John Peter Demarin], *A Treatise upon the Trade from Great Britain to Africa*, 7, as cited in Anstey, *Atlantic Slave Trade*, 36–37.
25. Edwards, *Equiano's Travels*, 25–26, as cited in Anstey, *Atlantic Slave Trade*, 27–28.

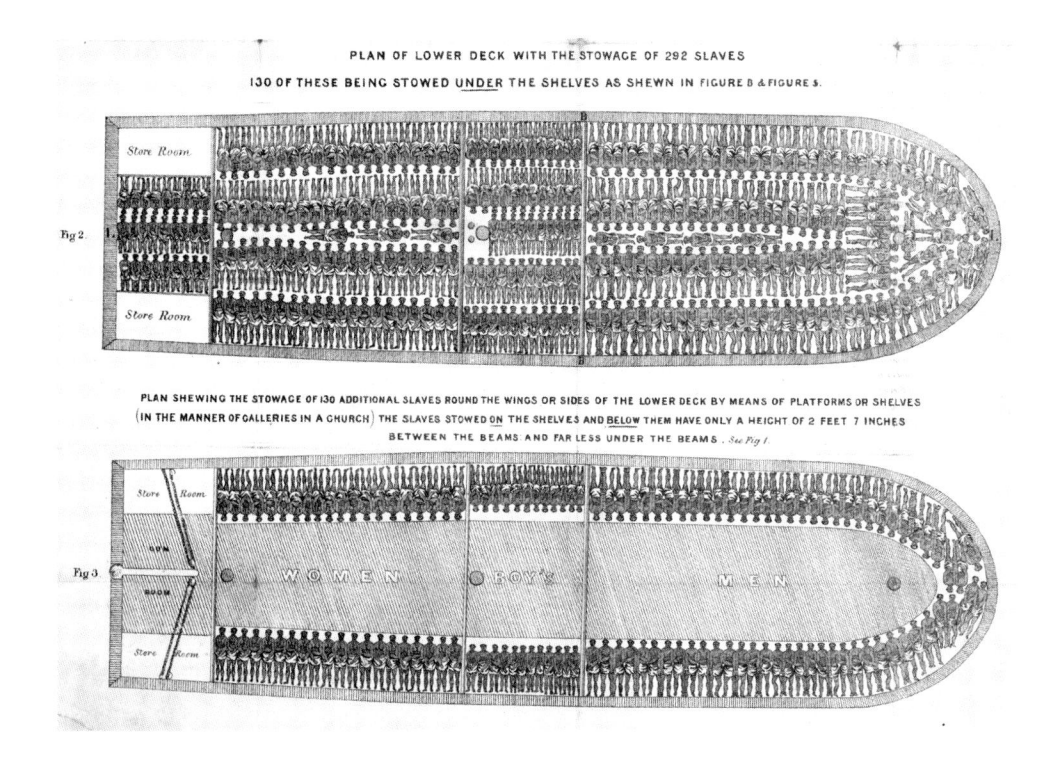

Atlantic slave-trade ship. *Stowage of the British Slave Ship Brookes under the Regulated Slave Trade Act of 1788*, published by the Plymouth Chapter of the Society for Effecting the Abolition of the Slave Trade.

And if Britain's House of Commons Subcommittee reports are to be believed, some atrocities border on the incredible, as described in the following 1764 account by one crew member:

> What were the circumstances of this child's ill-treatment? The child took sulk and would not eat. . . . The captain took the child up in his hand, and flogged it with the cat. Do you remember anything more about this child? Yes; the child had swelled feet; the captain desired the cook to put on some water to heat to see if he could abate the swelling and it was done. He then ordered the child's feet to be put into the water, and the cook putting his finger into the water, said, "Sir, it is too hot." The captain said, "Damn it, never mind it, put the feet in," and so doing the skin and nails came off, and he got some sweet oil and cloths and wrapped round the feet in order to take the fire out of them; and I myself bathed the feet with oil, and wrapped cloths around; and laying the child on the quarter deck in the afternoon at mess time, I gave the child some victuals, but it would not eat; the captain took the child up again, and flogged it, and said, "Damn you, I will make you eat," and so he continued in that way for four or five days at mess time, when the child would not eat, and flogged it, and he tied a log of mango, eighteen or twenty inches long,

and about twelve or thirteen pound weight, to the child by a string round its neck. The last time he took the child up and flogged it, and let it drop out of his hands, "Damn you (says he) I will make you eat, or I will be the death of you;" and in three quarters of an hour after that the child died. He would not suffer any of the people that were on the quarter deck to heave the child overboard, but he called the mother of the child to heave it overboard. She was not willing to do so, and I think he flogged her; but I am sure that he beat her in some way for refusing to throw the child overboard; at last he made her take the child up, and she took it in her hand, and went to the ship's side, holding her head on one side, because she would not see the child go out of her hand, and she dropped the child overboard. She seemed to be very sorry, and cried for several hours.[26]

Wilberforce was not the first to decry the sordid spectacle of the slave trade. A groundswell of opposition had been developing for decades. Samuel Johnson, Charles Montesquieu, John Wesley, William Paley, Edmund Burke, Adam Smith, Jean-Jacques Rousseau, François-Marie Arouet (Voltaire), and scores of other eighteenth-century writers, philosophers, and religionists were adamantly opposed to it. Leaders of the French Revolution also roundly condemned slavery as a vicious attack on human rights and staunchly criticized the Roman Catholic Church for idly standing by in quiet sanction of a human abomination.

Most scholars agree, however, that the practice was so ensconced in the popular mind, so highly profitable to British and European colonial interests, so defended by various religionists as a decree of God and sanctioned by biblical slavery that only a well-financed, highly sustained, and inspired movement of widespread popular reform could ever discredit and destroy it. The Crown was too complacent, and the Church of England was ill-disposed to take on the fight, as were also the universities and capitalists. The labor movement led by William Cobbett was too busy with its own agenda (see chapter 7). As long as other European powers and America profited therefrom, why shouldn't England? To abolish the slave trade would cause undue economic hardship to port cities all over Great Britain. The trade's stout defenders, most often Tories and astute businessmen, increasingly articulated their concerns in direct proportion to the rising chorus of their critics. Thus, it would take nothing less than a nationwide religious crusade to dislodge the slave trade—which is precisely what happened.

Even before his conversion to evangelical Christianity, Wilberforce had been schooled in the inhumanities of the slave trade. Reverend Newton had seen to that. But Wilberforce was also greatly affected by James Ramsay's disturbingly frank and critical *Essay on the Treatment . . . of Slaves in the British Sugar Colonies*.[27] When Wilberforce began his antislavery efforts in earnest in 1787, he remarked, "I confess to you . . . so enormous, so dreadful, so

---

26. A crew member, "Britain's House of Commons Subcommittee Report," as cited in Anstey, *Atlantic Slave Trade*, 33.
27. Ramsey, *Essay on the Treatment . . . of Slaves*.

irremediable did its wickedness appear, that my own mind was completely made up for the abolition."[28]

The coalition for change and reform began in 1790 with the Clapham Sect (Clapham was a small suburb of London), made up of such leading and influential evangelical Christians as Wilberforce (MP), Henry Thornton (MP) (1760–1815), the Reverend John Venn, Charles Grant, Isaac Milner, Zachary Macaulay (1768–1839), Thomas Babbington, Lord Teignmouth, and Hannah More. The Clapham Sect became a formidable agent for improving society in many ways but took initial and special aim at slavery. Christ died for *all* humankind, they asserted, and his Atonement applied to all. Because he came to free humankind from spiritual bondage, how could physical bondage ever be biblically condoned? And with the same fervency with which many believed they had been saved from their own shackles of sin, so they would now attack the shackles of human slavery at whatever the cost to personal fame or reputation. If slavery's defenders drew on the Old Testament for support, the evangelical Christian drew upon the New Testament to denounce it. And while some may disagree that religion was the driving force behind British abolitionism, it was, as one of the foremost scholars on the slave trade put it, "precisely because of [Wilberforce's] predominantly spiritual concern that he was so sensitive to the slavery issue." These evangelical Christians came to see a "superintending Providence," a kind of urgent, ever-intensifying "continuing divine revelation" from a God intent on change. And they believed ardently, as did the Reverend Newton, that England would forever stand condemned of God until and unless this curse was lifted.[29]

To the work of the Clapham Sect must be added that of another powerful religious influence—the Society of Friends, better known as the Quakers. Although in 1806 there were only some fifty thousand Quakers then living in England and another forty thousand in the United States (mostly in Pennsylvania), their moral influence and reputation for integrity, equality, and fairness far outweighed their numbers. Believing in true brotherly love and Christian charity and piety and opposed to war and conflict, the Quakers believed that all men were created equal and that slavery was an immoral affront to God. Led by such leaders as Anthony Benezet (1713–84) and John Woolman (1720–72), the Quakers had begun attacking slavery as early as 1750. Perhaps their greatest role was one of adding an early and deeply moral conscience and inspiration to the crusade.

Religious arguments alone, however, could hardly have turned the tide. There were also changing political and economic factors at play that an astute Wilberforce, situated as he was as a close friend of Pitt and as an ever more highly respected member of Parliament, could see and understand and use to full advantage. The campaign for abolition lasted for twenty years (1787–1807) before culminating in the passage of the Abolition Act in 1807. The fundamental reasons for its success may be attributed to the following: (1) publicity and the power of the press; (2) a highly successful grassroots organization; (3) intensive research

---

28. Belmonte, *William Wilberforce*, 109.
29. Anstey, *Atlantic Slave Trade*, 191, 198.

into the abuses of the trade; and above all (4) Wilberforce's powerful and winsome personality, his reputation for integrity, and his ever increasing popularity among the rich, powerful, and influential classes of society. Religious but not preachy, converted but warmly sociable, secure in his faith but a friend to all, Wilberforce spoke the language of the Bible and of the barroom equally well.

Poets and pamphleteers, printers and publishers lent their talents to publicizing the wrongs of slavery. Of all these many writers, none was as widely read, respected, and revered as Hannah More, arguably more popular than William Wordsworth, Samuel T. Coleridge, or Sir Walter Scott, at least for a time. More was the primary pamphleteer and moralist of the age, and in her poem "The Slave Trade," published in 1787, she captured the injustices of slavery as perhaps none of her colleagues could have ever done. Appealing to the British sense of fair play and love of liberty, she quietly rallied millions to abolition's banner as is perhaps most keenly felt in her poem "The Slave Trade," from *Thoughts on the Importance of the Manners of the Great to General Society*.

"The Slave Trade"
. . . Perish the illiberal thought which would debase
The native genius of the sable race!
Perish the proud philosophy, which sought
To rob them of the powers of equal thought!
Does then the immortal principle within
Change with the casual colour of a skin?
Does matter govern spirit? or is mind
Degraded by the form to which 'tis join'd?
No, they have heads to think, and hearts to feel,
And souls to act, with firm though erring zeal,
For they have keen affections, kind desires,
Love strong as death, and active patriot fires.

. . . Whene'er to Africa's shores I turn my eyes,
Horrors of deepest, deadliest guilt arise;
I see, by more than fancy's mirror shown,
The burning village, and the blazing town:
See the dire victim torn from social life
The shrieking babe, the agonizing wife;
She, wretch forlorn! is dragged by hostile hands,
To distant tyrants sold, in distant lands!
Transmitted miseries, and successive chains,
The sole sad heritage her child obtains!

> . . . What wrongs, what injuries, does oppression plead
> To smooth the crime and sanctify the deed?
> What strange offence, what aggravated sin?
> They stand convicted—of a darker skin!
>
> . . . Though dark and savage, ignorant and blind,
> They claim the common privilege of kind;
> Let malice strip them of each other plea,
> They still are men, and men should still be free.
>
> . . . Shall Britain, where the soul of freedom reigns,
> Forge chains for others she herself disdains?
> Forbid it, Heaven! O let the nations know
> The liberty she loves she will bestow;
> Not to herself the glorious gift confined
> She spreads the blessing wide as humankind;
> And, scorning narrow views of time and place,
> Bids all be free in earth's extended space.[30]

While the writings of Hannah More, Reverend Newton, Thomas Clarkson, Anthony Benezet, William Cowper ("The Negro Complaint," 1788), and John Wesley (*Thoughts upon Slavery*, 1774) were becoming ever more popular in the broadways of thought, the careful organization of the abolitionist campaign at the town and village level—the capillaries of society—was likewise critical to its success. Often borrowing from Methodist organizations and their successes, local abolition committees (usually led by Quakers and evangelical Christians) promoted the cause through correspondents, informal meetings, house visits, speaking tours, local petitions, and the active dissemination of abolitionist literature. Gradually the very conscience of the nation became tormented.

Yet for all of this, there was persistently strong opposition to the abolitionist movement, and a cacophony of arguments was raised against it. The propertied and capitalist classes of society, so well represented in the Tory Party, maintained that slavery was in the best economic interests of western England, particularly for such port cities as Bristol, Liverpool, and Lancashire. They argued that chimney sweeps and dairymaids were treated far worse than slaves; that Africa was overpopulated; that many more blacks suffered and were butchered to death in the Congo than in the plantations of the Caribbean; that if England unilaterally withdrew from the trade, far less principled American, French, and Spanish slave interests would predominate and ruin the British colonies; and that with the Napoleonic Wars about to break out, there were more important matters to debate. Even if the abolitionist crusade was morally right, this was no time for change.[31]

---

30. In the *Miscellaneous Works of Hannah More*, 1:209–11.
31. Anstey, *The Atlantic Slave Trade*, 303.

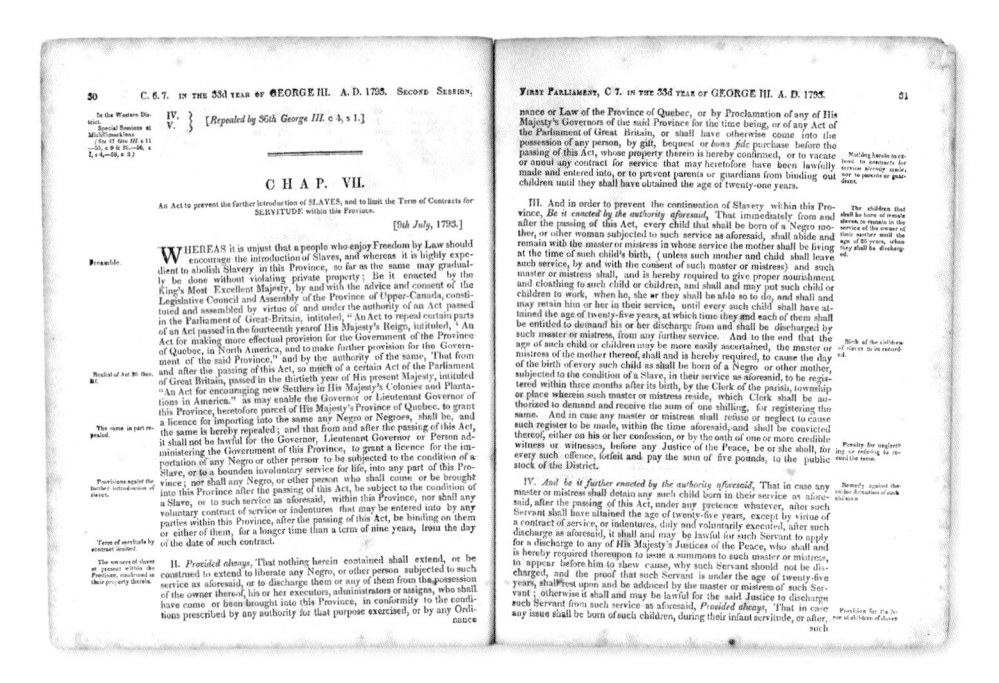

An Act to Prevent the Further Introduction of Slaves and to Limit the Term of Contracts for Servitude within This Province, Legislative Assembly of Upper Canada.

Because of these and related reasons, the abolitionist movement stalled time after time. Hard-liners against Napoléon branded the abolitionists, including Wilberforce and the Whigs, as pro-French revolutionaries for wanting to weaken the labor force of British colonies for the benefit of France. When word arrived of a Nat Turner–like slave uprising and bloody rebellion on the British isles of Grenada, Dominica, and St. Vincent in 1795 in which slaves killed many of their white masters, the movement almost failed entirely. Time after time Wilberforce tabled a bill for abolition—often to the embarrassment of his fellow Tories—only to see it defeated by significant majorities.

However, with French and Spanish privateers importing West Indian sugar at much cheaper prices than the English colonies could ever sell it for, with Napoléon's European embargo making English trade on the continent ever more difficult, and with the Tory defeat in 1806, the abolitionist campaign began to catch its stride. The final death knell of the pro-slavery economic argument may well have been Lord Horatio Nelson's (1758–1805) stunning victory at Trafalgar in 1805 and the subsequent British naval mastery of the seas. Why continue to use British slave ships to supply labor to French and Spanish colonial possessions in Central and South America? In a word, why abet the enemy?

When the ultimate passage of the Foreign Slave Trade Bill finally occurred in a cheering House of Commons on 23 February 1807, it came by "a more overwhelming" vote than anyone could have ever predicted—283 to 16—a moral, humanitarian, and religious victory over the long combined forces of economic and political self-interest. Exactly one month later, the bill passed the House of Lords by a vote of 100 to 34 and received royal assent on 25 March with the act taking effect on 1 May 1807. A long, dark night had finally come to an end. The abolition of the British slave trade eventually proved the death knell for slavery in Britain and in all its colonies. Twenty-six years later, another bill was passed—the Slavery Abolition Act of 1833—that freed over eight hundred thousand slaves and effectively abolished slavery forever in the British Empire.

BISHOP IN PETTICOATS: HANNAH MORE

While Wilberforce was changing attitudes in the House of Commons, Hannah More was reaching the houses of commoners all over Britain. Born in Stapleton in 1745 to a strong-willed Protestant schoolmaster father who taught in poor country districts near Bristol in west England, More was the fourth of five sisters, all of whom were well educated and groomed to become teachers themselves. Believing that women should be educated beyond the traditional domestic roles, her oldest sister, Mary, began a very successful boarding school in Bristol in 1758 for girls of wealthy families and invited the likes of Charles and John Wesley, the astronomer James Ferguson, and William Wilberforce to come and lecture. "The Sisterhood," as the More sisters came to be known, were "men's women" in that they were strong-minded, energetic, deeply religious, and committed to educating young women and young men.[32]

Like her sisters, Hannah never married, so dedicated were they to their work and to one another. However, her wealthy onetime fiancé, Edward Turner (1788–1837), set up an annuity for her of £200 as a way of extricating himself from the engagement, helping finance her later writing career. Her first love was the theater, and in the 1770s, Bristol, then rich in wealth from the overseas triangular trade, was the busiest theater city outside of London. At age sixteen Hannah wrote her first play, *The Search after Happiness: A Pastoral Drama*" (1773), a work that showed her early interests in promoting Christian virtues and innocent amusements, especially among young women. Before long, she took to writing tragedies (*The Inflexible Captive*

Mrs. Hannah More, Popular Graphic Arts.

---

32. Hopkins, *Hannah More and Her Circle*, 25.

[1775], *Percy, A Tragedy* [1777], and more complex plots), leading her to London, where she became an enthusiastic admirer of the immensely popular David Garrick (1717–79), whom many considered the greatest actor of his age. She even wrote "Ode to Dragon" as a poetic tribute to Garrick upon his 1777 retirement from the stage. While in London she became acquainted with Dr. Samuel Johnson (1709–84), the renowned writer and critic, who favored her work. He called her "the most powerful versificatrix" in England and encouraged her to pursue a literary and theatrical career.[33] She had other admirers as well—the critic Horace Walpole (1717–97), the historian Edward Gibbon (1796–1862), and the statesman Edmund Burke (1729–97). Even Coleridge dedicated one of his plays to her, and John Wesley encouraged her in her literary pursuits.

Garrick's death in 1778 devastated the young poet and playwright, and though she remained in contact with Mrs. Eva Garrick, More "gradually turned against the stage" and the oftentimes sordid living of many in the theater business, convinced that there were better avenues for her increasingly moralistic and deep-toned religious convictions.[34] As one of her recent biographers put it, she realized that "the theater was ineffective in propagating godliness."[35]

Returning to live and work with her three sisters (Elizabeth, Mary, and Martha More), she resumed teaching in the country schools near Bristol, but with a difference from before. Following the example of Robert Raikes (1736–1811) of Gloucester, who had founded the nondenominational Sunday School movement in 1780, she and her sister Martha (1747–1819) began their Cheddar school in October 1789 with financial backing from Wilberforce and other Clapham reformers. Raikes's amazingly successful and rapidly expanding system of Sunday Schools, which were usually held in homes or barns on Sunday afternoons or evenings, taught destitute boys and girls how to read by studying from the Bible and singing gospel hymns, how to dress in clean clothes, and how to learn to be honest and morally upright. It was a grassroots, primarily evangelical movement that struck an extremely responsive chord all over Great Britain.[36] It stirred the imagination of educators like the Mores while embarrassing and frustrating the established but out-of-touch church that, once again misreading the needs of the people, saw it all as little less than Methodist propaganda.

The Cheddar school represented a blended form of secular and religious education and was aimed primarily at educating poor children with financial support of the lords of the manor and of others who had means. Held on Sundays as a Sunday School and on some

---

33. Brown, *Fathers of the Victorians*, 76–77.
34. Hopkins, *Hannah More*, 102–3.
35. Ford, *Hannah More*, 43.
36. Royle, "Evangelicals and Education," in Wolffe, *Evangelical Faith and Public Zeal*, 121. In 1800 the number of students enrolled in British Sunday Schools barely reached 200,000. By 1851 there were over two million, and by 1881 there were 5.7 million! The Sunday School movement later inspired the rise of elementary schools after 1840. Richard Ballantyne (1817–98), a Scottish convert, founded the Sunday School of The Church of Jesus Christ of Latter-day Saints in December 1848 and which continues to the present time.

weeknights for training in various literary skills, personal behavior, domestic arts, and more, the Cheddar school proved highly popular and soon expanded into the nearby coal-mining districts. Some of the weekday classes were held to teach mothers how to read as well as to instruct them in knitting, sewing, and other domestic skills.

Committed to remaining steadfastly single, Hannah adhered to a very rigid, almost puritan form of personal conduct, including strict Sabbath observance, no playing cards, no dancing, strict temperance, a concentrated study of the scriptures and little else, and a carefully self-scrutinized form of individual obedience. As she once phrased it, "My Bible has been meat, drink and company to me."[37]

Hannah More's religious convictions were deeply rooted in her belief in the Fall of Adam and the need for Christ as a personal Savior. In a letter she wrote in 1820 she said:

> I cannot conceive that the most enchanting beauties of nature, or the most splendid production of the fine arts, have any necessary connection with religion. . . . Adam sinned in a garden too beautiful for us to have any conception of it. . . . The distinctive nature of Christianity [means] a deep and abiding sense in the heart of our fallen nature; of our actual and personal sinfulness; of our low state, but for the redemption wrought for us by Jesus Christ; and of our universal necessity of a change of heart and the connection that this change can only be effected by the influence of the Holy Spirit.[38]

Religious commitment meant far more to her than merely accepting Christ—it meant consistently living a life of personal holiness and consecration. "The two great principles on which our salvation must be founded are faith and holiness; faith, without which it is impossible to please God, and holiness, without which no man can see the Lord."[39] Given to severe headaches and repeated bouts of depression, Hannah retreated into the life of a virtual religious hypochondriac. Keeping detailed notes of all her sins and shortcomings, "she was never sure that she had won what she passionately desired—God's complete approval."[40]

Committed to humanitarian causes, Hannah gravitated toward the Clapham Sect and the rapidly expanding evangelical and antislavery movement. Aware of her talents as a writer, Wilberforce and the Anglican bishop of London and private chaplain to King George III, Beilby Porteus (1731–1809), urged her to get out of herself and write popular moralistic stories and uplifting ballads to support the aims of the Clapham Sect. Such was the beginning of her early tract writing that soon mushroomed into scores of inexpensive Repository Tracts, which sold for mere shillings with a reading audience soon in the millions. By 1795 "the great Evangelical propagandist," as she was coming to be known, was writing a new tract every month, published on coarse brown paper with lively woodcuts, the likes of which

---

37. More, *The Shepherd of Salisbury Plain*, 15.
38. Hannah More to Mr. and Mrs. Huber, 1820. In Roberts, *Memories of the Life and Correspondence of Mrs. Hannah More*, 4:139.
39. Roberts, *Memories*, 4:147.
40. Hopkins, *Hannah More*, 199.

included *Village Politics, by Will Chip, a Country Carpenter*; *The History of Idle Jack Brown*; *The Story of Sinful Sally*; and by far her best-known work, *The Shepherd of Salisbury Plain*, based on a true character (which sold two million copies in four years!). In just three years' time, she wrote thirty-nine Repository Tracts, becoming both rich and famous in the process.

She also found time to write several popular books of essays of similar tone and purpose, including *Thoughts on the Importance of the Manners of the Great and General Society* (1788), *An Estimate of the Religion of the Fashionable World* (1790), *Hints for Forming the Character of a Young Princess* (1805), and her most famous book and only novel, *Coelebs in Search of a Wife* (1809), an essay on how to choose a good wife, which went through twelve editions its first year. Deeply religious, platitudinous, and highly moralistic in tone, her writings established her reputation as "the most greatly respected woman of the Christian world."[41]

Her book *Thoughts on the Importance of Manners*, which appeared in seven editions in one year, took special aim at the rich and powerful classes of society, "the good kind of people" who were "the makers of manners," and gently admonished them in how to live true Christian lives and help the less privileged to do the same. "Believe and forgive me," she pleaded, "reformation must begin with the great or it will never be effectual."[42]

If her essays took aim at the rich, her tracts were designed in large part to convince the poor to find better ways to live than to criticize the rich and wish for a better world. "Be honest, be industrious—Anything is better than idleness, sir." "Pay down your debts, count your blessings, submit to the lot God has appointed you, and be content with all that you have save your sins." As her poor Shepherd on Salisbury Plain put it to the rich nobleman: "My cottage is a palace!" and "I have health, peace, and liberty, and no man maketh me afraid." "God is pleased to contrive to make things more equal than we poor, ignorant, short-sighted creatures are apt to think."[43]

More's fabulously popular *The Importance of Manners* called not just for improving manners but also for acquiring a new religious disposition. While complimenting on the one hand—"A good spirit seems to be at work. . . . We have a pious King; a wise and virtuous [prime] minister, very many respectable . . . clergy," and "an increasing desire to instruct the poor"—she could be blisteringly critical on the other: "May I venture to be a little paradoxical," she asked while rebuking the "shining counterfeit" of many doing good but not really changing. "Is it not almost ridiculous to observe the zeal we have for doing good at a distance, while we neglect the little, obvious, every day domestic duties?"[44] "What is morally wrong can never be politically right," she chided. "Reformation must begin with the great, or it will never be effectual. Their example is the fountain whence the vulgar draw their habits,

---

41. Brown, *Fathers of the Victorians*, 98.
42. Brown, *Fathers of the Victorians*, 101.
43. More, *'Tis All for the Best*, in *The Shepherd of Salisbury Plain and Other Narratives*, 45, 50, 52.
44. More, *'Tis All for the Best*, in *The Shepherd of Salisbury Plain and Other Narratives*, 45, 50, 52.

actions and characters. To expect to reform the poor while the opulent are corrupt, is to throw odours into the stream while the springs are poisoned."[45]

In her *Estimate of the Religion of the Fashionable World*, More showed herself far more than a poet or a storyteller or admonisher for good, but a highly intelligent defender of Christianity. Scolding those whose "practical irreligion" saw Christianity as merely a perfect system of morals, while they deny its divine authority," she wrote: "As noble as the principle itself is, [it] has engendered a dangerous notion, that all error is innocent. Whether it be owing to this, or to whatever other cause, it is certain that the discriminating features of the Christian religion are every day growing into less repute; and it is become the fashion, even among the better sort, to evade, to lower, or to generalize, its most distinguishing peculiarities."[46]

Believing there was little of Christ in the Christianity of her day, she asserted that Christianity was more than merely doing good: "It is a disposition, a habit, a temper; it is not a name, but a nature."[47] Strict obedience, whether keeping the Sabbath holy or daily reading the scriptures, is what brings "perfect freedom." "It is a folly to talk of being too holy, too strict, or too good," any more than it is to be "too wise, too strong, or too healthy," for the heart must change. To More, Christianity was all-encompassing, a religion that "must be embraced entirely, if it be received at all." If it is to be anything, "we must allow it to be everything."[48]

What explains More's meteoric rise in popularity? To answer this question is to capture the prevailing mood of contemporary English society. England was a religious country, anxious to get more religion than the established church knew how to give. Most people were the rural poor and the uneducated and identified more with her plain and powerful stories and parables than they did with the erudite and distant sermon. Having seen firsthand the sufferings of the poor, More spoke to their poverty, their family conditions, their longings—in a word, she understood them.

While calling on the rich to do much more to provide for the poor, she also criticized the lower classes for their greediness, for regarding appearances too much, for even thinking of revolting against the system—inviting them to be happy and content with what God has provided and look to a better world hereafter. "To fear God and honour the King—to meddle not with them who are given to change—To not speak evil of dignitaries—to render honour to whom honour is due."[49] Above all, More preached with paper and pen that "sin is the great cause and source of every existing evil," that "sin is a greater evil than poverty, that personal reformation, not political revolution, was all that most mattered."[50] Her lively,

---

45. More, *Importance of Manners*, 293.
46. More, *Estimate of the Religion of the Fashionable World*, in *Miscellaneous Works of Hannah More*, 1:302.
47. More, *Fashionable World*, 306.
48. More, *Fashionable World*, 333–34.
49. From *The Shepherd of Salisbury Plain*, as cited in Brown, *Fathers of the Victorians*, 144.
50. Brown, *Fathers of the Victorians*, 155.

simple, and persuasive style of writing inspired many readers, especially women, to improve their literacy and education while tending the hearth and home. Although she was more of a religious family traditionalist than many modern feminist scholars might prefer, More was nevertheless ahead of her time as an educator, religious spokeswoman, and philanthropist.

Yet there was more to Hannah More's writing than religion: not a political agitator, she nonetheless had very strong economic, political, and patriotic convictions. She believed the gentry had a God-given duty to look after the worthy poor, that government had no social responsibilities to feed the poor, and that God, who knows best, will provide in his own time and way. She despised the French Revolution and Napoléon's growing sinister shadow, Tom Paine's *Rights of Man* and the anti-British aims of the recent American Revolution, and the secular humanitarian Robert Owen.[51]

More staunchly believed that British royalty was a God-given institution despite its flaws. Such a stance explains her popularity with even the upper classes. Likewise, she feared that the rising trade union and democratic movements and wrenching agricultural changes in England would destroy an established and trusted way of life. In her mind, there was no pressing need for a social or political gospel that emphasized widespread societal improvements. What was most needed was changing one's individual life for the better through daily acts of strictly chaste and righteous living: "A man can't talk like a saint and live like a sinner."[52] She urged discontent with personal sins more than society's problems and finding happiness in personal reformation, not public revolution. Outliving all her sisters, More spent her declining years at Barley Wood in the Mendy's Hills and later in Clifton, where her home became a shrine for thousands of admirers who came from all over Britain, the Continent, and North America. Until the end, she was an inveterate letter writer, and copies of her correspondence are now scattered in libraries and archives all over the Western world. Disposing of most of her fortune to various charities and religious societies, she died 7 September 1833 at the age of eighty-eight and was buried with her sisters in Wrington churchyard.[53]

---

51 Thomas Paine (1737–1809), an Englishman who moved to America to save his life, was a radical critic of establishment politics and religion. His essays *Common Sense* (1776), *The Rights of Man* (1791), and *The Age of Reason* (1794/95) rejected revealed religion and Christianity and became "major works of popular atheism." His dream of a radically democratic state was too much for an England that still maintained an established church. Royle, "Secularists and Rationalists," 407.

   Robert Owen (1771–1858) of Scotland was a benevolent factory master who believed in education reform and fairer working conditions for the working class. Regarding himself as "the prophet of the new age," Owen was a deist, a socialist, and a rationalist thinker who gave little regard to Christianity. He believed that if ever a new world order or millennium were to come, it would be built by man, human reason, and humanitarianism, not by the return of a savior. Royle, "Secularists and Rationalists," 408 (see chapter 7 herein).

52. More, *Religion of the Fashionable World*, 329.
53. M. K. Smith, "Hannah More: Sunday Schools, Education and Youth Work," in *The Encyclopedia of Informal Education*.

REAL CHRISTIANITY

One year before the appearance of More's *Importance of Manners*, Wilberforce published his own Christian manifesto titled *A Practical View of the Prevailing Religious System of Professed Christians in the Higher and Middle Classes in the Country, Contrasted with Real Christianity* (1797). An enduring classic in modern Christian literature, *Real Christianity* is a stirring, book-length essay on deep-seated, evangelical Christian faith and a thoroughly scripture-based invitation—and warning—to the British upper classes to come unto Christ and change their worldly ways. Reminiscent of Martin Luther's "Here I Stand" declaration over two centuries before, and Coleridge's later *Aids to Reflection*, *Real Christianity* was Wilberforce's personal declaration of belief. Written between 1789 and 1797 while Wilberforce was a sitting member of Parliament, *Real Christianity* might have branded a lesser man as a Christian do-gooder and mere moralistic preacher. Instead, the book was quickly revered as a reflection of the highly respected character of the author and, as such, a work to be seriously regarded. As England's most esteemed humanitarian in the war against the slave trade, child labor, and the exploitation of women in the work force, Wilberforce was a highly respected figure. Unlike More or even Wesley, Wilberforce was more intellectually and artistically in the world than out of it, more connected to the rich and the socially influential, and thus spoke with a powerful credibility other religionists could not then feign to obtain.

In some superficial ways, Wilberforce echoed More's writings. He, too, criticized Sabbath breakers, the debauchery of the theater, the writing of corrupt and evil novels, and other outward manifestations of sin. Yet, as a patron of the arts (he had cofounded the National Galleries), Wilberforce was no narrow-minded religious zealot. While decrying mere "nominal," "geographic," and "general" Christians (a nation Christian in name only), Wilberforce probed deeper than had Hannah More in deciphering the true nature of what he called "a religion of motives," a "radical or essential Christianity." While complimenting royalty and the influential classes for their benevolence and good desires, he, like Coleridge, believed that most people "advance principles and maintain opinions altogether opposite to the genius

Memorial to William Wilberforce, by Samuel Joseph.

and character of Christianity" and that too many neglected the Bible and turned from the gospel "as a thing of no estimation."[54]

His work emphasized four principal elements: the root cause of societal decay, the essential Christian solution, a call for voluntary change and a whole-scale reformation, and finally, a warning. The primary reason for England's malaise, or "fatal malignancy" as he viewed it, was the sin of pride, which he defined as "a disposition in each individual to make self the grand centre and end of his desires and enjoyments."[55] To have lost the sense of guilt and the evil of sin and its malignancy was sin enough, but to revel and rebel in "that proud self-complacency so apt to grow upon the human heart" was humanity's great weakness.[56] In words later echoed by twentieth-century writer C. S. Lewis (1898–1963), Wilberforce believed that "we do not set ourselves in earnest to the work of self-examination." And humility, the "vital principle of Christianity, [is] its only antidote."[57] Pride inoculated one from changing, and those guilty of it viewed Christianity as nothing more than "a cold compilation of restraints and prohibitions, . . . a set of penal statutes" that "stressed external actions rather than the habits of the mind."[58] Because of pride, "a system of decent selfishness is avowedly established" and the sensual pleasures predominate. He observed that England's main desire was "to multiply the comforts of affluence, to provide for the gratification of appetite, to [have] . . . magnificent houses, grand equipages, high and fashionable connexions [sic]." England's heart is "set on these things."[59] Pride, he argued, is the very opposite of love, whereas humility "will prevent a thousand difficulties," and it "changes all to gold."[60]

Thus the "main object and chief concern of Christianity" was "to root out our national selfishness,"[61] to counter it with benevolence, moderation, humility, and meekness. This solution and societal change would come not by conforming to outward rules and laws but by confirming the affections of the fallen heart on Jesus Christ, the "blessed Savior" and "Redeemer." "For all our moral superiority, . . . we are altogether indebted to the unmerited goodness of God"[62] and his "undeserved grace."[63] Through the "atoning sacrifice" of Jesus Christ and his death at the cross, "Christianity became far more than a creed, a rational system of ethics or morality, but the perfect contrast to Epicurean selfishness, . . . stoical pride, . . . and cynical brutality."[64]

---

54. Wilberforce, *Real Christianity*, 9–14.
55. Wilberforce, *Real Christianity*, 337.
56. Wilberforce, *Practical View*, 137.
57. Wilberforce, *Real Christianity*, 251, 375.
58. Wilberforce, *Real Christianity*, 156, 159.
59. Wilberforce, *Real Christianity*, 144, 147.
60. Wilberforce, *Real Christianity*, 376–77.
61. Wilberforce, *Real Christianity*, 340.
62. Wilberforce, *Real Christianity*, 180.
63. Wilberforce, *Real Christianity*, 253.
64. Wilberforce, *Real Christianity*, 208.

To all the above admonitions, he sounded this note of warning: if England and its higher classes in particular do not reform and repent, no amount of military or financial strength will ever save her. A sterling patriot, Wilberforce nonetheless said, "My only solid hopes for the well-being of my country depend not so much on her fleets and armies, not so much on the wisdom of her rulers, or the spirit of her people, as on the persuasions that she still contains many who love and obey the Gospel of Christ." "We bear upon us too plainly the marks of a declining empire," and "God will be disposed to favour the nation to which his servants belong."[65] England must no longer be Christian in name only. "Every effort should be used to raise the depressed tone of public morals" or else a France-like state of "moral deprivation" will ensue.[66] Without such changes, the time will soon come, he warned, "when Christianity will be almost as openly disavowed in the language, as in fact it is already supposed to have disappeared from the conduct of men; when infidelity will be held to be the necessary appendage of a man of fashion and to behave will be deemed the indication of a feeble mind and a contracted understanding."[67]

Of all the important accomplishments of our age of 1820, few were as momentous as the abolition of the British slave trade and, in its wake, the eradication of slavery within the British Empire. Against insuperable odds, William Wilberforce, Hannah More, and a host of other humanitarian leaders successfully waged a war against prejudice, bigotry, economic disparity, and human degradation in its meanest expressions. Theirs was a victory for the ages, and it characterized the strivings and struggles of the period of our study for a better world. And in the process, they also stamped on the coming Victorian age an expectation of a new order of Christian living, a change of heart and mind that far transcended the commonplace and the ordinary.

In retrospect, one has to wonder how The Church of Jesus Christ of Latter-day Saints could ever have made the inroads it did in Great Britain in the late 1830s and early 1840s without John Wesley's religious preparation among the poorer classes of society. For it is a well-known fact that a majority of its early converts were Methodists of one kind or another, and many were discontent with their social and ecomonic lot in a rapidly changing British society.

Furthermore, the untiring efforts of Wilberforce, More, and countless others toward the successful abolition of the slave trade gradually resulted in a growing spirit of emancipation, tolerance, and respect that would slowly counter long-held attitudes of pride and prejudice, even among those who considered themselves devoutly Christian.

---

65. Wilberforce, *Real Christianity*, 411.
66. Wilberforce, *Real Christianity*, 349–50.
67. Wilberforce, *Real Christianity*, 317.

Simón Bolívar. *El Libertador (Bolívar diplomático)*, Rita Matilde de la Peñuela.

EL LIBERTADOR

SIMÓN BOLÍVAR AND THE SPANISH AMERICAN INDEPENDENCE MOVEMENT

"It would be far too tedious to describe in detail . . . the labors performed by the troops of the Army of Liberation. . . . The winter on the flooded plains, the frozen peaks of the Andes, the sudden changes of climate, an army twice inured to war and in control of the best military positions of South America—these and many other obstacles we managed to overcome at Paya, Gámeza, Vargas, Boyacá and Popayán, in order to liberate in less than three months twelve provinces of New Granada."[1] So spoke Simón Bolívar, liberator of much of South America, after his 1,000-mile march with 2,500 battle-tested soldiers from Angostura, Venezuela, up the Orinoco River, and ultimately over the towering 13,000-foot Andes to Nueva Granada (present-day Colombia) in the summer of 1819. His daring campaign still stands as one of the most challenging and forbidding military expeditions of all time. As one South American historian wrote, "Other crossings of mountains may have been more adroit and of a more exemplary strategy, [but] none so audacious, so heroic and legendary."[2] Without this expedition, the ensuing Battle of Boyacá in August 1819 would never have been fought and won, and Bolívar's dream of a free and independent South America would never have come to pass. His surprising victory cleared the pathway to independence for Venezuela, New Granada, Bolivia, Ecuador, and eventually Peru.

---

1. "Message to the Congress of Angostura," 14 December 1819, in Lecuna, *Selected Writings of Bolívar*, 1:211, item 80 (hereafter *Selected Writings*).
2. J. E. Rodó, as cited in Sherwell, *Simón Bolívar*, 125.

A LIFE IN PREPARATION

Simón Bolívar y Palacios, the youngest of four children, was born in Caracas, Venezuela, on 24 July 1783. He came from a wealthy aristocratic family whose Spanish ancestry in South America extended back seven generations to an earlier Simón Bolívar who had immigrated to Venezuela in 1578. A nervous, idealistic man whose parents both died young, young Bolívar inherited his family's fortune and learned to fend for himself, to think and act independently, and to run the family ranch and plantations. From Hipólita, his childhood nurse who was an enslaved black woman, he learned compassion, fairness, and a respect for races other than his own. "I never knew any father but her," Bolívar later said of her.[3] An early tutor, Andrés Bello, who was one of South America's finest men of letters, taught him how to read and appreciate literature and the arts.

From Simón Rodríguez, his other teacher and lifelong friend, he gained an intellectual appreciation for Rousseau, Montesquieu, Voltaire, the lofty aims of the French Revolution, and the recent conquests of Napoléon. Rodríguez instilled in Bolívar an iron will and a penchant for health, hiking, and horsemanship. From him Bolívar also learned early to read voraciously, write clearly, converse intelligently, and believe in himself and his innate abilities. Years later, Bolívar referred to Rodríguez as his personal Robinson Crusoe for discovering within him oceans of self-confidence, islands of inspiration, and waves of personal motivation. He learned also to be an incessant talker. "He talked to everyone, always, anywhere, throughout his life," and this was at a time when revolution against the ruling Spanish power was becoming the table talk of all Venezuela.[4]

Although his family were Creoles, or white South Americans of European Spanish derivation, they suffered from many of the same inequities and injustices that lower classes in society were then experiencing. The rigid class system descended from the Creole to the mestizos, those with mixed white and indigenous ancestry; to the *pardos*, those with mixed white and black ancestry; to the blacks, of whom many were slaves; and to the *zambos*, who were a mixture of black and indigenous ancestry. At the bottom of the social ladder were the indigenous slave populations. They had suffered most acutely at the hands of their Spanish overseers since Hernán Cortés had defeated Montezuma and his Aztec empire in Mexico in 1521 and since Francisco Pizarro's conquest of the Incas in gold-laden Peru in 1533. Pursuing a Machiavellian policy that at first consisted of a single government over all of South America and Mexico and centered in Peru, Spanish authorities over time had established a system of viceroys in New Granada, Buenos Aires, and elsewhere throughout the continent. These agents of Spanish colonial power wielded despotic power, and their injustices and cruelty defy comprehension.[5] In Peru alone, the El Dorado of South America, Spanish

---

3. As cited in Trend, *Bolívar*, 28.
4. Rourke, *Man of Glory*, 19.
5. As of 1800, the Spanish viceroyalties in Spanish America were New Spain (the western USA and most of Central America), New Granada, Peru, Río de la Plata (consisting of much of Argentina), and Chile. Brazil was a Portuguese colony. (See map on page 210.)

authorities operated fourteen hundred gold mines, where indigenous peoples were forced to labor for months at a time as beasts of burden under the most degrading and dehumanizing circumstances. One scholar has estimated that eight million native South American natives died working in such hellholes in Peru—many were buried alive. "Oppression, violence, and arbitrariness were the only laws that ruled in [the Spanish colonies]," and whole tribes committed suicide rather than work under such oppressive circumstances.[6] Consider this consequence of resistance, as one of tens of thousands discovered in 1780:

> His wife and children, as well as his brother-in-law Bastidas, were put to death before his eyes, his tongue was cut out, and he was torn to pieces by four horses; his body was reduced to ashes and his legs and arms were sent to the towns that had revolted. His house was razed, his property confiscated, his family was declared infamous forever, and one of his brothers was sent to Spain and condemned to the galleys, where he remained thirty years. The Indians [native peoples] were deprived of their privileges, if any remained, their festivals and meetings were abolished, and it was forbidden that any one should take the title of Inca.[7]

In the century after Cortés and Pizarro, a staggering twenty million natives may have perished due to Spanish colonial inhumanity, warfare, trade in alcohol, and the importation of smallpox from Europe and yellow fever from African slaves. Peru's native populations declined by 90 percent, and Brazil's by 95 percent. "In the Caribbean, the indigenous population was virtually annihilated."[8] Little wonder that by the time of Bolívar much of the continent—including Brazil, whose Portuguese overseers were just as cruel as their Spanish counterparts—was a revolution in waiting, fueled by centuries of ensconced tyranny, malignant neglect, and unjust oppression. It was a terror that ranks with the Holocaust of the twentieth century in its demonizing inhumanity.

Through prominent business leaders and plantation owners, the Creole establishment was forced to trade its cocoa, tobacco, cotton, indigo, coffee, and other crops with only the Caracas Company, which was granted a monopoly by Madrid over almost all Venezuelan trade. While permitting a Creole aristocracy, authorities denied it opportunities for education, international travel, a free press, and even reading—in short, "denying it the privileges an aristocracy demand." Add to this volatile mix prohibitively high taxes, pervasive racial animosities, and the vagaries of a system of justice that would not guarantee due process of

---

6. Jones, *History of South America*, 75, 81. The term then in use was *encomienda*, a grant from the Spanish crown to colonists in America conferring the right to demand tribute and labor from the native populations in return for providing supposed education, Christianization, and protection.
7. Jones, *History of South America*, 83.
8. Sowell, *Conquests and Cultures*, 257.

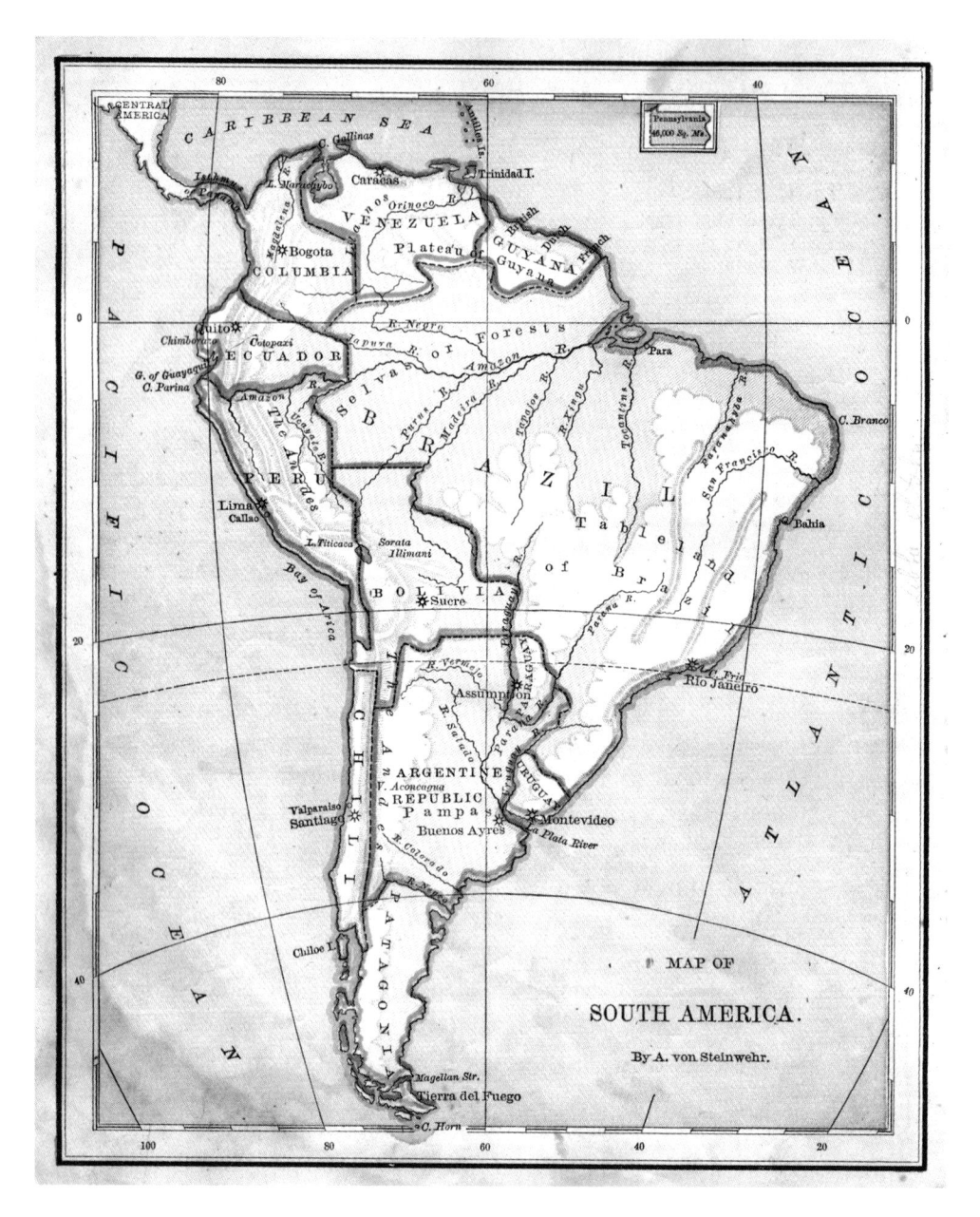

Map of South America, by A. von Steinwehr. iStock Photo by Getty Images.

law, and it is not surprising that Spain was "on a powder keg to which she herself had applied the slow match."[9]

---

9. Rourke, *Man of Glory*, 6–7.

Stirred to destroy this centuries-long Spanish oppression, the young Simón Bolívar penned the following diatribe: "The fierce Spaniard, spewed upon the shores of Colombia, proceeded to transform Nature's loveliest of territories into a vast and odious empire of cruelty and plunder. . . . He signalized his entrance into the New World by death and desolation. He annihilated the original inhabitants, and, when his raging fury found no others left to destroy, he turned upon his own sons whom he had brought forth in the land that he had usurped. . . . Would that we were not compelled by cruel necessity to exterminate these foul murderers!"[10]

However, it would have to be a controlled and careful revolution. The Creoles, while sympathetic, feared the disruption of commerce and trade and the potential for slave insurrections if the taste of freedom took hold too quickly. And what of retribution from Spain if the revolution failed? Who, then, would pay the price? Preserving the status quo may not have been desirable, but it was at least the easy way, safe and known.

As for the church, its sympathies were conservative and distinctly loyalist. The Jesuits, especially, were critical of revolutionary talk, and some of them were believed to double as spies for the Spanish viceroyalties. While Bolívar himself was more a skeptic than an atheist, more a deist than a Christian, he always attended mass but was at best a guarded Catholic. Over time, he came to regard the church as a rapacious agent of the old regime and thus became a deist, disinclined toward theology and bent more toward the study of history and philosophy.

In 1798 Bolívar's uncle sent him, at the age of fifteen, to Spain to gain a better education than Venezuela could offer him. In Madrid he lived under the roof of another uncle, Esteban Palacios, the first stable influence in his life, and in this uncle's spacious library, Bolívar continued his studies of history, mathematics, and languages, like Napoléon. In the process, Bolívar began to formulate his life's philosophy and a lifelong love of books and serious reading of both classical and modern Age of Reason authors including Homer, Locke, Montesquieu, Rousseau, and Voltaire. Young, impressionable, and possessing an inquiring, independent mind, he came to believe that the sovereignty of the people, the division of powers, civil liberty, prohibition of slavery, the abolition of monarchy, and a written constitution were greatly preferable—and inevitable—forms of government.[11]

His stay in Europe, coming at a most momentous time in history, taught him firsthand about the rising power of Napoléon, the importance of sea power, the supremacy of the British navy, and the declining influence of a French-occupied Spain. If George Washington's America could overthrow imperial British occupation, by what right and by what reduced power did Spain remain in control of South America? As much as he came to dislike Napoléon's lust for power, personal ambition, and despotism, Bolívar was nonetheless inspired by the awe and acclaim *Le Petit Caporal* generated wherever he went. Like Beethoven, Bolívar revered the Napoléon he also came to detest. "What seems great to me," Bolívar later admitted, "was

---

10. Simón Bolívar to James Cockburn, 2 October 1813, in *Selected Writings*, item 16, 1:39, 42.
11. Lynch, *Simón Bolívar*, 29.

the universal acclaim and interest that his person inspired. This, I confess, made me think of my country's slavery and the glory in store for the man who would free her."[12]

At age seventeen, he met and married his charming fourth cousin, the nineteen-year-old María Teresa Rodríguez del Toro y Alayza, in 1802. Sadly, just eight months later and shortly after their return to Venezuela, she died of a malignant fever, leaving a deep romantic yearning in Bolivar's heart that a long line of later mistresses could hardly fulfill. Returning to Europe in 1803 to drown his youthful sorrows, he gave free rein to his desires. Handsome, rich, daring, independent, a meticulous dresser, and a dashing dancer, Bolívar was a Zorro-like temptation some women could not resist. The stories of his later affairs are the things of love and legend. He was a frequent visitor to Paris's notorious Palais-Royal, where honor and virtue were left at the door.

Yet, if forever attracted to beautiful women, he would never remarry. María's untimely death was, as J. B. Trend has argued, the "crucial point" in Bolívar's career. It turned him to a life of power, politics, and patriotism. "I loved my wife," he admitted twenty-five years later. "When she died I swore that I would never marry again and I have kept my word. If I had not lost her, my whole life might have been different. I should not have been General Bolívar or the Liberator."[13] Sex was an enjoyable interlude, not his dominant passion. He reserved that for love of country and freedom.

In company with Simón Rodríguez, Bolívar walked all over Europe. While in Paris, Bolívar missed Napoléon's coronation as emperor in 1804, but he did see Napoléon in full field uniform and military array at the Battle of Marengo near Turin, Italy, and saw him later crowned king of Italy. While in Paris, he may have dined with Alexander von Humboldt (see chapter 12), just back from his amazing archaeological expeditions throughout Central and South America. Some argue that Humboldt encouraged the young Bolívar to return and spread the cry of South American freedom. Later, at Monte Sacro, a hillside just outside of Rome, the twenty-three-year-old Bolívar, freshly stirred by the Napoléon conquests, in a moment of inspiration and personal deduction, uttered his famous life-changing oath: "I swear by the God of my forefathers, I swear by my forefathers, I swear by my native land, that I shall never allow my hands to be idle nor my soul to rest until I have broken the shackles which bind us to Spain."[14]

Years later, Bolívar wrote an endearing letter to Rodríguez. "Do you recall how we went together to the Monte Sacro at Rome, to pledge upon that holy ground the freedom of our country?" he asked. "You molded my heart for liberty, justice, greatness, and beauty. I have followed the path you traced for me. You were my pilot, though you remained upon the shores of Europe. You cannot imagine how deeply and engraved upon my heart are the lessons you taught me. Never could I delete so much as a comma from the great precepts that

---

12. De Lacroix, *Diario de Bucaramanga*, 64–66, as cited in Lynch, *Simón Bolívar*, 25.
13. As cited in Trend, *Bolívar*, 38.
14. Rourke, *Man of Glory*, 32.

you set before me. They have been ever present in my mind's eye: I have followed them as infallible guides."[15]

Bolívar believed that "only democracy . . . is amenable to absolute liberty"[16]—but a democracy founded on and guaranteed by a written constitution and with it a strong constitutional executive (though not a monarchy) and an elected legislative form of government. "Nothing in our fundamental laws would have to be altered were we to adopt a legislative power similar to that held by the British Parliament," he further said.[17] And with such a free democracy, slavery could not be maintained but rather abolished.

On returning to Caracas, Bolívar sensed the time was ripe for revolt against a Spain preoccupied with waging a civil war against Napoléon's puppet brother, King Joseph, who came to power in May 1808. Lord Nelson had destroyed the combined French and Spanish fleets at Trafalgar, and Britain, a cautious ally, now controlled the waves. All over South America, as if on cue, juntas and provincial assemblies began to rise up in rebellion, declaring feigned allegiance on the one hand to Fernando VII of Spain—a son of Charles IV who had been forced by Napoléon to renounce his rule over Spain—while on the other hand plotting schemes of independence. Such a backdoor, boring-from-within revolutionary movement manifested a pretext of loyalty to the Spanish king while cloaking its real purpose.

The newly formed Venezuelan or Caracas Junta—led by Bolívar, José Félix Ribas, Mariano and Tomás Montilla, and others—secretly began meeting at Bolívar's plantation home in veiled conspiracy while publicly proclaiming Spanish allegiance. Their forceful deportation from Caracas of the Spanish vice-regent, Captain General Vicente Emparán in April 1810, was the powder keg of Venezuelan revolution. The first independent government in South America came into being in Caracas, and on 5 July 1811 the city council of Caracas and the newly formed congress declared Venezuelan independence. By the end of the year, the same pattern held true in many other South American countries, with independent governments established in Buenos Aires (25 May), Bogotá (20 July), and Santiago, Chile (18 September). Said Bolívar, "What do we care if Spain submits to Napoléon, if we have decided to be free? Let us without fear lay the cornerstone of South American freedom. To hesitate is to die."[18]

Bolívar was by all accounts an exceptionally complex man who reveled in his own sense of independence. As the scholar, Eduard Fueter, said of him almost a century ago, Bolívar was an oxymoron, "a born hero of freedom, a logical idealist, absolutely unselfish, incomparably energetic, and ahead of his time," a man in a hurry who, while in quest of personal glory, disdained the idea of dictatorial rule, whether his or that of anyone else. Like Napoléon, he possessed supreme self-confidence. If he did not have Napoléon's military genius, he shared his tranquility and composure when under attack. A master at guerilla

---

15. Bolívar to Simón Rodríguez, 19 January 1824, in *Selected Writings*, 2:424, 449.
16. Address delivered by Simon Bolívar at the Inauguration of the Second National Congress of Venezuela in Angostura, 15 February 1819, in *Selected Writings*, item 50, 1:178.
17. Address delivered by Simon Bolívar at the Inauguration of the Second National Congress of Venezuela in Angostura, 15 February 1819, in *Selected Writings*, item 50, 1:185.
18. As cited in Sherwell, *Simón Bolívar*, 31.

warfare, he proved his military mettle time and time again. His calm but firm decisiveness served him well on the battlefield and in the halls of congress or parliament. A man of vision, he created his own opportunities. At the brink of becoming a dictator, he always shrank back to exercising mere presidential, constitutional powers and privileges. Highly creative and deeply intelligent, he was an intellectual in uniform, a philosopher in politics, and an objective and impartial thinker blessed with the power of persuasion. A keen student of human nature, he had "a will of iron, strengthened, not weakened, by adversity and was above pettiness."[19]

Almost immediately, the new provisional government dispatched Bolívar to London to seek foreign recognition and to gain a British blockade of the Spanish Main, or northern coasts of South America. While in London, Bolívar met up with General Francisco de Miranda (1750–1816), who two years earlier had launched an abortive effort to jump-start Venezuelan independence. Called an "apostle of human liberty," Miranda had the vision to free all of South America and unite the continent into one or two federalist nations. A native Venezuelan by birth, a popular soldier with Lafayette in the American Revolutionary

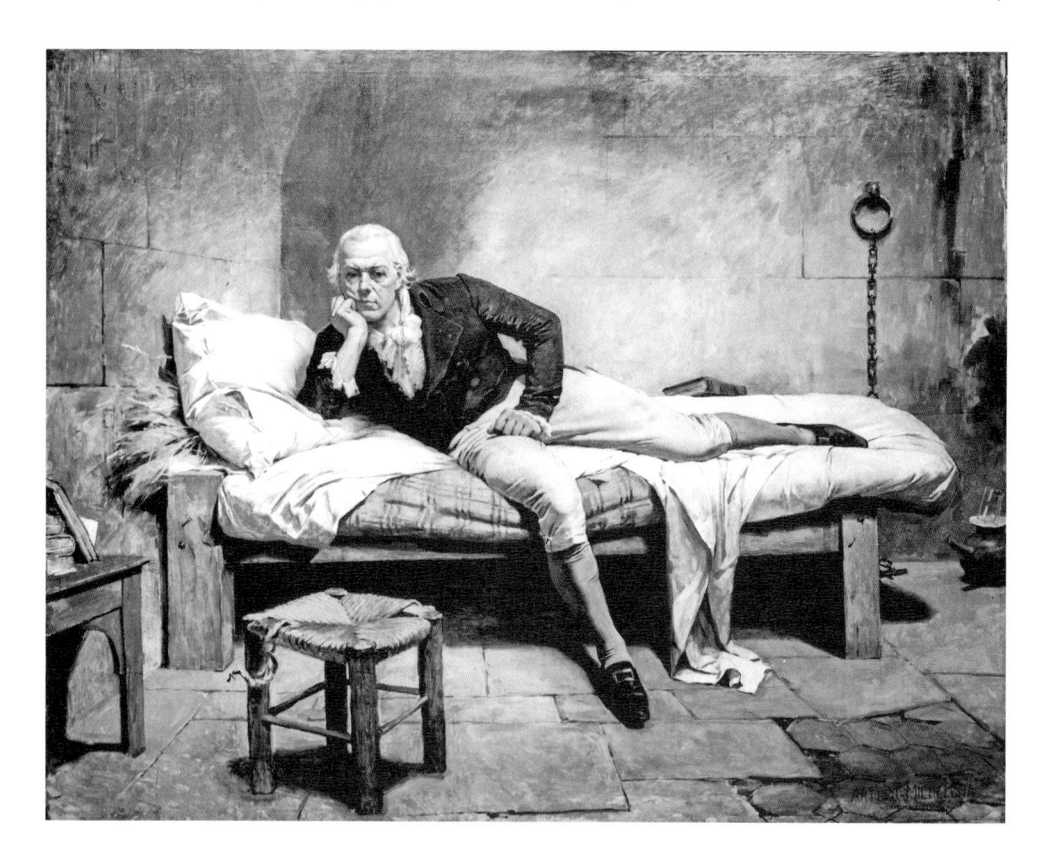

Miranda en la Carraca (1896), by Arturo Michelena.

---

19. Salcedo-Bastardo, *Bolívar*, 34.

War, and later a general in Napoléon's Grande Armée, Miranda was an avid supporter of, if not the inspiration for, Venezuelan political independence. His ill-timed 1806 three-boat invasion of Coro, Venezuela, was too little and too soon. Intercepted by Spanish warships, Miranda barely got away to British-controlled Barbados, where he raised another small force to await a more favorable tide.

In London, Bolívar and Miranda together sought out British help for the Venezuelan independence movement. Lord Wellesley (the Duke of Wellington), then British secretary of foreign affairs, played a very careful hand. He was reluctant to offend Spain, their ally in fighting Napoléon, but anxious to gain economic and political influence in the South American independence movement. He chose not to meet them in his public office but only privately at home. He could not openly support Venezuelan independence but promised assistance if French interference became manifest. Bolívar also met William Wilberforce, who encouraged him in his plans to eradicate slavery from the continent.

Enthusiasm aside, a successful independence movement was far from certain, primarily for economic, social, and military purposes. Bolívar's own Venezuelan aristocracy, or Creoles and plantation owners, were fearful that a revolution against Spain would so advance the cause of abolition among the slave populations that it would go too far and foster widespread dissatisfaction, even insurrection, among less-privileged classes. Furthermore, if Great Britain became involved there was no assurance that it would honor Creole monopolies and controls over trade. Labor costs would accelerate, with slave labor becoming a thing of the past. And lest one forget, Spain still had well-trained and well-equipped royalist armies all over much of South America. Thus, when the sixty-year-old General Miranda made his third and final invasion, he overestimated the support he thought he would receive from local Venezuelan leaders.

A far better field soldier than politician, Miranda also mistakenly shunned the guerilla warfare his circumstances required. His temerity, poor planning, and overestimation of local support forced him to surrender to Spanish forces in July 1812. Sensing that the time to confront Spanish control had not yet arrived, Bolívar declared Miranda's surrender was treasonable and thwarted Miranda's attempt to escape, eventually handing him over to the Spanish Royal Army. A concert with Miranda at this premature stage, Bolívar reasoned, would have doomed the liberation movement at the start. Bolívar has been roundly criticized for his actions against Miranda ever since. Soon captured and deported, Miranda rotted away, chained to a wall in a dark Spanish dungeon in Cádiz. He died four years later on 14 July 1816, all the while convinced that Bolívar had betrayed him and the cause of revolution by failing to confront and defeat the local Spanish royalist forces.[20] An unfortunate early casualty of Venezuela's independence movement, Miranda is still honored as a martyr and revered as a guiding force and lover of liberty in Spanish American history.

---

20. An oil painting by artist Arturo Michelena titled *Miranda en la Carraca* (1896) portrays the hero in prison, a graphic symbol in Venezuelan history.

Meanwhile Bolívar, after being questioned and detained by Spanish forces, soon found himself at the head of the independence forces. As a former second lieutenant in his father's local militia, did he really have the soldiering skills to fight a war against General Domingo de Monteverde and his battle-tested army of 12,000-plus Spanish soldiers?

Miranda's defeat was actually the second ill omen; the first was an act of God—at least the Catholic clergy thought so. On 26 March 1812, Holy Thursday, a devastating earthquake destroyed virtually the entire city of Caracas, killing more than twenty thousand people, including entire regiments of the newly formed revolutionary army, while inextricably sparing most royalist forces. "Whose side was God on anyway?" asked many who had quietly supported the rebel cause. Defying nature's apparent decree, an unsuperstitious Bolívar worked in the ruins round the clock, saving the lives of many cramped or crushed in the debris. With the Catholic Church blaming the revolutionary junta for bringing down God's wrath, an emboldened Monteverde took the offensive and won. Viewed as the real ringleader of the revolutionaries, Bolívar fled to Cartagena, New Granada (Colombia). Round one of Venezuela's quest for independence ended with the First Republic, like Caracas itself, in ruins.

The atrocities visited upon revolutionary sympathizers by Monteverde and his royalist troops were Inquisition-like in their savage butchery and ferocity. "Spare no one over seven years," he decreed. Thousands of men, women, and children were impaled or hacked to death and their heads fastened to fence posts as gruesome reminders of the fate of anyone disloyal to Spain. However, in the long run, Monteverde's atrocities in his antirevolutionary *Guerra a Muerte*, or "War to the Death," proved damaging to the royalist cause, causing some in the Creole establishment to look more favorably on Bolívar's cause.

Bolívar now concluded that if liberty was to be achieved, he alone had the passion and self-confidence to accomplish it. He may have been right. As historian J. B. Trend has again argued, Bolívar saw himself as a practical revolutionary and a logical dreamer who understood the Venezuelan mind and soul and who would carefully outmaneuver militarily and outflank his enemy politically.[21] Enlisting the kind of local sympathy and support Miranda had failed to do, Bolívar rallied military support in New Granada for his fragile cause. His rapidly growing forces of both men and not a few women fought six pitched battles, defeated five armies, and marched seven hundred miles in a three-month period. Using surprise attacks, he eventually regained Caracas and, as the newly christened Savior of the Country and Liberator of Venezuela, he proclaimed the rebirth of the republic on 6 August 1813. Hailed by adoring crowds and maidens dressed in white who threw garlands at his feet, Bolívar took especial delight in one Josefina Machado, who became his acknowledged mistress for the next five years.

Not wanting to make the same mistakes in this Second Republic as in the first, Bolívar trusted few, if anyone. He could be as vengeful and merciless as his enemies, ordering the retaliatory execution of over eight hundred Spanish prisoners in his Decree of War to the

---

21. Trend, *Bolívar*, 94.

Death. "The time has come at last to repay the Spaniards torture for torture," he said, "and to drown that race of annihilators in its own blood or in the sea."[22]

The main body of Spanish forces, however, had only retreated to the plains further south, where they formed an uneasy alliance with the llaneros, feared but fickle bandit horsemen of the plains, who were mostly blacks and *pardos*. Meanwhile General José Tomás Boves replaced Monteverde, who returned to Spain. More monstrous in cruelty than his predecessors, Boves launched a counteroffensive in which thousands more were massacred and dismembered, and he roundly defeated Bolívar's smaller and less equipped forces at Aragua in August 1813. For the second time, Bolívar escaped to New Granada, Washington-like in his tactical retreat. He learned how to turn military misfortune into a strength. "The novice soldier believes all is lost when he has once been routed. Experience has not proved to him that bravery, skill and perseverance can mend misfortune."[23] Realizing more than ever that their brightest hope for permanent independence now lay with Bolívar, New Granada made him captain general of the Army of Confederation.

A new Spanish general field marshal, Pablo Morillo, fresh from Spain with forty-two transports of thousands of additional troops, continued the offensive with a comprehensive strategy to conquer New Granada, destroy Bolívar, march to Peru and Buenos Aries, and extinguish once and for all the entire simmering South American independence movement. By the end of 1814, all of Venezuela lay in Morilla's grasp, and within three months he had conquered New Granada, subjecting it to the same kind of cruelty and punishment Monteverde and Boves had inflicted on Venezuela. Bolívar barely escaped, this time to the British isle of Jamaica.

In forced exile, Bolívar, shaken—though not defeated—penned his famous "Jamaica Letter" on 6 September 1815, soon after hearing news of the Battle of Waterloo. This document was a requiem to past failures, as John Lynch described it, a celebration of future victories, and a justification for continued warfare.[24] Sensing the need to more fully justify and explain to local supporters and foreign allies alike his political vision that had engulfed his homeland into a nightmarish bloody civil war, he put down his sword and took up his pen.

Bolívar's "Jamaica Letter" was an urgent cry for help, a reiteration of the inevitability of independence, and a vision for his future of South America. Written at the nadir of his revolutionary cause and addressed to his fellow countrymen, potential allies, and even his enemies, the document remains a landmark in South American independence history.

First and foremost, he argued that Spain had brought this disaster upon itself. Its history of abject cruelty, continued mismanagement, and painful oppression since the time of Cortés and Pizarro were so atrocious that they "appear to be beyond the human capacity

---

22. Simón Bolívar, "Reply of a South American to a Gentleman of this Island (Jamaica)" (frequently titled "Jamaica Letter"), 6 September 1815, in *Selected Writings*, letter 41, 1:106–7.
23. "Memorial to the Citizens of New Granada by a Citizen of Caracas," 15 December 1812, in *Selected Writings*, item 9, 1:20.
24. Lynch, *Simón Bolívar*, 91.

for evil."[25] He wrote that Spanish absolutism has not only "deprived us of our rights but has kept us in a sort of permanent infancy with regard to public affairs[,] . . . no better than that of serfs."[26] The result is "the hatred that the Peninsula has inspired in us is greater than the ocean between us. It would be easier to have the two continents meet than to reconcile the spirits of the two countries."[27] Nor could the clock turn back. Now that the Americas had begun to taste freedom and seen the light, "it is not our desire to be thrust back into darkness. The chains have been broken; [and] we have been freed."[28]

While seeking aid, the letter was also a supremely confident reiteration of ultimate and inevitable victory. "We must not lose faith," Bolívar wrote, and "success will crown our efforts" if for no other reason than that Spain is a weak and declining European power, "a phantom nation" lacking manufacturers, agricultural products, crafts and sciences, and even policies. Spain is an "aged serpent, bent only on satisfying its venomous rage [and] devouring the fairest part of our globe. . . . What madness for our enemy to hope to reconquer America when she has no navy, no funds, and almost no soldiers!"[29]

Seeking financial and military support from both Europe and "our brothers of the North [who] have been apathetic bystanders in this struggle," Bolívar argued that a free and independent South America would eventually promise far greater trading opportunities with the United States and other nations than Spanish colonial rule had ever provided.[30] As a declaration of independence and an intellectual attempt to institutionalize the revolution, the "Jamaica Letter" promised a free society founded on the principles of justice, liberty, and equality. The various juntas already established on the continent had elected free and democratic governments based on a constitutional system of checks and balances that would protect civil liberties and ensure the rights of men.[31]

To Bolívar, independence and freedom alone were not enough; his extended vision was for some kind of unity or, at the very least, a strong democratic confederation of South American nations governed not by a monarch but by a strong centralized executive and congress resident in one of the greater nations, perhaps Mexico. "It is a grandiose idea to think of consolidating the New World into a single nation," he realistically admitted. "This is not possible," for "[South] America is separated by climatic differences, geographical diversity, conflicting interests, and dissimilar characteristics."[32] "The American states need the care of paternal governments to heal the sores and wounds of despotism and war."[33] An

---

25. "Reply of a South American," 1:104.
26. "Reply of a South American," 1:111.
27. "Reply of a South American," 1:104–5.
28. "Reply of a South American," 1:105.
29. "Reply of a South American," 1:104–7.
30. "Reply of a South American," 1:108.
31. "Reply of a South American," 1:111–15.
32. "Reply of a South American," 1:118.
33. "Reply of a South American," 1:115.

exceptionally complex man, a "liberator who scorned liberalism," and a "soldier who disparaged militarism," Bolívar was both realist and idealist wrapped in an "uneasy rivalry."[34]

With only a few hundred men and enough arms for six thousand more provided by Jamaica and Haiti, the intrepid Bolívar returned to undertake the impossible. This time, however, he would proclaim freedom for the slaves while encouraging them to take up the cause. After a failed landing and a forced return to Haiti, Bolívar returned for the fourth time on 1 January 1817, this time for good.

Rather than confronting Morillo head-on in Caracas, Bolívar scoured the jungles to the east in search of support from *pardos* and former slaves. Seeking refuge, his growing band of multiracial followers and British mercenaries gravitated eastward to Angostura, where Bolívar suffered his most stunning defeat at the Battle of La Puerta in early 1818. Bolívar began to professionalize his army with clear rankings and sound discipline. In February 1819 he reconvened a new Venezuelan republican government at the Congress of Angostura, where he proclaimed a new constitution while awaiting the arrival of much-needed reinforcements. One such new recruit, a former British officer turned mercenary, later took time to describe his new commander. "We had long wished to see this celebrated man," he wrote,

> whose extraordinary energy and perseverance, under every disadvantage, have since effected the liberty of a large portion of South America. . . . He was then about 35, but looked upwards of 40; in stature, short—perhaps five feet five or six,—but well proportioned and remarkably active. His countenance, even then, was thin, and evidently careworn, with an expression of patient endurance under adversity, . . . however his fiery temper may at times have appeared to contradict the supposition. His manners not only appeared elegant, surrounded as he was by men far his inferiors in birth and education, but must have been intrinsically so; . . . [dressed in] a plain round jacket of blue cloth, with red cuffs, and three rows of gilt sugar-loaf buttons; course blue trousers; and *alpargates*, or sandals (the soles of which are made of the fibres of the aloe plaited), completed his dress. He carried in his hand a light lance, with a small black banner, having embroidered on it a white skull and crossed bones, with the motto "*Muerte ò Libertàd!*"[35]

Recognizing the utter futility of a frontal attack on Morillo's expanding army, Bolívar hit upon a daring and most dangerous strategy.[36] Leaving behind a small battalion to veil his true intent, he set out on 27 May 1819 with twenty-one hundred men on a circle-the-mountains strategy. His aim was to travel up the Orinoco River, traverse the savannah

---

34. Lynch, "Simón Bolívar," 6. Bolívar wrote: "My greatest weakness is my love of liberty: this leads me to forget even my desire for glory. I will undergo anything, abandon all my hopes, rather than pass for a tyrant, or even be suspected of it. My ruling passion, my one aspiration, is to be known as a *lover of liberty*." *Obrus Complete*, as cited in Salcedo-Bastardo, *Bolívar*, 36.
35. Vowell and Mahoney, *Campaigns and Cruises*, 1:65–67.
36. For a map of the 1819 campaign, see *Selected Writings*, 1:199.

of Casanare, scale the mighty Andes far to the west, overpower Spanish garrisons in New Granada, and finally march east from Caracas to Venezuela, surprising and challenging Morillo's rear. With a fall and wintertime march of some 1,500 miles over the most rugged terrain imaginable, his daring strategy owed everything to stealth, speed, and surprise.

The well-watered savannahs of the upper Orinoco—with their small islands, swamps, and lagoons extending as far as the eye could see—posed the first formidable obstacle. Infested with panthers, jaguars, and swarms of biting insects and plagued with pestilential diseases, oppressive heat, and sudden torrential rains, the region posed a never-ending challenge. For days they marched in water up to their armpits and fended off giant water snakes and alligators. The local boatmen took pains to avoid sailing under the trees that overhung the river lest the mast dislodge giant serpents from the branches. And many native tribes, such as the Yanomami, were unfriendly. To complicate matters, many towns along the route were predominantly royalist in sentiment. At El Morichal, a band of women came close to assassinating Bolívar as he returned from early mass by attempting to stab him to death with daggers they had concealed under their mantillas. By the time the army reached the village of Socha, their uniforms were in tatters, their boots long gone, and many officers literally without trousers, forced to cover themselves with pieces of blankets or whatever else they could obtain. Local women offered their own clothes to the tattered soldiers. And as bad as the first month had been, now stood before them the almost impassable wall of the towering Andes, as described by one of Bolívar's trusted and keenly observant British officers:

> The snowy peaks of the Andes were now frequently seen . . . ; and . . . opposed an inaccessible barrier to [our] entrance into New Granada. The more, indeed, a stranger gazes on them, the less he can conceive the practicability of passing them. The narrow paths leading to the *Paramos*, wind among wild mountains, which are totally uninhabited, and covered with immense forests, overhanging the road, and almost excluding the light of day. . . . An incessant drizzling rain . . . had rendered the paths so slippery, when our army passed, that they became excessively dangerous; especially to the few tired mules and bullocks, that yet survived the fatigues of [our] march. . . . Multitudes of small crosses are fixed in the rocks, by some pious hands, in memory of former travelers who have died here; and along the path are strewed fragments of saddlery, trunks, and various articles, that have been abandoned, and resemble the traces of a routed army. Huge pinnacles of granite overhang many parts of these passes, apparently tottering, and on the point of overwhelming the daring traveler; while terrific chasms . . . yawn far beneath, as if to receive him. A sense of extreme loneliness, and remoteness from the world, seizes on his mind, and is heightened by the dead silence that prevails; not a sound being heard, but the scream of the *condòr*, and the monotonous murmur of the distant water-falls.[37]

---

37. Vowell, *Campaigns and Cruises*, 1:161–62, 164.

While scores of his men died along the way, the persistent, self-confident Libertador, in Hannibal-like fashion, finally succeeded in crossing the 13,000-foot Paramo de Pisba Pass and reaching New Granada. There he and General Santander of Cartagena combined forces to win the decisive Battle of Boyaca on 7 August 1819 against a far larger, thoroughly surprised, and unprepared royalist army.

From there Bolívar moved on to Bogotá, which the loyalists had deserted, liberating the heart of New Granada. Bolívar then completed his circuit march to Caracas, where he overpowered the Spanish army (whose more liberal officers had mutinied against their leaders) and ultimately returned in triumph to Angostura in December 1819. General Morillo, recognizing

Bolívar's Troops in the Cordillera Oriental, by Archibald Forbes.

he had been outfoxed by Bolívar, surrendered but not before saying of his foe, "What, that little man in the blue frock-coat and forage cap riding a mule?"[38] Morillo's successor, General Manuel de la Torre, was soon afterward defeated at the Battle of Carabobo on 24 June 1821, and Venezuela's ten-year struggle for independence was finally secured.

Hailed the *padre de la patria* (father of the country), destroyer of oppression, and victor over tyranny, Bolívar, in proclaiming the Fourth Republic, let his enthusiasm outpace the political realities. He proclaimed not only Venezuela's permanent independence but also the unification of all the old viceroyalties of Venezuela, Ecuador, and Nueva Granada into the single state of the Republic of Colombia. Spain soon signed an armistice treaty (partly at General Morillo's insistence back at the Spanish court), recognizing once and for all the legitimacy of Bolívar's stunningly successful independence movement.[39]

Bolívar's amazing success soon caught the kind of international attention he had intended. Not only did England approve, but in the United States Senator Henry Clay proposed in the American Congress that Colombia be recognized as a free country, "worthy for many reasons to stand side by side with the most illustrious peoples of the world."[40] Clay's support affirmed America's Monroe Doctrine of 1820 that had declared against any and all extensions of European powers into the Western Hemisphere (see chapter 11). It was a

---

38. O'Leary, *Narración*, 2:58, as cited in Lynch, *Simón Bolívar*, 137.
39. Trend, *Bolívar*, 151.
40. Sherwell, *Simón Bolívar*, 136.

The Battle of Boyacá, by Martín Tovar y Tovar (1890).

welcome sign of American support and a promise not to intervene. Mexico and Panama announced their independence at the same time.

IN SEARCH OF SOUTH AMERICAN UNIFICATION

Bolívar soon left Angostura for Bogotá, where he determined to take the revolution southward, eventually to Peru, the last bastion of Spanish rule. Without Peru, Spanish forces could still destabilize the hard-fought gains of the independence movement all over the continent. Defeating Peru, however, would prove challenging. Bolívar, unable to go by sea for fear of Spanish ships, left Bogotá on 13 December 1821, choosing to cross volcanic mountains and gorges of an even higher mountain range to reach Quito (Ecuador). Meanwhile, General Antonio José de Sucre and his army, marched south along the coast. After winning the battle of Bombona in April and then the Battle of Pichincha in May 1822, Bolívar marched into Quito, where a dozen young women in white crowned him in laurels. Bolívar wasted little time incorporating the so-called presidency of Ecuador into Greater Colombia.

Still a bachelor, Bolívar caught the eye of not only foreign observers. Since his wife's death some eighteen years before, he had had many mistresses—such as Josefina Machado and Joaquina Garaycoa, to name but two. Yet for years he did not find another woman he could love as he had María. That all began to change, however, during his eventful victory parade into Quito. Watching from her balcony, the twenty-two-year-old Manuela Sáenz saw Bolívar for the first time. A passionate supporter of the republican cause, she quickly caught Bolívar's eye. An excellent equestrian and a skilled sharpshooter with a strongly independent mind, Manuela was "attractive and shapely, her oval face, pearl complexion, dark eyes and flowing hair the epitome of South American beauty."[41] That evening at the victory ball, they danced the night away. The fact that Manuela was already married to a wealthy British merchant meant little to her in the light of this new romance. "What fire of love burns in my breast for you," she wrote to Bolívar soon afterward. "In fact we are all rivals in love with you."[42]

The two fell madly in love. She soon wrote to her "dull" husband without a tinge of regret: "I do not live by social rules, invented only to torment. So leave me alone. . . . We will marry again when we are in heaven but not on earth. . . . You are boring, like your nation. . . . I will never return to you." But to her new lover: "I want to see you, to touch you, feel you, taste you, to join me in complete union. . . . Love me and don't go away, not even with God himself."[43]

Writing back, Bolívar said, "I think of you and your situation every moment. Yes, I adore you. . . . You beg me to tell you that I do not love anyone but you. No. I do not love anyone else, nor shall I ever love another."[44] Years after they met, their letters were as passionate as ever. One day his newfound lover, who was almost always by his side, would even save his life. In many respects, Manuela was, as many called her, "La Libertadora."

Peru posed a particular challenge to the independence movement. As scholar Timothy Anna has noted, José Fernando de Abascal, Spanish viceroy of Peru from 1806 to 1816, had almost single-handedly stopped the spread of independence throughout much of the continent. A more just and enlightened administrator than any of his peers, Abascal was "a pillar of rectitude, honesty, clear thinking and leadership."[45] And although silver mine production had peaked some twenty years before, the nation was gripped in poverty. Abascal was respected by many for his sound administrative abilities, his love of humanity, and hard work. Thus, the war of independence, despite the Tupac Amaru uprising of a generation earlier, reached Peru last and did not create an organized underground or groundswell of popular opinion as in New Granada or Venezuela. Even the most liberal of Peru's enlightenment thinkers never actually advocated rebellion and did not join the cause for independence until after 1820. Except for tracts and leaflets imported from outside, insurgent literature did

---

41. Lynch, *Simón Bolívar*, 179.
42. Lynch, *Simón Bolívar*, 180.
43. Lynch, *Simón Bolívar*, 181–82.
44. As cited in introduction to *Selected Writings*, xxvi. After Bolívar's death, she eked out an existence in the small Peruvian port of Paita, selling sweets until her death. Her biography remains to be written.
45. Anna, *Fall of the Royal Government*, 27.

not appear in any significant numbers until 1820. In short, Bolívar needed to convince Peru it was time for independence.[46]

Several unexpected things happened, however, that played into his hands. The first was the economic collapse of Abascal's successor government of Viceroy Joaquín de la Pezuela that was brought on by the total cessation of Spanish shipping. Second, General José de San Martín—commanding officer of the United Provinces, liberator of southern South America, and arguably the finest military genius in South America—had already crossed the higher Andes to the south. After winning the battle of Chacabuco in 1817, he had liberated Santiago and eventually all Chile from royalist control. By July 1821, San Martín had subdued southern Peru and achieved possession of the capital city, Lima. Declaring, "¡Viva la patria! ¡Viva la libertad! ¡Viva la independencia!," San Martín unfurled for the first time the flag of independent Peru on 28 July 1821.

Manuela Sáenz, by unknown artist.

Yet outside Lima, much of the country still lay firm in royalist hands. The two liberators met for the first time in Guayaquil. San Martín was suffering from a malicious malady and, having lost some of his earlier military influence, seemed anxious to leave Peru. While the two men agreed on the aims of independence, they differed on what form of government—monarchical or republican—Peru would eventually have. A better soldier than diplomat, San Martín quit his position of protector of Peru, ceded the new political arena in Peru to Bolívar, and retired to Argentina and eventually to Europe.[47]

Chile's independence and that of many other South American states was further secured by the recruiting of a most valuable asset—the brave and resourceful English naval admiral Lord Thomas Cochrane (1775–1860). His bravery, skill, and daring exploits, so well proven in the Napoleonic Wars, were now put to the test in South America. Sailing under the Chilean flag, he blockaded ports, disrupted Spanish trade, and destroyed Spanish naval influence from the Spanish Main to Cape Horn. Called "El Diablo" by his Spanish enemies, Cochrane was to the sea what Bolívar and San Martín were on land. Peru's independence could not

---

46. Anna, *Fall of the Royal Government*, 31–33.
47. Robertson, *Rise of the Spanish-American Republic*, 200.

have been secured without Cochrane's naval transports and control of the sea.[48]

The fourth unexpected factor was the inevitable spread of revolution to Spain itself in 1820. Spain was redefining itself, motivated in part by the liberal aims of the French and American Revolutions and a conscious rejection of royal absolutist power, being increasingly unsupportive of a repugnant South American policy it could no longer support financially or morally. The Spanish uprising spread throughout most military possessions in Spain that spring of 1820, fueled by a deteriorating economy that lagged far behind England's and the rest of postwar Europe. The king soon had to rewrite the constitution and withdraw financial support of many military activities overseas.

José de San Martín, by unknown artist (1827 or 1829).

Finally, Bolívar's three-year military campaign against Peru's stubborn, resistant royalist forces, especially in the north, may also have failed without the splendid efforts of General Antonio José de Sucre. Winning one cavalry-charged battle after another, reminiscent of the brilliance of Marshal Ney, Sucre and his patriot army went on to defeat the Peruvian royalists at the key Battle of Ayacucho in December 1824—the last battle fought by Spanish military power in South America.

Now firmly and finally in command of all "El Dorado," in August 1825 Bolívar divided the eastern or upper region of Peru to form Bolivia (named in his honor), called for the end of slavery, proclaimed religious liberty, and established a new constitution with a president or chief executive and three chambers of congress. Sucre became the first president of Bolivia, and Bolívar of Peru. In 1827 Bolívar, acting with virtual dictatorial authority, drafted the Peruvian constitution along much the same lines as that of Bolivia's and Venezuela's. Bolívar's constitutions and government were patterned more along the British model, with a strong and highly centralized government, and less on that of the United States, which vested considerable power in the legislature and in the states. Although he was not a monarchist, Bolívar preferred a very strong executive unfettered by congressional authority.[49]

---

48. Robertson, *Rise of the Spanish-American Republic*, 213–14. For a comprehensive new study, see Harvey, *Cochrane*.
49. Rodríguez, *Independence of Spanish America*, 190.

Now in a position to wield absolute power, Bolívar was an unwilling dictator. In Peru as in Venezuela and elsewhere, he occupied the chair of first president only temporarily and was content to relinquish supreme political control as soon as possible. The thought of becoming a king or emperor, à la Napoléon, was antithetical to his native republican and egalitarian instincts. He respected the rule of law and the voice of the people. However, he admittedly preferred a strong, almost absolutist executive, a weaker legislature, and a more limited form of democracy.

Ironically, despite his deep desire for social reform, his new republics failed to ensure the abolition of slavery and a true equality among all peoples, which were ever his ambitions. "Nothing is nearer to the condition of beasts," he once declared, "than to view free men everywhere and not be free. Men in this position are the enemies of society, and, if large in number, they are dangerous. . . . It is, therefore, borne out by the mission of politics and derived from the examples of history that any free government which commits the folly of maintaining slavery is repaid with rebellion and sometimes with collapse."[50]

To Bolívar's way of thinking, it was "madness that a revolution for liberty should try to maintain slavery."[51] However, there still existed far too many vested economic interests, too many long-entrenched racial prejudices for Bolívar's egalitarian aims to be secured so quickly. Abolished on paper, slavery endured for at least another fifty years as forced servile labor.

If Bolívar failed to eliminate slavery, his other major disappointment was the lost dream of Spanish-American unification. "We have indeed driven out our oppressors, smashed the tablets of their tyrannical laws, and established legitimate institutions," he wrote in an 1822 letter to General Bernardo O'Higgins, revolutionary leader in Chile: "But we have yet to lay the foundation of the pact of union that will make of this part of the world a nation of republics. . . . The union of the five great states of America is itself so sublime that I do not doubt but that it will come to be the cause of amazement in Europe. . . . Who shall oppose an America united in heart, subject to one law, and guided by the torch of liberty?"[52]

Without the creation of a colossus of South American power into a single national body, as George Washington had done in North America, Latin America would never stand up or be equal to the other great world powers, nor successfully stifle divisions from within. "Unless we centralize our American governments, our enemies will gain every advantage," Bolívar had said years before. "We will inevitably be involved in the horrors of civil strife and [be] miserably defeated by that handful of bandits who infest our territories."[53]

By 1828 the Liberator of Venezuela, Colombia, Ecuador, Bolivia, and finally Peru had arrived at the reluctant conclusion that such a plan of unity was impossible. The forces of

---

50. Bolívar to General Francisco de Paula Santander, 20 April 1820, in *Selected Writings*, item 85, 1:223.
51. Lynch, *Simón Bolívar*, 151.
52. Bolívar to General Bernardo O'Higgins, 8 January 1822, in *Selected Writings*, item 124, 1:289.
53. "Memorial to the Citizens of New Granada by a Citizen of Caracas," 15 December 1812, in *Selected Writings*, item 9, 1:22.

separation; the immense and varied geographies that were barriers to travel and easy communication; the racial, social, and economic divides; the weak central governments; and the strong suspicions, if not hatreds, among classes, tribes, and even nations all proved too resistant in the long run to coalition and unification. "I am ashamed to admit it," Bolívar said to the Congress of Colombia, "but independence is the only benefit we have gained, at the cost of everything else."[54]

Bolívar's final years proved difficult and disappointing. He was finally getting weary of serving and of having his mind in constant turmoil. "Not even success can induce me to bear the burden any longer. . . . You cannot imagine how I long for rest."[55] He barely survived an assassination attempt in Peru, thanks to his lover, Manuela, who shot and killed the intruder. Sucre, his loyal lieutenant, was murdered. Small and intermittent insurrections continued to break out here and there. Beginning in 1828, Bolívar contracted tuberculosis, and seven months after stepping down as president of Colombia, Bolívar died at Santa Marta on 17 December 1830. He was forty-seven.

If one of the prevailing themes of this book has been that of liberation, freedom, and wars of independence, then surely the political history of South America fits that pattern. And in the rest of Latin America, the same liberating forces discussed above were simultaneously at work nearly everywhere. As shown, Bolívar was certainly not alone in pursuing the dream of South American freedoms. Argentina gained its independence in 1820. That same year, Brazil finally threw off centuries of Portuguese monarchical rule in a revolution of its own that Lisbon reluctantly recognized five years later. After years of fighting, Agustín de Iturbide successfully declared Mexico a free and independent state in 1821, with Guatemala doing the same. Uruguay accomplished its independence in 1828. And the list goes on.

Yet of all those men and movements, few if any equaled Bolívar, although he would not have said so. "In the midst of that sea of troubles, I was but a mere plaything in the hurricane of revolution that tossed me about like so much straw. I could do neither good nor evil. Irresistible forces directed the course of our events. To attribute these forces to me would not be just, for it would place upon me an importance that I do not merit."[56]

Nevertheless, he was, as San Martín called him, "the most extraordinary personage that South America has produced."[57] As a military commander, he was surpassed by few for his prowess, his self-confidence, and his bravery and skill on the battlefield. He defied overwhelming odds and intimidating mountain ranges. Like America's George Washington, he learned how to retreat strategically and regroup successfully. In the process, he brought independence to almost all northern South America and brought glory to himself. He

---

54. "Message to the Constituent Congress of the Republic of Colombia," 20 January 1830, in *Proclamas y Discursus del Libertador*, 298, as cited in Lynch, *Simón Bolívar*, 212.
55. Bolívar to General Francisco de Paula Santander, 9 February 1825, item 206, in *Selected Writings*, 2:468.
56. "Address Delivered at the Inauguration of the Second National Congress of Venezuela in Angostura," 15 February 1819, in *Selected Writings*, item 70, 1:173–74.
57. Robertson, *Rise of the Spanish-American Republic*, 312.

established new constitutions, governments, and republics and worked hard at abolishing slavery and ensuring the rights of the individual. If neither a dictator nor an emperor, he was a controlling liberator who tended toward imperialism and favored strong executive powers in all his new nations. Although he failed to establish a unity of South American states, he was acclaimed father of their independence and the inspiration for democracy, equality, and the dignity of human rights.

Bolívar was to South America what Napoléon had been to Europe. He despised the hated and corrupt Spanish rule that had terrorized much of the continent for almost three hundred years. He tried to tear down slavery wherever he found it, established new constitutions, reduced the powers of the Catholic clergy, and created an independence movement that set many South American nations on a path of self-rule. His accomplishments also made possible modern freedom of religion in many parts of the continent, paving the way for the astonishing spread of evangelicalism, Pentacostalism, The Church of Jesus Christ of Latter-day Saints, and other religions in the latter half of the twentieth century. Without Bolívar and the liberties he promoted over the ensconced political and ecclesiastical powers of his day, modern religious freedoms in South America might never have come to pass.

The Rev. John Williams, the Martyr of Erromanga, with a Landscape of the Mission House and Grounds of Rarotonga, by George Baxter.

"TO EXTEND THE BOUNDARIES OF ZION"

THE LONDON MISSIONARY SOCIETY AND REV. JOHN WILLIAMS, "APOSTLE OF POLYNESIA"

"Some were tattooed from head to foot; some were painted most fantastically, with pipe-clay and yellow and red-ochre; others were smeared all over with charcoal; and in this state were dancing, shouting, and exhibiting the most frantic gestures."[1] Upon welcoming Chief Tamatoa on board his vessel, the twenty-five-year-old Reverend John Williams found he could converse readily with the chief in his own language and told him of the Christianizing influences then happening in the Tahitian and Society Islands. "He asked me, very significantly, where great Tangaroa was? I told him that he, with all the other gods, was burned. He then inquired where Koro of Raiatea was? I replied, that he too was consumed of fire; and that I had brought two teachers to instruct him and his people in the word and knowledge of the true God." The two men were pressing noses in greeting when the chief suddenly spotted the minister's four-year-old boy, the first European white child he had ever seen. The child "attracted so much notice, that every native wished to rub noses with the little fellow" and begged John Williams to give the child to them, to make him king. But the mother and child quickly hastened away to the ship's cabin, fearful of possible kidnapping, torture, or worse.[2]

The above account was written by the Reverend John Williams of his first encounter with the native islanders of Aitutaki, an island that is part of the Cook Islands in the South Pacific, in the year 1821. It was but one of scores this illustrious "apostle of Polynesia" from

---

1. Williams, *Narrative of Missionary Enterprises*, 12–13.
2. Williams, *Narrative of Missionary Enterprises*, 14.

the London Missionary Society (LMS) would write during a lifetime of dedicated missionary service among the peoples of the South Pacific. His was a life that many years later would end tragically on the shores of yet another beautiful, mysterious South Sea island.

The Christian evangelization of indigenous Pacific peoples is a hotly debated topic among many modern scholars. Some argue that it was an exercise in western paternalism, a "cultural" or "Christian imperialism," expressed in how Christian missionary societies looked down upon their distant counterparts with thinly veiled disdain and all but replaced their native cultures. To this school of thinking, the Western missionary agenda was a "treacherous" exercise, one "inseparably linked to a broad and deliberate effort to dismantle" local cultures.[3] Such efforts were viewed as nothing short of the imposition of one, supposedly more advanced empire, on a far less advanced, "heathen" society, more of a disservice than a blessing. These Christian missionaries, and quite often their wives, feared intimacy with the locals, refused to send their children to native schools, and in other ways refused "going native."[4] As Emily Conroy-Krutz has likewise argued, such missionaries obeying the Great Commission may have seen themselves as "servants of Christ" but were actually "partisans of a particular Anglo-American style of civilization."[5]

There may well have been some Christian missionaries who thought this way, who harbored prejudices, fears, and biases toward the islanders and their way of life. Certainly, Christian missionaries saw some islander practices as destructive, particularly slavery, human sacrifice, infanticide, and polygamy, and were committed to eliminating such practices. These missionaries were equally critical of the drunken European or American beachcomber and the lascivious buccaneer influences that proved harmful and degrading to so many in the islands.[6] For those missionaries who spent much of their adult lives among the islands of the Pacific, they could not have succeeded without the love and respect of the people they had set out to teach and convert. Their main intention was not so much to supplant one empire with another, but to educate, evangelize, and make safer the world about them. Some even translated local beliefs and customs to send back home, to give the so-called civilized world the best of a distant culture in what was sometimes a two-way beneficial process of learning. Admittedly, not all missionaries were respectful of, or "Christian," to the island

---

3. Herbert, *Culture and Anomie*, 165. Herbert continued: "Despite the ambition to inculcate right beliefs, deeds—and the passage from one set of practices to another was the only markers available for missionaries to gauge conversion. In fact, missionaries spent far less time worrying about beliefs than they did regulating conduct." *Culture and Anomie*, 58.
4. Maffly-Kipp, "Assembling Bodies and Souls: Missionary Practices on the Pacific-Frontier," in Maffly-Kipp, Schmidt, and Valeri, *Practicing Protestants*, 62–63, 71.
5. Conroy-Krutz, *Christian Imperialism*, 15. To be Christian, he insisted, "one had to be civilized." *Christian Imperialism*, 210.
6. "The cultural-imperialist narrative . . . has not yielded fruitful explanation for why non-Western resisters embraced Christianity with such confounding enthusiasm that they now outnumber the Western imposters." Case, *Unpredictable Gospel*, 5.

peoples; however, the fact is men and women like the Williams were highly esteemed by their native counterparts who sought to learn what they knew and believed.

If every age must have its heroes, then the name that had captured the imagination of the people of the late eighteenth and early nineteenth century was the adventurous circumnavigator and intrepid British explorer Captain James Cook (1728–79). On board his famous ships *HMS Endeavor* and later *HMS Revolution*, this incomparable seaman conducted three memorable voyages: first of the southern seas and two later on of the entire Pacific Ocean, from 1768 to 1779. His vivid journal descriptions of majestically beautiful, faraway islands and accompanying traditions of native life proved irresistibly popular to both English and European audiences. By circumnavigating the southern waters around Antarctica, Cook was the first to map the entire coastline of New Zealand, to find several island chains in the South Pacific, to map much of eastern New South Wales (Australia), to found Botany Bay, and to prove the nonexistence of a habitable southern continent. Cook was also the first European to have widespread and sustained contact with the various native peoples of the Pacific and was the first to argue that there was an anthropological relationship among them. He was also the first to successfully combat scurvy, the sailor's dreaded scourge, through the use of such fresh citrus as lemons and limes.

Sailing the vast Pacific Ocean from east to west and then from south to north, Cook mapped the entire coastline of northwestern North America (north of Nootka Sound to Alaska) and proved the impenetrability of the ice-jammed Bering Sea and, with it, the improbability of an easy Northwest Passage connecting the Atlantic to the Pacific. While returning from his third voyage, he landed on the Hawaiian Islands, which he promptly christened the Sandwich Islands, where unfortunately he was killed by native islanders in 1779. His tragic death stirred his many readers, some of whom vowed someday to spread the gospel to these same beautiful, faraway isles of the sea. In praise of the great navigator, Rev. Williams said, "[His] name I never mention but with feelings of veneration and regret."[7]

Born 29 June 1796 at Tottenham High Cross, a suburb of London, John Williams was a child of the Industrial Revolution. Although his mother insisted that he receive a religious upbringing, his apprenticeship at the age of fourteen to an ironmaker by the name of Enoch Tonkin brought out his native interests in the mechanical arts. Particularly adept at blowing at the forge, hammering out new tools, and repairing and recasting a myriad of mechanical parts, young Williams soon "became a skillful workman, and was able to finish more perfectly than many whose lives had been devoted to the attainment."[8]

Thanks to Mrs. Tonkin, Williams also experienced a Christian conversion in 1814 during his eighteenth year as he listened to a sermon by the Reverend Timothy East. "What is a man profited, if he shall gain the whole world, and lose his own soul?" the minister had demanded. "From that hour my blind eyes were opened," Williams later recalled, "and I beheld wondrous things out of God's law. I diligently attended the means of grace. I saw the

---

7. Williams, *Narrative of Missionary Enterprises*, 2.
8. Prout, *Memoirs*, 9.

beauty and reality in religion which I had never seen before. My love to it and delight in it increased, . . . and I grew in grace, and in the knowledge of my Lord and Saviour, Jesus Christ."[9] Soon afterward, young Williams became an avid Sunday School teacher.

Upon learning of the LMS, he applied in July 1816 to become one of their missionaries. The LMS had just learned of the amazing evangelical successes of the Reverend Henry Nott in Tahiti and was desperately seeking young new missionaries—preferably married. In late October 1816, Williams married Mary Chauner, "the ornament of a meek and quiet spirit,"[10] who was as equally committed to promoting the Christian gospel as he was. Just weeks later, on 17 November 1816, John and Mary Williams set sail on board the *Harriett* on a five-month voyage to Sydney, New South Wales, and on a twenty-five-year mission to the South Pacific. Theirs was destined to become one of the most successful Christianizing missions of the nineteenth century. The work of John and Mary Williams cannot be fully appreciated without first placing it within the larger context of the tract and Bible societies of which the London Missionary Society was so much a part.

"THIS IS THE AGE OF SOCIETIES"

"This is the age of societies," wrote the British historian Thomas Macaulay in 1823.[11] It expressed itself in ways that crossed over many cultures and in many fields of endeavor, foreign or domestic. Some such societies were formed to establish universal peace, to Christianize the Jews, or to improve upon the family. This surging humanitarian and religious impulse was neither government-sponsored nor denominationally directed. Instead, it was a local, spontaneous, Protestant-inspired groundswell spreading from England that was in many ways a reaction to the irreligious spirit of the French Revolution.

Some of the societies that contributed to this era of change were designed solely for women—the Institution for the Protection of Young Country Girls; the Ladies' Association for the Benefit of Gentlewomen of Good Family, Reduced in Fortune Below the State of Comfort to Which They Have Been Accustomed; and the Friendly Female Society for the Relief of Poor, Infirm, Aged Widows and Single Women of Good Character Who Have Seen Better Days. Others catered generally to the poor—the so-called mendicity orders—including the Climbing Boy Society (aiding young chimney sweeps), the General Benevolent Institution for the Relief of Decayed Artists of the United Kingdom, and the Clothing Society for the Benefit of Poor Pious Clergymen.

Far more than casual afternoon tea get-togethers, such societies were strongly supported by the Quakers, the orthodox clergy, evangelicals, and many in the upper classes of society, depending on the cause. The Small Debts Society, for instance, helped discharge twenty-four thousand men and women from debtors' prisons by 1808 at a cost of sixty-six thousand

---

9. Prout, *Memoirs*, 8, 13–14.
10. Prout, *Memoirs*, 23.
11. Brown, *Fathers of the Victorians*, 317.

pounds.[12] And some, like the Young Men's Christian Association (YMCA) and the Society for the Prevention of Cruelty to Animals have survived to the present day.

Of all the many religious societies, three kinds or groupings are especially relevant to our discussion: the religious tract societies, the Bible societies, and finally, the missionary societies. Inspired in large measure by the *Cheap Repository Tracts* of Hannah More, as well as the spectacular rise in popularity of the Sunday School movement of Robert Raikes (see chapter 8), the dual aim of most of these tract societies was to counter the concomitant rise of popular vile and vulgar literature, especially among the poorer classes. They also set out to improve moral behavior in England and abroad and to spread Christianity worldwide through the power of the pen. Although religious tract societies had been in existence in England since 1647, the Society for Promoting Christian Knowledge Among the Poor in England (instituted in 1799) was the parent of the religious tract phenomenon.

Other tract societies soon sprang up all over England and later in the United States and British North America (Canada) and as far away as India, China, and Ceylon. The London Religious Tract Society (established in 1799) became the most ambitious of them all, distributing an astonishing thirty million tracts by 1820 and creating 999 branches and 4,595 auxiliaries.[13] "Your Tracts instruct the ignorant in the Sunday School," one religious paper exulted in 1820, "in the factory, in the fields, in the mines, by the docks, and on the public way. Your tracts enter the cottages of the poor, the chamber of disease, the cell of the condemned, and yield consolation and hope to the wretched and the dying; and perhaps, in many instances, unknown to us . . . they are the means of saving knowledge and eternal life."[14]

In North America, the New England Religious Tract Society, established in 1814, became the most famous of all American tract societies. By 1855 it had distributed 800,000 tracts of its own, containing over ten million pages.[15] These North American tracts, like their English counterparts, included hymns, stories for children in Sunday Schools, scriptures, sermon extracts, prayers, and more.

"WITHOUT NOTE OR COMMENT"

These religious tract societies served well as indispensable aids to the far-flung missionary efforts and became the essential precursor to the even more spectacularly successful Bible societies. However, the spark that ignited the Bible movement was the desperate lack of Bibles in northern Wales, most poignantly felt by a sweet Welsh maiden. Since 1791, Wales had been experiencing a religious awakening and among the converts was one Mary Jones, then a girl of about ten years of age. She walked two miles every Saturday to a relative's home to read from the nearest Bible. Over the next several years, she tried hard to save enough

---

12. Brown, *Fathers of the Victorians*, 350.
13. *The Weekly Recorder* (London), 9 February 1820.
14. *The Weekly Recorder* (London), 16 February 1820.
15. American Tract Society, *Brief History of the Organization*, 5–10.

money to finally purchase her own set of scriptures, which she did when seventeen years old, after walking twenty-eight miles barefoot to buy her first Bible from the good reverend Thomas Charles. As the popular story goes, "He reached her a copy, she paid him the money and there [they] stood, their hearts too full for utterance, and their tears streaming from their eyes."[16]

Inspired by the young girl's devotion, Rev. Charles traveled to London in 1802 in quest of ten thousand Welsh Bibles from the almost moribund Society for Promoting Christian Knowledge, an Anglican Bible Society that had begun in 1698.[17] Its representatives declined his request. He then approached the LMS and Religious Tract Society. Rev. Joseph Hughes of the latter society wondered why no such vibrant Bible society existed. Subsequently, he, along with Rev. C. Steinkopf of the German Lutherans, Rev. John Owen (chaplain to the Anglican bishop of London), Samuel Mills, Zachary Macauley, William Wilberforce, Granville Sharp, and some three hundred others set about organizing the founding meeting of the Society for Promoting a More Extensive Circulation of the Scriptures at Home and Abroad on 7 March 1804 at 123 Bishopsgate Street in London. Soon renamed the British and Foreign Bible Society (BFBS), the BFBS immediately garnered interdenominational, panevangelical support, with its first three secretaries acting as a triumvirate: John Owen, Anglican; Joseph Hughes, evangelist or Nonconformist; and Carl F. Steinkopf, foreign. The respected John Shore, Lord Teignmouth, was appointed president, an office he would hold for thirty years. Its purpose was "to encourage a wider dispersion of the Holy Scriptures through the British Dominions and to other countries whether Christian, Mahomedan, or Pagan."[18] Thus was born "a society for furnishing the means of religion, but not a religious society."[19] In short order, the BFBS printed twenty thousand Welsh Bibles and in the space of only three years, printed, and distributed 1,816,000 Bibles, testaments, and portions thereof in sixty-six languages.[20]

What accounts for this remarkable success? Most scholars rightly point to the BFBS's multidenominational organization and support as a critical positive factor. While some Anglican clergy in particular bemoaned the absence of the Book of Common Prayer, and later arguments erupted over whether or not to include the Apocrypha, virtually everyone

---

16. Canton, *History of the British and Foreign Bible Society*, 1:466. See also Owen, *History of the Origin and First Ten Years*, 15. The above famous account was first published in the Bible Society's *Monthly Reporter*, January 1867.

17. The Society for Promoting Christian Knowledge had distributed some copies of the Bible in England, Wales, India, and Arabia. In 1701 the Society for the Propagation of the Gospel in Foreign Parts commenced, with special emphasis on the American Colonies. The year 1750 saw the startup of the Scottish Society for Propagating Christian Knowledge Among the Poor, and in 1780 the Naval and Military Bible Society began. See *The Catholic Encyclopedia*, New Advent, http://www.newadvent.org/cathen/02544a.htm.

18. Browne, *History of the British and Foreign Bible Society*, 1:10.

19. Canton, *History of the British and Foreign Bible Society*, 2:359.

20. Canton, *History of the British and Foreign Bible Society*, 1:318.

rallied around its constitution, the seminal first article of which mandated that its Bibles (then only the King James Version) be distributed "without note or comment." Prefaces, explanatory notes, and particular creeds and theologies "were explicitly forbidden."[21] The conviction reigned that the power of the word was sufficient enough to inspire, reprove, correct, and instruct "in righteousness" (2 Timothy 3:16).

While the original leadership was deeply religious, they were also tough-minded business people, innovators, and risk-takers with a global perspective. Soon after the society's formation and in the wake of Napoléon's recent defeat in 1812, Secretary Steinkopf embarked on incredibly ambitious tours of Prussia, Denmark, Russia, Sweden, Finland, and even the Middle East. Unforeseen by these founders was the remarkable and immediate popularity of what rapidly became a thriving business and a vast, international grass-roots movement. The rapid multiplication of auxiliaries and associations, in chain-reaction style in virtually every county in the United Kingdom, throughout Europe (including France), in Russia, in North America, and even in parts of the Orient, was a critical element of the society's success.[22] Its phenomenal expansion was clear evidence of the popular desire for Bibles at home and abroad.[23]

The British and Foreign Bible Society, London. From *A History of the The British and Foreign Bible Society*, by William Canton.

---

21. Howsam, *Cheap Bibles*, 6.
22. Within fourteen years of the establishment of the British and Foreign Bible Society, the following societies had been organized in imitation of the BFBS: the Basel Bible Society (Nuremberg, 1804), the Prussian Bible Society (1895), the Swedish Evangelical Society (1808), the Dorpat British Society (1811), the Riga Bible Society (1812), the Finnish Bible Society (1812), the Hungarian Bible Institution (1812), the Russian Bible Society (1812), the Swedish Bible Society (1814), the Danish Bible Society (1814), the Saxon Bible Society (1814), the Hanover Bible Society (1814), the Netherlands Bible Society (1814), the American Bible Society (1816), and the Norwegian Bible Society (1817). By 1817 these societies had printed 436,000 copies of the scriptures (Bibles and testaments) and had received gifts of sixty-two thousand volumes from the parent British and Foreign Bible Society. See "Bible Societies," https://www.encyclopedia.com/philosophy-and-religion/christianity/protestant-denominations/bible-societies.
23. As one early historian of the society put it, "This augmented demand for the English Scriptures [in Britain] was stimulated by the discoveries successively made of the want of them existing

Local leaders of various Christian faiths, including Roman Catholic priests in several areas, with independent boards soon joined in promoting subscriptions, appointing agents, and receiving and filling orders for scriptures.[24] This capillary action, extending down to the hosts of volunteer "home visitors" and colporteurs (traveling salesmen) who went from house to house, skirted the traditional bookseller method of distribution. At this level, women served by the thousands, often appointing their own auxiliaries with their own presidents, officers, and appointments. The ladies' associations were "enormously more successful and widespread than those of gentlemen" in distributing both tracts and Bibles.

> No gentleman could be found, who would undertake the task of going from house to house, to receive the subscriptions, and to make the necessary inquiries into the actual want of Bibles; but . . . [the ladies] immediately set to work with cheerfulness and courage, not minding the cold and even unfriendly reception which they met with here and there. . . . On entering a room whence an old woman was about to dismiss them with repulsive language, a poor girl, who had earnestly listened to their representation, arose from her spinning wheel, saying, in a cheerful tone, "I believe I have a few halfpence in my box; most gladly will I give them for so blessed a design." She fetched them, and they were her little all. Her conduct softened the old woman, and she likewise came forward with a few pence.[25]

By 1819, the BFBS counted 629 such auxiliaries, and in 1820 women home visitors in Liverpool alone made 20,800 Bible visits.[26]

The critical barrier, however, to popular ownership of the Bible in the United Kingdom and elsewhere was not so much ignorance, illiteracy, indifference, or even Catholic resistance but poverty—abject and universal. As late as 1812, British bishops estimated that at least half the population of the United Kingdom was destitute of Bibles.[27] In Ireland and other more impoverished countries, the percentage was steeply higher.

Thanks to the significant contributions of hundreds of wealthy philanthropists and the thousands of small donations from supporters everywhere, the BFBS vigorously financed ways to reduce the costs of production. By former royal decree, Cambridge University,

---

in a degree that could hardly have been conceived." Strickland, *History of the American Bible Society*, 55.

24. Despite the fact that the pope issued a bull against Bible societies as a weapon of Protestant evangelism that was "immensely dangerous to the faith," many Catholics supported local Bible society initiatives. "Religious Intelligence," *American Monthly Magazine and Critical Review* (New York) 1, no. 3 (July 1817): 202.
25. From the *16th Report of the British and Foreign Bible Society*, 102, as cited in Howsam, *Cheap Bibles*, 53. Whenever possible, the societies sought to sell their Bibles, rather than merely give them away.
26. Browne, *History of the British and Foreign Bible Society*, 1:76.
27. As one bishop lamented, "Half the population of the labouring classes in the metropolis of the British Empire were destitute of the Holy Scriptures." Browne, *History of the British and Foreign Bible Society*, 1:60.

Oxford Press, and the King's Printer owned the charters for printing the authorized King James Version of the Bible, if for no other reason than to ensure accuracy and dependability. But by ordering vast quantities, using such new advances as steam-power presses and stereotype printing (a process by which pages of type were cast as permanent metal plates and stored for reprinting),[28] using cheaper paper and binding, and printing in smaller quarto size volumes, the society continued to reduce the costs of its Bibles. A Bible that once cost a day's wages now sold for twenty-five shillings, within reach of most family incomes.

The proliferation in Bibles was not just a matter of reduced cost. The society early on vigorously sought to translate the scriptures into foreign languages, beginning with Mohawk language for those in Upper Canada (Ontario). Other early translations soon followed, including Italian (1807), Portuguese (1809), Dutch (1809), Danish (1809), French (1811), and Greek (1814). As one contemporary put it: "The most extraordinary disposition of the whole, however, is the remarkable exertions in translating the Bible into so many different languages—in 17 languages in the Russian Empire alone. . . . This is an extraordinary event. The like, in all circumstances, has never taken place in the world before."[29]

Yet even this winning combination of affordability, sound leadership, excellent organization, spirited volunteers, and a distribution system using Great Britain's Royal Navy does not fully explain the phenomenon. The fact is, in this prescientific epoch, the times were right for this new holy war. Many interpreted the successful termination of the Napoleonic Wars as a victory of Christian thought against the godless secularism of the French Revolution, a divine approbation of the expanding British Empire. They saw it as a new "Age of Light" of blessed opportunities, a "New Morality."[30] "Since the glorious period of the Reformation," wrote one American observer in 1818, "no age has been distinguished with such remarkable and important changes."[31]

---

28. Howsam, *Cheap Bibles*, 79.
29. *Remembrancer*, 22 January 1820, 88. Serious consideration was given early on to translating the Bible into the languages of India; however, the East India Company was for many years resistant to missionary work and Bible distribution for fear of possible revolt. See Browne, *History of the British and Foreign Bible Society*, 1:166–72, 273.
30. As Briggs put it, "The wars against France reinforced the movements for the reformation of manners and the enforcement of a strict morality; in many ways they widened the 'moral gap' between Britain and the Continent, as much as they widened the economic gap. . . . Only moral standards, supported by 'vital religion' were guarantees of social order, national greatness, and individual salvation." Briggs, *Age of Improvement*, 172.
31. *Evangelical Recorder*, 31 January 1818, 1. And from another, writing in February 1820: "We are labouring in a pacified world! The sword is beaten into the plough share, and the spear into the pruning hook. . . . The spirit of enterprize, nurtured in a protracted contest, is bursting forth in the discovery of new nations. The relations of Commerce, broken by war, are renewed; and are extending themselves on all sides. Every shore of the world is accessible to our Christian efforts. The civil and military servants of the Crown throughout its foreign possessions . . . are freely offering their labour and their influence to aid the benevolent designs of Christians. . . . Let us offer, then, as we have never yet offered. Let us meet the openings of Divine Providence." From

What had started inauspiciously quickly exceeded every expectation of the society's founders. Speaking in the spring of 1820, the Right Honourable Lord Teignmouth, former governor general of the British East India Company and president of the BFBS, took justifiable pride in the society's spectacular accomplishments:

> Never has the benign spirit of our holy religion appeared with a brighter or a more attractive luster, since the Apostolic times, then in the zeal and efforts displayed during the last sixteen years for disseminating the records of divine truth and knowledge. The benefit of these exertions has already extended to millions, and when we contemplate the vast machinery now in action for the unlimited diffusion of the Holy Scriptures, the energy which impels its movements, and the accession of power which it is constantly receiving, we cannot but indulge the exhilarating hope, "that the Angel, having the everlasting Gospel to preach to them that are upon the earth" has commenced his auspicious career. Even now, the light of divine revelation has dawned in the horizon of regions which it never before illuminated, and is becoming visible in others in which it had suffered a disastrous eclipse. . . . By His special favour the Bible Institution has proved a blessing to man-kind, and with the continuance of it . . . it will be hailed by future generations as one of the greatest blessings, next to that of divine Revelation itself, ever conferred on the human race.[32]

As of 1834 the BFBS had distributed 8,549,000 Bibles in 157 different languages.[33] By 1900 that figure had grown to 229,000,000 volumes of scripture in 418 languages. And by 1965 it had printed 723,000,000 volumes in 829 languages![34]

"ERRAND OF MERCY": THE AMERICAN BIBLE SOCIETY

In America, the need for Bibles was no less real and immediate. Up until 1780 almost all Bibles circulating in America had been printed in Great Britain. The Puritans had brought with them their Geneva Bible, first published in 1560, with its notes and teachings by John Calvin. Other immigrants brought the so-called Bishops' Bible, published by the Church of England in 1568.[35] With the suspension of British imports during the Revolutionary War,

---

"Extract from the 10th Report of the Church Missionary Society." *Remembrancer*, 12 February 1820, 99.

32. From a speech by The Right Hon. Lord Teignmouth, President, at the Sixteenth Anniversary of the Society, 3 May 1820, *Sixteenth Report of the British and Foreign Bible Society*, 223, 225.
33. From a speech by The Right Hon. Lord Teignmouth, President, at the Sixteenth Anniversary of the Society, 3 May 1820, *Sixteenth Report of the British and Foreign Bible Society*, 223, 225.
34. "List of Contributing Institutions," Mundus: Gateway to Missionary Collection in the United Kingdom, http://workbook.wordherders.net/2005/01/mundus-database-of-missionary-collections-in-the-uk.html.
35. Jackson, "Joseph Smith's Cooperstown Bible," 41. For an excellent study of the history of the Bible in America, see Gutjahr, *American Bible*.

there developed a "famine of Bibles" in America, one of the many ills which "a distracted Congress was called upon promptly to remedy."[36] Scottish-born Robert Aitken, at the direction of Congress, became America's first Bible publisher in 1781. Isaiah Thomas printed the first folio Bible from an American press ten years later. The Quaker Isaac Collins began printing his Bibles, known for their accuracy, that same year. The Irish-American Matthew Carey became the best-known Bible printer in early America, publishing more than sixty different editions in the early 1800s.[37] Between 1777 and 1820, propelled in part by the Second Great Awakening, the formation of Bible societies, and the aim of evangelizing the West,[38] four hundred new American editions of Bibles and New Testaments had been issued. By 1830 that number had climbed to seven hundred.[39]

Such increased production could not, however, keep up with population growth. Between 1790 and 1830, America's population skyrocketed from 3.9 to 9.6 million, with a very large number of people still not owning their own Bibles. For instance, an 1824 Bible society report from Rochester, New York, reported that in Monroe County alone some twenty-three hundred families were without Bibles.[40] An 1825 report stated at least 20 percent of Ohio families were without Bibles, and in Alabama, out of its thirty-six counties, half of the population did not own scriptures. In that same year, a reported ten thousand people in Maine were without Bibles, and in North Carolina there "cannot be less than 10,000 families . . . without the Bible." Even large metropolitan areas, such as New York and Philadelphia, were reported as seriously lacking.[41]

Such lack had been the reason for the organization of the Philadelphia Bible Society in 1808, the Connecticut and Massachusetts Bible Societies in 1809, and the New York Bible Society in that same year. Scores of others followed throughout New England and in the South. Yet even with these, many feared not "famine of bread, not a thirst for water, but of hearing the words of the Lord" (Amos 8:11). Among these was the intrepid reverend Samuel J. Mills, who viewed the Louisiana Purchase and the opening of a vast new western frontier as a potential new "valley of the shadow of death" (Psalm 23:4) in a future America

---

36. Dwight, *Centennial History of the American Bible Society*, 3.
37. Daniell, *Bible in English*, 594–96, 598–99, 627–29.
38. For a comprehensive and detailed study of the various American Bible editions, see Hills, *English Bible in America*.
39. Daniell, *Bible in English*, 639.
40. Dwight, *Centennial History*, 85. It may be worth noting that the Bible, "which fed the soul of Abraham Lincoln in the Kentucky log cabin of his boyhood, was one of those cheap little Bibles imported from London." Dwight, *Centennial History*, 3.
41. Lacy, *Word-Carrying Giant*, 50. See also Dwight, *Centennial History*, 84. See also American Bible Society, *Brief Analysis of the System of the American Bible Society*, 45. The following report is from an agent in Long Island, New York: "I am confident no region will be found in a Christian land where Bibles are more needed. There are here multitudes of people but just able to live, and who live and die almost as ignorant of the gospel as the Heathen. Many observe no Sabbaths, enjoy no religious ordinances, and have no religion, and they value them not, for they have no Bibles." Lacy, *Word-Carrying Giant*, 41.

unschooled in the Bible. In a series of tours and travels throughout the Ohio and Mississippi Valleys, Mills spread his message of Christian revivalism. More than any other person, Mills was the inspiration for the establishment of the American Bible Society (ABS).[42]

Seeing the need for cheaper American Bibles at a convention of American Bible societies in New York, Samuel Mills, Lyman Beecher, Thomas Biggs, Jedediah Morse, John E. Caldwell, William Jay, and several others presided over the formation of the ABS in May 1816. Elias Boudinot, of Cherokee descent and a former New Jersey delegate to the Continental Congress, presided over the society in its infant years. Soon forty-two other smaller state and regional societies merged under its expanding banner.[43]

Like its British parent and model, the ABS had as its sole object "to encourage a wider circulation of the Holy Scriptures without note or comment."[44] In what was called the "General Supply," the aim of the ABS was to furnish or "supply all the destitute families in the United States with the Holy Scriptures that may be willing to purchase or receive them."[45] It also aimed at resisting Thomas Paine's godless *Age of Reason*, a work that the ABS viewed as a "type of infection" and a flood of infidelity.[46] In addition to its primary goal of disseminating scriptures, it also served as a catalyst for local religious revivals and very much supported evangelistic activities and temperance movements.[47] Initially headquartered on Nassau Street in New York City, the ABS constantly enlarged its facilities to keep up with demand as well as advances in technology. Stereotype plates facilitated the printing process; auxiliaries soon spread to most American cities (301 by 1821); and every effort was made to put copies of the scriptures in every home. Among its many early translations were French, Spanish, and some Native American languages, the first of which was Delaware. After just four years in operation, the ABS had printed and distributed 231,552 Bibles and New Testaments.[48] By 1830 the numbers had climbed to 1,084,000.[49] By 1848 that figure would reach 5,860,000. And by 1916, after its first century, the corresponding figure stood at 115,000,000 volumes of scripture printed in 164 different languages.[50] Where the Smith family found its Bible that came to have such enormous influence on the boy prophet, Joseph Smith, is unknown (see chapter 13); however, it may well have come from the efforts of the American Bible Society. Without such a set of scriptures in his home, it is doubtful he would have ever been led to

---

42. Lacy, *Word-Carrying Giant*, 49.
43. "The First Annual Report of the Board of Managers of the American Bible Society, presented May 8, 1817." *Evangelical Guardian and Review* (New York), July 1817, 137.
44. Strickland, *History of the American Bible Society*, 31.
45. Lacy, *Word-Carrying Giant*, 51.
46. Few, *Bible Cause*, 28.
47. Few, *Bible Cause*, 52.
48. "First Report of the American Bible Society, Presented at the Annual Meeting, May 10, 1821," *Methodist Magazine*, August 1821, 312.
49. *Brief Analysis of the System of the American Bible Society*, 33.
50. Dwight, *Centennial History*, 521.

reading the scripture that changed his life—James 1:5–6—or made the invocations that led to a whole new religion.

"GO YE INTO ALL THE WORLD": THE AGE OF MISSIONARIES

As impressive as were the accomplishments of these tract and Bible societies, it was the dedicated men and women of the reinvigorated missionary societies who, in spending their lives in the cause, "extend[ed] the boundaries of Zion" in so real and permanent a way. Their stories of devotion and adventure, hardship and suffering—both in the home missions within England as well as those far afield—would fill volumes.

The Reverend John Williams characterized this as the "Great Century" of modern missions. While Catholicism had its full share of intrepid Jesuit missionaries in the form of St. Jean de Baptiste (1686–1770), Pierre Jean de Smet (1801–73), and many others, the Protestant initiatives were launched by William Carey (1761–1834), "the father of modern missions."[51] A masterful linguist, agriculturalist, botanist, and lover of books and learning, Carey authored the famed *Enquiry into the Obligations of the Christians to the Means for the Conversion of the Heathen.*" Carey devoted forty years of unbroken service as a Baptist missionary in India, beginning in tiger-infested jungles of Sunderbund, south of Calcutta, and later in Serampore, north of Calcutta. Carey mastered not only the languages but also the literature in Sanskrit, Punjabi, Bangali, and Mindi. He also translated and published the Bible from English into forty languages and dialects of India and Southeast Asia. A careful and wise administrator, he discreetly handled the antagonism of both local Indian officials opposed to Christianity, as well as the opposition of the East India Company (at least until its charter, guaranteeing religious freedom, was renewed in 1813), which worried that religious tampering might threaten its profits. Carey established a lasting reputation as a Christian educator who fell in love with his adopted country. Though an ardent proponent of Christianity, he founded Serampore College in Bengal in 1819 and became "an architect of secular education and social reformation in India."[52] What made his college so successful a role model and one so far ahead of its time was the policy of imparting all instruction in both English and local languages, of teaching the most modern Western sciences and classic Western literature in combination with a respect for Indian literature and culture, and of including a faculty of Christian theology. No less a pioneering feat in what was then a rigid caste-bound society, his college was "open admission to all persons, irrespective of caste, creed, color or religion."[53]

Suffering the loss of his wife, Dorothy, and two of his children, Carey soldiered on until his own death in June 1834. By that time, there were thirty missionaries in India, forty-five native teachers, forty-five stations, and over six hundred Christian converts. More than

---

51. Kane, *Concise History of the Christian World Mission*, 83.
52. Ngapkynta, *William Carey*, i.
53. Ngapkynta, *William Carey*, 105.

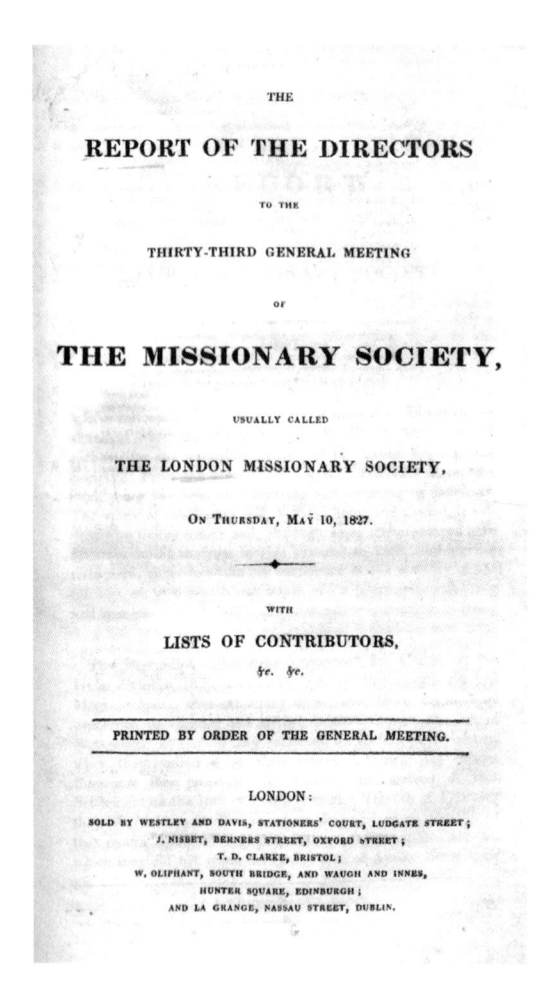

Report of the Directors to the Twenty-Third General Meeting of the Missionary Society, in London, on Thursday, May 15, 1827.

anyone else, Carey inspired the formation of the LMS in 1795 and the Church Missionary Society in 1799. Carey "inaugurated a new era of united, organized and systematic operations" that have persisted to the present day.[54]

Carey's pioneering counterpart in China was the Reverend Robert Morrison (1782–1834). Having learned Chinese before his mission departure in 1807, he worked for the East India Company for a time before becoming a resident of China. A narrow survivor of the emperor's 1812 edict that forbid the printing of any Christian books on pain of death, Morrison completed his translation of the New Testament into Chinese in 1814. After twenty-seven years of persecution, "incessant labour and of great loneliness for the Master's sake," deprivation of family for several years, and subsistence living on a diet of only Irish stew and dried roots, Morrison baptized only ten persons.[55] Yet, despite almost every conceivable discouragement, he produced his English-Chinese dictionary, established the Anglo-Chinese College at Malacca, and finally translated the entire Bible into Chinese.[56]

---

54. Kane, *Progress of World-Wide Missions*, 59.
55. Lovett, *History of the London Missionary Society, 1795–1895*, 2:422. Of the religious persecutions in China, the following 1815 letter from a Catholic missionary there affords some details: "Every European priest that is discovered, is instantly seized and put to death; Chinese Christian priests undergo the same fate. Christians of the laity, unless they will apostatize, are first dreadfully tortured, and then banished. . . . This year, in the prisons of one province alone, (Sutchen) two hundred Christians were expecting the orders for their exile. A Christian Chinese priest has just been strangled, and two others were also under sentence of death." "Persecution in China," *American Masonic Register* 1, no. 1 (September 1820): 73.
56. A man of encyclopedic interests and one who respected other faiths, Morrison also translated Buddha's biography from Chinese into English: entitled *Account of Foe: The Deified Founder of a Chinese Sect*. This translation, published in 1812, gave Europeans a direct sense of the

Besides the Far East, three other areas of special concern for the LMS were the British West Indies (Jamaica and British Guiana), Africa, and the South Pacific. The Reverend John Smith will ever be remembered for his Christianizing, courageous, and liberalizing efforts among the much-abused and tortured slaves of Demerara, Berbice, Jamaica, and elsewhere in the West Indies. What Smith opposed was a culture of atrocity and inhuman cruelty to enslaved people, which included lack of medical treatment, the prohibition of marriage, gross licentiousness, whippings, indiscriminate and defenseless murdering, black holes of endless punishments, insufficient nourishment, and excessive work demands.[57] Despised on the one hand by many white plantation owners for fomenting ideas of freedom, equality, and human dignity, he was cherished on the other hand by the native populations who welcomed his liberating spirit, sense of human justice, unflinching honor, integrity, and Christian zeal. Tragically, Rev. Smith was imprisoned in hideous circumstances. He perished in 1824, a martyr to his cause, and is buried in an unmarked grave somewhere on the beautiful isle of Jamaica.[58]

William Carey, by unknown artist.

Dr. J. T. Vanderkemp, MD, was the first LMS missionary to South Africa, arriving there in 1797, just two years after the British seizure of the former Dutch colonies there. Distrusted by both disgruntled Dutch farmers and nervous British overseers and administrators for believing in "equal rights for blacks and whites, for Kafir [natives] and Boer, for Hottentot and colonist," Vanderkemp spread the Christian gospel to native and colonist alike and in the process founded Bethelsdorp, a Dutch colony. He died in Cape Town at age sixty-three in 1811.

He was succeeded by the Reverend John Campbell in 1812 and Dr. John Philip in 1819, both of whom were vilified by British and Dutch established interests for their "ceaseless,

---

religion and contributions of Buddha in a biographical setting. See Wu and Wilkinson, *Reinventing the Tripitaka*, 12.
57. Lovett, *History of the London Missionary Society*, 2:337–45.
58. Wallbridge, *Demerara Martyr*.

energetic, and successful toil on behalf of the native races" and for confronting the evils of slavery, racial prejudice, opium trafficking and addiction.[59] While the stated objective of the LMS was "to spread the knowledge of Christ among heathen and other unenlightened nations" and to do so without regard to denominationalism, LMS missionaries confronted social and cultural evils whenever and wherever they encountered them. While they generally stayed out of local politics and governance, they believed that "if the government of a country allies itself with cruelty, social wrongs, and oppression, the Christian missionary, working within the sphere of such government, must find himself in active opposition to such things."[60]

Gradually the proselytizing efforts of the LMS in Africa moved northward through the efforts of Rev. Robert Moffat at Kuruman, a missionary outpost in South Africa north of the Orange River, eventually culminating in the multiyear explorations and evangelical efforts of the famed Scotsman Dr. David Livingstone (1813–73). Both Kuruman and Livingstone were anxious to rid Africa of the slave trade. During Livingstone's expeditions across Africa from the Atlantic to the Indian Oceans, and later northward into the African interior in search of the source of the Nile, he identified twenty-eight previously unknown tribes. He died of malaria at the village of Ilala in Zambia in central Africa years later in 1873 and today lies buried in Westminster Abbey. In America the Calvinist-oriented Boston Mission, or American Board of Commissioners for Foreign Missions (ABCFM), began in 1810 and concentrated its early efforts on Native Americans and Hawaiians, with its first missionaries disembarking there in the spring of 1820.

David Livingstone, by Thomas Annan.

What turned the attention of the LMS to the Polynesian Islands (literally meaning "many islands") was a combination of several factors. These included Carey's own interests in the region; the Reverend Henry Nott's (1774–1844) recent proselyting successes in Tahiti; the tragic death of Captain Cook in Hawaii; "its conflicting if not mysterious scenes of incredible beauty, adventure and human degradation"; the success of the Wesleyan Missionary Society in Tonga, Australia, and New Zealand;

---

59. Lovett, *History of the London Missionary Society*, 2:541.
60. Lovett, *History of the London Missionary Society*, 2:544.

and concern over a renewal of post-Revolution, French-sponsored, Roman Catholic missionary endeavors.[61]

After sailing 13,820 miles aboard the sailing ship *Duff*, Rev. Nott first set foot on the island of Tahiti on 5 March 1797, along with twenty-nine other missionaries. A bricklayer by trade, Nott applied himself to learning the native language and to teaching the gospel without ceasing, refusing to give up when many of his minister colleagues became discouraged and returned home. A natural peacemaker, he negotiated a remarkable peace between warring tribes in the island of Tutuai. Nott's greatest breakthrough came in 1813 with the conversion of Otu, King Pōmare in 1813 and his victory over the island's pagan chiefs. Pōmare's conversion resulted in the eventual Christianization of most of Tahiti, the destruction of pagan temples and of the pagan idol Oro, and erection of the 730-foot-long, 54-foot-wide Royal Mission Chapel at Papaoa, which opened in 1819. Pōmare baptized some five thousand of his people in June 1819, and Christian churches and chapels began springing up all over Tahiti. Before Nott's death of a stroke in 1844, he had translated the entire Bible into Tahitian. The islanders' rapid conversion to Christianity persuaded many of the missionaries as well as the native populations that the Polynesians descended from the ten tribes of Israel.[62] Tahiti remained in English hands until the time of the French interventions in 1838 and the coming of large numbers of Roman Catholic priests. Even though Tahiti became a French protectorate in 1847, much of Protestantism has endured there to this day.

"WE MUST BRANCH OUT TO THE RIGHT AND LEFT"

We must now return to our apostle of Polynesia. Nott's impressive success inspired young John Williams to apply to serve in the LMS in the first place. "A man of restless energy, of sunny temperament, of strong self-confidence, of bold initiative, [and] of resolute faith," Williams and his wife, Mary, arrived in Tahiti on 16 November 1817, twelve long months to the day after leaving England's shores.[63] Two months later their first child, a boy, was born, one of the first European babies born in Tahiti. Mary found companionship with the wives of other missionaries and tried to adjust to raising a newborn and living a half a globe away from home. Mail took months to arrive, and a twenty-week-old newspaper was about as current as could be expected.

Unlike Rev. Nott, who had confined himself throughout his forty-seven years of missionary service almost exclusively to Tahiti, Williams was a restless sort who would spread his nets wide across the many islands and vast distances of Polynesia. "I never considered [Tahiti] alone as worthy of the lives and labours of the number of missionaries who have been employed there," he later wrote. "I cannot content myself within the narrow limits of a

---

61. Smith, *History of the Establishment and Progress*, 108. Peru had sent Catholic missionaries to Tahiti in the early 1770s but with little effect.
62. Koskinen, "Missionary Influence as a Political Factor in the Pacific Islands," 101–2.
63. Lovett, *History of the London Missionary Society*, 2:238.

single reef," and "we must branch out to the right and left."[64] Oftentimes called the ironmonger apostle, "the apostolic skipper," and "Polynesian apostle," Rev. Williams would spread the Protestant Christian gospel from Tahiti and Raiatea of the Society Islands and other islands of what today is French Polynesia to the Samoan (Navigator) Islands, where his pioneering missionary efforts reached crowning success.

Williams and his wife knew full well the dangers they were up against. The work of converting these peoples was challenging. A highly intelligent, remarkably curious, cheerful, and inquisitive people, the natives of these many islands had accumulated over the centuries many customs that were strange and offensive to Europeans. Oro, the god of war, seemed to rule everywhere, at least in the Society Islands, and his priests delighted in offering human sacrifice. Their constant interisland wars, which lasted with atrocious vengeance from one generation to the next, featured wholesale massacres at sea or on land and human dismemberment, with captives slain and cannibalized on the spot or burned alive in giant bonfires. One of the great evils of the islands was the existence of Ono, a systematic revenge for the killing of a family member. "It was a legacy bequeathed from father to son to avenge that injury, even if an opportunity did not occur until the third or fourth generation."[65]

The idolatry of these islands was fearful and legendary. The creator god was Tangaroa, sometimies called Taaroa, or Taau, god of thunder. There were deities of snakes, lizards, dogs, and almost every other creature on land and in the sea—be it turtles, sharks, and even eels. To appease the anger of these myriad divinities, human sacrifice or disfigurements often took place in their island temples, or marae. Each island had its own oracle or priestly class to divine the will of the gods through their incessant prayers or *ubu*, chants and drum beating. Witchcraft and sorcery were also common, as were divinations and exorcisms.[66]

These islands were as dangerous and unpredictable as they were beautiful. Many of Williams's missionary colleagues disappeared, either at sea or on land. Others of the less courageous makeup gave up and returned with their families to England. The natives' social customs and codes of conduct could be harsh. Thieves caught in the act were sometimes cut in pieces and their limbs hung up in different parts of the *kainga*, or farm. Even young children caught stealing could be thrown into the sea with a heavy stone attached to one or both legs. The sick and the elderly were often buried alive because they were seen as a troubling nuisance.

On some islands, women were considered to be a necessary evil. As Williams described it, "Females were looked upon as so polluting, that they were never allowed to enter the sacred precincts (idol temples); and even the presence of the pigs in the enclosure was not considered so dreadful a desecration as that of women."[67] Immorality and polygamy were rampant. Many of a chief's young polygamous wives were purchased, and "if a sufficient

---

64. Lovett, *History of the London Missionary Society*, 2:254, 378.
65. Williams, *Narrative of Missionary Enterprises*, 64.
66. Smith, *History of the Establishment and Progress*, 60–97.
67. Williams, *Narrative of Missionary Enterprises*, 83.

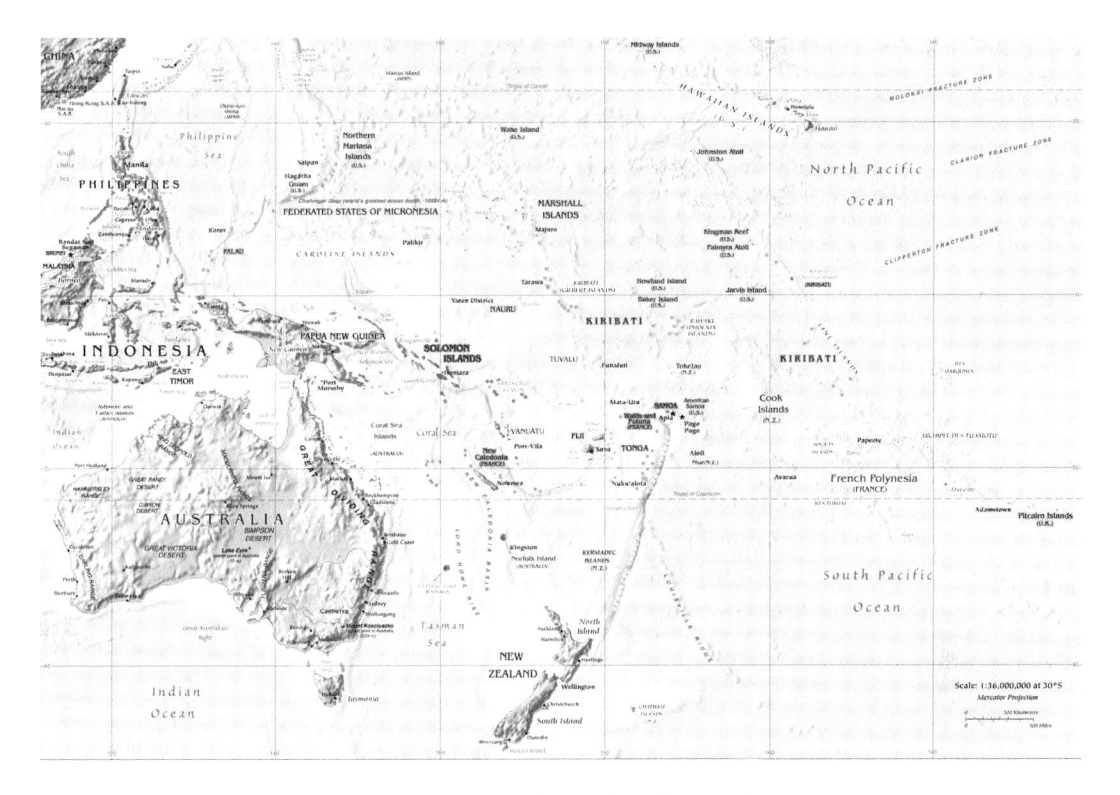

A Map Covering Most of Oceania. Courtesy of Cental Intelligence Agency.

price is paid to the relatives, the young woman seldom refuses to go, though the purchaser be ever so old and unlovely."[68] Many older wives were abandoned. In Fiji when a chief died, all his wives were executed one by one, much like the custom of Suttee in India.

Abortions and infanticide were considered to be among the worst of the practices. In a society and culture that emphasized violence and criminality and minimized conscience, such atrocities were especially rampant in the Society and Georgian Islands. Mothers would sometimes kill their own children if they and their husbands were of inferior rank one to another, if the nursing of a child was seen as reducing a mother's beauty, or if they feared their children would be killed or sacrificed as a by-product of an impending war. They would either break their bones and limbs and bury them alive in a hole or else strangle them to death. There are accounts of many women who had killed at least five of their own children. One woman killed sixteen of her children. Such atrocities particularly bothered Mrs. Williams, who worked to improve their morality and to abandon violent practices.[69]

As frightful as many of these customs were to the eyes of these early missionaries, they were made worse by runaway sailors and escaped convicts (beachcombers) who performed

---

68. Williams, *Narrative of Missionary Enterprises*, 91.
69. Prout, *Memoirs*, 280–90. See also Williams, *Narrative of Missionary Enterprises*, 65–83.

"incalculable mischief." Their acts of murder, kidnapping, cruelty, and "harbour prostitution" made the missionary efforts all the more difficult. They spread a religion of a very selfish and destructive kind. Ship captains of one nation or another often unloaded barrels of alcohol of every variety in exchange for booty and to buy the support of one tribe or another in interior island conflicts. John and Mary Williams despised the beachcombers and fought to lessen their damaging influence.[70]

Rev. Williams employed many of the proven tactics of the more successful missionaries of the LMS, plus several of his own variety. Like William Carey in India, Williams had a remarkable aptitude for learning the native languages and possessed an unfailing memory. An intense observer, he astounded even the natives by how quickly he learned the inflection and accentuations of their languages and dialects, which, at least west of the Melanesia Islands, bore a striking similarity one to another. He soon was sermonizing in their languages, and translated the scriptures into native languages. He taught in their new Christian schools and introduced new and more powerful medicines. He also taught them of the advances in agriculture and showed them new crops to grow—sugar and tobacco—but how to make the necessary tools to plant and harvest their crops. A definite hands-on kind of educator and minister, he delivered many of his best sermons at the plow rather than the pulpit. He taught with scythe as well as scripture and carried within him an uncommonly deep respect for the island culture and people, their native cheerfulness, trusting disposition, and sense of gratitude. He appreciated their unbounding curiosity, inquisitiveness, and strong intelligence; their eagerness to learn and to improve; and their native humility. Because of such endearing qualities, wherever he sailed, he soon came to be loved and respected.

Williams did not stay long in Tahiti. Perhaps the work done there by Rev. Nott, their file leader, left little room for a young, ambitious soldier of the cross. Williams and his young family sailed to a new field of endeavor in the island of Raiatea in September 1818, with its magnificent natural harbor and two-thousand-foot-high, cloud-enshrined mountains rising majestically from the blue watery carpet of the surrounding sea. Recently devastated by plague and epidemic, Raiatea was particularly disposed to hear of a powerful religion.

Though Raiatea had been the center of the worship of Ono and of human sacrifices, King Tamatoa had already met Rev. Williams and invited him to come. Soon after arriving, Williams set about erecting a fine new dwelling house for his wife and family unlike anything the islanders had ever seen before. It was sixty by thirty feet with seven rooms and their own handcrafted furniture. The natives loved to visit and have tea. The women were as impressed with Mary's long dresses and sunbonnets as the men were with Rev. Williams's feats of carpentry. Once Williams had finished the house, he went to work teaching the islanders the practical gospel of mechanical arts: carpentry, smithing, plastering, and other aspects of house building as well as gardening. The natives learned these newfound skills

---

70. Williams, *Narrative of Missionary* Enterprises, 119–20.

quickly. Williams knew that a new house was as good as a homily in changing old ways. He lived by the motto "Expect great things and attempt them."[71]

Williams taught his new island friends not only mechanical skills but also how to read and write in the best Sunday School tradition. Attendance at their Sabbath sermons and Bible-reading services Sunday morning and evening significantly increased, and many learned English by ponderously reading aloud the Gospel of Luke. Williams and his wife both loved to sing, and hearing the islanders sing "Abide with Me" was a new experience. Although he sermonized from the Christian gospels, Williams followed LMS policy in not establishing new codes of laws or imposing a new political system in his growing number of followers. He keenly sensed the delicate balance between teaching a new religion and imposing a new political order.[72] However, he did teach about the Decalogue and the Bible, a new respect for life, and other important laws prohibiting criminal and unduly cruel behavior. In this broader sense, he became one of "the legislators of the islands."[73]

" And the idols he shall utterly abolish."—Isaiah ii. 18. (See page 30.)

The Reverend John Williams and his wife watching as natives give up their idols. From *Narrative of Missionary Enterprises*, engraving by George Baxter.

---

71. Prout, *Memoirs*, 68.
72. Williams, *Narrative of Missionary Enterprises*, 36–37.
73. Koskinen, *Missionary Influence*, 58.

To accommodate his growing number of followers, Williams next did what was characteristic of most LMS missionaries: he constructed a chapel. With the help of many of the natives, anxious to show off their new skills, he built a massive 191- by 44-foot chapel with strong pillars, pulpits, and glorious candle-bearing chandeliers in the winter of 1819–20. At its opening on 11 May 1820, 2,400 Raiateans crowded in, and hundreds of them were soon baptized. The birth of the Williams's second child that same season gave cause for the entire island to celebrate, with women bearing so many gifts of coconuts and plants to Mrs. Williams that their home could not contain them all.

A particular attraction of Christianity to the Polynesians was the Christian doctrine of redemption of sin and the common belief in the afterlife. "The fate of their departed ancestors was to them a subject of painful interest. 'Have none of the former inhabitants of these islands gone to heaven?' many often asked."[74] Indeed, one primary reason for tattooing was to perpetuate the memory of a beloved and departed relative.[75]

Leaving Mary in Raiatea and having established a winning pattern, Williams sailed to Ruruta in 1821, where he met a supreme test. The local priests invited William to a large feast. Feeding pork, turtle, and other substances of unknown content to the guests, the priests predicted some would die, especially those sitting at unknown, prearranged seating places. Those who sickened, would themselves be sacrificed and eaten. However, if no one sustained any injury or illness, they would destroy their idols. "They met accordingly; and after satisfying their appetites without any injuries being sustained, they arose; boldly seized their gods; set fire to the three sacred houses, the residences of their godships; and then proceeded to demolish the maraes."[76] Relieved and highly encouraged, Williams promptly set about building a new Christian chapel.

Still, not all of their news that year was good. Their worst sadness that year was the unexpected death of their second child, a devastating blow especially for Mary, who was growing weary of her husband's island hopping. Later that year, William visited the island of Aitutaki, pressed noses with the chiefs, and told the islanders of the overthrow and destruction of Raiatea's gods. Convinced that Williams's god was more powerful than all their idols, the natives of Aitutaki proved especially receptive to the Christian gospel, in part because of Williams's particularly effective evangelizing tactic of leaving behind indigenous island mission teachers as pastors to teach their own people.[77]

With the death of his mother in 1819, Williams had used part of her estate to purchase a boat in Sydney, New South Wales, which he named the *Endeavor*, in remembrance of Captain Cook. While still recovering from giving birth to her second stillborn child, Mary joined her husband on yet another Christian conquest in 1823, this time to Rarotonga.

---

74. Smith, *History of the Establishment and Progress*, 222.
75. Williams, *Narrative of Missionary Enterprises*, 139–40.
76. Lovett, *History of the London Missionary Society*, 252.
77. Boutilier, "'We Fear Not the Ultimate Triumph,'" in Miller, *Missions and Missionaries in the Pacific*, 38–39. "Indigenous Christians, Not the Missionaries, Were the Experts." Case, *Unpredictable Gospel*, 8.

Kindly received by King Makea as a healer and builder, Williams went right to work erecting another massive chapel as big as the Royal Chapel at Tahiti. Built without nails or any ironwork it was large enough to accommodate three thousand new converts.

The Rarotongans soon learned to love their island apostle. His biggest obstacle proved not to be the islanders but the LMS itself. Somehow persuaded that Williams was becoming more of a merchantman than a missionary, his overseers demanded that he surrender his ship, which he had no choice but to do. His wife firmly at his side, Williams felt that he was misunderstood. After two years in Rarotonga, he hoped to set sail aboard the next vessel for Samoa in the Navigators' Islands. This time, Mary demurred. Not one to complain, she felt she could go no further. "How can you suppose that I can give my consent to such a strange proposition?" she asked. "You will be 1800 miles away, six months absent, and among the most savage people we are acquainted with; and if you should lose your life in the attempt, I shall be left a widow with my fatherless children, 20,000 miles from my friends and my home."

No doubt such pioneering missionary work took its toll on marriage and family life. Although the LMS pursued a policy of married couples going out together, such service was extremely demanding. William Carey's wife lost her mind; other wives became alcoholics; not a few returned homesick and heartbroken to England. Education for missionary children was always a grave concern.

One particular trial bears mentioning. Although an island of exquisite beauty, Rarotonga was overridden with rats. There were so many of them that when eating, two or more people had to knock them off the table. When kneeling in family prayer, the Williamses had to fight off rats that would run over them from all directions. They reported, "We found much difficulty in keeping them out of our beds."[78] One night the rats even devoured Mary's shoes. The infestation continued until Williams brought back from a nearby island a shipload of cats and hogs that in short order decimated the rat populations.[79]

Mary soon came down with a terrible fever and took deathly ill. Miraculously, she recovered. In her still faithful way, she chose to see it as a sign, a trial sent from God for her stubbornness. Turning to her husband, who had put off his Samoan plans indefinitely, she said, "From this time your desire has my full concurrence; and when you go, I shall follow you every day with my prayers, that God may preserve you from danger, crown your attempt with success, and bring you back in safety."[80]

Buoyed by his wife's support and confidence, and waiting in frustration for a passing ship that would never dare come to such a feared island, Williams set upon a new course of action. He resolved, in Robinson Crusoe fashion, to build one himself. Applying all the iron-making, woodworking, and other mechanical skills he had ever learned, the resourceful Williams crafted a set of bellows out of goatskins, a variety of machine pumps, a lathe,

---

78. Williams, *Narrative of Missionary Enterprises*, 40.
79. Williams, *Narrative of Missionary Enterprises*, 40.
80. Williams, *Narrative of Missionary Enterprises*, 37–38.

pincers, tongs, rope-spinning machinery, cordage, sails, oakum, pitch, paint, anchors, and rudder. With iron in short supply and a lack of saws and nails, he used wedges to split the wood and wooden pins or treenails to fasten boards together. For sails, he used the mats on which the natives slept. Fortunately, he had his own compass and quadrant. To the fascination and delight of the native islanders that winter of 1827–28, who rushed to help him out and called it all "godly mechanicks," the new ship-builder of Rarotonga fashioned in three months' time a seaworthy vessel of some fifty to sixty tons' displacement that he christened the *Messenger of Peace*. Some of his amazed missionary colleagues preferred to see it as "the finger of God."[81] In evaluating his success, Williams later provided this insight: "There are two little words in our language which I always admired, try and trust. You know not what you can or cannot effect, until you try; and if you make your trials in the exercise of trust in God, mountains of imaginary difficulties will vanish as you approach them, and facilities will be afforded you never anticipated."[82]

The Williamses' return to Raiatea in 1828 was not without disappointment: the death of yet another infant child. Leaving Mary behind but with her support, Rev. Williams finally realized his long-standing dream of spreading the gospel to the Samoan Islands. With few, if any, of the idols and temples with the reputation for cruelties and human sacrifices, Samoa was a favored destination. The absence of a priestly hierarchy (unlike Tahiti) worked to Williams's advantage. And as fortune had it, the leading antagonist chief against Christianity died just days before Williams disembarked. The new chief, Malietoa, welcomed him and allowed him to preach his message. The result was that "a wide and effectual door was here opened for the gospel."[83] Rev. Williams's successful work in converting virtually the entire Samoan Islands was no less an accomplishment than what Nott had done previously in Tahiti and will ever remain Williams's crowning missionary achievement.

After seventeen years in the islands, John and Mary and family returned to England for two years to reacquaint themselves with family, write, publish a book of their missionary experience, buy a bigger boat, and complete the translation and printing of the Bible into the Rarotongan tongue. They also used this opportunity to raise much-needed funds from selling the book and lecturing throughout Great Britain on their experiences. Little did they know that this would be the last time John Williams would see England.

The Williamses returned to Rarotonga in February 1839 on board the *Camden*, a much bigger ship that the islanders, eagerly awaiting their return, promptly renamed "the praying ship."[84] Williams's determination was to move to the islands further west to proselyte in the New Hebrides because he was convinced they were the key to successfully proselyting New Caledonia, New Guinea, and the whole of western Polynesia.

---

81. Prout, *Memoirs*, 176. See also Boutilier, "'We Fear Not the Ultimate Triumph,'" 34.
82. Williams, *Narrative of Missionary Enterprises*, 93.
83. Prout, *Memoirs*, 220.
84. Prout, *Memoirs*, 330.

The Messenger of Peace Leaving Aitutak (London, Snow, 1837), engraving by George Baxter.

His dream never materialized. On 20 November 1839, while on a surveying mission to the island of Erromango, an island in Vanuatu, everything began to go terribly wrong. The islanders there spoke a language Williams did not know and were very shy and of a more untrusting demeanor. Not long before, European traders in search of sandalwood had invaded the island and committed several atrocities against the natives, particularly the women. Sailing on a small whaleboat to the shore, Williams noticed yet another ominous sign: the absence of women, who almost always were made absent when hostilities seemed imminent. He and a missionary companion, Mr. Harris, disembarked and attempted to give their presents to their frowning hosts. Suddenly, a large number of shouting islanders charged out from behind the trees, setting the two men scrambling for the sea. Both were brutally clubbed before being pierced with several arrows, their blood staining the sandy shoreline. A distraught Captain Robert C. Morgan and the other sailors aboard the *Camden* were powerless to help and could not even retrieve the bodies, which were soon stripped and hauled inland. Three months later, Captain Morgan returned on board *The Favorite*, a British man-of-war, to recover their bodies, only to learn the sordid tale that the islanders "had devoured the bodies, of which nothing remained but some of the bones."[85] Wrote Captain Morgan in his ship's log: "Thus died a great and good man, like a soldier standing to his post: a heavy loss to his

---

85. Williams, *Narrative of Missionary Enterprises*, 394.

Apolima Island, Samoa, by Alfred T. Agate (ca. 1840). Courtesy of Naval History and Heritage Command.

beloved wife and three children. He was a faithful and successful laborer among the islands of these seas. . . . I have lost a father, a brother, a valuable friend and advisor."[86]

The news of his tragic death devastated his wife and children and set the islanders of Samoa, Rarotonga, Raiatea, Hitataki, and a score of other islands into an extended period of sorrow and mourning. Gone was their teacher and guide, their missionary friend and builder, their kind exemplar and devoted servant. At his wife's instructions, his few remains were buried in Apia, Samoa. She eventually returned to England, a sad and lonely woman who died faithful to the Christian cause in 1852, two years after the first Latter-day Saint missionaries arrived in the Sandwich Islands.

The pioneering efforts of men and women like John and Mary Williams paved the way for the later arrival of the Latter-day Saint missionaries. Latter-day Saint historian Fred E. Woods may have summed up their contributions best:

> Although there was a vying for native converts, the LDS missionaries benefited from the preparatory work of the LMS, which had launched Christianity in this region at the end of the eighteenth century. Further, primary evidence reveals that although there was certainly friction between representatives of these two denominations, some degree of

---

86. Williams, *Narrative of Missionary Enterprises*, 392.

mutual respect occurred when the missionaries from each party discussed their personal beliefs while meeting in private. . . . Surely the Mormons recognized how LMS work laid the groundwork for their own, just as Paul wrote: "I have planted, Apollos watered; but God gave the increase" (1 Cor. 3:6).[87]

The fire of religious fervor that characterized our age of 1820 found expression in hundreds of different kinds of improvement societies that sprang up almost spontaneously, first in Great Britain and then later in America and elsewhere. This chapter has emphasized three kinds of Christian societies in particular that wielded such astonishing influence worldwide that their story had to be told: the religious tract societies, the British Foreign Bible Society and its Americana counterpart, the American Bible Society, and their incredible success in disseminating scripture, and most noteworthy the London Missionary Society. Their efforts led to millions of people having copies of the Holy Bible in their home, and may even have resulted in the Joseph Smith family having one such set of scriptures at their kitchen table.

Yet it was the faith and sacrifice of men and women like the faithful Rev. John Williams, the "apostle of Polynesia," and his devoted wife, Mary, who really made it happen. Their proselytizing efforts among the islanders struck a responsive chord. They were particularly successful because they taught practical skills as well as religious convictions, because they respected island culture while teaching them new ways of behavior, and because they loved and were loved in return.

The Massacre of the Lamented Missionary the Rev. J. Williams and Mr. Harris, by George Baxter (1841).

---

87. Woods, "Latter-day Saint Missionaries Encounter the London Missionary Society," 124.

Henry Clay, by Matthew Harris Jouett.

"WE NEVER HAD SO OMINOUS A QUESTION"

HENRY CLAY, THE RISE OF AMERICA, AND THE VALUE OF POLITICAL COMPROMISE

"We should become the center of a system which would constitute the rallying-point of human freedom against all the despotism of the old world."[1] So wrote Henry Clay, one of America's finest patriots and most successful compromisers, who on several different occasions would run for president of the United States. Although he was never elected to that high office, his most fascinating life and his many contributions to his native country will serve as a springboard for the following short study of American history in the age of 1820.

In the year of our Lord 1820, the young and emboldened United States of America increasingly viewed itself as the rising bastion of liberty and equality for all the world to see, the last, great hope of better things to come. Yet it almost dismembered itself in a cacophony of harsh-sounding warnings and epithets that reverberated through the halls of Congress and all across the land in debates over admission of its first state west of the Mississippi River. This stunning controversy, what Thomas Jefferson called "a fire bell in the night," marked the greatest crisis in America's short history up until that time.[2] Had it not been for the statesmanship of one particular Kentucky politician, the bloodbath of the American Civil War may well have begun forty years ahead of its time and perhaps with a much different outcome.

---

1. Henry Clay, 10 May 1820, in Colton, *Life, Correspondence, and Speeches of Henry Clay*, 5:243.
2. Moore, *Missouri Controversy*, 1.

At issue was the admission of Missouri into the Union and the fractious controversy over slavery. Warned Senator Freeman Walker of Georgia in a speech he delivered in Congress on 19 January 1820:

> I fear—much do I fear—that the imposition of restrictions on the refusal to admit [Missouri] unconditionally, into the Union, will excite a tempest, whose fury will not be easily allayed. It is, perhaps, wrong to predict or anticipate evil, but he must be badly acquainted with the signs of the times, who does not perceive a storm portending; and callous to all the finer feelings must he be, who does not dread the bursting of that storm. . . .
>
> I behold the father armed against the son, and the son against the father. I perceive a brother's sword crimsoned with a brother's blood. I perceive our houses wrapped in flames, and our wives and infant children driven from their homes. . . . I trust in God, that this creature of the imagination may never be realized. But if Congress persist[s] in the determination to impose the restriction contemplated, I fear there is too much cause to apprehend that consequences fatal to the peace and harmony of this Union will be the inevitable result.[3]

As Representative Thomas W. Cobb, also of Georgia, phrased it, "We have kindled a fire which all the waters of the ocean cannot put out, which seas of blood can only extinguish."[4]

Speaking for the majority in the House of Representatives that strongly opposed Missouri's entrance into the Union as a slave state, an exasperated and emotional James Tallmadge of New York fervently responded: "Sir, if a dissolution of the Union must take place, let it be so! If civil war, which gentlemen so much threatens, must come, I can only say, let it come! My hold on life is probably as frail as that of any man who now hears me; but while that hold lasts, it shall be devoted to the service of my country—to the freedom of man. . . . Now is the time. [Slavery] must now be met, and the extension of the evil must now be prevented, or the occasion is irrevocably lost."[5]

Meanwhile, several thousand miles away, in Göttingen, Germany, two young American students were studying abroad, oblivious to the rancorous debates then paralyzing Washington. They raised their glasses in a 4 July 1820 toast to the goodness, greatness, and divine destiny of their glorious, young American republic. One of them, nineteen-year-old George Bancroft of Worcester, Massachusetts, who would become one of America's most towering nineteenth-century future historians and intellects, read the honor roll of George Washington, Thomas Jefferson, John Adams, and President James Monroe. He then proclaimed his allegiance to his native land: "The great forests of the west, the hum of business,

---

3. US Congress, *Abridgment of the Debates of Congress, from 1789 to 1856*, 16th Congress, 1st Session, Senate Papers, 6:400.
4. As cited in Jones, "Henry Clay and Continental Expansion," 244.
5. From a speech by Mr. James Tallmadge (New York), 16 February 1819, 15th Congress, 2nd Session, House of Representatives, *Debates of Congress*, 6:351–52.

the vessels of commerce, the American Eagle, 'the sweet nymph of liberty,' the abolition of slavery, and last of all, 'Our country—the asylum of the oppressed.'"[6]

The year 1820 therefore marked both a dream and a warning, an unfolding promise of liberty in a land that had grown sixfold from a mere 1.6 million in 1760 to 9.6 million in 1820, an unmistakable warning of the unbridgeable divide over the existence and attempted extension of that peculiar institution of slavery. Bancroft's optimism was surely tempered by Senator Walker's gloomy prophecies. This tug of war of expectations forms the entry point for our following discussion on the rise of America and its place on the world stage.

"WAS EVER A PEOPLE MORE BLESSED?"

If the age of 1820 was one of rights and revolutions, of liberty and rising equality, of congresses and enduring peace agreements, and of continuing exploration and discovery, then the story of America fits well into this larger historical pattern. These impulses were far more than a national or American expression; they were of universal origins, but they played out remarkably well on a national scale in the New World.

The American dream was not to be obscured or dominated by its fears. Said Henry Clay: "But if one dark spot exists on our political horizon, is it not obscured by the bright and effulgent and cheering light that beams all around us? Was ever a people so blessed as we are, if true to ourselves? Did any other nation contain within its bosom so many elements of prosperity, of greatness, and of glory?"[7] Or, as Jefferson so optimistically painted it in his first inaugural address, "[America] is a chosen country, with room enough for our descendants to the thousandth and thousandth generation."[8]

A native son of the American Revolution, Henry Clay was born near Richmond, Hanover County, Virginia, on 12 April 1777. He was the son of John Clay and Elizabeth Hudson, both of English descent. His father, a Baptist minister, died young, and his mother remarried Captain Henry Watkins. Clay's early formal schooling came under the hand of an itinerant Englishman, Peter Deacon, at the old field schoolhouse. It was a very meager education, however, as it was ever interrupted by clearing, planting, plowing, harvesting, and every other chore expected of a healthy boy growing up on a farm. Clay always regretted not learning more about history, literature, and the classics. "I never studied half enough," he lamented later in life,[9] What he did learn was how to write legibly, how to work hard, how to debate, how to ride horses, and how to play the fiddle and have a good time. He made friends easily and could drink and party with the best of them. Nothing in these early years indicated anything more than an average young man with a normal future.

---

6. Howe, *Life and Letters of George Bancroft*, 75–76. See also Nye, *George Bancroft*, 45.
7. From a speech by Henry Clay in the U.S. Senate, 7 February 1839, in Colton, *Life, Correspondence, and Speeches of Henry Clay*, 6:157.
8. As cited in Cunliffe, *Nation Takes Shape*, 70.
9. Remini, *Henry Clay*, 6.

Clay grew up in a most exciting time and place, with the sounds of the Revolutionary War in his backyard. He could remember Lt. Tarleton's British regulars ransacking his home and running their swords into the newly made graves of his father and grandfather in search of buried goods. Clay thus grew up with a deep wellspring of patriotic devotion to his country and an intense hatred of the British. He viewed General George Washington as his childhood military hero and Thomas Jefferson as God's architect of American independence.

Clay doubtless heard at the dinner table, fireplace, and schoolroom about the inequities of the British Parliament's Stamp Act of 1765, the resultant Virginia Resolutions spearheaded by that fiery patriot Patrick Henry, the Boston Massacre of 1770, and the Boston Tea Party of December 1773, which led to the well-known American battle cry of "No taxation without representation." When Great Britain responded with a set of harsh measures that included the suspension of the Charter of Massachusetts, the other colonies made the Boston cause their own and assembled together in Philadelphia nine months later in Samuel Adams's First Continental Congress.

Then in April 1775 a large body of British troops stationed in Boston, while seeking stores and supplies outside the city, met armed colonial resistance for the first time at Concord and at Lexington. A similarly armed confrontation soon followed at Bunker Hill and Breed's Hill, where British forces lost 1,500 men in a Pyrrhic victory over the well-armed colonialist defenders. When the Second Continental Congress convened in Philadelphia in May 1775, it appointed George Washington of Virginia as commander-in-chief of the American forces, drafted the Articles of Confederation, and adopted Thomas Jefferson's Locke-inspired Declaration of Independence, which was passed and signed on 4 July 1776, the birthdate of the United States of America.

The details of the ensuing Revolutionary War, from Washington's tactical retreats to the eventual surrender of General Cornwallis and seven thousand British regulars at Yorktown in 1781—all these and more were surely not lost on young Clay. The ultimate result was British recognition of American independence and the birth of a new nation. Two years later, in 1783, Great Britain ceded to the United States the vast territory between the Alleghenies and the Mississippi River. Four years later the Continental Congress passed the Ordinance of 1787, which allowed for the ultimate organization of six new states on equal basis with the original thirteen states in what was then considered the Northwest, with slavery expressly forbidden therein.

The Articles of Confederation failed, however, in one critically important aspect—passing legislation for the federal government to raise money and to control commerce. The goal was "a more perfect union" that balanced the unique needs of the new nation with the vested interests of the several states. For this purpose, a new Federal Convention convened in Philadelphia in May 1787 when Clay was only ten years old. After months of toiling through a long, hot summer, the several delegates crafted a new Constitution of the United States with seven articles that, among other things, called for a tripartite form of government—the executive branch, with an elected president; the legislative or congressional branch, with a bicameral elected House and Senate; and the judicial branch, with a Supreme Court nominated by the president and ratified by Congress. The Constitution provided Congress power to lay and collect taxes and pay debts, allowed for a difficult but possible amendment process, and ensured elected representation, with two representatives per state in the Senate and with proportional representation by population in the House. When it was ultimately approved by the individual states, several amendments were incorporated that limited the powers of Congress, the first of which became the Bill of Rights. These preserved the freedoms of religion, speech, press, and the right to assemble and reserved to the states those powers not expressly delegated to the federal government. With New Hampshire's ratification vote in June 1788, the Constitution became the supreme law of the land.

In contrast with the almost simultaneous French Revolution (see chapter 1), the American Revolution, which in many ways inspired the French uprisings, was a much less bloody affair. Unlike France, which regurgitated the accumulated abuses of a corrupt caste system over a millennia, the American Revolution was directed at its mother country and resulted in a far more peaceful transition from one form of parliamentary democracy to a republican style of government. While both the French and American republics chose military figures as their first leaders, the United States was spared the bloody wars of liberation that soon engulfed the European continent. Fifty-seven-year-old general George Washington, "Columbia's Savior" and the man most highly regarded in all the land, was unanimously elected America's first president and inaugurated in 1789.

"FUN TO HAVE AROUND": HENRY CLAY'S FORMATIVE YEARS

Washington had been president for only three years when fifteen-year-old Clay began working as a clerk in Peter Tinsley's prestigious law office in Richmond, Virginia, in 1792. An "extraordinarily intelligent and diligent worker, and friendly and fun to have around," Clay soon gained the attention of George Wythe, chancellor of the Virginia High Court of Chancery.[10] Wythe was himself a signer of the Declaration of Independence, the most learned jurist in Virginia, and the law professor to Jefferson, Chief Justice John Marshall, and James Monroe. He was also a firm opponent of slavery. Wythe took Clay under his wing as his amanuensis and student for the next four years, introducing him to great literature and encouraging the development of his debating skills. As historian Robert Remini put it, Wythe "was the father Henry Clay never had."[11] For a few months Clay even worked for Robert Brooke, former governor and later attorney general of Virginia.

Clay was tall and thin and as confident, relaxed, and self-assured as he was singularly unattractive, "loosely put together." Although he developed a devastating wit, a biting sarcasm, and an overbearing arrogance, his native charm and unfailing sense of humor easily made him a great many friends. Never a loner, he played as hard as he worked, spending as many hours in backroom gambling halls with convivial company playing whist and poker

---

10. Remini, *Henry Clay*, 9.
11. Remini, *Henry Clay*, 9–10.

as he did in the barrooms of the law. He developed a love for gambling, hard drink, and beautiful women. As he once admitted, "I have always paid peculiar homage to the fickle goddess."[12] But he knew his limits. After a late-night reverie, he was almost always back at his law desk the next morning. He was quick to apologize to anyone he had offended the night before. And after his marriage to Lucretia Hart in 1799, he was ever faithful to her.

Even before he was admitted to the Virginia bar at the age of twenty, Clay had formed his own political convictions. His time with Wythe and Brooke had endeared him to the Jeffersonian doctrine of states' rights, agrarian democracy, the French Revolution, the ideals of a limited interpretation of the Constitution, and a commitment to the Republican Party. James Madison became another one of his heroes.

Following his mother and stepfather, he moved from Virginia to Lexington, Kentucky—then a town of two thousand—in 1797, five years before Kentucky became America's fifteenth state. He soon gained admission to the Kentucky bar, whereupon he opened a law office, specializing in criminal law. Save for farming, law was the only career he ever seriously considered. A superb actor, Clay loved to debate and developed a flair for the theatrical. His voice had a wonderful musical tone that could rise and fall as if on cue. With such talent, the courtroom soon became his stage.

Yet there was much more to Clay than sound, fury, and histrionics. He earned his reputation as a very good defense attorney because of the clarity of his arguments, his careful preparations, and his highly intelligent reasonings based on comparisons, contrasts, and common sense. There was always enormous substance in what he had to say, and he genuinely persuaded gentlemen and juries to his way of thinking.[13]

Often accepting land as payment for his legal services, while at the same time running his wealthy father-in-law's—Colonel Thomas Hart—many businesses, Clay soon owned several thousand acres, some of which he eventually developed into his Ashland estate, just a mile or two out of town. He soon gained a reputation as a successful land developer. Clay enjoyed farming, horse breeding, and his estate, where he later retreated often for rest and inspiration. Like many other Kentucky farmers, he owned several slaves, some of whom he had inherited from his father and grandfather. Thanks to his wife who was as good if not a better manager of money than he was, Ashland usually prospered. Although theirs would be a happy marriage, it was constantly beset with deep sorrow. All six of their daughters and two of their sons would predecease them, and two of their other boys would spend time in insane asylums. Though Clay was a believer in God, he deliberately refrained from joining any organized religion until much later in life, when he became an Episcopalian.

An exciting new era in American history began to unfold with the election of Jefferson as the country's third president in 1800. An intellectual, philosopher, science enthusiast, and careful constrictionist in constitutional matters, Jefferson will ever be remembered as much for expanding the nation as for defining it in writing. Ironically, for one so committed to

---

12. Van Deusen, *Life of Henry Clay*, 25.
13. Remini, *Henry Clay*, 20.

performing no more than what the Constitution allowed, it was Jefferson who exercised unstated power to secure the vast Louisiana Purchase from Napoléon in 1803. For a sum of fifteen million dollars, which was then a staggering amount of money, and with one stroke of the presidential pen, America's land mass almost doubled, extending from West Florida (Louisiana and Mississippi) all the way to the Rocky Mountains, although the precise boundaries of the purchase were not yet determined.

Jefferson also dispatched Lewis and Clark on their famous expedition up the Missouri River, to the Yellowstone and Columbia Rivers, and eventually to Oregon in 1804–6, thereby laying tentative American claim to the great Pacific Northwest. Soon other intrepid explorers like Zebulon M. Pike, Henry M. Breckenridge, and Stephen H. Long further defined the exciting vastness of the American West and described the territory west of the Mississippi River to the Rockies as the Great American Desert. America's frontiers were moving relentlessly westward while Europe was sinking into the abyss of the Napoleonic Wars.

An Engraving of "Ashland," Henry Clay's Home near Lexington, Kentucky, by Carl Schurz, in *Life of Henry Clay* (Boston: Houghton, Mifflin & Co., 1899), vol. 2, secondary frontispiece.

It wasn't long before rugged pioneers and restless farmers were seeking out new lands and opportunities in the new American West. Many were anxious to escape the cold and rocky terrain of New England. Others wanted to leave the overly aggressive cotton plantation owners of Georgia and the Carolinas. And some fled the economic and political exigencies in Great Britain and Europe. Fiercely individualistic, highly ambitious, antielitist, and intolerant of indigenous claims of any kind, the new American commoner would not be denied. Vermont was accepted into the Union in 1792 as the fourteenth state, followed by Kentucky (the same year), Tennessee (1796), Ohio (1803), Louisiana (1812), Indiana (1816), Mississippi (1817), Illinois (1818), Alabama (1819), and Maine (1820).

In 1803, during Jefferson's presidency, Clay entered politics as an elected assemblyman in the first Kentucky legislature. A Jeffersonian Republican by leaning, he was nonetheless astute enough to support the manufacturing and mercantile interests of his new adopted state, and he recognized the need for active government participation in its economic behalf. The peculiar genius of Clay was that he was as much pragmatic as he was idealistic; he was a conciliator who could see the value of opposing political interests. Early on, he learned that the art of compromise was necessary if anything lasting were to be accomplished. In large part, his role in having the state step in and save the ailing Bank of Kentucky led to the legislature electing him to the United States Senate to replace John Adair, who had unexpectedly resigned his seat. Clay was only twenty-nine years old at the time, one year younger than the required age of thirty, but no one cared to ask.

Never known for bashfulness, the aspiring young senator soon made a name for himself on the Senate floor as a skilled orator and debater. Even federalist senator John Quincy Adams of Massachusetts took notice of Clay and his Jeffersonian ideals: "Quite a young man—an orator—a Republican of the first fire."[14] Clay strongly argued for the federal government to take the lead in making better internal improvements such as roads, bridges, and canals, and levying the requisite taxes and tariffs to make them all possible. Such would lead to a continental home market, further westward expansion, and promotion of new manufacturing possibilities. In such arguments lay the kernel of his later famous "American System" economic plan. A pragmatic Republican who championed states' rights, he nonetheless saw the need for a strong national government and sound banking principles. Clay blended the ideals of Jefferson with the financial practicalities of Alexander Hamilton.

Clay owned that wonderful political asset of not taking personally the jibes and jostlings of congressional debate. He usually rose above personal injury, but there were occasions when he felt his honor and good name were so impugned that he would fight back. Such was the case in 1809. Believing in the cult of honor, then still prevalent in the South, Clay could have suffered the same fate as Alexander Hamilton, who died in a duel with Aaron Burr in 1804. In 1809, Clay and former US senator Humphrey Marshall, a cousin of Chief Justice John Marshall, went to the wall in a duel of their own. Although wounded in the thigh, Clay was fortunate to survive. Marshall suffered only a few bruises and went on to write a two-volume history of Kentucky.

The following year, his wounds healed, Clay returned to the Senate at a time when strong congressional pressure was being exerted on Jefferson's successor, President James Madison, to declare war once more on Great Britain. Upon quitting the Senate, Clay returned home, where he was elected a member of the House of Representatives, which he greatly preferred over the staid Senate. In short order, largely because of his anti-British stance, he was elected Speaker of the House in 1811 at the age of thirty-four, perhaps the only freshman Congressman ever to be so honored. Soon dubbed "the Western Star," Clay, then as much a war hawk as any other elected official from the West and South, soon joined forces with those who saw conflict as the preferred resolution. Concluded Josiah Quincy, the Boston federalist, Clay "was the man whose influence and power more than that of any other produced the War of 1812 between the United States and Great Britain."[15]

---

14. Adams, *Memoirs*, 1:44, in Van Deusen, *Life of Henry Clay*, 46.
15. Quincy, *Life of Josiah Quincy*, 259, in Remini, 413.

AMERICA'S "SECOND WAR OF INDEPENDENCE"

The War of 1812 was but an echo of that much greater conflict then raging on the European continent. Napoléon and his Grande Armée were marching on Moscow in their last, great campaign. The French had placed embargos on British and foreign trade all across Europe, and in return Great Britain, supreme ruler on the sea, was blockading marine trade in and out of Europe. America was a hapless neutral power that was eventually shut off from foreign trade and commerce. New England manufactories and Southern cotton producers were especially hard-hit. The resulting war was essentially an unnecessary conflict, born of the hysteria of the time, that solved nothing. As Edward Channing dryly put it, "The War of 1812 was waged by one free people against another free people in the interest of Napoleon, the real enemy of them both."[16]

Of particular annoyance to America was the humiliating British habit of impressment. American ships were captured and their American sailors were impressed, or sworn into forceful duty aboard British navy vessels, often in sight of the American seacoast. This practice of "inalienable allegiance" was, at base, a deliberate mockery of American citizenship, and it demonstrated, perhaps more than anything else, British arrogance and contempt for the new nation. When President Jefferson foolishly retaliated with an embargo of his own in 1807, it only made things worse for American trade and commerce.

America's anglophobia at home was no less galling to the British, whose hands were full fighting Napoléon. The upstart American, particularly in the western frontier states, suspected British collusion with angry, displaced Native American tribes who felt cheated by unfair American land treaties that increasingly deprived them of their long-held homes and hunting lands. American Indian warriors like Tecumseh and his brother "The Prophet" were difficult to defeat, even with the full force of General William Henry Harrison and the United States Army.

While the Americans distinguished themselves at sea and on the waters of the Great Lakes during the War of 1812, they generally failed miserably on land. American losses at Niagara, Lundy's Lane, and Detroit were as much the result of state militias refusing to obey national orders as from British general Isaac Brock's and other British generals' superlative field strategies. The American goal of the conquest of Canada backfired, with British raiders burning Washington, DC On 24 December 1814 the peace treaty of Ghent was signed in Belgium. News was slow to travel, so the brightest moment for American land forces—General Andrew Jackson's brilliant 1815 victory in New Orleans against a vastly superior army of British regulars—came two weeks after the signing of the treaty. The utter futility of the war is apparent in that none of the issues that started the war—impressment, squabbles over fisheries, and British demands for navigation of the Mississippi River—were even mentioned in the final treaty.

The manner of ending the War of 1812 accomplished three very important things. First, the Treaty of Ghent was the first formal international recognition of American nationality.

---

16. Channing, *United States of America*, 1765–1865, 189. For the most recent study of the War of 1812, see Alan Taylor, *Civil War of 1812*.

Capture and Burning of Washington by the British, in 1814 (wood engraving, 1876), by unknown artist.

For this reason, the War of 1812 has been called America's "Second War of Independence." The fact that America had taken on such a vastly superior power and held its own, if not more so after Jackson's stunning victory, instilled a sense of pride in many Americans and established a lasting peace that would endure for half a century. Shortly afterward, in a separate treaty, Spain forfeited all its claims to East or modern Florida, consenting to sell what she could no longer defend.

Second, the pro-English Federalist Party found itself on the losing end of popular support as the war dragged on, and by 1820 it had virtually disappeared from off the American political landscape. Commensurate with its decline came the "Era of Good Feelings," in which federalist partisan politics, at least on the surface, had given way to Jeffersonian principles.

Third, because of America's failure to win the war, Canada, then better known as British North America, was now assured of a great, new future of its own. While Upper Canada (Ontario) and Lower Canada (Quebec) still held on to vastly different cultures, religions, and languages—the one province English and the other French—the war and its treaty ensured their future as well as those of the maritime provinces—New Brunswick, Nova Scotia, and Prince Edward Island. In 1820, William Lyon Mackenzie (1795–1861) and Sir John A. Macdonald (1815–91)—two men synonymous with Canadian independence and later confederation—immigrated from Scotland and soon began their own careers in Toronto (York) and Kingston, respectively. With the later signing of the Rush-Bagot Treaty, recognizing the 49th parallel as the border between the United States and Rupert's Land, extending from the Lake-of-the-Woods to the Rocky Mountains, the possibility of another great nation from sea to shining sea was all but assured. Some forty-three years later, the Dominion of Canada did indeed come into being on 1 July 1867.

As one of the five American peace commissioners assigned to Ghent to hammer out the treaty ending the war, Clay played a greater role forging the peace than he had ever done supporting the war, despite the fact that he had spearheaded a new conscription bill to raise thousands of troops. Clay clashed more, through his compulsive gambling, with his fellow commissioners, including John Quincy Adams—the senior American statesman, than he ever did with his British counterparts, who were mere puppets of Lord Castlereagh anyway. Distrustful of Tsar Alexander's "unholy alliance" and of growing Russian hegemony and its potential alliance with America, Castlereagh preferred to forge a separate peace treaty with America. Still young and brash, Clay's sometimes erratic behavior offended some, but he was unbending in preventing the surrender of any American territory. In the end, the war concluded on the basis of the "status quo ante bellum," or things as they were before the war, and both the United States and British Canada preserved all their former territories.

"SETTLE AND SELL, SETTLE AND SELL"

In many ways, Henry Clay epitomized the America of 1820. He was incurably optimistic, ardently if not irritably patriotic, and restlessly ambitious, seeking new lands, wealth, and limitless opportunities in the ever-expanding westward reaches of the confident, young nation. With the Revolutionary War over and won, the Louisiana Purchase completed, and the War of 1812 now behind them, Americans looked forward to what many would soon call their Manifest Destiny.

At its most dynamic core was the family. One may speak of the spirit of equality and American democracy, as Alexis de Tocqueville so brilliantly did in his magisterial book *Democracy in America* (1832); the predominantly rural and agricultural way of life, as so many British travelers described America at this time; and the changing and challenging economics. Yet at its base, America rose on the shoulders of the family—its greatest strength. "Marriage," Tocqueville observed, was more "highly regarded" in America than in any other nation.[17]

From his early childhood, a young man was trained to tame the wilderness. "Every man, or nearly every man," one female traveler noted, "knows how to handle the axe, the hammer, the plane, all the mechanic tools in short, besides the musket, to the use of which he

---

17. Tocqueville, *Democracy in America*, 1:303.

Westward the Course of Empire Takes Its Way, by Emanuel Leutze.

is not only regularly trained as a man but practiced as a boy."[18] Raised to be independent and self-reliant, the American farmer—with his skills, tools, practices, ambitions, and a coarse common sense—was expected to make a living. A young farmer's hardest work was in felling trees, burning stumps, clearing the land, fencing, planting, and harvesting. Split-rail fences stretched everywhere, demarcating one farm from the other. Families often grew their own food in tended gardens. And as they prospered, log cabins with dirt floors gave way to painted houses and cottages with larger rooms, better chimneys, larger stables, and painted barns. The spirit of improvement seemed everywhere.

While a basic elementary education was more or less universally accessible, education beyond that was not particularly valued. Most Americans cared more about the practicalities of making a living than the generalities of abstract thinking. They were far more interested in business and politics than they were in music and literature. Higher education was almost an anomaly, with more energy devoted to heated argument and debate than to idle book reading, at least among young men. For those who did find time to read, the historical novels of Sir Walter Scott were very popular, and Hannah More was more widely read than Shakespeare. The works of American writers such as James Fenimore Cooper and

---

18. Letter XVI, September 1819, in Wright, *Views of Society and Manners in America*, 150.

Washington Irving bespoke the rise of American literature dominated by such publishing houses as Carey & Lea in Philadelphia and Harper & Brothers in New York.

There was little time for recreation or diversion. Organized sports were a future luxury. Many found entertainment in hunting and fishing and in rough-and-tumble fighting in the bar or tavern. If chewing tobacco was an everyday experience, drinking was even more constant, even among the young women. If outright drunkenness was rare, "constant tippling" was everywhere.[19]

At the risk of overgeneralizing, the America of 1820 was always on the move in a state of restless agitation, eyeing more and better land westward, as if afraid of finding insufficient room for growing families. And with the new land system of 1800 that divided townships into thirty-six square miles and subdivided them into sections of 640 acres, one could buy small or large acreages at very competitive prices. It was, as one scholar has described, a time of "settle and sell, settle and sell."[20]

America was thus predominantly rural and agricultural. The largest cities were New York City (pop. 122,000), Philadelphia (64,000), Boston (43,000), Charleston (25,000), and other eastern seaboard cities and towns with internal riverside cities such as Pittsburgh and Cincinnati, which were in their industrial infancy. What manufacturing did exist was centered primarily in New England, with as many women working in the new cotton mills and factories as men. Labor unions were nonexistent, and many, such as President Jefferson, believed manufacturing was far more apt to corrupt personal morality than a life on the land could ever do.

Patterns and pathways of transportation were in their infancy. Families traveled over ill-marked paths and byways by wagons or carts, often migrating in groups of family caravans. From Auburn, New York, in April 1815 came the statement that "during the past winter our roads have been thronged with families moving westerly. It has been remarked by our oldest settlers, that they never before witnessed so great a number of teams passing, laden with women, children, furniture, etc. to people the fertile forests of New York, Pennsylvania, and Ohio."[21] Tens of thousands were on the move in what the *Niles Register*, one of America's most popular American newspaper magazines of the day, referred to as "The Great Migration." "Old America seems to be breaking up, and moving westward," wrote Morris Birkbeck in 1817 while on the road to Pittsburgh. "We are seldom out of sight, as we travel on this grand track towards the Ohio, of family groups, behind and before us."[22] By 1820 there were nearly 1,140,000 more people living west of the Allegheny Mountains than in 1810.

Roads were often impassable, with few inns or conveniences along the way. The Genesee Road west of Utica to Buffalo, New York, and the Forbes Road over the Allegheny Ridge and across Pennsylvania were rough precursors to the National or Cumberland Road, which

---

19. Mesick, *English Traveller*, 73–75.
20. Boorstin, *Americans*, 91.
21. Clark, *West in American History*, 173.
22. Clark, *West in American History*, 175.

stretched from Cumberland, Maryland, to Wheeling, West Virginia, and over the mountain passes that for so long had held back westward migrations. The 363-mile Erie Canal, completed in 1825, connected the Hudson River in the east to Lake Erie in the west, greatly facilitating trade and travel. It opened up settlement of the old Northwest; promised the rise of Chicago, Cleveland, Milwaukee, and other great lake ports; and guaranteed the place of New York as America's largest city and commercial center. The invention of Robert Fulton's river steamboat in 1806 ushered in a new industrial age of sea and river travel. And with the organization of the Baltimore and Ohio Railroad in 1828, travel to places far removed from rivers would soon become possible. Americans were in haste and on the move, and there seemed to be a confused clamor of new trails and travels and innovations and opportunities, as if Washington Irving's Rip Van Winkle were just waking up to the morning of a bright new day.

The nation then was enjoying another form of liberty—a country virtually out of debt. As a country without income tax, the United States relied on income from the sale of public lands and from duties (or tariffs) on imported goods. The debts incurred by the Revolutionary War and the War of 1812 were virtually eliminated by the late 1820s, and the government was running a balanced budget by 1823.[23]

Yet people were moving just to eke out a living. Though many sought wealth, few found it. There were very few millionaires in 1820. Foreign markets for American products and produce were hard to come by, and distribution systems within the country were few and poorly developed. America's greatest internal debate, other than that of slavery, was surely the murky issue of banking and finance. Since the collapse of the unpopular federalist-inspired First National Bank in 1811, financial chaos had ensued. Despite the bank being rechartered in 1816, this was a time of serious recession. Without a recognized standard national currency and sufficient hard specie, foreign coins and cut money abounded with "half bits" or "quarter bits" of Spanish gold or silver dollars. Small, local wildcat banks proliferated to fill the void, each issuing its own paper money, often accepted at a fraction of its value by the larger eastern banks. The notes of unchartered banks were especially discounted. In 1819, many state banks collapsed, and enormous amounts of Western real estate were foreclosed by the Bank of the United States. Not until 1823 would the economy finally pull out of the nation's first economic depression. America's banking and currency system was in chaos, with no federal reserve system, no deposit insurance programs, no uniformity, and precious little regulation and oversight, resulting in a general lack of trust and confidence. The two great political parties that followed the Era of Good Feelings—Democratic and Republican—debated the issue for years, with Henry Clay favoring and Andrew Jackson vehemently opposing the concept of a national bank, which he believed was a dangerous, cruel, and useless monopoly. It would take years and other panics and depressions before the American banking system finally stabilized.

While it was the province of young men to learn the professional arts and sciences and the rigors of law, medicine, and business, young women were generally educated in such

---

23. Mesick, *English Traveller*, 190–96.

domestic arts as spinning, weaving, cooking, reading, writing, and other skills considered necessary to build a home. It was customary for women to marry young—often only between the ages of twelve to fourteen—and to have a family of six or more children before the age of twenty-five. Divorce was a rarity, and large families the order of the day. The politics of America was, at base, the economics of the home. The spirit of democracy, independence, and equality that colored governmental politics emanated in large measure from the log cabins and houses of the nation, the very capillaries of society.

However, it took consistent, backbreaking labor of both husband and wife, working equally hard together, to tame the wilderness and make a living as the following traveler's account will show of one young New York family who had turned their cabin into an inn.

> Alighting at the little tavern, we found the only public apartment sufficiently occupied and accordingly made bold to enter a small room, which by the cheering blaze of an oak fire, we discovered to be the kitchen and, for the time being, the peculiar residence of the family of the house. An unusual inundation of travelers had thrown all into confusion. The busy matron, nursing an infant with one arm and cooking with the other, seemed worked out of strength and almost out of temper. A tribe of young urchins, kept from their rest by the unusual stir, were lying half asleep, some on the floor and some upon the bed, which filled a third of the apartment. We were sufficed to establish ourselves by the fire, and having relieved the troubled hostess from her chief incumbrance, she recovered good humour and presently prepared our supper. While rocking the infant, it was with pleasure that I observed its healthy cheeks and those of the drowsy imps scattered around.[24]

This same female traveler opined that the future of woman in America was bright indeed.

> I must remark that in no particular is the liberal philosophy of the Americans more honorably evinced than in the place which is awarded to women. . . . [They] are assuming their place as thinking beings, not in despite of the men, but chiefly in consequence of their enlarged views and exertions as fathers and legislators. It strikes me that it would be impossible for women to stand in higher estimation than they do here [in America]. The deference that is paid to them at all times and in all places has often occasioned [in] me as much surprise as pleasure . . . and as their education shall become more and more the concern of the state, their character may aspire in each succeeding generation to a higher standard.[25]

As for dress, men were giving up wigs and powder and exchanging breeches and silk stockings for pantaloons. Women were also wearing more practical and modest attire. As one observer wrote: "Their light hair is tastefully turned up behind in the modern style and fastened with a comb. Their dress is neat, simple and genteel, usually consisting of a printed

---

24. Letter XIII, September 1819, in Wright, *Views of Society*, 123.
25. Letter XXIII, March 1820, in Wright, *Views of Society*, 218–19, 221.

cotton jacket with long sleeves, a petticoat of the same, with a colored cotton apron or pin cloth without sleeves, tied tight and covering the lower part of the bosom. This seemed to be the prevailing dress in the country places."[26]

In the political sphere, America proudly took ownership of their system of government in a way Europeans never did. "He's *our* president," "*our* governor," "*our* senator," US citizens would often say. The love of family, liberty, individuality, democracy, majority rule, and equality were very real fruits of a young America. There exuded a strong feeling of independence, a reverence for the power and sovereignty of the people and their beloved Constitution bordering on religious fervor. As Tocqueville put it, "Nothing struck me more forcibly than the general equality of condition among the people," a people "eminently democratic," seeking "heaven in the world beyond . . . and liberty in this one."[27] Indeed, many interpreted the death of Thomas Jefferson and John Adams on the very same day, 4 July 1826, as a "palpable sign of divine favor," a country called of, and created by, Providence.[28] The new nation was the political showcase of the world, and Americans never stopped talking about it. America was coming into her own and, in Clay's words, "gaining that height to which God and nature have destined it."[29]

"WE NEVER HAD SO OMINOUS A QUESTION": THE MISSOURI COMPROMISE OF 1819–21

Yet ever lurking beneath these times of good feelings and positive advancement was the loathsome legacy of slavery—America's shadow in the sunlight. It was countenanced by the Founding Fathers as a necessary evil; increasingly condemned by the North, which viewed it as a stain upon America's conscience; and ever more rigorously defended by the South as a property right protected in the Constitution.

The antebellum South had a mind of its own, a culture and character very distinct from that of the northern states. While it is true that tens of thousands of people in Virginia and the Carolinas were moving westward in parallel migrations to those in the North, their destinations were usually to the more southerly regions of Arkansas, Mississippi, Texas, and Missouri, where they hoped to perpetuate their unique way of life. Most were also lower middle-class farmers in search of richer opportunities. One Missouri observer in 1818 counted over one hundred persons a day, for many days in succession, passing through St. Charles, Missouri. He saw a train of "nine wagons harnessed with four to six horses. We may allow a hundred cattle, besides hogs, horses, and sheep, to each wagon; and from three to four to twenty slaves. The whole appearance of the train, the cattle with their hundred bells; the negroes with delight in their countenances, for their labors are suspended and their

---

26. Mesick, *English Traveller*, 2:323.
27. Tocqueville, *Democracy in America*, 1:3, 43, 46.
28. Boorstin, *Americans*, 387.
29. Van Deusen, *Life of Henry Clay*, 109.

imaginations excited; the wagons, after carrying two or three tons, so loaded that the mistress and children are strolling carelessly along . . . the whole group occupies three quarters of a mile."[30]

The climate was hotter and the pace of life slower in the South. If more committed to church attendance and Bible reading, the South was less open to rapid change and unfriendly to novelties in law and technology. Less affected by the rapid rise in European emigration, the South was fiercely individualistic. It proudly preserved its ancestral ties, where family honor, dignity, and moral conduct led to an unwritten code of honor that, as we have already seen with Clay, sometimes led to the fatal custom of dueling to retain the good opinion of one's equals. There was in the South a strong streak of violence and an unwritten law of vigilante justice to address old grievances and simmering arguments.

Since the invention of the cotton gin in 1793 and the rise of "King Cotton," the lower South had witnessed a growing number of plantation owners, along with an increase in tobacco growers, both of which demanded increased slave labor. As W. J. Cash has argued, "It was actually 1820 before the plantation was fully on the march, striding over the hills of Carolina to Mississippi."[31] In the mind of the South, slavery was essential to its economic well-being and a property right guaranteed under the Constitution. Such views led to a prevailing political philosophy that put a premium on states' rights and sectional interests. Southern interests of the state were above those of the nation, and the true power of the country lay in the individual states' consenting to a confederation of all the other states. Residing in the sovereignty of such states' rights was the ultimate legal authority and constitutional provision to secede—that the creators were greater than the creation. No consortium of other states or prevailing popular opinion elsewhere could overrule the conviction or rights of any one state. Abraham Lincoln's later vision of an indissoluble union was not the Southern view. The South had imposed its limitation on a new national membership from the beginning.

With the British abolition of the slave trade in 1807, through the work of William Wilberforce (see chapter 8), and the eradication of slavery in the North (New York abolished slavery in 1817), the number of newly enslaved blacks brought to America declined. However, interstate slave trade and illicit slave smuggling activities increased into a thriving business, with many plantation owners purchasing as many enslaved people at auction as possible, even renting enslaved people from other owners on a seasonal or monthly basis. Long lines of chained slaves could be heard mournfully singing and trudging along the dusty Southern roads under a hot summer sun.

Slave auctions occurred regularly in many major cities and presented such a sight that few outsiders could refrain from describing them. "The usual process differs in nothing from that of selling a horse," wrote one observer. "The poor object of traffic is mounted on a table, intending purchasers examine his points, and put questions as to his age, health, etc. The auctioneer dilates on his value, enumerates his accomplishments, and when the hammer at

---

30. Clark, *West in American History*, 175.
31. Cash, *Mind of the South*, 10.

length falls, protests in the usual place that poor Sambo has been absolutely thrown away. When a woman is sold, he usually puts his audience in good humor by a few indecent jokes."[32]

Slaves were often treated as chattel and separated from family members, not allowed or encouraged to marry, and forbidden from going to church or gaining an education. They were treated unkindly or kindly depending on the attitudes of their owner and his family. Slave communities worshipped in "hush harbors," densely forested areas away from the plantations, to shield their secret religious meetings.[33] There were, of course, both good and bad masters, but the incidents of abuse—the floggings, lynchings, tortures, dismemberments, and other forms of inhuman treatment—left a scar and a stain so deep and profound on the American conscience that not even a future Civil War could remove it.

The spirit of America in 1820 with respect to the "peculiar institution" was one of accommodation, not emancipation. While there was a rising spirit of indignation in the North,

Buying Slaves, Havana, Cuba, 1837, in Arthur Thomas Quiller-Couch, ed., *The Story of the Sea*, 2:440. Courtesy of *Slavery Images: A Visual Record of the African Slave Trade and Slave Life in the Early African Diaspora*.

---

32. Hamilton, *Men and Manners in America*, 2:216, as cited in Mesick, *English Traveller*, 139–40.
33. Hucks, "Black Church," in *Encyclopedia of American Cultural and Intellectual History*, 1:230.

the nation was too young, tender, and unprepared for a national conflict. The nation's collective social conscience had not yet reached a strong enough point to take on the evil of slavery. Resolving that issue was a horror reserved for a later generation.

As early as 1790, Southern congressmen like William Smith of North Carolina were stoutly condemning Northern arguments, petitions, and memorials to limit or abolish slavery. Smith saw such as attacks on the integrity of the South that represented a spirit of persecution. It was not the business of the Quakers, abolitionists, or any other antislavery Northern voices "to be busy bodies above their stations." Claiming that enslaved Africans were "an indolent people, improvident, adverse to labor" and, if emancipated, "would either starve or plunder," Representative Williams argued that "the Northern states knew that slavery was so ingrafted into the policy of the Southern States, that it could not be eradicated without tearing up by the roots their happiness, tranquility, and prosperity; that if it was an evil, it was one for which there was no remedy."[34]

In 1790 the country counted 697,000 slaves and a "free colored population" of 59,000, the majority of whom lived in the North. Thirty years later, in 1820, those numbers had dramatically increased to 1,538,000 and 234,000 respectively.[35]

The admission of the several new states of the Union between 1790 and 1819 was a careful regional or sectional balancing act between slave and non-slave states. This was a deliberate attempt to maintain the status quo and provide the South equal representation—if not in the House of Representatives, whose members represented a population growth more rapid in the North, then certainly in the Senate, where each state, small or large, was guaranteed two senators under the Constitution.

This sectional balance, allowing for parity in the Senate, was achieved by the careful balancing act of accepting new states into the Union in a "their turn, our turn" manner (see table).

STATE ADMISSIONS INTO THE UNION, 1790–1819

Northern States	Southern States
Vermont (1792)	Kentucky (1792)
Ohio (1803)	Tennessee (1796)
Indiana (1816)	Louisiana (1812)
Illinois (1818)	Mississippi (1817)
Maine (1820)	Alabama (1819)

Table. From Clark, *West in American History*, 178.

---

34. Joseph Gales, debate of 17 March 1790, in *The Debates and Proceedings in the Congress of the United States*, 2:1503–4.
35. DeBow, *Statistical View of the United States*, 63, 82.

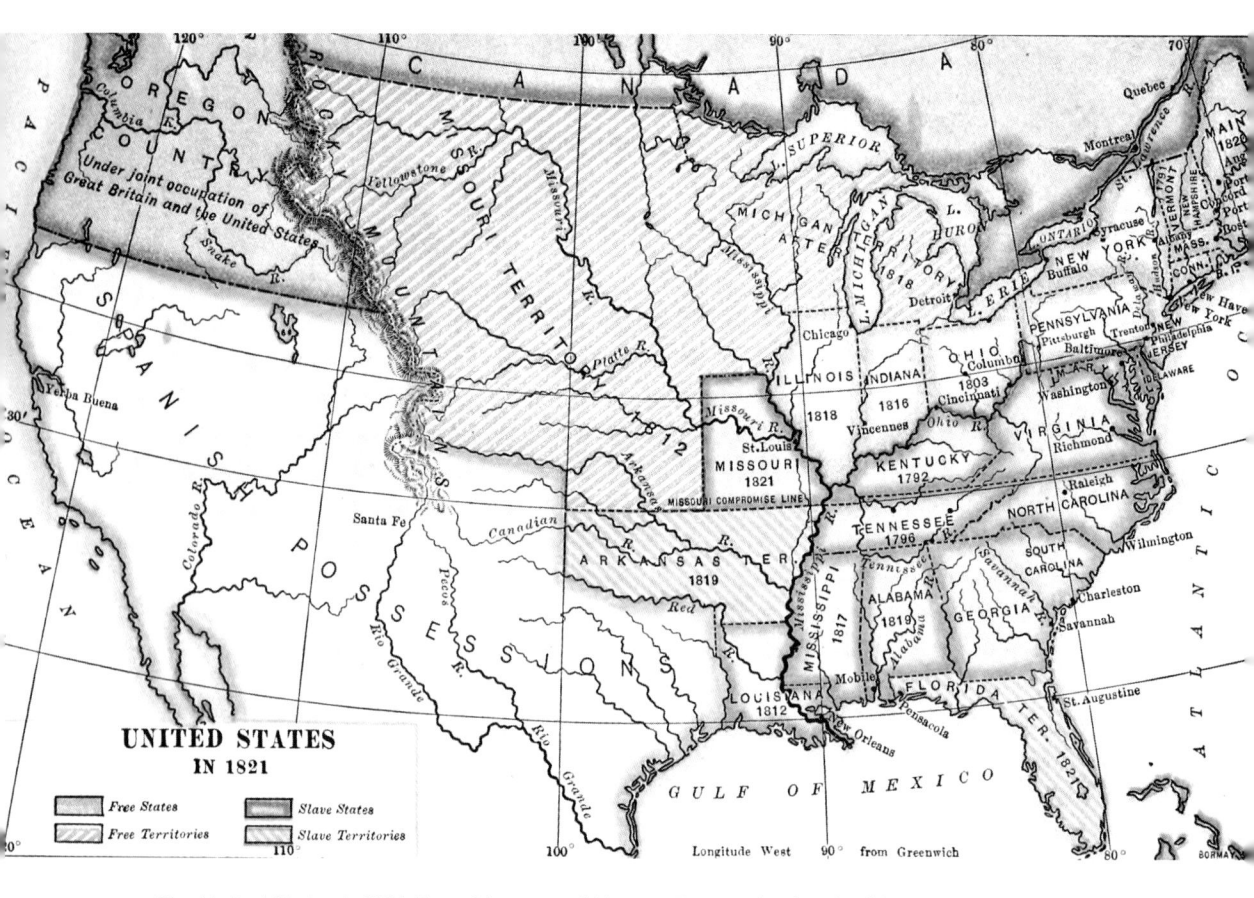

The United States in 1821. From Mowry and Mowry, *Essentials of United States History.*

The Territory of Missouri had been experiencing a rapid influx of settlers almost from the time Jefferson had signed the Louisiana Purchase. Most of them were streaming in from the Carolinas, Virginia, and other Southern states, and some were bringing their slaves with them. By 1820, several thousand slaves were living west of the Mississippi.[36] Jackson County and other areas in western Missouri had already gained the nickname "Little Dixie."

When the Territory of Missouri gained sufficient population, it petitioned Congress for statehood in January 1818, and most observers anticipated it would enter as a slave state. The trouble was, as shown in the table, that after Alabama had entered the Union in 1819, it was the North's turn to have a free state admitted. More to the point, a rising, ever louder, and more persistent antislavery sentiment in the North demanded an end to slavery, whatever the cost, due to their fear that slavery would extend far into the reaches of the Louisiana

---

36. See Moore, *Missouri Controversy*, chap. 1.

Purchase. To the North's way of thinking, slavery should never be allowed to extend west of the Mississippi River.[37]

The matter included more than whose turn it was to add a state or even the morality of slavery. Slavery was also seen as a constitutional issue. Was it the prerogative of Congress and the national government to determine whether an incoming state should be slavery friendly, or was it the right of those residing there to decide for themselves? Opponents of slavery argued that because Missouri was still a territory and not a state, it was subject to the control of Congress. After all, if Congress had previously legislated that no state carved out of the North-West Ordinance could come in as slave states, why could it not do the same in the Louisiana Purchase country?

Representative James Tallmadge of New York opposed the admission of Missouri as a slave state. Riding the rising humanitarian impulse sweeping over the North, Tallmadge proposed an amendment that would halt the importation of slaves and free the children of slaves already in the United States at age twenty-five. On the failure of this motion, another New York representative, John W. Taylor, fearing that if slavery were allowed in Missouri it would spread throughout the West "with all its baneful consequences,"[38] proposed something of a compromise. His motion allowed slavery in Missouri and west of the Mississippi River but forbade it in those regions or territory north of latitude 36° 30′ (a line westward corresponding to the southern border of Missouri).[39] To Northerners, the chief objection to Missouri's admission as a slave state was that it was in the same latitude with Ohio, Indiana, and Illinois. Stalled in conflict, Congress recessed without a resolution to the ongoing debate.

The acrimony engendered over the matter of Missouri can hardly be overstated. The South saw it as a Yankee conspiracy. "The Missouri question," wrote an aging Jefferson, "is a breaker on which we lose the Missouri country by revolt, and what more God only knows. From the battle of Bunker Hill to the Treaty of Paris, we never had so ominous a question."[40] John Quincy Adams, fearful that the present question was but "a preamble—a title page to a great tragic volume," recorded in January 1820 that "the Missouri or slave question . . . is beginning to shake this Union to its foundations."[41] Between sessions of Congress, public meetings were held all over the South and the North, and passions on both sides were running dangerously high.

When Congress reconvened in December 1819, during the severe economic depression discussed earlier, a new twist developed: Massachusetts consented to a division of its land mass, which allowed Maine to be admitted into the union as a new free state. To this proposition, the South agreed, so long as Congress would allow Missouri in as a slave state. When

---

37. Williams, *Historian's History of the World*, 23:347–50.
38. Moore, *Missouri Controversy*, 42.
39. It was generally understood that cotton could not grow north of latitude 36°.
40. Recited in Williams, *Historian's History*, 348.
41. Adams, *Memoirs of John Quincy Adams*, 5:502, 505.

the North refused on matters of principle, Southern representatives became ever more indignant, ever more bitter. "If you get Maine, why not Missouri for us?" came the Southern response. "If peace did not come, war would, and that soon."[42]

While outnumbered in the House, the South voted down almost every resolution in the Senate. The Senate united Maine and Missouri on the same bill and on the same terms, without any restriction upon slavery. Senator Jesse B. Thomas of Illinois then inserted the 36° 30′ clause proposed by Representative Taylor the year before. The House originally rejected the combination of Maine and Missouri in one bill but gradually gave way, and a committee of both houses of Congress reached a tentative compromise. President James Monroe signed the bill, allowing Maine admittance as the twenty-third state of the Union on 3 March 1820, and Missouri, once its constitution had been approved by Congress, was to follow shortly thereafter. The Missouri Compromise of 1820 was now assured—or was it?

Like a recurring nightmare, the conflict unfortunately erupted all over again and more loudly than before when the Territory of Missouri, either in a mood of spiteful defiance or shameful ignorance of the prevailing national sentiment, adopted a state constitution that

Senator Henry Clay Speaking about the Missouri Compromise in the Old Senate Chamber, by unknown artist.

---

42. Williams, *Historian's History*, 348.

denied citizenship rights to free blacks. Southern extremists called for immediate admission, while many Northerners desperately urged rejection of the state, constitution, and compromise. As Clay put it, "The flame which had been repressed during the previous session now burst forth with double violence."[43]

The debate revealed one of the fundamental causes of the entire controversy. As Glover Moore has well argued, "The desire of each great section of the nation [was] to spread its own type of civilization over the western country and appropriate the resources of the West for its own use."[44] It would take a man of towering intellect, courage, and political skills; one who had the ear and trust of politicians from both North and South; and one whose whole soul was bound up in the cause of the Union to untie the Gordian knot of Missouri's claim for admission into the Union.

"I KNOW NO SOUTH, NO NORTH, NO EAST, NO WEST": THE GREAT COMPROMISER

As Speaker of the House of Representatives from 1811 to 1820 and again from 1823 to 1825, Henry Clay, "the Great Pacificator," continued his own style of pragmatic Republicanism. He sought to create an American System, which would provide protection for business in the form of higher tariffs, a stronger military, a national bank, continued westward expansion, and a deep distrust of postwar Europe. Like Jefferson, he had been a strong supporter of the French Revolution and many of Napoléon's liberal policies and firmly believed that the Congress of Vienna, in seeking to restore constitutional monarchies, was "destructive of every principle of liberty." With the French monarchy restored, America was, he believed, now the only real bastion of liberty.[45]

Clay was also the most conversant and well-informed American politician in the doings of Simón Bolívar, San Martin, and the independence movements of South and Central America. He ardently believed that it was in America's best interest to do all it could to aid the revolutionary spirit then fanning across South America, and he constantly called upon Congress to render financial aid to their brothers in arms (see chapter 9). He believed, as one scholar has argued, that "continued Spanish dominion over Latin America was . . . a danger to the security of the United States, an impediment to possible trade relations, an affront to republican ideals, and probably of highest magnitude, a detriment to hemispheric influence."[46] He saw enormous trade opportunities in the Caribbean and with South America and believed the two continents could combine to form a counterpoise against European imperialism. Though eventually a supporter of the Monroe Doctrine, Clay overextended himself in attacking Monroe and secretary of state John Quincy Adams in their more reasoned approach

---

43. Colton, *Life, Correspondence, and Speeches of Henry Clay*, 3:334.
44. Moore, *Missouri Controversy*, 49.
45. Van Deuson, *Life of Henry Clay*, 117–18.
46. Wilkinson, "Henry Clay and South America," 15.

toward recognizing the emerging Spanish independencies. Yet there is no doubt that his fiery speeches emboldened Bolívar in his revolutionary efforts against Spain. As Clay said in 1816, "It would undoubtedly be good policy to take part with the patriots of South America."[47]

It was as Speaker of the House that Henry Clay forged a brilliant political career while leaving an indelible impression upon the functions of Congress. Ronald M. Peters has well argued that Clay was "the first strong Speaker" who carved a role for himself that has found no imitation in American history.[48] By dint of his own forceful personality, he demanded respect—and earned it. Even the boisterous and argumentative John Randolph of Virginia, who was an ardent proponent of slavery, highly regarded Clay. There was something in his voice and oratory, his honest, friendly demeanor, his courtesies and congeniality, his boldness, his respect for differing, even warring opinions, his earnest convictions, and his charismatic popularity that continually won the support of his colleagues in the House. It was more his winning and engaging personality and less his skills as a parliamentarian that made him so attractive. Ever more popular personally than the policies he espoused, Clay was never censured by the entire House or found to be out of order.

One particularly astute British observer had this to say of Clay at the height of the debate, "He seems, indeed, to unite all the qualities essential to an orator: animation, energy, high moral feeling, ardent patriotism, a subliminal love of liberty, a rapid flow of ideas and of language, a happy vein of irony, an action at once vehement and dignified, and a voice full, sonorous, distinct, and flexible . . . without exception the most masterly voice that I ever remember to have heard. . . . In conversation he is no less eloquent than in debate."[49]

The fact that he was from the South and that he owned slaves of his own back in Ashland endeared him to his Southern colleagues. Yet Clay was known for his temperate, antislavery sentiments, including his "gradual emancipationist" views. These views included either sending slaves back to Africa (he was president of the American Colonization Society for years) or having the government buy freedom for the slaves gradually from their masters. He opposed slavery, but not at the cost of the Union.

He had many Northern admirers as well because of his pro-Federalist stance in promoting higher tariffs, improving roads and bridges, and instituting the National Bank, a measure he pushed through Congress in 1816 to the discomfort of his fellow Republican colleagues. He was respected by friend and foe alike because he saw the value in all sides of almost any argument. The ideals of liberty and union were more important to him than ideology. Admitted John Quincy Adams, who often disagreed with his Kentucky colleague: "Clay is an eloquent man, with very popular manners and great political management. He is, like almost all the eminent men of this country, only half educated. His school has been the world, and in that he is proficient. His morals, public and private, are loose, but he has

---

47. Wilkinson, "Henry Clay and South America," 16.
48. Peters, *American Speakership*, 31–34.
49. Letter XXVIII, Washington, DC, April 1820, in Wright, *Views of Society and Manners in America*, 262–63.

all the virtues, indispensable to be a popular man."[50] He was, in short, the right person at the right time, with the right blend of philosophy, personality, background, and political skill.

His success as Speaker and as the eventual broker of the Missouri Compromise owed much to his organizational and political skills. From the beginning, the House of Representatives had several standing committees, but they were not yet well developed. There were few fixed assignments and members often switched from one to another. Membership turnover on committees was high. Clay greatly expanded the number of both standing and select or specialized committees to handle the ever-increasing burden of new legislation. It can be argued that the standing committee system is a monument to Clay's efforts to mobilize the House.[51] He had an uncanny ability to put the best talents and interests of his colleagues to work most efficiently at a time when party politics were more regional and less ideologically rigid as today—even when he knew their politics and desired outcomes might very well differ from his own.[52] And they admired and respected him because of it. In short, he knew how to govern through committees and how to reach consensus out of argument, and he invented as many new committees as necessary to solve the problem at hand.

Such was the diplomatic magic he brought to bear to the Missouri Compromise debate, particularly on what scholars later termed the "Second Compromise of 1821," when the debate renewed after Missouri came back with that objectionable constitution. Even though Clay was not then Speaker, having temporarily resigned to take care of financial problems back home in Ashland, he was still the most influential member of the House. He clearly and unmistakably saw the nature and deep peril in the debate at hand. All looked to him for a resolution. He begged and beseeched, with all his powers of persuasion, for all to compromise. And then he put his organization skills to work. If one joint committee of thirteen from both the House and Senate failed to break the impasse, he requested another, this time of twenty-three. Gradually and with great patience, like a mother with squabbling children, he won over his colleagues. All were given voice; all were respected by Clay as committee chairman. Said Clay: "I am for something practical, something conclusive, something decisive upon this agitating question, and it should be carried by a good majority. How will you vote, Mr. A.? how will you vote, Mr. B? how will you vote, Mr. C?"[53] Reducing the logjam to its simplest common denominator—a skill few others could imitate so often and so well—Clay finally put it thus: "Shall not Missouri be admitted into this Union on an equal footing with the original states in all respects whatever so long as the Constitution of the United States is paramount over the local Constitution of any one of the states of the Union?"[54]

Who could disagree with such a resolution? This second compromise was, therefore, achieved on 2 March 1821. The pledge was secured, and on 10 August 1821, Missouri became

---

50. Adams, *Memoirs of John Quincy Adams*, 5:325.
51. Peters, *American Speakership*, 38.
52. Peters, *American Speakership*, 38.
53. Colton, *Life, Correspondence, and Speeches of Henry Clay*, 3:336.
54. Colton, *Life, Correspondence, and Speeches of Henry Clay*, 3:337.

the United States' twenty-fourth state. Such was the work of the Great Compromiser, who believed that "the art of politics consists only in the possible."[55]

CONCLUSION

Henry Clay served as senator from Kentucky for most of the rest of his life. As ambitious as he was respected, Clay never attained his long-sought prize of the presidency, despite the fact he ran for the post three different times in 1824, 1832, and 1844. He came closest when he lost to John Quincy Adams in 1824 who then appointed him in what some felt was an act of collusion as his Secretary of State. Riding a tide of anti-banking democratic anger, Jackson was elected in 1828. Then in 1832, Clay suffered his worst loss to his old nemesis "Old Hickory," who was then up for reelection, one of the few men Clay thoroughly distrusted personally and utterly despised politically, as one unfit for the presidency. Clay, however, lacked Jackson's populist instinct and democratic impulse and underestimated Jackson's appeal to rural America. Jackson's dismantling of the National Bank of the United States in 1834, his harsh Indian Removal policies, his contempt of the "American System" of higher tariffs and internal improvements, and his imperious nature were all anathema to Clay.

Next to Jackson, if there was another man in Congress Clay resisted the most, it was John C. Calhoun of South Carolina, not on account of his personality—they got along reasonably well—but because of his ideology. Calhoun was the embodiment of the principle of states' rights to the point, as seen in the Nullification Crisis of 1833, that states' rights were more important than the preservation of the Union. To this viewpoint, Clay could never agree. His stand on the preservation of the Union later earned him the accolades of a new congressman from Illinois—Abraham Lincoln.

Clay may have shown ambivalence towards the slavery question, as James Klotter and others have well argued, but the essential point to make is that at center, he stood firmly for the preservation of the Union. "Union was his motto; conciliation his maxim."[56] "I know no South, no North, no East, no West," he said on another occasion.[57] He believed that where at all possible, war must be avoided. Once a war hawk, he had witnessed firsthand the terrible burden the War of 1812 had been to the nation and how costly, ruinous, and totally unpredictable wars could be. Truth is, he feared a civil war and what the unknown results of it might be. "If there be any who want civil war . . . I am not one of them. I wish to see war of no kind; but, above all, I do not desire to see civil war." He continued:

> When war begins, whether civil or foreign, no human sight is competent to foresee when, or how, or where it is to terminate. But when a civil war shall be lighted up in the bosom of our own happy land, and armies are marching and commanders are winning their

---

55. For an excellent, succinct study on this topic, see Lightfoot, "Henry Clay and the Missouri Question," 143–65.
56. Klein, "Henry Clay, Nationalist," 229.
57. Klein, "Henry Clay, Nationalist," 238.

victories, and fleets are in motion on our coast; tell me, if you can, tell me, if any human beings can tell the duration. God alone knows where such a war would end. In what a state will our institutions be left? In what state our liberties? I want no war; above all, no war at home.[58]

The question of Missouri is probably more relevant to the Latter-day Saints than almost any other Christian denomination in America, for in Joseph Smith's budding theology Independence, Jackson County, Missouri, was to be the center stake of Zion, where thousands were to gather in imminent expectation of the Second Coming of Christ. If Missouri had become part of a new Southern confederacy in the early 1820s, could a church then made up predominantly of northerners and not a few abolitionists have thrived in such a place?

Fact is, Latter-day Saints encountered enormous problems in Missouri when it *was* part of the Union. As historian Stephen LeSueur has well shown, the fundamental causes for the Mormon-Missouri conflict were multiple but certainly included religious incompatibilities and prejudices; a restless anxiety that the Saints, as predominantly northerners, would inevitably tamper with the "peculiar institution" of slavery; a lingering suspicion that they would stir up, if not align themselves with, the Native American tribes, whom the Saints regarded were of the House of Israel; a resentment of Mormon-style economics, with its emphasis on consecration and internal trade; and finally, a fear that the Saints would "dominate local politics to the exclusion of all non-Mormons."[59] Had war broken out and had the South won that war, such fears and suspicions would very likely have been even further exacerbated. Furthermore, if the South had seceded in 1820 and if war had followed, what impact would such events have had on missionary work, on the gathering, and on the entire mission of the Church? Admittedly, these are impossible questions to answer, but this chapter has tried to show that Henry Clay had so developed his unique talents and political skills that he played a pivotal role in the preservation of the Union in 1820, which preservation was likely very beneficial to the cause of the Restoration.

Missouri finally came into the Union in 1821, and the Civil War was avoided for over forty years in large measure because of the statesmanship of Henry Clay. Trusted by both North and South, respected in both the House and the Senate, and revered by millions, the Great Compromiser has been overlooked and underappreciated in American history. He not only forged the Compromise of 1820–21 but also helped dissolve the Nullification Crisis of 1832–33 and brokered yet another compromise between bitter factions in 1850. The forces of enmity and irreconciliation eventually overwhelmed his efforts at peaceful resolution, but for our time and age he represents the best in American politics—a nation-building age of hope and optimism.

---

58. Register of Debates, 22nd Congress, 2nd Session, 472, as quoted in Klein, "Henry Clay, Nationalist," 213.
59. LeSueur, *1838 Mormon War in Missouri*, 17. See also Alex Baugh, "Call to Arms."

Portrait of Alexander von Humboldt, by Friedrich Georg Weitsch.

"HE, LIKE ANOTHER SUN, ILLUMINES EVERYTHING I BEHOLD"

ALEXANDER VON HUMBOLDT AND THE NEW AGE OF SCIENTIFIC INQUIRY

"The first impression made by Humboldt's face was that of broad, genial humanity. His massive brow bent forward, overhung his chest like a ripe ear of corn, but as you looked below it, a pair of clear blue eyes, almost as bright and steady as a child's, met your own. You trusted him utterly at first glance. I had approached him with a natural feeling of reverence, but in five minutes I found that I loved him." So remembered the American traveler Bayard Taylor (1825–78) of the man Thomas Jefferson declared to be "the most scientific man of his age."[1] The American transcendentalist poet Ralph Waldo Emerson (1803–82) went even further, calling Humboldt "one of those wonders of the world, like Aristotle, like Julius Caesar, . . . who appear from time to time, as if to show us the possibilities of the human mind, the force and the range of the faculties—a universal man."[2] Even Charles Darwin (1809–82) considered Humboldt his mentor and tutor in the ways of science. "I formerly admired Humboldt, I now almost adore him."[3] "He, like another sun, illumines everything I behold."[4] "I shall never forget that my whole course of life is due to having read and re-read as a youth his [book] *Personal Narrative*."[5] One can well argue that Humboldt was to the nineteenth

---

1. Botting, *Humboldt and the Cosmos*, 279; and Nichols, "Why Was Humboldt Forgotten?," 2.
2. Walls, *Passage to Cosmos*, 254–56.
3. Charles Darwin, as cited in Buttimer, "Bridging the Americas," vii, and Walls, *Passage to Cosmos*, viii.
4. Charles Darwin, as cited in Walls, *Passage to Cosmos*, viii.
5. Helferich, *Humboldt's Cosmos*, xxi.

century what Albert Einstein (1879–1955) became to the twentieth century: "the iconic scientist, whose intellect was so far beyond the ordinary as to seem mystical, superhuman, fabulous, yet curiously benign."[6]

Such tributes as these could be multiplied for the man who personifies the scientific spirit of the time and who, during the age of 1820, was at the apex of his brilliant career. More than any other of his prestigious colleagues, Humboldt brought the study of science into the realm of popular respectability and paved the way for Darwin and the modern age of enlightened scientific inquiry.

And yet there was so much of the enigmatic in the character of this great Prussian who despised his native land and adored his adopted France instead, who loved many but never married, and who comprehended the deepest recesses of space and nature but may have failed to understand himself. Although he was a mentor to thousands and the key supporter of a whole new generation of scientists, Humboldt—the "Napoléon of science"—was essentially a loner. Mysteriously, modern history has all but forgotten him. This chapter will challenge that omission by reclaiming one of the finest minds of the nineteenth century and, while so doing, introduce other contemporary pillars of science whose discoveries and inventions continue to influence modern society.

"THE LITTLE APOTHECARY": HUMBOLDT'S CHILDHOOD AND EARLY LIFE

Friedrich Wilhelm Karl Heinrich Alexander von Humboldt was born in Berlin on 14 September 1769, the same birth year as Napoléon, Lord Wellington, and William Wilberforce. His father, Major Alexander Georg von Humboldt (1720–79), married Marie-Elisabeth von Colomb (1741–96) a forlorn widow of Huguenot descent who had inherited from her first husband an estate at Schloss Tegel, twelve miles north of Berlin. Unfortunately, young Alexander's father, a jolly, imaginative, and life-affirming soul, died young when Alexander was only ten years old, and his aristocratic mother—a cold, distant, self-sufficient Calvinist and a puritanical woman—raised him and his slightly older brother, Wilhelm von Humboldt (1767–1835), in what one of his leading biographers, Douglas Botting, calls "an emotional wasteland."[7]

Frau Humboldt did, however, see to it that her two sons received the very best education. Privately tutored first by Joachim Campe (1746–1818) and later by Gottlob Kunth (1757–1829), both boys developed early on a love of languages, mathematics, history, and the liberal ideals later enshrined in the French Revolution. Young Alexander grew up in the intellectual shadow of his older brother, who showed outstanding promise as a linguist, politician, and diplomat. Wilhelm soon became the idol of the household for his remarkable intellectual prowess, and his mother saw to it he that he was trained for high office.

---

6. Nichols, "Why Was Humboldt Forgotten?," 412n1.
7. Botting, *Humboldt and the Cosmos*, 11.

Alexander, on the other hand, seemed destined for lesser things. He was slower or at least more deliberate, more reserved, and certainly more aloof, guarded, and reflective. In fact, there was nothing in his childhood bespeaking exceptional talent or hinting of true genius, save for three telling characteristics: his vivid, yearning imagination; an incredibly keen sense of observation; and a boundless passion for reading. His most enjoyable outlet was to escape from the castle boredom at Tegel and wander the delightful grounds and nearby gardens, studying and collecting, cataloging and drawing various leaves and flowers, butterflies, and beetles, so much so that he was nicknamed "the little apothecary."

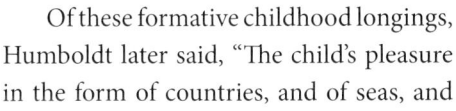

Of these formative childhood longings, Humboldt later said, "The child's pleasure in the form of countries, and of seas, and lakes as delineated in maps; the desire to behold the southern stars; . . . the representation of palms and cedars of Lebanon as depicted in our illustrated bibles, may all implant in the mind the first impulse to travel into distant countries."[8] He had "a peculiar predilection for the sea."[9] With a mother who remained distant and detached, the two brothers became intensely close, showering visitors and the occasional playmates with nonstop chatter and animated conversation. The emotional deficit the two Humboldt brothers felt from their mother was one that Wilhelm overcame through a most felicitous marriage to Karoline von Dacheröden (1766–1829) in 1791, but one that Alexander, restless and emotionally insecure, could never fill.

Missing from their education, as for most young men of the age, were any lessons in science. In fact, the word *scientist* had not even entered the language. It was a subject not then part of the cultural and educational environment, and had Alexander, at the age of sixteen, not had the good fortune to meet Marcus Herz (1747–1803), a Jewish physician who had studied Kant, he may never have gone on to become a scientist. Alexander owned the uncanny ability of meeting the right person at the right time, especially in his early life. Herz presented a series of stimulating illustrated lectures at his home on physics and philosophy

Portrait of Alexander von Humboldt, by Joseph Karl Stieler.

---

8. Humboldt, Cosmos, 1878 ed., 2:370.
9. Humboldt, *Cosmos*, 1878 ed., 1:310.

in which he elaborated upon the latest scientific breakthroughs, theories, and discoveries, including Benjamin Franklin's lightning conductor. Humboldt sat enthralled.

Two years later, in October 1787, the two Humboldt brothers, accompanied by their watchful guardian, Kunth, began their university education at nearby Frankfurt an der Oder. Soon they transferred to the far more prestigious Göttingen University, where Wilhelm read law. Uncertain and still searching his own interests, Alexander dropped out of school for a year to collect his thoughts and regroup. During that time, he became a close friend of Karl Ludwig Willdenow (1765–1812), four years his senior, who had just published his *Flora of Berlin*. Until Willdenow, Alexander had never even heard the word *botany*.

In the spring of 1789, Alexander rejoined Wilhelm at the University of Göttingen, where he shared a room with Count Metternich, the future Austrian prime minister who would play so dominant a role in the Congress of Vienna (see chapter 3). That same year, Alexander made his first trip of exploration up the Rhine to Heidelberg. While studying at Göttingen, Alexander met Georg Forster (1754–94), his true mentor and guiding star, and, although Forster was twice Alexander's age, he became the most important single influence on Alexander's life.[10] Forster had sailed with Captain James Cook on his second around-the-world voyage, where he mastered the business of careful, systematic note-taking. Upon his return, Forster wrote up his findings and adventures in his elegantly written, highly popular *A Voyage Round the World* (1777).

Anxious to return to London to secure a publisher for a second book, Forster invited his new young friend and protégé to come along. In 1790, the two men traveled down the Rhine and arrived in Paris during the apex of a celebration for the hard-fought gains of the French Revolution. From there they traveled westward through Holland and Belgium, where at Dunkerque (Dunkirk), Alexander gazed out at the sea for the first time—a childhood dream fulfilled but a longing never satiated. All along the way, Forster taught his traveling companion the importance of making careful observations of everything from ferns to factories and meticulously recording nearly all they saw and experienced.[11]

Although Forster failed to find a publisher for his book, he did promote his young Prussian friend to such leading lights as William Bligh (1754–1817), the cast-off captain of the *Bounty* on Cook's third and final voyage; Henry Cavendish (1731–1810), prominent physicist and chemist who had determined the density of the earth and established that water is a compound; Sir William Herschel (1738–1822), the foremost astronomer of his day; and Sir Joseph Banks (1743–1820), a leading English naturalist and longtime president of the

---

10. Botting, *Humboldt and the Cosmos*, 16–19.
11. For more on Forster's profound influence, see Ackerknecht, "George Forster," 83–95. "Forster was able to impress upon Humboldt some of his basic approaches: his all-embracing tendency in science and his combined literary and scientific method. The influence of Forster's 'Voyage' is easily recognized in Humboldt's 'Voyage.' Humboldt's famous 'Kosmos' is a grandiose elaboration of Forster's 'Blick ins Ganze der Natur.' Forster remained the better writer, while Humboldt became by far the greater scientist. Nobody has been more explicit as to his indebtedness to Forster than Humboldt himself." Ackerknecht, "George Forster," 87.

Royal Society. Banks immediately recognized in the young Humboldt a kindred spirit. An avid botanist and inveterate collector, Banks had also accompanied Captain Cook aboard the *Endeavour* and later sailed to Iceland and Newfoundland. He became a lead player in establishing the Royal Botanic Gardens at Kew, near London. Banks took special tutorial delight in showing his younger visitors his magnificent herbarium (then the largest in the world) and his vast botanical library.

Upon their return to their homeland, Forster could not refrain from preaching the liberal reforms and ideals of the French Revolution to a wary, suspicious, and much more autocratic Prussia, so much so that he was arrested and branded a traitor to Germany. Tragically Forster died not long afterward in miserable circumstances at the age of forty.

Forster's sad end taught Alexander a stark lesson of another kind—to separate science and the study of nature from the more unpredictable, unforgiving, and unsavory variables of human politics. While he may have held deep liberal convictions, he understood that discretion would be the better part of discovery and quiet, measured common sense the best friend of scientific observation. He saw early in his career that science had its enemies, be they the jealousies and political intrigues among nations and peoples or the long-established doctrines and traditions of some religions that resisted any new theories or findings that might cast doubt on their particular claims to biblical authority.

Alexander became "almost manic about learning," spending his days and nights reading and researching, comparing and analyzing, working late into the night, rising early, eating quickly, and forging study habits that would last a lifetime. Before he was twenty-five, he had authored three books and a dozen articles. He thrived on doing many things at once. As Wilhelm put it, "Alexander maintains a horror of the single fact. He tries to take in everything."[12] And as Alexander himself admitted, "There is a drive in me that, at times, makes me feel as though I am losing my mind."[13]

Rather than follow his mother's wishes for him to prepare for a career as a civil servant, in 1791 he opted to study mining and geology at the Frieberg Mining Academy under the tutelage of the highly popular Professor Abraham Gottlob Werner (1749–1817), a founder of German mineralogy and the Neptune school of geology. Alexander completed this normally three-year course of instruction in less than twelve months, whereupon he became a mining inspector, though of a distinctly different sort than most. While mastering the practical problems of subsurface mining, he was always recommending improvements, including safer gas masks and better safety lamps. While wandering the drifts and stopes below ground, he was as much geologist as he was mining engineer. He studied plant crystallizations underground with the same furious interest and avidity as he did plant clusters above ground. It was while working underground that he began to formulate correlations between the world above and the one below, between living plants and their petrified cousins, and between subterranean gases and the quality of the atmosphere. Because of his sensationally

---

12. Helferich, *Humboldt's Cosmos*, 9.
13. Helferich, *Humboldt's Cosmos*, 14.

detailed reports and "heroic perseverance and exuberance," Humboldt quickly gained the respect of his supervisors and became assessor in the Prussian Mining Service at age twenty-two. Before long, he became superintendent of mines in two duchies and found time to write a mining textbook.[14]

In 1794, the famed German poet Johann Wolfgang von Goethe (1749–1832) sought Humboldt out. Though he was yet to write *Faust*, Goethe had already fashioned an almost godlike reputation. The two men hit it off famously. Alexander's zest for discovery and the accurate recording of scientific data led Goethe to describe him as "our conqueror of the world." Goethe gushed in saying, "what Alexander says in one hour could not be read in eight days reading."[15] Alexander rekindled Goethe's interest in plants and biology, while Goethe, for his part, instilled in his new friend the Romantic ideal that a "primeval principle"[16] and essential unity infused all nature and that nature needed more than mere measurement—it required contemplation, deep enjoyment, and poetic expression.

Goethe's colleague, the Romantic poet Friedrich Schiller (1759–1805), was far less impressed. Coarchitect of the natural philosophy school of thought, Schiller believed that the scientific measurement of nature was an irreverent distraction from its primary purpose of shedding inspiration and revelation on the human soul. Any effort to simply study and measure nature in a scientific way was to him mere rubbish and a waste of time, like measuring the dimensions of the *Mona Lisa* without savoring the sublime beauty of the painting.

For his part, Humboldt considered Schiller and the natural philosophy school of thought to be sentimental sloppiness. Humboldt was a man given to facts and careful observations, not to poetry and vacant imaginations, what Botting called "the difference between a romantic poet and an empirical scientist."[17] Yet such a contrast is probably overblown. For the truth is, Alexander was deeply impressionable. For him, the quest for the scientific knowledge of nature was inspiration enough. He and Goethe would remain in contact one with another for years to come.

"HIS APPRENTICESHIP WAS OVER": IN SEARCH OF A MISSION

In 1796, when Humboldt's mother died of breast cancer, he found it hard to grieve her passing. "My heart could not have been much pained by this event," he later admitted, "for we were always strangers to each other."[18] Her death, however, opened new and unlimited horizons for him and his brother, Wilhelm, because they inherited the family estate and a sizable fortune.

---

14. McCrory, *Nature's Interpreter*, 36–40.
15. McCrory, *Nature's Interpreter*, 51.
16. McCrory, *Nature's Interpreter*, 50.
17. Botting, *Humboldt and the Cosmos*, 40.
18. Helferich, *Humboldt's Cosmos*, 16.

Gladly quitting his mining position, Humboldt, then only twenty-seven, visited his brother and family in Jena, climbed Mount Vesuvius in Italy, then eyed a trip to the West Indies. In gleeful preparation for further adventures, he purchased a vast assortment of the latest magnetic, geographical, and meteorological instruments. He also spent time in Austria and Paris in company with such other leading scientists as Professor Franz Porth and the eccentric geologist Leopold von Buch (1774–1853). Buch taught him how to use a sextant, how to calculate elevation and precise readings of longitude and latitude, how to measure barometric pressure and fluctuations in temperature, how to determine the oxygen and carbon dioxide content of the air, and much more. It was an outdoor schooling in the Tyrolean Mountains of meteorology at its scientific best. Because of it, Humboldt developed a program of readings that was to become "the universally accepted procedure for meteorological observations all over the world."[19]

When word came that the English Navy, wary of Napoléon's intentions, had barricaded the West Indies, Humboldt was invited to join the notorious Lord Bristol, bishop of Derry (1730–1803), on a caravaning expedition up the Nile. But Napoléon's massive military buildup and surprise 1798 invasion of Egypt spoiled even that attempt.

All dressed up with nowhere to go, a frustrated but still determined Humboldt returned to his beloved Paris. As the intellectual, artistic, and social capital of Europe, the city was teeming with artists and scientists from all over the world, many of whom were already acquainted with his work. Georges Cuvier (1769–1832), founder of comparative anatomy, had just published his *Tableau élémentaire de l'histoire naturelle des animaux* (1798) on the classification of various groups of animals. Cuvier would go on to become famous for studying extinct mammals and reptiles, and by 1820 he had laid the foundation for modern paleontology. Cuvier advised Humboldt on equipment purchases and drew his attention to the need of studying the earth's magnetic fields. With plenty of time on his hands, Humboldt also studied with Jean-Baptiste Delambre (1749–1822), a leading mathematician and historian of astronomy; Claude Louis Berthollet (1748–1822), a chemist; and the famed Jean-Baptiste Lamarck (1744–1829), a renowned zoologist, botanist, early evolutionist, and chair of zoology at the Jardin du Roi. Lamarck's study of invertebrates—a term of his own invention—and his conclusion that "the production of a new organ in an animal body results from a new need" foreshadowed Darwin's evolutionary thesis by fifty years.[20]

Meanwhile, the busy Paris rumor mill had it that the French government was about to dispatch the famous navigator and explorer Louis-Antoine de Bougainville (1729–1811) on a five-year voyage of discovery to the Pacific Ocean, the unchartered waters of Antarctica, and the lands of South America, Mexico, California, and Africa. Bougainville, one of Humboldt's childhood heroes and one who had fought in 1759 with Louis-Joseph de Montcalm-Grozon, marquis de Montcalm, against Major General James Wolfe and the British at the Plains of Abraham, approached Humboldt and invited him to join his scientific staff. Overjoyed at the

---

19. Botting, *Humboldt and the Cosmos*, 53.
20. Williams, *Biographical Dictionary of Scientists*, 303.

prospect, Humboldt eagerly agreed but at the moment of departure, Bougainville was suddenly replaced by the much lesser known Captain Nicolas Baudin (1754–1803). Humboldt's dreams of discovery were shattered once again when Napoléon invaded Austria and diverted the monies that had been earmarked for the expedition into supporting his military conquests. No one walked down the ship's gangplank with a heavier heart than did our crestfallen Humboldt.

Determined not to let a minor detail such as Napoléon's conquest of Europe get in his way, Humboldt hurriedly made other plans. While staying at L'Hotel Boston in Paris, he had the good fortune of meeting Baudin's ship doctor and botanist, Aimé Jacques Alexandre Bonpland (1773–1858), four years his junior. A cheery sort of man with dreams of adventure almost as bold as Humboldt's, Bonpland would prove the perfect partner. The two men soon became fast friends and together planned to make their own kind of conquests by sailing to Algeria on board a neutral Swedish packet boat and then on to Cairo to join up with Napoléon's army of scientists, where they would then travel up the Nile (see chapter 2).

Alas, that plan also failed to materialize when the promised vessel ran aground off of Portugal. So now what? Paris was a troop encampment, Berlin was braced for a coming invasion, London was madly preparing for war, and Algeria was imprisoning French civilians—where else to go but Spain? It was worth a try, so the two men, with their bulky instruments, quit Marseilles and crossed over the Pyrenees on foot. In the best Forster tradition, they took more careful scientific observations of the Spanish peninsula than had ever before existed. Their expedition proved that Spain's interior was one high continuous plateau, and in the process, Humboldt and Bonpland earned a reputation for themselves as Europe's "most meticulous and well-trained travelers." As Botting succinctly concluded, "Humboldt's apprenticeship was over."[21]

Once Humboldt and Bonpland arrived in Madrid, the Saxon ambassador to Spain, Baron Philippe de Forell (1756–1819), introduced Humboldt to the Spanish prime minister, Mariano Luis de Urguijo (1769–1817), who in turn introduced Humboldt and Bonpland, as Humboldt's "secretary," to King Carlos IV (1748–1819) and Queen Maria Luisa (1751–1819) at the Court of Aranjuez in March 1799. Sensing that this was the opportunity of a thousand lifetimes, Humboldt determined to make the best of it. Speaking fluent Spanish and showing his wonderfully detailed new maps of Spain, he proposed a plan to visit the Spanish-American colonies and the Philippines and to make key studies and observations for the Spanish crown, all at his own expense, if necessary.

Convinced that they were not spies, the king listened sympathetically, but for other reasons. Humboldt's reputation as a mining engineer and explorer had preceded him, and the king, sensing that Spain was lagging behind the other European powers in science and technology, saw in Humboldt the potential for charting new territories, encouraging science, and discovering new gold and silver mines. So here we find this incredible spectacle of a Prussian Protestant and a French sailor being granted royal passports and unlimited

---

21. Botting, *Humboldt and the Cosmos*, 62.

Alexander von Humboldt and Aimé Bonpland at the Foot of the Chimborazo Volcano, by Friedrich Georg Weitsch (1806).

permission to visit, study, and observe every Spanish colony from Cape Horn to California—the entire Spanish Catholic empire in the Americas! And all at Spain's expense! And Humboldt, who was not given to religious devotions, could only kneel in gratitude. In over three hundred years of Spanish rule, no other man had ever been given such permission and such an incomparable opportunity.

THE SCIENTIFIC DISCOVERY OF THE NEW WORLD

Humboldt's and Bonpland's five-year exploration of South America and Mexico was to Latin America what Lewis and Clark's expedition became to the United States and what Alexander Mackenzie's expedition became to Canada—a portent of the discovery and creation of a national identity. But similar to Captain James Cook, Humboldt's and Bonpland's quest for pure scientific knowledge, their meticulous observations, and their careful mathematical readings and measurements established a standard of excellence, a strident methodology for all such future expeditions. Far more than mere travelers and explorers, Humboldt and Bonpland became the prototype of scientific adventure. They laid the cornerstones of climatology, meteorology, oceanography, geomagnetism, anthropology, geology, and modern plant science. Rapidly becoming the leading naturalists of their day, they would set a standard for all to follow.

Humboldt's devotion to writing and illustrating his adventures and discoveries and their publication in newspapers all over Europe and in North America made him an international celebrity. He popularized the world of scientific observation as never before. To this day, more places on the earth and on the moon are named after him than any other figure in history.[22] Humboldt's and Bonpland's adventure is, indeed, one for the history books. They set sail from A Coruña, Spain, on 5 June 1799 on board the corvette *Pizarro*, bound for the New World like a modern Columbus.

Laden with sextants and quadrants, balances and compasses, barometers and thermometers, telescopes and microscopes, hygrometers and magnetometers, rain gauges and theodolites, Humboldt and his loyal assistant proved a fascinating spectacle for sailors and sojourners alike—a veritable floating scientific laboratory. And Humboldt soon lived up to his reputation. Spending his days and nights sounding sea depths and ocean salinity, making astronomical readings, and gauging changing ocean temperatures, Humboldt kept meticulous notes on most everything. He was especially interested in studying and mapping ocean currents, those rivers of moving waters—like jet streams—beneath the surface of the sea that moderate temperatures and affect sea life throughout the oceans. "Every motion is the cause of another motion in the vast basin of the seas,"[23] he penned. When once the ship captain ordered all lanterns out lest they be detected by nearby British naval ships, no one was more frustrated at this waste of time than Humboldt was. So he went on deck and studied the starry firmament.

At their first port of call in the Canary Islands, dressed in his customary open-necked shirt, loose striped trousers, short jacket, high black hat, and tall boots with the tops turned over, Humboldt gave hint of things to come when he spent his shore leave climbing the 12,200-foot volcano Mount Teide on the isle of Tenerife—his first volcano climb of many. Twenty days later, after picking up the trade winds and following the same route of Columbus's first voyage, they crossed the equator into the southern hemisphere. One night, while out on deck, Humboldt put down his telescope to record his feelings at seeing the Southern Cross constellation for the first time. "Nothing awakens in the traveler a livelier semblance of the immense distance by which he is separated from his country, than the aspect of an unknown firmament."[24] When at length they reached the West Indies, they chose not to disembark at Havana, Cuba, as per their original plan, because of a typhus epidemic. The ship changed course, reaching Cumaná, Venezuela, on 16 July 1799, the oldest continuously inhabited settlement in South America.

---

22. Helferich, *Humboldt's Cosmos*, xvii, 25.
23. Humboldt and Bonpland, *Personal Narrative*, 1:19.
24. Humboldt and Bonpland, *Personal Narrative*, 1:134.

Humboldt and Bonpland were giddy with excitement at having seen the tropics and the southern night sky for the first time. The sights and sounds, fruits and flowers, and rocks and mountains of the New World beckoned them onward. There they began to collect the first of what would be tens of thousands of plant specimens to eventually take or send back to Paris, many of which had never before been classified. "It might be said," Humboldt recorded, "that the earth, overloaded with plants, does not allow them space enough to unfold themselves."[25] The only thing that marred their stay at Cumaná were the notorious slave markets, a spectacle of human indignity that the liberal-minded Humboldt detested and decried. He hated slavery and racial prejudice of any kind but was careful not to mix politics with science, lest their ever-watchful Spanish authorities renounce their passports.

From Cumaná the expedition moved on to Caracas, where, after a short stay, they temporarily gave up the idea of going to Cuba and instead set out southward to explore the rain forests of the Amazon and the upper reaches of the Orinoco River. The Orinoco was to Venezuela what the Amazon was to Brazil, and local legend had it that "he who goes to the Orinoco either dies or comes back mad."[26] To reach their goal, they would first have to traverse the feared Llanos, a plains region larger than France. Come the rainy season, it was transformed into a sea of infinite archipelagos teeming with crocodiles, snakes, electric eels (*tembladores*), giant rodents, jaguars, venomous bats, piranhas, mosquitoes, and millions of other insects—not a journey for the fainthearted, as even Bolívar discovered. When their horses were crossing a stream, they were stung almost to paralysis by swarms of electric eels. Humboldt once picked up one of the eels barehanded to measure the six-hundred-volt transfer. It almost killed him. Their security dogs were sometimes carried off at night by prowling jaguars, and only their nighttime bonfires kept hungry crocodiles and deadly vipers at bay. While on the rivers, they traveled with natives in large canoes (*lanchas*) through piranha-infested waters, their makeshift, screen-covered cabin headquarters at the rear, often with anacondas swimming at their sides. For Humboldt, who could not swim, the rivers proved most challenging, and those on the expedition were indeed fortunate to survive. As one scholar has rightly noted, "Against some of the most inclement conditions to be found anywhere on earth they were armed with nothing but their sense of humour, their *joie de vivre*, and their unquenchable enthusiasm for scientific discovery."[27]

Choosing not to sail down the Amazon into Brazil, a Portuguese colony that would not have recognized their Spanish passports and likely would have thrown both Humboldt and Bonpland into jail, they explored the Río Negro (see map on p. 210), portaging around great cataracts and endless rapids. They eventually proved the existence of the Casiquiare Canal, which connected the Orinoco River basin with the Amazon River Basin. At almost every stop, Humboldt recorded his observations in such a hurried scrawl and in so many different languages (though mainly in French) that few others besides himself would be able to

---

25. Humboldt and Bonpland, *Personal Narrative*, 1:216.
26. Helferich, *Humboldt's Cosmos*, 124.
27. Botting, *Humboldt and the Cosmos*, 104.

decipher them.[28] Seventy-five days and 1,500 miles later, they finally reached the port city of Nueva Barcelona at the end of August 1800 with a collection of twelve thousand specimens of plant and animal life—and almost an equal number of stories to tell.

After sending his manuscripts, herbariums, geological specimens, native skeletons, caged monkeys, and much more back home to Europe on three different ships for fear of the British naval blockade, sinkings, piratings, and any number of other potential calamities, Humboldt and Bonpland set sail for Cuba, their original destination.[29] From there Humboldt's plans were to explore Mexico, the west coasts of America, the Philippines, and the East Indies before returning home.

En route to Havana, Bonpland and Humboldt had the hair-raising misfortune of being attacked and seized by pirates but then the great fortune of being liberated almost immediately thereafter by a British sloop of war under the command of a Captain Garnier. As fate would have it, Captain Garnier was a devotee of his celebrated prisoner, having read almost every newspaper account of Humboldt's South American exploits. Spending hours together, the two men became fast *bons amis* and relished in their mutual good fortune.

Upon reaching Cuba near the close of 1800, Humboldt spent several weeks surveying the entire island, recalculating local latitudes and longitudes, improving and correcting maps, sounding out depth readings of Havana harbor, studying sugar cane and slave-holding plantations, and completing enough other studies to eventually publish his *Political Essay on the Island of Cuba* (1828). Never had anyone so carefully studied the "pearl of the Antilles" as did this "second discoverer of Cuba."[30]

When word came that Captain Baudin's around-the-world exploration had been funded after all, Humboldt abandoned his North American plans. The projection now was that after a three months' exploration of the Andes and some of the highest volcanoes in the world, they would rendezvous with Baudin in Lima, Peru. So they turned around and set sail for South America once again.

Humboldt had a clear plan of what he wanted to accomplish in his "Andes project." By carefully studying volcanoes, Humboldt planned on correlating what species of plant life existed at similar elevations and in comparable climates. He planned to test his theory of isothermal ranges of plant geography and hoped to show cartographically that similar plant life existed at the same elevations, zones, and temperatures all over the world in surprisingly consistent isothermal lines and patterns. Later publishing his findings in his *Essay on the Geography of Plants* (1807), complete with its stunning tables and illustrations, he was the first to systematically study why different plants grew where they did, such as deciduous and broadleaf trees on lower hills and conifers at higher altitudes.

---

28. Helferich, *Humboldt's Cosmos*, 142.
29. His collection of insects was lost at sea, and another collection was captured by the British Navy, but thanks to Sir Joseph Banks it was eventually returned to its rightful owner.
30. Helferich, *Humboldt's Cosmos*, 203.

As for volcanoes, to Humboldt, each merited study. Comparing their perpendicular heights to their base circumferences and climbing and exploring almost every foot of terrain, the intrepid Humboldt was most interested in studying lava formations and outcrops at all levels of the mountainside, since currents of volcanic lava as often as not poured out of the cracks at the base of such mountains as at the top. His daring solo climb of Mount Chimborazo, at 20,702 feet then considered the highest mountain in the world, and of Mount Pichincha and others earned him lasting fame as the world's foremost mountain climber and one whose hands were often frost bit from the cold air but whose feet were on fire from the heat of the volcano.

From his many ascents, Humboldt revolutionized the science of geology by arguing in his three-volume *Personal Narrative of Travels to the Equinoctial Regions of America* (1818) that the "Neptune theory" of volcanic origin, that is that volcanoes were ancient accidents of subterranean coal fires, was false. Rather, Humboldt proposed that volcanoes are the result of far more modern, even current, extensive and interconnected worldwide geological activity and that they originated as violent lava upheavals from fissures or cracks along the crust or platelets deep within the earth. This explained why volcanoes were often found in clusters or series, such as along the west coasts of the Americas. Humboldt thus came to espouse uniformitarianism, the scientific theory that the processes that shaped the earth are still at work, constantly changing the earth's landscape and topography. His findings anticipated those of Sir Charles Lyell (1797–1875), the most famous geologist of the later nineteenth century, and Darwin's more zoological-based study of ever-evolving organic species and life formations.[31] While studying in Peruvian mountaintops, Humboldt also discovered the location of the earth's magnetic equator and the existence of magnetic storms, which are caused by sudden releases of ultraviolet radiation from the sun.

Eventually reaching Lima, Peru, in October 1802, some 1,600 miles from Cartagena, a leaner, lighter Humboldt and his well-nigh exhausted partner, Bonpland—who had foregone the pleasure of volcanic climbing for collecting plants at lower altitudes—rested, but not for very long. Upon learning that Baudin had changed courses and was not coming after all, the ever-resourceful Humboldt took the disappointing news in stride by studying intently the ancient Incan civilizations, starting at the palace Tapayupangi. Although it had been conquered relatively recently by Pizarro and the Spanish conquistadores in the 1530s,

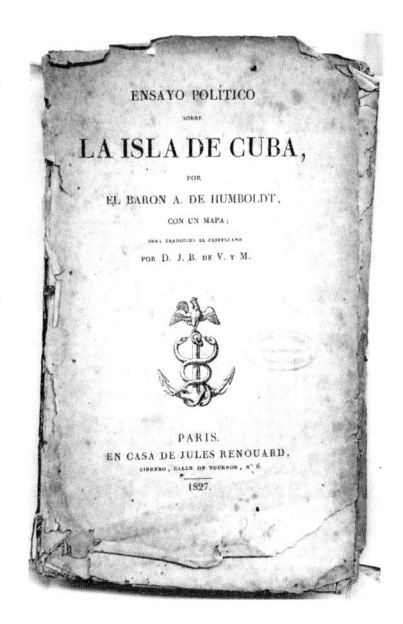

Political Essay on the Island of Cuba, by Alexander von Humboldt.

---

31. Helferich, *Humboldt's Cosmos*, 231.

the ingenious Incas had once wielded enormous power and influence in establishing their civilizations in the very tops of the Andes. From his careful study of their language, and miles and miles of roads, architecture, and gardens, Humboldt argued that such peoples were not the blighted and backward natives some insisted on but rather were once "a very advanced civilization."[32]

Humboldt was among the first to argue that these indigenous people had migrated from eastern Asia long ago, likely crossing the Behring Straits and establishing colonies of various advanced civilizations from north to south and along the western coastal regions of the hemisphere. "A darker shade of skin color [was] not a badge of inferiority," he asserted. His writings speak less of differences between races and more of similarities. He saw all humankind, whether ancient Egyptians or the more modern Incas, as brothers and sisters in one vast network of humankind. More than a casual anthropologist, this "self-proclaimed child of the French Revolution" was "the first prominent European to appreciate the great indigenous cultures of the New World."[33]

Humboldt pursued the same kind of anthropological studies among the Aztec ruins of New Spain (or Mexico)—the crown jewel of Spain's New World—where he and Bonpland arrived in late March 1803. After spending most of the year studying gold and silver mines, Humboldt made several recommendations for King Carlos IV on how Mexico—then a country of 5.2 million people—could be even more productive and profitable. Just as he had done previously in Spain and in Cuba, his careful land and typographical surveys of Mexico from Acapulco to Mexico City and eventually to the east coast city of Veracruz formed the basis of future cartographic Mexican studies for decades to come. As much as he saw a bold future in Mexican mining, he saw even more potential and wealth in developing Mexican agriculture. Humboldt's work left such a profound impression on Mexico that he was offered a ministerial position in the government. Just fifteen years later in 1820, leaders of Mexico's independence movement adopted Humboldt as their national hero because of his republican ideals and faith in their future, calling him the "benefactor of the nation."[34]

One of his primary interests in Mexico was his study of the ancient Aztec empire and its people. Like the Incas, the Aztec empire flowered relatively recently, with Montezuma II on his temple throne in their capital city of Tenochtitlán—later Mexico City. A violent and religious people, the Aztecs had once sacrificed hundreds of thousands of hapless victims to their great sun god on the steps of their soaring temples. Like the Incas, the Aztecs had no wheeled vehicles, no arches, and no metal tools, but they were magnificent builders and astronomers. Especially advanced in reckoning time and the movements of the earth around the sun, the Aztecs had devised a solar calendar year of 365 days, divided into 18 months, each of 20 days, with the final five days of the year added at year's end. Each day of the month

---

32. McCrory, *Nature's Interpreter*, 101.
33. Helferich, *Humboldt's Cosmos*, 261–62.
34. Helferich, *Humboldt's Cosmos,* 291–92. For a much fuller discussion of Humboldt's contributions to "New Spain" (Mexico), see Helferich, *Humboldt's Cosmos,* 264–87.

had its own name. The Aztecan festivals were all based on their solar calendar.[35] Conquered by a ruthless Cortes in 1519, which resulted in the slaughter of some 250,000 people, the Aztecs quickly declined and their past glory was but a memory by Humboldt's time. A fan of neither Pizarro nor Cortes, Humboldt was just as critical of their Roman Catholic successors, whose dogma and ceremonies, he believed, were no better than those that lay at his feet in ruins.

Humboldt was to ancient Latin America what Champollion had become to ancient Egypt—the pioneer of discovery (see chapter 2). From his careful study of Aztecan art and writings, Humboldt concluded that they were "the debased remnants of a more advanced nation."[36] He also believed that their hieroglyphics, if not an alphabet, were a system of symbols to perpetuate memories of their past as well as to represent the state of the soul after death. His careful studies became the inspiration for a long list of later scholars who were interested in uncovering the deeper secrets of the ancient Aztec Empire.[37]

In his *Political Essay on the Kingdom of New Spain* (1814), Humboldt wrote that the "nations of America . . . form a single race," that they crossed over the Behring Straits, and that they owned a striking resemblance to the Mongol nations from which they most likely

Storming of the Teocalli by Cortez and His Troops, by Emanuel Leutze.

---

35. Humboldt, *Researches*, 1:390–93.
36. Helferich, *Humboldt's Cosmos*, 237.
37. Humboldt, *Researches*, 1:147, 160.

sprang.[38] He ended his study of modern Mexican native populations with a plea for equality: "The prosperity of the whites is intimately connected with that of the copper-colored race, and there can be no durable prosperity for the two Americas till this unfortunate race, humiliated but not degraded, shall participate in all the advantages resulting from the progress of civilization and the improvement of the social order."[39]

"HALF AN AMERICAN"

Humboldt's six-week visit to the United States of America on his way home to Europe left an indelible impression on the young republic. An ardent admirer of the aims and ideals of the American Revolution and of President Thomas Jefferson (1743–1826), who was a student of science himself, Humboldt first visited the American Philosophical Society in Philadelphia. There he met with such leading American naturalists, linguists, and scholars as Caspar Wistar and Samuel Latham Mitchill, the latter of whom was arguably America's foremost naturalist and whom Jefferson once called "a chaos of knowledge."[40]

Humboldt and Bonpland then traveled on to Washington, DC, the nation's capital since only 1800. Humboldt and Jefferson spent many hours together in Washington and at Monticello. Jefferson, who had just completed the Louisiana Purchase and whose own Lewis and Clark expedition was then exploring its way up the Missouri River, had intently followed Humboldt's Latin American exploits and was particularly interested in his maps of Mexico and his studies of Mexican land claims, extremely valuable information which Humboldt freely shared. To Humboldt's way of thinking, all scientific knowledge should be freely communicated. From this brief meeting, a lifelong friendship developed between Humboldt and Jefferson, to be marked by a lively exchange of ideas in twenty years of correspondence.[41] Of their meetings Humboldt wrote, "I have had the good fortune to see the first Magistrate of this great republic living with the simplicity of a philosopher who received me with that profound kindness that makes for a lasting friendship."[42]

Humboldt saw in America a political model for the realization of his liberal ideals. Furthermore, he greatly admired the new republic's rapid progress in the sciences, education, and culture. As Humboldt often said of himself, he was "half an American."[43] Only the

---

38. Humboldt, *Researches*, 1:147.
39. Humboldt, *Political Essay*, 240.
40. This same Professor Samuel L. Mitchill in February 1828 met with Martin Harris, early scribe to Joseph Smith's translation of the Book of Mormon. Mitchill compared the characters that Harris showed to him and to his younger colleague, Charles Anthon, to the writings of Champollion, and set them down to an ancient, "delicate" people who once lived in the America's but who long ago had been destroyed by the "Tartars," a more warlike Asiatic people. For more, see Bennett, "'Read This I Pray Thee," 178–216.
41. Rebok, "Enlightened Correspondents," 328–69.
42. Malone, *Jefferson the President*, 421–22.
43. Rebok, "Enlightened Correspondents," 333.

continued existence of slavery—America's tragic flaw—marred his otherwise glowing regard of the new nation.

Humboldt's work would live on in America for years to come. Henry Thoreau (1817–62), Washington Irving (1783–1859), Walt Whitman (1819–92), Ralph Waldo Emerson (1803–82), and Albert Gallatin (1761–1849), Jefferson's secretary of state, studied Humboldt intently. He became the inspiration for the expedition of Zebulon Pike of 1806, and his work with the Aztecs later motivated John Lloyd Stephens (1805–52) to rediscover the Mayas. The great American landscape painter Frederic Church (1826–1900), of the Hudson River School (see chapter 5), owed much of his inspiration for his masterpiece *Heart of the Andes* and other paintings to Humboldt. Humboldt's reputation in America lived on till as late as 1869, when Oliver Wendell Holmes called him the "hero of knowledge" and the "peaceful conqueror."[44] It would take the decline of transcendentalism, two world wars against Germany, and the rise of anti-German xenophobia to dismantle and disfigure America's nineteenth-century admiration for the great Prussian discoverer.[45]

Humboldt had come to personify the careful study of nature, the making of discoveries, and the laying down of new scientific laws that had caught the imagination not only of Americans but of the whole world. Many since have called his approach Humboldtian science, with its key elements being exploring, collecting, measuring, and connecting.[46] To these he would later add publishing, lecturing, promoting, and encouraging. Just as Charles Lindbergh (1902–74) would herald a new age of international flight and aeronautics in the twentieth century, Humboldt was changing the way the early nineteenth century looked at science by trusting in those new discoveries and emerging technologies that would change the world.

THE BUDDING AGE OF SCIENCE

Our study of Humboldt begs at least a cursory overview of the world of science as it stood in the era of 1820. Professional scientific journals were just beginning to appear, and scientific associations were forming on a broad international scale. The age was witnessing the beginnings of a new era of accelerated revolutionary advances and discoveries, only a few of which can be studied here.

Nineteenth-century astronomy obtained its most spectacular results in positional astronomy. This included the study of celestial mechanics—with its mathematical research into the perturbations of planetary motion and the motion of the sun—of stellar distances and of the charting of stars, galaxies, new nebulae, and even black holes. Best remembered for his fundamental contributions to mathematical physics and celestial mechanics and for

---

44. Walls, *Passage to Cosmos*, 310.
45. Walls, *Passage to Cosmos*, 129, 165–67, 224, 252, 268, 302, 310. Walls's work is probably the most definitive study yet written on Humboldt's influence on American thought.
46. Walls, *Passage to Cosmos*, 126–27.

proving the stability of the solar system was Pierre-Simon Laplace (1749–1827). A worthy successor of Sir Isaac Newton (1642–1727), Laplace developed stunning mathematical methods for calculating the disturbances of planets and moons by their gravitational forces. His work included the development of lunar and tidal theory and a careful study of the moon's gravitational impact on the motion of the earth and on the long-term stability of the solar system. In his *Mécanique Céleste* and his *Théorie analytique des probabilités*, the latter published in five volumes between 1799 and 1825, Laplace developed the "calculus of probability" based on his theory of "enchained probabilities," upon which nearly all later developments in the theory of probability are based.

Karl Friedrich Gauss (1777–1855), the "prince of mathematics," must be compared to Archimedes and Newton. "With few peers and none in the theory of numbers," Gauss was led to the study of advanced algebra and differential and hyperbolic geometry. Director of the Göttingen Observatory for many years, Gauss fathered the Quadratic Reciprocity Theorem. Much of modern mathematical physics and Einstein's theory of gravitation would hardly have been possible without Gauss's pioneering mathematical work.[47] Gauss's calculations in astronomy led to his discovery of a wide band of asteroids and planetoids between the orbits of Mars and Jupiter and to the eventual mathematical discovery of the planet Neptune.

The leading figure in nineteenth-century astronomy was undoubtedly the German-born Sir William Herschel (1738–1822). A professional optician, Herschel developed a passion for the study of mirrors and for constructing bigger and better telescopes. Peering through his seven-foot telescope, he discovered the planet Uranus in 1781. Later on, with his twenty-foot telescope, he embarked upon a lifelong, systematic quest to catalogue and classify the distribution of the stars by their brightness down to the fourteenth magnitude. Herschel named and located over five thousand new stars, and his stellar maps and minute study of the Milky Way are foundational to the mapping of modern astronomy. He furthermore suggested the name *asteroids* for those tiny fragments of planets long ago shattered by explosions. Through careful, persistent charting of the heavens, he proved that the sun and stars are not fixed but are moving through space.[48]

The year 1790 began one of the "most brilliant periods in the history of science," culminating in the discovery of the battery and current electricity and of the relationship between electricity and magnetism—in short, "the birth of the modern electrical industry."[49] One could argue that the present-day computer age, based as it is on electricity, began in this age 1820. The four leading pioneers in this scientific revolution were Italy's Alessandro Volta (1745–1827), Denmark's Hans Christian Ørsted (1777–1851), France's André-Marie Ampère (1775–1836), and England's Michael Faraday (1791–1867).

While electricity was well known before the nineteenth century, it had never before been created in a laboratory setting. No other source for it besides the atmosphere and lightning

---

47. Williams, *Biographical Dictionary of Scientists*, 207–9.
48. Taton, *History of Science*, 102–28.
49. Taton, *History of Science*, 178.

had yet been discovered. Thus, any continuous or controlled use of it had not been achieved. It was Alessandro Volta who harnessed, controlled, and generated electricity as never before. Building on the earlier experiments of his fellow countryman Luigi Galvani (1737–89), who worked on the electrical stimulation of animal muscles, Volta discovered in 1796 that certain series of metals (zinc, carbon, and copper) suspended in an aqueous acidulated solution could create a steady current of electricity. His voltaic pile, or early electric battery, provided a steady and reliable new source of energy that allowed for the study of the phenomena of flowing electricity and what could be accomplished and achieved with it. With his electrometer and condenser, Volta was able to measure the flow and intensity of atmospheric electricity. Some contend that his letter of discovery on 20 March 1800 to the Royal Society of London ushered in the age of electricity.[50]

Sir William Herschel and Caroline Herschel, by A. Diethe.

Hans Christian Ørsted's subsequent accidental discovery of the magnetic effects of electric currents in 1819 owed much to Volta's battery. Ørsted clearly saw that the newly discovered electrical currents moved in circles around the conductor, thus showing that an electric current produces a circular magnetic effect as it flows through a wire. Electricity, therefore, and magnetism were intimately related one to another.

André-Marie Ampère of Lyons took Volta's and Ørsted's pioneering work to the next level. While Volta supplied a new reliable source for electricity and Ørsted a new way to apply it, Ampère found in September 1820 that parallel currents in the same direction attract one another, while those in opposite directions repel one another. From this discovery he demonstrated that parallel currents acted as magnetic poles and that currents could be made to attract or repel one another, thereby changing the direction of the flow of electricity. With wires bent into circular form and with coils consisting of many circular windings, Ampère was able to set contrasting magnets into spinning motion, giving rise to the study of electrodynamics. The potential applications of his discovery were enormous.

---

50. Lenard, *Great Men of Science*, 158–67.

In the following year, thirty-year-old Michael Faraday, carried out a series of magnificent experiments on electromagnetic rotation. A laboratory assistant of Sir Humphrey Davy, Faraday proved that a magnetic pole can be made to spin or rotate around a wire carrying an electric current. He thus essentially produced electricity from magnetism and in the process created the first electric motor. His work with electromagnetic induction led him into an investigation of the laws of electrolysis, an entirely new method of producing electric currents that opened the way to the new world of electrodynamism.[51]

Contemporaneous advances in chemistry were hardly less impressive than those in astronomy and electricity. The Quaker John Dalton (1766–1844) in his *New System of Chemistry* proposed his "atomic hypothesis," where he stated that each atom within a certain chemical compound has a "characteristic relative weight."[52] Dalton concluded that heat is not so much the result of friction as it is the property of gases, thus providing for "the classical hypothesis of the atomic constitution of matter."[53] This laid the foundation for the modern constitutional theories of chemistry.

Using the Voltaic battery and building upon Dalton's studies, Jacob Berzelius (1779–1848) of Sweden was the first to show that properties of the atom appeared capable of deduction and that atoms of a particular element are held together in molecules by electric forces.[54] Berzelius is credited for devising the modern chemical tables so popular today when in 1818 he published his *Essays on the Cause of Chemical Proportions*, which contained a table of Latin initial letters of atomic weights with the combination of gases by volume—for example, H_2O or CO_2.

Humphrey Davy (1778–1829), a friend of Southey and Coleridge (see chapter 6) and as much a poet as he was a scientist, was already well known for his studies with nitrous oxide, or laughing gas. By using Volta's new source of battery-powered electricity, Davy was enabled in 1807 to separate chemical elements on a scale larger and at speeds faster than ever before. His pioneering work with electrochemistry led to isolating elements never before separated and inspired his discovery of potassium and the separation of sodium from many chemical combinations. Davy discovered that light was not a modification of heat as much as it was a constituent of oxygen and that heat was not a substance but a form of motion. Thus, Davy was a pioneer in the study of electrolysis, which has led to such modern activities as copper, silver, and gold refining, electroplating, electrotyping, and other beneficial commercial processes.[55]

In the field of light and fundamental optics was Thomas Young (1773–1829), who competed with Champollion in decoding the Rosetta Stone (see chapter 2). Building on Newton's *Optics* and the earlier works of Pierre Bouguer and Joseph von Fraunhofer's spectrum

---

51. Kendall, *Michael Faraday*, 114–20.
52. Taton, *History of Science*, 270–73.
53. Greenaway, *John Dalton and the Atom*, 3.
54. Lenard, *Great Men of Science*, 195.
55. Hart, *Makers of Science*, 227.

analysis, Young pursued lengthy studies of light and its various inherent colors. Young is to be credited for the discovery of light waves.

In the budding field of photography, in 1816 Nicéphore Niépce (1765–1833) laid the groundwork for successfully fixing images on paper coated with silver chloride, and in 1826 he obtained the first permanent photograph. Eleven years later, his partner, Louis Daguerre (1787–1851), developed a process that included a silver-plated copper sheet that was coated with silver iodide that led to daguerreotypes, the earliest stable and enduring photographic images.

Meanwhile, the development of the binocular microscope was to zoology what the telescope had become to astronomy. Herschel's equal in the biological sciences was Carl von Linné, often referred to by his Latin name Linnaeus (1707–78). In his encyclopedic *Systema Naturae*, first published in 1735, Linné not only counted thousands of new species of animals but also catalogued and divided them by way of a whole new system of nomenclature. Using binomial Latin terms such as *homo sapiens* and *plantago lanceolata*, he subdivided the major classes of life-forms—such as Mammalia, Aves (birds), Amphibian (including reptiles), and Pisces (fish)—into a much more specific, comprehensive, and convenient system of nomenclature.

As the numbers of discovered species of both plants and animals skyrocketed in the early nineteenth century (some seventy-two thousand new species of plants were found and described between 1798 and 1850), interest in zoology and botany intensified from mere classification and description to the inevitable study of their origins. Jean-Baptiste Lamarck, who coined the term *biology*, was as much a geologist as he was a biologist. Through his careful studies of plants, especially invertebrate fossils in widely separated geological strata, he recognized more clearly than many the enormous age of the earth and nature's slow and continuous process of change. An early evolutionist, Lamarck gradually abandoned his belief in the immutability of species and adopted a view that stressed activity and "processes of small extent acting over vast periods of time to produce immense effects."[56]

His rival and fellow countryman was Georges Cuvier. Cuvier is considered the father of modern paleontology and comparative anatomy on account of his masterful comprehensive study of the whole animal kingdom, living and dead. He successfully argued for the principle of "organic correlation" and the interrelationship of one internal organ to another. Cuvier likewise recognized that species had changed over time and that many had become extinct. In contrast to Lamarck, however, Cuvier believed in the "fixity of species," positing a theory of catastrophism in which change came suddenly and not gradually over millions of years.

It was Lamarck's view, however, that gained the ascendancy. Lamarck's courage in presenting an evolutionary uniformitarian view of geology clearly "prepared the public consciousness" for Darwin's later *Origin of the Species*[57] and his theory of organic evolution

---

56. Jack, "Jean Lamarck," 16.
57. Jack, "Jean Lamarck," 31.

based on natural selection, variations within species, competition, and the "survival of the fittest" concept.[58]

In 1795, L'Académie des Sciences in Paris became the focus of French science. Four years later, Benjamin Thompson (1753–1814), aided by Sir Joseph Banks, founded the Royal Institution of Great Britain for the "promotion, diffusion, and extension of science and useful knowledge." In 1815 the Swiss Natural Science Association began. In America, where technology advanced more rapidly than the study of pure science, the American Geological Society was formed in 1819. And in 1829, James Smithson, a British chemist, gave 100,000 pounds to establish the Smithsonian Institute in Washington DC.

Napoléon's defeat, however, and with it the defeat of many of the aims of the French Revolution, played into the hands of those scientists who were perceived to be opposed to religion, and arguably led to a decline in scientific research post-1820. In France and Prussia, during decades of ensuing conservative monarchial rule, scientific progress slowed to a virtual crawl.[59] For the rest of his life, Humboldt, to whom we must now return, fought a rearguard battle with reactionary forces bent on turning back the clock.

"THE NAPOLÉON OF SCIENCE"

By the time the thirty-five-year-old Humboldt returned home to Europe in the summer of 1804, his name had become a household word, "a blend of mental brilliance and physical daring," thanks to the numerous published accounts that had preceded him.[60] Humboldt was welcomed first in Bordeaux and then in Paris by large and adoring crowds as a conquering hero, revered by all—except Napoléon. The two men met for their first and only time in December at a gala ball right after Bonaparte's coronation. "So I understand you collect plants," the emperor brusquely said. "So does my wife."[61] And with that preemptory remark, he turned his back and walked contemptuously away. Feigning suspicion that he thought Humboldt was a Prussian or Spanish spy, the truth is Napoléon was jealous of sharing the national spotlight with anyone—especially a Prussian. Thereafter Humboldt adamantly refused to attend any of Napoléon's weekly receptions.

During the week of Napoléon's coronation, Humboldt crossed paths with yet another man destined to change the world of 1820—Simón Bolívar—whose exploits and accomplishments we have already examined (see chapter 10). Bolívar was but a very young man

---

58. Humboldt very much encouraged Darwin. "You have an excellent future ahead of you," Humboldt wrote in an 1839 letter to the younger scientist. "Your work is remarkable for the number of new and ingenious observations on the geographical distribution of organisms, the physiognomy of plants, the geographical structure of the earth's crusts. . . . What progress indeed has been made in science by those who like you are eloquent interpreters of it." Barrett and Corcos, "Letter from Alexander von Humboldt," 163, 165.
59. Taton, *Science in the Nineteenth Century*, 550–70.
60. Helferich, *Humboldt's Cosmos*, 300–301.
61. Botting, *Humboldt and the Cosmos*, 179.

at the time. The two men shared similar republican views, and Humboldt came away impressed. Bolívar never forgot their encounter and counted himself a friend and admirer of Humboldt, lauding him as "the true discoverer of South America."[62]

It is tempting to argue that at this point Humboldt's greatest contributions were behind him when, in truth, his finest works still lay ahead. In mid-October 1804, he presented the first of many reports to the Institut Nationale des Sciences et Arts and the following year was elected a member of the Berlin Academy of Sciences. After spending the next two years visiting Switzerland, Italy, and Berlin, Humboldt returned to Paris to begin the task of writing up what he had seen and accomplished in the New World. What he initially believed would be three volumes over three years eventually took thirty years and thirty volumes and earned him the title of "Napoléon of Science."

Relying on his voluminous field notes, written mostly in French scrawl with types of scribbled shorthand only he or a Champollion could ever decipher, he went feverishly to work. His first volume was *Essays on the Geography of Plants* (1807). The year 1808 saw the publication of his immensely popular *Views of Nature*, and in 1810 he published *Research, Concerning the Institution & Monuments of the Ancient Inhabitants of America*. The following year his three-volume *Political Essay on the Kingdom of New Spain* appeared. His most popular work—*Personal Narrative of Travels to the Equinoctial Regions of the New Continent*—came out in three volumes between 1815 and 1819. A perfectionist with an inner frenzy to achieve, Humboldt spent his fortune having his works carefully edited, paying friends and respected colleagues for peer reviews, and employing artists and designers for hundreds of exquisite sketches and engravings, plates, prints, and maps.

Had it not been for Napoléon's invasion of Moscow and his resultant inglorious retreat in 1814, Humboldt may well have seen his other dream fulfilled of visiting Russia, Tibet, China, India, and the Himalayas. Instead of leaving Paris, Humboldt—"never the patriot, always the scientist"—found himself welcoming Tsar Alexander I and Wilhelm, Humboldt's brother, now Prussian ambassador, as part of the conquering Russian-Prussian-Austrian forces as they marched into Paris in April 1814. Had it not been for Humboldt literally barring the doors, Alexander's conquering armies would likely have ransacked and destroyed the Académie des Sciences and other great Paris museums.[63]

For much of the rest of his life, Humboldt was forced into the lucrative role of tutor, academic adviser, and chamberlain to the king of Prussia. It was a mutually beneficial relationship. Humboldt needed the money since by now his family fortune had been long spent. Ironically, King Wilhelm III (1770–1840) of Prussia and later his successor, King Wilhelm IV

---

62. Helferich, *Humboldt's Cosmos*, 303.
63. Wilhelm went on to participate in the Congress of Vienna as a special Prussian envoy. Later, in 1819, he became Prussia's Minister for Home Affairs, but his more liberal views led to his dismissal in 1820. Kellner, "Return to Berlin," in *Alexander von Humboldt*. Though Wilhelm was much more pro-Germany than his brother, he and Alexander remained in close contact with one another throughout their lives. Wilhelm's death in 1835 was a devastating blow to Humboldt.

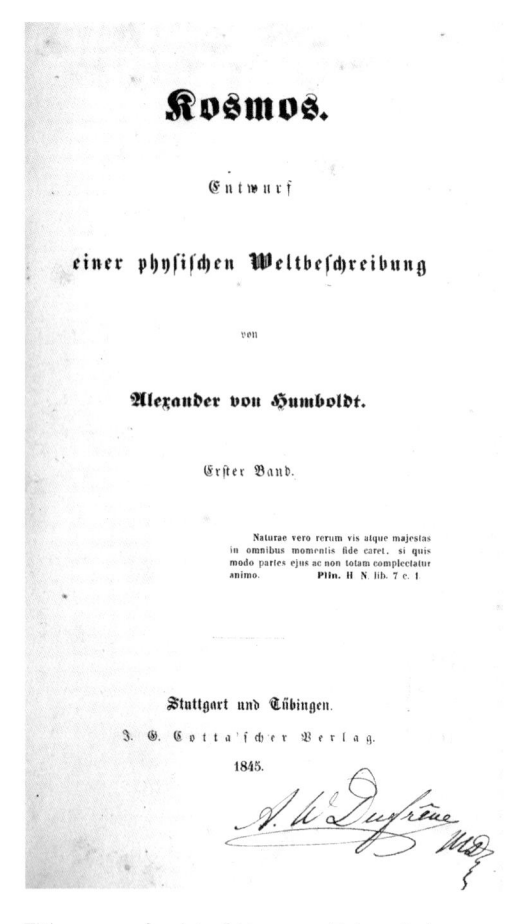

Title page of vol. 1 of *Kosmos: Entwurf einer physischen Weltbeschreibung,* by Alexander von Humboldt (Stuttgart and Tübingen: Cotta, 1845–62).

(1795–1861), trusted him implicitly, while the Prussian secret police suspected his French-leaning, revolutionary sympathies. King Wilhelm indulged Humboldt's desire to spend much of his time in Paris, but by 1827 the king insisted that Humboldt return to live permanently in Berlin.

That same year Humboldt's long-cherished dream to travel to Asia began to be realized when the new Russian tsar, Nicholas I (1796–1855), invited him to make a six-month summer expedition to create a series of new maps of Russia and to study mining and geology in the Urals and further east, all at Russian expense. Two years later, Humboldt embarked upon the second great expedition of his life, one that eventually took him, like a modern Marco Polo, to the gates of China. Braving late winter blizzards, ice flows, spring floods, terrible roads, and never-ending changes in horses and wagons, Humboldt and his entourage of three dozen Russian mining officials and local politicians forged their way across the Siberian steppes, discovering iron, copper, topaz, gold, platinum, and even diamond mineral deposits in the process. These were the first diamonds ever found outside the tropics. Within ten years of Humboldt's visit, Russia would become the world's top exporter of gold. He finally reached the Russian-Chinese border in late August 1829 before turning abruptly west and heading home, lest the expedition become trapped in a Siberian winter. Arriving back in Moscow on 3 November, after a grueling journey of 9,700 miles—much of it on foot—the sixty-year-old Humboldt was widely honored and acclaimed "as the Prometheus of our day."[64] "Your sojourn in Russia has been the cause of immense progress in my country," Tsar Nicholas I exulted. "Wherever you go you spread a life-giving influence."[65] As was his custom, Humboldt would later publish a three-volume recitation of his Russian exploits and adventures in his *Asie Centrale* (1843).

---

64. Kellner, *Alexander von Humboldt*, 139.
65. Botting, *Humboldt and the Cosmos*, 252.

Humboldt's Russian expedition paid rich dividends. Besides his mining discoveries, he proposed the establishment of a chain of geomagnetic, meteorological observation stations all across Russia and eventually throughout the British Empire, including Canada, Australia, and New Zealand. Such stations recorded magnetic dips and declinations, isothermal readings, barometric pressure, temperature and humidity readings, wind directions, and moisture levels—all of which laid the foundation for modern meteorology and zonal geography.

As for Bonpland, Humboldt's trusted and loyal assistant, he proved a much better field botanist than a writer. Sadly, the two men gradually drifted apart. After working as a gardener to Napoléon's wife and empress, Bonpland returned to South America, where he married a native woman, raised a family, and lived in Uruguay, if not in poverty, certainly in obscurity. Humboldt eventually secured a government pension for his longtime friend, who believed he never got the full credit he deserved as Humboldt's partner. "Unmourned and unsung, but loving life to the last," Bonpland died in 1858 at the age of eighty-five.[66]

Despite Napoléon's defeat and Wilhelm's constant invitation to return to Berlin, Humboldt soldiered on in his beloved Paris. Confirmed bachelor that he was, Humboldt craved companionship, especially from men. Much has been written, often of a speculative and psychological nature, of his alleged homosexuality. The evidence is inconclusive. His language of love and affection is not altogether out of character of the wording many used at this time to describe two men working in close and harmonious relationships. Throughout Humboldt's life he had many intense friendships with other men, but perhaps none more fervent that that he forged with Dominique François Arago (1786–1853). Arago was a friend of Ampère and a leading physicist whom Humboldt met in 1809. Although the two men communicated with each other for forty-four years, in the end, it was also the most disappointing relationship of Humboldt's life.

The sadness of their relationship sprang from its lopsidedness and inequality of affection. For every letter Arago wrote Humboldt, Humboldt wrote back ten. "Could it be that you ever doubted my invariable attachment?" Arago once said to Humboldt. "Be it known to you that I should consider the slightest doubt upon this point a most cruel offense. Beyond the immediate circle of my own family, you are, without comparison, the person whom, of all others, I love the most dearly."[67] After Arago's marriage, the distance between the two men lengthened, while Humboldt desperately held on, as if to a dream or will-o'-the-wisp. When Arago died in 1853, Humboldt, starving for affection, lived on in loneliness and retracted further into himself.

Humboldt still remains something of an enigma. On the one hand, he developed "a true genius in friendship."[68] An infallible judge of scientific talent and an avid supporter and benefactor of hundreds of scholars all over the world, Humboldt became a living legend. Free of jealousy or rancor of any kind, he enjoyed the success of others. Importuned for

---

66. Botting, *Humboldt and the Cosmos*, 207.
67. Francois Arago to Humboldt, 12 March 1841, in Kapp, *Letters of Alexander von Humboldt*, 94.
68. Ackernecht, "George Forster," 93.

money, advice, and references virtually daily, Humboldt spent much of his influence and fortune helping the unknown and the poor, protecting the persecuted and bringing recognition to those who deserved it.

On the other hand, the greatest emptiness in what otherwise was a remarkably full life was his failure to form close human relationships. Blame it on his cold and indifferent mother or on a father who died too young—whatever the cause, Humboldt never found lasting happiness in any other human being. He never married. His closest friends were men, many of whom took advantage of his kind support and interest. The tragedy of his life is that while he understood nature, he never did, or never could, allow another human being to venture too close. In the end, nature was his mistress.

COSMOS

Humboldt could easily have spent the remainder of his days supporting and encouraging his fellow scientists had it not been for his flint-like determination to depict in a single work the entire material universe—from the phenomena of heaven and earth to the tiniest plants and organisms. Thus Humboldt set out as early as 1820 to write his most enduring masterpiece—*Cosmos*.

A study in five volumes, the first of which appeared in 1845 and the last of which appeared posthumously, *Cosmos* (taken from the Greek word *Kosmos*, meaning heaven and earth) was an intensely scholarly attempt to regard all nature as part of one majestic, unifying whole. His primary purpose was to show that one spirit "animates the whole of Nature," including stones, plants, animals, and even humankind itself, and that everything is in relation to something else, "which is the reason for its being."[69] *Cosmos* showed that Humboldt was a scientist with Goethe-inspired romantic convictions. He believed that nature, from Dalton's atoms to Herschel's solar system, functioned according to unified and unifying principles. Though his book never mentions God or a creator—indeed, Humboldt never let religion influence his scientific conclusions—it was all about intelligent design. Humboldt saw nature as a harmoniously ordered unit. If there was not divine design in the creation of nature, there was nonetheless an essential unity or unifying force among all life-forms, botanical and zoological. His pioneering work ironically led to specialization, but he himself was a towering generalist, a universal polymath who yearned to see the interrelatedness of everything and an endless series of cause and effect in nature. Far more than the mere sum of its parts, nature manifested a unifying, undergirding, and all-enveloping wholeness that only poets could fully fathom. As Humboldt understood, nature was a "harmoniously ordered whole," a "unity in diversity of phenomena; a harmony, blending together all created things, however dissimilar in form and attributes; one great whole animated by the breath of life."[70]

---

69. McCrory, *Nature's Interpreter*, 122–23.
70. Humboldt, *Cosmos*, 1877 ed., 1:24.

Though there was more to the cosmos of nature and its beauty than what is beheld by one's senses, Humboldt believed it was the "inward mirror of the sensitive mind which reflects the true and living image of the natural world." Almost Platonic in his views, he thought there was as much reality of nature or essential meaning in the human soul as on a distant landscape and that there was a mysterious communion between the beholder and the beheld, with place for both scientific observation and artistic expression, poet and scientist, language and mathematics.[71]

As one of his biographers has concluded, *Cosmos* was "the last great work of the last great universal man: It captured all of Humboldt's thoughts and discoveries from South America to Siberia, and the discoveries of the many other leading scientists of his age."[72] Though later superseded by the modern era of scientific specialization, *Cosmos*, in its attempt to discover the overriding realities of all of nature, must go down still as one of the greatest works of the nineteenth century.

The book also captured his sometimes hidden, or at least unexpressed, social and political convictions. Liberal, democratic, and cosmopolitan in his thinking, Humboldt, ever the humanist, stood for freedom, equality, and justice—a German prince of the ideals of the French Revolution. He opposed colonialism and despised slavery and racism in all their sordid expressions. Like Wilberforce, More, and Bolívar, he regarded slavery as the vilest of all the evils that afflict humanity. He argued for the unity of humanity, calling different races "varieties" of humankind and rejecting all and every notion of superior or inferior races. "While we maintain the unity of the human species," he wrote, "we at the same time repel the depressing assumption of superior and inferior races of men. . . . All are in like design, designed for freedom."[73] Whether discussing the Aztecs of Mexico, the enslaved blacks of the Southern states, or any other relegated and despised people, Humboldt preached the gospel of human dignity and racial equality.

Some may argue that Humboldt, supported in his expeditions by such autocratic and totalitarian regimes as Spain and Russia, was either too timid or two-faced in waiting so long in his career to make his genuine feelings and criticisms widely known. In his defense, he was, we must remember, a careful diplomat whose first love was science, not politics. He was astute enough not to criticize his followers and sponsors. Fortunately, he lived long enough to make his true feelings known, and with his reputation at a lifelong high, his criticisms took on even greater meaning. Likewise, he deplored the destruction of the environment. Arguably the founder of the modern ecological movement, Humboldt fought for the preservation and respect of nature everywhere.

Cosmos was an instant popular success and reprinted in multiple editions, with sales in the tens of thousands. By the late 1850s, it was the most translated book in the world next to the Bible. Still writing almost every day until three in the morning, Humboldt suffered

---

71. Humboldt, *Aspects of Nature*, 2:208.
72. Botting, *Humboldt and the Cosmos*, 260.
73. Humboldt, *Cosmos*, 1877 ed., 1:358.

Study of Alexander von Humboldt in Berlin, Oranienburger Steet, 67, by Eduard Hildebrandt.

a small stroke in 1858. Johann Siefert, his servant to the last, ran Humboldt's household arbitrarily and decided who could or could not see the great scientist. Tragically, most of Humboldt's correspondence was inexplicably destroyed. Finally on 6 May 1859, twenty-four years after his brother Wilhelm's passing, Humboldt died of completely natural causes at age eighty-nine, almost penniless. His dying words were: "What glorious beams of sunlight! They seem to be calling the earth up to heaven."[74] He was buried back in his childhood haunt: Tegel. His many lingering debts were quietly paid for by the king.

It has been said that when a great man dies a library burns down. In Humboldt's case, he gave rise to a whole series of new libraries full of a great many discoveries and findings from a remarkably rich and varied life. His lasting contributions were the sheer magnitude of his writings and the highly measured and captivating appeal of his scientific studies to an uninformed but interested reading public. Capturing the essence and the mystery of faraway places, with the "courage to become the hero of his own life,"[75] he drew a generation of readers into his scientific world. A path breaker and a giant, gentle genius, Humboldt made sense of science and brought it out of the realm of suspicion into a bright new day of acceptance. In

---

74. McCrory, *Nature's Interpreter,* 216.
75. Helferich, *Humboldt's Cosmos,* xxii.

so many ways he was the catalyst for modern science. Ultrareligionists castigated him for not speaking of God and of his creation, yet Humboldt was neither atheistic nor anti-Christian. He simply religiously adhered to what can be seen, measured, and known by the senses. Yet he always believed in "an underlying cosmic intelligence" that governs all.[76]

The prophet and pioneer of the scientific investigator, Humboldt presaged the coming age of science. One can argue that the age of 1820 saw the discrediting of religion amongst the educated, that the "vision of all" lay in fostering the future of scientific discovery, not in preserving the past of religious tradition. It is certain that for some religionists, the coming controversies over creation, evolution, and the very meaning of human existence would spell endless debate, doubts, and anxiety. Nevertheless, those new revelations that saw little or no conflict between science and faith, that encouraged the seeking of truth no matter where it is found, welcomed and embraced the many and varied beneficial advances in science and every other field as heralds of a new and better day. As one of Joseph Smith's early revelations stated: "Teach ye diligently . . . of things both in heaven and in the earth, and under the earth; things which have been, things which are, things which must shortly come to pass, things which are abroad, . . . and a knowledge also of countries and of kingdoms—that ye may be prepared in all things" (Doctrine and Covenants 88:78–80).

The cult of Humboldt reached its zenith in America in 1869 in honor of his hundredth birthday, with celebrations everywhere, from Boston to San Francisco. Banquets and banners, concerts and parades, speeches and celebrations all heralded him as the greatest man of the century, with Oliver Wendell Holmes calling him "the hero of knowledge" and "the peaceful conqueror."[77] Humboldt's reputation soon faded, however, as Darwin's discoveries took hold and the age of specialization replaced Humboldt's more generalized approach to the study of science. Furthermore, the First and Second World Wars poisoned negative attitudes in America toward all things German. However, today Humboldt's reputation, like that of Napoléon, is deservedly on the ascendancy.

Humboldt was a towering intellect, a man who constantly overcame one obstacle after another to fulfill his deepest dreams and ambitions. A person of enormous discipline, courage, restlessness, and conviction who loved nature, Humboldt changed the world and the way we look upon it. He regarded everyone through the lens of dignity, humanity, and equality. As one of his most recent biographers has concluded, Humboldt "pointed to the future, not to the past: to universal peace and healing after decades of war and revolutions, to the reign of reason, to the liberation of the human mind, to the dawn of a new age."[78]

---

76. McCrory, *Nature's Interpreter*, 185.
77. Walls, *Passage to Cosmos*, 310.
78. Walls, *Passage to Cosmos*, 312.

Joseph Smith Jr., by Alvin Gittins. Courtesy of Church History Library.

FROM PLYMOUTH ROCK TO PALMYRA

JOSEPH SMITH JR., THE SECOND GREAT AWAKENING, AND THE QUEST FOR DIVINE TRUTH

"Some time in the second year after our removal to Manchester [New York], there was in the place where we lived an unusual excitement on the subject of religion. It commenced with the Methodists, but soon became general among all the sects in that region of country. Indeed, the whole district of country seemed affected by it, and great multitudes united themselves to the different religious parties, which created no small stir and division amongst the people, some crying 'Lo, here!' and others, 'Lo, there.'"[1] So wrote the Latter-day Saint prophet Joseph Smith Jr. (1805–44) of the scenes of religious intensity, turmoil, and confusion that permeated much of western upstate New York in the winter of 1819–20. "I was at this time in my fifteenth year," he further recalled.

> My father's family was proselyted to the Presbyterian faith, and four of them joined that church, namely, my mother, Lucy; my brothers Hyrum and Samuel Harrison; and my sister Sophronia. . . .
>
> In process of time my mind became somewhat partial to the Methodist sect, . . . but so great were the confusion and strife among the different denominations, that it was impossible for a person young as I was, and so unacquainted with men and things, to come to any certain conclusion who was right and who was wrong. . . .
>
> I at length came to the determination to "ask of God."[2]

---

1. Joseph Smith—History 1:5.
2. Joseph Smith—History 1:7–8, 13.

This book culminates in a study of an early American boy prophet's quest for divine truth, but will do so by endeavoring to place it within the larger context of American religious history. In the words of Jan Shipps, Joseph Smith may have begun "a great new religious tradition," but he was very much a product of his family, time, and place.[3]

"I COVENANTED WITH GOD"

Joseph Smith Jr. was born in a crude cabin on a cold, wintry 23 December 1805 in the town of Sharon, Windsor County, Vermont, the fourth child of his farmer father, Joseph Smith (1771–1840), and devout mother, Lucy Mack Smith (1775–1856). A determined, hardworking, and deeply religious woman, Lucy had found God in her own difficult life for at least three reasons. The first was her father, Solomon; the second was a painful near-death experience; and the third was her husband's own quest for spiritual truth.

The youngest of eight children, Lucy was the daughter of Solomon Mack (1735–1820), son of Ebenezer Mack. Solomon was born in Connecticut and had fought in the king's service during the French and Indian War (1754–63), barely escaping with his life at the bloody Battle of Ticonderoga in 1758. Later he fought against the British in the American Revolutionary War as a naval gunner. Marrying young schoolteacher Lydia Gates in 1759, Solomon failed at almost everything in life—whether as a farmer, seafarer, or businessman. Prone to accidents and even shipwrecks, and vulnerable to swindlers and poor judgment generally, Solomon lived a careless and profligate lifestyle for most of his adult life, barely able to support his family in their various moves from one part of New England to another. When afflicted with a terrible siege of rheumatism in the winter of 1810–11 at the age of seventy-five, however, his life was dramatically transformed as he prayed as never before for his health, forgiveness, and salvation. In a forty-eight-page self-published autobiography titled *A Narrative of the Life of Solomon Mack*, a penitent Solomon wrote:

> I prayed to the Lord, as if he was with me, that I might know it by this token—that my pains might all be eased for that night. And blessed be the Lord, I was entirely free from pain that night. And I rejoiced in the God of my salvation—and found Christ's promises verified.... Everything appeared new and beautiful. Oh how I loved my neighbors. How I loved my enemies—I could pray for them.... The love of Christ is beautiful. There is more satisfaction to be taken in the enjoyment of Christ [in] one day than in half a century serving our master, the devil.[4]

Solomon spent his declining years in service to God, family, and friends before his death in Gilsum, New Hampshire, in August 1820.

---

3. Shipps, *Mormonism*, x.
4. Mack, *Narrative of the Life of Solomon Mack*, 23–24.

Some few years before her father's conversion, Lucy had undergone a near-death experience of her own. While living in Randolph, Vermont, a few years after her marriage, Lucy came down with "a hectic fever" sometime in the fall of 1802 that almost claimed her life. Freely admitting that at the time she was unprepared to die, she sensed "a dark and lonely chasm between [herself] and Christ that [she] dared not attempt to cross." After her husband and several doctors gave her up to die, the twenty-seven-year-old Lucy desperately covenanted with God that if he would let her live, she would endeavor "to get religion that would enable [her] to serve him right, whether it was in the Bible or wherever it might be found, even if it was to be obtained from heaven by prayer and faith."[5] On hearing a voice declare, "Seek, and ye shall find; knock, and it shall be opened unto you," Lucy miraculously recovered from her illness.[6] As a seeker of true religion, she began attending one church after another, favoring at first the Methodists but finally finding a minister who baptized her but left her free from membership in any particular church. Right up to the Palmyra area revivals of 1819–20, Lucy, though firm in her Christian devotions, was looking for something more. She ultimately joined the Presbyterians.

In addition to her own conversion as well as her father's changed life, Lucy came to religion by yet another way. Historians have commonly described her husband, Joseph Smith Sr., as a nondenominational, almost Universalist in his religious leanings, as was certainly the case with his father, Asael Smith. However, Joseph Sr., unlike others in his family, was a man of recurring dreams and visions.

Joseph Sr. was a descendant of Robert Smith, who emigrated from England in 1638 at the height of the Puritan immigration and settled in Topsfield, eight miles north of Salem, Massachusetts. Robert's son, Samuel, was a highly esteemed citizen, and his grandson Asael briefly fought in the Revolutionary War. A Congregationalist with Universalist leanings, Asael "owned the [Congregationalist] covenant" and "promised to live an upright and moral life."[7] Asael's marriage to Mary Duty in 1767 resulted in a large family, including Joseph Sr., who was born in 1771.

At age twenty-five, Joseph Sr. married Lucy Mack in 1796 in Tunbridge, Vermont, where their two oldest children, Alvin and Hyrum, were born before moving to Royalton and then later, Sharon, where Joseph Jr. was born. Their marriage was off to a promising economic start until Lucy's husband was swindled out of almost all they owned, owing to an overseas ginseng trade deal that went sour.[8] Moving seven times in fourteen years from one rented farm to another, Joseph Sr. finally resolved to pull up stakes and moved to greener pastures

---

5. Proctor and Proctor, *Revised and Enhanced History*, 48.
6. Smith, *History of Joseph Smith by His Mother*, 47–50.
7. Bushman, *Joseph Smith and the Beginnings of Mormonism*, 26.
8. The root of the ginseng, which grows wild in parts of Vermont, is prized in China as a panacea for cancer, rheumatism, diabetes, and other ailments. To this day, the lucrative ginseng trade is still active in parts of Vermont. Smith, *History of Joseph Smith by His Mother*, 57.

in 1816 after the "year without a summer."⁹ After locating a new rented farm, he sent word to Lucy to bring the family to start a new life in Palmyra, New York, some thirty-five miles southeast of Rochester.

When Lucy told of their early efforts in Palmyra to eke out a living, eventually making a modest down payment on a hundred-acre farm straddling the townships of Palmyra and Manchester, she also referred to her husband's dreams and religious searching. In 1808 a series of religious revivals engulfed the Royalton, Vermont, region, so much so that Father Smith became "much excited" on the subject of religion. As he "contemplated the confusion and discord that were extant" among the various Christian religions, he "contended for the ancient order"¹⁰ of religious truth—embarking on a spiritual quest very similar to that which his son would later follow.

Joseph Smith Sr. had at least seven dreams, the earliest of which Lucy called "The First Vision of Joseph Smith, Sr." Most of them shared a common element of a field, a spiritual guide, a broad and narrow path, a stream or river of water, a rope running along its banks, a large building in the distance, and a tree, "exceedingly handsome" and beautiful with fruit of "dazzling whiteness."¹¹ It was after his seventh dream in 1819 during a great revival near Palmyra in which his guide said, "There is but one thing that you lack," that his son Joseph Jr. set out on his own prayer of discovery.¹² Thus family dynamics and a sincere, deep-seated family quest for religious truth prepared their son Joseph Jr. for a religious quest of his own. Yet there were other broader factors at play more general and far-sweeping than the intimate family inquiries described above, for 1820 was by all accounts a very special year in American religious history.

"A CITY UPON A HILL"

Speaking of the "peculiar benignity of a superintending Providence" in a sermon delivered in New York City in 1820, the Reverend Gardiner Spring (1785–1873) reminded his congregation that the year 1820 marked the two hundredth anniversary of the coming of the Pilgrims to Plymouth Rock in 1620. Taking as his text Psalm 107:7, which reads "And he led them forth by the right way, that they might go to a city of habitation," Dr. Spring rehearsed with deep devotion the causes and details of the Puritans' coming so long before. He saw it, as did many others before him, as fulfillment of a divine grand design. Quoting the Reverend Jonathan Edwards, he said, "We may well look upon the discovery of so great a part of the world as America, and bringing the Gospel into it, as one thing by which Divine Providence

---

9. Smith, *History of Joseph Smith by His Mother*, 81. Volcanic ash in the atmosphere, caused by the eruption of Mount Tambora in Indonesia more than twelve thousand miles away, devastated what few crops remained in New England and drove thousands of dispirited New Englanders west to the Finger Lakes region of western New York, where farmers raised wheat in abundance.
10. Smith, *History of Joseph Smith by His Mother*, 63.
11. Smith, *History of Joseph Smith by His Mother*, 65–66.
12. Smith, *History of Joseph Smith by His Mother*, 94.

is preparing the way for those glorious times, when Satan's kingdom shall be overthrown throughout the whole habitable globe."[13]

While lauding the Puritans and their immediate descendants who had made the New England wilderness "blossom as the rose" and made the desert "become as the garden of the Lord," Spring decried the decay in faith since those earlier days. In so doing he lamented the apostasy of these latter times, "an apostasy that involved the rejection of all the essential articles of the Christian faith; all that is binding in the plenary of the Holy Scriptures; all that is precious in the hopes of the Gospel; and all that is holy in a Christian walk and conversation; and all that is solemn in the retributions of the eternal world."[14]

Rev. Spring's sermon embodied a recurring sentiment expressed in American religious thought in both the Great Awakening of the 1740s, centered in New England, and its sequel, the Second Great Awakening from 1800 to 1830 farther west and south: to remind America of its deeply Christian roots, to revive the covenant of grace that brought the Puritans to New Plymouth in the first place, and to reclaim and convert to Christ a new generation of Americans who had lost their way in the wilderness. To look back, therefore, on American religious history was characteristic of 1820.

The Puritans who came to New England's rocky coast in 1620 were unquestionably a deeply Christian people. Derisively labeled Puritans by their English persecutors, who felt their desires to purify the Anglican Church were overly zealous, more than eight hundred of these wandering Pilgrims, or Separatists, sought refuge first in Amsterdam in 1606 and later in Leyden, Holland. In their view, King Henry VIII had not gone nearly far enough in distancing the Church of England from the apostate rituals, corrupt priesthood, and unholy performances of the clergy of the Roman Catholic Church.[15]

Fundamental to the Puritan argument was the centrality of individual spiritual experience and the supremacy of the Bible over the "tyranny of the Papacy." Puritanism was "an emotional dissent," or, as Patrick Collinson described it, "a hotter sort of Protestantism."[16] The mainspring "of all their protests," as historian George Ellis has argued, was "the simplicity that was in Christ," "the word versus the Church," and *sola scriptura*—that is, the scriptures were the sole and final religious authority, not a Roman Catholic pope or an English archbishop.[17] They wanted a reversion to simplicity and to the "first principles" of gospel living and envisioned a church without priesthood hierarchy, superstition, or ceremony. Queen Elizabeth I and her successor, King James I of Scotland, had done precious little to make needed ecclesiastical change, and when King James decreed in 1603, "No Bishop, No King," the Puritans saw no other solution but exile.

---

13. Brainerd and Brainerd, *New England Society Orations*, 1:30.
14. Brainerd and Brainerd, *New England Society Orations*, 1:34, 45–46.
15. For a helpful, if dated, primer on the Puritans, see Skelton, *Story of New England*. The less religious term *Pilgrim* was much later applied to these early settlers.
16. Heimert and Delbanco, *Puritans in America*, 14.
17. Ellis, "The Religious Element in the Settlement of New England," in Winsor, *English Explorations*, 3:225–29.

Embarkation of the Pilgrims, by Robert W. Weir.

Fearing the loss of their English customs and language, if not their religious convictions, and promising the king full obedience, the Puritans secured a patent from the new Virginia Company, England's first American colony of 1606, to establish their colony in the New World.[18] Sailing aboard the *Mayflower*, 102 would-be settlers left Southampton on 5 August and made the transatlantic voyage under difficult and crowded circumstances before finally anchoring off Plymouth Rock on 26 December 1620. Plagued by sickness and malnutrition, many perished in their rather crude settlement that first harsh winter, including their original governor, John Carver. Surely more would have died had it not been for the "social compact" they had signed to assist and govern one another. By 1630 New Plymouth had grown from a single plantation to eight towns along the shore of Cape Cod, consisting of 2,500 souls.

A second wave of Puritans, less persecuted and less strident than the first but still called Nonconformists, arrived in Massachusetts Bay beginning in 1624 and continuing until 1628 under the direction of the Cambridge-educated John Winthrop (1588–1649). Though

---

18. The "Council for New England" was incorporated in November 1620 for the original Plymouth Colony. It was a Crown-approved reincorporation of the earlier adventures of the "Northern Colony of Virginia," under which authority Jamestown had been established in 1607. See Deane, "New England."

Governor Winthrop and his Massachusetts Bay Colony of planters denied any intention of separating formally from the Church of England, after moving to Salem they soon established the Congregational Church and abandoned use of the Book of Common Prayer. Decimated by scurvy and malnutrition like the Plymouth Colony settlers some sixty miles to the south, they too barely survived their first winter. Still, they did not regret their coming. "I do hope that our days of affliction will soon have an end," Winthrop wrote in a letter to his wife. "We here enjoy God and Jesus Christ. Is not this enough? What would we have more? I thank God. I like so well to be here, as I do not repent my coming."[19] In 1642, four years after Robert Smith, Joseph Smith's great-great-grandfather, immigrated to America, the two Pilgrim colonies, now numbering more than thirty thousand, combined into the United Colonies of New England.

Winthrop fervently believed that God had led them to the New World not to found a new nation but to reform the old in their new Zion community. "Through a special overvaluing providence," their coming was, in Winthrop's famous words, "to be better preserved from the common corruptions of this evil world, to serve the Lord and work out our own salvation under the power and purity of his holy ordinances." And they would do so by covenant. "Thus stands the cause between God and us. We are entered into covenant with him for this work. We have taken out a commission."[20] Their keeping of such a "covenant of grace" with the God of the New Testament and their "being knit together by this bond of love" would result either in permanent blessings or in endless damnations. "We must consider that we shall be as a city upon a hill," Winthrop wrote in *A Model for Christian Charity*.[21] But if righteously obedient they would bless themselves, England, and the whole world by hastening the time of the Second Coming of Christ and by ushering in the long-sought-for millennial day.[22]

John Cotton (1584–1652), who arrived in Boston in 1633 with another eight hundred settlers and who became the generally recognized spiritual leader of the colony, likewise saw it all as God's doing. "The placing of people in this or that country is from God's sovereignty over all the earth," he said.[23] Edward Johnson (1598–1672), who wrote the first history of New England in 1648, said, "These are but the beginnings of Christ's glorious reformation and restoration of his churches to a more glorious splendor than ever. . . . Will you not believe that a nation can be born in a day?"[24] Peter Bulkeley (1583–1659) reiterated their covenant theology when he too wrote of their being "a city on a hill," "a special people," a New Jerusalem in the making. "Heaven and earth . . . will cry shame upon us, if we walk contrary to the covenant which we have professed and promised to walk in."[25]

---

19. Adair, *Founding Fathers*, 14–15.
20. Heimert and Delbanco, *Puritans in America*, 89–91.
21. Heimert and Delbanco, *Puritans in America*, 91.
22. Heimert and Delbanco, *Puritans in America*, 9.
23. Heimert and Delbanco, *Puritans in America*, 77.
24. Heimert and Delbanco, *Puritans in America*, 116.
25. Heimert and Delbanco, *Puritans in America*, 120.

Such a covenant required strict conformity to the Puritan way of Christian living and thought. It would not countenance dissent of any kind. Anne Hutchinson (1591–1643) and Roger Williams (1603–83) found that out the hard way. Critical of many of her Puritan leaders for what she perceived as their lack of spiritual zeal and an increasingly works-and-rewards-driven soteriology, Hutchinson soon found herself banished to that new colony for outcasts—Rhode Island. Roger Williams, a strident Separatist, soon followed her for believing that John Cotton and other Puritan divines were liberalizing the purity of the faith and minimizing a "by grace only" salvation.

"ERRAND INTO THE WILDERNESS"

With the passage of time, however, the earlier passion of conversion became increasingly hard to maintain. By 1670 some second-generation Puritans sensed that much had gone wrong with what the Reverend Samuel Danforth called "New England's Errand into the Wilderness." Increase Mather and other second-generation Puritan leaders began speaking of a growing "apostasy," while Michael Wigglesworth (1631–1705) called it "God's controversy with New England."

There were reasons for such drift. In 1662 King Charles II reaffirmed the Massachusetts Bay Charter but, in lessening Puritan authority, demanded that all but the openly reprobate be granted baptism and other sacraments. Many new settlers were Anglicans who resisted Puritan Congregationalism. Thomas Hooker (1586–1647) formed a new colony in Hartford, up the Connecticut River, in 1636. Though the Massachusetts Bay and Connecticut colonies were equally religious and devout, fissures were beginning to appear in Puritan solidarity.

And though Puritanism was essentially Calvinistic in its theology, as scholar Perry Miller has noticed, the Calvinist belief in election or predestination, the transcendent sovereignty and redeeming grace of God in Christ, and humankind's total depravity were gradually being modified to allow for a more Arminian belief in human free will, the saving value of good works, and heartfelt faith and repentance.[26] The constant struggle for survival in the harsh wilderness led inexorably to a sense of accomplishment, of achievement, of well-deserved profits, and of a grateful reliance tinged with personal pride. As Thomas Morton (1575–1646) wrote, "If this land is not rich, then is the whole world poor."[27] Taming the wilderness bred a new frontier-style individualism and sense of personal accomplishment that balked at a theology of absolute determinism and humankind's nothingness.[28]

These and other factors led to the adoption of the so-called Half-Way Covenant of 1662, a watershed moment in Puritanism's decline. This compromise essentially was a begrudging

---

26. Jacobus Arminius, a seventeenth-century Dutch theologian, had taught that God's grace is conditional on the free-will obedience of man, that the works of faith and repentance are essential to salvation.
27. Heimert and Delbanco, *Puritans in America*, 50.
28. Miller, *Errand into the Wilderness*, 35–57.

admission that a great many second-generation settlers had never made the profession of faith required for full membership in the Congregationalist Church. Before 1662, children of such halfway members could not be baptized, but with the Half-Way Covenant they would now at least be treated as church members, even if they had not experienced the same soul-changing experience that had qualified their fathers. It was a religious rapprochement, a regression that allowed membership for new generations of members like Joseph Smith's ancestors, Samuel and Asael Smith, but did not guarantee them the right to partake of the Lord's Supper.

JONATHAN EDWARDS AND THE GREAT COLONIAL AWAKENING

Jonathan Edwards (1703–58) of Northampton, Massachusetts, a child of both Puritanism and the wilderness, kindled an unparalleled revival of religious fervor in 1739–40.[29] Edwards called this religious phenomenon "a flash of lightning" on "the hearts of the people."[30] Blessed with an uncanny ability to infuse old doctrines with new meanings through a radical reformulation of language and metaphor, Edwards was both a caring pastor and a towering intellect. His lasting work, *A Treatise Concerning Religious Affections*, called for deep emotion in one's conversion, not mere stylistic conviction. Arguing that "the heart of true religion is holy affection," Edwards believed in the love and beauty of God and the need for believers to *feel* their way to Christ and conversion.[31] As he once said: "He that has doctrinal knowledge and speculation only, without affection, never is engaged in the business of religion. . . . True religion is a powerful thing, . . . a ferment, a vigorous engagedness of the heart."[32] Through his

Jonathan Edwards, by unknown artist.

---

29. For the most complete biography of Edwards, see Marsden, *Jonathan Edwards*. For a comprehensive new study of Edwards's complex theology, see McClymond and McDermott, *Theology of Jonathan Edwards*. The authors contend that Edwards, "the greatest religious thinker in the history of America," believed in the beauty of God and his creation, in the charismatic gifts of the Spirit, and in salvation coming through a mixture of faith and love. McClymond and McDermott, *Theology of Jonathan Edwards*, 23.
30. Bushman, *From Puritan to Yankee*, 183.
31. Sweet, *Revivalism in America*, 30; emphasis added.
32. Sweet, *Revivalism in America*, xvii.

masterful sermonizing, including his famous "Sinners in the Hands of an Angry God" (1741), Edwards convinced thousands of the unchurched and halfway religionists to repent of their sins and convert to the Christ of their Puritan forefathers. With his blending of a fear for God but belief in a God who loved, Edwards made religion and religious emotion "theologically and intellectually respectable."[33]

Calling on George Whitefield (1714–70), the well-known English Methodist itinerant preacher and spell-binding orator, to help push the work forward with him, Edwards fathered the Great Awakening all over New England and the Atlantic Seaboard and as far south as Virginia, the Carolinas, and Georgia.[34] Other evangelists included Theodore J. Frelinghuysen (ca. 1691–ca. 1747), a Dutch Reformed minister in New Jersey, and Gilbert Tennent (1703–64), of Pennsylvania. As Richard Bushman has written, "People could not get enough of preaching."[35] And this from Benjamin Franklin: "It seemed as if all the world were growing religious; so that one could not walk through the town in an evening without hearing Psalms sung in different families of every street."[36]

The message was much the same as before, but with a softer tone: All were sinners, if not enemies of God, bound for damnation; no amount of their good works could ever save them; all were justified by faith alone; and their increasing New England prosperity served only to augment a guilty conscience. Edwards and company emphasized more than before eternal rescue through the freely accepted grace of Christ, a salvation that "dissolved uncertainty and fear" and ensured to every true seeker the joy of rebirth.[37] The Great Awakening taught a much more optimistic expression of Christian faith than Puritanism ever did, and for many their conversion brought about a new sense of peace and joy that would last a lifetime.

Aimed at all classes of people, the Great Awakening was an awakening of another sort. It was, arguably, a democratic movement.[38] As Perry Miller has argued, it was a revolution,

---

33. Sweet, *Revivalism in America*, 85.
34. Though an ordained priest in the Church of England, George Whitefield converted to a form of "personalized" Calvinism. Between 1738 and 1770, he made seven voyages to America, preaching from Georgia to Maine. Sometimes called "the flaming apostle," he preached to far more American colonists than did anyone else. Ministers and congregations welcomed him everywhere as the crystalizing force that galvanized the "here and there awakenings into a continent-wide renewal." Rutman, *Great Awakening*, 35. One would err, however, in concluding that the colonial Great Awakening owed its origins to the British Wesleyan Methodist movement, since that effort blossomed in Great Britain after the time of the Great Awakening. For more on Wakefield and the British Wesleyan Methodist Movement, see chapter 8.
35. Bushman, *From Puritan to Yankee*, 185.
36. Rutman, *Great Awakening*, 36.
37. Bushman, *From Puritan to Yankee*, 187–95.
38. Miller, *Errand into the Wilderness*, 162–63. Religious historian William Sweet observed, "They sowed the basic seeds of democracy more widely than any other single influence." Sweet, *Revivalism in America*, 41. Richard Bushman likewise contends that the institutional church lost power and authority while individuals gained a new "investiture of authority" through

a populist movement, an awakening to the power and influence of the people as a whole to demand a more personalized religion that spoke to all of them, not just a favored few. Edwards must be seen as a transitional figure in the rise of individualism and democracy in the colonies because he gave the people a voice.[39]

By midcentury the Great Awakening had subsided, but not before converting tens of thousands, if not hundreds of thousands, while also giving rise to Rutgers, Dartmouth, Princeton, and Brown universities—all based on a deeply Christian premise.[40]

"INCREASING APATHY AND COLDNESS": 1750–1800

For all its profound impact, the Great Awakening could last only so long and reach only so many people. In fact, some scholars are now arguing that it never did have the influence many have long assumed, that it was far more localized and scattered in nature than a general outpouring of the Holy Spirit.[41] This debate promises to continue, but it is generally agreed that during the ensuing years in the last half of the eighteenth century, other urgent priorities and compelling schools of thought were competing for the hearts and minds of the American colonists. These cultural forces might best be categorized in three ways: intellectual, political, and social.

Rising in opposition to the Calvinist Puritan doctrines of the total depravity of humankind, God's election of grace, and the sovereignty of God in Christ Jesus was deism—that theological product of the Enlightenment, the French Revolution, and the age of reason. As opposed to atheism, deism provided place for a creator God, but one who, after creation, left the world on its own without interfering collectively or individually in the affairs of

---

experiencing the joy and liberty of personal spiritual experience and conversion. Bushman, *From Puritan to Yankee*, 220. Not all scholars today, however, accept Sweet and Bushman's view that such religionists contributed to the rise of democracy and the fire of the American Revolution.

39. Miller, *Errand into the Wilderness*, 162–64,
40. Weisberger, *They Gathered at the River*, 54–60. Harvard College was founded by the Reverend John Harvard in 1639, and Yale University, in 1701, both religious schools.
41. One revisionist branch of scholarship asserts that the term *Great Awakening* was an overstatement and oversimplification, that it was not nearly so great or widespread as many historians have long assumed. One of the first to make this argument was Jon Butler, "Enthusiasm Described and Decried: The Great Awakening as Interpretive Fiction," 305–25. More recently, Frank Lambert claims it was at best "a creation of a particular group of evangelicals," that it was far more localized and scattered in scope, and that its religious publicists generated a false image of a widespread, interconnected religious movement. Lambert goes so far as to call the Great Awakening "an invention," an overstatement and oversimplification, and not a widespread movement. It was all just an "ordinary occurrence," more local than general. See Lambert, *Inventing the "Great Awakening,"* 6–8, 11, and 255. From my own limited research on the topic, however, I have found compelling evidence that the Great Awakening was both a widespread and a very intense religious movement.

humankind. Rejecting a belief in the Trinity, human depravity, the need of a Savior, and miracles and revelations, deism claimed that one came to truth by way of reason, not by revealed religion, and that man was the source of his or her own salvation. The devotion of Voltaire and Thomas Paine, deism was human-centered and democratic in its tendencies and counted such famous early American disciples as George Washington, John Adams, Benjamin Franklin, and Thomas Jefferson. Believing in God's benevolence, generosity and all-forgiving nature, deists practiced, as Bernard Weisberger has written, a nice "rational religion."[42]

A sort of halfway house between deism and Puritan Calvinism was Unitarianism. It attempted to "reconcile the lion of God's almighty power" and majesty with God's affection for his children or creations on the one hand and humanity's use of intellect on the other. In trying to unite both ends of the God-man spectrum, Unitarianism was essentially a difficult compromise between revealed Christianity on the one hand and the religion of reason on the other. By 1820 Unitarianism had gained a particularly strong foothold at Harvard and Yale as a favored religion of the more highly educated.[43]

In the political realm, the rising spirit of democracy and a growing climate of restless independence led inexorably to the American Revolutionary War. Ironically, the Great Awakening, with its message of obedience and dependency on God, may well have contributed to the Revolutionary War by instilling in its adherents a sense of power, personal liberty, and conviction and a resistance to former authorities and institutions.[44]

The political results of the war are well known; no less far-reaching were its religious ramifications. The Church of England, which supported the Loyalist cause (as did the Quakers), fell out of favor with many Americans and was disestablished as the government-supported religion. So too Congregationalism was eventually disestablished in New Hampshire (1817), Connecticut (1818), and Massachusetts (1833). Meanwhile, Unitarianism and deism flourished, as did a new liberal religious expression—Universalism—and its contention that in the end, all humanity would be universally saved anyway.

As regards the social realm, historians generally agree that during the closing years of the eighteenth century, church attendance noticeably declined throughout the new American nation. As Catharine Cleveland noted over a century ago, since the American Revolution an "increasing apathy and coldness" in church involvement and devotion, coupled with rising immorality, had filled religious leaders with "apprehension and alarm."[45]

Many of these independent thinkers moved to the expanding frontier of the United States of America. Others, like the Loyalists, fled to the British colonies of Upper Canada, Nova Scotia, and New Brunswick, resulting in the emptying of more churches in New England and the Eastern Seaboard states than any other factor. And with what Reverend

---

42. Weisberger, *They Gathered at the River*, 7.
43. Weisberger, *They Gathered at the River*, 15.
44. Bushman, *From Puritan to Yankee*, 267–71.
45. Cleveland, *Great Revival in the West*, 30.

Timothy Wright of Yale University once called an "unregenerate frontier," many turned to violence and alcohol, "the haunt of vicious men."[46]

THE SECOND GREAT AWAKENING

Ironically, this westward migration sowed the seeds of the Second Great Awakening (ca. 1798–ca. 1835), a term evangelists deliberately employed to link them and their work to the former Great Awakening of Jonathan Edwards, George Whitefield, and William Tennant. This new generation of evangelists saw their day as an age of reformation and restoration and of preparing anew for Christ's Second Coming.[47] Christianity was hardly dead in the new republic. The Church of England, Congregationalism, and Presbyterianism all survived the war, but they were eclipsed on the rural frontier by the vitality, flexibility, and relevancy of the Baptists and more especially the Wesleyan Methodists.

To the Baptists, religion was not a formal profession or a hierarchical institution but rather a passionate expression of one's faith in Christ. The unlicensed and relatively uneducated Baptist farm preachers were very effective revivalists, particularly in the South, and appealed most to the common people, the illiterate and the unschooled. Samuel Harris and James Ireland were just two of many well-known contemporary Baptist preachers.[48]

Methodism, transplanted from Great Britain in about 1765, was particularly suited to the American frontier, both doctrinally and structurally. Emphatically individualistic, Methodism taught a modified form of Arminianism by stressing that salvation, though originating in Christ, was in part conditional, depending on one's behavior. Those who had come to rely on their own hard work to forge a living on the frontier resonated with a doctrine that put stock in individual effort and obedience.

Furthermore, the structures of Methodism were successful and appealing. While well organized and controlled, with a top-down chain of ecclesiastical command and authority, Methodism's army of relatively uneducated circuit riders or itinerant traveling evangelical ministers made the critical difference. They went almost anywhere at any time and, in doing so, created an atmosphere of intensity and religious zeal that largely accounts for Methodism's spectacular growth from a mere 15,000 in 1785 to 850,000 by 1840.[49]

Sometimes called "sons of thunder," these itinerant preachers underwent two years of training and then stayed out on the hustings for one or two years at a time. Lorenzo Dow was one of the better known Methodist circuit riders. Dressed in a broad-brimmed hat, a round-breasted frock coat, and breeches, many with hair to their shoulders, these "saddlebag

---

46. Weisberger, *They Gathered at the River*, 11.
47. Scott, *Evangelicalism, Revivalism, and the Second Great Awakening*.
48. Sweet, *Revivalism in America*, 93–95.
49. Weisberger, *They Gathered at the River*, 46.

preachers" often slept on the hard floor of a pioneer's cabin or out under the stars, "a saddle for their pillow and the sky their coverlet."[50]

Following a highly demanding lifestyle, by day they forded rivers and streams on horseback; rode through storms in capes and with umbrellas; braved blistering summer heat, Native American conflicts, and endless mosquitoes; and still persevered. The key to their success was that they brought their Methodist religion and their well-worn Bibles and Methodist hymnals and the works and music of John and Charles Wesley to the doorsteps of frontier America. As in England (see chapter 8), Methodism delighted in coming to the people, not the other way around. Excellent record keepers who preached with such earnestness that even devils may have stopped to listen, these "brush preachers" were indefatigable missionaries of the frontier's "personal religion."[51]

And they almost always found a ready audience. To the backwoods frontiersman, fear of death by Native American attacks, lawlessness, and even starvation was all too real. The "possibility of sudden death," as historian Charles A. Johnson has noted, "made the question of one's eternal destiny a matter of great concern."[52] The frontier was no place for mild homilies; rather, it demanded rigorous, forceful preaching, often with great bodily gestures. Immorality, intemperance, tobacco use, gambling, card playing, Sabbath breaking—all came under condemnation. Standing in awful earnestness at a flickering fireplace and preaching in solemn tones to a farmer and his family sitting on the floor and leaning against the cabin wall, the Methodist itinerant preacher had found his most intimate stage and most effective pulpit. It was one such Methodist preacher that had visited Joseph Smith's mother, Lucy Mack Smith, during her sickness in 1802.

Methodism succeeded for another reason: its belief in what Methodist scholar John H. Wigger calls "the efficacy of prophetic dreams, visions, and supernatural impressions," not unlike those experienced by Joseph Smith Jr. Referencing the conversion accounts of Thomas Rankin and Freeborn and Catherine Livingston Garrettson, Wigger has shown that the "quest for the supernatural in everyday life" was "the key theological characteristic of early American Methodism." Adherents put great stock in "signs, wonders, and ecstatic experiences." Wigger makes a strong point when he writes, "Early Methodism without such spiritual enthusiasm would be like *Hamlet*, not without the prince, but without the Ghost."[53]

Surprisingly, it was not only the Methodists who fanned the flames of the Second Great Awakening; it was also the Presbyterians who, under the Reverend James McGready of Pennsylvania, introduced the camp meeting concept of public religious expression. Having

---

50. Johnson, *Frontier Camp Meeting*, 156.
51. Johnson, *Frontier Camp Meeting*, 158–67. From one circuit rider came this representative report of February 1820: "I shall here state for the benefit of the society, that I have visited and preached in seventy towns, travelled three thousand six hundred and seventy miles, (in about eight months) and preached two hundred and forty sermons." Joseph A. Merrill, from a letter dated 15 February 1820, in *The Methodist Magazine*, April 1820.
52. Johnson, *Frontier Camp Meeting*, 170–71.
53. Wigger, "Taking Heaven by Storm," 167–94; see especially 170, 173, 191.

Sacramental Scene in a Western Forest, by unknown artist.

moved to Kentucky in 1798, McGready employed a powerful, if unpolished, preaching style that attracted so many followers that no single edifice could begin to hold them all. In the ensuing Western (or Kentucky) Great Revival, which almost amounted to "godly hysteria," McGready and his fellow preachers conceived the idea of a religious service of several days' length held outdoors and for vast numbers of followers who were obliged to eat and find shelter far from home.[54] Best remembered was his monster meeting at Cane Ridge in 1801 where some twenty thousand people congregated for days on end to listen to one sermon after another. With preachers standing, shouting, and exhorting from wagons or tree stumps, something was bound to happen. People spontaneously began shrieking and groaning and singing amens and hallelujahs with thunder, lightning, and horses' whinnying all thrown in for good measure. Soon such a grand cacophony of bustle and noise erupted that some described it as a "sound like the roar of Niagara."

The camp meeting movement soon spread like wildfire. Reported one eyewitness:

> The woods and paths seemed alive with people, and the number reported as attending is almost incredible. The laborer quitted his task; age snatched his crutch; youth forgot his pastime; the plow was left in the furrow; the deer enjoyed a respite upon the mountains; business of all kinds was suspended; dwelling houses were deserted; whole neighborhoods were emptied; bold hunters and sober matrons, young women and maidens,

---

54. Weisberger, *They Gathered at the River*, 21–28.

and little children, flocked to the common center of attraction; every difficulty was surmounted, every risk ventured, to be present at the camp meeting.[55]

This unbridled spirit of camp meeting enthusiasm quickly rolled out over Kentucky, Tennessee, Georgia, the Carolinas, Virginia, and eventually north to Pennsylvania, Ohio, New England, and New York, though not without some resistance. McCready and other "New Lights," as they were called, or revivalists who put stock in experiential, "felt" religion, offended many "Old Light" Presbyterians, who favored a more subdued and traditional form of sacred worship, preachers like the Reverend Barton Stone and Richard McNemar. Rigid Calvinism, as Bernard Weisberger has argued, could not "coexist with revivalism."[56] Such contrasting points of view caused deep schisms within the Presbyterian clergy.

If Presbyterianism had trouble constraining the passions of the revival, "Methodism was made for it."[57] By 1805, Joseph Smith Jr.'s birth year, the Methodists had taken over most camp meetings and, in their penchant for organization, gave them new structure, a more defined purpose, and much more careful planning and preparation. By so doing, the Methodist camp meeting regularly attracted crowds commonly in excess of twenty thousand people, often for days at a time.[58]

The central physical feature of the Methodist camp meetings was the wooden pulpit, often placed under roofed platforms and set up at one or both ends of an outdoor amphitheater, facing parallel rows of circular or horizontal hewn-log seating. The "mourning bench" or "anxious seat" was conspicuously placed in front of the pulpit and was used for sinners seeking forgiveness. The aisles and rows were filled with straw to make kneeling prayer more comfortable. Beyond the benches were their many tents, wagons, carriages, and horses to which the crowds reverted at night or between meetings for meals, rest, and refreshment. Lighting came from flickering lamps, candles, tent fires, and torches attached to trees or set on six-foot-high wooden tripods throughout the camp, allowing for meetings to last far into the night. Women sat on the right and the men on the left, always with scriptures in hand. Depending on the size of the crowd, there could be several adjacent arenas or amphitheaters prepared with as many as twenty to thirty ministers, several preaching simultaneously.

Usually these camp meetings lasted four days, from Friday until Monday and from dawn to dusk. With the sound of a trumpet at an early hour, all were to have concluded their tent family prayers and breakfast before the first meeting of the day at 8:00 a.m. Then came the "main event" at 11:00 a.m., another "handshake ceremony" at 3:00 p.m., and finally the candlelight confessionals—often the most stirring of all—from 7:00 p.m. to whenever the

---

55. Davidson, *History of the Presbyterian Church*, 136–37, as cited in Sweet, *Revivalism in America*, 123.
56. Weisberger, *They Gathered at the River*, 83.
57. Weisberger, *They Gathered at the River*, 42.
58. See Jones, "Power and Form of Godliness," 88–114. See also Fleming, "John Wesley," 131–49.

Spirit dictated. Services began with prayer, much singing, and a stirring sermon one to two hours long. Sundays featured communion services with the sacramental tables covered in sheets. "Prayer circles" or "prayer rings" materialized, usually between meetings when laymen and preachers joined hands to form a "circle of brotherly love" and where sinners too shy to walk to the anxious seat could come for encouragement, support, and acceptance.

Everything about these outdoor assemblies was carefully designed to convict people of their sins, to turn their hearts to Christ, and to have them confess and repent. Their songs and sermons were often unforgettable, usually full of fear, hellfire, and damnation but always with the promise of redemption. Shall we listen in?

The opening hymn might well have been "A Mighty Fortress," "Fairest Lord Jesus," "Come, Thou Fount of Every Blessing," or the ever-popular "Come and Taste Along with Me" as found in well-worn copies of *The Wesleyan Camp Meeting Hymn-Book*:

> When I hear the pleasing sound
> Of weeping mourners just converted,
> The dead's alive, the lost is found.
> The Lord has healed the broken-hearted.
>
> When I join to sing his praise,
> The heart, in holy raptures use;
> I view Immanuel's land afar,
> I shout and wish my spirit there.
> Glory, honor and salvation;
> What I feel is past expression.[59]

As for the sermons, they were of the urgent, thunderous, introspective, and enthusiastic variety, given spontaneously and without notes, and often concentrated on a single passage of scripture. As one "soul-melting minister" followed after another, they earnestly called on everyone within the sound of their voice and within the scope of their fierce eye to repentance before it became everlastingly too late. "If therefore your mind is more intent on the possession of this world than on your soul's welfare," exhorted one minister in one such camp meeting west of Schenectady, New York in 1820,

> If you are more anxious to make gain than to honor God with your substance; if your thought and desires are more conversant about the body than about the soul, you must be satisfied that you seek your portion in this world and are numbered with the wicked....
>
> If therefore you do not sincerely mourn for your sins, if you do not hate your sins, and desire above all things to be delivered from their burthen, you are ranked with those

---

59. *The Wesleyan Camp Meeting Hymn-Book*, as cited in Johnson, *Frontier Camp Meeting*, 135. I am indebted to Charles Johnson for his excellent study of everything pertaining to the order, structure, and sentiment of the camp meetings.

> who must be cast out, who must perish because you are wicked. . . . If therefore you do not put your trust in the Lord Jesus Christ as your only hope, if you do not renounce all dependence on your own supposed goodness or your deeds of morality and trust entirely in the obedience and death of Christ as the only [means of] acceptance with God, if you do not receive him as your Lord and Savior and neglect to live devoted to his service, you are numbered with them who are . . . wicked and must be so accounted in the great day.[60]

Such sermonizing condemned not only the sinners but also the would-be saints who were content to think they had lived sufficiently righteously and had worked their way into the good graces of an all-forgiving God.

At the end of such rounds of preaching, with or without invitation, the assembled throngs would often stand and break out in singing another favorite, soul-stirring hymn, such as "Shout Old Satan's Kingdom Down."

Camp-Meeting, by Harry T. Peters. Courtesy of National Museum of American History, "America on Stone" Lithography Collection.

---

60. From an unpublished sermon titled "Woe unto the Wicked," by the Reverend Andrew Yates (1772–1844) and delivered 21 March 1813 and in 1820 at or near Schenectady, New York.

This day my soul has caught new fire—Hallelujah!
I feel that heaven is coming nearer, O glory Hallelujah!
(Chorus)
Shout, shout, we're gaining ground, Hallelujah!
We'll shout old Satan's kingdom down, Hallelujah!
When Christians pray, the devil runs, Hallelujah!
And leaves the field to Zion's sons, O glory Hallelujah![61]

The effects wrought upon the vast assemblies by such powerful hymn singing and hand-wringing, soul-shaking sermons defy simple explanation. Many a convicted sinner could not wait to walk up to the mourner's bench. As one Methodist leader, John McGee, said, "The people were differently exercised all over the ground, some exhorting, some crying for mercy, while others lay as dead men on the ground."[62]

The different exercises McGee referred to included a large number of unexplainable, Pentecostal-like behaviors that affected hundreds of people both young and old, male and female, simultaneously or intermittently. Speaking in tongues (glossolalia) for hours at a time was common, as were other manifestations of the gifts of the Spirit. In the falling exercise, women and men shouted out praises to God and suddenly, as if on cue, fell to the ground lifeless, only to rise up hours later with stirring accounts of dreams and visions of the Almighty. With others, their necks and limbs began to twitch and jerk so violently that they fell down, doubled up, and rolled over and over in somersault fashion, rolling like a wheel. Others began to laugh uncontrollably or dance so vigorously that they whirled around fifty times a minute before collapsing in exhaustion, while still others, particularly women, began singing and chanting in melodious beautiful tones not from their mouths and throats, but, strangely, from deep within their breasts. Some laughed, most cried, and some even began to gather at the trunk of a nearby tree and bark in short guttural sounds while falling on all fours and "treeing the devil." There are even accounts of a "running exercise" in which those who tried to run away, either for fear or disbelief, suddenly stopped and began to shout praises to their God before falling down and later awakening confirmed in the faith. Little children spoke and sang in tongues, while others, never known to speak with erudition, preached powerful sermons and often "so loud that they might be heard at a distance of a mile."[63]

Such camp meetings were open to ministers of all denominations since the demand for preachers far exceeded the local Methodist supply. Usually they took on the personality of the leading preacher. Some were more subdued, some more unrestrained, some given to the great fear of the Lord, others to solemn gratitude and joy. While their messages more or less agreed one with another, not infrequently great debates and shouting matches broke

---

61. From Mead, *Hymns and Spiritual Songs*. See also Scott, *New and Improved Camp Meeting Hymnbook*, as cited by Sweet, *Revivalism in America*, 144.
62. Words of John McGee, 1800, as cited in Johnson, *Frontier Camp Meeting*, 57.
63. Letter by Rev. Thomas Moore, Ten Mile, Pennsylvania, 9 March 1803, in the *Massachusetts Missionary Magazine*, 198–99, as cited in Cleveland, *Great Revival in the West*, 95–96.

out between the warring sides. Bitterly sectarian sermons were common, particularly at the eleven o'clock meetings, as many a preacher waxed loquacious and dogmatic on matters of creed. During one 1822 setting, the well-known reverend Peter Cartwright held his audience spellbound and long past their lunchtime with a three-hour diatribe against the Baptists. His remarks prompted a visiting Baptist minister to quit the field in disgust.[64] Other ministers often got into fierce debates and shouting matches one with another to such a degree that in such emotionally charged settings, many wondered who was right and who was wrong. When Joseph Smith Jr. referenced so great a scene of "confusion and strife among the different denominations," he could not have been more accurate.[65]

This spirit of religious revivalism eventually spilled into western upstate New York and in such a sustained and pronounced fashion that historian Whitney Cross called it "the burned-over district."[66] So many men of the cloth were vying for converts, so many revivals and torch-lit camp meetings were staged, that the area was burned over with religious excess. Said Joseph Smith, "There was in the place where we lived an unusual excitement on the subject of religion"[67]—an understatement, to say the least.

It would be an egregious error, however, to paint the burned-over district revivals with only the loud zealotry and emotional excesses of the camp meeting. Many new converts came to their own spiritual encounters in a much more subdued and reflective way. As noted previously, Joseph Smith's mother, Lucy, converted to the Presbyterian faith. This may not be too surprising, considering her own previous covenant with God for sparing her life, her father Solomon Mack's sudden conversion, and a sense that all their hard work had failed to get her and her indigent family any further ahead financially. Despite all this, Lucy Mack nurtured an abiding belief in God's overarching purposes. However, there may well have been another reason for her Calvinist tendencies and the contrasting style of Presbyterian revivals in western New York state in 1819–20 as personified in the work of the Reverend Asahel Nettleton (1783–1844).

Born in 1783 in North Killingworth, Connecticut, to parents of the Half-Way Covenant, Nettleton had converted to Christianity at age eighteen in 1800 after spending many a night in prayer in nearby fields and forests. In 1805 he entered Yale College, where he

---

64. Johnson, *Frontier Camp Meeting*, 126.
65. Joseph Smith—History, 1:8. One minister, in speaking of sectarian strife in 1819, reported as follows: "The Rev. Simeon Snow was employed 26 weeks, chiefly in the [New York] counties of Oneida, Otsego, and Delaware. The people in those parts were much divided by sectarian prejudices. . . . At Lewiston, [Niagara County] . . . the Rev. David M. Smith has a pastoral charge. . . . When the small number of praying people have been cheered with the prospects and hopes of a revival, a sectarian spirit, under the impulse of ignorance and a passionate zeal for proselyting, has grievously disappointed their pleasing expectations." In Genesee County in particular, "sectarian bigotry divided the people." Missionary Society of Connecticut, *21st Annual Narrative of Missions*, 4.
66. Cross, *Burned-Over District*.
67. Joseph Smith—History, 1:5.

came to know both Timothy Dwight and the writings of Jonathan Edwards well. Graduating in 1811 as an ordained Presbyterian minister, Nettleton declined a life of foreign missionary service in favor of pursuing Christian revivalism closer to home. Kind and courteous, conscientious and exemplary, unassuming and unostentatious, the Reverend Nettleton began his ministry in New Haven, where his congregants soon regarded him as their "spiritual father."[68]

As the fire of the Second Great Awakening swept into upstate New York, Nettleton, now in increasing demand, accepted offers to conduct revivals in Schenectady, Nassau, Malta, Galway, and several other communities in the Finger Lakes region in early 1820. Wherever he went his style of preaching converted many, some say as many as thirty thousand.[69] When at the pulpit, "he was remarkably clear and forcible in his illustration of the sinner's total depravity, and in his utter inability to procure salvation by unregenerate works, or any desperate efforts. . . . Absolute, unconditional submission to a sovereign God, was the first thing to be done."[70] As to his quiet effectiveness, one of his disciples wrote: "This evening we met in the school house. The room was crowded, and the meeting was exceedingly joyful. Every word that was spoken, seemed to find a place in some heart. 'Old things are passed away, and all things are become new.'"[71]

Asahel Nettleton, by Samuel Lovett Waldo and William Jewett.

The key to Nettleton's success was not only his plain, simple style of instructive preaching but also his fatherly care and concern for the individual. Shying away from large, camp-meeting–style assemblies as those just described, Nettleton discouraged fanaticism, alcohol, confusion, and disorder of any kind, choosing the more intimate paths to individual conversion. Consequently, many felt free and easy with him, as if he were some long-tried friend. His idea of an "anxious meeting" was to pray and fast with others one-on-one, often walking home with both sinners and saved, listening and supporting. One man spoke reverently of their private conversations eighteen years after the fact. "I have found Him, I have found Him, and He is a precious Savior," he confided to Nettleton. And in words similar to those describing the conversion of Solomon Mack, Lucy's father, he further said: "That night I could not sleep for joy. I do not think I closed my eyes. I found myself singing several times in the night. In the morning all nature seemed in a new dress and vocal with the praises of

---

68. Tyler, *Memoirs*, 91.
69. Cheek, "Revivalism: A Study of Asahel Nettleton."
70. Tyler, *Memoirs*, 156.
71. Tyler, *Memoirs*, 106.

a God all glorious. Everything seemed changed, and I could scarcely realize that one, only yesterday so wretched, was now so happy."[72]

A confirmed bachelor throughout his life, Nettleton was a wise, caring evangelist who died in May 1844, just one month before Joseph Smith died. Whether Reverend Nettleton ever preached in or near the Smith home in Palmyra is not yet known, but his style of Presbyterian preaching, his house-to-house visits, and his caring concern paint a very different picture from that of the loud, Methodist-dominated camp meeting. The one was as still as the other was boisterous and may beg a revision to what some readers assume was the spirit of revivalism. Considering Lucy's serious frame of mind and convictions, her conversion to Presbyterianism likely came through a Nettleton-like revival experience.[73]

Much of the spirit of Presbyterian evangelicalism in upstate New York in early 1820 began with Nettleton's visit to Union College in Schenectady, where the sudden death of a young student in the third week of January sparked a revival of religion. In addition to Nettleton, professors like the Reverend E. Nott, president of the college, T. McAuley, Walter Monteith, Halsey A. Wood, and Elisha Yale began fanning out in all directions in what was a case of a college-inspired educated revival.

During 1820 in Saratoga, New York, Nettleton added fifty-five converts to the local church. In Malta, New York, the awakening spread over different parts of the town until almost all were affected. "Every house exhibited the solemnity and silence of a continued Sabbath; so profound was this stillness and solemnity, that a recent death could have added nothing to it in many families." And in Stillwater, New York, "in a large district, though harassed by sectarian contention, there is now scarcely one house where daily prayer is not want to be made. . . . Boatmen, tipplers, infidels and atheists, were mixed with the unholy multitude, . . . [and all] felt the power of the Holy Ghost, and yielded to his influence." By the end of March, more than twelve hundred people had converted in Stillwater alone.[74]

Unlike outdoor camp meetings, these Presbyterian-led revivals occurred during the dead of winter, after the harvests and before the busy springtime planting season, as evidenced in this March 1820 report from Amsterdam, New York:

> An awe! A stillness! An oppressive silence, which cannot be described. . . . It was the sinking of the wounded heart! . . . Many who visited these meetings from motives of curiosity,

---

72. Tyler, *Memoirs*, 172.
73. William Smith, a younger brother to Joseph Smith, remembered that it was his mother, Lucy Mack Smith, who "prevailed on us to attend the meetings, and almost the whole family became interested in the matter, and seekers after truth." She continued her importunities and exertions to interest us in the importance of seeking for the salvation of our immortal souls, until almost all the family became either converted or seriously inclined." Smith, *William Smith on Mormonism*, 6–7. I am indebted to Kyle R. Walker for bringing this remembrance to my attention. For more on revivalism near the Smith Palmyra home, see Backman, *Joseph Smith's First Vision*. For a more current study, Harper, *Joseph Smith's First Vision*.
74. *What Hath God Wrought?*, 6–10, 22.

Going to Church, by George Henry Durrie.

totally careless! Beholding the mighty power of God, were terrified at their own hard and impenitent hearts; convicted of sin; awakened to a sense of the misery of their state. . . .

Sometimes, sleigh loads of convinced sinners, after leaving the meeting, and riding half a mile, or a mile, homewards, would turn back again to the place of prayer, to hear still more about the salvation of Jesus! And they often did this too, through lanes and ways and snows, that would have been deemed by persons in any other state of mind, to have been impassible.[75]

Women were key to the success of revivals. Many, particularly widows, visited from house to house encouraging family and individual prayers, holding anxious meetings of whispering or conversing individually with God, reading scriptures, and in other intimate ways furthering the flame of the local revival by challenging individuals to change course. Women clearly were a numerical majority among Methodist and Presbyterian adherents and formed the backbone of these revivals.[76]

Another highly effective mode of visitation was to hold meetings of as many as possible of one sex where they would discuss their most perplexing concerns and the deep issue of

---

75. *What Hath God Wrought?*, 17.
76. Wigger, *Taking Heaven by Storm*, 184.

personal conversion. These visits were sometimes made to male heads of families, sometimes to the female heads, sometimes to young men or young women, sometimes to Native Americans and people of color, "which gave an unembarrassed opportunity of suiting an address to the persons present."[77]

And it was among the youth, young men, and young women where revivals of all kinds bore the greatest fruit. One Baptist minister writing in January 1820 in speaking of mass conversions in Cornish, New York, told of "a number of young children" from "thirteen down to seven years of age" singing hosannas to the Son of David.[78]

Another Baptist minister in Bristol, Rhode Island, reported:

> There are as many as four or five crowded meetings at once, at almost every hour of the day, from an early hour in the morning, until late at night. And even at the corners of our streets, you will scarcely see two or three persons together, but the great concern of the salvation of the soul is the subject of their conversation....
>
> Were I to attempt to tell you the number of young converts, who in a judgment of charity, have been brought out of darkness into God's marvelous light, it would be utterly impossible.[79]

It was not uncommon for ministers of all faiths to report from the field that "two thirds of [the] whole number of converts are under 20 years of age."[80]

Often "a sound of a going" was heard, and entire schoolhouses emptied their anxious students, who scattered out into the nearby fields and quiet groves to pray to God above. In so doing, they usually took their Bibles with them and were encouraged to pray over a single verse or specific passage of scripture in their soliciting heaven for the salvation of their souls. Once in their quiet place of meditation, they would then stand and see the workings of heaven. "There you are at the place of meeting between the Spirit of God and your own spirit," one minister reported in 1819. "You may have to wait, as if at the pool of Siloam; but the many calls of the Bible to wait upon God, to wait upon him with patience, to wait, and to be of good courage, all prove that this waiting is a frequent and a familiar part of that process by which a sinner finds his way out of darkness into the marvelous light of the gospel."[81]

---

77. *What Hath God Wrought?*, 23.
78. Letter from Ariel Kendrick to the editors, January 1820, in *American Baptist Magazine* 2, no. 8 (March 1820): 297.
79. Letter from L. W. B., 7 April 1820, to Rev. Dr. Baldwin, in *American Baptist Magazine* 2, no. 9 (May 1820): 343. For a fine treatment of the role of youth in the Second Great Awakening, see Wright, "'Your Sons and Your Daughters Shall Prophesy,'" 147–50. Wright demonstrates both qualitatively and quantitatively that youth were more than passive onlookers in these religious revivals but were very active participants.
80. Letter from R. Maddocks to the editors, in *American Baptist Magazine* 2, no. 11 (September 1820): 407.
81. Chalmers, *Sermons Preached in the Iron Church*, 68.

And such waiting on the Lord often bore remarkable fruit, as the following 1820 letter by a young lady to her minister friend attests:

> From the age of 13 years I was blessed with the strivings of the Holy Spirit; but alas, I did not yield until your voice, by the Power of God, reached my heart. From that time I resolved to repent and forsake my most pleasing sins, if haply I might find that peaceful but unknown way. While in the sacred grove on the 14th of August 1818, my incessant cries reached the Father of mercies, and my benighted soul received the dawn of heaven. My confidence in God, through the atoning blood of the Dear Redeemer, has grown stronger and stronger.[82]

"I BECAME CONVICTED OF MY SINS"

If the outcome of Joseph Smith's sacred grove experience resulted in his vision of God the Father and the Son and in the birth of a new American religion, the pathway to that theophany was very much in consonance with the religious strivings and experience of his time and place.

As he explained it in his original account:

> At about the age of twelve years my mind became seriously impressed with regard to the all important concerns for the welfare of my immortal Soul which led me to searching the scriptures. . . . I became convicted of my sins and by searching the scriptures I found that mankind did not come unto the Lord, but that they had apostatized from the true and living faith and there was no society or denomination that built upon the Gospel of Jesus Christ as recorded in the New Testament and I felt to mourn for my own sins and for the sins of the world.[83]

It is beyond the scope of this study to look at the result of his erstwhile prayers and strivings. Many readers know full well of his succeeding visions and revelations, his ensuing translation and publication of the Book of Mormon in 1829–30; his organization of the "Church of Christ" in April 1830 and its early growth in Ohio, Missouri, and in Illinois; and of Joseph Smith's ultimate death in Carthage, Illinois, in 1844 at the hand of mobs and persecutors. These all derived from what happened in 1820. Rather, what this concluding chapter has endeavored to do is to show that Joseph Smith's prayerful, deeply faithful yearnings did not emerge from a vacuum. There is no question that he was very much exercised over religion and his own salvation, and that he possessed extraordinary faith. What this chapter has tried to do is to place his religious quest within a long and fascinating American religious

---

82. Letter of Miss Eliza Higgins, 30 October 1820, *Methodist Magazine* (August 1822): 291. For much more on the important role women played in the conversion process during this time, see Cope, "'In Some Places a Few Drops.'"
83. 1832 Recital of the First Vision, in Backman, *Joseph Smith's First Vision*, 156.

Sacred Grove, photograph by George Edward Anderson. Courtesy of Church History Library.

context, one that began with the Puritans and continued through one apostasy and one great awakening after another. Such earlier lights as John Winthrop and Jonathan Edwards, James McGready and Asahel Nettleton, Solomon and Lucy Mack, and Joseph Smith Sr. in their own time and place uniquely prepared the way for his First Vision experience.

Hence it was, he wrote, "in accordance with this, my determination to ask of God," to seek forgiveness, and, like his mother and father, to know which church to join, that young Joseph Smith Jr. "retired to the woods to make the attempt. It was on the morning of a beautiful, clear day, early in the spring of eighteen hundred and twenty."[84]

---

84. Joseph Smith—History 1:14.

BIBLIOGRAPHY

The works listed below are cited in the text or otherwise proved highly valuable to the writing of the book.

Ackerknecht, Erwin H. "George Forster, Alexander von Humboldt, and Ethnology." *ISIS* 46, no. 2 (June 1955): 83–95.

Adair, John. *Founding Fathers: The Puritans in England and America.* London: J. M. Dent & Sons, 1982.

Adams, John Quincy. *Memoirs of John Quincy Adams, Comprising Portions of His Diary from 1795 to 1848,* edited by Charles Francis Adams. 12 vols. Philadelphia, PA: J. B. Lippincott & Co., 1874–77.

Adkins, Lesley and Roy A. Adkins. *The Keys of Egypt: The Obsession to Decipher Egyptian Hieroglyphs.* New York: HarperCollins, 2000.

Allen, James B., Ronald K. Esplin, and David J. Whittaker. *Men with a Mission, 1837–1841: The Quorum of the Twelve Apostles in the British Isles.* Salt Lake City: Deseret Book, 1992.

American Baptist Magazine, March 1820.

American Baptist Magazine, May 1820.

American Baptist Magazine, September 1820.

American Bible Society. *A Brief Analysis of the System of the American Bible Society: Containing a Full Account of Its Principles and Operations, and of the Manner of Organizing and Conducting Auxiliary, Branch, and Ladies' Bible Societies: Published by the Direction of the Board of Managers, and under the Inspection of a Committee Appointed by the Same.* New York: Daniel Fanshaw, 1830.

The American Monthly Magazine and Critical Review, July 1817.

American Tract Society. *A Brief History of the Organization and Work of the American Tract Society*. Boston: American Tract Society, 1855.

Anna, Timothy E. *The Fall of the Royal Government in Peru*. Lincoln: University of Nebraska Press, 1979.

Anstey, Roger. *The Atlantic Slave Trade and British Abolition, 1760–1810*. London: Macmillan, 1975.

Arago, Francois. Francois Arago to Alexander von Humboldt, March 12, 1841. In *Letters of Alexander von Humboldt to Varnhagen von Ense, 1827 to 1858*. Translated by Friedrich Kapp. New York: Rudd and Carleton, 1860.

Armajani, Yahya, and Thomas M. Riches. *The Middle East: Past and Present*. Englewood Cliffs, NJ: Prentice Hall, 1986.

Arrington, Leonard J. "James Gordon Bennett's Report on 'The Mormonites.'" *BYU Studies* 10, no. 3 (July 1970): 353–65.

Artz, Frederick Binkerd. *From the Renaissance to Romanticism: Trends in Style in Art, Literature, and Music, 1300–1830*. Chicago: University of Chicago Press, 1975.

Ashton, Rosemary. *The Life of Samuel Taylor Coleridge: A Critical Biography*. Oxford: Blackwell Publishers, 1996.

Aspland, Robert B. *The Rise, Progress, and Present Influence of Wesleyan Methodism*. London: n.p., 1831.

d'Athanasi, Giovanni. *A Brief Account of the Researches and Discoveries in Upper Egypt, Made Under the Direction of Henry Salt, Esq.* London: John Hearse, 1836.

Aubry, Octave. *St. Helena*. Translated by Arthur Livingstone. Philadelphia: J. B. Lippencott, 1936.

Austin, Paul Britten. *1812: Napoleon in Moscow*. London: Greenhill Books, 1995.

Babbington, Anthony. *Military Intervention in Britain: From the Gordon Riots to the Gibraltar Incident*. London: Routledge, 1990.

Backman, Milton V., Jr. *Joseph Smith's First Vision: The First Vision in its Historical Context*. Salt Lake City: Bookcraft, 1971.

Badura-Skoda, Paul, ed. *Uber den Richtingen Vortrag der Samtlichen Beethoven'schen Klavierwerke*. Vienna: Universal Edition, 1963.

Baker, Frank. "Wesley Brothers." In *The Encyclopedia of Religion*. Edited by Mircea Eliade. New York: Macmillan, 1987.

Baker, Kenneth. "George IV: A Sketch." *History Today* 55, no. 10 (October 2005): 30–36.

Ballard, Colin R. *Napoleon: An Outline.* Freeport, NY: Books for Libraries Press, 1971.

Bancroft, George. *History of the United States of America from the Discovery of the American Continent.* 10 vols. New York: D. Appleton, 1885.

Barrett, Paul H., and Alain F. Corcos. "A Letter from Alexander von Humboldt to Charles Darwin." *Journal of the History of Medicine and Allied Sciences* 27, no. 2 (April 1972): 159–172.

Baugh, Alexander L. "A Call to Arms: The 1838 Mormon Defense of Northern Missouri." PhD diss. Brigham Young University, 1996.

Becke, A. F. *Napoleon's Waterloo: The Emperor's Campaign with the Armée du Nord, 1815.* London: Kegan Paul, Trench, Trubner & Co., 1939.

Bednarski, Andrew, ed. and trans., with contributions by Philippe Mainterot. *The Lost Manuscript of Frederic Cailliaud: Arts and Crafts of the Ancient Egyptians, Nubians, and Ethiopians.* Cairo: American University in Cairo Press, 2014.

Beers, Henry A. *A History of English Romanticism in the 18th Century.* New York: Henry Holt & Co., 1906.

Belmonte, Kevin. *William Wilberforce: A Hero for Humanity.* Grand Rapids, MI: Zondervan, 2007.

"Belzoni's Discoveries in Egypt and Nubia." *Saturday Magazine,* August 11, 1821.

Bennett, James Gordon. "Mormon Religion—Clerical Ambition—Western New York—The Mormonites Gone to Ohio," *Morning Courier and New-York Enquirer,* September 1, 1831.

Bennett, Richard E. "'Read This I Pray Thee': Martin Harris and the Three Wise Men of the East." *Journal of Mormon History* 36, no. 1 (Winter 2010): 178–216.

Berger, Klaus. *Gericault: Drawings and Watercolors.* New York: H. Bittner & Company, 1946.

Bernbaum, Ernest, ed. *Blake, Coleridge, Wordsworth, Lamb and Hazlitt.* Vol. 3 of *Anthology of Romanticism and Guide through the Romantic Movement.* New York: Thomas Nelson and Sons, 1933.

Blackburn, Julia. *The Emperor's Last Island.* New York: Pantheon Books, 1991.

Blumenkranz, Bernhard "Bible Societies." *Encyclopaedia Judaica.* https://www.encyclopedia.com/religion/encyclopedias-almanacs-transcripts-and-maps/bible-societies

Blunden, Edmund, and Earl Leslie Griggs, eds. *Coleridge Studies by Several Hands on the Anniversary of His Death.* London: Constable and Co., 1934.

Bolívar, Simón, and Rufino Blanco-Fombona, *Discursos y proclamas*. N.p.: Garnier Hermanos, 1913.

Boorstin, Daniel J. *The Americans: The National Experience*. New York: Vintage Books, 1965.

Botting, Douglas. *Humboldt and the Cosmos*. New York: Harper & Row, 1973.

de Bourrienne, Louis Antoine Fauvelet. *Memoirs of Napoleon Bonaparte, Volume 16*. Edited by R. W. Phipps. New York: Charles Scribner's Sons, 1891.

Boutilier, James A. "We Fear Not the Ultimate Triumph: Factors Effecting the Conversion Phase of 19th Century Missionary Enterprises." In *Missions and Missionaries in the Pacific*. Edited by Char Miller. Vol. 14 of *Symposium Series*. New York: Edwin Mellen Press, 1985: 13–63.

Bowle, John. *The English Experience: A Survey of English History from Early to Modern Times*. London: Weidenfeld and Nicolson, 1971.

Bradish, Luther. Papers. New York Historical Society. New York City.

Brainerd, Cephas, and Eveline Werner Brainerd, eds. *The New England Society Orations: Addresses, Sermons and Poems Delivered Before the New England Society in the City of New York 1820–1885, Volume 1*. New York: The Century Company, 1901.

Brett, R. L., and A. R. Jones. *Lyrical Ballads: Wordsworth and Coleridge*. London: Methuen & Co., 1963.

Briggs, Asa. *The Age of Improvement, 1783–1867*. 2nd ed. Harlow, England: Longman & Pearson Education, 2000.

Brion, Marcel. *Art of the Romantic Era: Romanticism, Classicism, Realism*. New York: Frederick A. Praeger, 1966.

British and Foreign Bible Society. *16th Report of the British and Foreign Bible Society 1820*. London: Benjamin Beasley, 1820.

British and Foreign Unitarian Association. *The Rise, Progress, and Present Influence of Wesleyan Methodism*. London: Hackney, 1831.

Broers, Michael. "The Empire behind the Lines." *History Today* 48, no. 1 (January 1998): 20–26.

Brooke, John. *King George III*. London: Constable and Company, 1972.

Brown, Christopher Leslie. *Moral Capital: Foundations of British Abolitionism*. Chapel Hill: North Carolina Press, 2006.

Brown, Ford K. *Fathers of the Victorians: The Age of Wilberforce*. Cambridge: Cambridge University Press, 1961.

Browne, George. *The History of the British and Foreign Bible Society, From Its Institution in 1804, to the Close of Its Jubilee in 1854*. 2 vols. London: Bagster and Sons, 1859.

Browning, Oscar. *The Boyhood and Youth of Napoleon: Some Chapters on the Life of Bonaparte, 1769–1793*. New York: John Lane and Company, 1906.

Brownsword, A. "Extracts of Journals," *The Primitive Methodist Magazine*, 1821.

Bruhn, Mark J. *Wordsworth before Coleridge: The Growth of the Poet's Philosophical Mind, 1785–1797*. New York: Routledge, 2018.

Budge, E. A. Wallis. *The Rosetta Stone*. London: Harrison and Sons, 1913.

Buichard, Sylvie, ed. *Lettere di Bernardino Drovetti Console di Francia ad Alessandria d'Egitto (1803–1830)*. Torino, Italy: Academia delle Scienze di Torino, 2005.

Bushman, Richard L. *From Puritan to Yankee: Character and the Social Order in Connecticut, 1690–1765*. New York: W. W. Norton & Company, 1967.

Bushman, Richard L. *Joseph Smith and the Beginnings of Mormonism*. Chicago: University of Illinois Press, 1984.

Butler, Jon. "Enthusiasm Described and Decried: The Great Awakening as Interpretive Fiction." *Journal of American History* 69, no. 2 (September 1982): 305–25.

Buttimer, Anne. "Bridging the Americas: Humboldtian Legacies." *Geographical Review* 96, no. 3 (July 2006): vi–ix.

Byman, Daniel L., and Kenneth M. Pollack. "Let Us Now Praise Great Men: Bringing the Statesman Back In." *International Security* 25, no. 4 (Spring 2001): 107–46.

Cailliaud, M. Frédéric. *Travels in the Oasis of Thebes and in the Deserts Situated East and West of the Thebaid: In the Years 1815, 16, 17, and 18*. Edited by M. Jomard. London: Sir Richard Phillips and Company, 1822.

Caine, Hall. *Life of Samuel Taylor Coleridge*. London: Walter Scott, 1887.

Cambridge History of English and American Literature. 8 vols. Cambridge: Cambridge University Press, 1907–21.

Campbell, James Dykes. *Samuel Taylor Coleridge: A Narrative of the Events of His Life*. New York: Macmillan, 1894.

Campbell, John Lord. *The Lives of the Lord Chancellors and Keepers of the Great Seal of England from the Earliest Times till the Reign of King George IV*. Third Series, vol. 7. London: John Murray, 1847.

Canton, William. *History of the British and Foreign Bible Society*. 2 vols. London: John Murray, 1904.

Carlyle, Thomas. *The Life of John Sterling*. London: Chapman and Hall, 1851.

Carter, Louise. "British Masculinities on Trial in the Queen Caroline Affair of 1820." *Gender and History* 20, no. 2 (August 2008): 248–69.

Case, Jay Riley. *An Unpredictable Gospel: American Evangelicals and World Christianity, 1812–1920*. Oxford: Oxford University Press, 2012.

Cash, W. J. *The Mind of the South*. New York: Alfred A. Knopf, 1957.

Chalmers, Thomas, D. D. *Sermons Preached in the Iron Church, Glasgow*. Glasgow: Kirk & Mercein, 1819.

Channing, Edward P. *The United States of America*. New York: Macmillan and Co., 1896. Part of the Cambridge Historical Series, edited by G. W. Prothero.

Chapman, Tim. *The Congress of Vienna: Origins, Processes and Results*. London: Routledge, 1998.

Cheek, Edison Gary, Jr. "Revivalism: A Study of Asahel Nettleton." Master's thesis. Dallas Theological Seminary, 1979.

Chenique, R. Michel B., and S. Laveissiere. *Géricault: Catalogue of Exhibition, Galeries nationales du Grand Palais*. Paris: Editions de la Reunion des Musees Nationaux, 1991–92.

Christian Disciple and Theological Review 1, no. 1 (January–February 1819).

The Christian Remembrancer (London), 22 January 1820.

Churchill, Winston S. *A History of the English-Speaking Peoples: The Great Democracies*. New York: Dodd, Mead & Company, 1971.

Clapham, J. H. *An Economic History of Modern Britain: The Early Railway Age, 1820–1850*. Cambridge: Cambridge University Press, 1950.

Clark, Dan Elbert. *The West in American History*. New York: Thomas Y. Crowell Co., 1937.

Clément, Charles. *Géricault: A Biographical and Critical Study*. New York: Da Capo, 1974.

Cleveland, Catharine C. *The Great Revival in the West, 1797–1805*. Chicago: The University of Chicago Press, 1916.

Cole, G. D. H., and Raymond Postgate, *The British People, 1746–1946*. London: Methuen, 1961.

Coleridge, Samuel Taylor. *Aids to Reflection*. London: Taylor and Hessey, 1825.

———. *Biographia Literaria*. Edited with its aesthetical essays by J. Shawcross. 2 vols. Oxford: Clarendon Press, 1907.

———. *The Collected Works of Samuel Taylor Coleridge Table Talk*. Recorded by Henry Nelson Coleridge & John Taylor Coleridge, edited by Carl Woodring. Routledge: Bollingen Series 75, Princeton University Press, 1990.

Colton, Calvin. *The Life, Correspondence, and Speeches of Henry Clay*. 6 vols. New York: A. S. Barnes & Co., 1857.

Le Comte de Forbin, M. *Voyage dans Le Levant*. Paris: de L'Imprimerie Royales, 1819. Translated by author.

Conroy-Krutz, Emily. *Christian Imperialism: Converting the World in the Early American Republic*. Vol. 15 of *The United States in the World*. Edited by Mark Philip Bradley, David C. Engerman, Amy S. Greenberg, and Paul A. Kramer. Ithaca: Cornell University Press, 2015.

Cooper, Martin. *Beethoven: The Last Decade, 1817–1827*. London: Oxford University Press, 1970.

Coote, Stephen. *Napoleon and the Hundred Days*. Boston: Da Capo Press, 2004.

Cope, Rachel. "'In Some Places a Few Drops and Other Places a Plentiful Shower': The Religious Impact of Revivalism on Early Nineteenth-Century New York Women." PhD dissertation: Syracuse University, 2009.

Cottle, Joseph. *Reminiscences of Samuel Taylor Coleridge and Robert Southey*. New York: Wiley and Putnam, 1847.

Crafts, N. F. R. *British Economic Growth During the Industrial Revolution*. Oxford: Clarendon Press, 1985.

Cronin, Vincent. *Napoleon*. London: William Collins Sons and Co., 1971.

Crook, Malcolm. *Napoleon Comes to Power: Democracy and Dictatorship in Revolutionary France, 1795–1804*. Cardiff: University of Wales Press, 1998.

Cross, Whitney R. *The Burned-Over District: The Social and Intellectual History of Enthusiastic Religion in Western New York, 1800–1850*. Utica, NY: Cornell University Press, 1950.

Cruden, R. P. *An Account of the Origin of Steam-boats in Spain, Great Britain, and America: And of Their Introduction and Employment Upon the River Thames, Between London and Gravesend, To the Present Time*. London: Effingham Wilson, 1831.

Cunliffe, Marcus. *The Nation Takes Shape, 1789–1837*. Chicago: University of Chicago Press, 1959.

Cunningham, William. *The Growth of English Industry and Commerce in Modern Times*. Cambridge: Cambridge University Press, 1929.

Crow, Thomas. "Classicism in Crisis." In Eisenman, et al. *Nineteenth Century Art: A Critical History*, 77–81. 3rd ed. London: Thomas & Hudson, 2007.

Crow, Thomas. "Patriotism and Virtue: David to the Young Ingres." In Stephen F. Eisenman, *Nineteenth Century Art: A Critical History*, 18–54. 3rd ed. London: Thomas & Hudson, 2007.

Cuvier, Georges. *Le Règne Animal distribué d'après son organisation pour servir de base à l'histoire naturelle des animaux et d'introduction à l'anatomie compare*, vol. 2. Hauman et compe., 1836.

Czerny, Carl. *Über den richtigen Vortrag der sämtlichen Beethoven'schen Klavierwerke*. Edited by Paul Badura-Skoda. Vienna: Universal Edition, 1963.

Dangerfield, George. *The Era of Good Feelings*. London: Methuen and Co., 1953.

Daniell, Christopher. *A Traveller's History of England*. New York: Interlink Books, 1996.

Daniell, David. *The Bible in English: Its History and Influence*. New Haven, CT: Yale University Press, 2003.

David, A. Rosalie. *The Experience of Ancient Egypt*. London: Routledge, 2000.

David, Jacques-Louis. *The Painting of the Sabines, as exhibited to the Republic at the National Palace of the Sciences and the Arts, Hall of the Former Academy of Art by The Citizen DAVID, member of the National Institute, Paris, Year VIII*, as cited in Elizabeth Gilmore Holt, ed., *From the Classicists to the Impressionists: Art and Architecture in the 19th Century*. Garden City, New York: Anchor Books, 1966.

Davidson, Robert. *History of the Presbyterian Church in the State of Kentucky: With A Preliminary Sketch of the Churches in the Valley of Virginia*. New York: R. Carter, 1848.

"Death of Napoleon Bonaparte." *Saturday Magazine*, 1 September 1821, 207–9.

Deane, Charles. "New England." In *Narrative and Critical History of America*, vol. 3, edited by Justin Winsor, 295–339. Boston: Houghton, Mifflin & Co., 1884.

DeBow, J. D. B. *Statistical View of the United States*. Washington: A. D. P. Nicholson, 1854.

Delderfield, Eric R., ed. and rev. *Kings and Queens of England and Great Britain*. New York: David & Charles Publishers, 1970.

Deutsch, Otto Erich. *Mozart: A Documentary Biography*. 3rd ed. Translated by Eric Blom, Peter Branscombe, and Jeremy Noble. New York: Simon & Schuster, 1990.

Drovetti, Bernardino Michel Marie. "Acquisition de la Collection Drovetti Transport Paiement." File 20144775/8. Les Archives Nationales de France, Paris, France.

———. Personal Dossier. Centre Historique des Archives (Militaire) a Vincennes, Paris, France. GR 2 YE 1242.

———. Personal Dossier. Centre Historique des Archives (Militaire) a Vincennes, Paris, France. GR 28 YC 441.

———. "Recommendation de M. de Forbin pour la Nomination de M. Drovetti, Consul General de France in Egypte." 19 May 1819. Archives Nationales de France, FD 20144775/24.

Dwight, Henry Otis. *The Centennial History of the American Bible Society*. New York: Macmillan, 1916.

Dwyer, Philip G. *Napoleon: Passion, Death and Resurrection, 1815–1840*. London: Bloomsbury Publishing, 2018.

———. "Napoleon Bonaparte as Hero and Saviour: Image, Rhetoric and Behaviour in the Construction of a Legend." *French History*, December 2004, 379–403.

Eastwood, David. "The Age of Uncertainty: Britain in the Early Nineteenth Century." In *Transactions of the Royal Historical Society*, 6th Series, vol. 8. Cambridge: University Press, 1998, 91–115.

Eisenman, Stephen, Thomas E. Crow, and Brian Lukacher. *Nineteenth Century Art: A Critical History*. 3rd ed. London: Thomas & Hudson, 2007.

Eitner, Lorenz. *Géricault: His Life and Work*. 1st ed. London: Orbis Publishing, 1983.

———. *Géricault's Raft of the Medusa*. London: Phaidon Press, 1972.

Eliade, Mircea. *The Encyclopedia of Religion*. New York: Macmillan Publishing Co., 1987.

Ellis, Geoffrey. *The Napoleonic Empire*. London: Palgrave Macmillan, 2003.

Emerson, Edwin, Jr. *A History of the Nineteenth Century, Year by Year*. 3 vols. New York: P. F. Collier and Son, 1901.

Equiano, Olaudah. *Equiano's Travels: His Autobiography. The Interesting Narrative of the Life of Olaudah Equiano or Gustavus Vassa, the African*. Edited by Paul Edwards. London: Heinamann, 1967.

Evangelical Guardian and Review. New York. July 1817.

Evangelical Recorder and Missionary Chronicle. No. 1 (31 January 1818): 1.

"Extract from the 10th Report of the Church Missionary Society." *Remembrancer*, 12 February 1920, 99.

Fagan, Brian M., ed. *Eyewitness to Discovery: Fifty-Person Accounts of More Than Fifty of the World's Greatest Archaeological Discoveries*. Oxford: Oxford University Press, 1996.

Few, John. *The Bible Cause: A History of the American Bible Society*. New York: Oxford Press, 2016.

"First Report of the American Bible Society, Presented at the Annual Meeting, May 10, 1821." *The Methodist Magazine*. New York. N. Bangs, and J. Emory for the Methodist Episcopal Church, at the Conference Office. August 1821.

Fleming, Stephen J. "John Wesley: A Methodist Foundation for the Restoration." *Religious Educator: Perspectives on the Restored Gospel* 9, no. 3 (2008): 131–49.

Forbes, Elliot, ed. *Thayer's Life of Beethoven*. Princeton, NJ: Princeton University Press, 1967.

Ford, Charles Howard. *Hannah More: A Critical Biography*. New York: Peter Lang, 1996.

Foreign Affairs. The National Register, 21 November 1818.

Fraser, Antonia, ed. *The Lives of the Kings and Queens of England*. New York: Alfred A. Knopf, 1975.

Fraser, Flora. *The Unruly Queen: The Life of Queen Caroline*. New York: Alfred A. Knopf, 1996.

Frederickson, O. J. "Alexander I and His League to End Wars." *Russian Review* 3, no. 1 (Autumn 1943): 10–22.

Frye, Northrop. *A Study of English Romanticism*. Chicago: The University of Chicago Press, 1968.

Fueter, Eduard. *World History, 1815–1920*. Translated by Sidney B. Fay. New York: Harcourt, Brace and Co., 1922.

Gales, Joseph. *The Debates and Proceedings in the Congress of the United States.* 2 vols. Washington: Gales & Seaton, 1834.

Gibbs, Christopher M. *The Life of Schubert.* Cambridge: Cambridge University Press, 2000.

Gilbert, Alan D. *Religion and Society in Industrial England*: Church Chapel and Social Change, *1740–1914.* London: Longman Group, 1976.

Gilley, Sheridan. "The Church of England in the 19th Century." In *A History of Religion in Britain: Practice and Belief from Pre-Roman Times to the Present*, edited by Sheridan Gilley and W. J. Shields, 291–305. Oxford: Blackwell Publishers, 1994.

Gilley, Sheridan, and W. J. Shields. *A History of Religion in Britain.* Oxford: Blackwell Publishers, 1994.

Gordon, Cyrus H. *Forgotten Scripts: Their Ongoing Discovery and Decipherment.* Rev. ed. New York: Basic Books, 1982.

Grab, Alexander. *Napoleon and the Transformation of Europe.* New York: Palgrave Macmillan, 2003.

Greenaway, Frank. *John Dalton and the Atom.* Ithaca, NY: Cornell University Press, 1966.

Greenspan, Alan. *The 14th Adam Smith Lecture.* St. Bryce Kirk, Fife College, Kirkcaldy, Scotland, 6 February 2005.

Griggs, Earl Leslie, ed., *Collected Letters of Samuel Taylor Coleridge.* Vol. 4. Oxford: Clarendon Press, 1959.

Gutjahr, Paul C. *An American Bible: A History of the Good Book in the United States, 1777–1880.* Stanford: University of Stanford Press, 1999.

Gutman, Robert W. *Mozart: A Cultural Biography.* New York: Harcourt Brace, 1999.

Halévy, Elie. *The Birth of Methodism in England.* Translated by Bernard Semmel. Chicago: University of Chicago Press, 1971.

Hall, Caine. *Life of Samuel Taylor Coleridge.* London: Walter Scott, 1887.

Hallberg, Charles W. *The Suez Canal: Its History and Diplomatic Importance.* New York: Octagon Books, 1974.

Halls, J. J. *The Life and Correspondence of Henry Salt, Esq. F. R. S.* 2 vols. London: Richard Bentley, 1834.

Hamburger, Michael, ed. and trans. *Beethoven: Letters, Journals, and Conversations.* Westport, CT: Greenwood Press, 1951.

Hamilton, Thomas. *Men and Manners in America.* 2 vols. Edinburgh: W. Blackwood and Sons, 1843.

Hammerton, Sir John, and Dr. Henry Elmer Barnes, eds. *The Illustrated World History: A Record of World Events from Earliest Historical Times to the Present Day.* New York: William H. Wise and Co., 1937.

Hankins, Thomas L. "In Defense of Biography: The Use of Biography in the History of Science." *History of Science* 17, no. 1 (1979): 1–16.

"Hannah More: Sunday Schools, Education and Youth Work." In *The Encyclopaedia of Informal Education*. http://infed.org/mobi/hannah-more-sunday-schools-education-and-youth-work/.

Harper, Steven C. *Joseph Smith's First Vision: A Guide to the Historical Accounts*. Salt Lake City: Deseret Book, 2012.

Harper, Steven C., Andrew Hedges, Patty Smith, Thomas R. Valletta, and Fred E. Woods. *Prelude to the Restoration: From Apostasy to the Restored Church*. Provo, UT: Religious Studies Center, Brigham Young University; Salt Lake City: Deseret Book; 2004.

Hart, Ivor B. *Makers of Science: Mathematics, Physics, Astronomy*. London: Oxford University Press, 1924.

Harvey, Robert. *Cochrane: The Life and Exploits of a Fighting Captain*. New York: Carroll and Graf, 2000.

Harwood, George H. *The History of Wesleyan Methodism*. London: Whittaker and Co., 1854.

Hazareesingh, Sudhir. "Napoleonic Memory in Nineteenth-Century France: The Making of a Liberal Legend." *MLN* 120, no. 4 (2005): 747–73.

Heimert, Alan, and Andrew Delbanco. *The Puritans in America: A Narrative Anthology*. Cambridge, MA: Harvard University Press, 1985.

Helferich, Gerard. *Humboldt's Cosmos: Alexander von Humboldt and the Latin American Journey that Changed the Way We See the World*. New York: Gotham Books, 2004.

Hempton, David. "Evangelicalism and Reform, c. 1780–1832." In *Evangelical Faith and Public Zeal: Evangelicals and Society in Britain, 1780–1890*, edited by John Wolffe, 17–37. London: SPCK, 1995.

Hennelling, Ronald C. *Coleridge's Progress to Christianity: Experience and Authority in Religious Faith*. London: Associated University Presses, 1995.

Herbert, Christopher. *Culture and Anomie: Ethnographic Imagination in the 19th Century*. Chicago. University of Chicago Press, 1991.

Herford, C. H. *The Age of Wordsworth*. London: G. Bell and Sons, 1925.

Higgins, Eliza. "Memoir of Miss Eliza Higgins." *Methodist Magazine* 5 (August 1822): 289–94.

Hills, Margaret T. *The English Bible in America: A Bibliography of Editions of the Bible and the New Testament Published in America 1777–1957*. New York: American Bible Society, 1962.

Holmes, Richard. *Coleridge: Darker Reflections, 1804–1834*. New York: Pantheon Books, 1998.

Holt, Elizabeth Gilmore, comp. and ed. *From the Classicists to the Impressionists: A Documentary History of Art and Architecture in the 19th Century*. Garden City, New York: Anchor Books, Doubleday & Co., 1966.

Honour, Hugh. *Romanticism*. New York: Harper and Row, 1979.

Hopkins, Mary Alden. *Hannah More and Her Circle*. New York: Green & Co., 1947.

Hoskin. Michael A. *William Herschel and the Construction of the Heavens*. New York: W. W. Norton and Company, 1963.

House of Commons, Parliament. Great Britain. Report of the Minutes of Evidence Taken Before the Select Committee on the State of the Children Employed in the Manufactories of the United Kingdom: 25 April–18 June, 1816. London: House of Commons, 1816.

Howe, M. A. De Wolfe. *The Life and Letters of George Bancroft*. New York: Charles Scribner's Sons, 1908.

Howsam, Leslie. *Cheap Bibles: Nineteenth-Century Publishing and the British and Foreign Bible Society*. Cambridge: Cambridge University Press, 1991.

Hucks, Tracey E. "The Black Church: Invisible and Visible." *Encyclopedia of American Cultural and Intellectual History*. Vol. 1. New York: Charles Scribner's Sons, 2001.

von Humboldt, Alexander. *Aspects of Nature, in Different Lands and Different Cultures: With Specific Elucidations*. 2 vols. Translated by Mrs. [Elizabeth Juliana] Sabine. London: Longman, Brown, Green, and Longmans, 1849.

———. *Cosmos: A Sketch of a Physical Description of the Universe*. Vol. 2. London: George Bell & Sons, 1878.

———. *Cosmos: A Sketch of a Physical Disruption of the Universe*. Translated by E. C. Otté. New York: Harper and Brothers, 1877.

———. *Political Essay on the Kingdom of New Spain*. Translated by John Black (abridged). Edited by Mary Maples Dunn. Norman, OK: University of Oklahoma Press, 1988.

———. *Researches, Concerning the Inhabitants and Monuments of the Ancient Inhabitants of America*. 2 vols. Translated by Helen Maria Williams. London: Longman, Hurst, Rees, Orme, and Brown, 1814.

———. *Letters of Alexander von Humboldt to Varnhagen von Ense 1827 to 1858*. Translated by Friedrich Kapp. New York: Rudd and Carleton, 1860.

von Humboldt, Alexander and Aimé Bonpland. *Personal Narrative of Travels to the Equinoctial Regions of America, During the Years 1799–1804*. 3 vols. Translated and edited by Thomasina Ross. London: Henry G. Bohn, 1852.

von Humboldt, Wilhelm. *Gesammelte Werke*. Edited by Alexander von Humboldt. Berlin: Reimer, 1841.

Hunt, Jocelyn. *The French Revolution*. London: Routledge, 1998.

Jack, K. M. "Jean Lamarck, 1744–1829." In *Late 18th Century European Scientists*, vol. 2, edited by R. C. Olby, 5–32. Oxford: Pergamon Press, 1966.

Jackson, Kent P. "Joseph Smith's Cooperstown Bible: The Historical Context of the Bible Used in the Joseph Smith Translation." *BYU Studies* 40, no. 1 (Winter 2001): 41–70.

Jackson, Stephen T., and Laura Dassow Walls, eds. *Views of Nature: Alexander Von Humboldt*. Translated by Mark W. Person. Chicago: The University of Chicago Press, 2014.

James, T. G. H. *Egypt Revealed: Artist-Travellers in an Antique Land*. London: The Folio Society, 1997.

Jenner, Heather. *Royal Wives*. London: Ebenezer Baylis & Son, 1967.

Johnson, Charles A. *The Frontier Camp Meeting: Religion's Harvest Time*. Dallas: Southern Methodist University, 1955.

Johnson, Dorothy. *David to Delacroix: The Rise of Romantic Mythology*. Chapel Hill: University of North Carolina Press, 2011.

Johnson, Douglas, Alan Taylor, and Robert Winter. *The Beethoven Sketchbooks: History, Reconstruction, Inventory*. Berkeley and Los Angeles: University of California Press, 1985.

Johnson, Paul. *The Birth of the Modern: World Society, 1815–1830*. New York: HarperCollins Publishers, 1991.

———. *Napoleon: A Life*. New York: Viking Penguin, 2002.

Jones, Adnah D. *The History of South America: From Discovery to the Present Time*. London: Swan Sonnenschein & Co., Ltd., 1899.

Jones, Christopher C. "The Power and Form of Godliness: Methodist Conversion Narratives and Joseph Smith's First Vision Narratives." *Journal of Mormon History* 37, no. 2 (Spring 2011): 88–114.

Jones, P. M. *The French Revolution, 1787–1804*. London: Pearson Education, 2003.

Jones, R. Ben. *The French Revolution*. New York: Funk and Wagnalls, 1967.

Jones, Thomas B. "Henry Clay and Continental Expansion, 1820–1844." *The Register of the Kentucky Historical Society* 73, no. 3 (July 1975): 241–62.

Kane, J. Herbert. *A Concise History of the Christian World Mission: A Panoramic View of Missions from Pentecost to the Present*. Grand Rapids, MI: Baker Book House, 1982.

Kane, J. Herbert. *The Progress of World-Wide Missions*. New York: Harper & Brothers, 1960.

Kapp, Friedrich, trans. *Letters of Alexander von Humboldt to Barhagen von Ense, 1827 to 1858*. New York: Rudd and Caleton, 1860.

Katz, Ruth. "The Egalitarian Waltz." *Comparative Studies in Society and History* 15, no. 3 (June 1973: 368–77.

Kellner, L. *Alexander von Humboldt*. London: Oxford University Press, 1963.

Kendall, James. *Michael Faraday: Man of Simplicity*. London: Faber & Faber, 1954.

Kendrick, Ariel. "Letter to the Editors, January 1820." *American Baptist Magazine*, March 1820, 29.

Kinderman, William. *Beethoven*. Berkeley: University of California Press, 1995.

Kissinger, Henry A. *A World Restored: Metternich, Castlereagh and the Problems of Peace, 1812–22*. Cambridge: Riverside Press, 1957.

Klaits, Joseph, and Michael Haltzel, eds. *The Global Ramification of the French Revolution*. Woodrow Wilson Series. Cambridge: Cambridge University Press, 1994.

Klein, Larry Dean. "Henry Clay, Nationalist." PhD diss., University of Kentucky, 1977.

Klimenko, Michael. *Notes of Alexander I, Emperor of Russia*. Vol. 3 of *American University Studies, Series XII, Slavic Languages and Literature*. New York: Peter Lang, 1989.

———. *Tsar Alexander I: Portrait of an Autocrat*. Tenafly, NJ: Hermitage Publishers, 2002.

Koskinen, Aarne A. "Missionary Influence as a Political Factor in the Pacific Islands." PhD diss., University of Helsinki, 1953.

Kramer, Lloyd S. "The French Revolution and the Creation of American Culture." In *The Global Ramification of the French Revolution*, edited by Joseph Klaits and Michael Halzel, 26–54. Woodrow Wilson Series. Cambridge, England: Cambridge University Press, 1994.

von Kreissle, Heinrich. *The Life of Franz Schubert*. 2 vols. London: Longmans, Green, and Company, 1869.

Labaume, Eugène. *A Circumstantial Narrative of the Campaign in Russia: Embellished with Plans of the Battles of Moskwa and Malo-Jaroslavits*, 3rd ed. London: Samuel Leigh, 1815.

Lack, H. Walter. *Alexander Von Humboldt and the Botanical Exploration of the Americas*. Munich: Prestel, 2009.

De Lacroix, Peru L. *Diario de Bucaramanga: Vida pública y privada del Libertador Simón Bolívar*. Medellín: Editorial Bedout, 1967.

Lacy, Creighton. *The Word-Carrying Giant: The Growth of the American Bible Society (1816–1966)*. South Pasadena, CA: William Carey Library, 1977.

The Ladies' Literary Cabinet: Being a Repository of Miscellaneous Literary Productions, Original and Selected, in Prose and Verse. New York: Woodworth and Heustis, 1819–22.

Lambert, Frank. *Inventing the "Great Awakening."* Princeton, NJ: Princeton University Press, 1999.

Landon, H. C. Robbins, comp. and ed. *Beethoven: His Life, Work and World*. Translated by Richard Wadleigh and Eugene Hartzell. London: Thames and Hudson, 1970.

Lansley, Charles Morris. *Charles Darwin's Debt to the Romantics: How Alexander von Humboldt, Goethe, and Wordsworth Helped Shape Darwin's View of Nature*. New York: Oxford University Press, 2018.

Laven, David, and Lucy Riall, eds. "Restoration Government and the Legacy of Napoleon." In *Napoleon's Legacy: Problems of Government in Restoration Europe*, 1–26. Oxford: Berg, 2000.

Laven, David, and Lucy Riall, eds. *Napoleon's Legacy: Problems of Government in Restoration Europe*. Oxford: Berg, 2000.

Lecuna, Vicente, comp. *Proclamas y Discursos del Libertador*. Caracas, 1939.

———. *Selected Writings of Bolívar*. 2 vols. Edited by Harold A. Bierck Jr. Translated by Lewis Bertrand. New York: Colonial Press, 1951.

Lenard, Phillip. *Great Men of Science: A History of Scientific Progress*. Translated by H. Stafford Hatfield. New York: Macmillan, 1934.

LeSueur, Stephen C. *The 1838 Mormon War in Missouri*. Columbia, MO: University of Missouri Press, 1987.

Letter from L. W. B., 7 April 1820 to the Rev. Dr. Baldwin. *American Baptist Magazine* 2, no. 9 (May 1820): 343.

Levy, David Benjamin. *Beethoven: The Ninth Symphony*. New York: Schirmer Books, 1995.

Lieven, Dominic. *Russia Against Napoleon: The True Story of the Campaigns of War and Peace*. New York: Viking, 2010.

Lightfoot, Alfred. "Henry Clay and the Missouri Question 1819–1821." *Missouri Historical Review* 61, no. 2 (January 1967):143–65.

Lockwood, Lewis. *Beethoven: The Music and the Life*. New York: W. W. Norton and Co., 2003.

The London Literary Gazette and Journal of Belles Lettres, Arts, Sciences, etc. no. 180 (1 July 1820): 427. Quoted in Eitner, Lorenz. *Géricault's Raft of the Medusa*. London: Phaidon Press, 1972.

Lovett, Richard. *The History of the London Missionary Society, 1795–1895*. 2 vols. London: Henry Frowde, 1899.

Lukacher, Brian. "Landscape Art and Romantic Nationalism in Germany and America." *Nineteenth Century Art: A Critical History* (2002): 143–59.

———. "Visionary History Painting: Blake and His Contemporaries." In Stephen Eisenman, Thomas E. Crow, and Brian Luckacher, *Nineteenth Century Art: A Critical History*, 119–41. London: Thames & Hudson, 2007.

Luvaas, Jay. "Napoleon on the Art of Command." *Parameters: Journal of the U.S. Army War College* 15, no. 2 (Summer 1985): 30–36.

Lynch, John. *Simón Bolívar: A Life*. New Haven: Yale University Press, 2006.

———. "Simón Bolívar and the Spanish American Revolution." *History Today* 33, no. 7 (July 1983): 5–10.

Mack, Solomon. *A Narrative of the Life of Solomon Mack, Containing an Account of the Many Severe Accidents He Met with During a Long Series of Years, Together with the Extraordinary Manner in Which He was Converted to the Christian Faith*. Windsor, VT: self-published, 1811.

Maddocks, R. "Letter to the Editors." *American Baptist Magazine*, September 1820, 407.

Maffly-Kipp, Laurie F., Leigh E. Schmidt, and Mark Valeri, eds. *Practicing Protestants: Histories of Christian Life in America, 1630–1965*. Baltimore: Johns Hopkins University Press, 2006.

Malone, Dumas. *Jefferson the President, 1801–1805*. Vol. 4 of *Jefferson and His Times*. Boston: Little, Brown and Co., 1970.

Maness, Lonnie Edward. "Henry Clay and the Problem of Slavery." PhD diss. Memphis State University, 1980.

Markham, Felix. *Napoleon*. New York: New American Library, 1963.

Markham, J. David. *Imperial Glory in The Bulletins of Napoleon's Grande Armée, 1805–1814*. London: Greenhill Books, 2003.

Marriott, J. A. R. *England Since Waterloo*. London: Methuen & Co., 1913.

Marsden, George M. *Jonathan Edwards: A Life*. New Haven & London: Yale University Press, 2003.

McClymond, Michael J., and Gerald R. McDermott. *The Theology of Jonathan Edwards*. New York: Oxford University Press, 2012.

McConnell, Allen. *Tsar Alexander I: Paternalistic Reformer*. New York: Thomas Y. Crowell, 1970.

McCrory, Donald. *Nature's Interpreter: The Life and Times of Alexander von Humboldt*. Cambridge, UK: Lutterworth Press, 2010.

McCullough, David. *1776*. New York: Simon and Schuster, 2005.

Mead, Stith. *A General Selection of the Newest and Most Admired Hymns and Spiritual Songs Now in Use*. Richmond: Seaton Grantland, 1807.

Meinhardt, Maren. *A Longing for Wide and Unknown Things: The Life of Alexander von Humboldt*. London: Hurst and Company, 2018.

Merriam, Joseph, comp. *The Wesleyan Camp Meeting Hymn-Book*. 4th ed. Wendell, MA: J. Metcalf, 1829.

Merrill, Joseph A. Letter in *The Methodist Magazine* (April 1820).

Mesick, Jane Louise. *The English Traveller in America, 1785–1835*. Westport, CT: Greenwood Press, 1970.

Miller, Perry. *Errand into the Wilderness*. Cambridge: The Belknap Press of Harvard University Press, 1956.

"The Minutes or Journal of the Conference of the People Called Methodists." Vol. 2. Unpublished MSS, The Methodist Archives and Research Centre, The John Rylands University Library, University of Manchester, Oxford Rd., Manchester England.

Missionary Society of Connecticut. *21st Annual Narrative of Missions Directed by the Trustees of the Missionary Society of Connecticut in 1819.* New Haven, CT: Yale, 1819.

Mitchill, Catherine. Papers. Library of Congress, MSS Division, Washington, D.C.

Mitchill, Samuel L. Papers. University Archives. Columbia University, New York.

Monthly Reporter of the British and Foreign Bible Society. London: William Mavor Watts, 1867.

Moore, Glover. *The Missouri Controversy, 1819–1821.* Lexington: University of Kentucky Press, 1953.

Moore, Rev. Thomas. Letter to his father, Deacon Israel Moore. 9 March 1803, Ten Mile Pennsylvania.

More, Hannah. *The Miscellaneous Works of Hannah More.* 2 vols. London: Thomas Tegg, 1840.

———. *The Shepherd of Salisbury Plain and Other Narratives.* London: The Religious Tract Society, 1866.

———. *Thoughts on the Importance of the Manners of the Great and General Society.* London: T. Cadell, 1788.

Morrison, Robert. *Account of Foe: The Deified Founder of a Chinese Sect.* London: n.p., 1817.

Muhlestein, Kerry. "Prelude to the Past: Sweeping Events Leading to the Discovery of the Book of Abraham." In *Prelude to the Restoration: From Apostasy to the Restored Church*, 130–41. Provo, UT: Religious Studies Center; Salt Lake City: Deseret Book, 2004.

Muirhead, John H. "Metaphysician or Mystic?" In *Coleridge: Studies by Several Hands on the Hundredth Anniversary of His Death*, edited by Edmund Blunden and Earl Leslie Griggs, 177–98. London: n.p., 1934.

Mundus database of missionary collections in the UK. http://workbook.wordherders.net/2005/01/mundus-database of missionary-collections-in-the-uk.html.

New Advent. http://www.newadvent.org/cathen/02544a.htm.

Newbould, Brian. *Schubert: The Music and the Man.* Berkeley: The University of California Press, 1999.

Newton, John. "Amazing Grace," hymnal.net, https://www.hymnal.net/en/hymn/h/313.

Ngapkynta, Hamlet Bareh. *William Carey in a New Perspective.* Guwahati, India: Spectrum Publications, 2004.

Nichols, Sandra. "Why Was Humboldt Forgotten in the United States?" *Geographical Review* 96, no. 3 (July 2006): 399–415.

Nottebohm, Gustav. *Two Beethoven Sketchbooks: A Description with Musical Extracts.* London: Gollancz, 1979.

Nye, Russell B. *George Bancroft: Brahmin Rebel.* New York: Alfred A. Knopf, 1944.

d'Odeleben, M. Le Baron, and Aubert de Vitry. "Review of *Relation Circonstancice de la Campagne de 1813 en Saxe.*" *Edinburgh Review* 32 (July 1819): 208–31.

Olby, R. C., ed. *Late 18th Century European Scientists.* Oxford: Pergamon Press, 1966.

O'Leary, Daniel Florencio. *Memorias del General Daniel Florencio O'Leary.* Caracas, Venezuela: Emprenta de la Gazeta Oficial, 1881.

Osborne, Richard. *Rossini.* London: J. M. Dent & Sons, 1986.

———. *Rossini: His Life and Works.* Oxford: Oxford University Press, 2007.

Owen, John. *The History of the Origin and First Ten Years of the British and Foreign Bible Society.* New York: James Eastburn & Co., 1817.

Paine, Thomas. *The Age of Reason: Part the Second, Being an Investigation of True and of Fabulous Theology.* Philadelphia: Benjamin Franklin Bache, 1796.

———. *Common Sense: The Crisis.* London: John Brooks, 1831.

———. *Rights of Man, Part the First, Being an Answer to Mr. Burke's Attack on the French Revolution.* New-York: Berry, Rogers, and Berry, 1792.

Palmer, Alan. *Alexander I: Tsar of War and Peace.* London: Weidenfeld and Nicolson, 1974.

Parissien, Steven. "George IV and Posterity." *History Today* 51 no. 3 (March 2001): 9–15.

Parkinson, R. B. *Cracking Codes: The Rosetta Stone and Decipherment.* Berkeley: University of California Press, 1999.

Perkin, Harold James. *The Origins of Modern English Society, 1780–1880.* London: Routledge & K. Paul; Toronto: University of Toronto Publishing, 1969.

Perry, Seamus. *Samuel Taylor Coleridge.* Oxford: Oxford University Press, 2003.

"Persecution in China." *The American Masonic Register and Ladies' and Gentlemen's Magazine* 1, no. 1 (1 September 1820): 73.

Peters, Ronald M., Jr., *The American Speakership: The Office in Historical Perspective.* 2nd ed. Baltimore: Johns Hopkins University Press, 1997.

Peterson, H. Donl. *The Story of the Book of Abraham: Mummies, Manuscripts, and Mormonism.* Salt Lake City: Deseret Book, 1995.

Pinel, Philippe, and Henry Maudsley. *Treatise on Insanity: Responsibility in Mental Disease.* Edited by Henry Maudsley and Daniel N. Robinson. Significant Contributions to the History of Psychology, 1750–1920, Series C, Medical Psychology, vol. 3. Washington: University Publications of America, 1977.

Pope, Maurice. *The Story of Decipherment: From Egyptian Hieroglyphs to Maya Script.* Rev. edition. London: Thames and Hudson, 1999.

Popkin, Jeremy D. *A Short History of the French Revolution*. 4th ed. Upper Saddle River, NJ: Pearson Prentice-Hall, 2006.

Porter, Bruce H. "Antonio Lebolo: His Life and Contributions to Egyptology." Unpublished paper in possession of the author.

Proctor, Scot Facer, and Maurine Jensen Proctor, eds. *The Revised and Enhanced History of Joseph Smith by His Mother*. Salt Lake City: Bookcraft, 1996.

Prout, Ebenezer. *Memoirs of the Life of the Rev. John Williams, Missionary to Polynesia*. Andover: Allen, Morrill and Wardwell, 1843.

Quincy, Josiah. *Memoir of the Life of Josiah Quincy*. Philadelphia: J. B. Lippincott and Co., 1875.

Raeff, Marc. *Michael Speransky. Statesman of Imperial Russia, 1772–1839*. The Hague: Martinus Nijhoft, 1969.

Ramsey, James. *An Essay on the Treatment and Conversion of African Slaves in the British Sugar Colonies*. London: J. Phillips, 1784.

Reardon, Bernard M. G. *Religious Thought in the Victorian Age: A Survey from Coleridge to Gore*. 2nd ed. London: Longman, 1995.

Rebok, Sandra. "Enlightened Correspondents: The Transatlantic Dialogue of Thomas Jefferson and Alexander von Humboldt." *Virginia Magazine of History and Biography* 116, no. 4 (2008): 328–69.

Reid, Donald Malcolm. *Whose Pharaohs? Archaeology, Museums and Egyptian National Identity from Napoleon to World War 1*. Berkeley: University of California Press, 2003.

"Religious Intelligence." *American Monthly Magazine and Critical Review*, July 1817.

Remini, Robert V. *Henry Clay: Statesman for the Union*. New York: W. W. Norton, 1991.

Richards, Robert J. "The Role of Biography in Intellectual History." *KNOW: A Journal on the Formation of Knowledge* 1, no. 2 (2017): 295–318.

Richardson, Joanna. *The Disastrous Marriage: A Study of George IV and Caroline of Brunswick*. Westport, CT: Greenwood Press, 1960.

Rifaud, Jean-Jacques. Papers. Book MS supplement 112, Fonds Rifaud, Bibliotheque de Genève, Switzerland.

"A Right Royal Scandal." *Economist* 381 (16 December 2006): 103–9.

Ringer, Alexander. Ed. *The Early Romantic Era Between Revolutions: 1789 and 1848*. Englewood Cliffs, NJ: Prentice Hall, 1991.

Robert, Warren. *Jacques-Louis David, Revolutionary Artist: Art, Politics, and the French Revolution*. Chapel Hill: University of North Carolina Press, 1989.

Roberts, Andrew. *Napoleon: A Life*. New York: Viking Penguin, 2014.

———. *Napoleon and Wellington*. London: Weidenfeld and Nicolson, 2001.

Roberts, B. H. *A Comprehensive History of the Church of Jesus Christ of Latter-day Saints, Century 1*. 6 vols. Salt Lake City: Deseret Book, 1965.

Roberts, William. *Memories of the Life and Correspondence of Mrs. Hannah More*. 4 vols. London: R. B. Seeley & W. Burnside, 1834.

Robertson, William Spence. *Rise of the Spanish-American Republic, As Told in the Lives of Their Liberators*. New York: D. Appleton & Co., 1918.

Robins, Jane. *The Trial of Queen Caroline: The Scandalous Affair That Nearly Ended a Monarchy*. New York: Free Press, 2006.

Rodriguez O., Jaime E. *The Independence of Spanish America*. Cambridge: Cambridge University Press, 1998.

Rosen, Charles, and Henri Zeiner. *Romanticism and Realism: The Mythology of Nineteenth Century Art*. New York: Viking Press, 1984.

Rosenblum, Robert. *19th Century Art*. New York: Harry N. Abrams, 1984.

Rourke, Thomas. *Man of Glory: Simón Bolívar*. New York: William Morrow & Co., 1939.

Royle, Edward. "Evangelicals and Education." In *Evangelical Faith and Public Zeal: Evangelicals and Society in Britain, 1780–1890*, edited by John Wolffe, 117–37. London: SPCK, 1995.

———. "Secularists and Rationalists, 1800–1940." In *A History of Religion in Britain: Practice and Belief from Pre-Roman Times to the Present*, edited by Sheridan Gilley and W. J. Shields, 406–22. Oxford: Blackwell Publishers, 1994.

Ruins of Sacred and Historic Lands. London: T. Nelson and Sons, 1857.

Rutman, Darrett B. *The Great Awakening: Event and Exegesis*. New York: John Wiley & Sons, 1970.

Sachs, Harvey. *The Ninth: Beethoven and the World in 1824*. New York: Random House, 2010.

Sadie, Stanley, ed. *The New Grove Dictionary of Music and Musicians*. 2nd ed. Vol. 3. London: Macmillan, 2001.

Salcedo-Bastardo, J. L. *Bolívar: A Continent and Its Destiny*. Edited and translated by Annella McDermott. Richmond, England: Richmond, 1977.

Sanders, Charles Richard. *Coleridge and the Broad Church Movement*. Durham, NC: Duke University Press, 1942.

Sanders, Margaret. *Intimate Letters of England's Kings*. London: Museum Press, 1959.

Scott, Donald. *Evangelicalism, Revivalism, and the Second Great Awakening*. New York: Queen's College, City University of New York, 2000.

Scott, Orange, comp. *The New and Improved Camp Meeting Hymn Book: Being a Choice Selection of Hymns from the West*. 3rd ed. Brookfield, MA: n.p., 1832.

Seward, Desmond. *Napoleon's Family*. New York: Viking Press, 1986.

Sherwell, Guillermo A. *Simón Bolívar: Patriot, Warrior, Statesman, Father of Five Nations*. Washington: Byron S. Adams, 1921.

Shinn, Rinn-Sup, ed. *Italy: A Country Study*, Washington, DC: Government Printing Office, 1987.

Shipps, Jan. *Mormonism: The Story of a New Religious Tradition*. Urbana: University of Illinois Press, 1985.

Siepmann, Jeremy. *Beethoven: His Life and Music*. Norfolk, England: Naxos Books, 2005.

Skelton, Edward Oliver. *The Story of New England: Being a Narrative of the Principal Events from the Arrival of the Pilgrims in 1620 and of the Puritans in 1624 to the Present Time*. Boston: Edward O. Skelton, 1910.

Smith, Adam. *An Inquiry into the Nature and Causes of the Wealth of Nations*. 1st ed. London: W. Strahan and T. Cottle, 1776.

Smith, Douglas. *Working the Rough Stone: Freemasonry and Society in Eighteenth Century Russia*. DeKalb, IL: Northern Illinois University Press, 1999.

Smith, E. A. *George IV*. New Haven, CT: Yale University Press, 1999.

Smith, Joseph. *The Pearl of Great Price. A Selection from the Revelations, Translations, and Narrations of Joseph Smith*. Salt Lake City: The Church of Jesus Christ of Latter-day Saints, 1979.

Smith, Lucy Mack. *History of Joseph Smith by His Mother*. Salt Lake City: Bookcraft, 1958.

Smith, M. K. "Hannah More: Sunday Schools, Education and Youth Work." *The Encyclopedia of Informal Education*. http://infed.org/mobi/hannah-more-sunday-schools-education-and-youth-work/.

Smith, Sarah Tappan. *History of the Establishment and Progress of the Christian Religion in the Islands of the South Seas*. Boston: Tappan & Dennet, 1841.

Smith, William. *William Smith on Mormonism*. Lamoni, IA: Herald House Steam Book & Job Office, 1883.

Snell, Robert. *Portraits of the Insane: Theodore Gericault and the Subject of Psychotherapy*. London: Karnac Books, 2017.

Society for Superseding the Necessity of Climbing Boys by Encouraging a New Method of Sweeping Chimneys, etc. *An Account of the Proceedings of the Society for Superseding the Necessity of Climbing Boys*. London: Baldwin, 1816.

Solomon, Maynard. *Beethoven*. 2nd rev. ed. New York: Schirmer Books, 1988.

———. "Beethoven's Ninth Symphony: The Sense of an Ending." *Critical Inquiry*, 17, no. 2 (Winter 1991): 289–305.

Southey, Robert. *Letters from England by Don Manuel Alvarez Espriella*. Edited by Carol Bolton. London: Routledge, 2016.

Sowell, Thomas. *Conquests and Cultures: An International History*. New York: Basic Books, 1998.

Stiebing, William H., Jr. *Uncovering the Past: A History of Archaeology*. New York: Oxford University Press, 1993.

"The Story of Giovanni Belzoni." *Harper's New Monthly Magazine* 2 (May 1851): 749–53.

Strawson, John. *The Duke and the Emperor: Wellington and Napoleon*. London: Constable and Company, 1994.

Strickland, W. P. *History of the American Bible Society from Its Organization to the Present Time*. New York: Harper and Brothers, 1849.

Sweet, Alfred Henry. *History of England*. Boston: D.C. Heath & Company, 1931.

Sweet, William Warren. *Revivalism in America: Its Origin, Growth, and Decline*. New York: Charles Scribner's Sons, 1944.

Tackett, Timothy. *The Coming of the Terror in the French Revolution*. Cambridge, MA: Belknap Press of Harvard University Press, 2015.

———. *When the King Took Flight*. Cambridge, MA: Harvard University Press, 2003.

Tallmadge, Mr. James (New York), 16 February 1819. *Debates of Congress*, 6:351–52, 15th Congress, 2nd Session, House of Representatives.

Tarbell, Ida M. *The Life of Napoleon Bonaparte*. New York: McClure, Phillips, and Company, 1903.

Taton, René, ed. *History of Science in the Nineteenth Century*. Translated by A. J. Pomerans. New York: Basic Book, 1965.

Taylor, Alan. *The Civil War of 1812: American Citizens, British Subjects, Irish Rebels, and Indian Allies*. New York: Vintage Books, 2010.

Teignmouth, Right Hon. Lord, President, at the Sixteenth Anniversary of the Society, 3 May 1820. *The Sixteenth Report of the British and Foreign Bible Society:* London: Benjamin Bensley, 1820.

Timar, Andrea. *A Modern Coleridge: Cultivation, Addiction, Habits*. New York: Palgrave Macmillan, 2015.

The Times (London), 1785–.

de Tocqueville, Alexis. *Democracy in America*. New York: A. A. Knopf, 1945.

Toynbee, Arnold. *Lectures on the Industrial Revolution of the 18th Century in England*. London: Longman, Green & Company, 1894.

A Treatise Upon the Trade from Great-Britain To Africa: Humbly Recommended to the Attention of Government. By an African Merchant. London: R. Baldwin, 1772.

Trend, John Brande. *Bolivar and the Independence of Spanish America*. Bolivarian Society of Venezuela, 1951.

Trevelyan, George Macaulay. *British History in the Nineteenth Century, 1782–1901*. London: Longmans, Green & Company, 1927.

Troubetzkoy, Alexis S. *Imperial Legend: The Mysterious Disappearance of Tsar Alexander I*. New York: Arcade Publishing, 2002.

Tulard, Jean. *Napoleon: The Myth of the Saviour*. Translated by Teresa Waugh. London: Weidenfield and Nicolson, 1984.

Tulloch, John. *Movements of Religious Thought in Britain During the Nineteenth Century*. New York: Lancaster University Press, 1971.

Turner, Jane, ed. *The Dictionary of Art*. 34 vols. London: Macmillan, 1996.

Tyler, Bennet. *Memoirs of the Life and Character of Rev. Asahel Nettleton, D. D.* 5th ed. Boston: Doctrinal Tract and Book Society, 1853.

US Congress. *Abridgment of the Debates of Congress, from 1789 to 1856*. New York: Appleton & Co., 1858, 16th Congress, 1st Session, Senate Papers, 6:400.

Usick, Patricia. *Adventures in Egypt and Nubia: The Travels of William John Bankes (1786–1855)*. London: British Museum Press, 2002.

Van Deusen, Glyndon G. *The Life of Henry Clay*. Boston: Little, Brown and Co., 1937.

Vaughan, William. *Romantic Art*. London: Thames and Hudson, 1978.

Vick, Brian E. *The Congress of Vienna: Power and Politics After Napoleon*. Cambridge, MA: Harvard University Press, 2014.

Vowell, Richard Longeville, and William D. Mahoney. *Campaigns and Cruises, in Venezuela and New Grenada, and in the Pacific Ocean: From 1817 to 1830*. Vol. 1. London: Longman and Company, 1831.

Walker, J. U. *History of Wesleyan Methodism In Halifax*. Halifax, England: Hartley and Walker, 1836.

Wallbridge, Edwin Angel. *The Demerara Martyr: Memoirs of the Rev. John Smith*. New York: Negro Universities Press, 1969.

Walls, Laura Dassow. *The Passage to Cosmos: Alexander von Humboldt and the Shaping of America*. Chicago: University of Chicago Press, 2009.

Ward, J. *A Brief Sketch of Methodism in Bridlington and Its Vicinity: With a List of All the Preachers Who Have Laboured in the Circuit from Its Commencement in 1791 to the Present Time*. Bridlington-Quay: John Varley, 1854.

The Weekly Recorder. London, 1820.

Weider, Ben, "Napoleon and the Jews." Presidential Forum Address, International Congress of the International Napoleonic Society. Alessandria, Italy, 21–26 June 1997. http://www.napoleon-series.org/ins/weider/c_jews.html.

Weinstock, Herbert. *Rossini: A Biography.* New York: Alfred A. Knopf, 1968.

Weisberger, Bernard. *They Gathered at the River: The Story of the Great Revivalists and Their Impact Upon Religion in America.* Boston: Little, Brown & Co., 1958.

Wellek, René. *Immanuel Kant in England, 1793–1938.* Princeton: Princeton University Press, 1931.

The Wesleyan Camp Meeting Hymn-Book. Compiled by Joseph Merriam. 4th ed. Wendell, MA; J. Metcalf, 1829.

What Hath God Wrought? A Narrative of the Revival of Religion, Within the Bounds of the Presbytery of Albany in the Year 1820. Philadelphia: S. Probasco, 1821.

Whitney, Wheelock. *Géricault in Italy.* New Haven: Yale University Press, 1997.

Wigger, John H. "Taking Heaven by Storm: Enthusiasm and Early American Methodism, 1770–1820." *Journal of the Early Republic* 14, no. 2 (Summer 1994): 167–94.

Wilberforce, William. *A Practical View of the Prevailing Religious System of Professed Christians in the Higher and Middle Classes in the Country, Contrasted with Real Christianity.* 4th ed. London: T. Cadell Jr. and W. Davies, 1811.

———. *Real Christianity.* 10th ed. London: T. Cadell and W. Davies, 1811.

Wilkinson, Dennis G. *Henry Clay and South America, 1810–1826: A Defeat for a Hemispheric Policy.* PhD dissertation, Southern Connecticut State College, 1974.

Williams, H. Noel. *The Women Bonapartes: The Mother and Three Sisters of Napoleon I.* New York: Charles Scribner's Sons, 1909.

Williams, Henry Smith. *The Historian's History of the World.* 25 vols. New York: The Outlook Co. and The History Association, 1904.

Williams, Rev. John. *A Narrative of Missionary Enterprises in the South Sea Islands: With Remarks Upon the Natural History of the Islands, Origin, Languages, Traditions, and Usages of the Inhabitants.* London: John Snow, 1840.

Williams, Trevor I., ed. *A Biographical Dictionary of Scientists.* 2nd ed. New York: Halsted Press, 1974.

Wills, John E., Jr. *1688: A Global History.* New York: W. W. Norton and Company, 2001.

Winsor, Justin. *English Explorations and Settlements in North America: 1497–1689.* Vol. 3 of *Narrative and Critical History of America.* Boston: Houghton, Mifflin & Co., 1884.

Wolffe, John, ed. *Evangelical Faith and Public Zeal: Evangelicals and Society in Britain, 1780–1890.* London: SPCK, 1995.

Woodring, Carl, ed. *The Collected Works of Samuel Taylor Coleridge: Table Talk.* Routledge: Bollingen Series LXXV, vol. 14, Princeton University Press, 1990.

Woods, Fred E. "Latter-day Saint Missionaries Encounter the London Missionary Society in the South Pacific, 1844–1852." *BYU Studies* 52, no. 3 (2013): 102–25.

Woodworth, Samuel, ed. *The Ladies' Literary Cabinet: Being a Repository of Miscellaneous Literary Productions, Original and Selected, in Prose and Verse.* New York: Woodworth and Heustis, 1819–22.

Wright, Frances. *Views of Society and Manners in America.* Cambridge: The Belknap Press of Harvard University Press, 1963.

Wright, Trevor J. "'Your Sons and Your Daughters Shall Prophesy . . . Your Young Men Shall See Visions': The Role of Youth in the Second Great Awakening, 1800–1850." Master's thesis, Brigham Young University, 2013.

Wu, Jiang, and Greg Wilkinson, eds. *Reinventing the Tripitaka: Transformation of the Buddhist Canon in Modern East Asia.* Lanham, MD: Lexington Books, 2017.

Wulf, Andrea. *The Invention of Nature: Alexander von Humboldt's New World.* 1st American ed. New York: Alfred A. Knopf, 2015.

Yates, Rev. Andrew. "Woe unto the Wicked." Sermon delivered 21 March 1813 and in 1820 at or near Schenectady, New York. In Andrew Yates Papers. Special Collections, Schaffer Library, Union College, Schenectady, New York.

Zacek, Judith Cohen. "The Russian Bible Society and the Russian Orthodox Church." *Church History* 35, no. 4 (December 1966): 411–37.

Zamoyski, Adam. *Moscow 1812: Napoleon's Fatal March.* New York: HarperCollins, 2004.

Zerner, Henri. *Géricault.* France: Liguge-Poitiers, 1997.

Zorin, Andrei, and Andrew L. Schlafly. "'Star of the East': The Holy Alliance and European Mysticism." *Kritika: Explorations in Russian and Eurasia History* 4, no. 2 (Spring 2003): 313–42.

ABOUT THE AUTHOR

Richard E. Bennett, professor of Church history and doctrine at Brigham Young University since 1997 and former president of the Mormon History Association, has published several books and over sixty articles on a wide range of topics in Latter-day Saint history. His award-winning *Mormons at the Missouri, 1846–1852* (University of Oklahoma) remains the definitive study of the Latter-day Saint experience at Winter Quarters (Nebraska), and his follow-up work, *We'll Find the Place: The Mormon Exodus, 1846–1848*, is an equally comprehensive study of Brigham Young's pioneering trek from Winter Quarters to the Salt Lake Valley. Born and raised in Sudbury, Ontario, Canada, he was also chair of the Department of Archives and Special Collections at the University of Manitoba in Winnipeg for twenty years. He and his wife, Patricia, have five children and several grandchildren.

INDEX

A

Abascal, José Fernando de, 223
Abolition Act (1807), 193–94
abolitionist movement, 181–82, 189–97, 199, 205–6
Abu Simbel, temple of, 50–51
Adam, Fall of, 149, 199
Adams, John Quincy, 266, 269, 274, 279, 282–83
Adams, Joseph, 142
agrarian revolution, 163–64
Aids to Reflection (Coleridge), 147
Aitutaki, 231–32, 252
Åkerblad, Johan David, 46
Alexander I, Tsar
    anointed emperor, 62
    Baroness Krüdener's influence on, 71–73
    battles against Napoléon, 64–66
    character of, 60–61
    and Congress of Vienna, 66–71, 74–76
    and death of Paul I, 61–62

Alexander I, Tsar (*continued*)
    final years and death of, 77–79
    impact and legacy of, xii
    invades Paris, 309
    marriage of, 59–60
    and Napoléon's Russian campaign of 1812, 17–19
    presents Holy Alliance, 73–74
    religious study of, 57–58
    and Treaty of Tilsit, 15
    upbringing of, 58–59
Ali, Muhammad, 36–37, 38
American Bible Society (ABS), 240–43
American Board of Commissioners for Foreign Missions (ABCFM), 246
American Revolution, 262–63, 328
Ampère, André-Marie, 305
ancien régime, 3–4
Anthon, Charles, 302n40
Arago, Dominique François, 311
Arakcheyev, Alexai, 77
astronomy, 303–4

atoms, 306
Austen, Jane, 130
Aztecs, 300–301

B

Bancroft, George, 260–61
Bankes, William John, 50
Bankes's obelisk, 49–50
banking and finance, 272
Banks, Joseph, 290–91
Barthélemy, Jean-Jacques, 46
Bastille, storming of (1789), 4
Battle of Austerlitz (1805), 12, 14–15, 64–65
Battle of Borodino (1812), 17–18
Battle of Boyacá (1819), 207, 221
Battle of Wagram (1809), 16
Battle of Waterloo (1815), 20–21
Beers, Henry, 130
Beethoven, Caspar Carl, 98
Beethoven, Johann van, 82–83
Beethoven, Karl, 97–98
Beethoven, Ludwig van
    childhood and adolescence of, 82–85
    composes Ninth Symphony, 99–102
    composition style of, 90–91
    death of, 102–3
    faith of, 96, 99
    first maturity of, 87–90
    guardianship of nephew of, 97–98
    hearing loss of, 93–94
    performs at Congress of Vienna, 81–82, 97
    personality of, 88–89, 92–93, 96–97
    second maturity of, 90–94
    third maturity of, 96–99
Bell, Henry, 166–67
Belzoni, Giovanni Battista, 37–41, 44–45
Bentham, Jeremy, 177
Berzelius, Jacob, 306
Bible, 54, 57–58, 148
Bible movement, 235–43
Bible societies, 234–35
Bill of Rights, 263
Biographia Literaria (Coleridge), 145

biography, as analytical approach to history, ix–xi
biology, 307–8
Blake, William, 112, 171
Blücher, Gebhard Leberecht von, 20, 22
Bolívar, Simón
    exile of, 217–18
    family and education of, 208, 211–13
    final years and death of, 227
    Humboldt meets, 308–9
    legacy of, xiii, 207, 227–28
    as military leader, 213–14, 216, 217
    on Napoléon, 211–12
    relationship between Manuela Sáenz and, 222–23
    and Second Republic, 216–17
    seeks British help in independence movement, 214–15
    and South American unification, 222–27
    on Spanish colonizers, 211
    success of, in revolution, 219–21
    and Venezuelan revolution, 213–14
    vision of, for South America, 218–19
Bolivia, 225
Bonaparte, Josephine, 11
Bonaparte, Marie-Louise, 11–12
Bonaparte, Napoléon
    and Alexander I, 60–61, 64–66
    and Beethoven, 84–85, 92
    Bolívar on, 211–12
    Champollion meets, 48
    death of, 25
    early years of, 1–2
    education of, 2–3
    as emperor, 10–11
    exile and final days of, 21–25, 74
    and French Revolution, 3–8
    Humboldt meets, 308
    impact and legacy of, xii, 25–29
    invades Egypt, 9–10, 32–34
    Jacques-Louis David and, 110
    marriages of, 11–12
    military skill and successes of, 12–16
    religion under, 28, 29, 32–33

Bonaparte, Napoléon (*continued*)
   religious beliefs of, 32–33
   returns to power, 19–21, 72, 74
   rise of, 8–10
   Russian campaign of 1812, 17–19
Bonpland, Aimé Jacques Alexandre, 294, 295–302, 311
Book of Abraham, 44
botany, 307
Bouchard (Boussard), Pierre-François, 34
Bougainville, Louis-Antoine de, 293–94
Boulton, Matthew, 165
Boves, José Tomás, 217
Bowden, Ann, 126
Bowyer, James, 126–27
Brentano, Bettina Antonie, 92
Brion, Marcel, 108–9
British and Foreign Bible Society (BFBS), 236–40
Broad Church Movement, 149
Brougham, Henry, 174
Buch, Leopold von, 293
Bulkeley, Peter, 323
Buonaparte, Carlo, 1–2
Buonaparte, Letizia, 1–2

C

Cailliaud, Frédéric, 44
Calhoun, John C., 284
Campbell, John, 245–46
camp meeting movement, 331–36
Canada, 268–69
Cane Ridge, 331
Canning, George, 176, 177
Carey, William, 243–44, 253
Carlos IV, King, 294
Carlyle, Thomas, 144, 147
Caroline, Queen, 154, 157–61, 173–76
Cartwright, Peter, 336
Caruel, Alexandrine-Modeste, 107–8, 117–19
Caruel, Jean-Baptiste, 107–8, 117
Castlereagh, Viscount, 67, 69, 71, 73, 154, 176, 269
Catherine the Great, 58–59
Cato Conspiracy (1820), 173

Chamber of Five Hundred, 8, 9
Champollion, Jacques-Joseph, 47, 48
Champollion, Jean-François
   education of, 46–48
   employment of, 48
   impact and legacy of, 29, 53–55
   relationships of, 48–49
   and translation of Rosetta Stone, 49–53
Charles, Thomas, 236
Charlotte, Queen, 158
Charlotte Augusta, Princess, 158–60
Chasseur de la Garde (*The Charging Light Cavalryman*) (Géricault), 116
Chatterton, Thomas, 130
Cheddar school, 198–99
chemistry, 306
child labor, 168–71
Chile, 224–25
chimney sweeps, 171
China, Morrison's missionary efforts in, 244
Church, Frederic E., 114, 303
Church of Jesus Christ of Latter-day Saints, The, vii, 44, 76, 153, 178–79, 198n36, 205, 285
"Civil Constitution of the Clergy," 6
Civil War, Clay on, 284–85
Clapham Sect, 193, 199
Clay, Henry
   childhood of, 261–62
   employment of, 264
   enters politics, 265–66
   legacy of, 259, 284–85
   and recognition of Colombia as free country, 221
   social context of, 269–74
   as Speaker and broker of Missouri Compromise, 281–84
   and Treaty of Ghent, 269
   young adulthood of, 263–64
Clay, John, 261
clothing, 273–74
coal mining, 166, 170
Cobb, Thomas W., 260
Cobbett, William, 172
Cochrane, Lord Thomas, 224–25

Coleridge, Derwent, 144
Coleridge, Hartley, 144
Coleridge, John, 126
Coleridge, Samuel Taylor
    conversion of, 125–26
    descent of, 137–42
    early years and education of, 126–28
    final years and death of, 143–50
    marriage of, 128–29
    personality of, 139–40
    religious beliefs of, 147–50
    Wordsworth and, 131–37
Coleridge, Sara, 144
Colombia, 221
Comet, 167
Committee of Public Safety, 6–8
Congress of Vienna (1814–15), 28, 66–72, 74–76, 81–82, 97
Constable, John, 113
Constitution of the United States, 262–63
Cook, James, Captain, 233, 246
Coptic language, 46, 49, 51
Cort, Henry, 166
Cosmos (Humboldt), 312–13
Cotton, John, 323
cotton mills, 165, 168–70
Cuirassier Blessé Quittant le Feu, Le (*The Wounded Heavy Cavalryman*) (Géricault), 116
Cuvier, Georges, 293, 307
Czerny, Carl, 96–97

D

Daguerre, Louis, 307
Dalton, John, 306
D'Angers, Pierre-Jean David, 116
David, Jacques-Louis, 109–11
Davy, Humphrey, 306
debt, federal, 272
deism, 327–28
"Dejection: An Ode" (Coleridge), 138
Delacroix, Eugène, 112
Demotic, 46, 49
Denon, Vivant, 33–34

de Quincey, Thomas, 139, 141
Dieudonné, Alexandre, 121
Drovetti, Bernardino, 41, 45, 52

E

education, 270–71
Edwards, Jonathan, 325–27
Egypt. *See also* Rosetta Stone
    British discoveries in, 36–41
    Champollion's expedition to, 53
    continuing study of, 54–55
    French discoveries in, 41–45
    French invasion of, 9–10, 32–34
electricity, 304–6
Elizaveta Alexeyovna, Grand Duchess, 59–60
Erie Canal, 272
Estimate of the Religion of the Fashionable World (More), 201
evangelical Christian movement, Coleridge on, 147
Evans, Mary, 127, 129
Evans, Tom, 127

F

Fall of Adam, 149, 199
family, 269
Faraday, Michael, 306
farming, 269–70
federal debt, 272
Fidelio (Beethoven), 91
Fifth Symphony (Beethoven), 94
Final Acts of Vienna (1815), 74
finance, 272
Fitzherbert, Maria, 156–57, 158, 178
Foreign Slave Trade Bill (1807), 196–97
Forster, Georg, 290–91
Fourier, Jean-Baptiste-Joseph, 47
Francis I, Emperor, 67–68
Frederickson, O. J., 76
Freemasonry, 63
French Revolution, 3–10, 27, 109, 110, 263, 281
Fricker, Sara, 128–29

Friedrich, Caspar David, 113–14
Friend, The: A Literary, Moral, and Political Weekly Paper, 140
Fuseli, Henry, 112–13

G

Gainsborough, Thomas, 115
Garrick, David, 198
Gauss, Karl Friedrich, 304
geology, 299
George III, King, 155, 157, 158, 160
George IV, King
    and Caroline's return to London, 154
    coronation of, 175
    criticism of, 155
    death of, 178
    early years of, 155–56
    legacy of, 177–78
    marital troubles of, 158–60, 161
    marriage of, 156–58
    path of, to throne, 160
Géricault, Théodore
    education of, 107–8
    final years and death of, 121–23
    legacy of, 123
    paints *The Raft of the Medusa*, 118–21
    studies art in Italy, 116–18
Gillman, James, 142, 143–44
Goethe, Johann Wolfgang von, 97, 292
gold plates, 53n46
Golitzen, Alexander, 57
Goya, Francisco de, 115–16
"grapeshot," 9
Great Awakening, 325–27
Great Britain, population growth in, 162–63
Great Migration, 271
Greek insurrections (Russia, 1821), 77–78
Grenville, Charles, 155
Grey, Charles, 154, 177
Grey, Thomas, 130
Grillparzer, Franz, 103
Gros, Antoine-Jean, 111
Guérin, Pierre-Narcisse, 108

H

Halévy, Elie, 182, 186
Half-Way Covenant (1662), 324–25
Hankins, Thomas L., x
Harris, Martin, 53n46, 302n40
Haydn, Joseph, 86, 87–88
Herschel, Sir William, 304
Herz, Marcus, 289–90
hieroglyphs, 46, 49–52
Hoffman, E. T. A., 102
Holy Alliance, 73–74, 76
Hooker, Thomas, 324
Hughes, Joseph, 236
Humboldt, Alexander Georg von, 288
Humboldt, Alexander von
    admiration for, 287–88
    death of, 314
    early years and education of, 288–92
    influence of, 303
    leads Russian expedition, 310–11
    legacy of, xiii, 303, 314–15
    personal relationships of, 311–12
    renown of, 308–10
    and scientific discovery of New World, 295–302
    seeks study opportunities, 292–95
    on task of historians, xi
    visits United States, 302–3
    writes *Cosmos*, 312–14
Humboldt, Marie-Elisabeth von Colomb von, 288–89, 292
Humboldt, Wilhelm von, 288–89, 290, 309
Hunt, Henry, 172–73
Hutchinson, Anne, 324
Hutchinson, Sara, 139, 140, 141
Huyot, Jean-Nicolas, 50

I

impressment, 267
Incas, 299–300
India, Carey's missionary efforts in, 243–44
Industrial Revolution, xiii, 153, 161–73, 178–79
infanticide, 248

iron making, 166
Isaac, Antoine, 46
itinerant preachers, 329–30

J

Jackson, Andrew, 284
Jacobins, 6
"Jamaica Letter" (Bolívar), 217–18
Jefferson, Thomas, 5n12, 262, 264–65, 274, 279, 302
Jerningham, Frances, 154
Jews, under Napoléon's government, 28
Johnson, Edward, 323
Johnson, Paul, 26, 86
Johnson, Samuel, 198

K

Kant, Immanuel, 85–86
Keats, John, 145
Kinderman, William, 84
Kircher, Athanassius, 46
Kissinger, Henry, 73, 74
Krüdener, Julie von, Baroness, 71–73

L

labor laws, 168–73, 176–77
ladies' associations, Bible movement and, 238
Lafayette, Gilbert du Motier, Marquis de, 21
La Harpe, Frédéric, 59
Lamarck, Jean-Baptiste, 293, 307–8
Lamb, Charles, 141, 144–45
Lambert, Frank, 327n41
Laplace, Pierre-Simon, 303–4
Lawrence, Thomas, 115
Lebolo, Antonio, 42–43, 44–45
Lepsius, Karl Richard, 53
Leym, Maria Magdalena, 82
light, study of, 306–7
"Lines Written a Few Miles above Tintern Abbey" (Wordsworth), 134
Linné, Carl von (Linnaeus), 307
Liszt, Franz, 96

Livingstone, David, 246
London Missionary Society (LMS), 234, 245–47, 250, 253
London Religious Tract Society, 235, 236
Louisiana Purchase, 241–42, 265
Louis XVI, King, 6
Louis XVIII, King, 120
Luxor, 38, 42
Lyrical Ballads (Coleridge and Wordsworth), 134–37

M

Macdonald, Sir John A., 269
Machado, Josefina, 216
Mack, Solomon, 318, 337–38
Mackenzie, William Lyon, 269
magnetism, 305–6
Maitland, Frederick, 22
Malmesbury, James Harris, 1st Earl of, 157
Maria Luisa, Queen, 294
Maria Naryshkina, Countess, 60
Marie-Antoinette, Queen, 6
marriage, 269
Marshall, Humphrey, 266
Martin, John, 113
Massachusetts Bay Colony, 322–23, 324
McAdam, John Loudon, 166
McCullough, David, viii–ix
McGready, James, 330–32
Méduse, La, 105–7. See also *Raft of the Medusa, The* (Géricault)
mental illness, 122–23
Methodism, 329–30, 332–35
Methodist movement, 182–87
Metternich, Klemens von, 29, 67, 69, 70–71, 73, 78, 290
Mexico, Humboldt's exploration of, 300–302
Michelet, Jules, 121
Mills, Samuel J., 241–42
Milner, Isaac, 189
Miranda, Francisco de, 214–15
Missa Solemnis in D Major (Beethoven), 99, 102
missionary age, 243–47

Missouri, relevance of, to Latter-day Saints, 285
Missouri Compromise (1820), 259–60, 274–81, 283–84
Mitchill, Catharine Akerly, 167
Mitchill, Samuel Latham, 53, 302
Moffat, Robert, 246
Monroe, James, 280
More, Hannah, 182, 194–95, 197–202
More, Martha, 198
More, Mary, 197–202
Morgan, Robert C., 255–56
Morillo, Pablo, 217
Morrison, Robert, 244
Mozart, Wolfgang Amadeus, 83–84, 86
musical age, 85–87
mysticism, 63

N

Napoléon. *See* Bonaparte, Napoléon
Napoleonic Code (1804), 10, 27, 69
Napoléon on the Battlefield of Eylau (Gros), 111
National Constituent Assembly, 4–6
Native Americans, 267
Neefe, Christian Gottlob, 83
Nelson, Horatio, 9, 10, 12, 32, 196
Nettleton, Asahel, 336–38
Newcomen, Thomas, 165
New England Religious Tract Society, 235
New Granada, 217, 221
New Plymouth, 322, 323
Newton, John, 181, 188, 192
Nicholas I, Tsar, 310
Niépce, Nicéphore, 307
Nile River regions, French survey of, 33–34
Ninth Symphony (Beethoven), 99–102
Nott, Henry, 246, 247

O

"Ode to Joy" (Beethoven), 99–102
Onions, Peter, 166
optics, 306–7

original sin, Coleridge on, 149
Orinoco River, 297
Ørsted, Hans Christian, 305
Owen, John, 236
Owen, Robert, 168, 170, 202

P

Paine, Tom, 202
"Pains of Sleep, The" (Coleridge), 141
Palacios, Esteban, 211
papyri, 42–43, 44, 45
Paul I, Tsar, 58, 61–62
Peel, Robert, 174, 176–77
Peninsular War (1809), 15–16
Percy, Thomas, 130
Pergami, Bartolomeu, 160–61, 174
Peru, and South American unification, 222–26
Peterloo Massacre (1819), 172–73
Petit, Claude, 121
Pezuela, Joaquín de la, 224
Philip, John, 245–46
photography, 307
Pinel, Philippe, 122–23
Pitt, William, 188
Plymouth Rock, 322
Polynesia
    Christian evangelization of, 232–33
    London Missionary Society's efforts in, 246–47
    Williams's missionary efforts in, 231–32, 247–55
Pōmare, King, 247
Practical View of the Prevailing Religious System of Professed Christians in the Higher and Middle Classes in the Country, Contrasted with Real Christianity, A (Wilberforce), 203–5
Presbyterianism, 330–32, 336–40
pride, Wilberforce on, 204
prostitution, 187
Puritans / Puritanism, 320–25

Q

Quakers, 193

R

Raft of the Medusa, The (Géricault), 107, 118–21
Raiatea, 250–52, 254
Raikes, Robert, 198
Ramsay, James, 192
Ramses II, 38
Rarotonga, 252–54
Real Christianity (Wilberforce), 203–5
reason, Coleridge on understanding versus, 149
redemption, Coleridge on, 149–50
Reform Bill of 1832, 177
Reid, Donald Malcolm, 36
Reign of Terror, 6–8
Reis, Ferdinand, 89, 97
Reiss, Johanna, 98
religious revivalism
    Great Awakening, 325–27
    impact of, xiv
    Methodist movement, 182–87
    in Russia, 62–63
    Second Great Awakening, 329–41
religious tract societies, 234–35
revelation, Coleridge on, 148–49
revivalism. *See* religious revivalism
revival meetings, 336–40
Revolutionary War, 262–63, 328
Richards, Robert J., x–xi
Rifaud, Jean-Jacques, 44
"Rime of the Ancient Mariner" (Coleridge), 135–36
roads, 271–72
Rodríguez, Simón, 208, 212–13
Rodríguez del Toro y Alayza, María Teresa, 212
Roman Catholic Church, 28
Romantics / Romanticism, xiii, 108–16, 129–31
Rosenblum, Robert, 111–12
Rosetta Stone, 34, 49–54
Rosignana, Josef, 42–43
Rossini, Gioachino, 86–87

Ruruta, 252
Russian Bible Society, 63

S

Sacy, Silvestre de, 46
Sáenz, Manuela, 222–23, 227
Salieri, Antonio, 88
Salt, Henry, 37, 42
Samoa, Williams's missionary efforts in, 254
San Martín, José de, 224
Savigny, Jean Baptiste Henri, 106
Schiller, Friedrich, 100, 292
Schlösser, Louis, 99–100
Schubert, Franz, 87
Schuppanzigh, Ignaz, 102
science, 303–8. *See also* Humboldt, Alexander von
Scott, Sir Walter, 131
Second Compromise of 1821, 283–84
Second Great Awakening, 329–41
Second Treaty of Paris (1815), 72–73, 74–76
Seventh Symphony (Beethoven), 82
slavery
    abolitionist movement, 181–82, 189–97, 199, 205–6
    Clay on, 282
    Humboldt on, 313
    and Missouri Compromise, 259–60, 274–81
    in South America, 208–9
    and Venezuelan independence movement, 215, 219, 226
Slavery Abolition Act (1833), 197
"Slave Trade, The" (More), 194–95
Smith, Adam, 167–68
Smith, Asael, 319
Smith, David M., 336n65
Smith, John, 245
Smith, Joseph, Jr., 242–43, 317–20, 341–42
Smith, Joseph, Sr., 319–20
Smith, Lucy Mack, 318–20, 336, 338n73
Smith, William, 277
Snow, Simeon, 336n65

Society for Promoting a More Extensive Circulation of the Scriptures at Home and Abroad, 236
Society of Friends (Quakers), 193
Solomon, Maynard, 87–88
South Africa, missionary efforts in, 245–46
South America. *See also* Venezuelan revolution
    Bolívar's vision for, 218–19
    factors inciting uprising in, 208–11
    Humboldt's exploration of, 295–302
    unification of, 222–27
Southey, Robert, 128–29, 138, 170
Spanish Revolution, 225
Speransky, Mikhail, 63–64
Spring, Gardiner, 320–21
steamships, 166–67
Steinkopf, Carl F., 236, 237
Stephenson, George, 166
Stiebing, William, Jr., 32
Sucre, Antonio José de, 225, 227
Suez Canal, 33n7
Sunday School movement, 198–99
Symphony No. 5 in C Minor, Opus 67 (Beethoven), 94

T

Tahiti, missionary efforts in, 247–48
Talleyrand-Périgord, Charles Maurice de, 29, 74
Tallmadge, James, Jr., 260, 279
Tapayupangi, 299–300
Tarbell, Ida, 25–26
Taylor, John W., 279
Teignmouth, John Shore, Lord, 236, 240
Telford, Thomas, 166
third estate, 3–4
Third Symphony (Beethoven), 91–92
Thomas, Jesse B., 280
Thoughts on the Importance of Manners (More), 200–201
Tinsley, Peter, 263
Tocqueville, Alexis de, 26, 269, 274
Tonkin, Enoch, 233
transportation, 271–72

Treaty of Fontainebleau (1814), 19, 66
Treaty of Ghent (1814), 267–69
Treaty of Tilsit (1807), 15, 65
Turner, Edward, 197
Turner, J. M. W., 113

U

Umlauf, Michael, 102
understanding, Coleridge on reason versus, 149
Unitarianism, 328
United States, Humboldt visits, 302–3
Urguijo, Mariano Luis de, 294

V

Valeriano, Pierio, 46
Vanderkemp, J. T., 245
Venezuelan revolution
    beginning of, 213–14
    Bolívar's success in, 219–21
    Bolívar's vision for, 218–19
    British aid for, 214–15
    Clay on, 281, 282
    and exile of Bolívar, 217–18
    and Second Republic, 216–17
Vernet, Carle, 108
volcanoes, 299
Volta, Alessandro, 305
Von Lieven, Dorothea, 154
Voyage dans la Basse et la Haute Egypte (Denon), 33–34

W

Walker, Freeman, 260
Warburton, William, 46
War of 1812, 266–69
War of the Consuls, 36–41
Washington, George, 262, 263
Watchman, The, 129
Watkins, Elizabeth Hudson Clay, 261
Watt, James, 165
Weber, Maria von, 97
Wellek, René, 145–46

Wellington, Arthur Wellesley, Duke of, 14, 15, 20–21, 26, 154, 155
Wesley, John, 183–86
Western Great Revival, 331–32
West Indies, Smith's missionary efforts in, 245
Whitefield, George, 184–85, 326
Wilberforce, William
    antislavery activism of, 182, 189–97, 205–6
    Bolívar meets, 215
    influences on, 187–89
    personality of, 189
    religious beliefs of, 203–5
Wilhelm III, King, 309–10
Wilhelm IV, King, 309–10
Wilkinson, John, 166
Willdenow, Karl Ludwig, 290
Williams, John
    context of missionary work of, 234–40
    conversion of, 233–34
    death of, 255–56
    first encounter with native islanders of Aitutaki, 231–32
    legacy of, 256–57

Williams, John (*continued*)
    on missionary age, 243
    missionary efforts of, in Polynesia, 247–55
Williams, Mary Chauner, 234, 247, 248, 252–53, 256, 257
Williams, Roger, 324
women
    Bible movement and, 238
    education and marriage of, 272–73
    labor exploitation of, 168–70
Woods, Fred E., 256–57
wool industry, 165, 168–70
Wordsworth, Dorothy, 131, 132, 137, 145
Wordsworth, Mary, 137
Wordsworth, William, 131–37, 140, 145
Wythe, George, 263

Y

Young, Thomas, 49, 50, 52, 306–7

Z

Zoëga, Georg, 46
zoology, 307